Texas
REAL ESTATE
Agency

EIGHTH EDITION

Donna K. Peeples, PhD, and Minor Peeples III, PhD,
and A. Sue Williams, MS, with Thomas C. Terrell
and Kathleen E. Terrell, CREI, Contributing Editors

Dearborn™
Real Estate Education

This publication is designed to provide accurate and authoritative information in regard to the subject matter covered. It is sold with the understanding that the publisher is not engaged in rendering legal, accounting, or other professional advice. If legal advice or other expert assistance is required, the services of a competent professional should be sought.

President: Dr. Andrew Temte
Chief Learning Officer: Dr. Tim Smaby
Executive Director, Real Estate Education: Melissa Kleeman-Moy
Development Editor: Julia Marti

TEXAS REAL ESTATE AGENCY EIGHTH EDITION
©2014 Kaplan, Inc.
Published by DF Institute, Inc., d/b/a Dearborn Real Estate Education
332 Front St. S., Suite 501
La Crosse, WI 54601

Printed in the United States of America
First revision, March 2016
ISBN: 978-1-4754-2809-4 / 1-4754-2809-X
PPN: 1560-0509

Contents

About the Authors

Donna K. Peeples (Katy), PhD, is an associate professor of management at Texas A&M-Corpus Christi and previous co-owner of the Real Estate Institute of Corpus Christi. She is licensed as a real estate broker in Texas, holds a BBA in finance, an MBA from Texas A&M University at Corpus Christi, and a PhD from Texas A&M University at College Station. Her real estate designations include the GRI, CRB, and the Texas Real Estate Teachers Association's (TRETA) CREI designation. Katy is a frequent public speaker on topics relating to business and real estate. Katy is a coauthor of *Prepare for the Texas Real Estate Exam* with Dr. Johnnie Rosenauer and Dr. Minor Peeples III, PhD.

Minor Peeples III, PhD, is cofounder, previous owner, and former CEO and principal instructor of the Real Estate Institute of Corpus Christi, Inc. Minor is a Texas real estate broker with extensive experience in the real estate business and has served as a content expert for various editions of the Texas real estate examination and as a member of the TREC MCE content committee. He is a coauthor of *Prepare for the Texas Real Estate Exam* with Dr. Johnnie Rosenauer and Dr. Katy Peeples. His educational background includes a BA in economics from Texas A&M at College Station, an MBA from Texas A&M-Corpus Christi, and a PhD from Texas A&M at College Station. Currently, Dr. Peeples offers consulting services to real estate brokerage companies and expert witness services in the area of agency law and is a frequent speaker at professional real estate meetings throughout south Texas.

A. Sue Williams, MS, GRI, served for over 20 years in the U.S. Navy in myriad assignments, ranging from associate professor of computer science at the U.S. Military Academy in West Point, New York, to commanding officer of the fleet ballistic missile (FBM) submarine base in Holy Loch, Scotland. She has been licensed as a real estate broker since 1996 in Texas and holds a BA in English from Texas State University in San Marcos and an MS in computer science from the Naval Postgraduate School in Monterey, California. Sue has been affiliated with the Real Estate Institute of Corpus Christi since 1994, serving full time as an instructor and writer of prelicensing and continuing education courses. She then stepped up to the position of executive director for several years before retiring in December 2010. She continues to author and teach mandatory continuing education (MCE) courses throughout the Coastal Bend and often contributes to the review and editing of real estate textbooks for Dearborn Real Estate Education, including previous editions of *Texas Real Estate Agency* and *Texas Real Estate Exam Prep, Third Edition*, and the writing of exam and chapter quiz rationales for *Modern Real Estate Practice in Texas, 13th Edition*. Sue is a member of the Texas Real Estate Teachers Association (TRETA) and the Real Estate Educator's Association (REEA).

Dearborn Real Estate Education would like to thank Katy Peeples, Minor Peeples, and Sue Williams for their dedication to Texas Real Estate Agency and its many students over the years. Their expertise in this field of study is truly admirable.

■ ABOUT THE CONTRIBUTING EDITORS

Thomas C. Terrell has been a licensed real estate salesperson since 1971 and a broker since 1976. He is an adjunct instructor at the University of North Texas, University of North Texas at Dallas, and Cedar Valley College, where he teaches real estate agency, contracts, principles of real estate, real estate math, and various continuing education topics. Tom is a former member of the Texas Real Estate Commission's Broker/Lawyer Committee, current member of the National Association of REALTORS®, Texas Association of REALTORS®, and the MetroTex Association of REALTORS®, and a life member of the Texas Real Estate Teacher Association (TRETA) and Texas Real Estate Buyer Agents Association (TRE-BAA), from which he received an award for Outstanding Consumer Advocate and Real Estate Agency Educator. In addition to his many other achievements, Tom is a graduate of the University of Oklahoma, completed post-graduate work at Southwestern Baptist Theological Seminary and Texas Wesleyan University School of Law, and attained the rank of Captain in the United States Marine Corps.

Kathleen E. Terrell, CREI, has held her Texas real estate broker license since 1978 and is co-owner of P.R.E.P.A.R.E. Real Estate and Real Estate Education Consultants. She is co-author of Texas Real Estate Principles I & II (Educational Textbook Company). She is a past president and board member of the Texas Real Estate Teachers Association (TRETA) and holds the Certified Real Estate Instructor (CREI) designation offered by TRETA. Kathy was named Educator of the Year in 1999 by the Texas Association of REALTORS®, and as Director of Education for the Dallas Association of REALTORS® (1986-2001), created education programs that were awarded Education Program of the Year in 1999 and 2000 by the Texas Association of REALTORS® and International Education Program of the Year in 2000 by the National Association of REALTORS®. Kathy is on the advisory board for the Real Estate Division of Cedar Valley College, and teaches real estate courses both in-class and online.

Acknowledgments

We wish to thank Loretta DeHay, former General Counsel, Texas Real Estate Commission, for her valuable contributions to this edition.

We also wish to thank the following reviewers for their valuable contributions to previous editions: Terri Macaluso, broker/manager, Ebby Halliday REALTORS®, Frisco, Texas, and associate faculty, Collin College; Ken Combs, professor (retired, Del Mar Junior College, Corpus Christi, Texas), GRI, CREI, MBA, Ken Combs Realty, Corpus Christi, Texas; Edd Price, owner, Century-21 Hallmark, Corpus Christi, Texas; James Wiedemer, BA, JD, DREI, CREI, State Bar Real Estate Forms Committee and author of several real estate textbooks; Harold E. Grimes, Tyler Real Estate College; Nanci Hawes, previous owner of Leonard-Hawes Real Estate School, now Kaplan Professional Schools; Phillip G. (L.) Schöewe, CREI, DREI, JD, adjunct professor San Jacinto College, managing broker HomeIndex, Int'l REALTY; Bob Reynolds, San Antonio College; Kenneth West, Tarrant County College; Patricia Banta, Collin County Community College; Dave Garcia, The Academy of Real Estate; James E. George, EdD, Professional Development Institute, University of North Texas (North Denton); Rick Knowles, Capital Real Estate Training; Randy McKechnie, RLM Consulting, Inc.; Joe C. Pickett, Academy of Real Estate (El Paso); Thomas E. Powell, Lee College; John Wesley Tomblin, J. Wesley Tomblin & Associates (Austin); and Cheryl Nance, EdD, DREI, CREI, author of *Modern Real Estate Practice in Texas*.

Preface

Knowledge of agency relationships is vital to a licensee's survival and ultimate success in the field of real estate. As clients and customers become more aware of their rights, real estate licensees are often expected to increase their level of service and are being held to higher standards of practice. In addition, because agency law is an evolving law, the practitioner must keep abreast of its changes. Many issues, such as those involving intermediary brokerage, buyer agency, or recent changes to the Texas Deceptive Trade Practices Act—Consumer Protection (DTPA) continue to evolve and be interpreted by the courts. The explanations in this text are consistent with the Texas Real Estate Commission's interpretations, but as more case law develops, these interpretations are subject to change.

This book is designed to help students seeking a real estate license and real estate practitioners understand relationships that are created in real estate transactions. Agency is a course of study required by The Real Estate License Act (TRELA) for all persons seeking a real estate license. This edition focuses on all statutory topics and ethical standards required by TRELA for a prelicensing core course in agency law.

This eighth edition of *Texas Real Estate Agency* retains many examples from previous editions to help students understand some of the new agency laws that have been enacted. Cases, used as learning tools, are meant to bring the real world into the study of agency and to give students the benefit of seeing how the courts interpret these issues.

Many references to TRELA and the rules of the Texas Real Estate Commission are included in the text to remind the reader that the law dictates much of our basic practice. Students who have a clear understanding of the basis of practice will usually have a clearer understanding of how and why certain practices exist.

While this text covers agency issues and may be used in Law of Agency core courses offered by colleges, universities, and proprietary level real estate schools, it is not intended to replace competent legal counsel. Each real estate transaction is unique; therefore, this text cannot be the source of law for any particular transaction. General direction that will guide a licensee's practice can be gained from study of the materials in this text; the licensee's sponsoring broker and legal counsel, who is retained to give advice, will decide specific practices.

CHAPTER 1

Agency Concepts

Of the many topics of study for the real estate professional, it is likely that no real estate topic receives more attention, heated dispute, and discussion than that of "agency".

One reason agency receives such great attention is because the term "agency" is so often applied in different ways in different contexts and the particular meaning must be inferred from its usage in its context.

Another reason agency receives so much attention and discussion is that the term is often frequently used incorrectly by real estate professionals and the public.

Yet a third, and most important, reason that agency is discussed so much in real estate can best be summed up by a quote from William D. North, former Executive Vice President and General Counsel for the National Association of REALTORS®, when he wrote the following in the preface to NAR's Legal Liability Series handbook on agency, *Who Is My Client?*:

> The legal concept of "Agency" is, **however, beyond question the most fundamental of all the legal concepts applicable to the real estate profession** [emphasis added] and professional. It is the very nature and function of the real estate broker, appraiser, and manager to be an agent. The law of agency literally defines the "species" and gives real estate practitioners their identity.

In other words, the reason agency is discussed and written about so much is because it is so important to the very identity of a real estate professional when acting for others in a real estate transaction. As North says, agency "literally defines" who the real estate professional is.

It might be said that when the concept and practice of agency is minimized, misunderstood, and misused by a real estate professional acting as an agent, a subtle and very dangerous form of "identity theft" has occurred. The real estate professional, in effect, has become a "secret agent," "double agent," "disloyal agent," or simply an incompetent agent.

It is critical today for real estate professionals to be well grounded in the fundamentals of agency law in order to perform the duties expected of them. Brokers must have a good understanding of the principles of agency law so that they may train their sales and broker associates properly. Sales and broker associates must likewise be able to communicate the principles of agency information to prospective customers and clients, whether they are buyers, tenants, or owners, in order for them to make informed decisions about the relationship that should be established with the broker that will best achieve the client's or customer's intended relationship.

This chapter introduces you to some basic agency concepts that will help you understand the larger, more complex issues introduced in succeeding chapters.

■ **LEARNING OBJECTIVES** *This chapter addresses the following:*

- ■ What Is Agency?
- ■ The Real Estate License Act, the TREC Rules, and You
  - — Laws Governing Licensee Conduct
  - — Protecting the Interests of the Agent's Clients/Principals
- ■ Roles People Play in Agency Relationships
- ■ Client or Customer?
- ■ Why Study Agency?
- ■ Relationships Between Principal and Agent

■ WHAT IS AGENCY?

In Webster's Encyclopedic Unabridged Dictionary of the English Language, the term "agency" is listed with 10 differing meanings or definitions. The word "agent" is listed with 15 different meanings and usages. Because so many situations and so many people hear and convey very different messages using the same term or terms, it is essential to clarify the appropriate and inappropriate uses of the terms in the real estate business and in the law that surrounds it.

The *Restatement of the Law of Agency* (3rd ed.) is a highly regarded reference and scholarly work by the American Law Institute containing a set of principles intended to set forth and clarify the current majority and minority opinions of courts in all 50 states and the U.S. federal court system on the subject of the law of agency.

The definition of *agency* as set forth in paragraph 1.01 of *Restatement* is as follows: "Agency is the fiduciary relationship that arises when one person (a 'principal') manifests assent to another person (an 'agent') that the agent shall act on the principal's behalf and subject to the principal's control, and the agent manifests or otherwise consents so to act."

That definition of agency itself has a loaded term in it: "fiduciary". What is a "fiduciary relationship"? What does the term "fiduciary" mean? Why do you need to know? You need to know because the Rules of the Texas Real Estate Commission (TREC) say that when you, as a broker or salesperson, act as an agent for another in a real estate transaction, you are a fiduciary.

As a noun, a fiduciary is a person who is entrusted, by another person, with property or power for the benefit of the person who entrusts the fiduciary with such power or property. It is important to note that the person would not become a fiduciary until the power or property has been entrusted to that individual.

The adjective *fiduciary* is used to describe the type of duty or capacity a person is operating on, or to describe the type of legal relation between an agent and the agent's principal. Note that in the real estate profession and almost 35 times in the TREC Rules, the principal that the fiduciary is serving, or owes loyalty to, is frequently called the "client," as distinct from a "customer" to whom fiduciary duties are not owed.

For centuries, people have engaged others to represent them in all types of situations. They may grant others the authority to act on their behalf in a single activity, in a specified group of activities, or in the ongoing operation of a business. Some agency relationships, like those in real estate, involve money and/or property and create a fiduciary relationship, in which one party is bound to act in the best interest of another. A fiduciary handles money or property for the client; therefore, special duties are created by operation of law, rather than by contract. (These special fiduciary duties are discussed in detail in a later chapter.) In any event, agents must at all times act in the best interest of the parties they represent, with a few exceptions, like the intermediary position. In the intermediary exception to traditional agency and fiduciary duties, an intermediary is prohibited by law from truly representing the interests of or protecting the interests of either of the intermediaries' two "clients" at the expense of the other. "Loyalty" and "full disclosure" are truncated in an intermediary transaction. Instead, the intermediary broker must, by law, remain impartial as to the interests of both principals/clients.

Today, a real estate professional must know what the agency and fiduciary priorities are—especially when a fiduciary relationship is triggered by an agency activity such as a real estate transaction, and even more so when the agency is "coupled with an interest".

Here is an example of the dangerous "agency coupled with an interest" situation:

> A and B are partners in the ownership of a duplex. B is a licensed real estate broker and lists the property for sale with A's consent. Where and with whom do B's fiduciary duties lie?
>
> If you are B, and something goes wrong and damages co-owner A's interests, you are likely to find out in court or even at a TREC hearing as to whose ownership rights you should have protected or whether

you breached your duties to act in A's best interest. The issue of a conflict of interest is bound to arise.

TREC Rules specifically address the licensing requirements for someone who acts as an agent in this situation. See Texas Real Estate Commission (TREC) Rule § 535.5(c), which states as follows:

> A person who owns property jointly may sell and convey title to his or her interest in the property, but to act for compensation or with the expectation of compensation as an agent for the other owner, the person must be licensed unless otherwise exempted by the Act.

■ THE REAL ESTATE LICENSE ACT, THE TREC RULES, AND YOU

To deal with the issues regarding agency relationships and other laws pertinent to real estate, the Texas Legislature passed the first law governing the activities of real estate professionals in 1939. At that time, it was called the Texas Real Estate Dealers Act. As we know it today, The Real Estate License Act (TRELA) has been amended numerous times. TRELA is the law that establishes the duties of real estate licensees to their clients, the public, and to TREC; it provides the legal framework within which each licensee operates. The law regarding agency and intermediary relationships, as it pertains to real estate licensees, is carefully detailed in the License Act. Each person licensed in Texas is obligated to be familiar with the Act and to conduct real estate transactions in strict accordance with the Act.

The Texas Real Estate Commission (TREC) was established by TRELA in 1949. In 2011, TREC became a self-directed, semi-independent agency no longer subject to the legislative budget and appropriations process at the state legislature. Instead, TREC conducts business using the licensing fees it collects, which exceed the agency's expenditures. TREC's mission statement has changed over the years. It remains the official agency in Texas for administering rules and regulations that govern real estate licensing and licensee conduct.

According to TREC's website (www.trec.state.tx.us/mission.asp), the mission and philosophy of TREC and the Texas Appraiser Licensing and Certification Board (TALCB) is as follows:

Mission & Philosophy

Mission of TREC/TALCB

The agency exists to safeguard the public interest and protect consumers of real estate services. In accord with state and federal laws, the agency oversees real estate brokerage, appraisal, inspection, home warranty and timeshare interest providers. Through education, licensing and regulation, the agency ensures the availability of qualified and ethical service providers, thereby facilitating economic growth and opportunity in Texas.

Philosophy of TREC/TALCB

To achieve its mission, the agency embraces these core values:

■ Provide exceptional customer service that is accessible, responsive and transparent
■ Demand integrity, accountability and high standards, both of license holders and ourselves
■ Strive continuously for excellence and efficiency

TREC is responsible for the administration of TRELA. TREC consists of nine members—six brokers and three public members—who serve staggered terms of six years each. The governor, with approval of the senate, appoints three replacement members every two years.

The commissioners may appoint an administrator and an assistant administrator who oversee the day-to-day operations of the commission. From a real estate licensee's perspective, some of the key functions of the TREC are

■ enforcing TRELA in a manner that protects the public,
■ overseeing the licensing process, and
■ monitoring and controlling the educational activities of approved providers of real estate education.

In the well-known Texas case of *Henry S. Miller Co. v. TREO Enterprises*, 585 S.W.2d 674 (Tex.1979) the court stated the following:

> It is settled that the Real Estate License Act, Tex.Rev.Civ.Stat.Ann. art 6573a, is a valid exercise of the State's police power to regulate a private business which affects the public interest. The purpose of the statute is to **eliminate or reduce fraud** that might be occasioned on the public **by unlicensed, unscrupulous, or unqualified persons**. (emphasis added)

TREC's duty is to carry out these purposes of the Act.

If the commission receives a complaint about the practice of a licensee who has violated TRELA, it may investigate the complaint and take the appropriate action, which could result in fines and/or suspension or revocation of the license. The wise practitioner never forgets that TREC is a consumer protection agency.

TRELA provides that TREC is authorized to establish rules and regulations necessary to administer the act (TRELA § 1101.151(b)). Typically, each legislative session results in new and revised statutes that affect real estate practice. Following the legislative session, the commission is then empowered by the License Act to adopt the necessary rules and regulations to implement the legislation. Those new rules become a part of the Texas Administrative Code (TAC). The new provisions are then published at Title 22 of the TAC. These rules and regulations allow the law to be interpreted and enforced (see Figure 1.1). Throughout this text are references to specific sections of TRELA, as well as the Rules of the Texas Real Estate Commission, as adopted under the provisions of the TAC.

FIGURE 1.1

Statutes versus Rules

Real estate professionals in Texas are governed by both The Real Estate License Act (TRELA) and Title 22 of the Texas Administrative Code (TAC). Examples of both are provided as follows:

Example of statute (TRELA) complemented by a TREC Rule:

- TRELA § 1101.652(b)(14) states that TREC may suspend or revoke a license if the licensee "solicits, sells or offers for sale a real property by means of a lottery."
- 22 TAC § 535.149 defines and gives specific examples of what does and does not constitute a lottery. The same TREC Rule clarifies TRELA §1101.652(b)(15) by describing what is meant by a "deceptive practice."

It is important to note that Texas statutes such as the Texas Occupation Code (TOC), where TRELA is found, generally only change every two years when the legislature meets in the spring of odd years. However, the TREC Rules, contained in the Texas Administrative Code (TAC), as opposed to statutes passed by the legislature, are administrative regulations, and the Rules can change with as little as 30 days' notice anytime during any year. It is important for real estate professionals to know how quickly TREC regulations can change and to keep up with changes that might affect their real estate practice. The TREC website (www.trec .texas.gov) is kept up to date with recently adopted, amended, or repealed rules.

The Texas secretary of state's website (www.sos.state.tx.us) contains the following statement:

> The Texas Administrative Code (TAC) is a compilation of all state agency rules in Texas. There are 16 titles in the TAC. Each title represents a subject category and related agencies are assigned to the appropriate title.

The administrative agency that this text is concerned with is TREC. The sections of the TAC that contain TREC Rules begin with "Title 22. Examining Boards Part 23. Texas Real Estate Commission, Chapter 531, § 531.1. Canons of Professional Ethics and Conduct" and currently end with § 543.13.

According to the TREC website, TREC regulations affect

- real estate brokers and salespersons,
- education providers for real estate and inspection courses,
- inspectors,
- easement or right-of-way (ERW) agents,
- residential rental locators, (a.k.a. apartment locators)
- residential service companies (a.k.a. home warranty companies),
- and time-share developers.

Appraisers and Appraisal Management Companies (AMCs) are regulated by the Texas Appraiser Licensing and Certification Board (TALCB) Standards & Enforcement Services Division (SES) (see TOC § 1103 and § 1104; as well as the *Uniform Standards of Professional Appraisal Practice [USPAP]*). See also TALCB Rules.

Laws Governing Licensee Conduct

The two principal sources of laws governing the conduct of real estate licensees in Texas are The Real Estate License Act and the TREC Rules.

TRELA is not specifically called an "agency statute," as it was described in former TREC Rules. TRELA is the statute that created the Texas Real Estate Commission in order to administer and enforce TRELA. The Act gives TREC the responsibility and authority to create regulations to further the purposes of the Act. TREC is empowered to regulate and/or punish certain conduct by a broker or a salesperson. Some of the conduct prohibited by the Act and by the Rules violates long-held principles of common law relative to the duties expected of a licensee acting as an agent and certain fiduciary duties.

In fact, relative to the subject of agency, the first section of the TREC Rules actually begin with "The Canons of Profession Ethics and Conduct," which lay out the basic principles of agency duties.

In § 531.1. *Fidelity*, TREC specifically lays out the "fiduciary" duties required of a broker or salesperson acting as an agent for another in a real estate transaction:

> § 531.1. *Fidelity*. A real estate broker or salesperson, **while acting as an agent** for another, **is a fiduciary**. Special obligations are imposed when such fiduciary relationships are created. **They demand**:
>
> (1) that the **primary duty** of the real estate agent is to represent the interests of the agent's client, and the agent's position, in this respect, should be clear to all parties concerned in a real estate transaction; that, however, the agent, in performing duties to the client, shall treat other parties to a transaction fairly;
>
> (2) that the real estate agent be faithful and observant to trust placed in the agent, and be scrupulous and meticulous in performing the agent's functions; and
>
> (3) that the real estate agent place no personal interest above that of the agent's client.
>
> Amended to be effective May 21, 2014, 39 TexReg 3855.
>
> (emphasis added)

Protecting the Interests of the Agent's Clients/Principals

In addition, relative to fiduciary duties when acting as an agent, prospective holders or current license holders should be aware of these additional rules regarding the protection of clients' or principals' interests:

> **TREC Rule § 535.16. Listings; Net Listings**
>
> (a) A broker is obligated under a listing contract to negotiate the **best possible transaction** for the principal, the broker has agreed to represent. [Author's note: This cannot be done when the broker acts as an intermediary.]

(b) A "net listing" is a listing agreement in which the broker's commission is the difference ("net") between the sales proceeds and an amount desired by the owner of the real property. A broker may not take net listings unless the principal requires a net listing and the principal appears to be familiar with current market values of real property. The use of a net listing places an upper limit on the principal's expectancy and **places the broker's interest above the principal's interest** with reference to obtaining the best possible price. If a net listing is used, the listing agreement must assure the principal of not less than the principal's desired price and limit the broker to a specified maximum commission.

(c) A real estate licensee is **obligated** to provide a broker price opinion (BPO) or comparative market analysis (CMA) on a property **when negotiating a listing or offering to purchase the property for the licensee's own account** as a result of contact made while acting as a real estate agent.

TRELA § 1101.652(b)(2)

As grounds for TREC discipline, the License Act states that a licensee's license may be revoked if the licensee "engages in conduct that is dishonest or in bad faith or that demonstrates untrustworthiness."

TREC Rule § 156(a–c) Dishonesty; Bad Faith; Untrustworthiness

(a) A licensee's relationship with the licensee's principal **is that of a fiduciary**. A licensee shall convey to the principal all known information which would affect the principal's decision on whether or not to make, accept or reject offers; **however, if** the principal has agreed **in writing** that offers are not to be submitted after the principal has entered into a contract to buy, sell, rent, or lease a property, the licensee shall have no duty to submit offers to the principal after the principal has accepted an offer.

(b) The licensee must put the interest of the licensee's principal above the licensee's own interests. A licensee must deal honestly and fairly with all parties; however, the licensee represents only the principal and owes a duty of fidelity to such principal.

(c) A licensee has an affirmative duty to keep the principal informed at all times of significant information applicable to the transaction or transactions in which the licensee is acting as an agent for the principal.

(d) A licensee has a duty to convey accurate information to members of the public with whom the licensee deals.

TREC Rule § 537.11 Use of Standard Contract Forms

(a) When negotiating contracts binding the sale, exchange, option, lease or rental of any interest in real property, a real estate licensee shall use only those contract forms promulgated by the Texas Real

Estate Commission (the commission) for that kind of transaction with the following exceptions:

(1) transactions in which the licensee is functioning solely as a principal, not as an agent...

(b) A licensee may not: . . .

(3) give advice or opinions as to the legal effect of any contracts or other such instruments which may affect the title to real estate; . . .

(c) Nothing in this section shall be deemed to limit the licensee's **fiduciary obligation** to disclose to **the licensee's principals** all pertinent facts which are within the knowledge of the licensee, including such facts which might affect the status of or title to real estate.

(d) A licensee may not undertake to draw or prepare legal documents fixing and defining the legal rights of **the principals** to a real estate transaction. . . .

(f) When filling in a form authorized for use by this section, the licensee may only fill in the blanks provided and may not add to or strike matter from such form, except that licensees shall add factual statements and business details desired by the principals and shall strike only such matter as is desired by the principals and as is necessary to conform the instrument to the intent of the parties. . . .

(h) Nothing in this section shall be deemed to prevent the licensee from explaining to **the principals** the meaning of the factual statements and business details contained in the said instrument so long as the licensee does not offer or give legal advice. . . .

(l) Where it appears that, prior to the execution of any such instrument, there are unusual matters involved in the transaction which should be resolved by legal counsel **before** the instrument is executed or the instrument is to be acknowledged and filed for record, the licensee **shall** advise **the principals** that each should consult a lawyer of the principal's choice **before** executing same.

(m) A licensee may not employ, directly or indirectly, a lawyer nor pay for the services of a lawyer to represent **any principal** to a real estate transaction in which the licensee is acting as an agent. The licensee may employ and pay for the services of a lawyer to represent only the licensee in a real estate transaction, including preparation of the contract, agreement, or other legal instruments to be executed by **the principals** to the transactions.

(n) A licensee shall advise **the principals** that the instrument they are about to execute is binding on them.

(emphasis added)

■ ROLES PEOPLE PLAY IN AGENCY RELATIONSHIPS

In this book, we use many terms that describe the relationships created as a result of real estate transactions. The following list of terms will help you understand the roles that real estate professionals and other parties play and the terminology used in TRELA, TREC Rules, this book, the National Association of REALTORS® Code of Ethics, and in the real estate industry in general. You will notice that the terms may overlap at times, and several terms may apply to a single participant in a transaction.

Using correct terminology is essential in a real estate transaction to properly describe parties, roles, and actions. Using the wrong terminology can send the wrong message and cause confusion. Consider the following:

- Don't say "agent" when you mean "licensee."
- Don't say "contract" when you mean "offer."
- Don't say "my" customer when you mean "the" customer. Possessive pronouns may indicate to a court that an agency relationship exists when it was not intended. An agent or subagent who represents an owner should never refer to a buyer or tenant customer as "my customer" or "my buyer," but rather "the buyer" or "the tenant."
- Don't say "appointed agent" when you mean "appointed licensee" or "appointed license holder."
- Don't say "represent you both" when you mean "act as an intermediary between you both."
- Don't say "agency disclosure" or "disclosure of agency" when you mean "information about brokerage services." The Information About Brokerage Services (IABS) form is not a "disclosure of agency" form. There is no official form "disclosing an agency relationship" that you might have with any particular party to a transaction. The disclosure of your agency relationship may be done orally or in writing, and the IABS does neither.
- Don't say "REALTOR®" when you just mean a "broker" or "salesperson." The term *REALTOR*® can only be used to refer to someone who is a member of the National Association of REALTORS® (NAR).
- Don't say "cooperating agent" when you mean "buyer's agent" or "buyer broker."
- Don't say "selling agent" when you mean "buyer's agent" or "buyer broker."

> Buyer broker and buyer's broker refer to the same individual and are both commonly used in practice.

With that said, let's look at some roles and definitions and try to clarify some terms.

- **Broker**—For purposes of the TRELA, "Broker" means a person who in exchange **for a commission** or other valuable consideration or with expectation of receiving a commission or other valuable consideration **performs for another person** one of a list of many separate acts that constitute acting as a broker (see TRELA § 1101.002.(1)).
- **Unlicensed broker**—A person who performs any of the acts described in the TRELA definition of "Broker," for another person, for a fee or other valuable consideration without first obtaining a license as a broker. Such an act of a broker by a person who is not licensed as a broker violates the License Act and is punishable as a Class A misdemeanor and is also grounds for TREC to impose an administrative penalty under Subchapter O of TRELA § 1101.702 of up to $5,000 for each violation and "each day a violation continues may be considered a separate violation for purposes of imposing the penalty."

- **REALTOR®**—A licensed broker or salesperson who is a member of the National Association of REALTORS®. There are many licensees who are not members of NAR.
- **REALTIST®**—A member of the National Association of Real Estate Brokers (NAREB), the largest and oldest minority trade association in America.
- **Licensee (active)**—A person licensed by the Texas Real Estate Commission (TREC) to act as a broker or a salesperson in a real estate transaction. The definition also includes a licensee who may not necessarily be acting as a broker or a salesperson at that specific time.
- **Licensee (inactive)**—A person licensed by the Texas Real Estate Commission (TREC) but not authorized to conduct business as a broker or a salesperson until the license is converted to active status.
- **License holder**—A broker or a salesperson licensed by TREC; also called a licensee.
- **Agent**—(1) A broker who represents a seller, landlord, buyer, or tenant. (2) Salespersons or broker licensees who represent the broker with whom they are associated. (All references in the text to the broker's duties and responsibilities to the principal also apply to salespersons and broker associates in the firm, except where a broker acts an intermediary. In that case, an "appointed license holder" may have privileges that the broker does not have.)
- **Subagent**—A license holder not sponsored by or associated with the client's broker but who is representing the client through a cooperative agreement with the client's broker. (Like a buyer broker, a subagent may be referred to in a TREC-promulgated contract form as "other broker" to distinguish either a subagent or a buyer broker from being associated with the listing broker)
- **Dual agent**—Someone who represents both parties in a real estate transaction. As of June 1, 2003, "dual agency" is prohibited and is an illegal role for a real estate licensee to play in a real estate transaction. Instead, TRELA § 1101.561(b) states the following: "A broker **must agree to act as an intermediary** under this subchapter if the broker agrees to represent in a transaction (1) a buyer or tenant; **and** (2) a seller or landlord." (emphasis added). If the dual agency is undisclosed, the licensee acting as an undisclosed dual agent, could face charges of "constructive fraud" as well as loss of license.
- **Broker licensee**—An individual holding a broker's license issued by TREC. Brokers may act independently in conducting real estate transactions or may engage other broker or salesperson licensees to represent them in the conduct of their real estate business.
- **Sponsoring broker**—The broker through whom the salesperson's active license is issued and who assumes responsibility for the real estate brokerage activities of that salesperson.
- **Fiduciary**—As a noun, fiduciary means a person having the character of a trustee, who must act in scrupulous good faith and candor toward the person who has placed that trust in the fiduciary. As an adjective, fiduciary means that the duties owed have the characteristic of being analogous to a trust or being founded on a trust or confidence, as in a fiduciary duty of loyalty. As used in context by the Rules of the Texas Real Estate Commission (§ 531.1), the duties of a fiduciary include (1) representing the interests of the agent's client, (2) being faithful and observant to the trust placed in the agent,

(3) being scrupulous and meticulous in performing the agent's functions, and (4) placing no personal interest above that of the agent's client.

- **Salesperson licensee**—An individual holding a salesperson's license issued by TREC, an agent of the sponsoring broker. Salesperson licensees may conduct business only through and under the authority of their sponsoring brokers.
- **Broker associate**—A broker associated with and conducting business as an agent of another broker who accepts responsibility for the broker associate's brokerage activities.
- **Sales associate**—A salesperson licensee associated with and conducting business as an agent of the sponsoring broker.
- **Seller's agent**—A broker (and his agents) representing the seller in a real estate transaction. Also called seller's broker, listing broker, or listing agent.
- **Buyer's agent**—A broker representing the buyer in a real estate transaction.
- **Intermediary**—A statutorily modified and limited agency alternative permitting the broker to act as a modified agent for both a buyer-"client" and a seller-"client" in the same transaction. Note: The use of quotation marks around the term *client* is intended to denote that the term is being used in a modified sense not anticipated in TREC Rule § 531.1 but allowed under TRELA intermediary statutes.
- **Landlord's agent**—A broker and the broker's agents representing a landlord in a real estate transaction. Often called an owner's agent so that the same term can be used for both a seller and a landlord.
- **Tenant's agent**—A broker (and the broker's agents) representing a tenant in a real estate transaction.
- **Client**—A person, who in law is frequently called a principal, who engages services that include the professional advice and advocacy of another, called an agent, and whose interests are protected by the specific duties and loyalties of an agent in an agency relationship.
- **Client** (as used in NAR Code of Ethics)—"As used in this Code of Ethics, 'client' means the person(s) or entity(ies) with whom a REALTOR® or a REALTOR®'s firm has an agency **or legally recognized non-agency relationship**." (emphasis added)

  Under the NAR definition of client, both the seller and the buyer in an intermediary transaction could be called clients of the same broker in the same transaction; however, under the TREC-implied definition of client in § 531.1, they could not be called clients because primary duties of loyalty and full disclosure are missing in an intermediary transaction.
- **Customer**—A person who receives limited brokerage services without establishing an agency relationship. Specifically, advice, advocacy, and fiduciary relationships are not included in customer services. NAR's definition of a customer is "a party to a real estate transaction who receives information, services, or benefits **but has no contractual relationship** with the REALTOR® or the REALTOR®'s firm."
- **Other broker**—A broker involved as a broker in a real estate transaction who is not affiliated with the listing broker. "Other broker" is an agency-neutral term in that, by itself, it does not indicate who it is that the "other broker" represents. That is why it is now used in the TREC contract forms instead of "cooperating agent" or "selling agent," as previously was the case.

- **Appointed license holder**—An agent of a broker who is acting as intermediary. The appointed license holder may give opinions and advice to the party to whom the licensee is appointed, while the broker is prohibited by law from giving such advice and must remain "impartial." Such appointment must be made in writing and consented to by the parties. If appointments are not made or not made in writing with the approval of the two principals, then any licensees in the firm acting in the transaction must behave as though they are intermediaries and remain "impartial" and cannot give advice or opinions to either party. This is a role that is not well defined.

- **Party**—One of the principals to an agreement (e.g., the buyer or the seller). The broker is not a party to the real estate transaction; however, the broker is a party to the listing agreement or the buyer representation agreement.

- **Parties**—In a real estate transaction, both the buyer and the seller, or both the landlord and the tenant. Not the broker. However, in an owner or buyer/tenant representation agreement, the broker is one of the parties. The broker is a party in these types of agreements. Therefore, a broker is free to develop the kind of representation agreement he can get with an owner or a buyer. TREC, with minor exceptions, does not regulate the terms of these agreements.

- **"The** principals" versus "**the licensee's** principals," as used in TREC Rules—When the Rules use the phrase "**the** principals," they mean the two parties to the transaction, regardless of the licensee's agency relationship to them (e.g., the buyer **and** the seller, or the landlord **and** the tenant). When the TREC Rules use a possessive in front of the term "principals," they mean the one party that the licensee represents. (e.g., either the owner or the buyer/tenant, but not both)

- **Prospect**—As used in and for the purposes of NAR's Code, "prospect means a purchaser, seller, tenant, or landlord who is **not subject to a representation relationship** with the REALTOR® or REALTOR®'s firm." The term "prospect" is not defined in state law. However, in the Texas Association of REALTOR® "INTERMEDIARY RELATIONSHIP NOTICE," the term "'prospect' means the above named buyer or tenant for the Property." In this instance, the prospect is actually a client or principal of the broker and cannot be defined by the NAR definition of prospect.

- **Offeror**—The offeror is the person making the offer. The offeror may withdraw an offer at any time before its acceptance by the offeree.

- **Offeree**—The offeree is the person on the receiving end of the offer. The offeree, legally speaking, has the greater power because the offeree has the power to bind the offeror by accepting the offeror's offer. The offeree can also reject the offer.

- **Cooperating agent or cooperating broker**—A misleading and misused term of art that has no legal definition. It is a term that should describe only the broker or agent in a second brokerage firm in a transaction who brings a buyer to the transaction but is not a buyer's broker and is also not affiliated with the listing brokerage. The cooperating agent only operates as a subagent for the seller under agency law. Buyer agents don't cooperate, they compete. Buyer agents should not be thought of as selling agents. They are not assisting the seller in selling, they are assisting a buyer in buying or a purchaser in purchasing. They are more properly termed buyer's agents or purchasing agents.

The agency relationships that individuals playing these roles can enter into, and how they are to be entered into properly, are discussed in more detail in the following chapters. As you study the subject of agency, it is important that you pay close attention to the relationships that are created and begin to understand how these relationships and terms affect the way you will relate to the person or entity you are working with or for in your real estate transactions.

■ CLIENT OR CUSTOMER?

It is important to have a clear understanding of the difference between a client and a customer. The extent of services that a licensee can offer is determined by the legally recognized relationships established with buyers, tenants, and owners.

A real estate licensee who represents a party in a transaction is that party's agent. The party represented is the agent's principal and is frequently referred to as the agent's client. The person represented may be an owner, a buyer, or a tenant. For example, owner O wants to sell to buyer B. O is represented by broker X, and buyer B is represented by broker Y.

- To broker X, O is a client
- To broker X, B is a customer
- To broker Y, O is a customer
- To broker Y, B is a client.
- If buyer B is unrepresented, B is still a customer to broker X

Likewise, if owner O is a FSBO (For Sale by Owner), then broker Y will only negotiate for buyer B and O will have no agent and no representation.

X and Y can both give advice, opinions, and advocacy to each of their own clients but not to customers. Each must attempt to get the best price possible for each agent's own client.

X, as agent/fiduciary to owner O, should also see to it that, for the benefit of O, X transmits O's Seller Disclosure of Property Condition form to buyer B before O and B enter into a contract.

■ WHY STUDY AGENCY?

REASON 1: Increased Litigation Against Real Estate Licensees

There are many good reasons to study agency law, but a key explanation for the greater interest in agency is increasing litigation in this area of real estate practice. A real estate lawsuit usually results from something other than agency issues, such as breach of contract, misrepresentation, or a decision by one of the contracting parties to rescind a contract. After most lawsuits are filed, however, the issue of who represented whom frequently becomes the focal point. Licensees may not have adequately discussed or disclosed whom they represent. Therefore, a lawyer seeking to set aside a transaction may search for an undisclosed, often unintended, agency relationship. For example, a lawyer interviewing a buyer-client before filing an action based on misrepresentation or constructive fraud might ask the buyer the following:

- "How were you treated by the licensee who represented you?"
- "Did you think that the licensee was your agent?"
- "Did you sign a written agreement whereby the licensee agreed to represent you?"
- "Did you know that the licensee with whom you were working was really the legal agent of the seller?"
- "How do you feel about that now?"
- "Were the duties of an intermediary explained adequately to you?"
- "Did you give your written consent for the licensee to act as an intermediary before negotiations began or an offer was made?"
- "Did you give your written consent to have a licensee appointed to you and another to be appointed to the other party?"

An undisclosed or inadequately disclosed agency relationship might result in the licensee's representation of both parties without their permission to do so—a circumstance strictly prohibited by law. Such undisclosed relationships can be grounds for not paying a brokerage commission or may be used as a basis to rescind a purchase contract between a buyer and a seller. Many potential problems, even lawsuits, may be avoided by adherence to timely and accurate agency disclosure requirements. These same failures, if the subject of complaints to TREC, may also create grounds for disciplinary action from TREC, which could include loss of license, as well as substantial monetary penalties.

REASON 2: Confusion Regarding Whom the Licensee Represents

As implied in the introduction to this chapter, what at first may appear quite simple can be complex and confusing to the participants in a real estate transaction. In some transactions, the buyers and the sellers (and licensees as well) are not sure whether a licensee is an agent for the seller, the buyer, both, or neither. Why? Because it is the nature of a real estate licensee to be solicitous, friendly, and service driven. This behavior can be misconstrued as implying an agency relationship to a customer.

In 1995, the Texas State Legislature passed and made effective on January 1, 1996, TRELA § 1101.558(a);(b);(c);(d), which requires the exact language in a written statement about forms of agency relationships to be given to a party to a real estate transaction at the time of the first substantive dialogue with the party relating to a specific real property. There was no format prescribed for the statement in the Act, except that it must be in at least 10-point type. TREC then came up with an optional format that fulfilled the requirements of the Act and added the title Information About Brokerage Services (IABS) to the form, along with a few statements at the top of the form and a place for signatures of the persons receiving the form. None of those TREC additions to the form, including the name IABS were or are required by the Act or by TREC.

The required "written statement" (as contained in the IABS) does not disclose the licensee's agency relationship to anyone. The Act clearly states that the disclosure of the licensee's agency relationship may be made "orally or in writing" and that disclosure must be made at "first contact" with the other party to the transaction or to the agent of the other party.

The question of whether an agency relationship in a real estate transaction has been created is a question of fact—that is, one that a judge or a jury might be called on to determine. The particular circumstances of each case must be examined to determine whether the agent represents the buyer, the seller, or both. Because of the ease with which agency relationships may be created and in the absence of any required formalities or written agreements, a real estate licensee may be held to be an unwitting agent in a so-called unintended or accidental agency. In essence, if you act as the advisor for any party or give opinions to any party, you may find that you have unintentionally become the "agent" for that party. William D. North, past executive vice president of the National Association of REAL-TORS® (NAR), stated, "It's often hard to tell which party the broker represents, and both the buyer and seller are apt to visualize the broker as their broker."

A jury might find that the conduct of both the licensee and the consumer demonstrated that the consumer authorized the licensee to act on the consumer's behalf and that the licensee did so, thus creating a principal-agent relationship. Such a finding has serious legal, economic, and ethical consequences to brokers, salespersons, sellers, and buyers because both the Texas courts and the Texas Real Estate Commission tend to hold the licensee responsible should consumers misunderstand the role the licensee played in the transaction. TRELA § 1101.652(7) says that TREC can discipline a licensee who "fails to make clear to all parties to a real estate transaction the party for whom the license holder is acting." Notice here that language is not "tell," "inform," or "disclose," but instead is "fails to make clear to all parties."

REASON 3: Public Perceptions

Perhaps you have noticed the way the media portray real estate licensees. The image is often one of greedy, fast-talking salespersons whose primary purpose is to line their pockets with commissions while showing little regard for buyers and sellers. Granted, some licensees richly deserve such an image; however, many more try their best to be honest, knowledgeable professionals who make every effort to conduct their business in an ethical manner. An understanding of agency law is the foundation for sound business practices that will guide real estate professionals in their daily activities and help in changing public perceptions about the real estate industry.

REASON 4: Emotional Aspects

Unlike the purchase or sale of many items, a real estate transaction is frequently charged with emotion. Buyers, hopeful of realizing a part of the American dream through home ownership, are also faced with the prospect of a fearfully large financial obligation. Sellers, perhaps eager to improve their lifestyle, are sometimes struck with the prospect of leaving behind years of memories attached to the home they are selling. As a result of these high emotions, a small issue may blossom into a major event between the parties. Licensees who fail to understand and accommodate these emotional aspects will frequently lose the trust and confidence of the principals and have a difficult time becoming successful in the real estate business. Understanding the roles that licensees play also helps the professional maintain a clear sense of purpose and direction during such emotional periods.

REASON 5: Complexity

Buying a home is an investment decision, as well as a practical consideration. Transactions are becoming increasingly more complex in terms of property disclosures, inspection issues, land surveys, mineral interests, and of course financing. Today many consumers buy, sell, and buy again. Each time increases the consumer's understanding of the importance of receiving sound, objective advice and opinions, in addition to accurate information about the property under consideration. These repeat buyers and sellers recognize the distinction between advice and information, especially with so much money at stake. Many less experienced consumers, however, do not understand that as customers, they are entitled to any accurate, relevant information the licensee might possess, but as clients they are additionally entitled to advice and opinions, such as suggested negotiating strategies in light of the other party's marketing position.

REASON 6: Greater Consumer Expectations

Buyers seek representation more frequently in today's market because consumer education has led to their understanding the benefits of the agency relationship. Both the buyer and the seller increasingly have come to expect professionalism and competence from real estate licensees. After all, state licensing requirements demand a higher knowledge and competency level for brokers and salespersons than for the average person. A judicial trend has emerged away from the tradition of caveat emptor (let the buyer beware) and toward greater consumer protection and professional accountability on the part of the real estate licensee. Frequently, real estate licensees are the most visible experts in the transaction, and both the buyer and the seller tend to defer to the judgment and skill of the real estate professional. Seasoned real estate professionals are acutely aware of their importance and wisely know when to defer to another professional a matter not within the licensee's area of responsibility or expertise.

REASON 7: Use of More Than One Broker

A Federal Trade Commission (FTC) study on national residential brokerage practices noted that 66% of the home sales studied involved two brokers or salespersons, and more than half involved the services of two brokerage firms. With two brokers participating in one transaction, each working a different side of the transaction, it is not surprising that buyers and sellers sometimes question whom the participating brokers really represent. To some, it seems a natural division of labor for the listing broker to represent the seller and the other broker, the buyer. In practice, however, many buyers are surprised to learn that the salesperson they regard as "theirs" actually represents the seller. The surge in buyer brokerage is, no doubt, due in part to better information regarding the services available from brokers and more complete disclosure of agency relationships.

REASON 8: Greater Licensee Professionalism

In the past, the listing broker was hired primarily to find a buyer for the seller's property. Today, it is likely that another broker will find the buyer. Sellers look to listing brokers to protect their best financial interests in the form of professional advice and opinions as to the soundness of a buyer's offer. Buyers usually look to the licensees who introduce them to the property to provide the same service.

Many licensees now emphasize the variety and quality of services they offer rather than their salesmanship and matchmaking skills. Real estate licensees promote themselves as advisors, problem solvers, and data interpreters rather than solely as information providers. Licensees are expected to be generally knowledgeable in such areas as taxation, law, mortgage planning, contract preparation, investment analysis, finance, appraisal, and property management. The law and the industry itself are demanding higher standards of skill, care, and due diligence from brokers in promoting clients' best interests, in furnishing required disclosures, in treating everyone honestly, in spotting potential problems, and in recommending the use of experts when necessary.

REASON 9: State Agency Disclosure Laws

Nearly every state, including Texas, has passed legislation requiring real estate licensees to disclose whom they represent in each transaction. Some state laws permit simple oral disclosure; other laws mandate the use of specific disclosure forms. In all cases, the licensee faces the likelihood that the buyer or the seller will want to know what the licensee's role will be. Licensees who are not comfortable discussing their role may find the prospective client or customer seeking a more competent real estate licensee.

REASON 10: Required Topic of Study for Potential Licensees

For some, the most compelling reason to study agency law is the educational requirement mandated by the Texas legislature in 1993. The law, as implemented by TREC, requires that all applicants for licensure show evidence that a minimum of 30 clock hours (2 semester hours) in Law of Agency has been completed from an acceptable source of study.

■ RELATIONSHIPS BETWEEN PRINCIPAL AND AGENT

Numerous legal and practical relational roles occur in any given real estate transaction between a principal and the agent. It can be very difficult to know how law applies in every situation you encounter. What happens when you misunderstand how your daily conduct in the everyday business of acting as an agent violates law or your duty?

In any given part of a transaction, with any given party, there are three very important things to know:

- What to do
- How to do it
- When to do it

Real estate licensees have many roles in real estate transactions. At any given time in a transaction, they might act as advocates, negotiators (impartial negotiator "between" the parties, as well as agent/advocate negotiator "for" only one party), mediators, facilitators, arbitrators, counselors, and salespeople.

When is it appropriate to perform the duties associated with these roles?

When you are at an owner's property and are attempting to list that property for sale or lease, you are not an agent for the owner at that time. You are a negotiator for your own interests or the interests of your broker. You must deal honestly and fairly with the owner, but you are free, within limits, to negotiate numerous conditions of the listing. Some examples of these negotiating points are

- the price at which your firm will agree to take the listing,
- commissions,
- listing termination dates,
- extent of fiduciary duties,
- waivers of certain duties that would otherwise be required by operation of law. (e.g., loyalty may be waived in order to perform impartially as an intermediary), or
- duties to communicate all offers after the happening of certain events.

Once your negotiations for your broker's best interests in the listing agreement are complete and you have a signed listing agreement for your broker to become the agent for the owner, your role shifts as you now take on your broker's role as agent/fiduciary to the owner. You are no longer a salesperson trying to sell the owner your and your broker's services. From this point on, your interests and your broker's best interests in the transaction must be subordinated to the best interests of your client. Your broker's best interests have now been agreed to in the listing. You are no longer a negotiator for yourself or your broker but a negotiator for your owner/client against all other future buyer/tenant customers that may be interested in purchasing, leasing, or renting your client's property. You now become an advocate for your client's interests in all negotiations and a counselor to your client. You are not a mediator or arbitrator or mere facilitator, although some of the skills used in those roles will be evident in your professional conduct. Your duty is not to get a deal done so you can win a contest in your brokerage or a bonus for yourself or even just earn your commission so you can pay your bills. Your legal duty to your client is spelled out in TREC Rules § 156 (a–c), which are quoted previously in this chapter. It is so important that it bears repeating and reemphasizing throughout the text:

> (a) A licensee's relationship with the licensee's principal is that of a fiduciary. . . .
>
> (b) The licensee must put the interests of the licensee's principal above the licensee's own interests. . . . The licensee **represents only the principal and owes a duty of fidelity** to such principal.
>
> (c) A licensee has an affirmative duty to keep the principal informed at all times of significant information applicable to the transaction or transactions in which the licensee is acting as an agent for the principal.

Additionally, you have some other legal duties to the other party, the party that you **do not represent** in the transaction. Note that neither the TREC Rules nor TRELA refer to the other party as the customer. TREC Rule § 156(a) states that "a licensee must deal honestly and fairly with all parties." According to TRELA § 156 (d), "a licensee has a duty to convey accurate information to members of the public with whom the licensee deals."

Keep in mind that dealing honestly and fairly does not mean treating the nonclient "equally" relative to your client/principal.

Dealing honestly does not mean telling the non-client or the non-client's agent everything you know. For instance, you must give your client/principal your opinion regarding what the property could/should sell for, usually via a broker's price opinion (BPO) or a comparative market analysis (CMA, also known as a competitive market analysis). However, your fiduciary duties **do not permit** you to share those opinions with the other party nor with any other brokers or their agents representing other parties, or even with outside entities, **unless your client requires it or permits you to release such confidential information** to others. Any exceptions to the confidentiality of your price opinions should be stated in writing in your listing agreement, and you should make sure any releases from certain otherwise fiduciary duties are written and in nonambiguous, clear language.

Even in an intermediary situation, where, by law, some fiduciary duties, such as full disclosure and loyalty, cannot be carried out, the following rules apply regarding confidential information:

> **TRELA §1101.651(d)** A broker **and any broker or salesperson appointed** under §1101.560 **who acts as an intermediary** under subchapter 1 **may not**: (1) **disclose** to the buyer or tenant that the seller or landlord will accept a price less than the asking price, unless otherwise instructed in a separate writing by the seller or landlord; (2) **disclose** to the seller or landlord that the buyer or tenant will pay a price greater than the price submitted in a written offer to the seller or landlord, unless otherwise instructed in a separate writing by the buyer or tenant; (3) **disclose** any confidential information or any information a party specifically instructs the broker or salesperson in writing not to disclose, **unless**: (a) the broker or salesperson is otherwise instructed in a separate writing by the respective party; (b) the broker or salesperson is required to disclose the information by this chapter or a court order; or (c) the information materially relates to the condition of the property.

■ SUMMARY

From the most basic residential real estate transaction to the most complex commercial contract, it is important to understand whom the licensee represents and what services can or cannot be provided in accordance with Texas law. There exists an increased interest in clarifying agency issues, precipitated by agency disclosure laws, the growth in buyer agency, and the expanded professional liability lawsuits, as well as TREC discipline against real estate licensees resulting in larger and larger financial penalties against license holders.

By developing a positive and applied awareness of agency relationships, the real estate professional, when acting as an agent, will be able to adapt to consumer demands for greater and more professional representation in today's real estate marketplace.

■ KEY POINTS

■ An agent is one who acts on behalf of another—the principal or client.

■ The Real Estate License Act (TRELA) is the statutory law that establishes, to some extent, the duties of real estate licensees in Texas. To a greater extent, TRELA establishes the conduct a licensee is not permitted to engage in, and provides serious penalties for doing what is prohibited. The Texas Real Estate Commission (TREC) administers TRELA and is empowered by TRELA to make rules in furtherance of the statute. These rules are contained in the Texas Administrative Code (TAC). Many of the affirmative duties of real estate licensees, acting as agents, are contained in the Rules rather than TRELA.

■ A real estate licensee may work **for** a client in a principal-agent relationship or work **with** a customer in a nonagency relationship. A client has a legal right to expect accurate information, advice, informed opinions, and advocacy. A customer has a legal right to expect fair treatment, accurate information, referral to sources when advice or advocacy is demanded by the circumstance and the knowledge and sophistication of the consumer, and the seller's honest disclosure of a subject property's condition. The agent must also disclose defects in the property's condition, if the agent knows such information.

■ An undisclosed, underdisclosed, or accidental agency relationship may create an unauthorized representation of more than one party and could result in a lawsuit for rescission, forfeiture of commission, money damages, loss of license, or disciplinary action.

■ The study of agency is important because of misunderstandings among the public and licensees regarding agency issues, the complexities of real estate transactions, the presence of more than one broker in transactions, the growing demand for buyer representation, state disclosure laws, and the escalation of lawsuits resulting from problems in real estate transactions.

■ SUGGESTIONS FOR BROKERS

Develop a written company agency disclosure policy that emphasizes awareness of the various agency situations salespersons will encounter in daily practice. Establish training programs within your firm that will allow your sales staff to become comfortable in understanding and disclosing whom they represent (or don't represent), consistent with your established company policy. The lack of a clear company agency policy may easily lead to unlawful actions by the associated licensees of the broker. (The TREC holds the broker responsible for the professional acts of all licensees associated with the broker.) Train your agents in the proper use of terminology in real estate roles and duties.

CHAPTER 1 QUIZ

1. Agency is
   a. a real estate brokerage.
   b. the operation of a business.
   c. one person acting on behalf of another.
   d. one person giving advice to another person.

2. An agent works on behalf of
   a. a customer.
   b. a client.
   c. both a customer and a client.
   d. neither a customer nor a client.

3. TRELA
   a. enforces the License Act.
   b. may appoint an administrator for the TREC.
   c. is a primary law that regulates the conduct of real estate licensees.
   d. is the law established by the TREC in its rule-making authority.

4. The Texas Real Estate Commission
   a. does not hold the broker accountable for the actions of sponsored associates.
   b. holds the broker accountable for the professional actions of sponsored associates.
   c. holds buyers or sellers accountable for the acts of their real estate brokers and salespeople.
   d. holds the public accountable for the acts of real estate licensees.

5. B, a broker, is representing Smith, a buyer. In a real estate transaction, Smith is considered a(n)
   a. customer of B
   b. fiduciary of B
   c. client of B
   d. agent for B

6. A person who engages an agent to represent her interests in a transaction is called a client, or
   a. a customer of the agent.
   b. a seller.
   c. a buyer.
   d. the agent's principal.

7. A key distinction between the services given to clients versus those given to customers is that
   a. advice, opinions, and advocacy are given to clients, not customers.
   b. more advice and opinions are offered to the customer.
   c. customers get advice and opinions free, while clients must pay.
   d. clients must have a contract to receive services, while customers do not.

8. A licensee *NOT* associated with the listing broker who represents the seller through the listing broker is known as a(n)
   a. buyer's agent.
   b. intermediary.
   c. seller's agent.
   d. subagent.

9. One of the *BEST* ways a broker might protect against agency problems is to
   a. never represent buyers.
   b. never discuss agency issues with the parties.
   c. always treat both parties as valued customers and treat them fairly, giving them both the same level of service.
   d. develop a clear, written office policy regarding agency issues and require that it be followed by the broker's agents.

10. An important reason to study agency today is
    a. to better represent customers.
    b. the increased litigation against agents.
    c. to be able to settle legal disputes between buyers and sellers.
    d. that commissions are greater to the agent when agency law is followed.

DISCUSSION QUESTIONS

1. What types of services might a typical buyer expect of or from a licensee?

2. What types of services might a typical seller expect of or from a licensee?

3. What are some of the emotions that a buyer and a seller may experience in a real estate transaction?

4. What are some of the reasons for the increased interest in agency?

5. What is the essential difference between a client and a customer?

2

Basic Agency Relationships, Disclosure, and Duties to the Client

In real estate transactions, a variety of agency relationships may be created. For this reason, agency relationships must be clearly defined and recognized so they don't become a source of confusion and misunderstanding to buyers, sellers, real estate salespersons, brokers, lawyers, and judges. As discussed in Chapter 1, misunderstandings and preconceived notions about a party's right to representation or misunderstood and misapplied terminology often create roadblocks to greater understanding. They give rise to disagreements, lawsuits, TREC disciplinary actions, and even consumer complaints to professional real estate associations with accompanying disciplinary action on the part of these associations.

■ **LEARNING OBJECTIVES**   *This chapter addresses the following:*

- ■ Agency Defined
- ■ Authority of Agent
  - — Authority of Agent Under TRELA
- ■ Classifications of Agency
  - — Universal Agency
  - — General Agency
  - — Special Agency
  - — The Flow of Authority
- ■ Fiduciary Duties and Responsibilities
  - — Professional Codes and Texas Canons
  - — Reasonable Care and Diligence
  - — Obedience
  - — Loyalty
  - — Disclosure
  - — Confidentiality
  - — Accounting
  - — Minimum Service Requirements
- ■ Information About Brokerage Services and Disclosure of Representation

■ AGENCY DEFINED

As we learned in the previous chapter, agency occurs when one person, the agent, acts on behalf of another person, the principal, and under that person's control. The person in control of the agent's conduct is generally called the principal or "client." Many of the basic doctrines of agency are common to all businesses. Some agency duties differ in different types of business relations and are governed more by statute or regulation than by common law.

The term "licensee" includes both a licensed salesperson and a licensed broker. A salesperson/licensee is a general agent of a broker/licensee. Both the broker and the salesperson typically become special agents of any client/principal. TRELA itself has generally replaced the term "licensee" with the term "license holder." Either term can reference a broker or a salesperson.

It is worth noting here that real estate brokers or licensee associates should not be called agents when referring to them in relation to the public until an actual expressed agency relationship has been established. Of course, the licensees sponsored by or affiliated with the broker are always agents of the broker, but as far as the public is concerned, where no contract to represent a party has been formed, either by express or implied agreement with a public member, they are merely brokers, salespersons, licensees or license holders, but not agents.

After an agency relationship has been established between a member of the public and the broker, the broker is called the agent of the client and the licensee associates are called agents of the broker and act as agents of the broker's client. As agents of the broker, licensee associates (real estate salespersons or broker associates) owe the same duties to the broker's client/principal as the sponsoring broker owes to the client.

The agency relationship is established between the real estate broker and the broker's client/principal. All licensees in that office, as agents of the broker, are obligated to recognize that agency relationship and have the same duties to the principal as the broker. For instance, even the licensees in the firm who are not involved in the transaction must not divulge confidential information about the client to any other persons or parties.

The wise agent will not discuss a client's confidences, even with members of the brokerage. Even at sales meetings and luncheons. Confidential information should be kept on a strictly "need to know" basis within the firm.

The agents of the broker do not have "privity of contract" with the client because both the owner representation agreement and the buyer/tenant representation agreement are in the name of the broker. Why is that important? You, as your broker's agent, without privity of contract with the client, cannot sue the client for your commission. Only your broker can sue the client to enforce the commission agreement; however, you do have privity of contract with your broker. Your broker, as your principal, owes you the duty of compensation if you accomplish the tasks agreed to in your compensation agreement with your broker. If your broker will not enforce his rights to compensation under the listing agreement or buyer/tenant representation agreement, then you may attempt to enforce your rights to your commission against your broker. If you and your broker are REALTORS®, you may be prohibited from suing your broker and may have to submit your dispute to mediation or binding arbitration per Article 17 of the NAR Code of Ethics. TREC will not help you get your commission. That is not TREC's job. TREC Rule § 535.42 states, "The commission does not . . . mediate disputes between or among licensees concerning entitlement to sales commissions."

■ AUTHORITY OF AGENT

A very important and basic principle of agency and the authority of an agent is that "agency is always consensual." Both parties—the agent and the principal—must consent to the arrangement either by contract or by operation of law or both. The dangerous aspect of this consent principle is that the consent need not necessarily be express consent either orally or in writing. In some cases, a court may hold that the consent, though not expressed, was implied by the actions of the parties. In other cases, the courts may hold that an agent, in the absence of written or oral authority, had "apparent authority" and thus held to be an agent of the principal.

The authority of the agent always stems from, and derives its power from, the consent of both the principal and the agent. Whether that consent is found to be express authority by the principal and consent by the agent to accept the authority to be granted, or implied in fact or implied in law, is a matter for the courts to decide. An agency relationship is at its heart a form of contract and like a contract, to be valid, there must be offer and acceptance and mutual agreement. Whether the licensee is offering to list and sell or represent a party or whether the party is offering to allow the representation by the agent, the basic form is still that of contract. A key element of the agreement of an agent with a principal to be the principal's agent is that the principal is in control of the agent's conduct on the principal's behalf. With that control, comes the downside for the principal—liability for the conduct of the principal's agent when the agent is acting within the scope of the authority granted to the agent.

Let's look at an example of one of the practical consequences of consent or lack of consent in an everyday real estate situation:

> Broker Bre has listed owner Oliver's property for sale or lease on an exclusive agency agreement for a term of 180 days. Sixty days into the listing period, when Oliver learns that Bre refused to allow a buyer's broker's attempt to present an offer to Oliver, Oliver becomes highly dissatisfied with Bre's lack of activity, communications, and general nonperformance of Bre's promised duties to him. Oliver sends an email to Bre saying, "You're fired! I am terminating my listing with you." Bre responds, "You can't do that. I have a written agreement for a period of 180 days signed by you. I still have 120 days left, and I intend to keep marketing your property and get my commission if I produce an offer from a ready, willing, and able buyer or tenant under the terms of our agreement." Oliver does not respond.

> Is Bre legally allowed to continue to try to represent Oliver and act as his agent? No. Bre must cease all representation activities immediately upon receipt of Oliver's first email telling Bre she is fired, because Oliver withdrew his consent. Bre no longer has Oliver's authority to act as Oliver's agent. However, Bre is still bound by the fiduciary duty of confidentiality of all information relating to Oliver and any information derived from Oliver during the 60 days Bre was Oliver's agent. However, that may not be the end of the story. Bre now may have the ability to bring a lawsuit against Oliver for wrongful termination and ask the court to compel Oliver to compensate Bre for all the monetary damages incurred by Bre in pursuit of Oliver's objectives under the listing agreement. Regardless, Bre is still terminated and can no longer act as Oliver's agent.

> That still may not be the whole story. Bre now attempts to sue Oliver for Bre's commission under the terms of the previous listing agreement. At trial, Oliver proves Bre breached Bre's fiduciary duty of full disclosure concerning the previously non-disclosed offer from the buyer broker's client, and Bre's contractual duty under the listing agreement to "use reasonable efforts and act diligently to market the property for sale, procure a buyer, and negotiate the sale of the property." Oliver wins and owes Bre nothing. Oliver may countersue for damages caused by Bre's breach of fiduciary duty and breach of contract. Oliver may also report Bre to TREC for violations of TRELA § 1101.652(b)(1),(2) and TREC Rule § 535.156(a–c). In that case, Bre could also lose her real estate license or face other TREC penalties and fines.

> Bre should not have tried to insist that she still had the privilege to continue marketing Oliver's property.

Authority of the Agent Under TRELA

While TRELA cannot create the authority of a broker to be a particular person's or entity's agent in a real estate transaction, it does limit a broker's ability to act legally as anyone's agent in a real estate transaction. Here's the thing: You do not need a license to be a broker. You need a license to be a broker legally. Similarly, you don't need a license to be a driver; you just drive the car; however, you do need a license to drive a car legally. You are not arrested for being a driver; you are arrested for driving without a driver's license. According to TRELA § 1101.002(1), "'Broker' means a person who, in exchange **for a commission** or other valuable consideration, performs **for another person** one of the following acts . . ." The Act then makes it clear that an individual who performs certain acts for another person, for a fee or valuable consideration is a broker. Under the Act, you are a broker whether you have a license or not. It is just illegal to do those things under those conditions if you don't have a license.

Except for those persons listed in § 1101.005 of the Act, all other persons in Texas need a broker's license to "act as broker" in a real estate transaction. What are some conclusions that might be drawn from that premise?

1. A person could collect a commission in his own purchase without a broker's license because, in his own purchase he would be collecting a fee but not acting "for another person." Therefore, he doesn't meet the definition of "broker" in the Act and therefore needs no license to collect the fee.
2. A person could act as an agent for another person in a real estate transaction without being a broker or having a license to be a broker, if she did it gratuitously and not "in exchange for a commission or other valuable consideration or with the expectation of receiving a commission or other valuable consideration." However, in this case, even without the necessity of a license, she would still become the agent of, though not the broker for, the other person, which would include all the liabilities pertaining to the performance of the duties of a fiduciary. And for what? Nothing, because it was a "gratuitous agency."

■ CLASSIFICATIONS OF AGENCY

For real estate purposes, agency is typically classified into three categories based on the level of authority granted by the principal to the agent. The three categories of agency in real estate, in descending order of power granted, are as follows:

- Universal agency
- General agency
- Special agency

Each category has its own unique set of duties, responsibilities, and liabilities for both the principal and the agent, and even other parties. It is important for licensees to understand the scope of each type of agency so they can understand and comply with, and not exceed nor fall short of, the duties, obligations, and limits that agents are expected to be subject to in the course of conducting business for their client and their broker.

Universal Agency

Universal agency gives a very broad and general scope of power to the agent to act for the principal. With this type of agency, the agent is empowered to conduct every type of transaction that may be legally delegated by a principal to an agent. Such agency power may include acquisition and disposal of assets, expenditure of the principal's funds, and entering into contracts on behalf of the principal. This type of agency would hold a principal accountable for virtually any action by the agent. Universal agency is not very common in typical real estate transactions. An example of universal agency is an adult son or daughter who has been empowered by an elderly parent to conduct all personal and business transactions on the parent's behalf. In this case, the parent is accountable for the actions of the son or the daughter in conducting the parent's affairs. Unlike special agency, universal agency is never inferred or implied by conduct of the parties and must be created by clear and unequivocal language. Universal agency is not inferred from general expressions. As a real estate licensee, you will likely never play the role of universal agent, at least in your capacity as a real estate agent. Your broker would probably not consent to being placed in that position.

It is worth noting that in all the types of agency mentioned, before the principal can delegate any authority, the principal must legally possess that authority. A person's son cannot grant authority to you to sell the property owned by his father, unless the son has been granted authority from the father or a court to do so in some legal form such as power of attorney, guardian, receiver, and the like. In listing properties for sale, make sure that you always check the legal rights of the person or persons claiming to own the property and giving you the listing.

General Agency

The scope of authority in general agency is more restricted than in universal agency. The agent is authorized to conduct an ongoing series of transactions for the principals and can obligate them to certain types of contractual agreements. General agency is the relationship that most often exists between a broker and the broker's associates (broker licensees and salesperson licensees). Brokers authorize associates to act as broker's agents in the course of the brokerage operations. These agents are authorized to act for their brokers in any number of activities that are typical for a brokerage firm. Some of the most frequently performed activities are

- obtaining listings from sellers and landlords and signing the listing contract for the broker, but in the name of the broker only;
- conducting marketing activities for properties listed by the company;
- entering into buyer representation agreements, again, signing for the broker and in the name of the broker;
- showing properties to prospective buyers;
- preparing, presenting, and negotiating offers to purchase and to sell or lease properties; and
- maintaining and transferring a complete singular file of each transaction completed or otherwise terminated.

Considerable authority may be given to the agent by the broker. For example, an agent of the broker (such as an associate broker or a sponsored salesperson) can obligate the broker to a listing contract with a seller or to a buyer representation contract with a buyer. As with universal agency, the broker assumes a considerable amount of liability for the agent's actions. For example, if a broker's agent engages in inappropriate or illegal conduct while acting for the broker, the broker may be held responsible for those actions. In addition to liability under general agency law, TRELA also holds brokers accountable for the actions of their agents when the agents are acting within the scope of the general agency authority that was granted to them by the broker. (§ 1101.803; 22 TAC § 535.2(a)).

In rule 22 TAC § 535.2, TREC lays considerable responsibility on brokers for the conduct of their business activities. Because of this extensive responsibility, brokers are usually concerned with engaging conscientious associated licensees and training them to make good decisions and take actions that are not only within the scope of the law but also honest and ethical. Just one poorly trained or unethical associate who commits an illegal act can jeopardize a broker's entire business. For this reason, brokers must satisfy themselves as to the character and integrity of licensees who would like to be associated with the brokerage firm.

Another general agency relationship that frequently occurs in real estate practice is when a broker acts as a property manager for an owner. In most cases, the broker conducts a number of transactions for the owner, such as negotiating and signing lease contracts, contracting for maintenance, and initiating eviction lawsuits on behalf of the owner. Frequently, the owner is unwilling or unable to perform these functions; therefore, it is necessary to confer on the broker the full authority to carry out these activities. Property managers must conduct their business very carefully. The pages of the TREC enforcement actions are filled with property managers exceeding or mishandling the authority given to them by landlords. General agents wield a lot of power on a regular basis in property management. When any person has the power of the purse, the temptation to mishandle another's wealth is great.

Special Agency

Special agency, sometimes known as limited agency, authorizes the agent to perform only those acts permitted by the principal. When working for clients, real estate agents are most frequently acting as limited or special agents; their scope of authority usually does not extend beyond the terms of a listing agreement or a buyer-representation or tenant-representation agreement. A well-written listing agreement defines the duties of the broker and the client, and it uses distinct, well-defined terms rather than the broad, sweeping language of general agency agreements. However, keep in mind, that even when acting as a special agent to a buyer or a seller, you are still a general agent for your broker.

A listing agreement authorizes the broker to represent the seller in the marketing of the seller's property. The listing broker is authorized to find a ready, willing, and able buyer. Except in cases of property managers and leasing agents, the broker generally has no authority to sign sales contracts or lease agreements for the owner, to initial changes to an offer, to accept offers (even for the full purchase price) on behalf of the owner, or to permit early occupancy by a potential buyer or tenant. In the latter case, it is possible to have your licensed revoked or be subject to some other TREC disciplinary action, and/or be sued by your property owner/ client for allowing a buyer or a tenant to occupy a property before the contract authorizing possession has been fully consummated.

In exceptional cases, the broker may be appointed as attorney-in-fact under a separately granted power of attorney. Brokers are usually hesitant to accept a power of attorney because of potential conflicts or the appearance of impropriety that can arise because of the broker's interest in a transaction. Frequently a family member, a business associate, or an attorney will be granted the power of attorney when buyers or sellers are unable to be present to act in their own behalf. In the case of property managers and leasing agents, they frequently become general agents of the owners and are granted the power to commit the owner to leases, expend the owner's money for repairs or equipment, carry out evictions, and the like.

A buyer-representation or tenant-representation agreement authorizes the broker to represent the buyer as a special agent in purchasing or leasing a property. In the case of leases, most tenant representatives do not act as general agents for the buyer and are not authorized to commit a tenant to a lease by signing for the tenant. If that conduct was desired by a tenant, it probably should be done by executing a power of attorney limiting the agent to a specific property for a limited time. The agent seeks properties that meet the buyer's or the tenant's requirements and then will help negotiate the best contract terms and conditions for the buyer or the tenant.

■ **EXAMPLE**   In *Joseph v. James*, 2009 WL 3682608 (Tex. App. Austin 2009), the buyers had their agent fax an offer for $1,875,000 to the sellers' agent to purchase Joseph's home. The sellers' agent verbally informed the buyers' agent that the seller would not accept an offer for anything less than $2 million. The buyers' agent, after consulting with the buyers, changed the sales price to $2 million by crossing through the sales price on the contract and then, without obtaining the buyers' initials on the change, faxed the counteroffer to the sellers' agent. The sellers countered with several changes, including raising the sales price to $2,195,000. Each change was initialed by the sellers. The buyers' agent again altered the sales price, this time changing the total price to $2.1 million. Again, the buyers did not initial the changes. The buyers' agent attached the contract to an e-mail, along with a comment that the buyers loved the home and were countering at $2.1 million. The sellers' agent communicated a verbal counter from the sellers offering $2,125,000 and that the seller would leave several items of personal property. Hearing nothing back from the buyers, the sellers signed and initialed the latest written offer from the buyers' agent (for $2.1 million) and, without the knowledge of the seller's agent, asked the selling agent's assistant to send an e-mail acknowledging receipt and acceptance of the buyers' latest offer of $2.1 million.

When the transaction did not go forward, the buyers' agent apologized for the confusion, admitted he did not have the buyers' permission to make the changes and that the counteroffer of $2.1 million had been transmitted by mistake. The sellers sued for breach of contract and fraud (Texas Business and Commerce Code § 27.01. Fraud in Real Estate and Stock Transactions.)

■ **DISCUSSION**   The sellers argued that the buyers' agent had the authority to sign on behalf of the buyers. By sending the counteroffer, the buyers' agent therefore bound the buyers to the purchase contract. The court, however, granted summary judgment to the buyers, relying on a long line of Texas cases confirming the special agent relationship held in the typical real estate transaction. The sellers were unable to show that the buyers had signed or initialed the last counteroffer of $2.1

million, thus no contract had been created. A licensee, without a power of attorney, has no authority to bind a principal to a transaction. In the heat of negotiation, licensees feel pressured by their clients to expedite the negotiation by making verbal offers/ counteroffers. In this case, the buyers' agent attempted to simply make the change to the contract and fax the form without the buyers' initials. Without signatures and initials by the actual parties to the contract, according to the Texas statute of frauds (Texas Business and Commerce Code Section 26, Statute of Frauds), there is no binding contract.

■ **EXAMPLE**   In the similar *Mushtaha v. Kidd*, 2010 WL 5395694 (Tex. App. Houston [1 Dist.], 2010), a seller directed his agent to mark through the price offered by a buyer and substitute a higher price, which the broker did, and then initialed and delivered it to the buyer's broker. The seller then received a higher offer from a second buyer. Realizing a higher offer was on the table, the first buyer quickly signed the seller's counteroffer. The seller, however, signed the contract accepting the offer from the second buyer. The court ruled that no binding contract existed between the first buyer and the seller, again citing that the special agency relationship of a broker did not include the right to bind the owner.

Licensees must make clear to the parties that oral offers and counteroffers are simply not binding on the other party except in certain highly unusual situations. Furthermore, licensees should never attempt to sign offers or counteroffers or initial changes on behalf of their clients without benefit of a power of attorney.

However, can brokers' agents sign and/or initial for their brokers on listing agreements, buyer representation agreements, and management agreements? For instance: You are in the process of getting a listing agreement signed. The owner balks at signing as long as a particular paragraph is included. The owner lines through the unacceptable term, initials the change, and then signs the form, creating a counteroffer. Can you initial the change, sign the counteroffered listing agreement for your broker, and thereby commit your broker to the modified agreement? In the absence of specific office policies, probably yes. In fact, even if office policy does not allow you to do that, but the owner is not aware of the office policy, the broker may still be bound. However, this is not an advisable practice. It is best to make sure your broker is okay with the terms before committing your broker to them.

The Flow of Authority

As shown in Figure 2.1, a typical real estate transaction commonly consists of two levels of agency. One level of agency exists between the associated licensee and the sponsoring broker, and another level exists between the broker and the buyer or the seller. Real estate licensees associated with a broker have a general agency relationship with their broker for the operation of the brokerage firm, and brokers have a special agency relationship with buyers or sellers for the purchase or sale of property. Because these relationships can be complex and carry legal obligations, it is important that every principal and agent understand the concepts that surround agency relationships.

FIGURE   2.1

**The Flow of Authority in
Agency Relationships**

FIDUCIARY DUTIES AND RESPONSIBILITIES

Today the broker may play many roles—agent for a seller or a landlord, agent for a buyer or a tenant, subagent of a seller or a buyer, or intermediary. These roles are discussed in detail in later chapters, but for the moment, it is important to know that, regardless of the agency role assumed by the broker, a clear understanding of duties to the client is critical.

If an agency relationship exists, the real estate agent is held to be a fiduciary. In classic terms, a fiduciary responsibility implies a position of trust or confidence in which one person—the fiduciary—is usually entrusted to hold or manage the assets (in real estate, the property) of another—the principal or the client. Common examples of fiduciaries are trustees, executors, and guardians. In real estate terms, the client relies on the real estate agent, as a fiduciary, to give skilled and knowledgeable advice or opinions and to help negotiate the best price and terms possible for the client in dealings with a third party (the customer). (TREC Rule § 535.16(a)&(b))

Restatement (Third) of Agency, a widely accepted legal authority on the law of agency authored by the American Law Institute, states the following:

> Fiduciaries are held to the highest amount of good faith, are required to exclude all selfish interest, are prohibited from putting themselves in positions where personal interest and representative interest will conflict and must, in any direct dealing with the principal, make full disclosure of all relevant facts and give the latter an opportunity to obtain independent advice.

In lay terms, agents, as fiduciaries, generally have special skills and expertise that place them in a position of advantage over their principals. An important aspect of this relationship is that trust and confidence are on one side (the principal's), and superiority of knowledge and influence are on the other (the agent's). This is why the agent/fiduciary has special obligations to the principal. The most important obligations a fiduciary owes to a principal can be remembered by using the "OLD CAR" memory device:

- **O**bedience
- **L**oyalty
- **D**isclosure (Full disclosure)
- **C**onfidentiality
- **A**ccounting
- **R**easonable care and diligence

OLD CAR is only a mnemonic device. The order of the terms has no special significance. If there is an order of importance, loyalty is number one. Loyalty is the "prince" of the fiduciary duties. All others spring from it. It has been said that the distinguishing and highest duty of the person who acts as a fiduciary is the obligation of undivided loyalty. The United States Marine Corps has a motto that exemplifies this characteristic: "Semper Fidelis" or "Always Faithful." It is a good motto for agents to keep in mind relative to serving their principals' best interests.

It is important to note that the real estate licensee, when acting as an agent on behalf of either party in the transaction, owes these fiduciary duties in addition to whatever duties are specified in the listing contract with the seller, the buyer/tenant-representation agreement, property management agreement, TRELA, and/or the TREC Rules.

However, some of these specific duties, which are fiduciary in their nature and normally required of the agent, may be "contracted out of" or "contracted away" by the parties. For example, if the listing contract allows for the broker to act as an intermediary as described by TRELA, then fiduciary duties are severely attenuated and, in at least one scenario, made illegal to carry out. The duty of full disclosure of information required by common law and under TREC Rule § 535.156 (Dishonesty, Bad Faith; Untrustworthiness) cannot be accomplished by an intermediary or the appointed license holders acting for the intermediary broker. Rule § 535.156 states the following:

> "(a) A licensee's relationship with the licensee's principal is that of a fiduciary. A licensee **shall convey** to the principal **all known information** which would affect the principal's decision on whether or not to make, accept or reject offers." (emphasis added)

To the contrary, as described in TRELA § 1101.561 (Duties of Intermediary Prevail),

> (a) The duties of a license holder acting as an intermediary under this subchapter supersede the duties of a license holder established **under any other law, including common law** [emphasis added]."
>
> (b) A broker must agree to act as an intermediary under this subchapter if the broker agrees to represent in a transaction:
>
> > (1) a buyer or tenant; and
> >
> > (2) a seller or landlord.

As an example of this "superseding" law situation, consider two different scenarios:

Scenario 1: You have listed Mr. Allen's property and are working with a buyer broker outside of your brokerage who represents a buyer. The buyer broker tells you that his buyer has told him that he will pay up to $10,000 more than his offer price if he has to in order to acquire the property. Must you convey that information to Mr. Allen? Of course!

Scenario 2: You have listed Mr. Allen's property. A buyer who wants to purchase Mr. Allen's property is a client/principal of your brokerage brought to the transaction by one of your firm's other agents. Your fellow agent tells you about the buyer's statement that he will pay $10,000 more than stated in his current offer in order to get the property. Now what do you do? Assuming all the statutory requirements have been fulfilled to enter into an intermediary relationship, you are now forbidden by the law from disclosing that information with Mr. Allen. Had Mr. Allen known that, would he have given his consent? It is important for individuals to understand the limitations of the intermediary role before they consent to it.

TRELA § 1101.651 specifically addresses certain practices that are prohibited when a salesperson or broker acts as an intermediary.

> (d) A broker and any broker or salesperson appointed under Section 1101.560 **who acts as an intermediary** under Subchapter L **may not**:
>
>> (1) **disclose** to the buyer or tenant that the seller or landlord will accept a price less than the asking price, unless otherwise instructed in a separate writing by the seller or landlord;
>>
>> (2) **disclose** to the seller or landlord that the buyer or tenant will pay a price greater than the price submitted in a written offer to the seller or landlord, unless otherwise instructed in a separate writing by the buyer or tenant;
>>
>> (3) **disclose** any confidential information **or any information** a party specifically instructs the broker or salesperson in writing **not to disclose, unless**:
>>
>>> (A) the broker or salesperson is otherwise instructed in a separate writing by the respective party;
>>>
>>> (B) the broker or salesperson is required to disclose the information by this chapter or a court order; or
>>>
>>> (C) the information materially relates to the condition of the property;
>>
>> (4) **treat a party** to a transaction dishonestly (emphasis added)

Professional Codes and Texas Canons

Many licensees elect to join trade associations that provide specialized services and support to licensees in the industry. The largest is the National Association of REALTORS® (NAR), which was founded in 1908. In turn, NAR is composed of state (i.e., Texas Association of REALTORS® [TAR]) and local associations.

While the public tends to use the term REALTOR® synonymously with real estate agent, only a member of NAR may be called REALTOR®. All other licensees should be called real estate licensees, salespersons, brokers, or agents.

In addition to the Canons of Professional Ethics and Conduct, to which all Texas licensees are bound (22 TAC § 531), a licensee who is a REALTOR® owes additional ethical duties outlined in the REALTORS® Code of Ethics. The NAR Code of Ethics is generally recognized as representing reasonable and acceptable standards of conduct for any real estate licensee, REALTOR® or otherwise.

It is worth noting that other professional real estate organizations have professional codes of ethics that must be followed if you belong to and desire to retain your membership in any of these organizations.

Reasonable Care and Diligence

A broker, as an agent, is hired to do more than merely locate a property or find a ready, willing, and able buyer, and an agent's obligations extend beyond simply marketing or locating a property. Real estate licensees in Texas who act as agents are held to a standard of care that requires, among other things, that they be knowledgeable concerning the land, the title, and the physical characteristics of the property being sold or purchased.

According to TREC Rule § 531.1(2) fiduciary relationships **demand** "that the real estate agent . . . be scrupulous and meticulous in performing the agent's functions." Further, § 531.3 (Competency) states that

> it is the **obligation** of a real estate agent to be knowledgeable as a real estate brokerage practitioner. The agent should: (1) be **informed on market conditions** affecting the real estate business and pledged to continuing education in the intricacies involved in marketing real estate for others; (2) be **informed on** national, state, and local issues and **developments** in the real estate industry; and (3) **exercise judgment and skill** in the performance of the work.

As an agent for your client, whether an owner or a buyer or tenant, you must use reasonable care and due diligence in the performance of these duties:

- Guiding the owner-client to arrive at a reasonable listing price by the skillful and honest use of a BPO or a CMA and negotiating for the best possible price (see § 535.16(c) regarding obligation to use BPO or CMA when listing a property)
- Advising the buyer-client what a reasonable purchase-price offer might be in light of the current market by diligently preparing a BPO or CMA on a property on which your buyer wishes to make an offer but still assisting your buyer in getting the property for less if possible. Never forget that § 535.16's "best possible price" and "best possible transaction" goes for a buyer-client as well as a seller-client. Of course, if you are acting as a subagent of the seller, then you should not be preparing a BPO or a CMA for a buyer/customer.
- Making reasonable efforts to sell the property, such as holding open houses, advertising, listing with a multiple listing service (MLS), if customary and desired by your principal; and using whatever marketing and advertising means proven to be effective in the specific market area

- Seeking out and attempting to present to your buyer/tenant all properties in the market area of your agreement that meet your buyer/tenant /client's criteria for purchase or lease
- Affirmatively attempting to discover relevant facts about the property and surrounding area and disclosing these facts to the client
- Investigating the material facts related to the sale and asking the sellers questions (the duty to question) that will clarify the sellers' needs and protect their best interests (e.g., "Does your roof leak?")
- Preparing and explaining the provisions of the listing form, buyer representation agreement, purchase contract, lease agreement, and other relevant legal documents
- Recommending that the client seek independent expert advisers such as attorneys, inspectors, appraisers, and accountants, when appropriate
- Helping the principals meet deadlines and closing dates

Agents must exercise care by knowing the laws, financing options, and most importantly the level of knowledge and expertise the client possesses. An inexperienced client requires a significant amount -of information to make the best choices, while clients who have previously bought or sold properties usually are more aware of the basic concepts of ownership and intricacies of offers and acceptance. It is important for agents to give their clients the information they need to make informed decisions regarding the purchase, lease, or sale of real property.

However, once informed by the agent, the principal decides what course of action to take. Agents should take care not to assume a role as their principal's boss. You can and should advise your client as to what you think are the best options to achieve your clients' purposes, but you should not attempt to decide for them. On the other hand, if you have an unreasonable client who continues to ignore sound advice, you are generally free to terminate your agency relationship with such a client.

Suppose an agent sells a home one week after the listing is signed. Initially, the seller is thrilled. Later, however, the seller may complain that the agent lacked skill and care because the listing price was set too low. This example is not meant to suggest that homes that sell quickly are necessarily underpriced.

A seller might become angry after discovering that his own agent assisted the buyer-customer in obtaining financing that resulted in the seller's paying higher discount points when lower-discount-point options were available. If TREC's Third Party Financing Addendum for Credit Approval is used properly, this should not be a problem because the offer submitted should have the appropriate blanks filled in for paragraphs A, B, C, or D. If done properly by the agent submitting the offer, it would show the owner, beforehand, what he is agreeing to if he agrees to the payment of any of those costs for the buyer.

Likewise, a seller who unwittingly closes a transaction a few days before becoming eligible for favorable tax benefits could well complain that the agent failed to exercise reasonable skill by not informing the seller that an early closing would cost thousands of dollars in avoidable taxes. While questions regarding tax consequences of transactions should be referred to the client's CPA or tax attorney, it may be incumbent on you to at least warn your client to the problem and recommend your client seek competent tax counsel before signing a contract to sell.

Similarly, an agent who represents a buyer must exercise reasonable care and diligence on the buyer's behalf. This duty extends beyond giving honest information to a buyer/customer—it extends to rendering sound advice and advising the buyer to obtain assistance from experts when appropriate. At the very essence of the fiduciary concept is the fact that a true agent is an equity preserver for the client. A buyer's agent preserves equity for the buyer-client by using all the agent's specialized skills and knowledge in negotiating the lowest possible price with the best terms.

Agents do not have to meet the high standard of legal knowledge required of attorneys; however, agents do need a basic knowledge of real estate law to qualify for state licenses. Courts impose on agents a duty to know and to explain, in basic terms, the practical effects of key financing terms, contingency clauses, holding title, restrictions, and routine contract provisions. In short, agents must spot common problem areas and direct their clients to expert help when the clients require specific advice. (See TREC Rule § 537.11(c) which states, "Nothing in this section shall be deemed to limit the licensee's **fiduciary obligation** to disclose to the licensee's principals all pertinent facts which are within the knowledge of the licensee, including such facts which might affect the status of or title to real estate.")

Agents do more than act as fiduciaries. Typically, agents are hired to market property. Sometimes these dual responsibilities—marketing and advising—create practical and ethical dilemmas not normally experienced by other fiduciaries. Recognizing that the agent's income usually depends on a sale, the unprofessional agent could easily justify holding back information, based on the likelihood that the sale will proceed and that certain information would only cloud the client's decision. Nevertheless, the agent must disclose information to the client as part of the fiduciary duty required by law and ethics.

Unfortunately, an all too frequent example of this bad behavior occurs when some listing agents seem determined not to want to see the buyer's inspection report and don't want their owner client to see it either. These less-than-professional agents assume that if they or their client sellers don't see the inspection report, they won't have to reveal unpleasant property problems to the next buyer if the current transaction falls through. They may not realize that once the buyer's broker delivers the report to the listing office, both the agent and the seller will have constructive notice of all the information in the report even if they don't read it. That information will have to be disclosed to subsequent buyers as long the present transaction is not consummated. Exposure to the information about property defects will now require that the owner update the Seller's Disclosure of Property Condition in any current or future negotiations. While the inspection report itself does not have to be given to subsequent potential purchasers, the knowledge of the defects must be conveyed. Failure of the listing agent to convey the bad news could subject the agent to TREC discipline and subject the agent and the seller to a lawsuit for deceptive trade practice from future purchasers. (See § 535.156(a–d).)

A practical test applied by courts to decide whether an agent has used reasonable skill and care in a given case is, "Would a reasonably efficient broker in the community in a like situation use more care to protect the best interests of the client?" If the answer by the trier of fact (judge or jury) is yes, the agent has been negligent.

■ **EXAMPLE**   Salesperson Jane has just returned from a three-month vacation in Barbados. She immediately contacts her client, John, to see whether he is ready to list his property for sale. He informs her that his company has just finalized his transfer and that he needs to sell his property as soon as possible. She lists his property for $270,000, using her extensive list of prior sales in the neighborhood to determine property value. A full-price contract is submitted by a buyer's broker the same day the property is listed, and the seller eagerly signs the offer.

After signing the contract, John talks with a neighbor, Al, who is also under contract to sell his home. Their homes are very similar in style, amenities, and condition, so they compare their selling prices. Al's contract is for $295,000, with basically the same terms and conditions as John's, and he received his offer about 10 days after the property was listed.

■ **QUESTIONS**   1. Why do you think the sales price for John's home is $25,000 less than Al's? 2. What is Jane's liability, if any? 3. Would you do anything different if you were Jane? What? Explain.

Obedience

The agent has an obligation to follow the lawful instructions of the client. The agent frequently is asked to obtain a survey, obtain an appraisal, or arrange for an inspection for the client. It is important that the client make decisions about who will provide the services. The agent then can arrange for the services to be performed.

Because the agent cannot commit the principal to contractual obligations, doing such things as extending closing dates or loan approval dates is not allowed. Even with authorization by the principal, these types of contractual changes must be initialed or signed by the principal, unless the agent has been given power of attorney to commit the seller to such changes.

The agent is bound to follow the lawful instructions of the agent's client. Under no circumstances is an agent allowed to violate a law, even if told to do so by a client. Frequently, clients are unaware that an act being requested or required is illegal. If the client requests or requires an unlawful act, the agent should explain that the request is against the law and that all agents are required to adhere strictly to the law. If the client continues to insist upon the illegal act, the agent should withdraw from the transaction. For example, if a client desires to commit mortgage fraud, then the agent not only should withdraw from representation but also report the attempted or actual mortgage fraud to one of the many proper authorities. Failure to report the fraud, even when there is only a reasonable suspicion that a fraud is being or about to be committed could subject the licensee to serious state and federal penalties.

Mortgage fraud may be reported to the following:
- The broker
- The FBI (fbi.gov)
- TREC (trec.texas.gov)
- HUD (hud.gov)
- Texas Department of Savings and Mortgage Lending (sml.texas.gov)
- OCC (Office of the Comptroller of the Currency) (occ.gov)
- IRS (irs.gov)
- Texas attorney general (oag.texas.gov)
- FTC Federal Trade Commission (ftc.gov)
- CFPB Consumer Financial Protection Bureau (cfpb.gov)

See www.tdi.texas.gov/title/mortgagefraud.html. For a list of organizations to report mortgage fraud in Texas, see www.mortgagenewsdaily.com/mortgage_fraud /report_Texas.asp.

■ **EXAMPLE**   Jane has been asked by her good friend, Cecil, to list his property. Jane is delighted to take this listing because the home is in a great neighborhood, close to schools, in wonderful condition, and should have an excellent chance of selling quickly at the price and terms that Cecil desires.

After the listing agreement has been signed and Jane is preparing to leave, Cecil clears his throat and says, "Of course, you know how I feel about selling my home to a minority. I would like you to do whatever is necessary not to show my home to any of 'those folks.'"

At first Jane is stunned. She had no idea that Cecil would make this request. She would really like to take this listing; however, she knows that what he is asking is against the law. Jane has no experience in dealing with this type of situation, and she is very unsure how to proceed.

■ **QUESTIONS**   1. What should Jane do? 2. What could she say to convey her point and still be able to maintain the listing?

Loyalty

Agents must generally act in the best interest of their clients and be loyal to the trust placed in them (but remember the intermediary exception). Once an agreement has been reached between an agent (broker) and a client, all the associates of the firm, whether licensed as salespersons or broker associates, will represent the client through the principal broker. Thus, all licensees associated with the firm will have the same obligations as the broker and must represent the best interests of the client. This means striving to

■ obtain the best price and terms possible to satisfy the client's needs;
■ investigate and explain all offers;
■ obtain as much relevant information about the other party as possible;
■ disclose that information to the client; and
■ use "reasonable" or "best" efforts for the client's benefit, depending on what the law requires under the circumstance and what efforts or duties have been contravened by legally allowable contract terms in the agency agreement.

It is interesting to note at this point, that two of the most used representation agreements in Texas, one for buyer/tenant representation and the other for seller representation, require two different standards for the characterization of the effort required on the part of the broker to accomplish the clients' goals. One uses a paragraph titled "Broker's **Obligations**" and says the broker will use "best efforts to assist client. . . ." The other agreement titles the paragraph regarding broker's efforts "Broker's **Authority**" and states that the broker will use "reasonable efforts and act diligently to . . ." Whether there is a significant difference in the level of effort and accountability required of the broker under the differing contractual obligations could interest an attorney.

In any event, the agent who acts contrary to his legal or contractual duty is not acting in the best interests of the client. This is a requirement of Texas common law and the Texas Administrative Code (TAC), under the Rules of the Texas Real Estate Commission (22 TAC § 535.2(b), 535.156(a), (b), and (c)). Disloyalty to the principal or the client is not only unethical and unprofessional, it is forbidden under the law governing real estate licensees. Disloyalty may be grounds for forfeiture of commission, loss of the license to practice, lawsuit for damages incurred by the client, and possible rescission of the sales or lease contract itself.

■ **EXAMPLE**   Broker Nancy and her friend, George, owned homes in the same subdivision. Nancy listed George's home when George was transferred to Alaska. Nancy also placed her home on the market about the same time she listed George's home for sale. Nancy showed both her home and George's home to buyer Alicia. Alicia fell in love with George's home and expressed an immediate desire to purchase it for cash. Nancy then persuaded Alicia to purchase her own home instead.

■ **QUESTIONS**   1. Has Nancy breached her fiduciary duty of loyalty to George? 2. How could Nancy have avoided any question of a breach of her fiduciary duty?

Disclosure

A discussion of the duty of disclosure can be aptly introduced with TREC Rule § 535.2(b), which states the following:

> (b) A real estate broker acting as an agent owes the very highest fiduciary obligation to the agent's principal and is obliged to convey to the principal all information of which the agent has knowledge and which may affect the principal's decision.

A key point related to loyalty is the obligation of the agent to make a full, fair, **and timely** disclosure to the client of all known facts relevant or material to the transaction. A material fact is one that a reasonable person might feel is important in choosing a course of action. Recent changes to the Texas Deceptive Trade Practices—Consumer Protection Act (DTPA) clarify that real estate brokers are not subject to liability under that act unless the licensee has committed a misrepresentation of material facts, an unconscionable act, or a failure to disclose. The intent in the change to the DTPA, however, is that licensees should not be held liable under the DTPA for innocent acts of omission as long as the licensee can show that there was no attempt to defraud or deceive. However, the newer legislation does not relieve a licensee from being subject to § 17.46(b)(24) of the DTPA, which states that a person can be liable under the DTPA for

> failing to disclose information concerning goods or services which was known at the time of the transaction **if such failure to disclose such information was intended to induce** [emphasis added] the consumer into a transaction into which the consumer would not have entered had the information been disclosed.

■ **EXAMPLE**   Sam Broker knows that a client-owner's roof leaks badly and that black mold stains are evident. He touches up the stains with bleach and sells the house to Suzy Buyer. Between the purchase event and closing, Suzy's inspector arrives on a rainy day to discover the serious roof leak and the attempt to hide the mold and water stain problems. DTPA § 17.46(b)(24) is now very relevant. If the seller knew of Sam's misrepresentations, he will also be liable to Suzy and, depending on the other facts, may be liable whether he knew of Sam's misrepresentations or not.

The licensee continues to be at risk for even innocent acts of omission or commission under TRELA, the TREC Rules, and ethical standards dictated by various trade associations.

Important disclosures by an agent to a client include

- the relationship between the client's agent and other parties to the transaction;
- the existence of other offers and the status of the earnest money deposit (22 TAC § 535.156(a) and § 535.159(b));
- the buyer's financial condition;
- the agent's true opinion of the property's value (22 TAC § 535.16(c));
- any commission split between a listing broker and another broker;
- the meaning of factual statements and business details contained in the contract; and
- all known facts that might affect the status of title to real estate.

Clearly, an agent who has actual knowledge of a property defect is liable to both the client and the customer if the defect is not disclosed (§ 1101.652(b)(2)-(3); 22 TAC 535.156(a)). In addition, under TRELA and TREC Rules, liability may exist if agents fail to disclose facts that they should have known within the range of expertise expected of agents. Thus, a case can be made that in addition to disclosure of known material facts, the agent may have a duty of reasonable discovery and a duty to investigate the many aspects of the transaction as they affect the client's decision making. Texas courts, however, have held that the real estate agent is not liable for physical inspection of the property for defects. This is the realm of licensed inspectors, not of brokers and salespersons (*Kubinsky v. Van Zandt Realtors*, 811 S.W.2d 711 [Tex. 1991]) Keep in mind, that in this case the buyer had his own buyer broker and inspector and the listing agent was never shown to have had knowledge of the defects.

Some important facts affecting a client's decision do fall within the broker's domain. In one case, a buyer offered a seller a property as part of the down payment in the purchase of the seller's property; however, the listing broker failed to verify the appraised value of the property offered by the buyer. As a result, the broker was held liable for failure to disclose information that was important to the seller in making a decision to accept the buyer's offer.

Full Disclosure Relating to the Property   Full disclosure to the client is required, regardless of whether the fact is favorable or unfavorable, whether the fact is found before or after the purchase contract is signed, or whether disclosure might prevent the successful completion of the sale. Not only is the client entitled to know the same facts that the agent knows, but the client is generally assumed, by law, to know what the agent knows under the doctrine of imputed knowledge.

However, there are two notable exceptions to the imputed knowledge rule that could concern agents and their clients, especially in intermediary transactions. According to Marin R. Scordato in the *Fordham Journal of Corporate & Financial Law*, Volume 10, Issue 1, 2004, Article 5:

> There are two well recognized exceptions in agency law to the imputed knowledge rule. One is that a principal will not be imputed with knowledge possessed by an agent when the agent obtained the information from a third party to which the agent owes a duty of confidentiality. . . . The second exception to the imputed knowledge rule applies when the agent, whose knowledge a third party is seeking to impute to the principal, has acted adversely to the principal during the transaction in question.

Consider what these two exceptions might mean in an intermediary transaction when

- the buyer-client tells the intermediary broker that he, the buyer, intends to exercise his option to terminate the next day, and
- the intermediary broker knows that his seller-client is in receipt of another offer for a backup contract, and
- his seller-client is considering rejecting the second offer for the backup contract because the seller believes the first buyer is going to go through with the first contract.

What should the intermediary broker do with the information that the first buyer has expressed an intention to terminate? What if he does nothing? If he does nothing, the seller-client might reject the second offer, only to have the first buyer terminate his option the next day, in which case the seller-client is left with no contract at all.

Duty of Disclosure: Greater to Client Than to Customer   A buyer-customer is not legally entitled to, or legally privileged to, learn certain facts or opinions **from the agent** of the seller or from the seller about

- the seller's or the seller's broker's price opinions (CMA or BPO),
- how the listing price is justified,
- whether the seller will consider or possibly accept a lower price,
- whether the seller will agree to certain repairs or at what cost,
- how long the property has been on the market,
- the seller's reasons for selling,
- whether or not the sellers are planning a divorce,
- when the seller needs to be out of the house, or
- whether the seller has other offers.

The buyer has the right to ask about these things, but the agent just may not be legally entitled to answer in the way the buyer expects or desires.

Note that some listing agreements or seller representation agreements give the agent permission, but not the obligation, to disclose to buyer-customers and/or buyer-brokers certain information that would otherwise be confidential (like the information in the preceding list). Absent that contractual permission, however, the agent should remember that the duty of loyalty includes the duty to limit the information disclosed to any other party or parties unless required by the client, the law, or a court order.

The buyer-customer is entitled to information regarding material facts about the property, and the seller's agent and/or the seller must provide it. Those material facts include

- property defects,
- defects in the title,
- problems relating to the survey,
- floodplain information,
- rights of parties in possession (such as tenants), and
- environmental issues and/or property conditions that would affect the health or safety of occupants.

A client is entitled to all the items just listed plus full disclosure of information relating to the transaction and the other party to the transaction, such as

- the broker's opinion of the most appropriate or recommended sales price of the property via a CMA or BPO (but not an opinion of market value unless the broker is also an appraiser) (see TREC Rules §§ 535.16(c) and 535.17(a)-(d) regarding BPOs and CMAs),
- possible negotiating strategies or options available to the client,
- motivation of the other party to buy or sell, and
- financial condition of the other party.

It is important that an agent clearly understand the disclosure issues as they relate to a client or a customer. A key distinction is that the interest of the client is paramount, although the customer must, at the same time, be treated honestly and fairly. It should be noted that treating the customer honestly and fairly is usually in the best interest of the client. Remember that "fairly" does not mean "equally" when referring to the way you treat a customer relative to your treatment of your client-principal.

Full Disclosure of Relationships   The real estate agent must disclose to the client any special relationship that might exist between the broker and any of the broker's associates and the other parties in the transaction. Because the client may rely on the agent's loyal advice and counsel, it is important to know what interest any agent involved in the transaction may have in the other party's decision. The agent must disclose in writing, for example, whether the prospective buyer or seller is a relative or close friend of one of the broker's salespersons (§ 1101.652(a)(3); 22 TAC § 535.144(b)), whether the broker has an agreement with the buyer or the seller to be compensated if and when the property is resold, or whether the broker is loaning money to the buyer for the down payment.

The agent also must disclose to the owner or buyer/tenant whether any compensation is to be received from the referral of business to companies controlled by the broker or others, such as appraisal, termite control, lender, title, escrow, home warranty, or property inspection services (22 TAC § 535.148). It is not enough to disclose this information; permission to do so must be given by the owner/client or the buyer/tenant/client. Many brokers offer a number of these services in their offices, thus providing buyers and sellers with "one-stop shopping." When these services are discussed with the client or the customer, the agent must disclose that use of the broker-controlled services is optional.

Full Disclosure of Other Offers   Unless instructed otherwise by the seller, the listing agent should continue to present, or at least communicate, all offers until the transaction is closed. For rental property, the agent should continue to submit offers until the tenant takes possession of the premises. The agent must submit, or at least communicate, all offers and counteroffers to the client, even those that are believed to be too low or too high to warrant serious consideration. The offers may be oral or in writing or may or may not be accompanied by earnest money. The listing agent should disclose all offers presented after the acceptance of an offer to purchase or lease because the seller or the landlord may want to negotiate these offers as backup contracts. This decision is for the seller or the landlord to make, not the agent. See TREC Rule § 535.2(b). However, a typical real estate listing agreement may contain a provision that allows the listing broker to opt out of this provision.

Although TREC Rule 22; TAC § 535.156(a) states that the licensee has no duty to submit offers to the principal after the principal has accepted an offer, the contract forms promulgated by TREC over the years have routinely provided that "unless expressly prohibited by written agreement, Seller may continue to show the property and receive, negotiate, and accept back up offers." That provision remains in the One to Four Family Residential Contract (Resale) (20-12, paragraph 19). The buyer can object to this provision and attempt to negotiate with the seller to remove the property from the market. If the seller continues to offer the property for sale, it is recommended that the agent warn the seller to handle all subsequent offers strictly as offers for backup contracts to avoid the danger of lawsuits for breach of contract or for interfering with existing contracts. Once a contract has been agreed to by both the seller and the buyer, the buyer may have acquired "equitable title" or least an "equitable right to perform" on the contract to purchase the property. "Equitable title" and the "equitable right to perform" involve rights of the buyer to expect to complete the sale and receive title to the property once all the requirements of the contract are met: "Equitable title may be shown where the plaintiff proves it has paid the purchase price and fully performed the obligations under the contract." *Cullins v. Foster*, 171 S.W.3d 521, 533 (Tex. App.-Houston [14th Dist.] 2005, pet. denied).

Advise your client to consult an attorney in circumstances like this. The resolution of the issues may revolve around whether the contract is a contract for deed or a typical sales contract, and if a typical sales contract, whether or not the buyer has completely closed his side of the transaction (including the tendering of the sales price in escrow at closing), and the seller is simply refusing to sign the deed.

Full Disclosure of Information   Because their relationship with the client is that of a fiduciary, licensees must always place the interest of the client above that of their own interest, even if doing so directly or indirectly impacts on the agents' ultimate commission. Sellers' agents must disclose all information that would help sellers develop the best selling strategy, which means disclosing information that agents have about a buyer's level of price resistance or motivation to purchase. For instance, if a seller's agent is aware that a buyer is under pressure to complete a purchase in a short period, that information should be disclosed to the seller (22 TAC § 535.156).

Full Disclosure Regarding Status of Earnest Money Deposits   Many listing agreements authorize the seller's broker to accept and deposit earnest money in trust in accordance with a contract for the sale of the property. If the deposit is a postdated check or a promissory note, the broker must inform the seller. Otherwise, if the buyer defaults and the seller cannot collect on the note, the broker could be liable to the seller for the amount of the deposit to which the seller normally would be entitled.

According to the TREC-promulgated contract forms, the buyer, not either or any of the brokers, is responsible for depositing the earnest money with an escrow agent on final signing of the contract by all parties. In practice, in residential sales, it is common for the licensee delivering the contract of sale to the title company to also deliver the earnest money check because the title company is the most common holder of earnest money. For liability reasons regarding safeguarding of the earnest money, it is probably best for a seller and the seller's agent to not get involved in the handling of the earnest money under the current provisions of the TREC contract forms. The buyer should be responsible for getting the money to the escrow agent. If the buyer chooses to authorize his buyer broker to deliver it, that is probably safe. However, sellers' subagents should probably not be entrusted by either the buyer or the seller to handle the earnest money at all. For transactions involving other types of earnest money arrangements, it is incumbent on the seller's agent to check periodically with the escrow agent named in the contract to determine the status of the earnest money check in order to see if it was ever delivered to the escrow agent as required by the contract and if the check cleared the bank. The listing broker should keep the seller informed of all findings in this regard.

If the buyer asks the seller's broker to postpone the deposit of the earnest money check, the seller's broker should disclose this request to the seller and obtain written agreement between the parties to delay the deposit. Otherwise, the licensee holding the earnest money has one of two options: (1) to deposit it according to the contract or (2) to deposit it within a reasonable time, which is defined as "the close of business of the second working day after the execution of the contract by the principals" (22 TAC § 535.159(i)).

Full Disclosure of Buyer's Financial Condition   Frequently, a seller will make a decision to accept or reject a buyer's offer based on the buyer's financial standing. The seller's agent must disclose to the seller all information, good or bad, regarding the buyer's financial condition. This information is usually obtained directly from the buyer or the agent working with the buyer. The only exception is information that a licensee gains during the course of an agency relationship. For example, suppose the buyer had been represented by agent A in another transaction, and during this association, A came to know the buyer's financial condition. This information was gained in confidence and cannot be disclosed to the seller, even though the seller is now A's client.

Normally, the seller should make an independent evaluation of the buyer's finances on the basis of data collected from the buyer. Prudent sellers' agents or subagents will inform sellers that because they are not lenders or arrangers of credit, they are not in a position to verify or interpret the financial information supplied by the prospective buyer; however, they will use all possible skill to obtain such information for the seller's evaluation.

Sellers can obtain a copy of the Conditional Qualification Letter (Form A) from the Texas Department of Savings and Mortgage Lending (TDSML) and require that all offers be accompanied by this form, filled out by a reputable mortgage lender, and submitted along with any offers on the property offering evidence of buyer's financial ability. Of course, if the offer is a cash offer or contains no contingency on the buyer qualifying for a loan, this document would probably not be that helpful or necessary. The form can be obtained through the TDSML at http://info.sos.state.tx.us/fids/201401715-1.pdf.

Buyer brokers, on the other hand, should at least consider not even signing a buyer representation agreement with a buyer unless and until the buyer has applied for a loan and had the mortgage lender fill out the Conditional Qualification Letter setting out the buyer's qualifications for obtaining financing. If the buyer will be buying without needing a loan, the buyer broker needs to satisfy herself that the buyer has the necessary funds before undertaking a search for properties for the buyer. Nothing is more discouraging to a new agent than to drive an unqualified buyer around for two weeks and produce an offer that results in a contract, only to have the buyer unable to get the necessary financing for the purchase.

Because of the fiduciary relationship between the seller's agent, any subagents, and the seller, the seller's agent or subagents must disclose

■ any negative information that the agent has concerning the prospective buyer's financial situation. This is especially true when the seller is asked to carry a note for the buyer or allow an assumption of an existing loan that requires that the seller remain liable for repayment to the lender of the loan being assumed, or for the seller to take by a second lien on the property to minimize the buyer's down payment;
■ facts that the buyer states or that the agent has learned independently—for instance, that the buyer has other property that must be sold before closing on the seller's property; and
■ any information that affects the buyer's ability to obtain financing or gives the buyer an option to terminate the offer if financing is not obtained.

A buyer's agent has no duty to communicate negative information concerning the buyer's financial strength to the seller. Instead, the buyer's agent has a duty of confidentiality to not communicate to the seller the financial strength of the buyer's position unless given permission or direction to do so by the buyer-client. This does not mean the buyer's agent can misrepresent the buyer's financial strength by giving false or misleading information, only that information must not be disclosed unless the buyer gives specific permission.

Full Disclosure of Property Price Disclosure of the agent's opinion of the price of the property is a very important part of an agent's fiduciary duty to the client. Real estate agents have a duty to inform their clients of their opinion of the price of the real estate being listed or shown. Real estate licensees employ many of the same techniques for pricing property as professional appraisers do. Yet a real estate licensee may not perform an actual appraisal of real property unless also licensed or certified as an appraiser under Section 1103 of the Texas Occupations Code. Instead, real estate licensees provide a broker price opinion (BPO) or a comparative market analysis (CMA) to a consumer. That written opinion must include the statutory language indicating that the real estate licensee's opinion is not an actual appraisal (22 TAC § 535.17(b)). The opinion of a property's price is arrived at through studies of the sales of properties similar to the subject property, the price of the land and improvements, and/or the income the property might be expected to produce.

The agent is also liable for disclosure of sales prices of all comparable properties that the agent should have known through a reasonable review. An agent can be held liable to the client and customer for rendering a false price opinion because the agent is obligated to keep informed on market conditions. An agent is also liable for giving a wrong price opinion to a client or customer if the opinion was negligently based on inaccurate comparisons or inaccurate application of a broker price opinion or comparative market analysis methods (TRELA § 1101.652(b)(1); 22 TAC § 535.156(d); DTPA § 17.46(b)(5),(6),(7)). These duties and the law are especially relevant in cases in which the seller directs the listing agent to underprice or overprice a property to achieve the seller's objectives. For example, the seller may want a particularly fast sale and may suggest that the property be placed on the market for less than market price to achieve this goal. The listing agent should document this request to avoid future problems.

When a seller's agent learns of factors that change the price of the property after the listing is signed, disclosure of such factors must be made as soon as possible and certainly before the seller-client decides to accept or reject an offer. The price and terms of the listing may have to be adjusted in accordance with such changed conditions (TRELA § 1101.652(b)(2); TAC § 535.156(c),(d)).

An agent does not have the obligation to give a price opinion to a customer. Customers will usually form their opinions about the price of a particular property by comparing it with other properties they have seen for sale. Offers that customers submit generally reflect their perception of price based on all the properties they have seen. Seller's agents have an obligation to encourage buyers to submit offers that are favorable to the seller.

Occasionally, agents wish to purchase a property they have listed for a client. According to the rules of TREC, the agent must have given the seller-client a price opinion of property at the time of listing. If the seller's agent later attempts to negotiate an offer to purchase the seller-client's property for the agent's own account, it is particularly important to inform the seller of any change in the property's price. It may be particularly advisable for the seller or the broker to obtain an appraisal in these circumstances (22 TAC § 535.16 (c)).

Full Disclosure of Commission Split   The listing agent must disclose to the seller the existence of any fee-sharing arrangement with a cooperating broker (also known as the other broker). Although the exact amount of any split does not have to be revealed, it is better to disclose fully to the client the amounts to be split, with the rationale for doing so. This disclosure should be in writing, preferably in the listing agreement. (Note: It is a violation of TRELA § 1101.652(b)(11) for a broker to pay a commission or fees to or divide a commission or fees with anyone (including attorneys) not licensed as a real estate broker or a salesperson for compensation for services as a real estate agent; however, a broker is not prohibited from reducing a brokerage fee to either principal—buyer or seller.)

Full Disclosure of Contract Provisions   Before signing (executing) any document that is intended to be legally binding, the licensee is obligated to discuss the provisions of the contract with the client (22 TAC § 537.11(h)) and suggest that the client seek competent legal advice. Competent legal advice is especially important when there are unusual matters or areas of confusion that can best be handled by an attorney. In fact, where it appears that an unusual matter should be resolved by legal counsel or that the document is to be acknowledged and filed for record, the licensee is required, by Texas law, to advise both parties in the transaction to seek legal counsel. Failure to do so is grounds for loss of license (TRELA § 1101.654; 22 TAC § 537.11(b)).

Although licensees should not practice law or give legal advice, they are permitted, and in some cases required under their fiduciary obligation, to do at least the following:

- Explain the provisions of contracts
- Disclose all pertinent facts of which the licensee has knowledge, including such facts that might affect the status of or title to real estate
- Explain the meaning of factual or business details (22 TAC § 537.11(c)–(h)).

■ **EXAMPLE**   Buyer Brown is considering writing an offer to purchase a property that fits his idea of a perfect home. While reviewing the purchase contract, Brown asks agent Allen whether he will be obligated to purchase the property if he cannot obtain the financing he has stated as a condition in the contract. Allen explains the meaning of the paragraphs regarding financing and asks whether Brown would like to seek legal advice for further inquiries.

■ **QUESTIONS**   1. Did the agent practice law by explaining the terms relating to financing to the buyer? 2. Under what circumstances would the agent be practicing law?

Of course, licensees who are also licensed attorneys would be allowed to give legal advice. However, rendering legal advice in a transaction where the attorney is also participating as a real estate broker might create a conflict of interest within the Texas State Bar Association's Code of Ethics.

Confidentiality

The duty of loyalty requires that the agent keep confidential any discussions, facts, or information about the principal that should not be revealed to others. This is similar to the privileged information concept of a lawyer-client or doctor-patient relationship. The duty of confidentiality owed to a client extends to an affirmative responsibility to withhold from a party that the agent does not represent such confidential information as to his client's bargaining position, motivations for selling or buying, opinions of value, marketing and negotiating strategies, the seller's lowest acceptable price or the buyer's highest price, and the client's financial position (unless the client is aware of and consents to the disclosure of such information). Licensees are prohibited from disclosing any confidential information gained during an agency relationship even after the relationship has been terminated.

■ **EXAMPLE**   Agent Maxwell is Seller Brown's agent. Maxwell has been working with a buyer-customer Taylor for three weeks. Finally, they find the perfect property for Taylor's business, and he is ready to offer $215,000 for the property, which is $15,000 less than Seller Brown is asking. Maxwell believes that the owner would be happy to accept $195,000 and informs Taylor of his opinion.

■ **QUESTIONS**   1. Has Maxwell breached his duty of confidentiality? 2. If so, what should Maxwell have done to avoid a breach?

There are limits to the duty to maintain confidentiality. Laws and ethical standards prohibit a licensee from withholding information regarding the condition of the property, the condition of the title, and other material facts that any prudent person would need to make an informed decision to purchase. The duty of confidentiality is sometimes modified by a greater duty to the public.

Licensees have a legal requirement and duty to be honest and fair to the customer. For instance, it would be fair and honest for the seller's agent to reveal to the buyer any known hazardous conditions, such as the presence of lead-based paint. The customer has the right to pertinent information about the property but not to personal information about the seller.

Accounting

Money received by a broker as a result of transactions such as purchase contracts or property management agreements are trust funds and are frequently held by the broker for the benefit of the principal. The funds must be held in an account that is separate from the broker's own account(s)—one that does not pay interest unless specifically authorized by the parties. Brokers who hold both their own funds and trust funds in a single account are considered to be commingling funds. Commingling is strictly forbidden by TRELA and is grounds for suspension or revocation of the broker's license (§ 1101.652(b)(10)). To lessen the risk of unintended commingling, brokers might consider having separate trust accounts for sales and for rentals.

Once a contract has been fulfilled or terminated, the broker must deliver the trust funds to the principal or the appropriate party. If the funds have not been transferred within a reasonable time after a valid demand has been made, the broker may be subject to license revocation or suspension by TREC. In the event of a contract default, however, the broker or any other entity acting as escrow agent for earnest money may require that all parties sign releases before the earnest money is paid to either party. TREC addresses the details of setting up trust accounts and disbursement of funds from those accounts at 22 TAC § 535.159.

"Old timers" in the business remember when regular practice was for the listing broker to hold the earnest money in the broker's special trust account and then the broker would write a check to the title company for that amount at closing. Many problems came about as a result of this practice, such as commingling, disputes over the broker's improper release of those funds, whether the broker was truly a neutral escrow agent, and the like. As a result of these abuses and conflicts, general practice in Texas has evolved to the point that most brokers do not hold earnest money in their own trust accounts. Instead, they insist that the principals in the transaction agree on a truly neutral escrow agent to hold the earnest money. Generally, the escrow agent, for purposes of holding the earnest money, is selected by the parties in the sales contract and is the same title company that will close the transaction and provide the title insurance.

From 1975 to the present, as the first TREC-promulgated contract forms were periodically revised, the TREC rules allowed brokers to use contract forms other than TREC forms. Those exceptions to the use of TREC forms allow a licensee to use contract forms other than TREC forms and still avoid the charge of unauthorized practice of law if they are used correctly. The exceptions are clearly spelled out in TREC Rule § 537.11(a)(1–4). The use of any of the "exceptions" forms opens the door to many other parties writing the terms for the handling of earnest money. It is not up to the broker to determine these issues. For instance, a builder's contract form may require that the builder be the holder of the earnest money. Though dangerous for a buyer to allow, it is not up to the licensee to dictate how that should be done or who should hold the earnest money. The licensee should not engage in the unauthorized practice of law by trying to decide for the parties how those parties should handle earnest money. Licensees should not seek to control the parties as to the selection of an escrow agent (or any other service providers for that matter). The licensee who insists on the parties choosing an escrow agent of the licensee's preference may become liable for an escrow agent's wrongdoing and charge for "negligent referral."

If the buyer and the seller agree in writing that the broker is to act as the escrow agent for purposes of holding the earnest money, then TREC Rule § 535.159(a)-(k) Failing To Properly Deposit Escrow Monies should be carefully read and followed.

With regard to the handling of earnest money, the licensee, especially a broker, should become thoroughly familiar with TRELA and TREC Rules regarding the requirements for handling and penalties for mishandling those funds. (See TRELA § 1101.652(30)&(31) and TREC Rules § 535.146.)

Minimum Service Requirements

The preceding discussions address the general duties owed to the client in an agency relationship. TRELA § 1101.557 reinforces the idea that a broker who represents a party in a real estate transaction is that party's agent. Therefore, once the licensee accepts the responsibility of agency, the licensee, acting as an agent, has a fiduciary duty to provide certain defined minimum services to the client, services that cannot be passed to the other broker in the transaction.

For example, TRELA § 1101.652(b)(22) provides that a broker may not negotiate a transaction directly with a consumer if the broker knows that the consumer is already subject to an exclusive agency relationship with another broker. However, if the broker only has an open listing (i.e., nonexclusive listing) on the property, the new broker is not prohibited from negotiating a transaction directly with the consumer without contacting the first broker with the open listing. The September 1, 2005, amendment to Section 1101.557 clarifies that the mere delivery of an offer by one broker to the client of another broker would not violate TRELA. Thus, while a listing broker may not instruct a buyer's broker to deliver and negotiate the offer directly with the seller, the simple delivery of the offer to the seller would not violate TRELA as long as the buyer's broker did not also attempt to negotiate directly with the listing broker's seller.

TRELA § 1101.557(b) states that a broker representing a party or listing real estate for sale is that party's agent and

1. may not instruct another broker to directly or indirectly violate § 1101.652(b)(22);

2. must inform the party if the broker receives material information related to the transaction to list, buy, sell, or lease the party's real estate, including the receipt of an offer by the broker; and

3. shall, at a minimum, answer the party's questions and present any offer to or from the party.

■ INFORMATION ABOUT BROKERAGE SERVICES AND DISCLOSURE OF REPRESENTATION

There is generally a lot of confusion regarding the disclosure of agency and the information about agency that is required to be given to clients and customers. Missteps in this area can result in serious consequences, including the loss of a salesperson's or broker's license.

For decades, even centuries, it has been a common law rule, whether in real estate or not, for an agent to disclose whom the agent represents to all parties. As real estate license laws began to develop in the various states in the United States, it was apparent the law needed to address the issue of disclosure of agency. In Texas, the license law for real estate brokers made it clear that when licensees acted as agents in real estate transactions, they could lose their license or face other TREC disciplinary action for certain failures to act in conformance with various common law principles. One of those basic principles, converted to a statutory obligation, was the duty of a broker or salesperson to make clear to all parties to a real estate transaction the party for whom the license holder is acting. Although the language of this principle has been slightly modified in recent years, it is still the same concept. TRELA § 1101.652(b)(7) tells the license holder that failure to provide this clarity regarding whom the licensee represents is punishable by TREC action. (You can expect to see this type information on your state exam.)

The law requires that these notices be made timely so that **before** a transaction commences, or confidences are shared, and possibly irrevocable or costly decisions are made, everyone in the transaction will know who is on whose side. This is necessary so that each party can take appropriate precautions regarding confidential information, negotiating positions, and the like. Disclosure of your agency relationships after negotiations begin is too late and violates license law.

For decades, these disclosures were not required to be in writing and could be given orally. Proof that the disclosures were made was the problem. Based on giant lawsuits over undisclosed dual agency because of the failures to disclose representation, brokers began to lobby state real estate commissions to require written disclosure of agency.

In 1988, TREC started requiring seller agents to disclose to potential buyers that they, the broker, represented the seller only. That was in the days when virtually all licensees represented only sellers, either as agents or as subagents. Buyer brokers were few and far between. Six months later, TREC came out with a similar form for buyer agents (the TREC 2) to have to disclose to owners and owners' agents that they represented the buyer or tenant. A revolution for buyer representation and buyer brokerage was under way.

By 1993, formal legislation was introduced by real estate practitioners and passed by the state legislature allowing for a statutory form of dual agency. In response, TREC introduced TREC 3, which was a dual-purpose form providing two main things: (1) disclosure of whom the licensee represented, if any one, and (2) information about the services a broker could offer so that a consumer could understand the three different types of brokerage services available before making a choice of service desired.

By 1995, the dual agency provisions of TRELA were seen to be unworkable as far as the industry was concerned, so the industry lobbied the legislature again with another version of dual agency that they named intermediary. A new written statement to clarify the agency choices to include the intermediary option was written, by the legislature instead of TREC. This time, the requirement for a written disclosure of the licensee's representation of one of the parties was not included in the form and agents, after January 1, 1996, could make that disclosure "orally or in writing." The current wording of that statutorily required "written statement" is set forth in TRELA § 1101.558. That section also includes the conditions under which the written statement must be given. This is another area that the prospective licensee should expect to encounter on the state exam for licensure.

Then what is the IABS? Where did it get its name? Is the IABS ever required to be given?

To encourage compliance with § 1101.558 with regard to presenting the written statement to the consumers, TREC reproduced the statement in exactly the statutorily required font size and put it on a voluntary use form for licensees.

TREC named the form Information About Brokerage Services (IABS) and gave it an OP number. OP stands for optional and means you can use it if you want to. The form itself is not a mandatory use form. The IABS is not a disclosure of agency form combined with information about brokerage services form as the old TREC forms 1, 2, and 3 were. It is an information form only **and contains no disclosure of the licensee's actual representation of anyone.** You should not think of it as, or describe it as, an agency disclosure form. It contains only information about brokerage services.

Unless your brokerage requires a written disclosure, your oral disclosure is sufficient. In court or in a TREC disciplinary hearing, you may have to find some way of proving that you disclosed to an angry buyer or seller that you told them you represented the other party. And remember in "telling" them, you must make it "clear" to them. See TRELA § 1101.652(b)(7), Grounds for Suspension and Loss of License.

Only within the "statutory written statement," and in no other TREC Rule or place in TRELA, will you find the following statement: "Your payment of a fee to a broker does not necessarily establish that the broker represents you." That statement appears in the last paragraph of the IABS, fourth sentence. You might have to point that out to a buyer or a seller because the misconception exists that you work for the party that pays you.

What follows is the TRELA requirement under § 1101.558 for the use of the statutory written statement concerning agency choices:

Sec. 1101.558. REPRESENTATION DISCLOSURE.

(a) In this section, "substantive dialogue" means a meeting or written communication that involves a substantive discussion relating to specific real property. The term does not include:

> (1) a meeting that occurs at a property that is held open for any prospective buyer or tenant; or

> (2) a meeting or written communication that occurs after the parties to a real estate transaction have signed a contract to sell, buy, or lease the real property concerned.

(b) A license holder who represents a party in a proposed real estate transaction shall disclose, orally or in writing, that representation at the time of the license holder's first contact with:

> (1) another party to the transaction; or

> (2) another license holder who represents another party to the transaction.

(c) A license holder shall provide to a party to a real estate transaction at the time of the first substantive dialogue with the party the written statement prescribed by Subsection (d) unless:

> (1) the proposed transaction is for a residential lease for not more than one year and a sale is not being considered; or

(2) the license holder meets with a party who is represented by another license holder.

(d) The written statement required by Subsection (c) must be printed in a format that uses at least 10-point type and read as follows:

Before working with a real estate broker, you should know that the duties of a broker depend on whom the broker represents. If you are a prospective seller or landlord (owner) or a prospective buyer or tenant (buyer), you should know that the broker who lists the property for sale or lease is the owner's agent. A broker who acts as a subagent represents the owner in cooperation with the listing broker. A broker who acts as a buyer's agent represents the buyer. A broker may act as an intermediary between the parties if the parties consent in writing. A broker can assist you in locating a property, preparing a contract or lease, or obtaining financing without representing you. A broker is obligated by law to treat you honestly.

IF THE BROKER REPRESENTS THE OWNER: The broker becomes the owner's agent by entering into an agreement with the owner, usually through a written listing agreement, or by agreeing to act as a subagent by accepting an offer of subagency from the listing broker. A subagent may work in a different real estate office. A listing broker or subagent can assist the buyer but does not represent the buyer and must place the interests of the owner first. The buyer should not tell the owner's agent anything the buyer would not want the owner to know because an owner's agent must disclose to the owner any material information known to the agent.

IF THE BROKER REPRESENTS THE BUYER: The broker becomes the buyer's agent by entering into an agreement to represent the buyer, usually through a written buyer representation agreement. A buyer's agent can assist the owner but does not represent the owner and must place the interests of the buyer first. The owner should not tell a buyer's agent anything the owner would not want the buyer to know because a buyer's agent must disclose to the buyer any material information known to the agent.

IF THE BROKER ACTS AS AN INTERMEDIARY: A broker may act as an intermediary between the parties if the broker complies with The Texas Real Estate License Act. The broker must obtain the written consent of each party to the transaction to act as an intermediary. The written consent must state who will pay the broker and, in conspicuous bold or underlined print, set forth the broker's obligations as an intermediary. The broker is required to treat each party honestly and fairly and to comply with The Texas Real Estate License Act. A broker who acts as an intermediary in a transaction: (1) shall treat all parties honestly; (2) may not disclose that the owner will accept a price less than the asking price unless authorized in writing to do so by the owner; (3) may not disclose that the buyer will pay a price greater than the price submitted in a written offer unless authorized in writing to do so by the buyer; and (4) may not disclose any confidential information or any information that a party specifically instructs the broker in writing not to disclose unless authorized in writing to disclose the information or required to do so by The Texas Real Estate License Act or a court order or if the information materially relates to the condition of the property. With the parties' consent, a broker acting as an intermediary between the parties may appoint a person who is licensed under The Texas Real Estate License Act and associated with the broker to communicate with and carry out instructions of one party and another person who is licensed under that Act and associated with the broker to communicate with and carry out instructions of the other party.

If you choose to have a broker represent you, you should enter into a written agreement with the broker that clearly establishes the broker's obligations and your obligations. The agreement should state how and by whom the broker will be paid. You have the right to choose the type of representation, if any, you wish to receive. Your payment of a fee to a broker does not necessarily establish that the broker represents you. If you have any questions regarding the duties and responsibilities of the broker, you should resolve those questions before proceeding."

(e) The license holder may substitute "buyer" for "tenant" and "seller" for "landlord" as appropriate in the written statement prescribed by Subsection (d).

Remember, the "written statement" above is contained in TREC's Information About Brokerage Services form (see Figure 2.2) and you may use it instead of developing your own. Several brokers in Texas do not use the TREC form but choose to use their own. No matter whose form they use, it must comply with the minimum standards of the Act in terms of font size.

■ SUMMARY

In any given transaction, the decision to represent the seller exclusively, the buyer exclusively, or attempt to "represent" both of them at the same time is a serious matter. Agents must understand their fiduciary responsibilities to clients and their general duties of fairness, honesty, and good faith to customers. It is easy for salespersons in an automobile showroom to know whom they work for (client-employer) and whom they work with (customer). It is a more complex question in real estate, when salespersons can show a buyer in one day a property listed by their firm, an MLS listing of another firm, a For Sale by Owner (FSBO) property, or even the salesperson's own home. The various shifting relationships must be understood by all participants in the relationship. One way to understand these problem areas is to recognize how and when agency relationships are created and what the duties of an agency relationship are.

■ KEY POINTS

- Agency occurs when one person, the agent, acts on behalf of another person, the principal (or client).
- There are a variety of agency relationships for licensees, buyers, and sellers to consider in every transaction.
- The three general categories of agency are universal, general, and special. Each category has a unique set of duties, responsibilities, and liabilities for the principal and the agent..
- A general agency relationship is common between a broker and sponsored salespersons and affiliated broker associates. but uncommon between a broker and a client in a typical sales transaction.
- A general agency relationship is common in property management situations.
- A special agency relationship is common between the seller or the buyer and the broker for the purchase or sale of property.
- The agent owes the client the fiduciary obligations of obedience, loyalty, disclosure, confidentiality, accounting, and reasonable care and diligence (OLD CAR).
- As a fiduciary, a real estate agent owes greater duties to a client than to a customer, and thus the risk of liability is greater.
- A fiduciary for one party still owes a duty of fairness and honesty to the party for whom the agent is not a fiduciary.
- Principals and licensees are no longer vicariously liable for unknown misrepresentations of other parties in a transaction such as subagents, but brokers are liable for the acts of their agents while performing within the scope of the agent's authority. (TRELA §1101.805(c))
- A real estate licensee may not perform an appraisal of real property unless the licensee is licensed or certified as an appraiser under TOC § 1103.
- The IABS or its equivalent must be given to all parties in most cases.

■ SUGGESTIONS FOR BROKERS

Company training programs should stress the implications of agency relationships and the fiduciary duties imposed on the licensee acting as an agent. The broker's associates must understand that unless care is exercised, the firm may become an agent of a principal even when an agency relationship was not intended. The associate should be instructed on the type of agency relationships promoted by the firm, as well as the scope of authority when acting in those agency capacities. Brokers should be ever mindful that they are ultimately responsible for the acts of any broker associate or sales associate when those associates are acting within the scope of authority given to them by the broker. The broker may also become liable for the misrepresentations of a subagent if anyone in the listing broker's company is aware of the misrepresentation and allows it to go forward unchallenged and unexposed to both the clients and the customers.

FIGURE 2.2

Information About Brokerage Services

10-10-11

Approved by the Texas Real Estate Commission for Voluntary Use
Texas law requires all real estate licensees to give the following information about brokerage services to prospective buyers, tenants, sellers and landlords.

Information About Brokerage Services

Before working with a real estate broker, you should know that the duties of a broker depend on whom the broker represents. If you are a prospective seller or landlord (owner) or a prospective buyer or tenant (buyer), you should know that the broker who lists the property for sale or lease is the owner's agent.   A broker who acts as a subagent represents the owner in cooperation with the listing broker. A broker who acts as a buyer's agent represents the buyer. A broker may act as an intermediary between the parties if the parties consent in writing. A broker can assist you in locating a property, preparing a contract or lease, or obtaining financing without representing you.   A broker is obligated by law to treat you honestly.

IF THE BROKER REPRESENTS THE OWNER:
The broker becomes the owner's agent by entering into an agreement with the owner, usually through a written - listing agreement, or by agreeing to act as a subagent by accepting an offer of subagency from the listing broker. A subagent may work in a different real estate office. A listing broker or subagent can assist the buyer but does not   represent the buyer and must place the interests of the owner first. The buyer should not tell the owner's agent anything the buyer would not want the owner to know because an owner's agent must disclose to the owner any material information known to the agent.

IF THE BROKER REPRESENTS THE BUYER:
The broker becomes the buyer's agent by entering into an agreement to represent the buyer, usually through a written buyer representation agreement. A buyer's agent can assist the owner but does not represent the owner and must place the interests of the buyer first. The owner should not tell a buyer's agent anything the owner would not want the buyer to know because a buyer's agent must disclose to the buyer any material information known to the agent.

IF THE BROKER ACTS AS AN INTERMEDIARY:
A broker may act as an intermediary between the parties if the broker complies with The Texas Real Estate License Act. The broker must obtain the written consent of each party to the transaction to act as an intermediary. The written consent must state who will pay the broker and, in conspicuous bold or underlined print, set forth the broker's obligations as an intermediary. The broker is required to treat each party honestly and fairly and to comply with The Texas Real Estate License Act.   A broker who acts as an intermediary in a transaction:

(1) shall treat all parties honestly;

(2) may not disclose that the owner will accept a price less that the asking price unless authorized in writing to do so by the owner;

(3) may not disclose that the buyer will pay a price greater than the price submitted in a written offer unless authorized in writing to do so by the buyer; and

(4) may not disclose any confidential information or any information that a party specifically instructs the broker in writing not to disclose unless authorized in writing to disclose the information or required to do so by The Texas Real Estate License Act or a court order or if the information materially relates to the condition of the property.

With the parties' consent, a broker acting as an intermediary between the parties may appoint a person who is licensed under The Texas Real Estate License Act and associated with the broker to communicate with and carry out instructions of one party and another person who is licensed under that Act and associated with the broker to communicate with and carry out instructions of the other party.

If you choose to have a broker represent you, you should enter into a written agreement with the broker that clearly establishes the broker's obligations and your obligations. The agreement should state how and by whom the broker will be paid. You have the right to choose the type of representation, if any, you wish to receive. Your payment of a fee to a broker does not necessarily establish that the broker represents you. If you have any questions regarding the duties and responsibilities of the broker, you should resolve those questions before proceeding.

Real estate licensee asks that you acknowledge receipt of this information about brokerage services for the licensee's records.

_____

Buyer, Seller, Landlord or Tenant   Date

Texas Real Estate Brokers and Salespersons are licensed and regulated by the Texas Real Estate Commission (TREC). If you have a question or complaint regarding a real estate licensee, you should contact TREC at P.O. Box 12188, Austin, Texas 78711-2188 , 512-936-3000 (http://www.trec.texas.gov)

TREC No. OP-K

CHAPTER 2 QUIZ

1. An example of a general agency relationship would be one that exists between the
   a. seller and the broker.
   b. buyer and the broker.
   c. sales associates and the broker.
   d. selling broker and the listing broker.

2. Special agency occurs when
   a. the principals give an agent a limited authority to act on their behalf.
   b. the principals give an agent authority to act for them in the operation of a business.
   c. a person operates a real estate brokerage business.
   d. a person operates a special real estate brokerage business.

3. Brokers can buy a property listed with them under which of the following conditions?
   a. If a family member secretly purchases the property for more than the asking price
   b. Under no circumstances
   c. Only if the property is listed under an open listing
   d. Only if full disclosure is made to the seller of the broker's involvement as a purchaser

4. Which statement is *TRUE* of listing agents?
   a. They must communicate every offer, oral or written, to the owner.
   b. They may refuse to present an offer if it is too low.
   c. They must tell the buyer the seller's lowest acceptable price.
   d. They may tell the buyer the terms of a counteroffer the seller made yesterday.

5. A salesperson owes all of the following fiduciary duties *EXCEPT*
   a. inform the broker and the seller of material facts.
   b. be loyal to the best interests of the client.
   c. prepare a power of attorney for the buyer.
   d. obey the lawful instructions of the broker.

6. A listing agent tells a buyer-customer that the seller is under pressure to sell because of a recent contract to purchase another house in Idaho. Such disclosure is
   a. acceptable if it results in a sale.
   b. acceptable if no details of the move to Idaho are disclosed.
   c. unacceptable because of the fiduciary duty owed the owner.
   d. unacceptable because the listing broker is the agent of the buyer.

7. Sally, as an agent for the seller, listed and subsequently sold George's town house. She did not tell George that a major zoning change in progress would allow business use in the area, thus increasing property values. Which statement is *TRUE*?
   a. Sally was not required to disclose the change because George never asked her.
   b. Sally was not required to disclose the change if George received his full asking price.
   c. Sally was required to disclose the change because it was a material and pertinent fact.
   d. Sally was required to disclose the change because the zoning laws require notice to all interested persons.

8. Which is *NOT* a fiduciary obligation owed to a client?
   a. Obedience
   b. Confidentiality
   c. Accounting
   d. Inspection

9. A material fact is one that
   a. the client considers important.
   b. the customer considers important.
   c. a reasonable person might feel is important.
   d. the listing broker considers important.

10. According to TRELA § 1101.558, the written statement must be given at what time?
    a. At the first meeting with a consumer where a substantive dialog occurs
    b. A meeting at an open house
    c. After a contract is signed
    d. At the time of the first substantive dialog with a party relating to a specific real property

DISCUSSION QUESTIONS

1. What are the main duties a fiduciary owes to the principal?

2. As a broker, would you prefer to act for a client as a universal agent, general agent, or a special agent? Why?

3. Although brokers are permitted to act as escrow agents and maintain trust accounts, many choose not to do so. List some of the pros and cons of maintaining trust accounts for clients and customers.

4. If you act for the listing broker or as a subagent of the listing broker, how much information can you disclose to the buyer before you begin to act contrary to the best interests of your seller?

5. If you act for the buyer as a buyer's agent, how much information can you disclose to the seller or the sellers' agents before you begin to act contrary to the best interests of your buyer?

6. If you act as an intermediary, how much information can you disclose to either of the parties concerning the other party's position or information?

7. What are the exceptions to the necessity to give the written statement about agency choices (e.g., the IABS form)?

CHAPTER 3

Duties and Disclosures to Third Parties

In the previous chapter, we discussed fiduciary duties to clients, those parties the agent represents. The broker and the client (buyer or seller) are the parties to the agency contract; however, for the agency to be functional, a third party must be involved. A third party is the party to a transaction who is not represented by the agent. For example, if the licensee is representing an owner, the third party is the buyer or the tenant. Conversely, if the licensee represents a buyer or a tenant, the owner is the third party. In some transactions, both principals engage their own agent to represent their individual interests. In this case, the agent representing the seller would consider the buyer the third party. Likewise, the agent representing the buyer would consider the seller the third party. In any event, even though third parties are not clients, they are due certain duties by the licensees.

■ **LEARNING OBJECTIVES**   *This chapter addresses the following:*

- Nonfiduciary Duties
- General Duties of Honesty and Fairness
- Define Third Party and Obligations to Third Party
- Avoiding Disclosure and Misrepresentation Problems
- Section 5.008 of the Texas Property Code (Seller's Disclosure of Property Condition)
- Material Facts
  — Physical Material Facts
  — Material Facts Relating to Title Issues
  — Material Facts Relating to Survey Issues
- Stigmatized Properties
  — Purely Psychological Stigmas
  — Physical Stigmas
  — Guidelines for Disclosure of Stigmatized Properties
  — Prohibited Disclosures to Third Parties
- Liability for Misrepresentation

■ NONFIDUCIARY DUTIES

Nonfiduciary duties are duties that are owed to customers (nonclients) and to the general public (consumers). Although under Texas Law, a broker owes specific fiduciary duties to the client, a Texas broker also owes general duties of honesty and fairness to all parties in a transaction. The broker/agent of a principal is forbidden to be part of fraud on behalf of that principal against a third party or in conjunction with a third party against another third party. This includes not only parties to the sales agreement, but also third parties such as the lender, appraiser, service providers, and the like. For example, the agent cannot follow the instructions of the seller/client if the seller instructs his agent not to disclose known defects in the property to a prospective purchaser.

According to TREC's *MCE Broker Responsibility*, Edition 1.0, page 10, under "Duties to Third Parties":

> A broker is liable to third parties for misrepresentations, particularly for failure to disclose certain material defects that may affect the buyer's good judgment and sound business practice.

> Section 1101.652 of the Act requires at least 3 affirmative disclosures a broker must make to a third party under certain circumstances. These are

> - significant defects in the condition of the property under TX. Occ. Code §1101.652(b)(3) and (4),
> - advising a purchaser to have the abstract of title covering the real estate examined under TX. Occ. Code §1101.652(b)(29), and making clear to the parties of the transaction which party the broker is working for under TX. Occ. Code §1101.652(b)(7).

Additionally, all licensees, when engaging in a real estate transaction **on their own behalf**, [i.e., not representing another person] are obligated to inform any person with whom they deal that they are licensed (broker or salesperson) and shall not use their expertise to the disadvantage of a person with whom they deal, TREC Rules §535.144. If a broker or agent receives a request for a copy of a document from a person who signed the document, the licensee is obliged under TX. Occ. Code §1101.652(b)(28) to provide the requested document.

In the last instance concerning the giving of signed documents, a licensee should never leave a successful listing appointment or appointment for buyer representation with the only copy of the signed listing agreement or buyer/tenant representation agreement.

■ GENERAL DUTIES OF HONESTY AND FAIRNESS

A great deal of confusion concerns the use of the term *fairly*, as used twice in the TREC Rules and twice in the License Act. Perhaps more to the point for licensees, TREC Rules specify that while the primary duty of the agent is to protect the interests of the agent's client, the licensee "shall treat other parties to a transaction fairly" (22 TAC § 531.1(1)). Remember, *fairly* does not mean "equally" in the context of comparative duties owed to a client versus those owed to a customer. However, when fair or fairly is used in discussing the treatment of—and comparative duties owed to—one customer versus another customer, the concept of equal treatment is much more relevant. This is particularly germane when applying federal fair housing laws to the required treatment of members of protected classes.

When "fairly" is used in the context of a seller's broker dealing with two customers competing for the agent's seller's property, then the understanding of fairly as meaning equally is very important. Following is a list of illegal or unethical conduct of a listing broker toward two competing buyer-customers, Ms. Boyd and Mr. Cunningham, that demonstrates the opposite of treating all parties fairly.

> Shopping offers refers to giving one or more customers an unfair edge over competing customers.

- Shopping offers—"Mr. Cunningham, if you want to have the seller accept your offer for this property, you are going to have to beat Ms. Boyd's offer of $220,000." Who is this conduct unfair to? This conduct is unfair to Ms. Boyd. The broker is treating the two customers unfairly because she's giving Mr. Cunningham information about Ms. Boyd but not giving Ms. Boyd information about Mr. Cunningham.
- Illegal discrimination—Mr. Seller, I know Ms. Boyd's offer is better than Mr. Cunningham's, but since you are an atheist, I need to let you know that Ms. Boyd's mother and father are devout Irish Catholics." Who is this conduct unfair to? This conduct is unfair to Ms. Boyd because it's discriminating against her on the basis of religion.
- Questionable negotiating tactics—Mr. Cunningham, before you make your offer, I need to let you know that my seller is considering an offer from Ms. Boyd, but I can't discuss the price and terms of her offer." Who is this conduct unfair to? It's unfair if the broker hasn't told Ms. Boyd that Mr. Cunningham has made an offer (if he made an offer). Mr. Cunningham knows he has competition even if he doesn't know the price or terms, so he makes

an attractive offer to make it more likely it will be the accepted offer. It is best to tell customers, "Make your best offer the first time. I'm not going to tell you whether we have other offers or not."

Licensees have the duty of honesty to customers and consumers, members of the public (TREC Rules 535.156(d) and 1101.652(b)(3-7)). However, the licensee must balance the fiduciary duty of confidentiality with the duty of honesty. For example, a buyer-customer asks, "Will your seller take less than the list price?" You know that your seller has said that she would take up to $10,000 less, but your duty of confidentiality prevents you from being able to make that disclosure unless the seller has authorized you to say that. Being honest doesn't mean you have to give the person the answer he's looking for; in this case, being honest is telling the person that that information is confidential or that you are not allowed to discuss that information with anyone but your client.

■ DEFINE THIRD PARTY AND OBLIGATIONS TO THIRD PARTY

The distinction as to who is a party to a transaction is interesting. Years ago, it was common to see a contract starting with legalese like this:

> John Smith (hereinafter called The Party of the First Part) . . . and Suzy Jones (hereinafter called The Party of the Second Part) do hereby . . . .

So what do you call the other parties that may be affected by the agreement between the "party of the first part" and "the party of the second part," such as brokers, lenders, appraisers, inspectors, and the like?

Answer: third parties.

In a listing agreement for agency services, the two parties are the broker and the seller. Any buyer is a third party. The seller could have liability to the third party for the conduct of the seller's broker. The laws relating to obligations to and liabilities from third parties are extensive and filled with "except" and "unless" issues. That being so, we will identify only a few of the simpler situations.

The doctrine of caveat emptor or "let the buyer beware" has been steadily eroded and replaced with sellers and their brokers having duties to purchasers under theories of public policy, ethical codes, statutory obligations, or case law regarding malpractice and deceptive trade practice. In some cases, the pendulum has swung from caveat emptor to caveat vendor (let the seller beware). The reversal of rights in the old contract for deed in Texas is a good example. Under the old contract for deed, the owner/vendor had very substantial power or rights and the buyer/vendee had much less power or rights. Since the late 1990s, the Texas Legislature has gradually reversed those rights to balance what were considered the inequities of the old system. Similarly, the pendulum has swung in the direction of protecting the rights of third parties to transactions.

The listing broker owes a buyer or tenant customer duties of honesty, fairness, competency, good faith, and disclosure of all material facts. While these duties are nonfiduciary in nature, they are strong duties under Texas license law and regulation, professional association codes of ethics, tort law, and deceptive trade practice law.

Moreover, the listing broker and any seller's subagent broker owe the buyer certain statutory duties and other regulatory duties under TREC rules of fairness, such as promptly presenting all offers and avoiding misrepresentation and false promises. The fact that a buyer may be represented by a broker does not diminish the duties of the listing broker to the buyer, even through the buyer's broker.

The duties of fairness to customers are not clearly defined—except where specifically mandated in federal or state laws, such as in fair housing law. Nevertheless, a licensee must be honest at all times and in all situations when dealing with clients and customers.

Beware! Honesty to customers, or their brokers, **does not extend** to answering every question customers or their brokers ask. A customer and her broker ask you the following questions. Assume that you know specifically about every issue raised. Based on what you've learned so far, how would you answer them without lying and without breaching your fiduciary duties to your seller?

1. Why is your seller selling?
2. Will your seller consider a lower offer?
3. Is your seller currently considering other offers on the property?
4. If so, how much are the other buyers offering?
5. What is the square footage of the house?
6. By what date does your seller need to be out of the house?
7. Are your sellers getting a divorce?
8. Will your seller pay for repairs?
9. Will your seller do seller financing?
10. Does the roof leak?
11. Has your seller had an appraisal done?
12. Is your seller a "foreign person"?
13. How long has the house been on the market?
14. Do you have a CMA or BPO to justify the price your seller wants?

■ AVOIDING DISCLOSURE AND MISREPRESENTATION PROBLEMS

The most common complaint of buyers against brokers relates to misrepresentation by brokers or the brokers' associates. The National Association of REAL-TORS® (NAR) reports that nearly two-thirds of all complaints against members result from misrepresentation issues. Fraud is a type of misrepresentation where the misrepresentation is committed knowingly with the intent to deceive.

Misrepresentations may occur when a licensee or a party makes a false statement to a potential buyer or when a licensee or an owner fails to disclose to the buyer important facts about the property. Licensees and owners have a duty to disclose material facts, if they are aware of them, affecting the value and desirability of a property. A buyer frequently asks a broker to describe a property and make representations in connection with a sale. The most common complaint concerns a listing broker's failure to point out material defects or property conditions the broker is aware of. In California, court rulings have identified "red flags" that should put the broker on notice that a problem exists—and should be brought to the buyer's attention. Such red flags include evidence of recent mudslides, obvious building code violations, and drainage and soil settlement problems. In Texas, the broker, even if licensed as a real estate inspector, is neither expected nor even allowed to function as both broker and inspector in the same transaction. The licensee is, moreover, always responsible for revealing to a prospective buyer important negative facts about a property that the licensee knows about.

In most cases of liability, a threshold issue concerns the materiality of the issue and whether statements were facts or opinions. The materiality of the issue is based on misrepresentations of factual matters and whether such matters are important to reasonably prudent homebuyers in deciding to purchase.

Generally, statements of opinion are not considered appropriate grounds for a misrepresentation or fraud suit by a buyer or a seller. This is based on the belief that most buyers or sellers will not rely on a licensee's opinion as the basis for a decision to purchase or sell. Nevertheless, a licensee must take considerable care to clarify whether a statement is merely an opinion or a fact. For example, a licensee's opinion regarding easily verifiable factual matters such as property boundaries could be interpreted by the buyer as a statement of fact. Should the statement prove incorrect, the licensee may be held liable. The licensee is well advised to never give opinions about factual matters. Furthermore, when giving opinions about non-verifiable matters, the licensee should make it unequivocally clear that the statement is an opinion. A licensee must be especially careful when dealing with a topic that might be a primary purchasing or selling factor to the principals. In such cases, the licensee should suggest employing a professional, licensed if appropriate, and should not become the source of information outside the scope of real estate licensure or expertise of the licensee.

■ **EXAMPLE** Sally's client asks her about the local school district, and she responds by quoting the ratings that have been published by state education authorities. She goes on to say that her children attend a school in the district and that she believes it to be a good district. She then suggests that the buyers visit the school authorities in order to have the opportunity to explore any areas of concern or interest with them.

■ **QUESTIONS** 1. Was Sally's statement regarding the district rating fact or opinion? 2. How would you classify Sally's statements about her experience with the district?

■ **DISCUSSION** This example is typical of questions raised by buyers. If Sally raved about the district's rating and quality and later the buyer's children do not do well in school, Sally might be exposed to some liability. Although Sally is free to express her opinion based upon her experience, it is extremely important to support factual statements with proof (documentation from the state rating agency, in this case) and further suggest that the buyers personally visit the school officials to satisfy specific needs or questions.

■ SECTION 5.008 OF THE TEXAS PROPERTY CODE (SELLER'S DISCLOSURE OF PROPERTY CONDITION)

To provide better disclosures to buyers of single-family dwellings, Section 5.008 of the Texas Property Code (TPC) requires a written seller's disclosure notice for most single-family residential resale properties.

Specifically TPC § 5.008 states the following:

> A seller of residential real property comprising not more than one dwelling unit located in this state shall give to the purchaser of the property a written notice as prescribed by this section or a written notice substantially similar to the notice prescribed by this section which contains, at a minimum, all of the items in the notice prescribed by this section.

TREC has produced a form for licensees to help sellers meet the requirements under the Texas Property Code (see Figure 3.2). The form is called Seller's Disclosure of Property Condition, and while it is an option form and not a promulgated form, it is frequently used by licensees whose brokers do not have their own brokerage versions of the form. Firms that use their versions of the form contain many more disclosures than those required by TPC § 5.008 and used by the TREC optional form. Because the TPC indicates the form used by the seller must only read "substantially similar" to the TPC wording, members of the Texas Association of REALTORS® (TAR) routinely use a modified version of the TREC form provided by that trade association. According to TREC, this form "provides a vehicle for disclosure of defects or items in need of repair." Conditions such as the presence of lead-based paint, termite damage, and flooding are also addressed. The information required to be disclosed is frequently amended during Texas legislative sessions. The disclosures most recently added to the required information include those relating to the presence of smoke detectors, carbon monoxide alarms, emergency escape ladders, the previous use of the premises for manufacture of methamphetamines, liquid propane gas, blockable drains in pools, hot tubs, or spas, and rainwater harvesting systems.

The TREC form is generally updated every two years by TREC to reflect the legislative changes in the requirements. See Figure 3.1 for Texas Property Code § 5.008 wording concerning Seller's Disclosure of Property Condition and the requirements as to which sellers must give the disclosure (in whatever form) and what the remedy is for buyers who do not receive the information. Pay particular attention to which sellers are not required to give the information.

If the notice is not given before the effective date of the contract for sale, the purchaser may terminate the contract for any reason within seven days after receiving the notice. TREC contract forms help facilitate compliance with the law. Consistent and proper use of this form gives buyers better information about the property and can help prevent lawsuits against the broker, who is also tasked with disclosing material facts about properties to consumers.

Seller's Disclosure of Property Condition, Section 5.008 of the Texas Property Code

§ 5.008. SELLER'S DISCLOSURE OF PROPERTY CONDITION.

(a)A seller of residential real property comprising not more than one dwelling unit located in this state shall give to the purchaser of the property a written notice as prescribed by this section or a written notice substantially similar to the notice prescribed by this section which contains, at a minimum, all of the items in the notice prescribed by this section.

(b) The notice must be executed and must, at a minimum, read substantially similar to the following:

[See TREC No. OP-H at http://www.trec.state.tx.us/pdf/contracts/OP-H.pdf for text of disclosure notice.]

(c) A seller or seller's agent shall have no duty to make a disclosure or release information related to whether a death by natural causes, suicide, or accident unrelated to the condition of the property occurred on the property or whether a previous occupant had, may have had, has, or may have AIDS, HIV related illnesses, or HIV infection.

(d) The notice shall be completed to the best of seller's belief and knowledge as of the date the notice is completed and signed by the seller. If the information required by the notice is unknown to the seller, the seller shall indicate that fact on the notice, and by that act is in compliance with this section.

(e) This section does not apply to a transfer:

(1) pursuant to a court order or foreclosure sale;

(2) by a trustee in bankruptcy;

(3) to a mortgagee by a mortgagor or successor in interest, or to a beneficiary of a deed of trust by a trustor or successor in interest;

(4) by a mortgagee or a beneficiary under a deed of trust who has acquired the real property at a sale conducted pursuant to a power of sale under a deed of trust or a sale pursuant to a court ordered foreclosure or has acquired the real property by a deed in lieu of foreclosure;

(5) by a fiduciary in the course of the administration of a decedent's estate, guardianship, conservatorship, or trust;

(6) from one co-owner to one or more other co-owners;

(7) made to a spouse or to a person or persons in the lineal line of consanguinity of one or more of the transferors;

(8) between spouses resulting from a decree of dissolution of marriage or a decree of legal separation or from a property settlement agreement incidental to such a decree;

(9) to or from any governmental entity;

(10) of a new residence of not more than one dwelling unit which has not previously been occupied for residential purposes; or

(11) of real property where the value of any dwelling does not exceed five percent of the value of the property.

(f) The notice shall be delivered by the seller to the purchaser on or before the effective date of an executory contract binding the purchaser to purchase the property. If a contract is entered without the seller providing the notice required by this section, the purchaser may terminate the contract for any reason within seven days after receiving the notice.

Added by Acts 1993, 73rd Leg., ch. 356, § 1, eff. Jan. 1, 1994. Amended by Acts 2005, 79th Leg., ch. 728, § 17.001, eff. Sept. 1, 2005.

Licensees should use caution in presenting to the seller any version of the information their broker is using. Many larger brokerage operations use their own versions of the form and not the TREC version, and many brokerages use the TAR form for this purpose. If a brokerage is using anything other than the TREC form, there can be a problem in presenting the form to sellers and asking them to sign the form. Why? It is not uncommon to present the form by telling the seller, "The State of Texas requires you to fill out this form." If the broker is using anything other than the TREC version, there is a problem with that statement because Texas does not require the disclosure of the additional information these brokerages' forms call for. That is why the TAR version of the Seller's Disclosure of Property Condition form says in small, but bold, print at the top of the form words to the effect that TAR's form contains more disclosures than are required by the law. The broker should consider saying something like, "Our form contains more information to be disclosed than the minimal requirements of the statute. However, if you want our brokerage to market your home, my broker requires all our sellers to use our form or we cannot list their property." That is not a misrepresentation. It is a condition of listing the property with your broker's firm.

A review of Figure 3.2 will reveal that most of the listed items involve physical conditions of the property. The mistake made by many sellers and real estate licensees, therefore, is to presume that only items shown on the Seller's Disclosure of Property Condition need be addressed by the seller. Yet liability under the Texas Deceptive Trade Practices—Consumer Protection Act (DTPA) can accrue to a seller of property for failure to disclose any "material" fact that would influence a reasonable buyer's decision to purchase, whether or not the type of defect is listed on the form. That includes both physical defects and intangible facts or "psychological stigmas" which will be discussed later in this chapter. Remember, TPC § 5.008 states that the items listed on the form represent the "minimum" items required for a seller to identify in writing. As will be discussed in more detail later, once material facts are known by the licensee, even if not on the disclosure, the licensee also becomes liable for a cause of action under the DTPA if the information is not disclosed to the buyer.

Another difficulty is that additional statutorily mandated disclosure issues can only be addressed during a legislative session (every other year in Texas). Because ongoing litigation frequently results in disclosures of new information the courts deem important to reasonable purchasers under the common law, some argue that the TREC form lacks provisions of timely notice and may be less effective in avoiding litigation than the disclosure form prepared by TAR for its members, which contains such language. TAR may add items to its seller's disclosure form at any time the organization deems appropriate. As noted earlier, some brokerage operations have seller disclosure forms that are even more extensive than the TAR forms. Some cover almost three times the amount of information than TREC's minimum-disclosures version contains.

The listing agent will most likely obtain a complete factual disclosure of property issues from the seller by explaining to the seller the purpose and importance of the Seller's Disclosure of Property Condition form. The seller (not the agent) should complete the form, and the agent should carefully explain each section of the form to ensure complete compliance with the law. Generally, a good transaction starts with a good listing presentation that successfully encourages the seller to make a full disclosure of all material facts regarding the property. Ultimately, it is the seller's decision to give full disclosure, and the seller's attorney might actually advise the seller not to give it. If the seller refuses to complete a disclosure, the wise licensee should probably walk away from the listing and not become an agent for a seller who has a problem being candid. Note, however, that there are some possible liability reasons a seller's attorney might advise a seller to not put the disclosures in writing for fear of making a misstatement and then putting that misstatement in writing.

F I G U R E 3.2

Seller's Disclosure of Property Condition

10-23-2013

APPROVED BY THE TEXAS REAL ESTATE COMMISSION (TREC)

SELLER'S DISCLOSURE OF PROPERTY CONDITION

CONCERNING THE PROPERTY AT_____
(Street Address and City)

THIS NOTICE IS A DISCLOSURE OF SELLER'S KNOWLEDGE OF THE CONDITION OF THE PROPERTY AS OF THE DATE SIGNED BY SELLER AND IS NOT A SUBSTITUTE FOR ANY INSPECTIONS OR WARRANTIES THE PURCHASER MAY WISH TO OBTAIN. IT IS NOT A WARRANTY OF ANY KIND BY SELLER OR SELLER'S AGENTS.

Seller ☐ is ☐ is not occupying the Property. If unoccupied, how long since Seller has occupied the Property? _____

1. The Property has the items checked below [Write Yes (Y), No (N), or Unknown (U)]:

_____ Range	_____ Oven	_____ Microwave
_____ Dishwasher	_____ Trash Compactor	_____ Disposal
_____ Washer/Dryer Hookups	_____ Window Screens	_____ Rain Gutters
_____ Security System	_____ Fire Detection Equipment	_____ Intercom System
	_____ Smoke Detector	
	_____ Smoke Detector-Hearing Impaired	
	_____ Carbon Monoxide Alarm	
	_____ Emergency Escape Ladder(s)	
_____ TV Antenna	_____ Cable TV Wiring	_____ Satellite Dish
_____ Ceiling Fan(s)	_____ Attic Fan(s)	_____ Exhaust Fan(s)
_____ Central A/C	_____ Central Heating	_____ Wall/Window Air Conditioning
_____ Plumbing System	_____ Septic System	_____ Public Sewer System
_____ Patio/Decking	_____ Outdoor Grill	_____ Fences
_____ Pool	_____ Sauna	_____ Spa _____ Hot Tub
_____ Pool Equipment	_____ Pool Heater	_____ Automatic Lawn Sprinkler System
_____ Fireplace(s) & Chimney (Wood burning)		_____ Fireplace(s) & Chimney (Mock)
_____ Natural Gas Lines		_____ Gas Fixtures
_____ Liquid Propane Gas	_____ LP Community (Captive)	_____ LP on Property

Garage: _____ Attached   _____ Not Attached   _____ Carport

Garage Door Opener(s): _____ Electronic   _____ Control(s)

Water Heater: _____ Gas   _____ Electric

Water Supply: _____ City   _____ Well   _____ MUD   _____ Co-op

Roof Type:_____ Age:_____ (approx.)

Are you (Seller) aware of any of the above items that are not in working condition, that have known defects, or that are in need of repair? ☐ Yes   ☐ No   ☐ Unknown. If yes, then describe. (Attach additional sheets if necessary):_____

_____

_____

_____

TREC No. OP-H

FIGURE 3.2

Seller's Disclosure of Property Condition (continued)

Seller's Disclosure Notice Concerning the Property at _____ Page 2 10-23-2013
                                                      (Street Address and City)

2. Does the property have working smoke detectors installed in accordance with the smoke detector requirements of Chapter 776, Health and Safety Code? ☐ Yes ☐ No ☐ Unknown. If the answer to this question is no or unknown, explain (Attach additional sheets if necessary): _____

_____

_____

_____

*   Chapter 776 of the Health and Safety Code requires one-family or two-family dwellings to have working smoke detectors installed in accordance with the requirements of the building code in effect in the area in which the dwelling is located, including performance, location, and power source requirements. If you do not know the building code requirements in effect in your area, you may check unknown above or contact your local building official for more information. A buyer may require a seller to install smoke detectors for the hearing impaired if: (1) the buyer or a member of the buyer's family who will reside in the dwelling is hearing impaired; (2) the buyer gives the seller written evidence of the hearing impairment from a licensed physician; and (3) within 10 days after the effective date, the buyer makes a written request for the seller to install smoke detectors for the hearing impaired and specifies the locations for the installation. The parties may agree who will bear the cost of installing the smoke detectors and which brand of smoke detectors to install.

3. Are you (Seller) aware of any known defects/malfunctions in any of the following? Write Yes (Y) if you are aware, write No (N) if you are not aware.

_____ Interior Walls	_____ Ceilings	_____ Floors
_____ Exterior Walls	_____ Doors	_____ Windows
_____ Roof	_____ Foundation/Slab(s)	_____ Sidewalks
_____ Walls/Fences	_____ Driveways	_____ Intercom System
_____ Plumbing/Sewers/Septics	_____ Electrical Systems	_____ Lighting Fixtures

_____ Other Structural Components (Describe): _____

_____

_____

If the answer to any of the above is yes, explain. (Attach additional sheets if necessary):_____

_____

_____

4. Are you (Seller) aware of any of the following conditions? Write Yes (Y) if you are aware, write No (N) if you are not aware.

_____ Active Termites (includes wood destroying insects)	_____ Previous Structural or Roof Repair
_____ Termite or Wood Rot Damage Needing Repair	_____ Hazardous or Toxic Waste
_____ Previous Termite Damage	_____ Asbestos Components
_____ Previous Termite Treatment	_____ Urea-formaldehyde Insulation
_____ Previous Flooding	_____ Radon Gas
_____ Improper Drainage	_____ Lead Based Paint
_____ Water Penetration	_____ Aluminum Wiring
_____ Located in 100-Year Floodplain	_____ Previous Fires
_____ Present Flood Insurance Coverage	_____ Unplatted Easements
_____ Landfill, Settling, Soil Movement, Fault Lines	_____ Subsurface Structure or Pits
_____ Single Blockable Main Drain in Pool/Hot Tub/Spa	_____ Previous Use of Premises for Manufacture of Methamphetamine

If the answer to any of the above is yes, explain. (Attach additional sheets if necessary):_____

_____

_____

* A single blockable main drain may cause a section entrapment hazard for an individual.

TREC No. OP-H

FIGURE 3.2

Seller's Disclosure of Property Condition (continued)

Seller's Disclosure Notice Concerning the Property at _____ Page 3 10-23-2013
(Street Address and City)

5. Are you (Seller) aware of any item, equipment, or system in or on the Property that is in need of repair? ☐ Yes (if you are aware)
☐ No (if you are not aware) If yes, explain. (Attach additional sheets if necessary): _____

_____

_____

6. Are you (Seller) aware of any of the following? Write Yes (Y) if you are aware, write No (N) if you are not aware.

_____ Room additions, structural modifications, or other alterations or repairs made without necessary permits or not in compliance with building codes in effect at that time.

_____ Homeowners' Association or maintenance fees or assessments.

_____ Any "common area" (facilities such as pools, tennis courts, walkways, or other areas) co-owned in undivided interest with others.

_____ Any notices of violations of deed restrictions or governmental ordinances affecting the condition or use of the Property.

_____ Any lawsuits directly or indirectly affecting the Property.

_____ Any condition on the Property which materially affects the physical health or safety of an individual.

_____ Any rainwater harvesting system located on the property that is larger than 500 gallons and that uses a public water supply as an auxiliary water source.

If the answer to any of the above is yes, explain. (Attach additional sheets if necessary):_____

_____

_____

7. If the property is located in a costal area that is seaward of the Gulf Intracoastal Waterway or within 14,000 feet of the mean high tide bordering the Gulf of Mexico, the property may be subject to the Open Beaches Act or the Dune Protection Act (Chapter 61 or 63, Natural Resources Code, respectively) and a beachfront construction certificate or dune protection permit maybe required for repairs or improvements. Contact the local government with ordinance authority over construction adjacent to public beaches for more information.

_____ _____
Signature of Seller   Date   Signature of Seller   Date

The undersigned purchaser hereby acknowledges receipt of the foregoing notice.

_____ _____
Signature of Purchaser   Date   Signature of Purchaser   Date

TREC No. OP-H

The following case illustrates the importance of the seller's disclosure statement, as well as the issue of facts versus opinions.

■ **EXAMPLE** In *Kessler v. Fanning*, 953 S.W.2d 515 (Tex.App., Fort Worth 1997), the Fannings purchased a property after having received the proper Seller's Disclosure of Property Condition form, which indicated that there were no drainage problems. The Fannings had the property inspected, and no drainage problems were detected, even though it was raining at the time of the inspection. However, after moving into the property, the Fannings discovered drainage problems and sued the sellers, claiming violations of the DTPA for failing to disclose a material fact. The Fannings further claimed that they would not have purchased the home had they known of the drainage problems.

Although other issues had to be decided by the court, a key issue was whether the statements by the seller constituted misrepresentations or merely statements of opinion. The TREC disclosure form used by the sellers states that the form "is not a substitute for inspections or warranties" and that it contains "representations made by the owner(s) based on the owner's knowledge." The sellers claimed that the statements contained in the disclosure form were merely opinions and not statements of fact.

The court found, however, that the statements by the sellers met the three requirements for determining whether a statement is a fact rather than opinion in that

- the statements were specific rather than vague,
- the parties did not possess the same knowledge, and
- the representations pertained to past rather than future conditions.

As statements of fact, the representations contained in the disclosure form were considered deceptive and misleading. The court found in favor of the buyers.

■ **QUESTIONS** 1. Why was the broker not also found liable in this case? 2. The buyers had their own property inspector who indicated no drainage problems. Why was the seller not able to claim that the buyers relied on the inspector rather than on their statements?

■ **DISCUSSION** This case illustrates the importance of having the seller write a detailed disclosure of property condition. The broker was able to show that the statements were those of the seller and that the broker did not know about—nor was it reasonable that he would have known about—the drainage problems.

The argument that the buyer relied on the inspection report rather than on the seller's disclosure statements may be a defense under some circumstances when no fraud has occurred. Nevertheless, the law states that an independent inspection that might have uncovered fraud does not prevent the recovery for fraudulent misrepresentations.

That is precisely why a seller's attorney may advise the seller: "Don't fill this out." Don't attempt to give the seller legal advice on whether to fill it out or not. Filling it out may work to your and your broker's advantage, but not necessarily to the seller's advantage. If you and your broker are worried about your liability, don't take the listing. If the seller is willing to let the buyer walk away at the last minute before closing and receive his earnest money back rather than fill out the form, that is his decision. Your decision is whether or not to take the listing.

■ MATERIAL FACTS

One of the more vexing issues for licensees is determining what is, or is not, a material fact relating to a transaction. Why? Because the listing broker has a fiduciary responsibility to make clear to their principal that addressing only the items shown on the Seller's Disclosure of Property Condition does not absolve the seller from disclosing other material facts that may be of importance to a reasonable buyer's decision to purchase. Furthermore, once known by the licensee, the licensee has a legal and ethical responsibility to disclose the information to any buyer.

In the fifth edition of *The Language of Real Estate*, John W. Reilly defines and discusses a material fact as follows:

> [A material fact] is any fact that is relevant to a person making a decision. Agents must disclose all material facts to their clients. Agents must also disclose to buyers material facts about the condition of the property, such as known structural defects, building code violations, and hidden dangerous conditions. Brokers are often placed in a no-win situation of trying to evaluate whether a certain fact is material enough that it needs to be disclosed to a prospective buyer, such as the fact that a murder occurred on the property 10 years ago or the fact that the neighbors throw loud parties. It is sometimes difficult to distinguish between "fact" and "opinion." The statement "real property taxes are low" is different from "real property taxes are $500 per year." Even though brokers act in good faith, they may still be liable for failure to exercise reasonable care or competence in ascertaining and communicating pertinent facts that the broker knew or "should have known."

Physical Material Facts

Generally, the physical aspects of the property that may require disclosure are easier to identify than the nonphysical issues. Physical issues may relate to any negative condition of the property itself, such as

- foundation cracking or movement;
- previous flooding;
- roof problems;
- termite infestation or damage;
- electrical problems or wiring issues (e.g., aluminum wiring);
- plumbing;
- heating, ventilation, and air conditioning (HVAC);
- well-water contamination or insufficiency;
- septic drainage or stoppage;
- lack of smoke detectors/carbon monoxide alarms;
- propane gas tanks;
- rainwater harvesting systems; and
- blockable drains in pools/hot tubs/spas.

Obviously this list could include virtually any physical component of the property. When licensees know of problems in a property relating to these types of issues, disclosures must be made. As mentioned, the seller in the Seller's Disclosure of Property Condition should reveal the negative condition of any of these types of matters; nevertheless, a buyer should be advised not to rely solely on these disclosures and to hire licensed property inspectors and/or other professionals to inspect the property carefully. Further, the buyer should know that such inspections are not warranties and that they verify only that the inspected equipment was or was not functioning adequately at the time of inspection. The buyer and the seller should be informed that warranties are available through residential service companies (a.k.a. home warranty companies), which must be registered through TREC to offer such services in Texas. As is the case in a seller providing a policy of title insurance to a buyer, it is also a prudent seller protection and marketing strategy to provide a home warranty program for a buyer.

Material Facts Relating to Title Issues

Another important disclosure relates to the type and quality of title to be conveyed by the seller to the buyer. Types of title may include fee simple, defeasible fee, and life estate. Each of these types of ownership has a different value, and the persons acquiring the property should be fully informed about them. Quality of title is not the only issue. As strange as it might seem, sometimes "no title" is an issue. There are sellers who are not owners at all. Some of these sellers actually think they do own the property but don't; others know they do not own the property but pretend to.

In addition to the type of title a purchaser receives, there are concerns regarding the quality of the title. Licensees in Texas are required by TRELA §§ 1101.555 and .652(b)(29)(A)and(B) to advise buyers **in writing before the closing** of a real estate transaction that the buyer should

(A) have the abstract covering the real estate that is the subject of the contract examined by an attorney chosen by the buyer; or

(B) be provided with or obtain a title insurance policy.

All TREC sales contract forms already contain that notice. However, under TREC Rule § 537.11(a), there are four specific allowable exceptions to having to use a TREC-promulgated contract form. In those instances, you must provide the written notice to the buyer. Your license and your commission might be at risk if you do not provide such written notice to the buyer in a timely manner. See TRELA § 1101.555 and § 1101.806(b)(c)(d).

Abstracts of title are condensed versions of all records relating to the subject property, beginning with the initial transfer from a sovereign government forward to the present owner. The abstract contains a chronology of all instruments filed into the property records; this may include taxes, judgments, releases, and so on. Although abstractors make no judgments relative to the condition or quality of title, they are liable for failing to include or properly record all pertinent data. The abstract is then examined in detail by an attorney who evaluates the facts and submits a written report (opinion of title) on the condition of the title to the purchaser. The report is considered evidence of title for the current owner.

Because both abstractor and attorney have liability for mistakes, purchasers often believe that title insurance is not necessary. Purchasers should know, however, that the liability is only for mistakes made to properly filed, truthful records. For example, documents might have been forged, unrecorded claims might exist, unknown heirs might surface—in these instances, the property owner would have no recourse. If a purchaser seeks protection from such possibilities, the purchaser should obtain title insurance.

Title insurance is a contract between the insurance carrier and the policyholder to indemnify the holder for defects in title up to the policy limits. Note that the insurer does not guarantee continued ownership, only compensation for losses up to the policy limits. Title insurance companies are regulated by the Texas Department of Insurance (TDI) and are authorized to issue standard Texas policies. As a result of the 80th Texas legislative session in 2007, title insurance companies may also offer protection against defects in title for items of personal property, such as boats, RVs, automobiles, et cetera. The extension of coverage to personal property is particularly applicable in commercial real estate and farm and ranch, where lack of clear title and/or undisclosed liens to items such as office furnishings and equipment could be quite costly to the purchaser. The coverages, available endorsements, and exceptions relating to standard Texas policies that should be disclosed to buyers are shown in the following lists.

Standard coverage includes the following:

- Defects found in public records
- Forged documents
- Incompetent grantors
- Incorrect marital statements
- Improperly delivered deeds
- Lack of access to and from land
- Lack of good and indefeasible title

Standard exceptions in Texas policies are as follows:

- Deed restrictions or covenants
- Existing liens listed in policy
- Unrecorded title defects
- Governmental rights of limitation and eminent domain
- Shortages in area or discrepancies in boundaries, encroachments, or overlapping of improvements
- Issues relating to bankruptcy
- Taxes for the current and subsequent years

Additional coverage (endorsements) may be purchased to include the following:

- Property inspection
- Rights of parties in possession (such as tenant's rights)
- Examination of survey
- Unrecorded liens not known of by policyholder
- Environmental Protection Agency (EPA) lien endorsement (concerning claims related to EPA violations)
- Homestead or community property or survivorship rights

- Tax liability due to changes in land usage (rollback taxes)
- Title defects relating to personal property

Mortgagee's (Lender's) Title Insurance   Title coverage for the lender is available and usually required when the purchaser secures a new loan on the purchased property. This sometimes is confusing when buyers who have negotiated title policies to be furnished by sellers are charged for a mortgagee's title policy at closing. This policy is a separate policy to ensure that the lender has a valid lien against the property. The amount of coverage is for the original loan amount, and coverage decreases as the loan balance decreases, while the owner's title policy is for the sales price and remains constant. For these reasons, as well as the fact that the research is only required once, the price of a mortgagee's policy is considerably less when purchased in connection with an owner's title policy.

Material Facts Relating to Survey Issues

As with defects or flaws in the title to the property, any known problems relating to the physical description of the property must be disclosed. These problems may include discrepancies in the area of the property, boundary lines, encroachments, or the overlapping of improvements from one property onto the property of another. Note that these types of problems are specifically excepted from the standard title policy as shown.

Buyers should be advised not to rely on measurements furnished by the seller, measurements of a licensee, or their own measurements, but on the measurements of a registered professional land surveyor. Additionally, a buyer should be alerted that previous surveys, perhaps furnished by the seller, should not be relied on; the buyer should obtain a new survey. Surveys are generally required when

- conveying a portion of a given tract of land,
- obtaining a mortgage loan,
- government entities acquire land through condemnation procedures,
- showing the location of new or existing improvements, and
- determining legal descriptions of properties.

■ STIGMATIZED PROPERTIES

Another type of disclosure issue involves material facts related to stigmatized properties. Stigma refers to a perception of conditions or events (real or imagined) related to a property that reduces the marketability or value of the property. Stigmas may be classified as purely psychological stigmas or physical stigmas.

Purely Psychological Stigmas

Purely psychological stigmas are those that occur as a result of real or imagined events, at the property, that have no actual physical impact on the property or the occupants. An example of this type of stigma is a death occurring on the property as a result of natural causes, accident, murder, suicide, or an AIDS-related illness.

A stigma may also arise from a notorious event or individual associated with the property. Highly publicized and negatively stigmatized properties include the apartment building in which the serial killer Jeffrey Dahmer housed his victims;

the California home where Andrew Luster, the great-grandson of cosmetics magnate Max Factor and heir to a fortune, allegedly drugged and raped women; and the home of former football star O.J. Simpson in Buckingham Estate. The Dahmer and the Simpson houses were ultimately demolished because of severe stigma. In 2003, the Luster house finally sold for more than 20 percent below its non-stigmatized market value. Yet in none of the cases were the buildings physically impacted by the events. In the O.J. Simpson case, the alleged murder of his former wife and her friend did not even occur on the Buckingham property, but rather the stigma arose from the fact that Simpson, the accused murderer, lived in the house.

Curiously, one person's stigma can be another person's selling point. For example, after his shooting death on the steps of his own property, fashion designer Gianni Versace's mansion ultimately sold for $19 million, the highest price ever paid for a house in Miami-Dade County. Jacqueline Kennedy Onassis's apartment on Manhattan's Fifth Avenue, even though she died in the apartment, sold in 1995 for $9.5 million and listed as recently as 2006 for $32 million. So while the value of one property may be negatively impacted by horrific events (the Luster house), another property may represent the ultimate in glamour and style (Kennedy) to the purchaser.

It is important for licensees to accept that whether potential buyers will be concerned about death or horrific events on a property frequently relates to whether the previous owner was celebrated or disgraced, how long ago the event occurred, and the impact of the event on the public conscience. Furthermore, highly publicized stories such as the Dahmer, Versace, or Kennedy stories produce buyers who are fully aware of the property's reputation and know exactly what they are getting. But when deaths are private, buyers caught unaware tend to call their broker or attorney and ask, "Shouldn't we have been told this?" So purely psychological stigmas raise a number of issues for licensees, including materiality, fact or fiction, duration of the stigma, and laws relating to disclosure of certain events. Suppose it is rumored that satanic rites have been performed in a property by a previous occupant, or that a murder occurred at a property 10 years ago, or that a previous occupant had an AIDS-related illness—would these issues require disclosure? The answers to some of these questions may be found in Texas law. In 1993, the Texas legislature passed certain statutes relating to disclosure, later incorporated into The Real Estate License Act:

> § 1101.556. DISCLOSURE OF CERTAIN INFORMATION RELATING TO OCCUPANTS. Notwithstanding other law, a license holder is not required to inquire about, disclose, or release information relating to whether:
>
> (1) a previous or current occupant of real property had, may have had, has, or may have AIDS, an HIV-related illness, or an HIV infection as defined by the Centers for Disease Control and Prevention of the United States Public Health Service; or
>
> (2) a death occurred on a property by natural causes, suicide, or accident unrelated to the condition of the property.

It should be noted that on the issue of AIDS-related disclosures, TRELA does not prohibit disclosure; rather, it merely relieves the licensee of a duty to disclose. It is important, however, to note that TREC rules actually prohibit such disclosures

(22 TAC § 531.19) under the Canons of Professional Ethics and Conduct for Real Estate Licensees. Further guidelines on this issue may be found in the 1988 Fair Housing Amendment Act, which added persons with handicaps as a protected class. AIDS-HIV–related illnesses are included in the definition of a handicap. As a result, statements by the Department of Housing and Urban Development (HUD) make it illegal for licensees to make disclosures regarding an occupant or prior occupant with problems related to AIDS-HIV. In addition, HUD advises that licensees not respond to direct questions relating to these matters even if the licensee has actual knowledge that an occupant or prior occupant has, or has had, an AIDS-HIV–related illness. Although HUD has not produced an acceptable statement, the National Association of REALTORS®, in its Legal Liability Series relating to property disclosures as to previous occupants, recommends the following response when members are asked questions relating to these issues:

> It is the policy of our firm not to answer inquiries of this nature one way or the other since the firm feels that this information is not material to the transaction. In addition, any type of response to such inquiries by me or other salespeople of our firm may be a violation of the federal fair housing laws. If you believe that this information is relevant to your decision to buy the property, you must pursue this investigation on your own.

In relation to the four classifications of causes of death—natural causes, accident, suicide, and homicide—Texas law, as quoted here, requires that only a homicide be affirmatively disclosed. However, it is reasonable to believe that many buyers might be affected negatively if any type of death has occurred at the property. Remember that any type of death (or other issue) may be disclosed with permission of the client. A licensee who is concerned about such matters should discuss the issue with the seller and, if not satisfactorily resolved, should consider refusing the listing.

Under 22 TAC 535.156, the licensee is tasked with conveying to the client any information that would impact the client's decision to make, accept, or reject offers. Further, 22 TAC 535.2(b) obligates the agent to convey to the client "all information of which the agent has knowledge and which may affect the client's decision." It can therefore be reasonably argued that properties can be stigmatized by happenings not on but within the vicinity of the subject property that would also be material to a reasonable buyer's decision to purchase.

Nearby activities that might concern a reasonable purchaser include

- persistent criminal activity,
- drive-by shootings,
- planned rezoning of vacant lot,
- large airport considering extending its flight path over the neighborhood,
- numerous pet disappearances/killings,
- planned sewage treatment plant, and
- noisy, obnoxious neighbors.

Physical Stigmas

Physical stigmas arise when some negative or detrimental physical or environmental condition exists that may not directly affect the property but may affect the health or safety of the occupants. These conditions may have real or imagined health-related problems, but in either case the property suffers a loss in marketability or value. Problems in this area may include asbestos, lead hazards, electromagnetic fields (EMFs), radon, chlorofluorocarbon emissions, hazardous waste disposal, underground storage tanks, soil or groundwater contamination, and previous use of premises for manufacture of methamphetamines.

Although there is much conjecture regarding the true health risks of many of these problems, property values may be affected when the public becomes aware of such a condition. In her article "When Bad Things Happen to Good Properties" (Tierra Grande, April 1999), Jennifer Hoffman cites the asbestos scare of the 1970s as an example:

> The fibrous material was commonly used in the construction industry for decades until studies began to demonstrate that the asbestos fibers could infiltrate the lungs—a potentially fatal condition. Hitting the papers, this news caused a near panic in some real estate markets. "Many properties containing asbestos were stigmatized, becoming unmarketable virtually overnight," says Guntermann.
>
> With more scientific information available, public fear and concern in the real estate community dissipated and became more narrowly focused on a smaller sample of properties than originally suspected.

Although today the presence of asbestos requires disclosure to potential buyers, the stigma is much reduced due to better knowledge and understanding of remedies.

Guidelines for Disclosure of Stigmatized Properties

The National Association of REALTORS®, in its Legal Liability Series, offers members the following guidelines in the publication *Property Disclosures—What You Should Know*:

- **Determine whether the information is fact or fiction.** Investigate the validity of the information by checking sources such as newspaper accounts or reports from state or local agencies. Separate rumor from reality. If the stigma is based on rumor and not on facts that can be confirmed, there may be no obligation to disclose. If, on the other hand, the stigma turns out to be factual (e.g., there was in fact a murder on or near the property) you should proceed to the next step.
- **Check state law.** In Texas the law requires disclosure of all physical facts regarding the property. With nonphysical matters, the requirement to disclose will hinge on the materiality of the matter.
- **Determine materiality.** To analyze the materiality of a set of facts that may produce a stigma, one must determine whether knowledge of those facts would affect the willingness of a reasonable person in deciding whether to buy the property or the amount of money to offer or pay for the property. Most stigmatized property cases involve

stigmas that are less sensational than, for example, a multiple murder on the property. Less sensational stigmas may or may not impact the market value of the property. Whether or not the problem is a high-profile one, however, it is necessary to assess how reasonable persons would react to the information and if they are less likely to desire to purchase the property.

Alternately, one should consider how the "market" would judge such a property and whether it can be objectively concluded that the market value of the property is less because of the property's history. If this analysis results in the conclusion that the facts and stigma may have an impact on the buying decision of prospective purchasers, the facts creating the stigma are probably material and should be disclosed.

■ **Discuss disclosure with the sellers.** A listing agent who concludes that the physical or psychological stigma-producing facts are material and need to be disclosed should also discuss with sellers the basis for his conclusions and his intended course of action. The sellers need and deserve to understand the salesperson's analysis and why the particular facts may affect the marketing and sale of their property and, thus, must be disclosed. Often sellers can understand the problem better if they are asked to consider themselves in the position of a prospective purchaser and whether or not they would want the factual information before deciding to purchase or what to offer for the property. Discussing the matter with the sellers up front avoids objections and controversy later about why the particular facts were disclosed to prospective purchasers.

If the sellers refuse to agree to disclose what the listing broker (or a subagent working with the listing broker) has determined to be a material factor regarding the property, the agents should strongly consider terminating the listing or other involvement in the transaction.

Although such guidelines are helpful, the licensee should seek competent legal counsel whenever there is doubt regarding disclosure issues. Members of the Texas Association of REALTORS®, for example, may contact the TAR legal hotline for guidance. The following case illustrates the difficulty of determining the materiality of facts regarding stigmatized property.

■ **EXAMPLE**   In *Sanchez v. Guerrero*, 885 S.W.2d 487 (Tex. App.—El Paso, 1994), the Guerreros purchased a VA-foreclosed property through broker Sanchez. After closing, the Guerreros discovered that a prior occupant of the property had been indicted (although acquitted) of child molestation in the property. Upon learning this information, the new buyers moved out and later sold the property at a loss. The Guerreros then sued Sanchez, alleging that the broker was aware of the circumstance and willfully withheld the information in order to induce them to buy the property. The suit brought under the DTPA was won by the Guerreros, finding that the broker took advantage of the buyer's lack of knowledge of real estate to a grossly unfair degree and supported a claim for mental anguish, as well as damages. The jury awarded the Guerreros $120,000 in actual damages, $20,000 for closing costs, and $100,000 for mental anguish.

■ **QUESTIONS**   1. What implication does this have for licensees regarding disclosure of events that may not have happened but apparently created a stigmatized property? 2. What types of crimes that may or may not have occurred on the property must be disclosed? 3. Would the broker be exposed to a potential libel suit from the acquitted defendant for disclosing this information to the Guerreros?

■ **DISCUSSION**   Unfortunately, this case raises more questions than it resolves. The fact that a prior occupant had been accused of a notorious crime, even though acquitted, was sufficient to create a stigma that would have required disclosure by the broker. The broker admitted knowledge of the circumstances surrounding the property but felt that the alleged crime had no direct or physical impact on the property and therefore did not need to be disclosed. Further, the defendant argued that as the accused had been acquitted, it would have been inappropriate and potentially libelous to make such a disclosure. The court disagreed on the basis that the information was public knowledge and that the story had been reported in the media. All in all, a very troubling case for Texas brokers.

Megan's Law   An issue related to *Sanchez v. Guerrero* is the federal law concerning the registration of individuals convicted of child molestation and other dangerous sex crimes. The federal government now requires states to develop and implement registration procedures for released sex offenders living in their communities. The federal law requiring such registration is commonly known as Megan's Law.

Current Texas law enacted as a result requires a released sex offender to register with local law enforcement agencies and be photographed and fingerprinted. This information must be submitted to superintendents of public schools and to the administrators of private primary and secondary schools in the district where the offender resides. Additionally, enforcement officials must publish in a local newspaper information regarding the offender, including the name, age, and gender, a brief description of the offense, the street name, zip code, and municipality of residence, and the person's risk level, generally. If the individual is determined to be high risk (level 1), then notices must be mailed by the Texas Department of Public Safety (DPS) to each residential address within three blocks in a subdivided area, or within one mile in an area that is not subdivided.

Texas law exempts owners of single-family residences and real estate agents from a duty to disclose information relating to sex offenders to prospective buyers or tenants. Licensees should refer their buyer-clients to the DPS database to conduct their own research regarding sex offenders in the area.

Although the law does not require agents to make a sex offender disclosure, many licensees feel compelled to do so on ethical grounds. Further, it may be implied that when representing a buyer, a duty of care to the buyer would include disclosure of a released offender living in near proximity to a property being considered for purchase. When representing a seller who requests that such information not be disclosed, the broker should consider the advisability of offering brokerage services to the seller.

In any event, such disclosures should be approached with great care, citing the source of information and warning that the information may be incorrect or incomplete. A licensee is cautioned from making any related statements based on rumor or hearsay.

Even when a licensee has no specific knowledge that a sex offender lives in close proximity, it may be advisable to add this issue to a general checklist of items that may concern prospective buyers, including guidance on where to obtain such information. Such sources include local law enforcement agencies and lists published on websites. In Texas, sex offender information may be found at the Texas Department of Public Safety website, www.dps.texas.gov.

Prohibited Disclosures to Third Parties

Licensees should take care during disclosure to avoid volunteering information about or responding to questions relating to protected classes under federal, state, or local fair housing laws. Prohibited disclosures relate to race, color, religion, sex, national origin, familial status, or handicap. Such questions may be asked by buyers in relation to specific owners and/or properties, or neighborhoods in general. If the potential buyers have concerns relating to these matters, they should be advised to seek information through their own independent investigations. TREC Rule § 531.19(a) of the Canons of Ethics also prohibits licensees from discrimination based on ancestry.

In addition to the matters described, care must be taken not to volunteer to the buyer so much information that the client's negotiating position is compromised. Suppose the licensee knows that the sellers are anxious to sell because they have just completed the purchase of another home. If the owner's broker discloses this information and the prospective buyer chooses to offer substantially less than the listing price, the seller can claim that the listing broker acted contrary to the seller's best interests and cancel the listing. The buyer obviously would like to know that the seller is considering a price reduction, but the owner's broker is not privileged to release this information. On the other hand, a buyer broker who learns of this fact would be obligated to tell the buyer that information. Owners, as well as "loose lipped" owner's agents, frequently simply divulge too much to buyers and buyer brokers at open houses or elsewhere.

What if the seller orders the listing broker not to disclose a material fact, such as a basement that floods? If such an order is given early in the listing period, the broker should decline the listing and refuse to work with this seller. But if the order comes two days before closing, after the broker has fully performed all obligations, should the broker disregard the instruction, make the disclosure, and protect the earned commission, even if the disclosure prevents the sale? Whenever full and fair disclosure of a material fact is not made, the real estate agent is at risk. The broker has an independent duty to the buyer to take reasonable steps to avoid giving the buyer false information or concealing material facts. Seek immediate legal counsel in these situations. It is not a good idea to continue to market the property until you have resolved the problem.

■ LIABILITY FOR MISREPRESENTATION

Under the DTPA (Chapter 12), to file a successful misrepresentation claim against a broker, the plaintiff must prove that the

■ broker made a misstatement (oral or written) to the buyer or failed to disclose a known material fact to the buyer,
■ broker either knew or should have known that the statement was not accurate or that certain undisclosed information should have been disclosed,
■ buyer reasonably relied on such statement, and
■ buyer was damaged as a result.

Element of Reliance

Courts have held that the buyer is entitled to relief if the representation was a material inducement to the contract, even though the buyer may have made efforts to discover the truth and did not rely wholly on the representation. Also, agency is no defense; that is, it is generally not a defense that the broker merely passed along information that the seller provided—for example, the amount of taxes or the connection to the sewer system. The seller has a duty not to misrepresent, and the broker's duty stems from the seller's duty.

In fixing liability or in applying remedies, TRELA and various ethical codes make no distinction between whether the misrepresentation was intentional or negligent. Under changes made to the DTPA during the 82nd legislative session, however, legislators decided that licensees should not be held liable for innocent acts of misrepresentation. The difficulty arises when licensees are unable to prove they did not know or could not have known of the material fact.

Revisions to the DTPA in the 82nd Legislature (2011) also exclude the rendering of professional services from the purview of that act, meaning that a licensee's advice, opinion, or judgment cannot serve as a cause of action. However, the courts have not set precedence as to the meaning of "advice, opinion, or judgment" in the case of real estate licensees. Unfortunately, dissatisfied consumers tend to later remember a licensee's statement as being one of "fact" rather than "opinion," particularly if the decision to purchase was based on the statement and it turns out to be incorrect information.

Under a successful cause of action filed under the DTPA, plaintiff remedies include

■ monetary damages,
■ rescission of the contract, and
■ forfeiture of the broker's commission.

Under TRELA, enforcement actions against licensees include the following:

■ Criminal Prosecution (§ 1101.756)
■ State Civil Penalty (§ 1101.753)
■ Administrative Penalty (§ 1101.701)
■ Court Injunctions (§ 1101.751)

Watch What Is Said

Brokers must carefully consider their statements to consumers. The broker is considered the real estate expert; therefore, consumers rely on what the broker says, even when the broker is not acting as their agent. Following is a short list of broker statements that should never be made:

- No need to get a title search. I sold this same property last year, and there was no title problem.
- Don't worry, the seller told me by phone I could sign the contract for her.
- If it helps you make up your mind about the price to offer on my listing, the seller countered a $230,000 offer last week with $235,000.
- I won't be able to present your offer until the seller decides on the offer submitted yesterday.
- I can't present your offer yet. We have a contract working.
- I can't/won't present your offer with that type of contingency clause in there.
- Go ahead and make an offer. If you can't get financing, you don't have to buy anyway and you'll still get your earnest money back.
- I can't submit your offer without earnest money. It's not legal.
- Trust me. I can word a contingency clause in such a way that you can back out whenever you want.
- You don't have to disclose anything that is not listed on the Seller's Disclosure of Property Condition.

■ SUMMARY

In addition to the fiduciary duties owed to a client, a licensee must be aware of duties to third parties to the agency transaction. These duties include honesty, fairness, and a duty to disclose material facts regarding the property.

Material facts are important facts that may affect the decision to purchase or the price to offer. These facts may relate to physical attributes and title and survey problems, as well as certain stigmas that may have been attached to the property. These stigmas may be purely psychological, stemming from events that may have occurred in the property but that do not directly affect the structure, such as a death on the property. Other sources of stigma are physical psychological issues relating to environmental or other conditions surrounding the property that may affect the health or safety of the occupants, such as electromagnetic fields or radon gas.

Licensees should be constantly alert for circumstances or conditions that require disclosure and ensure that such disclosures are made in writing. In matters where the licensee is unsure of a disclosure issue, the licensee should consult a competent attorney.

■ KEY POINTS

- ■ An agency contract is a two-party agreement in which a client engages an agent to represent the client's interests; however, agency becomes functional when the agent represents her client with or toward a third party.

- ■ Licensees should take considerable care in avoiding misrepresentations to clients or third parties. Misrepresentations may occur by misstatements or by the omission of important facts by the licensee.

- ■ While duties owed to a third party are not fiduciary duties, they are strong and include a duty to treat the third party fairly and honestly. In addition, the licensee is obligated to disclose any material facts regarding the property that might affect the buyer's decision to purchase the property or the amount the buyer would be willing to pay.

- ■ Licensees should be certain that affected residential sellers complete the Seller's Disclosure of Property Condition form in complete detail and that, whenever possible, the potential buyer receives a copy before signing an offer to purchase.

- ■ Material facts are those facts that would affect a reasonable buyer's decision to buy, or the amount of money to be offered for the property, and include but are not limited to the following:
  - — Physical condition
  - — Title issues
  - — Survey issues
  - — Stigmatized properties

- ■ Stigmas may be created from purely psychological sources, such as the reaction of a purchaser to a death that may have occurred on the property, or from physical conditions outside the property that may have a negative health or safety effect on the occupants. Examples of physical stigmas are exposure to radon gas or electromagnetic fields.

The National Association of REALTORS® suggests the following guidelines when dealing with stigmatized properties:

- ■ Determine whether the information is fact or fiction.
- ■ Check state law.
- ■ Determine materiality.
- ■ Discuss disclosure with the seller.
- ■ Although a licensee has a duty to disclose material facts to a third party, care should be exercised not to disclose confidential nonmaterial information to a third party that could be detrimental to the best interest of the client.

■ SUGGESTIONS FOR BROKERS

Research indicates that a key reason for complaints against licensees across the nation relates to misrepresentation or omission of important information to clients and customers. In response to this problem, brokers should encourage associated licensees to participate in continuing education efforts in this area. Further, a well-designed, ongoing legal issue program is strongly recommended as part of company training. Keep in mind that the laws governing disclosure are dynamic and must be reviewed carefully and frequently.

CHAPTER 3 QUIZ

1. Title insurance companies in Texas are regulated by the
   a. Texas Department of Insurance.
   b. Texas Real Estate Commission.
   c. Texas attorney general.
   d. U.S. attorney general.

2. Title coverage for the lender is called
   a. mortgagor's title insurance.
   b. mortgage company title insurance.
   c. title commitment.
   d. mortgagee's title insurance.

3. The buyer should only rely on measurements furnished by
   a. the seller's previous survey.
   b. the listing agent.
   c. the registered professional land surveyor.
   d. all of these.

4. On the issue of AIDS-related disclosures,
   a. TREC rules and federal fair housing laws prohibit disclosure.
   b. TREC rules do not prohibit disclosure.
   c. licensees may follow their best judgment.
   d. HUD requires the licensee to respond to a direct question from the buyer.

5. Under Megan's Law, individual states
   a. may choose to ignore Megan's Law.
   b. must develop procedures for registering sex offenders.
   c. must require licensees to disclose registered sex offenders.
   d. are required to post a sign in the yard of the offender identifying the occupant as a sex offender.

6. What obligation does an agent have to disclose information regarding a convicted child molester in close proximity to a subject property?
   a. The agent is under no obligation to make this disclosure but could refer individuals to the DPS database.
   b. The agent is required to disclose if the seller gives authorization to disclose.
   c. The agent is required to disclose even if it is only rumor.
   d. The agent is required to disclose only if the buyer asks.

7. A seller states that he will list his home with you only if you do not reveal to prospective buyers that the police have twice raided the house next door for suspected drug activity. You should
   a. take the listing as long as there was no conviction.
   b. take the listing but reveal the information to prospective buyers.
   c. decline the listing and refuse to work with this seller.
   d. refer the seller to another agent in your office and take a referral fee.

8. The listing agent tells the buyer that the seller installed a new air conditioner as agreed in the contract, when in fact the seller only refurbished the existing air conditioner. Under TRELA, the licensee is
   a. not liable because the misrepresentation was not intentional.
   b. not liable because the misrepresentation was not negligent.
   c. not liable because he only passed on the seller's representation.
   d. liable.

9. A property whose value or marketability has been affected by conditions or events related to the property

    a. is considered unsalable.
    b. is considered stigmatized.
    c. is considered valueless by appraisers.
    d. may not legally be sold until the condition is corrected.

10. A property whose value has been diminished by a murder occurring on the property has suffered which of the following?

    a. Physical stigma
    b. Incurable obsolescence
    c. Curable obsolescence
    d. Purely psychological stigma

DISCUSSION QUESTIONS

1. Presume that you have learned from a neighbor that a property that you are attempting to list was the site of a death that occurred by natural causes. How would you approach the seller regarding this matter?

2. List the conditions or circumstances regarding a property that you consider important in making a decision to purchase. Compare your list with others.

3. In reference to question 2, how do the comparative lists illustrate the difficulty in determining the materiality of an issue?

CHAPTER

Seller Agency

Until the late 1990s, the traditional viewpoint in real estate brokerage was that the real estate licensee, when acting as an agent in a transaction, represented the seller. In fact, until 1988, when the first written agency disclosure was required in Texas, most licensees, clients, and customers gave very little thought to who represented whom. This agency disclosure requirement had the effect of raising the awareness of both the public and the licensees. Once consumers recognized that they were entitled to representation, more and more buyers began to actively seek brokers who were willing to offer advocacy to the purchaser. The growth in buyer representation in turn led to conflicting loyalties when brokers found themselves trying to offer agency/advocacy to both sides of the transaction. This, in turn, led to a very special and complex relationship involving dual representation. Consequently, with the increased awareness of the dynamics of the agency relationship came the necessity to first adequately identify the responsibilities agents assume by law when they agree to represent a single party to a real estate transaction. Brokers who represent only sellers or only buyers are practicing single agency; that is, they only have one client. The broker owes all fiduciary duties and all common law of agency duties only to the seller or buyer-client. In this chapter, we will explore the broker's responsibility when acting as an agent to the seller. This is called exclusive seller agency. We will identify how these agency responsibilities translate into our dealings with the buyer-customer-third party. In Chapter 5, we will deal with a similar type of single agency known as exclusive buyer agency. The more complex relationship, known as "intermediary," involves brokers who elect to provide representation to both a seller and a buyer in the same transaction and will be addressed in later chapters.

■ LISTING AGREEMENTS

The most common and easily recognized agency relationship in real estate is that between the seller (client) and the listing broker (agent). The relationship is usually evidenced by a written agreement called a listing agreement, typically an exclusive-right-to-sell listing. Listing agreements are generally used to establish the agency relationship between the seller and the broker. Although the actual listing agreement is frequently presented and signed by an associate of the broker on the broker's behalf, the agency relationship and all the rights and obligations of the agreement fall to the broker. These agency and contractual duties flow through the broker to all the associated licensees of the broker. Additionally, if other licensees not associated with the firm are permitted to represent the seller through the listing broker, the duties of the other licensees to the seller will be the same as those of the listing broker. This arrangement, although becoming much less common, is known as subagency.

Express and Implied Agreements

Listing agreements, as well as other agency agreements, may be either oral or in writing. TRELA § 1101.806 states that

> a person may not maintain an action in this state to recover a commission for the sale or purchase of real estate unless the promise or agreement on which the action is based, or a memorandum, is in writing and signed by the party against whom the action is brought or by a person authorized by that party to sign the document.

In other words, it is not illegal to take an oral listing on real property, but if the seller refuses to pay an orally agreed-on commission, the broker cannot look to the courts to compel the seller to pay. An oral listing agreement and commission entitlement may, however, be enforced against third parties who attempt to tortiously (wrongfully) interfere with them (for example, a licensee from another firm who attempts to list a property during the term of an oral listing).

Neither a written contract nor an oral agreement to pay a fee is necessary to create an agency relationship with the seller. As discussed earlier, the words and conduct of the parties may create an agency relationship. An agency relationship created in this manner is called an **implied agency,** and a broker may be surprised when a court determines there is an agency relationship when the broker intended none. The courts review the broker's words and actions to determine whether an agency relationship exists, even if there is no written agreement between the broker and the buyer or the seller. This implied agency could be a result of a previous relationship with the principal. For example, a licensee has represented a buyer in acquiring a new home and then unofficially helps the principal sell another property. Under these circumstances, it is assumed that the licensee has a close working relationship with the former client that is likely to continue after the previous contract is fulfilled or has terminated. Buyers who have been clients of a broker thus may continue to be clients when they subsequently sell a property with the unofficial help of the broker, even though no written listing agreement has been signed. What is the safest way to proceed, for both the broker and the seller or the buyer, when desiring to create an agency relationship? Answer: Create the agency agreement in writing, delineating all the rights and obligations of the parties to the agreement, thereby creating a written express agency.

Regardless of how the agency relationship originated, once created with the seller, the law imposes a number of fiduciary duties on the seller's agent (under the common law of agency, those duties include obedience, loyalty, disclosure, confidentiality, accounting, and reasonable care and diligence). One of the agent's most important duties to the seller is to protect and promote the best interests of the seller. The interests of the seller must be placed above those of anyone else, including the agent's own interests. The seller's agent owes absolute allegiance (loyalty) to the seller.

Types of Listing Agreements

The three generally recognized types of listing agreements that brokers and sellers can enter into are

- exclusive-right-to-sell listings,
- exclusive-agency listings, and
- open listings.

The type of listing the broker and the seller select depends on the circumstances surrounding the seller's motivation to sell and the broker's policies regarding listings.

Exclusive-Right-to-Sell Listing   The exclusive-right-to-sell listing offers the broker the greatest amount of protection and security, and, generally, offers the seller the greatest amount of service. Under this agreement, the broker is entitled to the contractually agreed fee or commission **no matter who sells the property— even if it is the seller.** The seller also benefits because by signing the exclusive-right-to-sell listing agreement, the seller is offering the maximum protection to the broker and the broker can then afford to invest time and money promoting the property with the assurance of payment regardless of who finds the buyer. It can be very costly for a broker to market listings and to operate a general brokerage business. The exclusive-right-to-sell listing agreement ensures payment to the listing broker, whether one of his agents procures a ready, willing, and able buyer for the seller's property, or whether another broker from a different company, or his sales associate brings in a ready, willing, and able buyer.

Most brokers avoid listings that do not have a reasonable chance to sell or that do not fairly compensate the broker for expenses. The brokerage business is just like any other business; it must pay for operations and give its investors a fair return on their money. The exclusive-right-to-sell listing gives the broker a greater opportunity to realize those goals. Brokers holding an exclusive-right-to-sell listing usually will agree to let other brokers negotiate with the seller through them. The listing broker typically agrees to pay the other broker some part or percentage of the commission paid by the seller. When brokers agree to cooperate in this manner, sellers gain wider exposure for their properties. Figure 4.1 shows the lines of communication and negotiation in an exclusive-right-to-sell listing.

FIGURE 4.1

Lines of Communication With an Exclusive-Right-to-Sell Listing

Figure 4.2 is the exclusive-right-to-sell listing agreement made available by the Texas Association of REALTORS® exclusively for use by its members. Notice that it states "USE OF THIS FORM BY PERSONS WHO ARE NOT MEMBERS OF THE TEXAS ASSOCIATION OF REALTORS® IS NOT AUTHORIZED." Forms establishing contractual business relationships between brokers and clients are not provided by TREC for licensee use. The TAR form is provided here, however, as an example of the types of contractual provisions that should be addressed when establishing an agency relationship with the seller of a residential property. When negotiating the listing agreement with the seller, the licensee, at this point, is not the agent of the seller and does not owe the seller any fiduciary duties. The licensee should carefully cover the agreement line by line, explaining the provisions of the document clearly. The moment the seller and the broker/broker associate sign the listing agreement, the agency relationship and the fiduciary duties of the broker begin. Examples of provisions that should be routinely addressed in a listing contract include the following:

■ Parties to the contract (paragraph 1)

- Legal description of the property (paragraph 2)
- Initial listing price of the property (paragraph 3)
- The term of the contract (beginning and ending date) (paragraph 4)
- Broker's compensation (paragraph 5)
  — How is it calculated?
  — When is it earned?
  — When is it payable?
  — Who pays it?
  — Are there miscellaneous fees?
  — Is there a protection period?
- Listing services the broker will provide (paragraph 6)
  — Will the broker place the listing in the MLS?
- Access to the property (paragraph 7)
  — Are there restrictions on the access times?
  — Are lockboxes permitted?
- Cooperation/fees involving other brokers (paragraph 8)
  — Will the seller permit cooperation with other brokers?
  — Will the seller permit licensees who are non-members of the multiple listing service (MLS) to show the property?
  — Will the seller permit both cooperating buyers' agents as well as sub-agents to show the property?
- Intermediary (paragraph 9)
  — On an in-house transaction will the seller permit the broker to also represent the buyer, and if so, how does that impact on the commission earned?
  — Can the seller still receive advice and opinion?

An exclusive-agency listing allows sellers to reserve the right to sell a property themselves without the obligation to pay a commission or fee, if successful. Under an exclusive-agency listing, a seller can do this and still have the property listed by a broker. If, however, another brokerage firm secures a buyer, it must present the contract through the listing brokerage; it cannot go directly to the seller. Hence the term *exclusive agency*—indicating that another real estate company cannot work directly with the seller. Caution: Do not confuse the term "agency" when used to denote a "business entity," with the term "agency" when used to declare a position of legal representation. Consider these examples:

- John Smith is the broker for ABC Brokerage, a real estate agency (business entity).
- Mary Jones, broker for XYZ Real Estate, Inc. is the listing agent and is in an agency relationship with Mr. Baxter (principal/client) in the sale of his home (position of legal representation).

FIGURE 4.2

Exclusive Right to Sell Listing Agreement

TEXAS ASSOCIATION OF REALTORS®

RESIDENTIAL REAL ESTATE LISTING AGREEMENT
EXCLUSIVE RIGHT TO SELL

USE OF THIS FORM BY PERSONS WHO ARE NOT MEMBERS OF THE TEXAS ASSOCIATION OF REALTORS® IS NOT AUTHORIZED.
©Texas Association of REALTORS®, Inc. 2014

1. **PARTIES:** The parties to this agreement (this Listing) are:

Seller: _____
_____
Address: _____
City, State, Zip: _____
Phone:_____Fax: _____
E-Mail: _____

Broker: _____
Address: _____
City, State, Zip: _____
Phone:_____Fax: _____
E-Mail: _____

Seller appoints Broker as Seller's sole and exclusive real estate agent and grants to Broker the exclusive right to sell the Property.

2. **PROPERTY:** "Property" means the land, improvements, and accessories described below, except for any described exclusions.

A. <u>Land:</u> Lot_____, Block_____, _____
_____ Addition, City of_____,
in _____ County, Texas known as _____
_____ (address/zip code),
or as described on attached exhibit. (If Property is a condominium, attach Condominium Addendum.)

B. <u>Improvements:</u> The house, garage and all other fixtures and improvements attached to the above-described real property, including without limitation, the following **permanently installed and built-in items,** if any: all equipment and appliances, valances, screens, shutters, awnings, wall-to-wall carpeting, mirrors, ceiling fans, attic fans, mail boxes, television antennas and satellite dish system and equipment, mounts and brackets for televisions and speakers, heating and air-conditioning units, security and fire detection equipment, wiring, plumbing and lighting fixtures, chandeliers, water softener system, kitchen equipment, garage door openers, cleaning equipment, shrubbery, landscaping, outdoor cooking equipment, and all other property owned by Seller and attached to the above-described real property.

C. <u>Accessories:</u> The following described related accessories, if any: window air conditioning units, stove, fireplace screens, curtains and rods, blinds, window shades, draperies and rods, door keys, mailbox keys, above-ground pool, swimming pool equipment and maintenance accessories, artificial fireplace logs, and controls for: (i) satellite dish systems, (ii) garage doors, (iii) entry gates, and (iv) other improvements and accessories.

(TAR-1101) 01-01-14   Initialed for Identification by Broker/Associate _____and Seller_____, _____   Page 1 of 10

F I G U R E 4.2

Exclusive Right to Sell Listing Agreement (continued)

Residential Listing concerning_____

    D. <u>Exclusions</u>: The following improvements and accessories will be retained by Seller and must be removed prior to delivery of possession: _____
_____.

    E. <u>Owners' Association</u>: The property ❑ is ❑ is not subject to mandatory membership in a property owners' association.

3. **LISTING PRICE:** Seller instructs Broker to market the Property at the following price: $_____ (Listing Price). Seller agrees to sell the Property for the Listing Price or any other price acceptable to Seller. Seller will pay all typical closing costs charged to sellers of residential real estate in Texas (seller's typical closing costs are those set forth in the residential contract forms promulgated by the Texas Real Estate Commission).

4. **TERM:**

    A. This Listing begins on _____ and ends at 11:59 p.m. on _____ .

    B. If Seller enters into a binding written contract to sell the Property before the date this Listing begins and the contract is binding on the date this Listing begins, this Listing will not commence and will be void.

5. **BROKER COMPENSATION:**

    A. When earned and payable, Seller will pay Broker:

    ❑ (1) _____% of the sales price.

    ❑ (2) _____.

    B. <u>Earned</u>: Broker's compensation is earned when any one of the following occurs during this Listing:
        (1) Seller sells, exchanges, options, agrees to sell, agrees to exchange, or agrees to option the Property to anyone at any price on any terms;
        (2) Broker individually or in cooperation with another broker procures a buyer ready, willing, and able to buy the Property at the Listing Price or at any other price acceptable to Seller; or
        (3) Seller breaches this Listing.

    C. <u>Payable</u>: Once earned, Broker's compensation is payable either during this Listing or after it ends at the earlier of:
        (1) the closing and funding of any sale or exchange of all or part of the Property;
        (2) Seller's refusal to sell the Property after Broker's compensation has been earned;
        (3) Seller's breach of this Listing; or
        (4) at such time as otherwise set forth in this Listing.

    Broker's compensation is <u>not</u> payable if a sale of the Property does not close or fund as a result of: (i) Seller's failure, without fault of Seller, to deliver to a buyer a deed or a title policy as required by the contract to sell; (ii) loss of ownership due to foreclosure or other legal proceeding; or (iii) Seller's failure to restore the Property, as a result of a casualty loss, to its previous condition by the closing date set forth in a contract for the sale of the Property.

    D. <u>Other Compensation</u>:

        (1) <u>Breach by Buyer Under a Contract</u>: If Seller collects earnest money, the sales price, or damages by suit, compromise, settlement, or otherwise from a buyer who breaches a contract for the sale of the Property entered into during this Listing, Seller will pay Broker, after deducting attorney's fees

Exclusive Right to Sell Listing Agreement (continued)

Residential Listing concerning_____

and collection expenses, an amount equal to the lesser of one-half of the amount collected after deductions or the amount of the Broker's Compensation stated in Paragraph 5A. Any amount paid under this Paragraph 5D(1) is in addition to any amount that Broker may be entitled to receive for subsequently selling the Property.

(2) <u>Service Providers</u>: If Broker refers Seller or a prospective buyer to a service provider (for example, mover, cable company, telecommunications provider, utility, or contractor) Broker may receive a fee from the service provider for the referral. Any referral fee Broker receives under this Paragraph 5D(2) is in addition to any other compensation Broker may receive under this Listing.

(3) <u>Other Fees and/or Reimbursable Expenses</u>: _____
_____
_____.

E. <u>Protection Period</u>:

(1) "Protection period" means that time starting the day after this Listing ends and continuing for _____ days. "Sell" means any transfer of any fee simple interest in the Property whether by oral or written agreement or option.

(2) Not later than 10 days after this Listing ends, Broker may send Seller written notice specifying the names of persons whose attention was called to the Property during this Listing. If Seller agrees to sell the Property during the protection period to a person named in the notice or to a relative of a person named in the notice, Seller will pay Broker, upon the closing of the sale, the amount Broker would have been entitled to receive if this Listing were still in effect.

(3) This Paragraph 5E survives termination of this Listing. This Paragraph 5E will not apply if:
   (a) Seller agrees to sell the Property during the protection period;
   (b) the Property is exclusively listed with another broker who is a member of the Texas Association of REALTORS® at the time the sale is negotiated; and
   (c) Seller is obligated to pay the other broker a fee for the sale.

F. <u>County</u>: All amounts payable to Broker are to be paid in cash in _____
_____ County, Texas.

G. <u>Escrow Authorization</u>: Seller authorizes, and Broker may so instruct, any escrow or closing agent authorized to close a transaction for the purchase or acquisition of the Property to collect and disburse to Broker all amounts payable to Broker under this Listing.

6. LISTING SERVICES:

❑ A. Broker will file this Listing with one or more Multiple Listing Services (MLS) by the earlier of the time required by MLS rules or 5 days after the date this Listing begins. Seller authorizes Broker to submit information about this Listing and the sale of the Property to the MLS.

   <u>Notice</u>: MLS rules require Broker to accurately and timely submit all information the MLS requires for participation including sold data. MLS rules may require that the information be submitted to the MLS throughout the time the Listing is in effect. Subscribers to the MLS may use the information for market evaluation or appraisal purposes. Subscribers are other brokers and other real estate professionals such as appraisers and may include the appraisal district. Any information filed with the MLS becomes the property of the MLS for all purposes. **Submission of information to MLS ensures that persons who use and benefit from the MLS also contribute information.**

F I G U R E   4.2

Exclusive Right to Sell Listing Agreement (continued)

Residential Listing concerning_____

❑ B. Seller instructs Broker not to file this Listing with one or more Multiple Listing Service (MLS) until ___ days after the date this Listing begins for the following purpose(s): _____
_____.

(NOTE: Do not check if prohibited by Multiple Listing Service(s).)

❑ C. Broker will not file this Listing with a Multiple Listing Service (MLS) or any other listing service.

Notice: Seller acknowledges and understands that if this option is checked: (1) Seller's Property will not be included in the MLS database available to real estate agents and brokers from other real estate offices who subscribe to and participate in the MLS, and their buyer clients may not be aware that Seller's Property is offered for sale; (2) Seller's Property will not be included in the MLS's download to various real estate Internet sites that are used by the public to search for property listings; and (3) real estate agents, brokers, and members of the public may be unaware of the terms and conditions under which Seller is marketing the Property.

7. ACCESS TO THE PROPERTY:

A. Authorizing Access: Authorizing access to the Property means giving permission to another person to enter the Property, disclosing to the other person any security codes necessary to enter the Property, and lending a key to the other person to enter the Property, directly or through a keybox. To facilitate the showing and sale of the Property, Seller instructs Broker to:
(1) access the Property at reasonable times;
(2) authorize other brokers, their associates, inspectors, appraisers, and contractors to access the Property at reasonable times; and
(3) duplicate keys to facilitate convenient and efficient showings of the Property.

B. Scheduling Companies: Broker may engage the following companies to schedule appointments and to authorize others to access the Property:_____.

C. Keybox: **A keybox is a locked container placed on the Property that holds a key to the Property. A keybox makes it more convenient for brokers, their associates, inspectors, appraisers, and contractors to show, inspect, or repair the Property. The keybox is opened by a special combination, key, or programmed device so that authorized persons may enter the Property, even in Seller's absence. Using a keybox will probably increase the number of showings, but involves risks (for example, unauthorized entry, theft, property damage, or personal injury). Neither the Association of REALTORS® nor MLS requires the use of a keybox.**

(1) Broker ❑ is ❑ is not   authorized to place a keybox on the Property.

(2) If a tenant occupies the Property at any time during this Listing, Seller will furnish Broker a written statement (for example, TAR No. 1411), signed by all tenants, authorizing the use of a keybox or Broker may remove the keybox from the Property.

D. Liability and Indemnification: When authorizing access to the Property, Broker, other brokers, their associates, any keybox provider, or any scheduling company are not responsible for personal injury or property loss to Seller or any other person. Seller assumes all risk of any loss, damage, or injury. **Except for a loss caused by Broker, Seller will indemnify and hold Broker harmless from any claim for personal injury, property damage, or other loss.**

8. COOPERATION WITH OTHER BROKERS: Broker will allow other brokers to show the Property to prospective buyers. Broker will offer to pay the other broker a fee as described below if the other broker procures a buyer that purchases the Property.

(TAR-1101) 01-01-14   Initialed for Identification by Broker/Associate_____ and Seller_____, _____   Page 4 of 10

F I G U R E   4.2

Exclusive Right to Sell Listing Agreement (continued)

Residential Listing concerning_____

    A. <u>MLS Participants</u>: If the other broker is a participant in the MLS in which this Listing is filed, Broker will offer to pay the other broker:
        (1) if the other broker represents the buyer: _____% of the sales price or $_____; and
        (2) if the other broker is a subagent: _____% of the sales price or $_____.

    B. <u>Non-MLS Brokers</u>: If the other broker is not a participant in the MLS in which this Listing is filed, Broker will offer to pay the other broker:
        (1) if the other broker represents the buyer: _____% of the sales price or $_____; and
        (2) if the other broker is a subagent: _____% of the sales price or $_____.

9. INTERMEDIARY: *(Check A or B only.)*

❏ A. <u>Intermediary Status</u>: Broker may show the Property to interested prospective buyers who Broker represents. If a prospective buyer who Broker represents offers to buy the Property, Seller authorizes Broker to act as an intermediary and Broker will notify Seller that Broker will service the parties in accordance with one of the following alternatives.

    (1) If a prospective buyer who Broker represents is serviced by an associate other than the associate servicing Seller under this Listing, Broker may notify Seller that Broker will: (a) appoint the associate then servicing Seller to communicate with, carry out instructions of, and provide opinions and advice during negotiations to Seller; and **(b)** appoint the associate then servicing the prospective buyer to the prospective buyer for the same purpose.

    (2) If a prospective buyer who Broker represents is serviced by the same associate who is servicing Seller, Broker may notify Seller that Broker will: (a) appoint another associate to communicate with, carry out instructions of, and provide opinions and advice during negotiations to the prospective buyer; and (b) appoint the associate servicing the Seller under this Listing to the Seller for the same purpose.

    (3) Broker may notify Seller that Broker will make no appointments as described under this Paragraph 9A and, in such an event, the associate servicing the parties will act solely as Broker's intermediary representative, who may facilitate the transaction but will not render opinions or advice during negotiations to either party.

❏ B. <u>No Intermediary Status</u>: Seller agrees that Broker will not show the Property to prospective buyers who Broker represents.

Notice: **If Broker acts as an intermediary under Paragraph 9A, Broker and Broker's associates:**
      ♦ **may not disclose to the prospective buyer that Seller will accept a price less than the asking price unless otherwise instructed in a separate writing by Seller;**
      ♦ **may not disclose to Seller that the prospective buyer will pay a price greater than the price submitted in a written offer to Seller unless otherwise instructed in a separate writing by the prospective buyer;**
      ♦ **may not disclose any confidential information or any information Seller or the prospective buyer specifically instructs Broker in writing not to disclose unless otherwise instructed in a separate writing by the respective party or required to disclose the information by the Real Estate License Act or a court order or if the information materially relates to the condition of the property;**
      ♦ **may not treat a party to the transaction dishonestly; and**
      ♦ **may not violate the Real Estate License Act.**

F I G U R E   4.2

Exclusive Right to Sell Listing Agreement (continued)

Residential Listing concerning_____

10. **CONFIDENTIAL INFORMATION:** During this Listing or after it ends, Broker may not knowingly disclose information obtained in confidence from Seller except as authorized by Seller or required by law. Broker may not disclose to Seller any confidential information regarding any other person Broker represents or previously represented except as required by law.

11. **BROKER'S AUTHORITY:**

A. Broker will use reasonable efforts and act diligently to market the Property for sale, procure a buyer, and negotiate the sale of the Property.

B. Broker is authorized to display this Listing on the Internet without limitation unless one of the following is checked:

   ❑   (1)   Seller does not want this Listing to be displayed on the Internet.
   ❑   (2)   Seller does not want the address of the Property to be displayed on the Internet.

   Notice: Seller understands and acknowledges that, if box 11B(1) is selected, consumers who conduct searches for listings on the Internet will not see information about this Listing in response to their search.

C. Broker is authorized to market the Property with the following financing options:

   ❑ (1) Conventional   ❑ (5) Texas Veterans Land Program
   ❑ (2) VA   ❑ (6) Owner Financing
   ❑ (3) FHA   ❑ (7) Other
   ❑ (4) Cash

D. In addition to other authority granted by this Listing, Broker may:
   (1) advertise the Property by means and methods as Broker determines, including but not limited to creating and placing advertisements with interior and exterior photographic and audio-visual images of the Property and related information in any media and the Internet;
   (2) place a "For Sale" sign on the Property and remove all other signs offering the Property for sale or lease;
   (3) furnish comparative marketing and sales information about other properties to prospective buyers;
   (4) disseminate information about the Property to other brokers and to prospective buyers, including applicable disclosures or notices that Seller is required to make under law or a contract;
   (5) obtain information from any holder of a note secured by a lien on the Property;
   (6) accept and deposit earnest money in trust in accordance with a contract for the sale of the Property;
   (7) disclose the sales price and terms of sale to other brokers, appraisers, or other real estate professionals;
   (8) in response to inquiries from prospective buyers and other brokers, disclose whether the Seller is considering more than one offer (Broker will not disclose the terms of any competing offer unless specifically instructed by Seller);
   (9) advertise, during or after this Listing ends, that Broker "sold" the Property; and
   (10) place information about this Listing, the Property, and a transaction for the Property on an electronic transaction platform (typically an Internet-based system where professionals related to the transaction such as title companies, lenders, and others may receive, view, and input information).

E. Broker is not authorized to execute any document in the name of or on behalf of Seller concerning the Property.

F I G U R E   4.2

Exclusive Right to Sell Listing Agreement (continued)

Residential Listing concerning_____

12. **SELLER'S REPRESENTATIONS:** Except as provided by Paragraph 15, Seller represents that:
   A. Seller has fee simple title to and peaceable possession of the Property and all its improvements and fixtures, unless rented, and the legal capacity to convey the Property;
   B. Seller is not bound by a listing agreement with another broker for the sale, exchange, or lease of the Property that is or will be in effect during this Listing;
   C. any pool or spa and any required enclosures, fences, gates, and latches comply with all applicable laws and ordinances;
   D. no person or entity has any right to purchase, lease, or acquire the Property by an option, right of refusal, or other agreement;
   E. Seller is current and not delinquent on all loans and all other financial obligations related to the Property, including but not limited to mortgages, home equity loans, home improvement loans, homeowner association fees, and taxes, except_____;
   F. Seller is not aware of any liens or other encumbrances against the Property, except_____ ;
   G. the Property is not subject to the jurisdiction of any court;
   H. all information relating to the Property Seller provides to Broker is true and correct to the best of Seller's knowledge; and
   I. the name of any employer, relocation company, or other entity that provides benefits to Seller when selling the Property is: _____.

13. **SELLER'S ADDITIONAL PROMISES:** Seller agrees to:
   A. cooperate with Broker to facilitate the showing, marketing, and sale of the Property;
   B. not rent or lease the Property during this Listing without Broker's prior written approval;
   C. not negotiate with any prospective buyer who may contact Seller directly, but refer all prospective buyers to Broker;
   D. not enter into a listing agreement with another broker for the sale, exchange, lease, or management of the Property to become effective during this Listing without Broker's prior written approval;
   E. maintain any pool and all required enclosures in compliance with all applicable laws and ordinances;
   F. provide Broker with copies of any leases or rental agreements pertaining to the Property and advise Broker of tenants moving in or out of the Property;
   G. complete any disclosures or notices required by law or a contract to sell the Property; and
   H. amend any applicable notices and disclosures if any material change occurs during this Listing.

14. **LIMITATION OF LIABILITY:**

   A. If the Property is or becomes vacant during this Listing, Seller must notify Seller's casualty insurance company and request a "vacancy clause" to cover the Property. Broker is not responsible for the security of the Property nor for inspecting the Property on any periodic basis.

   B. **Broker is not responsible or liable in any manner for personal injury to any person or for loss or damage to any person's real or personal property resulting from any act or omission not caused by Broker's negligence, including but not limited to injuries or damages caused by:**
      (1) other brokers, their associates, inspectors, appraisers, and contractors who are authorized to access the Property;
      (2) other brokers or their associates who may have information about the Property on their websites;
      (3) acts of third parties (for example, vandalism or theft);
      (4) freezing water pipes;
      (5) a dangerous condition on the Property;
      (6) the Property's non-compliance with any law or ordinance; or
      (7) Seller, negligently or otherwise.

FIGURE 4.2

Exclusive Right to Sell Listing Agreement (continued)

Residential Listing concerning_____

C. **Seller agrees to protect, defend, indemnify, and hold Broker harmless from any damage, costs, attorney's fees, and expenses that:**
   (1) are caused by Seller, negligently or otherwise;
   (2) arise from Seller's failure to disclose any material or relevant information about the Property; or
   (3) are caused by Seller giving incorrect information to any person.

15. **SPECIAL PROVISIONS:**

16. **DEFAULT:** If Seller breaches this Listing, Seller is in default and will be liable to Broker for the amount of the Broker's compensation specified in Paragraph 5A and any other compensation Broker is entitled to receive under this Listing. If a sales price is not determinable in the event of an exchange or breach of this Listing, the Listing Price will be the sales price for purposes of computing compensation. If Broker breaches this Listing, Broker is in default and Seller may exercise any remedy at law.

17. **MEDIATION:** The parties agree to negotiate in good faith in an effort to resolve any dispute related to this Listing that may arise between the parties. If the dispute cannot be resolved by negotiation, the dispute will be submitted to mediation. The parties to the dispute will choose a mutually acceptable mediator and will share the cost of mediation equally.

18. **ATTORNEY'S FEES:** If Seller or Broker is a prevailing party in any legal proceeding brought as a result of a dispute under this Listing or any transaction related to or contemplated by this Listing, such party will be entitled to recover from the non-prevailing party all costs of such proceeding and reasonable attorney's fees.

19. **ADDENDA AND OTHER DOCUMENTS:** Addenda that are part of this Listing and other documents that Seller may need to provide are:
   - [X] A. Information About Brokerage Services;
   - ☐ B. Seller Disclosure Notice (§5.008, Texas Property Code);
   - ☐ C. Addendum for Seller's Disclosure of Information on Lead-Based Paint and Lead-Based Paint Hazards (required if Property was built before 1978);
   - ☐ D. Residential Real Property Affidavit (T-47 Affidavit; related to existing survey);
   - ☐ E. MUD, Water District, or Statutory Tax District Disclosure Notice (Chapter 49, Texas Water Code);
   - ☐ F. Request for Information from an Owners' Association;
   - ☐ G. Request for Mortgage Information;
   - ☐ H. Information about Mineral Clauses in Contract Forms;
   - ☐ I. Information about On-Site Sewer Facility;
   - ☐ J. Information about Property Insurance for a Buyer or Seller;
   - ☐ K. Information about Special Flood Hazard Areas;
   - ☐ L. Condominium Addendum to Listing;
   - ☐ M. Keybox Authorization by Tenant;
   - ☐ N. Seller's Authorization to Release and Advertise Certain Information; and
   - ☐ O. _____
     _____.

F I G U R E   4.2

Exclusive Right to Sell Listing Agreement (continued)

Residential Listing concerning_____

20. AGREEMENT OF PARTIES:

A. <u>Entire Agreement</u>: This Listing is the entire agreement of the parties and may not be changed except by written agreement.

B. <u>Assignability</u>: Neither party may assign this Listing without the written consent of the other party.

C. <u>Binding Effect</u>: Seller's obligation to pay Broker earned compensation is binding upon Seller and Seller's heirs, administrators, executors, successors, and permitted assignees.

D. <u>Joint and Several</u>: All Sellers executing this Listing are jointly and severally liable for the performance of all its terms.

E. <u>Governing Law</u>: Texas law governs the interpretation, validity, performance, and enforcement of this Listing.

F. <u>Severability</u>: If a court finds any clause in this Listing invalid or unenforceable, the remainder of this Listing will not be affected and all other provisions of this Listing will remain valid and enforceable.

G. <u>Notices</u>: Notices between the parties must be in writing and are effective when sent to the receiving party's address, fax, or e-mail address specified in Paragraph 1.

21. ADDITIONAL NOTICES:

A. **Broker's compensation or the sharing of compensation between brokers is not fixed, controlled, recommended, suggested, or maintained by the Association of REALTORS®, MLS, or any listing service.**

B. **In accordance with fair housing laws and the National Association of REALTORS® Code of Ethics, Broker's services must be provided and the Property must be shown and made available to all persons without regard to race, color, religion, national origin, sex, disability, familial status, sexual orientation, or gender identity. Local ordinances may provide for additional protected classes (for example, creed, status as a student, marital status, or age).**

C. **Broker advises Seller to contact any mortgage lender or other lien holder to obtain information regarding payoff amounts for any existing mortgages or liens on the Property.**

D. **Broker advises Seller to review the information Broker submits to an MLS or other listing service.**

E. **Broker advises Seller to remove or secure jewelry, prescription drugs, other valuables, firearms and any other weapons.**

F. **Statutes or ordinances may regulate certain items on the Property (for example, swimming pools and septic systems). Non-compliance with the statutes or ordinances may delay a transaction and may result in fines, penalties, and liability to Seller.**

G. **If the Property was built before 1978, Federal law requires the Seller to: (1) provide the buyer with the federally approved pamphlet on lead poisoning prevention; (2) disclose the presence of any known lead-based paint or lead-based paint hazards in the Property; (3) deliver all records and reports to the buyer related to such paint or hazards; and (4) provide the buyer a period up to 10 days to have the Property inspected for such paint or hazards.**

F I G U R E   4.2

Exclusive Right to Sell Listing Agreement (continued)

H. Broker cannot give legal advice. READ THIS LISTING CAREFULLY. If you do not understand the effect of this Listing, consult an attorney BEFORE signing.

Broker's Printed Name   License No.

Seller's Printed Name

❑ Broker's Signature   Date
❑ Broker's Associate's Signature, as an authorized
     agent of Broker

Seller's Signature   Date

Broker's Associate's Printed Name, if applicable

Seller's Printed Name

Seller's Signature   Date

As with the exclusive-right-to-sell listing, listing brokers may allow other brokers to negotiate through them. Thus, if the listing broker or any other broker finds a buyer, the listing broker is entitled to a fee that will be shared with the selling broker if the listing broker has placed the seller's property in the MLS, and has offered compensation to a cooperating broker or has signed a separate compensation agreement with the cooperating broker. Sellers should be made aware that with this type of listing, the broker may not be able to justify the same level of advertising and promotion because the sellers still may secure their own buyer, in which case, the seller does not owe the broker any compensation. Figure 4.3 shows the lines of communication and negotiation in an exclusive-right-to-sell listing.

FIGURE 4.3

Lines of Communication and Negotiation With Exclusive-Agency Listing

The TAR listing agreement shown in Figure 4.2 can be easily amended to an exclusive agency agreement by adding the "Exclusive Agency Addendum" (TAR 1403 not provided).

Open Listing

A listing is generally considered an open listing unless its terms clearly indicate that both parties intend a more exclusive agreement. Open listings generally entitle brokers to compensation only if they are the procuring cause (the person who secures the offer from the buyer) of the sale or lease of the property. The open listing does not give any broker the exclusive right to offer the property for sale; rather, it allows the owner of the property to give one or more brokers the same opportunity simultaneously, but only the broker who produces an accepted contract is compensated. The open listing also allows the seller to continue to seek potential buyers and to negotiate independently of the broker. If successful, the seller does not owe any broker a commission.

Open listing agreements are rarely used in residential property sales, and are generally only used when commercial or farm and ranch property is being sold. For example, a vacant lot being sold in an area zoned for commercial property may have five different real estate brokerage signs on the property offering it for sale. Each of those brokers has an open listing on that lot with the owner. The broker producing a buyer who successfully purchases the property from the seller is the only broker who is due any compensation.

Depending on the terms of a specific open listing, the broker may be entitled to a commission if the broker produces an offer from a buyer that meets or exceeds the exact terms of the listing and the owner refuses to sell. This does not mean that the seller will be required to sell the home, but it does mean that if the broker with the open listing agreement produces a ready, willing, and able purchaser who meets the requirements of the seller, that broker is possibly due his compensation, even if the seller refuses to sell the property. Generally, in this circumstance, legal action will be required in order for the broker to successfully get paid. The buyer, however, has no rights under the broker's listing agreement to force the owner to sell the property, even if the buyer's offer meets or exceeds the terms of the listing agreement.

One disadvantage of the open listing is that a broker and the broker's associates may expend a great deal of energy and time advertising and showing a property, only to have another broker provide the actual buyer and receive the commission. For this reason, most brokers generally will not advertise open listings; however, they will show the properties to buyers in the course of showing other properties.

Most multiple listing service (MLS) systems refuse to take open listings because of the potential for disputes over procuring cause and commission entitlements. The only broker entitled to a commission under an open listing agreement is the one who procures the buyer. Any broker procuring a buyer for the seller who does not have an open listing agreement with that seller is merely a volunteer, as far as the seller is concerned.

Figure 4.4 shows the lines of communication and negotiation in an open listing.

FIGURE 4.4

Lines of Communication and Negotiation in an Open Listing

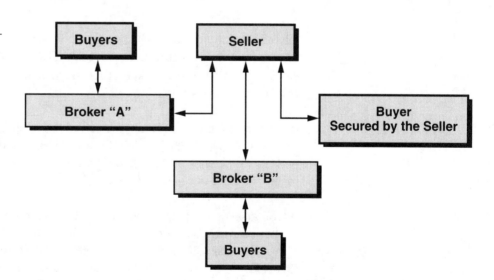

Net Listings

Any type of listing agreement (exclusive-right-to-sell, exclusive agency, and open listing) can be a net listing. Net listings relate to the **way the broker is paid rather than to the type of agency agreement**. Any of the agency agreements mentioned previously could be used in a net listing. With these types of listings, sellers determine the amount of money they will accept **after the costs of sale**; the broker receives the remainder as a commission.

This type of listing may present some legal and ethical problems, particularly with an inexperienced seller. Net listings are **not illegal in Texas**. However, two specific rules of the commission are especially designed to curb potential abuse:

This is very important. A broker may not take a net listing unless the client requires it and appears to be familiar with current market values of real property.

- 22 TAC § 535.16(b): A "net listing" is a listing agreement in which the broker's commission is the difference ("net") between the sales proceeds and an amount desired by the owner of the real property. A broker may not take net listings unless the principal requires a net listing and the principal appears to be familiar with current market values of real property. The use of a net listing places an upper limit on the principal's expectancy and places the broker's interest above the principal's interest with reference to obtaining the best possible price. If a net listing is used, the listing agreement must assure the principal of not less than the principal's desired price and to limit the broker to a specified maximum commission.
- 22 TAC § 535.16(c): A real estate licensee is obligated to provide a broker price opinion or comparative market analysis on a property when negotiating a listing or offering to purchase the property for the licensee's own account as a result of contact made while acting as a real estate agent.

TREC officially discourages taking net listings because of their possible manipulation and harm to the public, which TREC is designed to protect. In some cases, however, it is the broker rather than the seller who ends up with less money because of a net listing.

■ **EXAMPLE 1** Susan took a net listing on Gertrude's property. The asking price was $330,000, the closing costs were expected to be $15,000, and Gertrude had a loan balance of $269,000. The net listing agreement called for Gertrude to receive $23,000 in cash at closing.

After marketing the property for six months, Gertrude accepted an offer of $318,000 for her property. Susan received $11,000 as her brokerage fee because all costs of the sale ($269,000 note plus $15,000 closing costs) and the seller's agreed net ($23,000) were deducted before Susan's fee could be calculated. If Susan and Gertrude had agreed on the 5.5% commission her firm had established as its commission fee, she would have earned $17,490.

Most would agree that the broker in the preceding example should have been more careful to safeguard her position in the transaction. However, because a broker is considered to have the expertise to conduct business in a manner consistent with the desired outcomes, this transaction may have been one that met her objectives.

The situation that causes the greatest concern is one in which the broker earns an unusually large commission relative to the property being sold. The question in these cases is whether the broker took unfair advantage of a naive seller who was unaware of the real value of the property. Such actions by the broker would be regarded as clear examples of breaching the fiduciary duties owed to the client by the broker. The following example illustrates the problem that concerns most state regulators.

■ **EXAMPLE 2**   Phillip, the broker for Action Real Estate, has been called by Elvin and Elma Jones to list their property. The Joneses have lived in their present home for 60 years and have decided to move to California to be close to their grandchildren. During the listing presentation the Joneses tell Phillip that they would like to receive $420,000 cash for their home, and if he can guarantee them that amount, they will be absolutely delighted with the sale. In fact, they are quite willing for Phillip to keep whatever amount he can obtain over the $420,000, plus closing costs and repairs. Phillip attempts to tell the Joneses that he believes that the home will sell for at least $490,000, but the Joneses are not impressed and tell him, "Just get us $420,000 to take to California and we will be very happy." The Joneses sign the listing agreement. The home subsequently sells for $495,000. At closing, the Joneses receive their $420,000, the closing costs and repairs cost $22,000, and Phillip receives $53,000! One week later, the grandchildren call and threaten to bring a lawsuit against Action Real Estate for fraud.

■ **QUESTIONS**   1. How could Action Real Estate have avoided this situation? 2. Could Phillip refuse to take the listing for Action Real Estate?

■ **DISCUSSION**   This example appears to be a gross exaggeration; unfortunately, however, there have been many such situations. Action Real Estate could have avoided this problem by insisting on a percentage commission, especially because it was obvious that there was an enormous disparity between what the sellers desired to net and the potential net profit.

Action Real Estate should make sure that it has a clearly written policy regarding net listings that carefully follows TREC rules. At minimum, the broker should be notified by the associate that the sellers desire a net listing so that the final decision can be made by the broker, not the associate. If the sellers continue to insist on the net listing, the broker may refuse to enter into the agreement (knowing that a potential lawsuit is almost guaranteed) or give full disclosures that are signed by the sellers. The broker may suggest that family members enter into the discussion, although many sellers might reject this proposal, believing that it would be an unwelcome intrusion.

■ EXCLUSIVE SELLER AGENCY

Some real estate brokerage firms represent only sellers. In this situation, the seller is always the client and the buyer is always the customer. Until the increased acceptance of buyer agency, exclusive seller agency was the traditional and predominant type of practice. In Texas, some traditional brokerages have made the transition to other forms of agency representation, while other firms retain their commitment to represent sellers exclusively. These exclusive seller agencies encourage buyers and tenants, who want agency representation, to seek that representation by, hiring their own buyer broker, appraiser, or attorney. The broker usually offers to work with buyers or tenants in the purchase or lease of property as long as they realize that the broker and all licensed associates of the firm represent the interests of the sellers and the landlords. The exclusive seller representative has what is known as an "arm around" relationship with his seller-client, and an "arm's length" relationship with the buyer-customer.

Licensees working in firms representing sellers exclusively must be careful not to convey the impression that the buyer is being represented. A variety of situations can arise for licensees working in exclusive seller agency firms. Brokers and associates should have a clear understanding of their duties when conducting in-house sales, as well as cooperative sales involving other brokers.

It is possible for a broker to represent a person whether that person is in the capacity of buying a property or selling a property. In other words, the broker chooses to represent the individual throughout her real estate investment processes, rather than simply choosing to represent the person only when she is acting as a seller of property. A real estate broker may find that it is beneficial to represent people generally rather than people classified by their relationship to the property in question—that is, a broker may wish to represent a person whether that person sells, buys, or leases a property.

The listing agreement between the broker and the seller creates a written express agency relationship—it is essentially a broker's employment contract. Typically, this agreement is a contract that establishes the rights and obligations of both principals to the agreement—the seller and the broker. Because an agency relationship must always be consensual, the written listing agreement with the seller gives consent and authority to the broker to act as the seller's agent and generally agrees to pay a fee or commission for the service the broker renders. By signing the listing agreement, the broker mutually agrees to represent the seller; market the property; place the sellers' interests above all others, including the broker's own interest; and perform according to the listing contract. Compensation is usually conditioned on the broker producing a ready, willing, and able buyer at the price and terms stated in the listing agreement.

The parties to a listing contract are the broker and the seller. The listing contract is an agreement to market the property and to seek qualified buyers; it is not a contract in which the broker promises to sell the property. If the broker produces a ready, willing, and able purchaser who meets the terms and conditions of the seller, whether on the terms of the original listing or on negotiated terms with the buyer, the seller promises to pay the agreed amount stated in the listing agreement. Once a qualified buyer has submitted a contract that meets the price and terms stated in the listing contract, the broker has fulfilled any obligation. A seller who elects not to sell technically owes the broker the compensation stated in the listing agreement. The buyer has no recourse if the seller decides to remove the property from the market after the buyer has presented an offer but **before a contract of sale is signed**.

The only signed contract at this point is between the listing broker and the seller—no other parties (buyers or any other brokers involved) have the right to sue under the terms of the listing agreement because they do not have a signed contract with the seller. In other words, the parties to the listing agreement (broker and seller) have "privity of contract" to be able to seek legal remedies for a breach of contract by the other party. In the sales contract, the parties are the buyer and the seller, and they have privity of contract to be able to seek legal remedies for a breach of contract by the other party. Relative to the listing agreement, a sales associate of the broker who is working with the seller as the seller's agent does not have privity of contract to sue the seller. The broker is the owner of the listing agreement, not the sales associate. Any suit for breach of contract must be made by and through the broker.

■ **EXAMPLE**   Broker James, of Precision Realty, obtained a listing contract from Joyce to sell her home for $218,000 cash or with a conventional loan. James marketed the home, and three weeks after he listed the property, a full-price cash offer was submitted by a buyer with the resources to fulfill the terms of the offer. James met with Joyce later that evening and presented the offer. After discussing the terms and projected proceeds, it appeared that Joyce was prepared to sign the offer; however, at the last moment she had a change of heart and decided not to sell the property after all.

■ **QUESTIONS**   1. Is the broker entitled to a fee or commission? 2. If this contract offer was written by another agency, could the other broker sue Joyce? 3. What, if any, legal recourse might the buyer have against Joyce?

■ **DISCUSSION 1**   Under the terms of most listing contracts, the broker is entitled to a fee or commission once a ready, willing, and able buyer makes an offer that meets the price and terms stated in the listing contract. If the listing contract is in writing, the broker can seek the compensation and even go so far as to sue the seller, if necessary. If the contract is taken orally, the broker has no legal recourse.

■ **DISCUSSION 2**   If the purchase contract were written by another agency, Precision Realty would have the same right to seek compensation as it would if the sale had been in-house. However, the broker from the other firm would have no recourse because the listing contract was between Precision Realty and the seller. The decision to pursue the seller for compensation is one that can be made **only by the listing broker.**

Although the listing broker may have the right to bring legal action against the seller, this may not prove to be the best solution for the broker. The time, energy, expense, and possible damage to the broker's reputation may far outweigh the potential benefits.

Because the offer to purchase was not signed, the buyer has little recourse other than to pursue the seller on the basis of fraudulent advertising. While sellers can always remove their properties from the market, questions might be raised if they later sell the property to someone else under terms similar to the first contract offer. Of particular concern would be issues of discrimination, which could arise (under the Civil Rights Act) if it could be shown that the seller's reason for rejecting the first offer was based on the buyer's being a member of a protected class.

In-House Sales

A large number of residential real estate transactions involve the services of two brokers in a cooperative sale. However, a significant number of sales are in-house sales, especially in real estate firms with large market shares. In-house sales involve only one brokerage, although several associates from the same brokerage firm may participate. The buyer may be represented by the firm (in which case it should be an intermediary relationship) or not represented at all. A buyer who is not represented is treated as a customer.

Many brokers prefer to sell their listings in-house because of the control they maintain over the transactions and because of the prospect of earning the full commission. Some firms offer the selling associate a greater share of the commission as an incentive for producing an in-house sale. This incentive may motivate some associates to look primarily toward in-house listings, something that may not be in the best interests of every prospective buyer.

Exclusive Seller Agency in Practice

In the following examples, assume that Sally is a top salesperson for Bay Realty, a multi-office firm offering exclusive seller agency.

■ **EXAMPLE 1 Sally as the listing associate.** Sally successfully acquires for Bay Realty an exclusive listing of a three-bedroom town house from her friend George. At the first open house conducted by Sally, prospective buyer Betty discusses the property with Sally. Sally initially discloses to Betty that she is an agent of the seller and furnishes Betty with a written TREC statement regarding information about brokerage services. Later that night, Sally prepares an offer from Betty on George's property, which is later accepted by George.

■ **QUESTIONS** 1. Because Sally represents the seller through Bay Realty, must she suggest that Betty use another brokerage firm that would represent Betty's interest? 2. Would Bay Realty's agency role change if Betty were referred to a different licensee within the firm?

■ **DISCUSSION** In this case, Bay Realty clearly represents George only. No facts indicate that Bay Realty has become an implied agent of Betty because of any of Sally's actions. No law prohibits in-house sales or requires that Sally suggest that the buyer hire another broker to prepare the offer. Sally can show the property, explain its features, and deliver the buyer's offer without creating any implied agency with the buyer—in fact, that's her job. However, Sally must tell Betty at first contact regarding a specific property that she is the agent of the seller and that she does not represent Betty. Also, unless Betty is represented by an agent, Sally must present Betty with a written statement regarding representation responsibilities as required by § 1101.558(c). This statement must be presented during the first substantive discussion about a specific property between Sally and Betty. If Sally fails to provide the disclosure of her agency (i.e., whom she works for) and fails to provide the written statement regarding representation responsibilities of brokers generally, then Sally would expose herself to TREC disciplinary action and liability in a civil lawsuit.

TREC's Information About Brokerage Services includes this written statement.

■ **EXAMPLE 2   Sally as the selling associate with no prior relationship with the buyer.** Bay Realty has a policy of exclusive seller representation. Sally is the licensee on duty when Bob Brown walks in and asks about available properties. Sally checks Bay Realty's listings and finds a property on Main Street listed by Carol, from a branch office of Bay Realty, and one on King Street listed by Tom, from Southside Realty on the other side of town. Sally makes appointments to show Bob both properties.

■ **QUESTIONS**   1. Because Sally is not the listing agent on the Main Street property, will she be free to represent Bob on this property? 2. When Sally shows the properties, how will her duties to Bob and to the sellers differ when she shows the Main Street property from when she shows the King Street property?

■ **DISCUSSION**   Sally must remember that Bay Realty is the agent of the seller of the Main Street property and will be the subagent of the sellers of the King Street property. Even though an associated licensee other than Sally took the listing on the Main Street property, Sally is bound to act in the best interests of the seller. Because Bay Realty represents sellers exclusively, the same thing is true on the King Street property. Sally should be careful not to give Bob the impression that she can represent him in negotiations regarding any property. She can do this by giving Bob the written statement required by TRELA § 1101.558, discussing it with him, and disclosing her agency relationship with the sellers. In an exclusive seller agency firm, Sally should treat Bob as a customer, not as a client.

TREC's Information About Brokerage Services includes this written statement.

■ **EXAMPLE 3   Sally as the selling associate with prior relationship with buyer.** Sally, as listing agent, has just negotiated a completed sales contract on George's town house. She has opened escrow by placing the contract and earnest money with the escrow agent named in the contract. George is extremely pleased with Sally's professional attitude and skills and asks her to find a suitable replacement property. Sally is well aware of George's needs and wants, as well as his financial resources and favorite bargaining techniques. Sally knows a perfect property for George, and it happens to be listed with Bay Realty through Tom, another Bay Realty salesperson.

Sally knows from experience that when satisfied clients like George sell their homes and buy replacement properties in the same locality, the client typically works with the same listing agent (Sally, in this case). It is natural for George to think that Sally is still his agent. Sally recognizes that the seller of the new home might find it useful, in negotiations, to know how much cash George will receive from his recent sale and when George is planning to move. This seller, like most sellers, wants to learn as much information as possible from the agent about the buyer, especially if the offer is contingent on financing.

■ **QUESTIONS**   1. If Sally is to represent the new seller on behalf of Bay Realty, should Sally disclose these useful facts to the seller? 2. Would such disclosure surprise George or violate any fiduciary duty to him?

■ **DISCUSSION**   This in-house "turnaround" sale, so common in today's market, can present some confusing agency relationship questions. Is Bay Realty now representing two parties? Is George a client in the listing of his town house and a customer in buying the replacement property? Is it understandable for George to expect he'll continue to receive client-level services, even though his status has changed from seller to buyer?

It would be the path of least resistance for Sally to keep quiet, to avoid raising any of these questions, to simply proceed to do the best job for both parties, and to hope all goes well. This too often happens in the real world of real estate, especially with real estate licensees who regard themselves primarily as facilitators who help work out differences between buyers and sellers and bring a transaction to a successful close. The correct approach, though, is to clarify each relationship through discussion with and disclosure to the buyer and the seller.

Because Bay Realty represents sellers exclusively, George must be made fully aware that, in the purchase transaction, he will be receiving the reduced services extended to buyer-customers and will not enjoy client status. Sally also must inform the seller of the home that George is interested in purchasing that, because of a prior client relationship with George, there might be financial information known to Sally regarding George that she cannot disclose to the seller. Even with the informed consent of both parties, Bay Realty may be on shaky ground. Changing George's status from client to customer may be difficult at best.

If either George or the seller is not in agreement with Bay Realty's role in the transaction, Sally should not proceed until the agency issues are resolved. One possible alternative is to refer George to another firm offering buyer's brokerage services so he can get representation in the purchase of the home. In this scenario, Sally or any licensee within Bay Realty still would be prohibited from disclosing George's financial circumstances to the seller because that information was gained during a client relationship with George. Before continuing with the transaction, the seller must give informed consent to Sally and Bay Realty.

■ BENEFITS OF SELLER AGENCY RELATIONSHIPS

Agency Benefits to Seller or Landlord

The following are some of the benefits to sellers and landlords who are represented by agents instead of representing themselves in a sale or leasing transaction.

Reaching Buyers Through Broad Marketing   Reaching buyers through marketing efforts has long been one of the most valuable services that real estate professionals have offered sellers. Sellers generally do not have the expertise or the funds to advertise effectively. When a broker has numerous agency contracts with sellers, advertising can be combined to give each seller's property the greatest possible exposure to the market. Brokers who are members of the MLS also market to other real estate professionals in their areas through this medium. The internet is a powerful means for brokers to advertise their listings. Licensees and professional real estate organizations, have websites that provide valuable conduits for advertising. Although several internet listing services are available, the National Association of REALTORS® (NAR) site, www.realtor.com, has received considerable attention from real estate professionals and the public since it began posting listings from local boards of REALTORS® from around the country.

Analyzing the market appropriately and accurately to assist the seller in determining a list price is essential. One of the most important jobs the seller's agent has to accomplish is to accurately, thoroughly, and appropriately analyze the market in order to give the seller a broker's price opinion (BPO) or comparative market analysis (CMA). Providing the seller with data on properties that have sold within the last six months, that are within a radius of ½ to 1 mile of his home, if possible, and that are comparable to the style, size, number of rooms and amenities, as well as analyzing the comparable properties that are currently on the market in those areas, is essential to a successful sale.

Receiving Advice and Opinions That Inform the Seller or Landlord   Giving advice and opinions is another of the basic services that an agent offers to the seller. Licensees are considered experts in the field of real estate, and sellers and landlords are anxious to receive information about all aspects of listing and selling or leasing their properties. The information that licensees provide allows sellers to make informed decisions about their transactions. Licensees have an obligation to be knowledgeable about market conditions, financing conditions for buyers, rental information for tenants, and all other aspects of the real estate market that affect their clients.

Assistance in Contract Negotiations   Negotiating on behalf of the seller means that the seller's agent closely guards the equity of the seller. The agent plans, with the seller, the appropriate strategy for getting the highest possible price, best terms and conditions in the sale of the home. Skilled negotiations by the seller's agent can mean that the seller walks away from the closing of the transaction with the maximum amount of his equity from the property in his pocket. In addition, sellers' agents may be able to greatly assist sellers during negotiations by giving helpful advice relating to favorable financing options, counteroffers, and other terms and conditions of a sale. Many sellers are unprepared for the nuances and details of contract negotiations, making it vital that their agent be skilled in the art of preserving the equity and focusing on the goals of the seller.

Confidentiality   Once a licensee becomes an agent of her principal, she has an obligation of confidentiality under the law. Unless otherwise authorized by the seller, the seller's agent is required to keep all information of the seller-client confidential. If the agent shares confidential information of her seller-client with others, it is considered a breach of her fiduciary duties to the seller. Whether it is the seller's financial position, the fact that he has to be in California in two weeks for a new job, or many other issues that would affect the seller's negotiating strength, the agent has an obligation to maintain confidentiality to protect her client's bargaining position. There are times when the law requires that certain information be disclosed, such as the condition of the property or condition of the title to the property. In these instances, the agent is required to fully and honestly disclose that type of information.

When owners sell or rent their properties by themselves and a licensee has obtained information in a manner that was **not** confidential, that licensee is under no obligation to withhold the information from a prospective buyer-tenant. In fact, if the buyer-tenant is a client, that licensee has an affirmative duty to disclose all information that might be relevant in the client's decision to purchase or lease.

Benefits to Seller's or Landlord's Agents

The seller-landlord's agent can expect certain benefits from a seller-landlord agency relationship that would not be available to them when owners represent themselves.

Greater Understanding of the Circumstances of the Sale or Lease   As an agent for the seller, the licensee, by doing a detailed profile of the seller and the home when listing the property, gains insight into the motivations, needs, and desires of the seller-client. He gleans pertinent information that helps establish a thorough picture of the property and its conditions. He utilizes all this information to establish a solid marketing strategy and thus is able to confidently and skillfully prepare for successful negotiations with buyers and buyers agents. A licensee who is attempting to locate property for a buyer-customer will often show owner-listed properties. Without an understanding of the circumstance of the sale or the lease, the licensee may lose the potential sale or lease because of a lack of important information that would aid in facilitating the transaction.

Incentive to Market the Property   With an exclusive-right-to-sell, an exclusive-right-to-lease, or an exclusive-agency agreement, the agent will feel more comfortable marketing the property because there is a reasonable expectation that the property will sell or be leased and a commission will follow. Without some expectation of a return, as is often the case with an open listing, an agent may find it necessary to reserve scarce advertising dollars for other more promising opportunities. Sellers should be made aware of these limitations when choosing a type of listing agreement.

No Conflict of Loyalties   A seller-landlord's agent confidently, deliberately, and legally becomes an advocate for the seller-landlord. When seller representation is done properly, there is no conflict of interest when negotiating with buyer-customers because the agent's representation and loyalty belongs strictly to the owner; however, the agent must always be fair and honest with the buyer. The seller's agent will advocate for the best interests of his seller-client as his primary focus and will use all of his knowledge and skill to benefit his seller during the entire transaction. This allows for a clear delineation of loyalties and agency responsibilities. The seller's agent is the seller's agent only.

Limited Liability for the Acts of the Buyer's Broker   When buyers employ their own agent, the seller's/owner's agent is **not responsible for, and does not have vicarious liability for, the actions of that agent.** This can be particularly important when a buyer's agent gives misinformation or makes a misstatement of a material fact without the knowledge of the listing agent. Texas law gives some protection from the acts of other brokers and their agents; however, when buyers employ their own agent, there may be a more clearly defined separation of liability.

Options for Representing Sellers

Brokers have several options when deciding on company policy regarding seller agency:

■ *Exclusive seller representation*, in which brokers and associates represent sellers only, whether they are showing properties listed by their own companies (in-house sales) or properties listed by other brokers (cooperative sales)

■ *Nonexclusive seller representation*, in which brokers and their associates represent sellers on all in-house transactions but may represent buyers when selling the listings of **other brokers**

■ *Subagency*, which may involve permitting brokers and associates from other firms to represent a listing broker's sellers through their firms or permitting a broker's associates to represent sellers listed by other firms through those listing brokers

■ *Intermediary agency*, in which the broker may attempt to act as an agent of both buyer and seller in the same transaction, but with reduced representation to both while negotiating a transaction between the parties.

■ SUBAGENCY

Cooperative Sales With Buyer Agent or Subagents

Buyers frequently visit properties with another broker or a licensed associate of another broker, who might be called the other broker, cooperating broker, selling broker, or buyer's broker. Who is this other broker? Whom does the other broker represent?

Because significant numbers of transactions occur between two brokerage firms, particularly in large metropolitan areas with active MLSs, licensees must understand the roles they play in cooperative sales and how to conduct themselves appropriately. The misuse of terms, incorrect references to individuals, and the offering of information to a party who may not have the right to have that information, are all possible violations of an agent's fiduciary duties, or mistakes that could cause one or the other party harm, which could result in legal action by one or both of the parties. The role of a cooperating broker acting as a buyer's agent will be discussed in a later chapter. The cooperating brokers and all associates of those brokers who are working "with" rather than "for" the buyer (in other words they have not established an agency relationship with the buyer) should always seek to act as subagents of the listing broker's client when selling another broker's listing. TRELA § 1101.002 (8) gives the following definition:

(8) "Subagent" means a license holder who:

(A) represents a principal through cooperation with and the consent of a broker representing the principal and

(B) is not sponsored by or associated with the principal's broker.

In Figure 4.5, notice that associates of ABC Listing Broker are not subagents. They are agents, by way of their broker, for the seller. It is clear that the associates of XYZ Broker are agents for XYZ Broker and will function as subagents to the seller by way of XYZ Broker. The duties of ABC Broker and associates and XYZ Broker and associates include all of the OLDCAR (obedience, loyalty, disclosure, confidentiality, accounting, and reasonable care and diligence) duties, as well as common law agency duties.

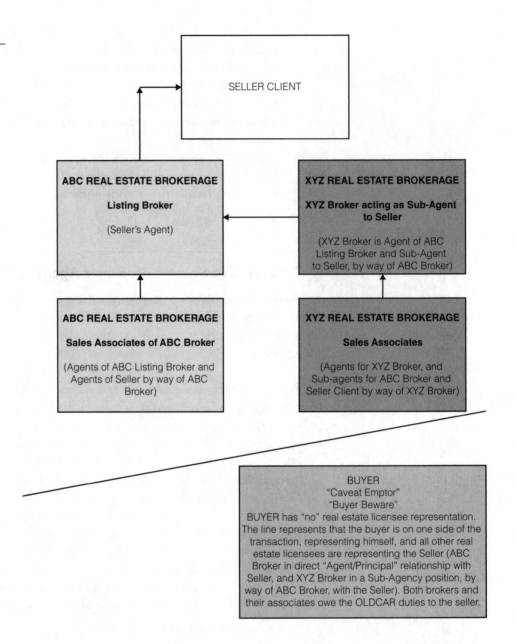

Offering Subagency   Like any agency relationship, the subagency relationship is created by the consent of those involved. Only when a valid subagency is created does the law impose fiduciary duties and liabilities on the subagent. Subagency may be created expressly by agreement or implicitly by words, conduct, or custom. Subagency may be created within or apart from the framework of an MLS. Even within the MLS, subagency is **not automatic**. The seller has the **option** to offer subagency. On the other hand, the listing broker has the option to condition the taking of a listing on whether the seller will allow or insist on subagency or some other form of representation. Also, any other broker in the transaction can reject any offer of subagency and can elect to work for the buyer on a client basis as the buyer's agent.

Creating Subagency   Subagency can be created outside the framework of an MLS. While many listing brokers are members of an MLS, thousands of listings in the small towns and rural areas of Texas have no MLS systems. Further, MLS systems do not require that certain types of properties be listed. Commercial properties, new project sales, business opportunities, long-term leases, and vacant land typically fall into this voluntary category. Still, listing brokers, at the direction of the seller, may work with other brokers on a selective basis to help in the search for buyers for these types of properties.

Rather than talk in terms of a formal offer of subagency, brokers may talk of cooperating in a transaction and sharing or splitting the commission. This type of informal understanding is particularly dangerous because it is often unclear as to whom the other broker represents or who is responsible for payment of compensation. In a recent case, a Texas commercial broker failed to recover a commission in a $9 million transaction because he was unable to convincingly establish whose agent he was, in whose best interests he acted, and who was supposed to pay him. Instead of the $270,000 commission he sued for, he settled for $40,000. Had the commercial broker known and practiced the principles set out by law, the outcome might have been decidedly different. A formal, well-written contractual agreement can and does help prevent fraud, misunderstandings, ambiguous oral conversations, and intentional misdirection.

Listing brokers and the other brokers involved in a transaction often have separate commission agreements among themselves that serve as a basis for the subagency relationship. Such agreements are often silent as to agency duties and tend to cover only how a commission is to be split. Brokers who work cooperatively frequently operate without any specific written or oral agreement; however, a written arrangement is preferable.

In seller subagency transactions, the broker working with but not for the buyer is in fact representing the seller through subagency. All of her fiduciary duties are due the seller, not the buyer. This subagent broker must fulfill her common law duties of agency (obedience, loyalty, disclosure, confidentiality, accounting, and reasonable care and diligence) on behalf of the seller as the seller's subagent. The buyer is not represented or contractually bound to any licensee and might be viewing properties with a number of brokers or salespersons and might even view the same property with more than one licensee. In these situations, where more than one broker works with a single nonrepresented buyer, the possibility exists that **procuring-cause** disputes may arise between different selling, cooperating, or other brokers, with two or more of the other brokers, each claiming a right to share the commission with the listing broker. However, from the listing broker's perspective, even though subagency may be offered to multiple brokers, only the subagent who procures the sale is entitled to a share of the commission as the procuring cause. Buyer subagency may also be created, but it is seen less often in the industry than seller subagency.

Because agency is consensual, the sellers may elect not to allow licensees from other offices to represent them in the sale of the property, particularly licensees they do not know. If this is the case and the broker is using the TAR Exclusive-Right-to-Sell Listing Agreement (see Figure 4.2), the listing broker would insert the elected commission to the cooperating broker in paragraph 8.A(1) and/or 8.B(1) and indicate "N/A" or "none" in the remaining blanks. If a listing broker doesn't offer subagency, a broker working with a buyer would not be able to show the buyer the property. Without an agreement to represent the buyer or a subagency agreement with the seller's agent, he is not an agent for either party. Therefore, if he wants compensation, he will have to refer the customer to the listing brokerage and ask for a finder's fee.

Fiduciary Duty Owed to the Seller   By accepting the listing broker's offer of subagency through the MLS or by some other agreement, the subagent broker and the subagent broker's associates owe complete fiduciary duties and loyalty to the seller. Any real estate agent acting as a subagent of the seller must relate to both buyer and seller exactly as though the subagent's company had taken the listing. The subagent must be careful not to act for the buyer in any manner adverse to the seller's best interests. This may be a problem if the subagent has developed close ties with the buyer. By the same token, the subagent rarely meets the seller and usually knows little about the seller's needs. The subagent's main source of information will be what is revealed in the MLS or what is discussed with the listing agent. This can be a challenge for the subagent of the seller because she is spending time with the buyer, learning about the buyer's family, and holding lengthy conversations with the buyer. A subagent for the seller must make it very clear to the buyer that everything that the buyer tells her must, by law, be communicated by the subagent to the seller. A legal line limiting representation is drawn between the seller's subagent and the buyer. Each is on the opposite side of that representation line. The seller's subagent serves the seller's interests. The buyer/customer serves his own interests without representation.

Liability and Ethics in Subagency   No one can make an informed decision to choose or not choose subagency without first becoming aware of the legal and practical consequences of a subagency relationship. Often, the outcome of a court case turns on whether the other broker is found to be a subagent of the seller or an agent of the buyer. Remember, agency can be created by actions as well as formal written agreements. Courts may declare a licensee an agent of a buyer due to his actions, even though the licensee intended to act as a subagent of the seller. Sellers and listing brokers sometimes refuse subagency because of potential liability created by a subagent over whom the listing broker may have no control or no knowledge. Some of these issues have recently been resolved by the Texas legislature, as shown in the following paragraphs.

TRELA addresses the concern some listing brokers have in regard to the liability (vicarious liability) that may attach to them for the acts of other parties and cooperating brokers, in this case, subagents:

> § 1101.805 LIABILITY FOR MISREPRESENTATON OR CONCEALMENT
>
> (a) In this section, "party" has the meaning assigned by Section 1101.551. [Emphasis by bolding has been added]
>
> (b) This section prevails over any other law, including common law.
>
> (c) This section does not diminish a broker's responsibility for the acts or omissions of a salesperson associated with or acting for the broker.

(d) A **party** is not liable for a misrepresentation or a concealment of a material fact made by a license holder in a real estate transaction unless the party:

(1) knew of the falsity of the misrepresentation or concealment; and

(2) failed to disclose the party's knowledge of the falsity of the misrepresentation or concealment.

(e) A **license holder** is not liable for a misrepresentation or a concealment of a material fact made by a party to a real estate transaction unless the license holder:

(1) knew of the falsity of the misrepresentation or concealment; and

(2) failed to disclose the license holder's knowledge of the falsity of the misrepresentation or concealment.

(f) A **party or a license holder** is not liable for a misrepresentation or a concealment of a material fact made by a subagent in a real estate transaction unless the party or license holder:

(1) knew of the falsity of the misrepresentation or concealment; and

(2) failed to disclose the party's or license holder's knowledge of the falsity of the misrepresentation or concealment.

■ NONEXCLUSIVE SELLER AGENCY

Rather than choosing to represent sellers exclusively, many firms wish to represent buyers and sellers, **but never in the same transaction**. This means that the brokerage firm will engage buyers in representation agreements but will show only properties listed by **other brokers** to their buyer-clients. In nonexclusive representation, the broker can offer representation services to buyers on properties not listed by the firm. On the other hand, this form of nonexclusive seller representation prohibits the broker from showing the buyer any property listed by his firm. This is because the broker already has a fiduciary relationship with the seller through the listing agreement he signed with the seller and owes his obedience, loyalty, disclosure, confidentiality, accounting, and reasonable care and diligence duties to the seller. The law recognizes that it is impossible to "serve two masters" at the same time, consequently the broker cannot give those same duties to both the seller and the buyer at the same time, in the same transaction. This may work to the disadvantage of the buyer, the seller, and the firm. That is, the buyer may not have access to a desirable property (one of the broker's listings), the seller may miss a sale because his listing broker cannot show his listed property to this buyer, and the firm is unable to earn a commission on one of its listings relative to this buyer.

In an effort to overcome the problem of not being able to show represented buyers properties listed in-house, some brokers have an understanding with buyers to show properties listed with their firms before entering into a buyer representation agreement. If after viewing the firm's listings, a suitable property has not been found, the broker and the buyers then enter into a buyer representation agreement in which the broker agrees to represent the buyers on all properties listed by other brokers. If such an arrangement is undertaken by the broker, the buyers must be made fully aware of the lack of representation that will occur if they choose to negotiate on any property listed by the brokerage firm. In addition, the broker who wishes to avoid situations that involve representing more than one party in a transaction must be prepared to deal with a possible dilemma if a buyer who has entered into a representation agreement later decides to negotiate on a listing held by the firm.

■ **EXAMPLE**   Broker Sally has 50 properties listed through exclusive-right-to-sell listing agreements. She promised each seller that she would attempt to get the highest price possible, the best terms and conditions possible for the property, would exclusively protect the best interests of the seller, and perform all fiduciary duties on behalf of her seller-client. Sally is the agent for each of these sellers.

Buyer Bob comes to Sally's office and asks to see her listed properties. Sally tells Bob that she is happy to show him the properties she has listed and carefully explains that she 1) is representing the seller, 2) her fiduciary responsibilities belong to the seller, 3) that all of her efforts will be to negotiate on behalf of the seller, and 4) that she is bound by law to reveal all information concerning Bob that she is made aware of, through communication or otherwise, to her seller-client. Bob acknowledges that he understands these limitations of the broker's services and agrees to work under the conditions of not having an agent represent his interests.

Bob does not find any property suitable to purchase in Sally's inventory of listed properties. However, Bob asks Sally to continue to work with him and asks her to research properties listed by other brokers that fit his needs and desires. Sally explains that she will be happy to do that but will require that Bob sign a buyer representation agreement before she takes him to see any properties listed by other brokers. Bob agrees to sign the buyer representation agreement. Sally is now the buyer's agent for Bob and owes all the fiduciary duties to Bob.

Sally can proceed without a conflict of interest as long as she does not take Bob to any of her listed properties and/or does not try to negotiate on a property listed by her, and does not reveal confidential information about any of her seller-clients (property or personal).

At this point, Sally is acting within the legal parameters of the agency relationships that have been created. However, if Bob does not like any of the properties he sees that are listed by other brokers and asks to go back to one of Sally's listed properties to try to negotiate with that seller for the purchase of his home, then there is a problem.

If she tries to show her listed property to Bob, Sally will be representing both the buyer and the seller in the same transaction and would owe full fiduciary duties to both parties, which the law does not allow. In addition, Sally already knows the privileged and confidential information about both the buyer and the seller and cannot bifurcate her brain so that one side of her brain does not reveal to the other side of her brain all the information she knows about each party. As a fiduciary, she is bound to tell everything she knows concerning the property, the third party, and the transaction to her client. In this circumstance, both the buyer and the seller are now her clients, which is a big problem.

If Broker Sally continues in this transaction under these circumstances, she has become a dual agent, which is no longer permitted under TRELA.

Sec. 1101.561. DUTIES OF INTERMEDIARY PREVAIL.

(a) The duties of a license holder acting as an intermediary under this subchapter supersede the duties of a license holder established under any other law, including common law.

(b) A broker must agree to act as an intermediary under this subchapter if the broker agrees to represent in a transaction:

(1) a buyer or tenant; and

(2) a seller or landlord.

(Added by Acts 2001, 77th Leg., ch. 1421, Sec. 2, eff. June 1, 2003. Amended by: Acts 2005, 79th Leg., Ch. 825, Sec. 8, eff. September 1, 2005.) (emphasis added)

Once begun, it is very hard to maintain the nonexclusive agency relationship if the broker is both taking listings and working with and then for a buyer. Just a few of the possible conflicts that begin to occur when practicing nonexclusive agency include 1) trying to track what information is known about the seller and the buyer, what information you can legally divulge in each circumstance or what information you must retain as confidential, and 2) maintaining a legal position within the scope of your agency relationship when negotiations begin. If done improperly, the broker sets herself up for possible serious legal consequences from the seller, the buyer, or both.

■ DISCLOSURE ISSUES

Disclosures of Seller's Agent to Seller

Before signing the listing agreement, the listing agent is required to provide the seller with the written statement required by TRELA § 1101.558, which describes the services that the seller may expect from a seller's agent, a buyer's agent, and an intermediary. TRELA **requires** that the listing agent provide this statement at the first substantive dialogue with the seller—that is, **the first meeting or written communication that involves a substantive discussion relating to specific real property.** In addition, the seller's agent should attempt to provide as much information to the seller as is reasonable to ensure that the seller is fully informed regarding matters such as

- general company policies regarding cooperating with other brokers;
- the fact that buyer/tenant agents represent the buyer/tenant, even if paid by the listing broker or the seller; and
- the possibility, if any, of the listing agent acting as an agent for both the seller and a buyer.

The licensee obtaining the listing also should discuss with the seller whether an MLS will be used and whether an offer allowing other brokers to represent the seller (subagency) through the listing broker will be permitted by the seller.

TREC rules require a real estate licensee to provide a broker's price opinion or comparative market analysis on the property at the time of negotiating a listing:

22TAC§535,16(c)

(c) A real estate licensee is obligated to provide a broker price opinion or comparative market analysis on a property when negotiating a listing or offering to purchase the property for the licensee's own account as a result of contact made while acting as a real estate agent.

22TAC§535.17 Broker Price Opinion or Competitive Market Analysis

(a) A real estate licensee may not perform an appraisal of real property unless the licensee is licensed or certified under Texas Occupations Code, Chapter 1103.

(b) If a real estate licensee provides a broker price opinion or comparative market analysis under §1101.002(1)(A)(xi) of the Act, the licensee shall also provide the person for whom the opinion or analysis is prepared with a written statement containing the following language: "THIS IS A BROKER PRICE OPINION OR COMPARATIVE MARKET ANALYSIS AND SHOULD NOT BE CONSIDERED AN APPRAISAL. In making any decision that relies upon my work, you should know that I have not followed the guidelines for development of an appraisal or analysis contained in the Uniform Standards of Professional Appraisal Practice of the Appraisal Foundation."

(c) The statement required by subsection (b) of this section must be made part of any written opinion or analysis report and must be reproduced verbatim.

(d) A salesperson may prepare, sign, and present a broker price opinion or comparative market analysis for the salesperson's sponsoring broker, but the salesperson must submit the broker price opinion or comparative market analysis in the broker's name and the broker is responsible for it.

If the licensee expects to receive compensation from more than one party or to represent buyers as well as the seller in a transaction, the source of compensation and consent to the arrangement must be expressed in writing (§ 1101.652(b)(8)). These and other disclosures can be made either in the listing agreement or in a special addendum to the listing agreement. It is grounds for loss of license under TRELA if the licensee does not comply with this requirement.

Disclosures of Seller's Agent to Buyer

The seller's agent must disclose to the buyer that the brokerage represents the seller, not the buyer. To facilitate this required disclosure, some firms have the buyer read and acknowledge a customer letter that outlines what the licensee can and cannot do for the buyer while acting as an agent of the seller. This letter could soften the tone of the disclosure, but it should not diminish the intent. Remember that the Information About Brokerage Services form is not a disclosure of agency.

It is simply information identifying to buyers or sellers what their business choices are relative to having representation or not having representation.

Early information and disclosure is the best policy. But keep in mind that state law prevails. If the buyer is not represented by an agent, the written information statement required by TRELA § 1101.558 must be provided at the **first substantive dialogue with the buyer**. This written statement, which is included in TREC's Information About Brokerage Services notice, contains state-mandated language relating to the various roles that a broker may play in a transaction. **In addition**, the agent must disclose to the buyer that the agent is the seller's representative at the time of the first contact with the buyer. This agency disclosure may be oral or written. Again, the Information About Brokerage Services form is not a disclosure of the licensee's agency relationship with any party.

Remember, the seller's agent dealing with a buyer cannot provide advice regarding the buyer's purchase decision that may be considered adverse to the seller's best interests unless it is information that the licensee is required, by law, to supply, such as a known defect in the property.

The seller's agent also should make clear to the buyer-customer that the licensee works on behalf of the seller in all negotiable issues. It is important to note at this point that almost every term or condition in any potential sales contract is fully negotiable between the buyer and the seller. The fact that TREC-promulgated forms for contracts may call for certain costs to be paid by the buyer and other costs to be paid by the seller in no way prohibits principals in the transaction from reallocating those costs to the other party through negotiation.

It is the licensee's legal obligation to make the contract conform to the intent of the principals. Therefore, licensees may add factual statements and business details desired by the principals and should strike from the contract only those items not desired by them (22 TAC § 537.11(f)). A fine line exists here between modifying the contract to "conform the instrument to the intent of the parties" and engaging in the unauthorized practice of law. All Texas licensees should be thoroughly familiar with the provisions and implications of TRELA § 1101.155; .252; .254; .652(a)(8); .654; and 22 TAC § 537.11 before they attempt to assist in contract negotiations.

A nonrepresented buyer should deal with the seller's agent as though dealing or negotiating directly with the seller. The buyer should be told in the initial interview not to disclose anything to the seller's agent that the buyer would not tell the seller. Additionally, the buyer should be told not to expect to receive any information from the seller's agent that the seller would not want to tell the buyer directly. The seller's agent must be careful in responding to questions such as "How low will the seller go?" "Will the seller take less?" "How can I get the seller to compromise on terms and come down in price?" Questions like these should elicit carefully rehearsed answers so that the agent appears professional and competent, replies honestly and fairly, and is not disloyal to the client or misleading to the customer.

▪ SUMMARY

The broker who consistently acts in the sole capacity of a seller's agent has little trouble distinguishing the client from the customer. Until the early 1990s, firms with large shares of the market often chose this type of relationship to lessen the risk of conflicts of loyalty in selling their own listings. However, with the passage of laws requiring better information and disclosures to the parties, buyers and sellers are becoming more aware of agency options. As a result, many Texas firms are experimenting with a variety of agency policies. Some firms have clearly stated policies of not offering cooperation with other brokers except on an individual, case-by-case basis. Great care should be exercised, both with in-house sales and cooperative sales, to avoid conduct that might be interpreted as creating implied agencies with the buyers where none is intended. Supervising brokers can and should develop policies and procedures and competently train licensed associates to act consistently within the parameters of company policy.

In most residential real estate transactions, an agent other than the listing agent procures the buyer. It is important to make an early decision about whether the other agent is a subagent of the seller or an agent of the buyer. This depends on whether subagency was offered and whether it was accepted. If accepted, the sub-agent owes client-level services to the seller and customer-level services to the buyer.

▪ KEY POINTS

- ▪ Expressed listing agreements can be written or oral.
- ▪ Implied listing agreements are created by words or conduct of the parties.
- ▪ Early disclosure of seller agency helps lessen the chance that the buyer will claim later that the broker also represented the buyer.
- ▪ Written disclosures and brochures help clarify that the buyer is the customer and the seller is the client. Warning: Do not substitute the word *impartially*, or *equally*, for the word *fairly* (which is sometimes used as a synonym for impartially or equally), in the context of how an agent for the seller-client will treat the buyer-customer. The customer must be treated fairly by law, but not impartially or equally, relative to the licensee's client.
- ▪ A seller's subagent owes a general duty of fairness and honesty to the buyer (customer) but owes full fiduciary duties to the seller (client).
- ▪ Under an MLS system, offering of subagency is optional. As a matter of routine, the listing office should clarify subagency status of any other broker.
- ▪ Some cooperating brokers prefer to treat certain buyers as customers, and thus, subagency to the seller is the appropriate relationship.
- ▪ It is dangerous to appear to treat buyers as clients if they are in fact "customers," leading the buyers to believe they are clients, and thus create an accidental undisclosed agency relationship.

■ SUGGESTIONS FOR BROKERS

Review with your licensed associates the types of services they can provide to accommodate at least some needs of the buyer while remembering that they act as agents of the seller.

To ensure that your licensed associates do not accidentally create an implied or accidental agency with the buyer, require that the associates have the buyer acknowledge **in writing** that your firm and your associates act as agents of the seller, not as agents of the buyer.

Develop a company policy regarding net listing that includes the TREC requirements for disclosure.

When you act as the nonlisting or other broker, decide whether you prefer to represent the buyer or to represent the seller as a subagent. Choose what works best for you, and to be safe, get the informed written consent of all parties to act in that manner. Because principals may incur some liability by the acts of their subagents, listing brokers should tell sellers of the risks, as well as the benefits, of using subagents.

CHAPTER 4 QUIZ

1. A listing broker owes which of the following duties to the prospective buyer-customer?
   a. Loyalty
   b. Obedience
   c. Agency disclosure
   d. All of these

2. Three different subagents show a property to the same buyer over a span of two weeks. Which subagent is entitled to a share of the commission?
   a. The subagent who procures the sale
   b. The subagent who first showed the property to the buyer
   c. The subagent who last showed the property to the buyer
   d. All three subagents in equal shares

3. A listing broker normally can do all of the following EXCEPT
   a. sell the listing broker's own listings.
   b. advertise listed properties.
   c. hold open houses.
   d. split fees with a buyer's broker without the seller's knowledge.

4. A buyer approaches broker Smith, an exclusive seller's agent, and asks to be represented in the purchase of a home. Smith should
   a. explain that there are no real benefits to buyer representation.
   b. explain that while he cannot personally work with the buyer, one of his associates may do so.
   c. describe the services that the buyer may receive as a customer, but if the buyer still wants representation, refer the buyer to a buyer's broker.
   d. show the buyer only properties listed by other brokers.

5. A net listing requires that the
   a. seller accept the net amount of money remaining after all costs of sale.
   b. seller independently determine the value of the property.
   c. agent advise the seller of the value of the property.
   d. agent limit the amount of commission charged.

6. The listing that allows the seller to list with several brokers is the
   a. exclusive right to sell.
   b. exclusive agency.
   c. open listing.
   d. net agency.

7. According to TRELA, brokers are responsible for the negligent acts of subagents
   a. under no circumstances.
   b. to the extent that they knew of the negligent acts.
   c. no matter whether they knew of the negligent acts or not.
   d. only when they encourage the subagent to commit a negligent act.

8. A subagent brings a full-priced offer to purchase to the listing broker but is later informed that the seller has elected not to sell the property. The subagent
   a. has no right to sue under the terms of the listing agreement.
   b. may file suit against the listing broker for his commission.
   c. may force the listing broker to file suit against his client.
   d. may file suit against the seller for his commission.

9. The seller says he will list with you as long as he gets enough to pay his loan balance and closing costs. Your commission will be anything above those costs. This is an example of a(n)
   a. open listing.
   b. one-time showing agreement.
   c. net listing.
   d. fixed commission listing.

10. A buyer asks a broker, who is the subagent of the listing broker, whether the seller would accept $4,000 less than the asking price. The listing broker already has told the subagent that the seller will take $5,000 less. Which is the *BEST* response for the subagent?

   a. "Go ahead and make the offer because the seller needs to sell before the bank forecloses."

   b. "You may make the offer, and we'll see what the seller says. But remember, you may want to make your very best offer the first time because we don't discuss the existence or nonexistence of other offers."

   c. "I can't present an offer that is less than the asking price."

   d. "If I get the seller to accept this low offer, I want a $1,000 bonus. But remember, you may want to make your very best offer the first time because we don't discuss the existence or nonexistence of other offers."

DISCUSSION QUESTIONS

1. Why can't licensed associates take listings with them when they transfer to new firms?

2. In exclusive seller agency brokerage firms, what is the best way to handle a transaction in which the seller wants help in finding a replacement property?

3. How would you offer to help a prospective buyer you meet at an open house and still remain loyal to the seller?

4. What should the associate of a listing broker say when the non-represented buyer asks common questions such as the following:

   ■ How low will the seller go?

   ■ Do you think the property is worth what the seller is asking?

   ■ Are there any other offers on the property?

   ■ Have you had any contracts that fell through?

5. Does a subagent owe the seller any different fiduciary duties from those owed by the listing broker?

6. Can a subagent sue the seller for a commission if the seller defaults and the listing broker elects not to sue? Why or why not?

7. What are the pros and cons of a seller offering subagency to other brokers?

8. What are some of the differences between client-level services and customer-level services?

9. Do you feel more effective as a real estate agent working with a buyer when you are a subagent or a buyer's broker?

CHAPTER

Buyer Agency

Although this chapter refers to buyer agency, it should be noted that tenants may be represented by brokers as well. By substituting tenant for buyer and landlord for seller, the licensee can apply the same principles to the leasing of real estate. Buyer agency exists when, through an oral or signed written agreement, through implied agency, or through the operation of law, a broker becomes the agent of a buyer or tenant, and the agency relationship focuses on the person who wishes to buy or lease property.

Buyer agency is not a revolutionary business practice. For decades, brokers have been employed to represent buyers. In fact, buyer representation in commercial real estate transactions is and always has been the rule rather than the exception. Brokers also have represented themselves, their business ventures, their relatives, and undisclosed principals in the acquisition of real estate. In residential transactions, however, it was not until the late 1990s in Texas that purchasers began to routinely employ a broker under written contract in the selection, negotiation, or acquisition of real estate. Attitudes have changed because of better consumer education and higher expectations and demand for advocacy.

Residential consumers recognize that they can benefit from client-quality representation, whether they are buyers or sellers. Once residential brokers began to offer their services to buyers, buyer agency rapidly became a growing market segment. Most brokers now offer client-level service to buyers. Although many brokers prefer not to take on the risks associated with dual representation, it is rare to find a brokerage office today that limits services to exclusive seller agency.

Many licensees do not understand the basic differences between conduct and duties of agency when representing sellers, buyers, or both. This chapter explores the factors that affect the broker's decision to treat certain buyers as clients (rather than as customers) or as one of two clients.

■ **LEARNING OBJECTIVES**   *This chapter addresses the following*

- ■ Buyer Representation Agreement
- ■ Deciding to Represent the Buyer
  - — Factors to Consider
- ■ The Creation of Buyer Agency
  - — Representation
  - — Advantages and Disadvantages of Exclusive Buyer Agency
- ■ Benefits of Buyer-Agency Relationships
  - — Agency Benefits to Buyer or Tenant
  - — Other Issues to Consider
  - — Example of Benefits to a Buyer
  - — Benefits to Buyers' Agents
- ■ Written Notification of Compensation to Broker and Fee Arrangements
  - — Procuring Cause
  - — Fee Arrangements
  - — Retainer Fee
  - — Seller-Paid Fee
  - — Commission Split
  - — Buyer-Paid Fee
  - — Net Purchase Price
  - — Gross Price
- ■ Buyer's Broker Disclosures
  - — Written Statement About Brokerage Services
  - — Disclosure of Agency Relationships
  - — Disclosure in Advertising
  - — Disclosure of Property Condition
  - — Disclosure of Pricing Opinions
  - — Disclosure of a Licensee's Position in Personal Real Estate Transactions
  - — No Requirement to Disclose HIV or HIV-Related Illnesses
  - — Disclosure of Client Information
  - — Fair Housing
  - — Buyers as Customers

■ BUYER REPRESENTATION AGREEMENT

To perform agency services to a buyer, it is recommended that the broker use a buyer representation agreement to delineate the rights and obligations of each party. A contractual agreement between the broker and the buyer serves to clarify all the issues agreed upon and prevents fraud or misrepresentation on the part of either party. The agreement that is used here is the Texas Association of REALTORS® (TAR) Residential Buyer/Tenant Representation Agreement (Figure 5.1). Only members of TAR may use TAR forms. Nonmember brokers might want to have an attorney create an agreement for the brokerage.

When presenting the agreement for the first time, it is recommended that the broker or sales associate of the broker cover it line by line to ensure that the buyer is completely familiar with the wording, the intent, and the ramifications of signing the agreement. Allowing the prospective buyer-client adequate time to ask questions and consider the implications of the concepts will forge a stronger relationship once the buyer is the broker's client.

F I G U R E   5.1

Buyer Representation Agreement

TEXAS ASSOCIATION OF REALTORS®
RESIDENTIAL BUYER/TENANT REPRESENTATION AGREEMENT
USE OF THIS FORM BY PERSONS WHO ARE NOT MEMBERS OF THE TEXAS ASSOCIATION OF REALTORS® IS NOT AUTHORIZED.
©Texas Association of REALTORS®, Inc.
2014

1. **PARTIES:** The parties to this agreement are:

Client:_____

   Address:_____
   City, State, Zip:_____
   Phone:_____Fax:_____
   E-Mail:_____

Broker:_____

   Address: _____
   City, State, Zip: _____
   Phone:_____Fax: _____
   E-Mail: _____

2. **APPOINTMENT:** Client grants to Broker the exclusive right to act as Client's real estate agent for the purpose of acquiring property in the market area.

3. **DEFINITIONS:**
   A. *"Acquire"* means to purchase or lease.
   B. *"Closing"* in a sale transaction means the date legal title to a property is conveyed to a purchaser of property under a contract to buy. *"Closing"* in a lease transaction means the date a landlord and tenant enter into a binding lease of a property.
   C. *"Market area"* means that area in the State of Texas within the perimeter boundaries of the following areas:_____
     _____
     _____
     _____.
   D. *"Property"* means any interest in real estate including but not limited to properties listed in a multiple listing service or other listing services, properties for sale by owners, and properties for sale by builders.

4. **TERM:** This agreement commences on _____ and ends at 11:59 p.m. on _____.

5. **BROKER'S OBLIGATIONS:** Broker will: (a) use Broker's best efforts to assist Client in acquiring property in the market area; (b) assist Client in negotiating the acquisition of property in the market area; and (c) comply with other provisions of this agreement.

6. **CLIENT'S OBLIGATIONS:** Client will: (a) work exclusively through Broker in acquiring property in the market area and negotiate the acquisition of property in the market area only through Broker; (b) inform other brokers, salespersons, sellers, and landlords with whom Client may have contact that Broker exclusively represents Client for the purpose of acquiring property in the market area and refer all such persons to Broker; and (c) comply with other provisions of this agreement.

Buyer Representation Agreement (continued)

Buyer/Tenant Representation Agreement between _____

7. REPRESENTATIONS:
   A. Each person signing this agreement represents that the person has the legal capacity and authority to bind the respective party to this agreement.
   B. Client represents that Client is not now a party to another buyer or tenant representation agreement with another broker for the acquisition of property in the market area
   C. Client represents that all information relating to Client's ability to acquire property in the market area Client gives to Broker is true and correct.
   D. Name any employer, relocation company, or other entity that will provide benefits to Client when acquiring property in the market area: _____.

8. INTERMEDIARY: *(Check A or B only.)*

❏ A. <u>Intermediary Status</u>: Client desires to see Broker's listings. If Client wishes to acquire one of Broker's listings, Client authorizes Broker to act as an intermediary and Broker will notify Client that Broker will service the parties in accordance with one of the following alternatives.
   1) If the owner of the property is serviced by an associate other than the associate servicing Client under this agreement, Broker may notify Client that Broker will: (a) appoint the associate then servicing the owner to communicate with, carry out instructions of, and provide opinions and advice during negotiations to the owner; and (b) appoint the associate then servicing Client to the Client for the same purpose.
   2) If the owner of the property is serviced by the same associate who is servicing Client, Broker may notify Client that Broker will: (a) appoint another associate to communicate with, carry out instructions of, and provide opinions and advice during negotiations to Client; and (b) appoint the associate servicing the owner under the listing to the owner for the same purpose.
   3) Broker may notify Client that Broker will make no appointments as described under this Paragraph 8A and, in such an event, the associate servicing the parties will act solely as Broker's intermediary representative, who may facilitate the transaction but will not render opinions or advice during negotiations to either party.

❏ B. <u>No Intermediary Status</u>: Client does not wish to be shown or acquire any of Broker's listings.

Notice: If Broker acts as an intermediary under Paragraph 8A, Broker and Broker's associates:
   ◆ **may not disclose to Client that the seller or landlord will accept a price less than the asking price unless otherwise instructed in a separate writing by the seller or landlord;**
   ◆ **may not disclose to the seller or landlord that Client will pay a price greater than the price submitted in a written offer to the seller or landlord unless otherwise instructed in a separate writing by Client;**
   ◆ **may not disclose any confidential information or any information a seller or landlord or Client specifically instructs Broker in writing not to disclose unless otherwise instructed in a separate writing by the respective party or required to disclose the information by the Real Estate License Act or a court order or if the information materially relates to the condition of the property;**
   ◆ **shall treat all parties to the transaction honestly; and**
   ◆ **shall comply with the Real Estate License Act.**

9. COMPETING CLIENTS: Client acknowledges that Broker may represent other prospective buyers or tenants who may seek to acquire properties that may be of interest to Client. Client agrees that Broker may, during the term of this agreement and after it ends, represent such other prospects, show the other prospects the same properties that Broker shows to Client, and act as a real estate broker for such other prospects in negotiating the acquisition of properties that Client may seek to acquire.

10. CONFIDENTIAL INFORMATION:
   A. During the term of this agreement or after its termination, Broker may not knowingly disclose information obtained in confidence from Client except as authorized by Client or required by law. Broker may not disclose to Client any information obtained in confidence regarding any other

F I G U R E   5.1

Buyer Representation Agreement (continued)

Buyer/Tenant Representation Agreement between _____

person Broker represents or may have represented except as required by law.

    B.   Unless otherwise agreed or required by law, a seller or the seller's agent is not obliged to keep the existence of an offer or its terms confidential. If a listing agent receives multiple offers, the listing agent is obliged to treat the competing buyers fairly.

11. BROKER'S FEES:

    A. Commission: The parties agree that Broker will receive a commission calculated as follows: (1) ____% of the gross sales price if Client agrees to purchase property in the market area; and (2) if Client agrees to lease property in the market area a fee equal to *(check only one box)*: ❑ _____% of one month's rent or ❑ _____% of all rents to be paid over the term of the lease.

    B. Source of Commission Payment: Broker will seek to obtain payment of the commission specified in Paragraph 11A first from the seller, landlord, or their agents. **If such persons refuse or fail to pay Broker the amount specified, Client will pay Broker the amount specified less any amounts Broker receives from such persons.**

    C. Earned and Payable: A person is not obligated to pay Broker a commission until such time as Broker's commission is *earned and payable*. Broker's commission is *earned* when: (1) Client enters into a contract to buy or lease property in the market area; or (2) Client breaches this agreement. Broker's commission is *payable*, either during the term of this agreement or after it ends, upon the earlier of: (1) the closing of the transaction to acquire the property; (2) Client's breach of a contract to buy or lease a property in the market area; or (3) Client's breach of this agreement. If Client acquires more than one property under this agreement, Broker's commissions for each property acquired are earned as each property is acquired and are payable at the closing of each acquisition.

    D. Additional Compensation: If a seller, landlord, or their agents offer compensation in excess of the amount stated in Paragraph 11A (including but not limited to marketing incentives or bonuses to cooperating brokers) Broker may retain the additional compensation in addition to the specified commission. Client is not obligated to pay any such additional compensation to Broker.

    E. Acquisition of Broker's Listing: Notwithstanding any provision to the contrary, if Client acquires a property listed by Broker, Broker will be paid in accordance with the terms of Broker's listing agreement with the owner and Client will have no obligation to pay Broker.

    F. In addition to the commission specified under Paragraph 11A, Broker is entitled to the following fees.
        1) Construction: If Client uses Broker's services to procure or negotiate the construction of improvements to property that Client owns or may acquire, Client ensures that Broker will receive from Client or the contractor(s) at the time the construction is substantially complete a fee equal to:_____.
        2) Service Providers: If Broker refers Client or any party to a transaction contemplated by this agreement to a service provider (for example, mover, cable company, telecommunications provider, utility, or contractor) Broker may receive a fee from the service provider for the referral.
        3) Other:_____
          _____
          _____.

    G. Protection Period: "Protection period" means that time starting the day after this agreement ends and continuing for _____ days. Not later than 10 days after this agreement ends, Broker may send Client written notice identifying the properties called to Client's attention during this agreement. If Client or a relative of Client agrees to acquire a property identified in the notice during the protection period, Client will pay Broker, upon closing, the amount Broker would have been entitled to receive if

F I G U R E   5.1

Buyer Representation Agreement (continued)

Buyer/Tenant Representation Agreement between _____

this agreement were still in effect. This Paragraph 11G survives termination of this agreement. This Paragraph 11G will not apply if Client is, during the protection period, bound under a representation agreement with another broker who is a member of the Texas Association of REALTORS® at the time the acquisition is negotiated and the other broker is paid a fee for negotiating the transaction.

H. <u>Escrow Authorization</u>: Client authorizes, and Broker may so instruct, any escrow or closing agent authorized to close a transaction for the acquisition of property contemplated by this agreement to collect and disburse to Broker all amounts payable to Broker.

I. <u>County</u>: Amounts payable to Broker are to be paid in cash in _____ County, Texas.

12. **MEDIATION:** The parties agree to negotiate in good faith in an effort to resolve any dispute that may arise related to this agreement or any transaction related to or contemplated by this agreement. If the dispute cannot be resolved by negotiation, the parties will submit the dispute to mediation before resorting to arbitration or litigation and will equally share the costs of a mutually acceptable mediator.

13. **DEFAULT**: If either party fails to comply with this agreement or makes a false representation in this agreement, the non-complying party is in default. If Client is in default, Client will be liable for the amount of compensation that Broker would have received under this agreement if Client was not in default. If Broker is in default, Client may exercise any remedy at law.

14. **ATTORNEY'S FEES**: If Client or Broker is a prevailing party in any legal proceeding brought as a result of a dispute under this agreement or any transaction related to this agreement, such party will be entitled to recover from the non-prevailing party all costs of such proceeding and reasonable attorney's fees.

15. **LIMITATION OF LIABILITY: Neither Broker nor any other broker, or their associates, is responsible or liable for any person's personal injuries or for any loss or damage to any person's property that is not caused by Broker. Client will hold broker, any other broker, and their associates, harmless from any such injuries or losses. Client will indemnify Broker against any claims for injury or damage that Client may cause to others or their property.**

16. **ADDENDA:** Addenda and other related documents which are part of this agreement are:
   - ☑ Information About Brokerage Services
   - ☐ Protecting Your Home from Mold
   - ☐ Information Concerning Property Insurance
   - ☐ General Information and Notice to a Buyer
   - ☐ Protect Your Family from Lead in Your Home
   - ☐ Information about Special Flood Hazard Areas
   - ☐ For Your Protection: Get a Home Inspection
   - ☐ _____

17. **SPECIAL PROVISIONS:**

18. **ADDITIONAL NOTICES:**

   A. **Broker's fees and the sharing of fees between brokers are not fixed, controlled, recommended, suggested, or maintained by the Association of REALTORS® or any listing service.**

   B. **In accordance with fair housing laws and the National Association of REALTORS® Code of Ethics, Broker's services must be provided without regard to race, color, religion, national origin, sex, disability, familial status, sexual orientation, or gender identity. Local ordinances may provide for additional protected classes (for example, creed, status as a student, marital status, or age).**

F I G U R E   5.1

Buyer Representation Agreement (continued)

Buyer/Tenant Representation Agreement between _____

    C. Broker is not a property inspector, surveyor, engineer, environmental assessor, or compliance inspector. Client should seek experts to render such services in any acquisition.

    D. If Client purchases property, Client should have an abstract covering the property examined by an attorney of Client's selection, or Client should be furnished with or obtain a title policy.

    E. Buyer may purchase a residential service contract. Buyer should review such service contract or the scope of coverage, exclusions, and limitations. The purchase of a residential service contract is optional. There are several residential service companies operating in Texas.

CONSULT AN ATTORNEY: Broker cannot give legal advice. This is a legally binding agreement. READ IT CAREFULLY. If you do not understand the effect of this agreement, consult your attorney BEFORE signing.

_____	_____
Broker's Printed Name License No.	Client's Printed Name

_____	_____
❑ Broker's Signature Date ❑ Broker's Associate's Signature, as an authorized agent of Broker	Client's Signature Date

_____	_____
Broker's Associate's Printed Name , if applicable	Client's Printed Name

	_____
	Client's Signature Date

■ DECIDING TO REPRESENT THE BUYER

When a prospective buyer enters a broker's office asking to see homes for sale, the broker does not necessarily have to represent the buyer in an agency capacity, even if the broker specializes in representing buyers. A seller's agent spends a considerable amount of time leading up to the listing of the seller's property. Likewise, an agent dealing with a prospective buyer spends time discussing the buyer's preferences and qualifications.

In some cases, a licensee may not feel comfortable in a fiduciary relationship with a particular buyer. This may be because of preexisting agency relationships the company has with sellers or because of an analysis of this particular buyer in terms of the buyer's cash, credit, or capacity to buy, motivation to buy, or incompatible personality traits. Nevertheless, the licensee still may want to serve that buyer as a customer. In addition, some licensees choose to spend time showing a buyer properties listed in the multiple listing service (MLS) with other brokers, or they choose to act as a subagent of the seller. It is not necessary that a broker create an agency relationship to help a buyer locate a property. In fact, some brokers, in order to avoid creating conflicting loyalties with their client-seller, prefer an office policy that dictates treating buyers as customers on in-house sales but as clients when working with listing brokers on cooperative sales, also known as nonexclusive single agency.

On the other hand, exclusive buyer agency has grown over the years, and some brokers have created companies that exclusively represent buyers. They have developed strategies for championing the cause and interests of the buyer and have mastered the concept of preserving equity on behalf of their buyer-clients. The focus of the exclusive buyer agent is to get the lowest possible price, and best possible terms and conditions for their buyer-client. They use their honed, professional skills to negotiate the most advantageous position for the buyer and work to preserve as much equity for the buyer possible. The buyer's agent preserves equity for the prospective buyer by negotiating a purchase price that is below market value and assisting the buyer in negotiating as many fees as possible, as the responsibility of the seller and not the buyer.

The exclusive buyer representative focuses on researching the available properties in the current market that meet the stated needs and desires of the buyer-client. By careful analysis of recently sold properties in close proximity to the subject property and properties that are currently on the market within that same radius, the buyer broker works diligently to give a professional broker's price opinion. The goal is to give the buyer-client as much information as possible so the buyer can make an informed decision to purchase or not purchase the property.

The professional licensee recognizes that adequately representing a buyer is a significant responsibility. Whether acting as a buyer's agent or as a seller's agent, the licensee is held to a higher standard of care when working with a client rather than with a customer. A buyer who feels the licensee has given poor advice may threaten to sue the agent for breach of fiduciary duty. The buyer might ask, "Who got me into this deal, anyway?" Deciding to offer client-level services, whether the client is the seller or the buyer, is a serious business decision with significant legal and economic consequences. For this reason, some brokers prefer to work with buyer prospects on a customer-level basis and with only select buyers on a client-level basis.

Factors to Consider

Unless company policy does not permit buyer representation, nothing prevents licensees from showing properties to a buyer as a client, provided the licensees clarify their role early in the transaction. When working with a buyer, licensees should decide, disclose, and obtain necessary consents to act. Licensees can act as agents of buyers, subagents of sellers (a licensee not associated with the listing broker but representing the seller through the listing broker), or in some cases, they may choose to act as an agent for both parties (intermediary). In deciding whether to represent the buyer, licensees should keep several points in mind:

The Broker Is the Primary Agent   The broker, not the licensed associate of the broker, is the primary agent of the buyer. If the broker already represents the seller, dual representation questions will arise if the broker's associate acts in such a way as to give the impression that the broker also represents the buyer.

The Buyer-Tenant Representation Agreement Belongs to the Broker   As with seller's listings, if the associated licensee who obtained a buyer's representation agreement leaves the brokerage firm, the agreement remains with the firm. A buyer's representation agreement cannot be transferred automatically to the new brokerage firm with which the licensee is now affiliated.

An Agency Relationship Is Not Required   The real estate licensee can, with proper disclosures, provide valuable services to a buyer without creating an agency relationship and without violating an already existing seller agency relationship. The existing seller agency representation produces an "arm around" relationship with the seller. The seller agent's relationship with the buyer-customer produces an "arm's length" relationship. As long as the licensee maintains these relationships, and his actions do not cross the line of "agency" with the buyer-customer, he is free to assist the buyer throughout the transaction, but not become an advocate for him or her. This is especially true with in-house sales. Real estate firms wishing to avoid representing more than one party develop ways to work "with" buyer customers, but not "for" buyer-customers, in a seller-oriented service business without crossing into agency representation of buyers.

Few Brokers Are Exclusive Buyers' Agents (EBA)   Even though some brokers start out representing buyers only, those brokers often find that satisfied buyers eventually turn into sellers and want the brokers to list their properties for sale. The practice of representing either buyers or sellers exclusively is known as **exclusive single agency,** and some brokers feel that this practice avoids potential conflicts that may arise when representing buyers and sellers.

A Buyer Broker Can Appoint Subagents   The buyer's broker can, with proper authority, appoint subagents to help in the search for the right property. This is especially useful in long-distance transactions—for example, when employees of nationwide companies are transferred and relocated. For example, broker Chris who runs an office in Dallas, Texas, has a buyer-client who desires to purchase a property located in Southlake, Texas. Chris does not usually assist buyers in finding properties in the Southlake area, but he has a buyer broker friend, Heather, who specializes in Southlake properties. Chris asks Heather if she would be willing to be a subagent in finding a property in Southlake for his buyer-client. Brokers will generally pay the subagent a finder's fee or will share a portion of the commission after it is earned and received.

■ THE CREATION OF BUYER AGENCY

As with seller-agency, a buyer-agency relationship can be created by implication, operation of law, or expressed agreement either orally or in writing. Texas requires only an intermediary agreement to be in writing (TRELA § 1101.559 (a)). The requirement that some note or memorandum of an agreement to pay a commission be in writing is a limiting requirement only if the Texas broker wishes to pursue legal action for the recovery of any agreed-upon commission (TRELA § 1101.806 (c)). In other words, it is not illegal to have an oral agreement between a broker and a buyer for the broker to be the buyer's agent. However, if the agreement is not written, the broker will generally not be able to use the Texas court system to sue the buyer for payment of compensation. While a written agreement is certainly preferable for any type of agency agreement, many express buyer agency and listing agreements are oral, with written confirmation noted in the sales contract. The best practice by licensees to assure that all parties clearly understand and agree to promises made, and the rights and obligations of the parties to an agency agreement, is to have it in writing and signed and dated by all parties to the agreement.

Representation

A buyer's agent should clarify the types of services to be offered to the buyer-client. These could include such tasks as

- creating a clear profile of the buyer's needs and desires to assist the broker in researching properties to fit those needs and desires
- providing a broker's price opinion (BPO) and/or a competitive market analysis from which the buyer may make an informed decision when making an offer on a property,
- assistance in determining favorable financing,
- structuring of the offer to purchase,
- explanation of contract documents and advice during contract negotiations,
- strongly and successfully advocating for the buyer when negotiating the buyer's offer,
- following the transaction from contract through closing to ensure that all contractual agreements are met before the buyer closes on the transaction, and
- assistance in investment analyses.

The buyer's agent should mention the potential need for the buyer to consult with legal, tax, and other expert advisers. All licensees are prohibited by TRELA from giving legal advice and from practicing law without a license to do so:

> **TRELA Sec. 1101.654. Suspension or Revocation of License or Certificate for Unauthorized Practice of Law.**
>
> (a) The commission shall suspend or revoke the license or certificate of registration of a license or certificate holder who is not a licensed attorney in this state and who, for consideration, a reward, or a

pecuniary benefit, present or anticipated, direct or indirect, or in connection with the person's employment, agency, or fiduciary relationship as a license or certificate holder:

(1) drafts an instrument, other than a form described by Section 1101.155, that transfers or otherwise affects an interest in real property; or

(2) advises a person regarding the validity or legal sufficiency of an instrument or the validity of title to real property.

(b) Notwithstanding any other law, a license or certificate holder who completes a contract form for the sale, exchange, option, or lease of an interest in real property incidental to acting as a **broker is not engaged in the unauthorized or illegal practice of law in this state** _if_ **the form was** [emphasis added]:

(1) adopted by the commission for the type of transaction for which the form is used;

(2) prepared by an attorney licensed in this state and approved by the attorney for the type of transaction for which the form is used; or

(3) prepared by the property owner or by an attorney and required by the property owner.

(Added by Acts 2001, 77th Leg., ch. 1421, Sec.2, eff. June 1, 2003.)

Buyer representation agreements can take many forms, depending on what the buyer and the buyer's agent want and are able to negotiate. Even if a licensee decides not to work as an agent with the buyer, the licensee and the buyer may enter into a general written understanding of their working relationship. This can be especially useful in large real estate firms that have many listings and need to avoid claims that the broker has illegally represented more than one party. Under one arrangement, the buyer agrees to work exclusively with the licensee and recognizes that the licensee renders specified customer-level services. Under this arrangement, the licensee is acting as an agent or a subagent of the seller and generally will be paid by the seller. Remember, however, that agency is not necessarily defined by who pays the licensee. Payment for the buyer representative may come from the seller through the seller's broker or from the buyer directly. The buyer representation agreement used to establish the agency relationship should spell out very clearly what responsibility the buyer has for the buyer broker's compensation.

Buyers' brokers frequently develop their own buyer representation agreement forms. Brokers who draft their working agreements without good legal counsel may be taking unnecessary risks, but they are not considered to be engaged in the unauthorized practice of law by doing so. In commercial transactions that involve large commissions, brokers often have their attorneys prepare comprehensive listing agreements. The Texas Real Estate Commission (TREC) has no state-approved or promulgated forms for agency agreements, listing agreements, buyer representation agreements, or agreements for representing more than one party. However, the Texas Association of REALTORS® (TAR) and local REALTORS® associations do have such forms, for use by their members only.

In some residential real estate transactions, the form used by the buyer's broker is not comprehensive, unlike those that may be found in big commercial transactions or the more carefully crafted agreements of the exclusive buyer's broker firms. These more generalized agreements are designed to encourage trust and understanding, **although they typically may not enable the real estate agent to prevail in a lawsuit**. Control of the client arises from the trust relationship itself, not from a supposedly ironclad agreement. Still, the form should be specific on essential items to minimize misunderstandings and disputes.

When deciding what type of agreement to use to establish an agency relationship of any kind, analyzing the purpose of the agreement is essential. The definition of a contract from the American Law Institute's Restatement (Second) of Contracts § 3 states: "A contract is a promise or a set of promises for the breach of which the law gives a remedy, or the performance of which the law in some way recognizes as a duty." It establishes the rights and duties of the parties to the contract, and it gives the parties to the contract the right to seek a legal remedy for any breach of an agreed duty of one of the parties. If necessary, the document may be used by one or both parties to sue the other party in a court of law. Otherwise, all agreements could simply be handshakes with good and honorable intentions by both parties. That is not always the case, and well written, comprehensive contractual agreements attempt to protect the parties from fraud, misunderstanding, and mistakes.

Some of the key points to consider in any buyer's broker agreements are

- exclusivity of representation;
- term of the agreement, including a specific calendar date for termination of the agreement;
- broker's obligations;
- client's obligations;
- representations of the parties;
- intermediary status and appointments (if appropriate);
- competing clients (i.e., more than one of your buyer-clients desire to make an offer on the same property);
- confidential information;
- conflicts of interest;
- mediation/no mediation;
- default of contract and remedies for default;
- compensation and/or fees; and
- special provisions.

This is by no means a comprehensive list. A broker would be wise to consult an attorney when contemplating creating a buyer representation agreement.

Well-written, comprehensive buyer representation agreements are as protective as well-written exclusive-right-to-sell listing agreements. For example, most buyer's agent agreements have an enforceable exclusive-right-to-purchase clause that allows the broker legal recourse for compensation if the buyer purchases a property without compensating the broker during the period of the agreement, even if the broker did not show the buyer the property.

Exclusive Right to Purchase   Paragraph 6 of TAR's Residential Buyer/Tenant Representation Agreement (Client's Obligations) clarifies that the buyer-client will work exclusively through her broker:

> Client will: (a) work exclusively through Broker in acquiring property in the market area and negotiate the acquisition of property in the market area only through Broker; (b) inform other brokers, salespersons, sellers, and landlords with whom Client may have contract that Broker exclusively represents Client for the purpose of acquiring property in the market area and refer all such persons to Broker; and (c) comply with other provisions of this agreement.

Novice buyers' agents are sometimes uncomfortable asking buyers to sign exclusive representation agreements. Some develop a nonexclusive agreement containing an automatic right-to-terminate provision. More experienced buyers' agents already have developed their counseling skills to a point where they are as comfortable in securing buyer's agent exclusive representation agreements as sellers' agents are in securing exclusive-right-to-sell listings from sellers.

Agents know that an exclusive-right-to-sell or exclusive-right-to-buy agreement means better control over the transaction and provides a better means for the buyer's agent to protect the agent's investment of time, energy, and skill. They also know that an "open" buyer-agency agreement can lead to the same type of procuring-cause disagreements between brokers and buyers as can occur in seller subagency or open-listing situations.

The buyer must make the same choice as the seller in an open listing: Does the buyer-client want more agents working on her behalf, but with less commitment, motivation, or knowledge of her needs? It is also much more important for the agent to have exclusive-agency rights when the agent is compensated by a contingent fee rather than by an hourly fee.

Termination Date

Both the agent and the buyer should be clear as to when the agency relationship will terminate. A specific termination date on any buyer representation contract is required by TRELA:

> **Sec. 1101.652. Grounds for Suspension or Revocation of License.**
>
> (a) The commission may suspend or revoke a license issued under this chapter or take other disciplinary action authorized by this chapter if the license holder: ...
>
> ...(12) fails to specify a definite termination date that is not subject to prior notice in a contract, other than a contract to perform property management services, in which the license holder agrees to perform services for which a license is required under this chapter

The expiration period is fully negotiable and can be longer or shorter than in a listing agreement with a seller. An agent who wants to be covered for a sale that takes place on a certain property after the agreement expires should insert an extending carryover clause to specify the protection period and the procedures for registering prospects. The agreement may be terminated anytime by mutual consent of the agent and principal.

Conflicts of Interest A problem exists if the buyer wants to purchase a property already listed by the broker or another associate in the same office. If the broker has a buyer representation agreement with the buyer, under Texas law, all licensees associated with that broker also represent the buyer and must act in that buyer's best interests in any transaction. To attempt to avoid conflicts that may result when representing more than one party in the same transaction, the buyer representation agreement may contain a withdrawal provision, whereby the agreement becomes void in any transaction in which a conflict arises. In this case, the buyer would be free to seek outside representation or counsel in making the offer and is not obligated to pay a fee or commission to the original broker representative. Compensation for the "new" buyer representative would come either from an obligation written into the new buyer representation agreement, or if agreed to by the seller, payment of the buyer broker compensation could come from the seller. The key is that the contractual agreement between the new buyer representative and the buyer should clearly set out the obligation of the buyer relative to payment of compensation.

Another method to consider is renouncing one or the other agency relationship. Some brokers use the LIFO approach (last in, first out), in which the broker represents, for a single transaction only, the buyer or the seller, depending on who signed the representation agreement **first**. The **last one in** can choose self-representation or find outside representation and is not obligated to pay the original broker any fee. All of these approaches have risks in that once agency has begun, it is not simple to disengage one part of the relationship or to avoid its consequences.

Some brokerage firms have developed a practice of representing buyers in the purchase of all properties except those listed with the firms. In this fashion, in-house listings are shown first, before buyer representation begins. The broker has an arm's-length relationship with the buyer-customer at this point. The broker must be very careful to represent the seller's interest and observe his fiduciary duties to the seller while in this position with the buyer-customer. If no acceptable in-house listings are found, the agent then enters into a buyer representation agreement and thereafter works solely as a buyer's agent when showing properties listed by other brokers. The broker is now in an "arm around" position with the buyer and owes the buyer all of the fiduciary duties and common law duties of agency (obedience, loyalty, disclosure, confidentiality, accounting, and reasonable care and diligence). As he approaches each seller, the broker is in an arm's-length position with each seller relative to his buyer-client. This practice reduces the possibility of transactions involving two represented parties while preserving the opportunity for the agent to make an in-house sale.

Caution: This can lead to an obvious problem if a buyer now represented by the firm wants to reconsider a property listed by the firm that had been seen earlier, or if a new listing acquired by the broker meets the buyer's needs. If the broker does not wish to represent both parties, either the buyer or the seller would have to agree to cancel the agency agreement and allow the agent to act as the sole agent of the other party.

Because some risk does arise when a party terminates agency and reverts to customer status, some agents may choose to terminate both agreements and refer the parties to other agents. From a practical perspective, few agents wish to lose business by referring their buyers and sellers to other agents. Instead, agents take measures to minimize their risk through careful practice, making sure the parties fully understand the changing roles of the agent.

Other firms that specialize in representing buyers take the position that they will not actively solicit listings to sell. They will, however, occasionally list a property for one of their satisfied buyer-clients who now wants to sell a property. They also will register a seller's property with the understanding that this property will be exposed to their buyer-clients. There is a clear disclaimer of agency with the seller, and no fee is required to register the property.

Another conflict may arise if more than one buyer-client is interested in the same property. This is the reverse of the situation of a listing broker working with a customer who is interested in more than one of the broker's listings in the same location. Some buyer representation agreements contain a disclosure that the buyer's agent may enter into agreements with other buyers to locate property, making it possible that two or more buyers will be interested in the same property. If this should occur, the buyer's agent might seek an agreement authorizing the broker to show the property to all buyer-clients, with the understanding that

- none of the buyer-clients will consider the arrangement to be a conflict of interest, and
- all such multiple interests will be strictly confidential to the agent.

TAR's Residential Buyer/Tenant Representation Agreement, paragraph 9 (Competing Clients) states the following:

> Client acknowledges that Broker may represent other prospective buyers or tenants who may seek to acquire properties that may be of interest to Client. Client agrees that Broker may, during the term of this agreement and after it ends, represent such other prospects, show the other prospects the same properties that Broker shows to Client, and act as a real estate broker for such other prospects in negotiating the acquisition of properties that Client may seek to acquire.

Remember that in the business of real estate, no form of agency is so pure that potential conflicts of interest cannot arise. If a broker decides beforehand how to handle possible conflicts, some serious problems may be avoided.

Advantages and Disadvantages of Exclusive Buyer Agency

There is a more dramatic solution to the previously discussed potential conflicts of interest: Some brokers have chosen to limit their practice to **exclusive buyer agency**. This indicates that the broker represents only buyers and will not list a seller's property for sale, whereas most brokers who offer buyer representation also will offer representation services to sellers. The brokers who practice exclusive buyer agency promote themselves to buyers both aggressively and successfully.

Some advantages of exclusive buyer agency include the following:

- It reduces the possibility of the unauthorized representation of more than one party because exclusive buyers' brokers do not take listings.
- Exclusive buyer agents develop and focus on methods, strategies, tools, concepts, techniques and systems to exclusively benefit a buyer-client.
- Buyers have greater confidence that they will see all the properties available from every source.
- Buyers have greater confidence that they will receive 100 percent undivided loyalty and expert advice on all property negotiations.
- Buyer loyalty to the agent increases under an exclusive buyer representation agreement.
- Exclusive buyer agency tends to prevent lapses or mistakes in negotiating objectives and styles that often occur when brokers switch back and forth from one role to the other, as do brokers who practice nonexclusive agency.
- An exclusive buyer's agent is more likely to be able to charge and collect retainer fees because buyers are sure of the 100% commitment they receive from the broker.

Some disadvantages of exclusive buyer agency include the following:

- Buyers sometimes want to sell and use brokers they're already familiar with; however, the exclusive buyer representative firm will not take the listings.
- Because the company has no listings, the possibility of earning commissions from both the listing side and the selling side of the business is eliminated. However, the conflict of interest that can occur when attempting to do both is also eliminated.
- A potential conflict of interest arises if two buyer-clients want to make offers on the same property.
- Exclusive buyer agency raises compensation issues, such as who pays the fee and whether listing brokers will cooperate and split any fees.
- In a For Sale By Owner (FSBO) situation, special care must be taken to disclose to the seller the position of agency between the broker and the buyer. In addition, the issue of compensation must be determined at two points: 1) at the time of the buyer representation agreement, and 2) at the time a buyer makes an offer to the seller. The wise exclusive buyer representative will require the buyer to sign a clearly written, comprehensive buyer representation agreement that spells out the obligations of the buyer to pay compensation to the buyer representative, before the buyer agent begins to do any work (i.e., research on available properties, showing available properties, giving in-depth and specific information, advocating for the buyer with third parties).

Single Property   A broker may wish to contract to represent a buyer with respect to a single property only. The situation could be handled in a way similar to the case of the unrepresented seller in a one-time-listing agreement). Remember, in a one-time-listing agreement, the licensee becomes the agent of the seller, but only for a specifically named buyer. This secures an agency relationship with at least one of the consumers in the transaction (the seller), while securing the ability to collect a commission should the transaction close.

In the original problem, what if the buyer-customer is interested in a specific property? If the seller is not represented by another broker or the seller is unrepresented and does not wish to enter into a one-time listing agreement, then the agent's status in the transaction is unclear. This could be resolved by having the buyer enter into a **one-time buyer representation agreement**, but only for the specifically named property. For example, using the TAR form, the market area indicated in paragraph 3C would be limited to the specifically named property rather than to a general market area, such as Texas or Nueces County. The buyer would revert to customer status for all other properties.

The one-time buyer representation agreement works particularly well when dealing with investors who ask a licensee to "be on the lookout" for particular types of properties. TREC would preclude the licensee from entering into a contract that had an open-ended termination date (§ 1101.652(b)(12)). To contractually represent a buyer in this case, the broker should prepare a brief letter agreement after first determining that the buyer is unaware of any similar property in the general location. For example, the agent might ask whether the buyer has been shown any large apartment buildings in the midtown area. If not, the investor-buyer agrees to a one-time buyer representation agreement but only for the specifically named property. The agent does not reveal the exact location of this property until the agreement is signed. This technique has proved helpful when the seller refuses to list a particular commercial property and the buyer does not want client status in regard to any other property except the one to be shown. Remember, the licensee must make clear to all parties which party he is representing in this transaction and secure a signature from the party agreeing to pay the commission (§ 1101.652(b)(7)–(8); .806(c)).

■ BENEFITS OF BUYER-AGENCY RELATIONSHIPS

Agency Benefits to Buyer or Tenant

Following are some of the benefits to a buyer (or tenant) who receives client-level services.

Tailored Buyer Representation Contract   In a buyer-representation (or tenant-representation) agreement with the broker, the buyer can tailor the agent's services to meet the buyer's needs and adjust the compensation accordingly. This applies not only to large national companies seeking housing for relocated employees or sites for chain stores or restaurants but also to purchasers seeking residences or investment opportunities. In some cases, the buyer has already identified the property and the financing and wants the agent to handle the negotiations. In addition, licensees should not stray outside their area of expertise. While generally familiar with local market issues and developments, a licensee may not wish to take on the responsibility of showing properties "anywhere in the state of Texas!" Using TAR's Residential Buyer/Tenant Representation Agreement (Figure 5.1) as an example, paragraph 3C could indicate "Nueces and San Patricio counties." The purchaser who wished to look at properties in another county would be free to enter into a buyer representation agreement with a broker from that county, as long as the other broker insures that agreement excludes Nueces and San Patricio counties.

Access to a Larger Marketplace   In practice, traditional agents frequently limit their search of properties to those in which the broker's commission is protected. Thus, they limit their search to properties listed in-house or in the MLS. The buyer's agent whose guarantee of commission is protected, although not necessarily paid, by a buyer-client is motivated to show the buyer all available properties that meet the stated requirements, including

- open-listing properties,
- properties exclusively listed with other brokers,
- For Sale by Owner properties,
- foreclosure and probate sales,
- sales by lenders of real estate–owned properties,
- sales by trusts and pension plans,
- properties owned by a government agency, and
- properties not yet on the market.

Stronger Negotiating Strategy   The buyer's agent views the entire transaction from the buyer's perspective, without the divided and diminished loyalty that would be demanded of an agent representing more than one party. Therefore, the buyer is in a stronger negotiating position. Also, the buyer may want the protection of an agent in dealings with an unrepresented owner. Some buyers fear that the reason an owner does not list with a broker is because something is wrong with the property.

Fiduciary Responsibility of the Agent   Under Texas licensing laws and common law, the buyer's agent is held to a higher standard of skill and care in dealing with the buyer than a subagent of the seller or the seller's listing agent, who works with the buyer on a customer basis. Buyers' agents have an affirmative duty to their clients to thoroughly investigate and completely disclose all facts that bear on a buyer's decision to buy. On the other hand, buyers' agents have a duty to be honest and deal fairly—not equally or impartially—with sellers, but they owe no duty to advise and counsel sellers.

The buyer's agent is held to the same standard of performance in dealing with the buyer that the listing broker is held to in dealing with the seller. There is nothing unique about the responsibility and duties of the buyer's agent. There is no new fiduciary duty or ethical responsibility that the buyer's agent must learn. What is different is that the agent owes conventional common, statutory, and administrative law fiduciary duties to a different group of participants, namely buyers. The quantity and quality of client-level services are at least the same as those a listing agent is required to give sellers. It is simply the other side of the representation coin. Buyers are not legally entitled to this level of service unless they retain their own real estate agents to represent them.

Confidentiality   Confidentiality can be especially important when the buyer wishes to remain anonymous. For example, Sarah, a movie star, considers purchasing a new mansion. If the seller learns the identity of the intended buyer, the seller may likely hold firm or increase the asking price. A buyer's agent acting for an undisclosed principal may be able to negotiate a better price and better terms for the anonymous buyer.

More Counseling, Less Selling   As opposed to persuasion or pressure to buy, the buyer who is represented by an agent can expect to receive more counseling, expert opinion, advocacy, and advice regarding the acquisition decision. When an agent is hired by a seller under an exclusive-right-to-sell listing, the agent's emphasis is on selling the property. When a buyer hires an agent under an exclusive-right-to-represent agreement, the agent does not sell a house but instead represents the buyer's best interests throughout the purchasing process of real property. In a very real sense, the buyer's agent is a purchasing agent, not a selling agent. This agent's emphasis is on helping the buyer-client evaluate different properties and alternative courses of action and then negotiating the best price, terms, and conditions possible once having elected to go forward with negotiations on a property.

A buyer's agent who takes his fiduciary responsibilities seriously is always looking for ways to supply his buyer-client with information and will provide recommendations designed to protect his buyer-client's interests. He is continually counseling the buyer using his professional knowledge and skill to accomplish his buyer-client's goals.

For instance, a buyer's agent might recommend that the buyer visit the neighborhood of a home he is interested in purchasing, at random times of the day, and suggest that the buyer inquire about the property with the neighbors to gain more complete information about the property or about the seller. Buyers' agents do their best to find out things about a property that the seller or the listing agent might not want to disclose or might not feel obligated to disclose, such as excess noise, sewage odors, high energy costs, traffic congestion, or unauthorized seller improvements.

Buyers expect their agents to counsel them when writing the offer on the seller's home, and review any counteroffers made by the seller. The buyer's agent reviews, line by line, the contract form used to make the offer, explains the wording, and answers the buyer's questions. The buyer's agent must be very careful to avoid giving legal advice but, at the same time, is required to use his knowledge and skill to guide the buyer in her decision making. He counsels the buyer by helping her identify "red flags" and areas where it would be in her best interest to hire an attorney for legal advice.

One of the most important tasks of the buyer's broker is to help the buyer locate properties that meet the buyer's needs and desires. If the buyer's agent does a good job during the initial interview with the buyer to clearly establish critical information concerning the desired property location, size, number and types of rooms, amenities, school district, and the like, he is then able to use specific search criteria to search for properties currently on the market that most nearly match the buyer's criteria.

A buyer's broker meets with inspectors, appraisers, repairmen, and other vendors on behalf of his buyer-client and is available to answer questions, as well as make sure that the buyer's interests are protected. His counseling covers many areas, and the buyer benefits greatly from having a buyer representative who is willing to spend valuable time sharing his expertise and guiding the buyer-client through a successful transaction.

Other Issues to Consider

When assisting a buyer with the preparation of an offer to purchase, the buyer's agent should keep in mind that

■ the agent is not an attorney and must avoid the unauthorized practice of law;
■ any complicated drafting should be left to an attorney, although it may be appropriate for the agent to suggest various negotiating strategies and certain contingencies and financing techniques that should be incorporated into the offer;
■ the offer should not be so one-sided that it is unfair or unrealistic; and
■ although the agent should help the buyer evaluate key contract terms, the agent should not decide what is best for the buyer.

What follows is a discussion of important items for the buyer's agent to consider before preparing an offer to purchase. Some items will influence price negotiations. Some states, including Texas, require the use of preapproved forms, and this requirement may affect the ability of a buyer's agent to use some of these suggestions.

Again, keep in mind that TREC contract forms may be adjusted to conform to the intent of the principals, not necessarily rigidly copied. It should be noted, however, that modifications to a promulgated form should be at the principal's direction—not at the agent's discretion. (Also remember that this chapter looks at these contract terms from the point of view of the buyer and the buyer's agent. Many of these statements would be reversed in the negotiating strategy of the seller's agent or the subagent.)

Earnest Money Deposit

In Texas, earnest money is not essential to the validity of a contract. A real estate contract in Texas is valid with or without earnest money. Earnest money is not the consideration necessary to make the contract valid. It is money or something else of value, usually to be held in escrow by a third party, to be given to the seller in the event of the buyer's default on the contract before closing.

Earnest money is meant to provide a nonjudicial remedy for damages incurred by the seller because of the buyer's default. It is an alternative remedy to a lawsuit for damages, specific performance, injunction, or other legal action. However, its major significance is that a seller does not have to go to court to get the earnest money; that is why earnest money is referred to as a nonjudicial remedy. Traditionally, the buyer gives the earnest money check to the broker to accompany the offer and to be deposited by the broker. Currently, TREC-promulgated forms do not indicate that necessity, stating only that the buyer must deposit the earnest money with the escrow agent named in the contract "upon execution of this contract by both parties."

Buyer's brokers should keep the following in mind when their clients agree to deposit earnest money in the course of a transaction:

- Discuss with the buyer-client the strategy of depositing a large amount of earnest money as a negotiation tool to drive down the sales price, giving an offer (in the eyes of the seller) an advantage over competing offers without such security. Remember, though, that a large deposit also increases the buyer-client's potential financial loss. A buyer-client who is risk-averse might want to keep the initial deposit low, with any additional deposit to be made 10–15 days (or some other acceptable period) after the seller accepts the offer. If a substantial deposit is made, suggest that the client consider the use of an interest-bearing account to benefit the buyer.

- Avoid giving the deposit directly to the seller. As previously noted, TREC contract forms do not provide for sellers or sellers' agents or subagents to deposit earnest money. Nor do they provide for earnest money checks to be carried back and forth with the contract documents. They are to be deposited by buyers or designated licensees on execution of the contract by both parties, unless otherwise agreed. If done differently, the contract should specify exactly how it will be handled. The selection of the escrow agent in the contract is a fully negotiable item; however, the issue must be agreed on by the parties or no enforceable contract exists.

- Where appropriate, request that the seller deposit a sufficient sum of earnest money to cover any closing and title cancellation charges, buyer's moving and storage expenses, and some money for the buyer's broker if the contract is terminated because of the seller's default. If the buyer representation agreement calls for the broker to get half of any earnest money put up and forfeited by the seller, the amount requested must be doubled; otherwise, the buyer will not receive enough to cover reasonable potential damages.

Discussing the purpose of earnest money and the contract document's wording relative to "earnest money" and "default" is an important part of the buyer broker's counsel. Earnest money, in the TREC One to Four Family Residential Contract (Resale) form is referred to as "liquidated damages." Liquidated damages, according to *The Language of Real Estate Seventh Edition,* by John W. Reilly with Marie S. Spodek, is "an amount predetermined by the parties to an agreement as the total amount of compensation an injured party should receive if the other party breaches a specified part of the contract."

Paragraph 15 of the One to Four Family Residential Contract (Resale) form says the following:

> 15. DEFAULT: If Buyer fails to comply with this contract, Buyer will be in default, and Seller may (a) enforce specific performance, seek such other relief as may be provided by law, or both, or (b) terminate this contract and receive the earnest money as liquidated damages, thereby releasing both parties from this contract. If Seller fails to comply with this contract, Seller will be in default and Buyer may (a) enforce specific performance, seek such other relief as may be provided by law, or both, or (b) terminate this contract and receive the earnest money, thereby releasing both parties from this contract.

The purpose of earnest money is to protect the seller in case the buyer defaults on promises made in the contract. It allows the seller to receive the earnest money as "liquidated damages," and not have to go to the courts for relief. It is very important that the buyer's agent discuss the strategy of how much to place in the earnest money blank of the contract form and explain the "demand" paragraph to the buyer-client.

Paragraph 18(C) of the One to Four Family Residential Contract (Resale) form states the following:

> 18(C) DEMAND: Upon termination of this contract, either party or the escrow agent may send a release of earnest money to each party and the parties shall execute counterparts of the release and deliver same to the escrow agent. If either party fails to execute the release, either party may make a written demand to the escrow agent for the earnest money. If only one party makes written demand for the earnest money, escrow agent shall promptly provide a copy of the demand to the other party. If escrow agent does not receive written objection to the demand from the other party within 15 days, escrow agent may disburse the earnest money to the party making demand reduced by the amount of unpaid expenses incurred on behalf of the party receiving the earnest money and escrow agent may pay the same to the creditors. If escrow agent complies with the provisions of this paragraph, each party hereby releases escrow agent from all adverse claims related to the disbursal of the earnest money.

Assignability

In Texas, most standard contracts are assignable unless otherwise stated. An assignable contract is one in which the rights to the contract can be given, or assigned, to some other party. Of course, the parties should understand this clearly before entering into any negotiations.

Seller Financing   If the buyer asks the seller to carry back a note and mortgage or a similar security instrument, such as a deed of trust or an installment sales contract, the buyer should specify in the purchase agreement the key provisions to be inserted in the financing document for the buyer's benefit. These might include

- no prepayment penalty,
- no due-on-sale clause,
- nonrecourse liability (the seller's remedy is to foreclose on the property without the buyer being personally liable for any deficiency),
- extended grace periods, and
- deferral of interest.

Depending on the terms of the seller-provided financing (maturity date, interest rate, and amount of down payment), the buyer should be flexible in selecting the offering price. These provisions are provided for in a TREC-promulgated addendum for seller financing that should be the only form used, unless the buyer's or the seller's attorney drafts another addendum. Don't try to create them in the special provisions paragraph of the contract. Such action is grounds for loss of license and a basis for lawsuit by the client if the terms are drafted incorrectly and lead to damage to the buyer. Notwithstanding this caution, the buyer-client, as a party to the purchase contract, has the right to insert any desired provision in a contract offer. The client's agent must follow the client's instructions, but when substantial modifications are made, the agent should advise the client to seek competent legal advice first.

Contract Acceptance

The seller's acceptance of the offer is effective only if delivered in writing to the buyer or the buyer's agent. This gives buyers the longest time possible in which to revoke an offer if they choose, for whatever reason.

Extended Closing

For their own protection, buyers should consider whether they want to be given the contractual right to extend closing dates beyond those in the TREC form if they have difficulty arranging financing or otherwise meeting the closing dates.

Inspection

The buyer's offer could be made contingent on one or more professional inspections. If there are problems with the condition of the property, the buyer may be justified in canceling the contract, based on the results of the inspection. The TREC-promulgated sales contracts provide for an option fee to be paid by the buyer to the seller, giving the buyer the unrestricted right to inspect and the unrestricted right to terminate the contract for some agreed-on period after the acceptance of the offer.

The contract provides boxes that may be checked indicating that if the property is purchased, the option fee will or will not be credited to the buyer. Buyers' agents or sellers' agents or subagents attempting to create their own version of this provision will be engaging in the unauthorized practice of law. Keep in mind, however, that a principal or an attorney acting for a client may use alternative inspection language in addenda. Likewise, professional organizations such as the Texas Association of REALTORS® may create alternative inspection addendum forms for optional use by their members.

Property Condition

The seller should submit a property condition disclosure report for the buyer's approval. A buyer's agent may counsel the buyer-client to require that the seller agree to the following:

- No personal property items will be substituted for those at the property when it was shown and that were expected, by the buyer, to be included in the purchase price.
- The property is in the same or the required improved condition at the time of possession by the buyer, as so contracted.
- The property is clear of debris, and the appliances and the plumbing, heating, and electrical systems are in good working condition.
- All required building permits have been issued.
- All adverse environmental conditions will be removed.
- The present use is lawful.

TREC contract forms already include some of these concerns. Texas law requires that most sellers furnish buyers with a Seller's Disclosure of Property Condition in accordance with Section 5.008 of the Texas Property Code. TREC has produced an approved, but not promulgated, form that licensees may use to meet this Property Code requirement. Sellers subject to this disclosure requirement to the buyer must do so by the time specified in the Property Code or the transaction may be subject to rescission by the buyer. A licensee who fails to make the client aware of the necessity and availability of this form for use could face a lawsuit from a damaged client and loss of license under TRELA § 1101.652(b)(1).

The condition of the property is obviously a critical part of the decision-making process, and the buyer's agent should pay close attention to the Seller's Disclosure of Property Condition document if and when it is provided to the buyer-client by the seller. The very purpose of this document is to have written documentation by the seller to the buyer, of the condition of the property, as of a specified date. § 5.008 of the Texas Property Code states the following:

> (a) A seller of residential real property comprising not more than one dwelling unit located in this state shall give to the purchaser of the property a written notice as prescribed by this section or a written notice substantially similar to the notice prescribed by this section which contains, at a minimum, all of the items in the notice prescribed by this section…

> (f) The notice shall be delivered by the seller to the purchaser on or before the effective date of an executory contract binding the purchaser to purchase the property. If a contract is entered without the seller providing the notice required by this section, the purchaser may terminate the contract for any reason within seven days after receiving the notice.

Caution: Generally, a licensee, whether a seller's agent or a buyer's agent, is not an expert in foundations, roofs, pools, structural conditions, electrical issues, plumbing, et cetera and must be careful to limit any discussion about these types of issues. Do not give advice or opinions about the condition of the property or how to specifically solve any defect.

In addition to carefully examining the Seller's Disclosure of Property Condition, the buyer's agent will discuss the possible advantage of his buyer-client hiring an inspector to conduct an inspection on the property in order to reveal any defects, whether structural, mechanical, or cosmetic. At this time, the number of days requested in paragraph 23 (Termination Period) of the One to Four Family Residential Contract (Resale) should be discussed with the buyer-client to ensure that the buyer has enough time to have the inspection (and any appraisal the buyer desires) completed before the end of the termination option period. This gives the buyer the greatest protection to be able to terminate the contract if he finds any reason not to purchase the property.

Paragraph 23 (Termination Period) of the One to Four Family Residential Contract (Resale) states the following:

> For nominal consideration, the receipt of which is hereby acknowledged by Seller, and Buyer's agreement to pay Seller $_____(Option Fee) within 2 days after the effective date of this contract, Seller grants Buyer the unrestricted right to terminate this contract by giving notice of termination to Seller within _____days after the effective date of this contract (Option Period). If no dollar amount is stated as the Option Fee or if buyer fails to pay the Option Fee to Seller within the time prescribed, this paragraph will not be a part of this contract and Buyer shall not have the unrestricted right to

terminate this contract. If Buyer gives notice of termination within the time prescribed, the Option Fee will not be refunded; however, any earnest money will be refunded to Buyer. The Option Fee ☐ will ☐ will not be credited to the Sales Price at closing. Time is of the essence for this paragraph and strict compliance with the time for performance is required.

The buyer's agent should also discuss the possibility of a residential service contract or other possible warranties. The One to Four Family Residential Contract (Resale) discusses this in paragraph 7.H (Residential Service Contracts):

> Buyer may purchase a residential service contract from a residential service company licensed by TREC. If Buyer purchases a residential service contract, Seller shall reimburse Buyer at closing for the cost of the residential service contract in an amount not exceeding $_____. Buyer should review any residential service contract for the scope of coverage, exclusions and limitations. The purchase of a residential service contract is optional. Similar coverage may be purchased from various companies authorized to do business in Texas.

Pests

The buyer may want to require that the seller agree to pay for a pest-clearance report from a licensed exterminator chosen by the buyer, and the seller may agree to repair all pest damage or to treat the home, if necessary. The seller may be required to treat for fleas and/or termites and other wood-infesting organisms, using care not to use chemicals that may make the dwelling unsafe after use.

Assessments

The seller should agree to pay all assessments at closing, on the theory that the enhanced value of these improvements has been reflected in the sales price. Suppose that an assessment is outstanding at a low interest rate (a $20,000 sewer assessment payable in 10 years at 6%, for example). Rather than have the seller pay off the assessment, consider having the buyer assume the assessment and lower the purchase price accordingly or credit the amount against the down payment.

Title Matters

The seller should agree to correct any title defect by a certain date; in fact, the closing can be postponed at the buyer's election to allow the defect to be cleared. The buyer may want to consider paying for the owner's title insurance policy to have the nonnegotiable right, under the Real Estate Settlement Procedures Act (RESPA), to choose the title insurer. Under RESPA, regardless of who pays for the title policy, the buyer cannot be required to use a specific title insurer as a condition of sale. By the same token, a seller cannot be forced to pay for a title policy. Thus, from a practical perspective, the party paying for the policy usually chooses the title insurer.

Financing and Other Contingencies

Financing contingencies should be structured so that the buyer has enough time to perform. It is appropriate to make the contract subject to the review and approval of the buyer's attorney or tax adviser. If the buyer cannot meet a contingency, such as obtaining loan approval, the buyer should have the choice to cancel, extend, or waive the condition and proceed to close, perhaps obtaining funds from another source.

If the property increases in value after the offer is accepted and before title transfers, the buyer who didn't qualify for financing could benefit by waiving the contingency and assigning her rights in the contract to another buyer for a profit. The buyer should use reasonable efforts to meet the contingency and not use the contingency clause as a bad-faith means to tie up the seller's property.

Miscellaneous Checklist

In a **seller's market**, the buyer may not be in a good position to demand too many concessions from the seller. The buyer's agent should consider reviewing some of the following items with the client for possible inclusion in a purchase contract for the buyer's benefit:

- The buyer is permitted occupancy before closing.
- The buyer is granted a right of first refusal to acquire any adjoining property owned by the seller.
- The buyer is given credit for any impound (escrow) accounts on assumed mortgages.
- The buyer is given the right to lock in points on a loan.
- The seller pays the appraisal fees and points on the loan.
- The buyer can extend the satisfaction date of any seller-provided financing.
- The buyer-borrower is given the right of first refusal if the seller discounts the sale of any purchase-money mortgage that the seller carried back.
- The seller agrees to allow the buyer-borrower to substitute collateral on any seller-provided financing.
- The seller provides a corporate resolution if the seller is a corporation, indicating, among other things, who is duly authorized by the corporation to sign all necessary documents on behalf of the corporation.
- The seller covers the buyer's expenses if the seller refuses to close on time.
- The seller permits the buyer to show the property to prospective tenants before closing.
- The seller allows the buyer reasonable access to the property to permit inspection by buyer's representatives such as interior designers and architects.

The seller's agent or subagent should urge the seller to consider resisting any or all of these concessions unless the seller-client gains some exceptional benefit in return. Sometimes an overly aggressive buyer's agent gives advice that works to the buyer's disadvantage in the negotiations. The buyer must keep in mind that each concession requested from the seller may result in refusal of an offer and the possible loss to the buyer of a desirable property. Similarly, overly aggressive listing agents may give sellers negotiating advice that will actually harm the sellers, such as rejecting an offer or encouraging sellers to make harsh counteroffers that are unacceptable to buyers. The agents in such cases may go beyond their legitimate roles and breach fiduciary duties to their clients.

Example of Benefits to a Buyer

To illustrate the level of service due a client, consider the following example.

■ **EXAMPLE**   George refers Betty, a buyer, to Sally, a broker for Bay Realty. Betty is interested in looking at properties, says she wants someone to represent her best interests, and if she works well with Sally, she will purchase other properties through Sally. Sally decides to work with Betty on a client basis. Betty indicates she will pay Sally for her help and advice or will see that Sally is paid by the seller as a condition of any subsequent contract. She signs an exclusive buyer representation agreement. Sally shows Betty, now the client, a country property listed in the MLS with Sam of Main Realty, and Betty decides to buy it. Sally properly notifies Sam, the seller's agent, that she disclaims any subagency to Sam and states that she and Bay Realty represent the buyer and not the seller.

■ **QUESTION**   In the course of negotiations, Sally, the buyer agent, deals with a number of important items, such as (1) price and appraised value, (2) seller financing, (3) earnest money, (4) condition of property, (5) contingencies, and (6) fixtures and inventory. How should Sally treat each item, recognizing that her primary allegiance is to Betty?

■ **DISCUSSION**   Sally must be honest and make appropriate disclosure to the seller; as Betty's agent, however, she owes a greater duty of skill, care, and disclosure to protect Betty's best interests. Sally can advise Betty how she might persuade the seller to modify the terms and reduce the selling price and what alternative courses of action Betty might take. Sally should handle each item as follows:

Price and appraised value. Sally should analyze the property and the seller's position to obtain the lowest realistic price for Betty. She is required to give her opinion of the estimated price of the property to her buyer-client, and will do a broker's price opinion (BPO) and/or comparative market analysis (CMA) on the property to accomplish that goal. Sally will consider getting Betty's permission to submit the CMA, along with any offer on the property from her client Betty, to the seller through Sam, the seller's agent. Sally is not obligated to give the seller any of Betty's confidential information, and especially if that information does not support her negotiating position. Sally, as the buyer's agent, legally negotiates with the seller through Sam, the seller's agent, for the best possible price, terms and conditions. She would not do so as a subagent. In a buyer's market, Sally might suggest that client Betty prepare two offers and not reveal the higher offer unless and until the seller rejects the first offer. Subagents of a seller who did that in this type of scenario would breach their fiduciary duties.

Seller financing. If the seller is financing any portion of the purchase of the home, Sally need not suggest that Betty submit tax returns and a credit report unless these are requested by the seller. Sally might suggest seeking legal advice regarding favorable financing terms, such as no due-on-sale clause, no prepayment penalty, liberal grace periods and minimal late charges, default remedies limited to judicial foreclosure with no deficiency against Betty (nonrecourse), or deferred interest.

Earnest money. Sally can suggest that the earnest money be relatively modest or be reflected in an unsecured note. Conversely, she might suggest a substantial earnest money deposit to convey the buyer's serious intent to purchase the property.

Condition of property. Sally should discuss with Betty the Seller's Disclosure of Property Condition, recommend an inspection, and discuss warranties available to her.

Caution: Generally, the licensee representing either a seller or a buyer does not have professional knowledge and skill in the financing area of a real estate transaction. A licensee/agent who lacks such professional knowledge and skill must be extremely careful about giving advice, counsel, recommendations, or absolutes relative to the financing of the purchase of the property.

Contingencies. Contingencies are placed in a contract so that either a particular event must take place or a particular act must occur in order for the contract to be binding. The contingency could be the ability of the buyer to obtain financing, sell an existing home, or any other issue. Sally can explain the meaning of standard contingency clauses as they appear in the many TREC-promulgated or approved addenda. Of course, she should be very careful not to engage in the unauthorized practice of law when dealing with contingencies and should never add any language of her own. (See 22TAC §537.11 (b)(c) & (d))

Fixtures and inventory. Sally may advise buyer-client Betty to request in her offer additional personal property for the same purchase price, such as paintings and Oriental rugs. Sally should review any written inventory list before the offer is prepared and check to see that no substitution of items occurs.

Other items. As a buyer's agent, Sally must be careful not to reveal to the seller or the listing agent facts regarding Betty's bargaining position—for example, plans to buy adjoining parcels or adjoining condominium apartment units or that a resale buyer waits in the wings. Sally has no duty to disclose the name of the buyer or that Sally might lend Betty money to make the down payment. However, in Texas, if Sally is being paid by her client Betty and **also** expects to be paid any compensation by Sam, the seller's agent, that fact must be clearly disclosed and consented to by all parties or Sally and/or Bay Realty could face TREC disciplinary hearings and possible loss of license (TRELA § 1101.652(b)(7); (8)).

Sally must use her skill to research and investigate the contemplated acquisition. She must advise her client Betty of any facts relevant to the purchase decision that can be used to negotiate better terms (for example, that the seller is near foreclosure, is filing for divorce, or has already bought a new home; the property is about to be rezoned; the neighbors are unruly; or the house was burglarized four times last year).

Sally can accept an incentive fee for obtaining a reduction in the listed price. But, again, **if Sally receives compensation from more than one party in the transaction, that fact must be agreed to by all parties**.

Sally must do more than produce copies of relevant documents for her client, Betty. She must be sure Betty understands the impact on her purchase decision of key provisions in the documents. If she feels it is necessary, Sally should recommend that Betty obtain legal, title, or property inspection advice from outside experts.

Sally has a duty to express any doubts she may have about the suitability of the property for Betty, especially if Sally feels that the property is overpriced.

Caution: Any personal property items that will be negotiated between the buyer and the seller can become a problem to the lender unless kept separate by using a form such as the approved TREC OP-M Non-Realty Items Addendum form. Using this form and referencing it in paragraph 22 of the One to Four Family Residential Contract (Resale) (Agreement of the Parties) makes the addendum a part of the main contract and keeps the negotiation of those personal property items separate from the "sales price." Now, the lender is not making a loan based on personal property items, but only the established market value of the real property.

Benefits to Buyers' Agents

The buyer's agent can expect certain benefits from an agency relationship with a buyer.

Greater Client Loyalty   Traditionally, real estate agents work with "wandering" buyers on the chance of earning a fee, sometimes even if the chance is remote. With an exclusive-right-to-purchase representation agreement, the agent has greater control and little fear of losing the buyer to an owner or to another brokerage. For many of the same reasons that traditional brokers seldom take open listings (oral or written) with sellers, buyers' agents may be reluctant to do so as well.

Avoid Conflict of Loyalty   The buyer's agent should feel no ethical discomfort or hesitancy in withholding from the seller-customer information on the buyer's future plans for the property, including immediate resale or obtaining options on adjoining properties. Nor should the buyer's agent be reluctant to disclose to the buyer the broker's opinion that the property is overpriced or that the seller's terms are unrealistic. As a matter of fact, the agent is duty-bound to express such opinions to a buyer-client.

Within the bounds of honesty and fairness to the seller-customer, the buyer's agent can develop with the buyer a negotiating strategy that promotes the buyer's best interests at all times and seeks to obtain concessions from the seller. Healthy and complete negotiations are not as likely in traditional real estate transactions where all the agents represent the sellers' interests only. While a buyer and a seller are not hostile in the sense of a plaintiff and a defendant in a lawsuit, they do have competing interests. The buyer's agent will be able to represent the buyer's best interests in this spirit of competition and negotiate honestly and vigorously to arrive at a transaction that accomplishes, as much as possible, the goals of the buyer-client. The negotiations may end with a "win-win" result; however, the goal of an advocate, who is preserving the equity of his buyer-client, is to negotiate for all the buyer-client's positions strongly and to place as many costs as possible onto the seller's side of the balance sheet, while getting the lowest possible price for the property.

In addition to price, many other items must be negotiated in every transaction. Among these are

- initial and additional earnest money deposits;
- down payment;
- seller financing;
- interest rate;
- due date;
- sales price;
- commissions;
- terms;
- home warranty;
- termite report;
- assessments;
- appraisal;
- closing costs;
- title report;
- possession date;
- impound, reserve, or escrow account on the seller's loan (in assumption situations);
- title and escrow agent;
- personal property and inventory;
- discount points;
- repairs;
- inspection contingencies;
- hazard insurance;
- default remedies; and
- extensions.

During the offer and counteroffer stage of the transaction, any one of these items can provide an opportunity for conflict between the buyer and the seller and, thus, a deal-making compromise. The buyer's agent is able to negotiate all these items on the buyer's behalf. Neither a listing agent nor a cooperating agent acting as the seller's subagent has the legal ability to negotiate on the buyer's behalf.

No Liability for Acts of the Listing Broker   Because a buyer's agent has no agency relationship with either the seller or the listing broker, the buyer's agent is not vicariously liable for their acts (TRELA § 1101.805(d)). In addition, buyers' agents tend either to verify information about the property given by the listing broker or to require that the seller give certain warranties or representations concerning such conditions of a property as roof, plumbing, and boundary concerns. This reduces the agent's exposure to claims for misrepresentation, for concealment of material defects, or for failure to ascertain material facts. Although changes in Texas law have reduced the broker's liability for the **unknown acts of other brokers**, it is felt that a buyer's agent is clearly separated from the acts of the listing broker. This may have the effect of further reducing the chance of the buyer's agent being sued for things that are not the agent's fault. However, in Texas, the buyer's agent has an increased responsibility to the buyer-client to use due diligence to discover problems that may adversely affect the client.

■ WRITTEN NOTIFICATION OF COMPENSATION TO BROKER AND FEE ARRANGEMENTS

Regardless of who will be responsible for the payment of fees or commissions to the broker, it is strongly advised that such agreements be in writing. Although Texas law does not require that listing contracts or buyer representation contracts be in writing, a broker will have no legal recourse against a seller or a buyer who refuses to pay a fee unless the agreement was written (TRELA § 1101.806(c)):

TRELA Sec. 1101.806 (Liability for Payment of Compensation or Commission) states:

(a) This section does not:

(1) apply to an agreement to share compensation among license holders; or

(2) limit a cause of action among brokers for interference with business relationships.

(b) A person may not maintain an action to collect compensation for an act as a broker or salesperson that is performed in this state unless the person alleges and proves that the person was:

(1) a license holder at the time the act was commenced; or

(2) an attorney licensed in any state.

(c) A person may not maintain an action in this state to recover a commission for the sale or purchase of real estate unless the promise or agreement on which the action is based, or a memorandum, is in writing and signed by the party against whom the action is brought or by a person authorized by that party to sign the document.

(d) A license holder who fails to advise a buyer as provided by Section 1101.555 may not receive payment of or recover any commission agreed to be paid on the sale.

The buyer's broker will generally seek compensation directly from the buyer-client through a buyer representation agreement. However, if the property is listed in the MLS system, and if the seller of the listed property has agreed, the listing broker will offer a share of his compensation to "other brokers" whose buyer successfully purchases the property.

In addition to written buyer or seller commission agreements, brokers are also advised to have written agreements relating to fee splits between cooperating brokers. Most MLSs require that listing brokers disclose all fee arrangements to other brokers when the property is published in the MLS. In addition, the Broker Information section (page 9) in the One to Four Family Residential Contract (Resale) references an already existing agreement between the listing broker and the other broker, and it identifies the percentage of the sales price that will be shared by the listing broker with the other broker. The broker information section appears after the seller's and buyer's signatures on the previous page, which means that the seller and the buyer are not agreeing, in the sales contract, to the payment of any compensation. Their agreement with their respective agents to pay compensation comes from a separate agreement, not from the sales contract. Generally, the written agreement for compensation to the buyer's agent appears in the buyer's representation agreement, and the written agreement for compensation to the seller's agent appears in the seller's listing agreement. The broker information page is for information only relative to the buyer and the seller. Relative to the brokers involved in the transaction, a final sentence appears at the end of the broker information section stating the following:

> Listing Broker has agreed to pay Other Broker _____ of the total sales price when the Listing Broker's fee is received. Escrow agent is authorized and directed to pay other Broker from Listing Broker's fee at closing.

FIGURE 5.2

Page 9 of the One to Four Family Residential Contract (Resale)

Contract Concerning _____ Page 9 of 9 4-28-2014
(Address of Property)

BROKER   INFORMATION
(Print name(s) only. Do not sign)

| Other Broker Firm | License No. | Listing Broker Firm | License No. |

represents ☐ Buyer only as Buyer's agent   represents ☐ Seller and Buyer as an intermediary
☐ Seller as Listing Broker's subagent   ☐ Seller only as Seller's agent

| Name of Associate's Licensed Supervisor | Telephone | Name of Associate's Licensed Supervisor | Telephone |

| Associate's Name | Telephone | Listing Associate's Name | Telephone |

| Other Broker's Address | Facsimile | Listing Broker's Office Address | Facsimile |

| City | State | Zip | City | State | Zip |

Associate's Email Address   Listing Associate's Email Address

| Selling Associate's Name | Telephone |

| Name of Selling Associate's Licensed Supervisor | Telephone |

| Selling Associate's Office Address | Facsimile |

| City | State | Zip |

Selling Associate's Email Address

Listing Broker has agreed to pay Other Broker_____of the total sales price when the Listing Broker's fee is received. Escrow agent is authorized and directed to pay other Broker from Listing Broker's fee at closing.

OPTION FEE RECEIPT

Receipt of $_____ (Option Fee) in the form of _____ is acknowledged.

_____   _____
Seller or Listing Broker   Date

CONTRACT AND EARNEST MONEY RECEIPT

Receipt of ☐Contract and ☐$_____Earnest Money in the form of _____
is acknowledged.

Escrow Agent: _____ Date: _____

By: _____
                                                    Email Address
_____   Telephone (____)_____
Address

                                                                              Facsimile: (____) _____
_____
City   State   Zip

This sentence alludes to the fact that the listing broker, either through the multiple listing service or through a separate broker-to-broker agreement, has promised to pay the other broker a percentage of the sales price at the time the listing broker's fee is received. This sentence, by itself, is not the actual "promise to pay" but is a reference to a separate agreement between the listing broker and the other broker. In addition, the listing broker gives authorization to the escrow agent (usually a title company) to pay the other broker out of the listing broker's compensation at the time of closing. If the TREC One to Four Family Residential Contract is used, upon execution of the sales contract by all the parties, the buyer is required to deposit the earnest money with the agreed escrow agent. Generally, at that time, a copy of the sales contract is also delivered to the escrow agent. This contract becomes the primary directive of the escrow agent relative to the promises made by the buyer and the seller.

Consider the following questions:

- What happens if the listing broker never receives compensation? The other broker/buyer broker may be out of luck. The other broker/buyer broker does not have privity of contract with the seller and cannot sue the seller over the seller's refusal to pay the listing broker. This is one of the reasons that it is essential that the buyer broker have a written agreement with the buyer to establish a contractual agreement and promise to pay directly with the buyer. If the buyer representative is able to help the buyer find a way to get "someone else" to pay his broker's compensation, all the better. But if, for whatever reason, the listing agent does not pay the buyer broker, the buyer is still responsible for payment of compensation to his agent.
- When is the compensation actually earned and payable according to the TAR Buyer/Tenant Representation Agreement? Paragraph 1.C. (Earned and Payable) states the following:

> A person is not obligated to pay Broker a commission until such time as Broker's commission is earned and payable. Broker's commission is earned when: (1) Client enters into a contract to buy or lease property in the market area; or (2) Client breaches this agreement. Broker's commission is payable, either during the term of this agreement or after it ends, upon the earlier of: (1) the closing of the transaction to acquire the property; (2) Client's breach of a contract to buy or lease a property in the market area; or (3) Client's breach of this agreement. If Client acquires more than one property under this agreement, Broker's commissions for each property acquired are earned as each property is acquired and are payable at the closing of each acquisition.

Why would any licensee take the risk of showing a buyer properties, giving valuable information, sharing negotiating strategies, or any other acts of a broker representing a buyer-client, without first obtaining the signature of the buyer on a buyer representation agreement? Usually, it is because they are afraid of losing the buyer if they require a written commitment and promise of loyalty from the buyer. It is a wise business practice to always require a buyer to sign a buyer representation agreement before doing any of the acts of a buyer broker on behalf of the buyer.

The following example shows the need for comprehensive commission agreements.

■ **EXAMPLE**   In *Trammel Crow Company No. 60, et al. v. William Jefferson Harkinson* (40 Tex. Sup. Ct. J. 425, 1997), a broker acting as a tenant's agent located a commercial rental space for the client. Subsequently, the client went around the broker and negotiated a lease directly with the property owner, who was represented by a different broker. The owner's agent was paid according to the representation agreement between the owner and the listing broker, which did not address payment of a commission to a tenant's broker.

The tenant's broker sought payment of a commission from the owner's broker. The state supreme court found that the tenant's broker was not entitled to a commission because there was no contract between the tenant's broker and the property owner.

Comment: If the tenant's broker had had a clause in the tenant's representation agreement that required payment by the tenant in the event the owner or the listing broker did not agree to pay, the tenant's broker may have had a legitimate claim for a commission from the tenant, unless other issues precluded payment. The new TAR Buyer/Tenant Representation Agreement does in fact include a paragraph that, if used, would have protected the tenant representative's right to a commission, and would have made the tenant responsible for payment of the commission to his tenant representative.

Procuring Cause

According to John Reilly's *The Language of Real Estate*, procuring cause is "that effort that brings about the desired result." Occasionally, more than one real estate licensee works with a buyer in locating a property. Without a clearly written agreement, disputes may arise over which licensee was the procuring cause of the sale and thus is entitled to a share of the commission. These disputes are sometimes resolved in arbitration using guidelines such as those developed by NAR.

In Texas, when a buyer or a tenant in a commercial or residential transaction desires representation and contracts with a buyer's broker or a tenant representative, procuring cause generally becomes a legal nonissue. This is true even if the buyer or the tenant was first shown a property by the listing or leasing agent or subagents and even if negotiations have begun. However, creating an agency relationship will not, in itself, prevent claims filed asserting procurement by another licensee.

Fee Arrangements

An entire book could be written on all the possible methods of compensating a buyer's broker. Keep in mind that the broker's first concern is to become comfortable with the agency relationship that exists and the types of services to be provided. The mechanics of compensation seem to fall into place once the agency relationship is clearly understood. Often, the buyer's broker's fee is paid out of the sales proceeds, either through an authorized commission split or through a credit from the seller to the buyer at closing. It is important for the buyer's broker to consider his position relative to the buyer, and relative to the seller and the seller's agent carefully in regards to his compensation.

Seller-oriented brokers can benefit from understanding the methods by which buyers' brokers structure their compensation arrangements. Because listing brokers may receive offers from buyers represented by their own brokerage/associated brokers, each listing broker should become acquainted with how the offers may be structured and how fees are handled. The following sections summarize the ways in which buyers' brokers can be paid for their services. The way in which fees are to be paid should be stated in writing and clearly understood well in advance to avoid conflict between the buyer and the broker. Remember: the broker is the owner of all listings and buyer representation agreements, and the broker is the one who will establish and structure the fees, commission payments, division of commission payments, and parties to receive those fees. Generally, the broker/owner of the company will provide all the firm's associates with a compensation agreement or some other document that clearly defines 1) the amount of payment, 2) when payment is considered earned, 3) when and how it will be paid, 4) any exceptions to payment, 5) any deductions that will be taken out before payment, 6) divisions of payments between sales associates working in the same transaction, 7) any bonuses, or 8) other compensation owed to a sales associate of the broker.

Retainer Fee

Although many brokers are willing to wait for their compensation until the closing of the transaction is concluded, some brokers feel more comfortable obtaining advance payments. This can serve as a screening device to determine whether a buyer is serious about buying. However, some states have extensive restrictions on advance fees. For example, in **California**, the broker cannot withdraw monies from retainer trust accounts to cover hourly fees until several days after an accounting has been made to a client for services performed, and statements must be sent every calendar quarter and at termination. **In Texas, however, no such requirement exists.**

If a retainer fee is to be taken, some benefit or service must accrue to the person paying the fee; **otherwise, it may be considered one of the two unconscionable acts under the Texas Deceptive Trade Practices—Consumer Protection Act (DTPA).** If no research is done for the client, no houses shown, no counseling, advising, or any other service performed and the client cancels the agreement, it may be difficult for the broker to justify keeping the retainer fee.

If the retainer fee from the buyer is retained by the broker and the transaction closes with the buyer's broker being compensated from the seller's side of the transaction, **the broker technically receives compensation from both parties, a fact that must be disclosed and consented to by all parties.** Some brokers choose to refund the retainer fee on closing to avoid this problem and make as much cash available for the buyer as possible. Tax counsel should be consulted regarding the deductibility of the retainer portion as a professional fee.

When deciding to require a retainer fee, the broker should establish a consistent office policy. In other words, the broker should not decide selectively that some buyers must pay a retainer fee and others will not be required to do so.

Seller-Paid Fee

No legal or ethical barriers prohibit the seller from paying the buyer's broker's fee or authorizing the listing broker to share fees with the buyer's broker. Either is a matter of contract and may be handled in advance by appropriate language in both the seller's listing agreement and the buyer representation agreement. Substantial legal authority backs up the proposition that the payment of fees does not determine whom a licensee represents. As long as the agency relationship is clear and explicit, it does not matter legally whether the buyer or the seller pays the fee. If the agency is unclear, however, a court will likely consider who paid the fee to be an important factor in determining who is the agent's principal.

Currently, in residential sales, the traditional commission-sharing arrangement between the listing broker and the other broker is the most widely accepted method of compensation for the buyer's broker. In essence, the seller is notified of the arrangement and agrees that the other broker represents the buyer and that the commission may be split between the listing broker and the buyer's broker. This tends to keep the transaction simple. However, some precedent exists to support the notion that this practice may create conflicts of interest and misunderstandings, especially regarding procuring-cause issues.

In Texas, some buyer's broker specialists are using and promoting the practice of the buyer's inserting a condition in the sales contract requiring that the seller pay the buyer's broker on behalf of the buyer or reimburse the buyer for brokerage expenses at closing so that the buyer may pay the broker. The broker should not draft these conditional terms. That may be considered practicing law without a license to do so.

Traditionally, the buyer's broker receives a share of the commission from the listing broker out of the sales proceeds. However, two alternative methods of providing compensation exist:

- The **listing broker** agrees to reduce the commission by the amount of the usual split with the cooperating broker so that the seller either can reduce the price by a like amount (the net offer approach) or can give an offsetting credit on the buyer's closing statement in the amount of the cooperating broker's share.
- The **buyer's broker** receives the amount of the fee negotiated with the buyer. If the amount offered by the seller to the cooperating broker exceeds the fee that the buyer is obligated to pay, any difference is credited to the buyer. If the amount is not sufficient to pay the fee, the buyer pays the difference to the broker.

When employing compensation methods differ from the traditional splitting of the listing broker's fee, cover letters should be drafted and then accompany the offer to explain this arrangement to both the listing agent and the seller. A possible problem with this approach is a lack of sophistication on the part of sellers, buyers, and some brokers, making such agreements difficult to negotiate, particularly in residential transactions.

Commission Split

In a number of states, real estate agents do not use formal written agreements to represent buyers. Commissions are normally paid out of an authorized commission split with the listing broker or by the seller's crediting the buyer with a specified amount out of the sales proceeds. There usually is a written acknowledgment of buyer representation in the state-required agency disclosure form, with a written confirmation also included in the purchase agreement. **(Note that Texas does not have such a form.)** The preferred practice in Texas is to use a formal written buyer representation agreement that addresses the issues of exclusivity, compensation, scope of services, termination, and conflicts of interest.

In Texas, no state-approved or state-promulgated form covers buyer representation, seller representation, or representation of more than one party. The Texas Association of REALTORS® (TAR), however, produces such forms for its membership (see Figures 4.2 and 5.1). Some larger local REALTOR® associations also have developed separate forms for their own local memberships.

A buyer's broker, if planning on a traditional fee-split method, must determine from the listing broker, at initial contact, whether the listing broker is authorized and willing to split the commission with the buyer's broker (as opposed to a subagent of the seller). If the listing broker is not authorized to split the commission, the buyer's broker should advise the buyer of that fact. If the buyer representation agreement requires that the buyer pay the buyer's broker's compensation, the fact that the seller does not allow for the listing broker to share the listing broker's compensation with the buyer's broker, will cause the buyer to have to pay his buyer broker "out of pocket" in addition to the purchase price, at the conclusion of the purchase.

The **buyer** then may decide to

- reduce the offering price to a net amount reflecting that the buyer is to pay his broker's fee; or
- simply pay the buyer broker's fee as agreed in the buyer representation agreement; and
- write a provision in the Special Provisions paragraph of the sales contract that the seller agrees to pay the buyer broker's compensation. (Note: The broker or broker's sales associate may not do this.)

If the seller agrees to pay the buyer broker's compensation, the seller will likely choose to negotiate with his listing broker to reduce the listing broker's commission. If the listing agreement stated

> 1) that the listing broker was owed 6% of the sales price from the seller, at the time the listing broker produced a ready, willing, and able buyer who purchases the property at the terms and conditions acceptable to the seller, and

> 2) if a buyer contracts with the seller to pay the buyer broker a 3% commission on the sales price at the time of closing the transaction, then

3) the seller is placed in a position of contractually owing a total of 9% on the sales price at the conclusion of the transaction instead of the 6% written into the listing agreement.

Generally, the listing agent will reduce the agreed 6% to a 3% fee from the seller to the listing broker. This allows the seller to pay the requested sales contract provision of 3% of the sales price to the buyer representative and pay his listing broker 3% of the sales price. In total, the seller will pay 6%. This is potentially the same amount the seller would have paid to the listing agent and then allow the listing agent to "split his commission" with the buyer broker.

Now that most MLSs accept listings in which sellers can offer cooperation regarding commissions but not subagency, there will be an increased general acceptance by sellers, buyers, and brokers of such commission-splitting arrangements. Sellers primarily are concerned with selling their property and netting a certain amount of money from the sales proceeds. Most sellers are much less concerned about whether their brokers split commissions with someone labeled as either a buyer's broker or a subagent of the seller. In fact, sellers often feel that the other broker, even if described as a subagent, actually works for the buyer. Some sellers feel that compensation for both the listing broker and the selling broker is already part of the listing and purchase price; that is, they feel there really are two fees—the listing fee and the selling fee.

■ **EXAMPLE**   In *LA&N Interests, Inc. v. Fish*, a buyer's broker and his licensed associate felt that they had been unjustly deprived of a commission in a transaction and sued their client and the competing broker to recover their commission and damages for interference with their buyer's brokerage agreement. The buyer-client bought a property with the assistance of another broker, and the buyer's broker was paid nothing, even though the buyer's broker had an exclusive-agency representation agreement with the buyer. The buyer's brokerage agreement with the buyer-client clearly stated that the client "shall have no liability or obligation to pay a Professional Service Fee to [the buyer's broker]" but rather that the seller would pay the buyer's broker fee. This flaw—assuming that some party other than the client would pay the commission—led to the broker's not being able to recover from his client. Neither was he able to sue the seller and recover any compensation from the seller because, in this case, the buyer's broker does not have "privity of contract" with the seller. There was no contractual agreement for the seller to pay the buyer's broker in the first place.

Although listing brokers typically voluntarily reduce their share of the commission if another broker, as **subagent** to the seller, finds the buyer, a few listing brokers adamantly resist such a reduction or split if a **buyer's broker** is involved. In the first instance, why should a seller or a listing broker consent to a split? Simply because it is more likely to lead to a sale of the listed property.

■ **EXAMPLE**   Assume that the seller signs an exclusive-right-to-sell listing agreement with a 7% commission. Most of the transaction participants expect that the 7% commission will cover all the sales commissions involved, with the listing broker and the other broker each earning 3.5%. Most sellers would refuse to sign if the total commissions were 10.5%, with the listing broker receiving 7%.

Why would a broker not consent to a split commission? The listing broker would not consent if there is an opportunity to obtain a full rather than a reduced commission.

If the listing agreement contains a clause permitting such a split with a buyer's broker, listing brokers who are REALTORS® should reconsider this refusal in view of the ethical restrictions in the NAR Code of Ethics. These articles require that the broker cooperate with other brokers and act in the best interests of the client at all times. If the listing broker's refusal to share commissions results in too low an offer, or no offer at all, the seller may have grounds for complaint, especially if it appears that the broker's sole motivation was to receive a larger fee than usual in a cooperative sale.

In any event, an agent's fiduciary duty of full disclosure to the client under TREC rules requires that the listing broker advise the seller of the general company policy regarding cooperation and compensation of buyers' agents. In brief, listing brokers should do everything possible to make it easy for the buyer's broker to show the seller's property and make an offer.

Buyer-Paid Fee

Buyers may elect to pay the commission directly to their broker. This may avoid any implication of seller agency or conflict of interest that may be present when the seller pays the brokerage fee. An experienced buyer's broker, not wanting a nonclient to control payment, may prefer being paid directly by the buyer rather than receive a commission split from the listing broker or be paid directly by the seller at closing. Buyer-paid compensation can take several forms, such as an hourly rate, a percentage fee, or a flat fee.

■ **EXAMPLE**   Sam, the listing broker, and Carol, the other broker representing the seller through the listing broker as a subagent of the seller, agree on a 50-50 commission split. The property is a commercial warehouse not listed in the MLS. The listing commission is 5%. The offer is submitted at $1 million on a $1.2 million listing. The seller accepts the offer, provided that Sam reduces his fee to 4%. Sam agrees to do so but fails to inform Carol. Carol now receives $20,000 instead of $30,000.

Hourly Rate   Under this arrangement, the agent is, in essence, a consultant, charging a noncontingent hourly rate. It is payable regardless of whether a title transfer is contemplated, for example, when a consultant advises on whether to develop a shopping center or a commercial office building. A variation may be an hourly fee applied against an incentive fee if the agent finds the right property for the buyer. This requires that an agent keep time sheets and be diligent in record-keeping and billing practices.

Percentage Fee   A buyer's agent may charge a percentage fee based on the selling price of the property bought by the client, just as most listing agents do. The obvious problem the percentage fee creates is the appearance of a potential conflict of interest because the higher the purchase price, the greater the fee—making the percentage fee seem seller-oriented. The prime benefit of the percentage fee is that real estate licensees and clients are accustomed to this arrangement.

Many buyers' agents begin by charging buyers on a percentage basis and later progress into charging flat fees (discussed below). Other agents combine an hourly rate with a percentage of the purchase price. Rates may vary when the seller is not represented by a listing broker because the buyer's agent may have to do more of the background work and handle negotiations with the seller.

Flat Fees (Contingent or Noncontingent)   A buyer's agent is sometimes compensated on a flat fee, payable if a buyer purchases a property located through the agent. The amount of the flat fee is based on the estimate by the agent of the work and skills involved, the potential fee that will be paid by the seller, and the probability of success.

A contingent flat fee often is based on what the buyer will pay for the agent's services, depending on the price range of the home or an estimate of the amount of work involved.

■ **EXAMPLE**   Betty is looking for a property in the $175,000 to $225,000 range. A cooperating broker might expect to receive a fee of $6,000 on a $200,000 sale. Carol, a buyer's broker, charges the buyer a $6,000 flat contingent fee. Whether Betty selects a property for $175,000 or for $225,000, the fee to Carol remains $6,000.

Another method is the noncontingent flat fee. The agent predicts the amount of work necessary to accomplish the client's objectives and then sets a flat fee. This approach is seldom used unless the agent has gained a great deal of experience in representing buyers.

Some buyer representation agreements provide that the buyer is obligated to pay the fee but is entitled to a credit for any amounts the seller agrees to pay. Thus, the buyer would not pay the buyer's broker fee in the usual MLS sale, although the buyer might pay the fee directly if the agent located an unlisted property, a builder-owned house, or a For Sale by Owner property. An experienced buyer's agent might encourage the client to make such a stipulation, just as the client might base a sale on the condition that the seller fixes the roof.

Disclosure of Fee   A buyer's broker paid directly by the buyer might disclose the exact amount of the fee on the offer to purchase. In this way, the seller and the listing broker have a clear understanding of what fees are being paid. It is easier for the seller to see that the net proceeds will be about the same with a gross price offer. The seller could be paying both brokers or could accept a net price offer, with the buyer paying the buyer's broker's commission and the seller paying the listing broker a reduced commission.

An argument can be made for not disclosing the amount of fees on the offer to purchase based on confidentiality. If, in fact, the buyer's broker has contracted to receive less than the typical commission split, the amount of the difference could accrue to the buyer's benefit.

Net Purchase Price

The net purchase price is the sales price reduced by the buyer's brokerage fee. A theory supporting the net price method is that the buyer has only a certain amount for the down payment. A portion of that money no longer will be deducted from the seller's proceeds to pay the other broker but now will be used to pay the buyer's broker. The restructured brokerage fees will not increase the acquisition costs. The overall transaction will not change, even if a loan is involved. If accepted, a net offer may result in lower title and closing costs, which are now based on the lower purchase price.

■ **E X A M P L E**   Betty makes a full-price offer to the seller on a $100,000 listing in the following way: a net purchase price of $97,300, plus Betty agrees to pay Carol, her buyer's broker, a cash fee of $2,700. The seller acknowledges that the buyer's broker represents the buyer and not the seller in this transaction. Carol inserts a provision in the sales contract that the buyer agrees to pay the sum of $97,300 to the seller and $2,700 to Carol for services rendered.

Lenders   The amount of a maximum loan is based on a percentage of the purchase price plus the buyer's broker's commission. The commission is thus paid from the loan proceeds rather than from the buyer's personal cash. A different approach is used in a net offer situation. So that a lender will add to the sales price a buyer's broker's commission as an acquisition cost, the broker might provide the lender with a copy of the purchase contract in which the buyer acknowledges the buyer's broker's commission. This makes it easier for a lender to visualize the economic adjustments made in the transaction.

Federal Housing Administration (FHA) regulations specifically authorize an add-back to the purchase price of the buyer's broker's fee under Section 532 of the National Housing Act. The notable exception is a Department of Veterans Affairs (VA) loan. The VA does not allow lenders to include buyer's broker's fees in the loans to be paid by veteran purchasers. This position is based on the belief that

■ the buyer's broker's fee may increase the acquisition cost;
■ buyers are adequately protected by the requirement to furnish a certificate of reasonable value and reasonable closing costs and by access to many properties through general advertising; and
■ selling brokers, although representing sellers, do not ignore buyers' interests.

Note that no VA rule prohibits the buyer's broker from receiving a seller-approved commission split from the listing broker. Thus, a VA transaction can include a buyer's broker, but the broker must be compensated by or through the seller. This is similar to the seller's paying the points on the buyer's loan.

Gross Price

An alternative method of buyer's broker compensation that is gaining some acceptance in residential sales transactions is the gross-price method. The buyer pays the gross purchase price. The purchase contract provides that the seller then pays the buyer's broker's commission. The seller acknowledges and accepts that the buyer's broker solely represents the buyer and not the seller, despite the payment of the fee by the seller. To ease the listing broker's and the seller's concerns, some brokers add that this fee is the sole compensation of the buyer's broker in the transaction. Texas licensees should recall that it is grounds for loss of license to be paid by more than one party to a transaction without the full knowledge and consent of all parties.

This method satisfies all outside participants in the transaction, such as appraisers, lenders, and insurers, and it is easier to finance the contract amount. This method helps reduce the concerns over excess commission expense and double charging, and it seems easier for the seller to understand and respond to a customary sales price offer. The seller's main difficulty is psychological: The seller and the listing broker may feel that while they pay the buyer's broker's fee, the buyer receives the services. This flaw is less serious when using the gross-price method of fee payment, where a buyer's broker's commission can be built into the contract price through the terms of the buyer's offer. As a consequence, the cash required, the mortgage amount, the net proceeds to the seller, and the sales price are approximately the same as they would be in the traditional sale, in which both brokers represent the seller and both commissions are included in the contract price. To avoid loan underwriting problems, some brokers include the following language in the purchase contract: "Seller credits $ [dollar amount] toward buyer's expenses listed on the closing statement."

Some advantages of sellers paying the commission are that it

- clears up questions of who works for whom and who pays whom;
- protects the buyer's agent from the listing agent's breaches and other chances of losing commissions because of badly crafted listing agreements;
- protects the buyer-client from having to pay the broker's commission at closing if the seller refuses to pay, but it provides the option to do so should the situation require;
- allows no reasonable basis for procuring-cause disputes;
- presents no suggestion of interfering with the listing broker's commission agreement with the seller;
- works equally well for listed, unlisted, builder, MLS, or non-MLS properties;
- places responsibility for securing the compensation of the buyer's broker directly on the shoulders of the client whose interests were served by the broker; and
- does not trigger the TRELA § 1101.652(b)(8) prohibition concerning payment from more than one party in the transaction without knowledge and consent of both, unless the buyer's broker has collected a retainer fee from the buyer in advance.

Some disadvantages are that it

- is relatively untested in the courts in Texas;
- may change expected tax advantages for the parties; and
- may cause some confusion among lenders until it is widely recognized, thus impeding some transactions.

It is important for brokers to understand compensation alternatives when they consider representing buyers. Many brokers working with buyer prospects now realize that they need not give away their time and expertise. Brokers should study the different methods of representation and develop their skills so that they can comfortably discuss with buyers and listing brokers the amounts and various methods of compensation. For assistance in this area, many buyers' broker books and seminars are helpful sources.

■ BUYER'S BROKER DISCLOSURES

Before, during, and after they become agents of a buyer/tenant or seller/landlord, real estate licensees must make certain disclosures to buyers, sellers, third parties, other licensees, and the general public. Some types of disclosures we will talk about in this section include the following:

> Remember, the written statement about brokerage services is *not* a disclosure of your agency relationships with any party.

- The statutory written statement about brokerage services (The TREC IABS form may be used for this purpose.)
- Disclosure of agency relationships
- Disclosure in advertising
- Disclosure of property condition
- Disclosure of pricing opinions
- Disclosure of title issues
- Disclosure of status as a real estate licensee in personal transactions

Written Statement About Brokerage Services

TRELA § 1101.558(c) requires that the broker provide the buyer with the statutory written statement describing seller agency, buyer agency, and intermediary brokerage. The TREC Information About Brokerage Services (IABS) form can be used to fulfill this requirement, but it is an optional form. Any form that meets the requirements of TRELA can be used for this purpose. TRELA §1101.558(c) states that

> a license holder shall provide to a party to a real estate transaction at the **time of the first substantive dialogue** [emphasis added] with the party the written statement prescribed by Subsection (d) unless:
>
> (1) the proposed transaction is for a residential lease for not more than one year and a sale is not being considered; or
>
> (2) the license holder meets with a party who is represented by another license holder.

The required language is included in TREC's IABS form (see Figure 5.3). This statutory written statement is NOT a disclosure of the licensee's agency; it is an information form that describes to buyers or sellers their business choices when deciding whether to hire an agent to represent them. The giving of this statutorily required written statement is not an option; it is a requirement. It must be given at the proper time "at the time of the first substantive dialogue with the party." As you can see in the law, there are two exceptions to this requirement:

- First exception: "If the proposed transaction is for a residential lease for not more than one year and a sale is not being considered." For example, if Sally is seeking a six-month lease with no option to purchase, neither the buyer broker nor the landlord's broker is required to give the written statement about agency choices to Sally.
- Second exception: "The license holder meets with a party who is represented by another license holder." For example, Sally is represented by George. When Sally meets with the landlord's agent, the landlord's agent does not have to give Sally the statutory written statement.

FIGURE 5.3

TREC's Information About Brokerage Services Form

10-10-11

Approved by the Texas Real Estate Commission for Voluntary Use
Texas law requires all real estate licensees to give the following information about brokerage services to prospective buyers, tenants, sellers and landlords.

Information About Brokerage Services

Before working with a real estate broker, you should know that the duties of a broker depend on whom the broker represents. If you are a prospective seller or landlord (owner) or a prospective buyer or tenant (buyer), you should know that the broker who lists the property for sale or lease is the owner's agent. A broker who acts as a subagent represents the owner in cooperation with the listing broker. A broker who acts as a buyer's agent represents the buyer. A broker may act as an intermediary between the parties if the parties consent in writing. A broker can assist you in locating a property, preparing a contract or lease, or obtaining financing without representing you. A broker is obligated by law to treat you honestly.

IF THE BROKER REPRESENTS THE OWNER:
The broker becomes the owner's agent by entering into an agreement with the owner, usually through a written - listing agreement, or by agreeing to act as a subagent by accepting an offer of subagency from the listing broker. A subagent may work in a different real estate office. A listing broker or subagent can assist the buyer but does not   represent the buyer and must place the interests of the owner first. The buyer should not tell the owner's agent anything the buyer would not want the owner to know because an owner's agent must disclose to the owner any material information known to the agent.

IF THE BROKER REPRESENTS THE BUYER:
The broker becomes the buyer's agent by entering into an agreement to represent the buyer, usually through a written buyer representation agreement. A buyer's agent can assist the owner but does not represent the owner and must place the interests of the buyer first. The owner should not tell a buyer's agent anything the owner would not want the buyer to know because a buyer's agent must disclose to the buyer any material information known to the agent.

IF THE BROKER ACTS AS AN INTERMEDIARY:
A broker may act as an intermediary between the parties if the broker complies with The Texas Real Estate License Act. The broker must obtain the written consent of each party to the transaction to act as an intermediary. The written consent must state who will pay the broker and, in conspicuous bold or underlined print, set forth the broker's obligations as an intermediary. The broker is required to treat each party honestly and fairly and to comply with The Texas Real Estate License Act.   A broker who acts as an intermediary in a transaction:

(1) shall treat all parties honestly;

(2) may not disclose that the owner will accept a price less that the asking price unless authorized in writing to do so by the owner;

(3) may not disclose that the buyer will pay a price greater than the price submitted in a written offer unless authorized in writing to do so by the buyer; and

(4) may not disclose any confidential information or any information that a party specifically instructs the broker in writing not to disclose unless authorized in writing to disclose the information or required to do so by The Texas Real Estate License Act or a court order or if the information materially relates to the condition of the property.

With the parties' consent, a broker acting as an intermediary between the parties may appoint a person who is licensed under The Texas Real Estate License Act and associated with the broker to communicate with and carry out instructions of one party and another person who is licensed under that Act and associated with the broker to communicate with and carry out instructions of the other party.

If you choose to have a broker represent you, you should enter into a written agreement with the broker that clearly establishes the broker's obligations and your obligations. The agreement should state how and by whom the broker will be paid. You have the right to choose the type of representation, if any, you wish to receive. Your payment of a fee to a broker does not necessarily establish that the broker represents you. If you have any questions regarding the duties and responsibilities of the broker, you should resolve those questions before proceeding.

Real estate licensee asks that you acknowledge receipt of this information about brokerage services for the licensee's records.

_____   _____
Buyer, Seller, Landlord or Tenant   Date

Texas Real Estate Brokers and Salespersons are licensed and regulated by the Texas Real Estate Commission (TREC). If you have a question or complaint regarding a real estate licensee, you should contact TREC at P.O. Box 12188, Austin, Texas 78711-2188 , 512-936-3000 (http://www.trec.texas.gov)

TREC No. OP-K

The TREC IABS form has a place at the bottom of the form for the signature of the buyer, the seller, the landlord or the tenant and a place for a date to be written in when one of these people receives the form. The law does not require that the person sign the statement. The signature of the party is only an acknowledgment that the party received the written statement. Many times the party receiving the form thinks that it obligates them in some way if they sign the form, and consequently they may refuse to sign. The sentence on the form above the party's signature states, "Real Estate licensee asks that you acknowledge receipt of the information about brokerage services for the licensee's records." That is the purpose of the party's signature and the date. By keeping a copy of the signed form, if one of the parties takes legal action against the licensee in the future, the licensee is able to prove that the written statement was given to the party.

Disclosure of Agency Relationships

The law requires that licensees make clear to all parties whom they are representing. Buyer brokers and all their associates are required under TRELA to be sure that any person on the opposite side of the transaction is made aware of their agency relationship with a buyer-client. The seller's agent has the same requirement.

The law provides this protection for buyers and sellers so they are made aware of the positions of advocacy of all licensees **before** they divulge any confidential information, or information that would inadvertently allow the other side a position of strength during the negotiations of the real estate transaction. For example, Sally, a seller, does not necessarily want the buyer's agent to know that she has a job waiting in California and has to sell her home quickly so that she can move to California in two weeks. That knowledge would give the buyer an advantage in the negotiations of any offer made by him. The buyer-agent would know that the seller is under pressure to move quickly and would share that information with his buyer-client, and likely encourage him to make a lower offer than the asking price. Consequently, the law requires disclosure by the buyer broker to Sally or Sally's agent of his agency relationship with the buyer, **at the time of the license holder's first contact with either or both of them**. Now, Sally and Sally's agent are aware of the position of the buyer broker, and Sally's agent can protect Sally's interests. Again, this is true, in reverse, concerning the seller's agent.

This disclosure must be given "at the time of the first substantive dialogue with the party."

According to TRELA § 1101.558 (a) and (b),

> (a) In this section "substantive dialogue" means a meeting or written communication that involves a substantive discussion relating to specific real property. The term does not include:
>
> > (1) a meeting that occurs at a property that is held open for any prospective buyer or tenant; or
> >
> > (2) a meeting or written communication that occurs after the parties to a real estate transaction have signed a contract to sell, buy, or lease the real property concerned.

(b) A license holder who represents a party in a proposed real estate transaction shall disclose, orally or in writing, that representation at the time of the license holder's first contact with:

(1) another party to the transaction; or

(2) another license holder who represents another party to the transaction.

Disclosure in Advertising

TRELA § 1101.652 (Grounds for Suspension or Revocation of License) states the following:

(a) The commission may suspend or revoke a license issued under this chapter or take other disciplinary action authorized by this chapter if the license holder: . . .

(b)(23) publishes or causes to be published an advertisement, including an advertisement by newspaper, radio, television, the Internet, or display, that misleads or is likely to deceive the public, tends to create a misleading impression, **or fails to identify the person causing the advertisement to be published as a licensed broker or agent** [emphasis added].

TRELA prohibits any advertising that is misleading and requires that all licensees identify themselves in the advertising they produce.

Fair housing advertising issues are also an important part of the requirements for disclosure (or non-disclosure). The Department of Housing and Urban Development (HUD) has extensive information available to assist real estate brokers and sales persons in meeting these requirements.

In the Rules of the Texas Real Estate Commission, § 535.154, it is clear that brokers are responsible for making sure all their sales associates are correctly producing any advertising. This advertising may be through electronic communications, billboards, yard signs, marketing flyers, facsimile, social media, and the like. Some companies hire an individual to scrutinize all advertising done by the sales associates in order to ensure that it complies with all TRELA and HUD regulations. The broker's name is required to be conspicuously mentioned in all advertising. Brokers who use an assumed name have 30 days to notify TREC if they changes that name, stop using that assumed name, or choose to use another name.

Disclosure of Property Condition

We previously discussed § 5.008 of the Property Code and the Seller's Disclosure of Property Condition, but the emphasis was placed on the requirement that the seller disclose the condition of the property. What does the law have to say about the broker or sales associate disclosing the condition of the seller's property to the buyer-client?

According to TRELA 1101.652(b)(4), the license of a broker or salesperson may be suspended or revoked if the licensee "fails to disclose to a potential buyer a defect . . . that is known to the license holder."

A licensee who is aware of any defects in the property, structural or otherwise, is obligated by law to make the defects known to a potential buyer. For protection, the licensee should document making the disclosure. Whether the seller gives the buyer the Seller's Disclosure of Property Condition form or not, the licensee is bound to disclose all known property defects.

Common areas of potential hazards in and on property for which a buyer may want to have an inspection:

- Asbestos
- Mold
- Lead and lead-based paint
- Radon
- Formaldehyde gas
- Underground storage tanks
- Electromagnetic fields (EMFs)
- Chlorofluorocarbons (CFCs)
- Hazardous wastes, et cetera.

TREC has an excellent Defect Disclosure FAQ section in the sixth edition of MCE *Ethics & Legal Update Manual*, which states the following:

What if, as a licensee, I learn that there is a defect, but the seller does not want it disclosed?

Inform the seller that you are obligated by statute to make the disclosure and that an attorney should be consulted if the seller chooses not to disclose the defect.

Why do multiple variations of the seller's disclosure notice exist?

The seller's disclosure notice statute requires that the seller use the form set out in the statute or a form that is substantially similar containing all of the items in the statutory form. The TREC Seller's Disclosure of Property Condition form is identical to the statutory form. TREC publishes the form as a convenience for brokers, sellers and buyers. Some professional associations also publish seller's disclosure notice forms that comply with the statute and contain additional disclosures that those groups have determined are relevant. Whichever form the seller uses, it must contain all items in and be substantially similar to the statutory form.

Must every seller deliver the seller's disclosure notice to a prospective buyer?

The seller's disclosure notice statute contains 11 narrow exemptions that most real estate brokers typically will not encounter on a regular basis. The most common exemption is the new home exemption or builder exemption. The next two most common exemptions are the trustee or executor exemption and the foreclosure exemption. Under these exemptions, the following are not required to complete the seller's disclosure notice:

- a builder of a new home,
- a trustee or executor of an estate, and
- a lender after it has foreclosed on a property.

Keep in mind, however, that while these sellers are exempt under Texas Property Code §5.008, they are still required under common law and other statutes to disclose any known defect. It is the mechanism of disclosure, namely the seller's disclosure notice, which is not mandated.

Is a relocation company required to deliver a seller's disclosure notice?

If the relocation company is the seller, it must deliver the seller's disclosure notice.

Must a seller disclose a previous death at a property?

The statute provides that neither a seller nor a broker must disclose deaths that occurred by natural causes, suicide, or accidents unrelated to the condition of the property [Texas Property Code §5.008(c)].

Must a seller disclose prior water penetration in a property?

If the prior water penetration has been cured and any ensuing damage from the prior water penetration has been cured, there is no longer a defect, and the seller would not be obligated to disclose the prior water penetration. However, if the prior water penetration has not been cured or the ensuing damage has not been cured, then such items would be considered defects.

Must a seller or broker disclose to a prospective buyer the fact that a registered sex offender resides in the neighborhood?

The Code of Criminal Procedures §62.056 provides that neither the owner of a single-family residential property nor real estate agents have a duty to disclose that a nearby resident is a registered sex offender. Texas Government Code §411.088 requires that DPS information about sex offender registrants be made available to the public at no cost over the Internet.

Is an off-site condition considered a defect (for example, roadways, landfills, feed lots, etc.)?

Generally, an off-site condition is not a defect with the property in question. However, the off-site condition might affect the property. If it affects the property in a physical way, it is possible that the off-site condition could be the source of a defect that has moved onto the property. For example, if a neighboring property contains underground tanks that leak, the contaminant might leak onto the property in question. 17

Must the listing broker or the seller provide a copy of a prior inspection report that they may have in their possession?

The seller and broker have a duty to disclose any known material defects. Possession of a prior inspection report may be evidence of the seller's or broker's knowledge of a known defect. There is no statute or other law that specifically states the prior inspection report must be provided. The question is whether the known material defect, which may be noted in the prior inspection report, has been disclosed. Most risk managers and defense attorneys suggest that the broker or seller provide the prior inspection report to avoid allegations of nondisclosure or mischaracterization of a purported defect.

May a listing agent instruct a buyer or buyer's agent not to provide a copy of the inspection report the buyer may obtain?

Yes. However, the instruction is simply a request. If the seller or seller's agent receives a copy of the inspection report, it will be unlikely that they may later disavow any knowledge of the inspection report.

Case Study

A buyer sued a seller for fraud and fraudulent inducement relating to the purchase of a store. Part of the letter of intent required the seller to produce all information in its possession to the buyer; however, the buyer alleged that the seller failed to disclose the declining credit status of the store. The purchase price was $7,667,000.00 for the property based on the absolute reported net income of $805,040.00 per year.

The seller claimed there was an "as is" provision and a merger clause, which prohibited the lawsuit, because the buyer agreed to take the property "as is," and the contract for sale specifically provided that there were no other agreements outside the contract.

The jury found that the seller committed fraud against the buyer and awarded damages in the amount of $3,961,524.60 and additional exemplary damages of $667,000.00. The judge overruled the jury's verdict.

The appellate court defined fraudulent inducement as "a species of fraud that arises only in the context of a contract and requires existence of a contract as part of its proof." A contract is subject to avoidance on the ground that it was induced by fraud (citing Italian Cowboy Partners, Ltd. vs. Prudential Ins. Co. of Am., 341 S.W.3d 323 (Tex. 2011). In this circumstance, failure to disclose information does not constitute fraud unless there is a duty to disclose the information.

The court concluded that the seller had a common law and contractual duty to provide the economic information that was concealed because of the agreement under the letter of intent. The court of appeals sustained the jury's findings on fraud, including the award of the damages, and remanded the case to the trial court with an order to render judgment on the verdict and pay the buyer's attorney fees. Fazio vs. Cypress/GR Houston I, L.P., ___ S.W.3d ___ (Tex.App.–Houston [1st Dist.] 2012)

Disclosure of Pricing Opinions

TREC Rule § 535.16(c) states that

> a real estate licensee is obligated to provide a **broker price opinion or comparative market analysis** [emphasis added] on a property when negotiating a listing or offering to purchase the property for the

licensee's own account as a result of contact made while acting as a real estate agent.

Although the rule does not specifically say that the buyer broker is to provide this same broker price opinion or comparative market analysis to his buyer-client, it is reasonable to extrapolate that the buyer broker has the same duty to give his opinion of the price of the property or provide a comparative property analysis to his buyer-client so that the buyer has the information necessary to make a sound decision on his offer price.

TREC Rule § 535.17 (Broker Price Opinion or Comparative Market Analysis) states the following:

(a) A real estate licensee may not perform an appraisal of real property unless the licensee is licensed or certified under Texas Occupations Code, Chapter 1103.

(b) If a real estate licensee provides a broker price opinion or comparative market analysis under §1101.002(1)(A)(xi) of the Act, the licensee shall also provide the person for whom the opinion or analysis is prepared with a written statement containing the following language: "THIS IS A BROKER PRICE OPINION OR COMPARATIVE MARKET ANALYSIS AND SHOULD NOT BE CONSIDERED AN APPRAISAL. In making any decision that relies upon my work, you should know that I have not followed the guidelines for development of an appraisal or analysis contained in the Uniform Standards of Professional Appraisal Practice of the Appraisal Foundation."

(c) The statement required by subsection (b) of this section must be made part of any written opinion or analysis report and must be reproduced verbatim.

(d) A salesperson may prepare, sign, and present a broker price opinion or comparative market analysis for the salesperson's sponsoring broker, but the salesperson must submit the broker price opinion or comparative market analysis in the broker's name and the broker is responsible for it.

The buyer is owed as much professional knowledge and skill as the buyer agent possesses relative to this real estate transaction. The buyer expects her buyer agent to locate the properties that best suit the buyer's needs and desires in a location of her choice, and she hired the buyer agent to use that knowledge and skill to assist in the negotiations to produce the lowest possible price, best terms and conditions. Evaluating and disclosing the price of the property is part of that analysis on behalf of the buyer-client.

Disclosure of a Licensee's Position in Personal Real Estate Transactions

Licensees have a duty to disclose their interest in real estate transactions. TREC Rules and TRELA address different concerns related to these circumstances.

TRELA Sec. 1101.652 (Grounds for Suspension or Revocation of License) states the following:

> (a) The commission may suspend or revoke a license issued under this chapter or take other disciplinary action authorized by this chapter if the license holder: . . .
>
> > (3) engages in misrepresentation, dishonesty, or fraud when selling, buying, trading, or leasing real property in the name of:
> >
> > > (A) the license holder;
> > >
> > > (B) the license holder's spouse; or
> > >
> > > (C) a person related to the license holder within the first degree by consanguinity.

TREC Rule § 535.144 (When Acquiring or Disposing of Own Property or Property of Spouse, Parent or Child) States this:

> (a) For purposes of § 1101.652(a)(3) of the Act:
>
> > (1) "a person related to the license holder within the first degree by consanguinity" means a license holder's parent or child; and
> >
> > (2) "license holder" includes a licensee acting on behalf of:
> >
> > > (A) the license holder's spouse;
> > >
> > > (B) a business entity in which the licensee is more than a 10% owner; or
> > >
> > > (C) a trust for which the licensee acts as trustee or of which the licensee or the licensee's spouse, parent or child is a beneficiary.
>
> (b) A license holder engaging in a real estate transaction on his or her own behalf or in a capacity defined in subsection (a) of this section, is obligated to disclose in writing that he or she is a licensed real estate broker or salesperson in any contract of sale or rental agreement or in any other writing given prior to entering into any contract of sale or rental agreement.
>
> (c) A license holder acting on his or her own behalf or in a capacity described under subsection (a) of this section or § 1101.652(a)(3) of the Act shall not use the license holder's expertise to the disadvantage of a person with whom the license holder deals.

A real estate broker or salesperson, when disposing of or acquiring property on her own behalf; on behalf of a business entity in which she owns more than 10%; or on behalf of her spouse, parent, or child is required by TRELA to disclose that fact "in writing" to anyone with whom the licensee deals. For example, broker Joy is a 75% owner of Realty One Investors. Joy is attempting to acquire a single-family residence on behalf of Realty One Investors. Joy must notify the seller and the seller's agent, and any person she is dealing with, in writing of the fact that 1) she is a licensed real estate broker, and 2) that she is acting on behalf of Realty One Investors. Joy must give this disclosure to the other party or parties in any contract of sale or rental agreement or in any other writing given before entering into any contract of sale or rental agreement.

No Requirement to Disclose HIV or HIV-Related Illnesses

TRELA Sec. 1101.802 (LIABILITY RELATING TO HIV INFECTION OR AIDS) states the following:

> Notwithstanding Section 1101.801, a person is not civilly or criminally liable because the person failed to inquire about, make a disclosure relating to, or release information relating to whether a previous or current occupant of real property had, may have had, has, or may have AIDS, an HIV-related illness, or HIV infection as defined by the Centers for Disease Control and Prevention of the United States Public Health Service.

The Texas Administrative Code actually prohibits this disclosure (22 TAC 531.19(a)(b)):

> (a) No real estate license holder shall inquire about, respond to or facilitate inquiries about, or make a disclosure of an owner, previous or current occupant, potential purchaser, lessor, or potential lessee of real property which indicates or is intended to indicate any preference, limitation, or discrimination based on the following:
>
> > (1) race;
> >
> > (2) color;
> >
> > (3) religion;
> >
> > (4) sex;
> >
> > (5) national origin;
> >
> > (6) ancestry;
> >
> > (7) familial status; or
> >
> > (8) disability.
>
> (b) For the purpose of this section, disability includes AIDS, HIV-related illnesses, or HIV infection as defined by the Centers for Disease Control of the United States Public Health Service.

Disclosure of Client Information

Even though we have covered this in several other areas of the text, a brief discussion of what information a seller's agent should disclose or not disclose to a buyer's agent, or a buyer's agent to a seller's agent, will act as a reminder.

Under the common law of agency duties of confidentiality and loyalty, each real estate agent, acting on behalf of a client, has the duty to keep confidential all confidential information. The agent also has a duty to be loyal to the buyer or seller-client. If the buyer has told his buyer agent personal information, financial situation, motivations for purchasing, strategies for the negotiations of his offer, or any other private information, the buyer agent is not at liberty to share this information with the seller or the seller's agent.

What if the seller's agent says to the buyer's agent, "My seller needs proof that your buyer-client is financially able to complete this transaction. She is asking for your buyer to provide evidence of his financial capability." The buyer agent is not required to give that information; however, the buyer-agent must make his buyer aware of the request from the seller's agent. The buyer now has to decide whether he, in fact, is going to give any financial information to the seller, or whether he is going to withhold that information and risk losing the opportunity to purchase the home.

Fair Housing

A real estate licensee is prohibited from illegally discriminating against any person in a real estate transaction based upon the race, color, religion, sex, national origin, ancestry, handicap status, or familial status of that person. For instance, if asked by her client to "find out if minority individuals live in the area," she must not comply, but instead help the client understand the fair housing regulations and laws and the licensee's duties under them. If buyers or sellers are not willing to comply with these laws, the licensee is well advised to refuse any representation relationship with that buyer or seller or terminate an existing relationship with a buyer or seller.

Buyers as Customers

Although this chapter has focused on buyer agency, remember that not every buyer wants or needs to be represented by an agent. Some buyers appreciate the flexibility of dealing with several brokers and avoiding commitments and loyalties to any one of them. Such buyers who work with a number of brokers may acquire enough facts to enable them to make a decision, such as information about property values and seller motivation, although they may be unaware of any fiduciary duties owed to the seller or landlord by the broker. Other buyers enjoy the "free ride" given by many brokers who hope that the buyer will make an offer to purchase through them. Still other buyers prefer to deal directly with the listing broker because they hope to obtain some inside information that they can use to make the best deal or because they fear they may lose the opportunity to buy the home they really want if they make an offer through another agent. This fear of missed opportunity may be based on the time factor involved in presenting an offer in a seller's market. Another concern is that an unprofessional listing agent might produce an equivalent or a better offer in-house after having first seen the buyer's offer submitted by the buyer's agent.

■ SUMMARY

In the past, in most real estate transactions, the seller was represented by a real estate agent, but the buyer was not. Today, primarily because of the better disclosures and information that agents are required to provide, many buyers now seek the same level of client service that sellers typically receive from agents. The decision to represent a buyer is a serious one because the agent will be held to a high standard of care and will owe fiduciary duties to the buyer. Both the agent and the buyer must weigh the various benefits of buyer representation. It is strongly recommended that brokers use a written buyer-agency agreement and carefully discuss alternative methods of compensation. In helping the buyer or the buyer's attorney prepare the purchase agreement, the agent should consider the negotiable aspects of the transaction from the buyer's perspective.

■ KEY POINTS

- ■ Whether to represent the buyer is an important decision because the agent then owes the full range of fiduciary responsibilities. The real estate licensee may want to be selective and not represent every buyer who walks in the front door.
- ■ Buyer brokerage does not mean that the broker is in the business of representing buyers only. Most buyers' agents regard buyer agency as one of the options available to them in single-agency or nonexclusive-agency practices.
- ■ Not every buyer wants or needs representation. Some prefer to represent themselves, especially those not wanting to risk a missed opportunity in a fast-moving seller's market.
- ■ Written buyer representation agreements are preferable to oral ones.
- ■ In showing buyers in-house listings, brokers must take care to avoid unintentional and unauthorized representation of more than one party. If such representation is to be authorized, the broker must make full disclosure of the potential conflicts of interest to both buyer and seller.
- ■ A buyer's agent must disclose to the listing broker at initial contact that the licensee is a buyer's agent and must clearly reject any offer of subagency. Frequently, the listing broker will be authorized to share fees with buyers' agents and allow them equal access to property for showing.
- ■ Buyers' agents in Texas should seriously consider the benefits and drawbacks of being compensated by buyers-tenants rather than by sellers-landlords, as is the most common practice in Texas today.

■ SUGGESTIONS FOR BROKERS

Establish an office policy on how to handle an offer received from a buyer's agent on one of your listings. Discuss with the seller the possibility that you will receive offers from buyers' agents and that these offers may require a commission split or an adjustment in the offering price when the buyer will pay the buyer's agent directly. Discuss the net effect these offers will have on the seller's position, and advise the seller accordingly.

CHAPTER 5 QUIZ

1. When a buyer's agent shows a property listed through an MLS, the agent is the fiduciary of which of the following?
   a. Buyer
   b. Buyer's broker
   c. Seller
   d. MLS

2. Buyer agency
   a. must be created with a written buyer representation agreement.
   b. may be created by the actions of a licensee, as well as by written agreements.
   c. while legal, is seldom practiced by brokers in Texas.
   d. excludes the possibility of a brokerage firm's obtaining listings from sellers.

3. Megan, a broker, entered into a buyer representation agreement with Sue, a buyer, using the TAR Residential Buyer/Tenant Representation Agreement (see Figure 5.1). The commission agreement under paragraph 11A was for 2.5%. Sue subsequently enters into a $210,000 purchase contract with a seller. The listing office agrees to pay a buyer's broker 2% of the sales price. How much commission is Megan entitled to at closing?
   a. $5,250 ($4,200 from the listing broker; $1,050 from Sue)
   b. $4,200 ($4,200 from the listing broker; zero from Sue)
   c. $9,450 ($4,200 from listing broker; $5,250 from Sue)
   d. $5,250 (zero from the listing broker; $5,250 from Sue)

4. Which requires that a buyer purchase only through a particular broker?
   a. The buyer pays the broker a commission.
   b. The buyer signed an exclusive representation agreement.
   c. The buyer asked the agent to help negotiate the purchase of an already identified property.
   d. The buyer signed an open buyer representation agreement.

5. Buyer representation agreements
   a. are promulgated forms available from TREC.
   b. impose duties on buyers' brokers similar to those that listing agreements impose on sellers' brokers.
   c. differ from listing agreements in that listings require definite termination dates while buyer representation agreements do not.
   d. in order to be binding, must provide that the buyer compensate the broker for the representation services.

6. The increase in buyer representation is due primarily to
   a. better disclosure and information required of brokers.
   b. the infusion of more buyers into the marketplace.
   c. brokers seeking and promoting compensation by both parties.
   d. all of these.

7. In which case must a real estate broker obtain a written agreement with a buyer?
   a. Broker to act as a buyer's agent
   b. Broker wishing to take legal action against a buyer for commission
   c. Both of these
   d. Neither of these

8. Which is a possible benefit of buyer agency?

    a. Greater client loyalty
    b. Better protection against conflicts of loyalty
    c. No liability for acts of the listing broker
    d. All of these

9. Which would be a disadvantage of exclusive buyer agency?

    a. The broker would not be able to list a property owned by the buyer-client.
    b. The broker could never earn full commission on an in-house sale.
    c. There is a potential conflict of interest if two buyer-clients wish to offer on the same property.
    d. All of these are potential disadvantages.

10. The listing broker has agreed to pay the cooperating broker a fee of 2% of the sales price. The buyer is represented and has agreed in writing to pay her broker a nonrefundable $2,000 flat fee. Which statement is *TRUE*?

    a. All parties must be notified of the compensation agreement between the buyer and her broker.
    b. As an agent of the buyer, the broker has no duty to disclose the dual compensation.
    c. The broker for the buyer may disclose the dual compensation only if authorized to do so by his client.
    d. The dual compensation must be disclosed only if it impacts on the ultimate tax advantage of the buyer.

DISCUSSION QUESTIONS

1. Can a buyer's broker participate in the MLS and receive a share of the listing broker's commission?

2. Why would a listing broker reduce a portion of the sales commission so the seller could credit that portion to the buyer for payment of the buyer's broker's commission?

3. How might a buyer's broker handle conflicts of interest involving in-house sales?

4. Name at least four important elements of a well-drafted buyer's broker-representation agreement.

5. Name at least five important points for a buyer's broker to cover in a purchase contract.

CHAPTER 6

Representing More Than One Party in a Transaction: Intermediary Brokerage

For decades, Texas brokers were accustomed to representing only one principal in a transaction. Traditionally, the seller was represented by an agent and treated as a client, whereas the buyer was not represented by an agent and was treated as a customer. The broker who worked with a buyer was generally a subagent of the listing broker.

The serious start and growth of buyer representation happened in the 1980s. During that time, buyer representation associations such as the Real Estate Buyer's Agent Council (REBAC®), the National Association of Exclusive Buyer Agents (NAEBA®), and in Texas, the Texas Real Estate Buyer Agents Association (TRE-BAA, which has since dissolved) began to develop and advocate "exclusive buyer agency" (EBA). This growth created new issues for "traditional brokers" who saw a threat to their commissions by this new development. Federal and state lawsuits alleging fraud against real estate brokerages for the practice of undisclosed dual agency brought the subject of agency and fiduciary duties to the forefront of enforcement agencies such as the Federal Trade Commission (FTC) and the Department of Justice (DOJ), the public, and brokers. The multi-million-dollar lawsuits that followed were even more threatening to these unethical and illegal practices.

The specter of representing both principals in a single transaction raises many questions about potentially conflicting duties. How, for example, can a broker place the interests of a client above all others if, in fact, there are two clients, each entitled to the fiduciary duties created by agency relationships with the broker?

This chapter explores the issues of multiple representation, the current status of intermediary brokerage as defined in the License Act, and the duties of the intermediary broker and appointed license holders. Students should have a clear understanding of these concepts before they become involved in a real estate transaction that involves representing more than one party.

■ **LEARNING OBJECTIVES**   *This chapter addresses the following:*

- The Path From Dual Agency to Intermediary Brokerage
- Representation of More Than One Party in a Transaction
    — Conflicting Positions in Representing More Than One Party in a Transaction
    — Common Law Dual Agency (Implied and Express)
    — Volatile Issues
- Intermediary Brokerage
    — General Concepts
    — The Appointment Process
    — Appointed Licensees—Who and When?
    — Status of Intermediary Brokers and Appointed Licensees
    — Concerns Related to Intermediary Practice
- Specialized Intermediary Applications
    — Exchanges
    — Syndications
    — Commercial Leasing Agent
- Intentional Versus Unintended Dual Representation
    — Prior Relationships
    — In-House Sale
    — Cooperating or Other Broker
    — Broker as Principal
    — Adopting the Buyer
    — Nonagency

■ THE PATH FROM DUAL AGENCY TO INTERMEDIARY BROKERAGE

Until 1993, the Real Estate License Act (TRELA) was silent on the subject of dual agency, which is the attempted representation of both parties to a transaction by one person acting as an agent for both.

Before 1993, Texas had always recognized the concept of common law dual agency. However, Texas courts frowned on dual agency applications in real-life situations because of the near impossibility of accomplishing a successful dual agency legally without betraying the interests of one party or the other.

One of several general approaches to law is "that which is not prohibited is permitted." Until 1993, that was the state of the law regarding dual agency in Texas. The general attitude among real estate professionals regarding dual agency was "Try it if you dare!" Strangely enough, agents are still trying dual agency today, even though it is now illegal, except through the intermediary provisions of TRELA.

Under common law, dual agency was not strictly illegal. However, for the leap to dual agency to be accomplished successfully, several precautions would have been beneficial and **might** have allowed a court to find that no breach of duty by the licensee had occurred. Some precautionary actions that could have or should have taken place include the following:

- Put the agreement to "represent" both parties in writing and have both parties sign it
- Have these OLDCAR fiduciary duties **specifically abrogated** or eliminated **by contract** because they are impossible to fulfill for parties on opposite ends of a transaction:
  — Obedience
  — Loyalty
  — Confidentiality
- Never have a conversation with one party when the other party is not present, or at least, on a conference call

> Current intermediary practice eliminates full disclosure and retains confidentiality.

The 1986 NAR pamphlet *Who Is My Client* aptly expressed the issue on pages 15–16, "As a practical matter, real estate brokers should avoid dual agency relationships. Creation of a lawful disclosed dual agency relationship is so difficult that the real estate broker who attempts to conduct his day-to-day affairs as a disclosed dual agent is playing the professional equivalent of Russian roulette."

Page 16 of the same pamphlet stated the following:

> **Dual agency** is a totally inappropriate agency relationship for real estate brokers to create as a matter of general business practice. **Undisclosed dual agency** is a clear breach of a broker's fiduciary duty to each of his principals and is generally viewed to be **an act of fraud**. (emphasis added)

Nevertheless, dual agency for real estate brokers was still permissible in Texas at that time.

With the growth in buyer-agency in the late 1980s and early '90s, more and more brokers attempted to profit from representing both sides in the transaction despite the lack of common law or statutory guidelines. Legal and TREC disciplinary actions mounted as brokers applied their own "how to" interpretation to common law cases. In 1993, the legislature, lobbied by the real estate industry, authorized a modified form of common law dual agency and created a statutory dual agency concept. Under industry pressure, the Texas Legislature amended TRELA to outline the specific duties of a broker who wished to function as a dual agent without the attendant legal and financial liability that flows from dual agency under common law. As a result of these efforts by the real estate industry, "statutory dual agency" was born and made effective in fall 1993.

> Texas was not the only state that struggled with this issue. See Figure 6.1 regarding an Oklahoma case.

Even with the new statutory dual agency laws, the Texas Association of REALTORS® still felt that this form of representation was inherently dangerous, both legally and financially. REALTORS® again lobbied for a change, from the statutory dual agency they had succeeded in having enacted two years before to a new concept: intermediary brokerage. On January 1, 1996, the new intermediary provisions of TRELA became effective.

The "How does it work?" aspect of the new law was so confusing that TREC called several meetings/information sessions around the state for all the educators/instructors/brokers teaching real estate agency and presented TREC's view (not legal position) relative to the new law and how TREC thought it would operate.

When the intermediary law replaced statutory dual agency on January 1, 1996, common law dual agency was resurrected because it was no longer specifically outlawed. On September 1, 2005, a new section was added to TRELA and common law dual agency was subsequently made legally impossible again.

TRELA § 1101.561 (Duties of Intermediary Prevail) states the following:

> (a) The duties of a license holder acting as an intermediary under this subchapter **supersede** the **duties** of a license holder established **under any other law, including common law.**
>
> (b) A broker **must agree to act as an intermediary** under this subchapter **if** the broker agrees to represent **in a transaction:**
>
> > (1) a buyer or tenant; **and**
> >
> > (2) a seller or landlord.
> >
> > (...eff. September 1, 2005) (emphasis added)

The preamble to the Code of Ethics and Standards of Practice of the National Association of REALTORS®), recognizes "that cooperation with other real estate professionals promotes the best interests of those who utilize their services. **REALTORS® urge exclusive representation of clients** [emphasis added]."

To understand the duties of a broker acting as an intermediary, it is helpful to trace the evolution of this status from its beginning and to understand the pressures and concepts that caused this evolution. From this starting point, it becomes evident why intermediary brokerage sometimes appears to have the same duties as the former statutory dual agency.

FIGURE 6.1

Snider v. Oklahoma Real Estate Commission

In a well known Oklahoma case on the efficacy of dual agency, *Snider v. Oklahoma Real Estate Commission*, apparently even OREC did not understand its own regulations or dual agency. The Oklahoma Supreme Court handed down a serious condemnation and rebuke of the OREC and the district court of civil appeals, for not understanding agency law and attempting to preempt the court's authority regarding interpretation and application of agency law. Snider, a buyer broker, published and distributed a pamphlet touting the advantages for a buyer in having an exclusive buyer agent (EBA) versus working with a dual agent or a seller's agent or seller's subagent. OREC sanctioned him and fined him $200. Snider appealed and lost in the district court and then appealed to Oklahoma Supreme Court for a resolution.

The Oklahoma Supreme Court stated the following, among other findings:

> ¶11 A review of the entire booklet from which the statement found false and misleading is taken reveals one premise. That premise is stated on page 2 of the booklet, and is that traditional real estate firms represent the seller, and that when they try to represent the seller and the buyer, they cannot meaningfully represent both. Page four of the booklet states that «By law, selling agents must negotiate in the best interest of their clients, not withhold information from them, and must present their property in a favorable manner.» It uses the illustration that one would not go to court using the same attorney who represents the opposing side. The booklet explains its reasons for these statements and the advantage to a buyer who is represented by an agent. The information in the booklet continuously refers to the law of agency. **Agency law is not an area in which the Oklahoma Real Estate Commission can claim expertise superior to the courts of Oklahoma.**

> ¶17 We find that the statement in the booklet for which the appellant was sanctioned is neither false nor misleading. **Sellers' agents and dual agents do not and cannot by law give a buyer the same degree of loyalty as an agent who acts on behalf of a buyer.** Sellers'' agents owe their allegiance to the seller. Dual agency invites a conflict of interest.[19] A buyer who relies on the seller's agent or on dual agency does not receive the same degree of legal protection as that afforded by an agent acting solely on behalf of the buyer. Accordingly, **we find that the order of the Oklahoma Real Estate Commission is clearly erroneous, contrary to its own rule, and without evidentiary support and must be set aside**" (emphasis added)

■ REPRESENTATION OF MORE THAN ONE PARTY IN A TRANSACTION

Conflicting Positions in Representing More Than One Party in a Transaction

The positions of buyer and seller are inherently in conflict, at least on some issues. A seller of a home and the buyer of that home present the perfect picture of two parties with adverse interests. In virtually any sale the buyer wants the lowest price and best terms achievable and the seller wishes to sell at the highest price with the best terms. True representation as we know it under common law and under TREC Rule § 531.1(1) is not possible under the intermediary relationship because of the statutory limitations and the abrogation of common law per TRELA § 1101.561(a). TRELA § 1101.559(c) says that an intermediary should act fairly and impartially.

Some brokers would say, "Agency just doesn't matter. . . . The buyer just wants to buy and the seller just wants to sell. . . . Who's on their side doesn't make any difference to them." While that might be true sometimes, it **will** make a difference as soon as the seller finds out he could easily have made $30,000 more on a $300,000 transaction if only "his agent" had told him the buyer was willing to pay more just to get the house. What happens if the buyer finds out after closing that the seller told the broker that the seller was willing to drop the price from $600,000 to $550,000 but the broker didn't pass that information on? In that situation, whose agent the broker was could make a big difference. Was the broker who received the information from the seller representing the seller (in which case he wouldn't pass along the information) or representing the buyer (in which case he would pass along the information)?

The buyer and the seller or a landlord and a tenant may be very friendly and share the goal of making a transaction work. In law, however, their interests are considered distinct and adverse, and each may need protection of these interests. The objectives of the buyer and the seller are very rarely identical in a transaction. The agent attempting to represent both parties is placed in the legally inadvisable position of using any knowledge about either side in a way to attempt to please both sides and complete the transaction. It may appear that one side does not receive full representation because the agent may find it impossible to remain completely neutral or impartial.

A disgruntled buyer or seller may decide at any time to challenge the agent's actions. In hindsight, either client may later assert that the agent violated the trust given the agent because the so called "representation" of both parties favored one "client" over the other "client" in some material degree. The provisions in a lease or sales contract that benefit one side may burden the other. If the agent wants to "represent" the interests of more than one party in a transaction, the agent is expected and required to maintain a position of impartiality and avoid the risk of favoring the interests of one client over the other. In this situation, the agent must get the parties' agreement to allow the broker to become an intermediary and follow the TRELA intermediary statutes.

Common Law Dual Agency (Implied and Express)

Chapter 7 discusses agency relationships that are created by actions or conduct in regard to a principal rather than by some express agreement. This is frequently called "implied agency," and the law imposes the full burden of agency duties on the agent. Sometimes this agency is implied in fact, and sometimes it's implied in law. The classic example of being implied in law is the situation in which a nonrepresented buyer believes that a licensee is acting as an agent for her, and the licensee fails to make it clear that he represents the seller either as an agent or subagent. When this occurs, a form of dual representation arises, known as undisclosed or nonconsensual dual agency. The effect is to create an illegal form of agency whereby the broker (through the broker's own actions or the actions of an associated licensee) unknowingly becomes an agent of both buyer and seller without their knowledge and consent. Interestingly, in most of these situations, the buyer, the seller, and the broker are unaware that dual representation is occurring. This situation exposes the broker to considerable liability from both principals and is clearly a position to be avoided by the broker, if not by the principals themselves.

Consensual dual agency in a real estate transaction involving a broker, wherein the broker knowingly becomes an agent of both principals with their express knowledge and consent, had long been established as a legal, albeit unwise, form of agency in Texas under common law. This form of agency is now illegal in Texas. Keep in mind that, although consensual dual agency is recognized under general agency law for agents in other types of legal situations, it is no longer a permitted form of representation by real estate brokers in real estate transactions in Texas. Dual agency in TRELA has been replaced by the intermediary provisions of TRELA.

Volatile Issues

As long as both buyer and seller are happy with the transaction, the question of the legality dual agency probably will not arise. However, if either party, for whatever reason, becomes unhappy, believes they were not represented fairly, or feels they were financially damaged, even months or perhaps years, after closing, the agent's multiple representation may provide the mechanism to

- unravel the transaction,
- recover commissions from the offending broker,
- seek money damages, and/or
- result in revocation of broker licensure.

It is a weak legal defense that the multiple representation was unintended or was performed with all good intentions to help both buyer and seller. Residential and commercial buyers, tenants, landlords, and sellers generally don't know and don't care much about agency law until one of them wants to back out of a transaction or seek damages, and consults an attorney, or reports the offending licensee to TREC, subjecting the agent to possible fines or even revocation of license.

It is after consulting an attorney that a principal often learns that the required (and appropriate) level of service was not received. Multiple representation cases have a high rate of success for plaintiffs (the person bringing the suit) and high monetary rewards.

Multiple representation might be risky even when disclosed and intended, even when the licensee can argue that both parties got what they wanted and neither party lost or was disadvantaged. For example, mutual gain might occur if the agent discloses the seller's urgency to sell and discloses the buyer's recent profitable cash sale of another property. These and other confidential disclosures might actually speed up acceptance of an agreement on price and terms acceptable to both parties. However, "acceptable" doesn't necessarily equate to "desired" or "desirable." One or both of the principals later may argue in court that the agent's loyalty was improperly directed and not in the clients' best interests.

■ INTERMEDIARY BROKERAGE

General Concepts

Recognizing the inherent shortcomings and the limitations created by the statutory dual agency, the real estate industry trade associations again lobbied the Texas Legislature and succeeded in having Senate Bill 489 passed, which, among other things, eliminated statutory dual agency (the old SB 314) and amended TRELA to substitute statutory intermediary brokerage for statutory dual agency. SB 489 failed to address common law dual agency, so common law dual agency emerged from the ashes and again became a legally permissible, even if ill-advised, form of multiple representation. Effective January 1, 1996, TRELA authorized brokers to act on behalf of both parties to a transaction in an intermediary role as follows:

§ 1101.559. BROKER ACTING AS INTERMEDIARY.

(a) A broker may act as an intermediary between parties to a real estate transaction **if**:

(1) the broker obtains **written consent** from each party for the broker to act as an intermediary in the transaction; and

(2) the written consent of the parties states the **source** of any expected **compensation** to the broker.

(b) A written listing agreement to represent a seller or landlord or a written agreement to represent a buyer or tenant that authorizes a broker to act as an intermediary in a real estate transaction is sufficient to establish written consent of the party to the transaction if the written agreement specifies in conspicuous bold or underlined print the conduct that is prohibited under Section 1101.651(d).

(c) An intermediary shall act **fairly and impartially**. Appointment by a broker acting as an intermediary of an associated license holder under Section 1101.560 to communicate with, carry out the instructions of, and provide opinions and advice to the parties to whom that associated license holder is appointed is a fair and impartial act. (emphasis added)

In addition, TRELA permits the appointment of associated licensees as follows:

§ 1101.560. ASSOCIATED LICENSE HOLDER ACTING AS INTERMEDIARY.

(a) A broker who complies with the written consent requirements of Section 1101.559 **may** appoint:

(1) a license holder associated with the broker to **communicate with** and **carry out instructions** of one party to a real estate transaction; and

(2) another license holder associated with the broker to communicate with and carry out instructions of any other party to the transaction.

(b) A license holder **may be appointed** under this section **only if**:

(1) the **written consent** of the parties under Section 1101.559 **authorizes** the broker to make the **appointment; and**

(2) the **broker provides written notice** of the appointment to all parties involved in the real estate transaction.

(c) A license holder appointed under this section **may provide opinions and advice** during negotiations to the party to whom the license holder is appointed. (emphasis added)

TRELA § 1101.651(d) provides specific prohibitions regarding acting as an intermediary as follows:

§ 1101.651. CERTAIN PRACTICES PROHIBITED.

(d) A broker and any broker or salesperson appointed under Section 1101.560 who acts as an intermediary under Subchapter L may not:

(1) disclose to the buyer or tenant that the seller or landlord will accept a price less than the asking price, unless otherwise instructed in a separate writing by the seller or landlord;

(2) disclose to the seller or landlord that the buyer or tenant will pay a price greater than the price submitted in a written offer to the seller or landlord, unless otherwise instructed in a separate writing by the buyer or tenant;

(3) disclose any confidential information or any information a party specifically instructs the broker or salesperson in writing not to disclose, unless:

(A) the broker or salesperson is otherwise instructed in a separate writing by the respective party;

(B) the broker or salesperson is required to disclose the information by this chapter or a court order; or

(C) the information materially relates to the condition of the property;

(4) treat a party to a transaction dishonestly; or

(5) violate this chapter.

One very important aspect of the License Act regarding intermediary brokerage activity is that the role of intermediary, as spelled out in TRELA, **prevails over common law** and **any other law**, including any part of the License Act or TREC Rules to the contrary. Both the old statutory dual agency and common law dual agency have been set aside and replaced by TRELA § 1101.561 as follows:

§1101.561. DUTIES OF INTERMEDIARY PREVAIL.

(a) The duties of a license holder acting as an intermediary under this subchapter **supersede** the **duties** of a license holder established **under any other law, including common law.**

(b) A broker **must agree** to act as an intermediary under this subchapter **if** the broker agrees to represent in a transaction:

(1) a buyer or tenant; and

(2) a seller or landlord. (emphasis added)

Consider how this might work in practice. The statute requires written permission from both parties before the broker may act as an intermediary, and the agreement must disclose any source of compensation expected by the broker. This may be accomplished in a listing contract with a seller (see Figure 4.2, paragraph 9) or a written buyer representation contract with a buyer (see Figure 5.1, paragraph 8). The respective agreements give the seller or the buyer the option of authorizing the broker to act as an intermediary. TREC considers these agreements sufficient, as long as the broker's compensation is clarified.

If the intermediary situation arises, the broker cannot disclose

■ the highest price a buyer might pay, until authorized to do so in writing;
■ the minimum price a seller will take, unless authorized to do so in writing; and
■ confidential information about either party, unless the parties authorize it or the law requires a disclosure.

Finally, the broker must treat all parties to the transaction honestly and fairly, while complying with the act.

Sound familiar? At least to this point, the intermediary brokerage language is almost identical to the former language regarding statutory dual agency. A broker accustomed to acting as a dual agent under the old statutory provisions would see no practical difference between the two. In fact, many brokers mistakenly believe that *intermediary* is simply another term for *dual agent*. However, the language in TRELA § 1101.560; .651 provides the major departure from the old dual-agency statute by providing for the appointment of licensees to assist buyers and sellers in an intermediary transaction by offering advice and opinions during negotiations.

The Appointment Process

The ability of the broker to make appointments is the *key difference* between the old, now illegal, statutory dual agency and the current intermediary status prescribed by TRELA. Under the intermediary practice, the appointed licensees may give opinions and advice.

Advice and Opinions From Appointed Licensees. In the intermediary transaction, if one or more licensees are appointed to the seller and different licensees are appointed to the buyer, the principals are able to receive services similar to, but not the same as, those of single agency. The three missing duties of an appointed licensee as opposed to a "true agent's" duties are those of loyalty, obedience, and disclosure. Nowhere in TRELA does the Act ascribe to an appointed licensee the duty or privilege of advocacy. The duty of confidentiality of information is still a duty of the appointed licensee, as much as it is for the intermediary. The appointed licensees (not the intermediary) may now give to the broker's respective principals to whom they have been appointed services that are at least more similar to those given when acting as a single agent. In other words, appointed licensees may give the party to whom they have been appointed advice and opinions that may not be in the best interest of the other party. For attorneys, this would be prohibited. Keep in mind, however, that the appointed licensee is still prohibited from disclosing how little a seller may accept, how much a buyer may be willing to pay, or any other confidential information about either party. In addition, appointees must treat the parties fairly and comply with TRELA.

Appointed Licensees—Who and When?

The appointment process raises several questions for brokers who wish to extend the company's services to buyer-clients and seller-clients through the appointment process. First, remember that before appointments may be made, the broker must have the written consent of both parties to act as an intermediary and their written permission to make appointments. The statute provides that, with this written consent, brokers may appoint one or more associated licensees to work with a buyer and different licensees to work with the seller. Brokers cannot appoint themselves to either client and must maintain the role of impartial intermediary in relation to both clients. Thus, brokers who work alone or brokers with only one associate cannot make appointments and must conduct such transactions as an intermediary without appointees.

To be able to appoint licensees to the buyer and the seller, the broker must

- have written consent to act as an intermediary and written consent to make appointments, and
- have at least two associates (in order to appoint one to the buyer and one to the seller).

Remember: Brokers cannot appoint themselves to a buyer or a seller. If a broker works alone or if a broker has only one associate, that broker is not allowed to make appointments.

To be able to give advice or opinions, licensees must have been appointed before negotiation. If the appointment happens after negotiation, the appointed licensee cannot give preferential advice or opinions and must act like the intermediary in the transaction. Once the broker becomes an intermediary, whether appointments have been made or not, the broker cannot give advice or opinions.

After the appointments have been made, the broker cannot give advice or opinions to the following:

- The licensee appointed to the buyer
- The buyer
- The licensee appointed to the seller
- The seller

The only person who acts **as** the intermediary is the broker, but all unappointed licensees must act **like** the intermediary (i.e., cannot provide advice or opinions to either party and must treat both parties impartially).

■ EXAMPLE: A THORNY PROBLEM

Fred, Sally, Suzy, and Jim are all agents of broker Bill.

Fred listed seller Sam's property at $225,000 for Fred's broker, Bill. Fred was then properly appointed in writing to Sam, while Jim, another agent in Bill's office, was properly appointed to the first buyer. There are a total of five offers for his seller's property, each of which arrived successively within 15 minutes of the previous offer.

The five offers were obtained by Fred and other licensees as follows:

1. A buyer Fred secured a buyer representation agreement with weeks before listing Sam's house

2. A buyer with whom another licensee, Sally, in Fred's firm secured a buyer representation agreement before showing Sam's property

3. A subagent with another firm

4. A buyer's broker from another firm

5. A buyer located by Suzy, another agent for Bill, who wanted to "represent himself" and would not sign a contract to be represented

What should Fred, Sally, Jim, and Suzy tell the buyers regarding whom they are working with or "representing"?

By the way, Fred, Sally, Jim, and Suzy all attended the sales meeting a few days earlier when Fred was complaining about how overpriced Sam's house was, and even though Fred's CMA showed the price should be $200,000, Sam was obstinate and would not list with him for less than $225,000. He took the listing anyway.

Timing of the Appointments and Notification to the Principals Is Important   Until a buyer who is represented by the firm wishes to negotiate on a property listed by the firm, no potential for an intermediary transaction exists and therefore appointments need not be made. Likewise, **if the broker has chosen not to make appointments,** the involved associates carry out the transaction as if they were intermediaries, offering neither advice nor opinions to buyer or seller during negotiations that might work to the disadvantage of the other party. This may prove to be a very difficult line to walk for the previous "true agent" of a buyer to now be reduced to not giving advice or opinions to the party he formerly fully represented. Questions like "What do you think I should offer?" or "Do you think the property is worth what they are asking?" now become impossible to answer in the way the client would previously have expected and been due.

It is extremely important that parties clearly understand that during an intermediary transaction, no preferential advice or opinions can be given by the associates working with the principals, unless appointments are made. If, however, the parties wish to have an associate appointed to each of them, thereby gaining the expanded advice and opinions of the associate, the **appointment must be made before such advice or opinions are given to either party.** The broker, or an authorized representative of the broker, must make the appointments, and written notification of these appointments must be given to both the buyer and the seller. Note that while the actual appointments of the licensees may be made orally, the notification to the parties announcing the appointments and identifying the appointees must be given to the buyer and the seller in writing. Neither the statute nor TREC provides specific language for the notification. Members of the Texas Association of REALTORS® may use form TAR 1409, Intermediary Relationship Notice (see Figure 6.2), to indicate that an intermediary transaction is occurring and whether appointments are to be made in order to identify the appointed licensees. Non-TAR members would have to have their own versions of these notices, seek permission from TAR to use them, or not use them at all and risk some fairly serious nondisclosure issues.

F I G U R E   6.2

Example of Intermediary Relationship Notice

TEXAS ASSOCIATION OF REALTORS®

INTERMEDIARY RELATIONSHIP NOTICE

USE OF THIS FORM BY PERSONS WHO ARE NOT MEMBERS OF THE TEXAS ASSOCIATION OF REALTORS® IS NOT AUTHORIZED.
©Texas Association of REALTORS®, Inc. 2004

To: _____ **(Seller or Landlord)**

and _____ **(Prospect)**

From: _____ **(Broker's Firm)**

Re: _____ **(Property)**

Date: _____

A. Under this notice, "owner" means the seller or landlord of the Property and "prospect" means the above-named prospective buyer or tenant for the Property.

B. Broker's firm represents the owner under a listing agreement and also represents the prospect under a buyer/tenant representation agreement.

C. In the written listing agreement and the written buyer/tenant representation agreement, both the owner and the prospect previously authorized Broker to act as an intermediary if a prospect who Broker represents desires to buy or lease a property that is listed by the Broker. When the prospect makes an offer to purchase or lease the Property, Broker will act in accordance with the authorizations granted in the listing agreement and in the buyer/tenant representation agreement.

D. Broker   ❑ will   ❑ will not   appoint licensed associates to communicate with, carry out instructions of, and provide opinions and advice during negotiations to each party. If Broker makes such appointments, Broker appoints:

_____ to the owner; and

_____ to the prospect.

E. By acknowledging receipt of this notice, the undersigned parties reaffirm their consent for broker to act as an intermediary.

F. <u>Additional Information:</u> *(Disclose material information related to Broker's relationship to the parties, such as personal relationships or prior or contemplated business relationships.)*

The undersigned acknowledge receipt of this notice

_____   _____   _____   _____
Seller or Landlord   Date   Prospect   Date

_____   _____   _____   _____
Seller or Landlord   Date   Prospect   Date

(TAR-1409) 1-7-04   Page 1 of 1

REALTORS® frequently refer to this form as the "second consent" form. Remember, if the clients agreed in the written listing or buyer representation contracts to permit the intermediary relationship should the buyer become interested in an in-house property, then the licensee has met the requirement under TRELA to obtain written consent. Considerable time may elapse, however, between the time their respective contracts were signed and when the buyer indicates a desire to begin negotiation on an in-house listing. The form also serves to meet the statutory requirement to identify the appointed licensees by name to all parties [§1101.560 (b)]. Licensees who are not members of TAR should develop in-house forms to give similar notice to the parties. Unless appointments are made, the broker is not required by statute to notify the parties that an intermediary transaction is occurring as long as the written consent to act as an intermediary was previously obtained, although the prudent broker will make it clear to the parties, preferably in writing, that an intermediary transaction is taking place.

An obvious timing problem may arise if an intermediary transaction occurs during the absence of the broker and no appointments have been made. If this occurred, the licensee associate could not give advice or opinions until the statutorily required appointment process had been completed. Clearly, this might be too late because the negotiations might be completed before the broker is available to make the required appointments. One solution might be for the broker to give the authority to make appointments to others in the firm. Another possibility could be to pre-appoint listing associates to work as appointees to sellers—and selling associates working under buyer representation contracts to work as appointees to buyers—should an intermediary transaction arise. Keep in mind that a pre-appointment would have no effect until an intermediary transaction actually occurred. The parties still would have to be furnished with written notice of the appointments, and consent to those appointments, before the intermediary transaction was undertaken.

Who Is to Be Appointed?   The appointees could be any licensees of the firm other than the broker. However, in a practical sense, it would be most common for the associate who obtained the listing to be appointed to the seller and the associate who obtained the buyer representation contract to be appointed to the buyer. Exceptions might be where listing agents sold their own listings to buyers with whom they were working under the terms of a buyer representation contract. For appointments to be made in these circumstances, a second licensee would be required to enter the transaction, to be appointed to either buyer or seller, because the statute requires that different licensees be appointed to buyer and seller. Would this indicate, then, that a licensee could not participate on both sides of the transaction and receive the increased commission? No; the practical solution might be for the broker to decline to make appointments and to instruct the associate to conduct the transaction as an intermediary transaction, giving no preferential advice or opinions to either party. However, how many individuals can, in good conscience and with skill, switch from an advocacy role and advisory role to a role requiring impartiality? How many can continue to work with two former clients who accepted and relied on the agent's advice and opinion for several weeks, only to be deprived of that professional advice at the last minute after finally locating the property they really want? It may be permissible, but is it advisable?

In any event, a broker should have a well-reasoned, written office policy to avoid confusion and conflict within the office regarding these matters.

The following examples and short questions and answers may help illustrate how and when an intermediary transaction may arise and when appointments may be made.

■ **EXAMPLE 1**   Broker Able has listed seller Sharp's house. The listing agreement permits Able to act as an intermediary if the occasion arises. Customer Jones, an unrepresented buyer, asks Able to present an offer on the Sharp property.

■ **QUESTION**   What kind of agency relationships will be operational?

■ **DISCUSSION**   Because Jones has no representation agreement, Able simply will act as the agent for the seller, giving Sharp full representation services, including advocacy, while treating Jones fairly and honestly but not advocating for his interests. Note in Figure 6.3 that the broker can give preferential advice and opinions to the seller, thereby tipping the scale in favor of the seller. It is important to understand that Able not only gives advice and opinion to Sharp, but also advocates Sharp's goals when meeting with Jones to discuss Jones's offer or Sharp's counteroffer. He tries to sell Jones on the idea of giving Sharp everything Sharp wants. Able should offer no seller concessions to Jones unless specifically authorized by his seller, Sharp. Some licensees in this position seem to act more like mediators than negotiators and just want to "get a deal" rather than vigorously attempt to achieve their client's objectives.

■ **EXAMPLE 2**   Broker Able has entered into a buyer representation agreement with buyer Baker. The buyer representation agreement permits Able to act as an intermediary should the occasion arise. Baker, a represented buyer, wishes to negotiate a contract on seller Sharp's house.

■ **QUESTION**   What is Able's position in the transaction?

■ **DISCUSSION**   Because the listing agreement with the seller and the written buyer representation agreement authorized Able to act as an intermediary, the intermediary brokerage relationship will become operational without requiring further notice to the principals. (Although the statutes do not require notice to the principals when the intermediary transaction begins, a prudent broker will advise the principals that an intermediary agency is in place.)

Throughout the transaction, Able must carefully adhere to the requirements of intermediary brokerage. Because Able operates alone, no appointments may be made, and the principals will receive the limited services permitted by the intermediary rules. Both parties must be treated honestly and fairly, but no advice or opinions may be given to either party in the negotiations. Observers of this transaction would see one key difference between this intermediary transaction and the former statutory dual-agency transaction if both were performed correctly. The difference would be between the two duties of confidentiality versus full disclosure. In the dual agency transaction, Able would have to disclose everything he knows to both Sharp and Jones. However in the Intermediary scenario, Able is required to keep everything he knows about both parties confidential.

Note that in example 2, the scale must be kept in balance, as shown in Figure 6.4. No preferential advice or opinions can be given to either seller or buyer.

FIGURE 6.3

Seller Representation Only

FIGURE 6.4

Broker as an Intermediary

■ **EXAMPLE 3**   Broker Able hires a new sales associate, Sally, who promptly engages buyer Smith in a buyer representation agreement. The written agreement authorizes Able to act as an intermediary and to make appointments when appropriate. Smith becomes interested in and wishes to make an offer to purchase seller Sharp's house, currently listed by Able.

■ **QUESTION**   What will be the roles of Able and Sally in the transaction?

■ **DISCUSSION**   Able will act as an intermediary and will direct Sally to act as Able's intermediary "agent" and carry out the duties of an intermediary, but she will not be considered "appointed." Both Able and Sally must remain impartial. No preferential advice or opinions may be given to either Smith or Sharp.

■ **QUESTION**   May Able make appointments in this transaction?

■ **DISCUSSION**   No. Able has only one sales associate; therefore, the appointment process is inappropriate. A broker with more than one associate may appoint different associates to the buyer and the seller; the broker cannot be appointed to either.

■ **QUESTION**   Could Able appoint Sally to Smith and simply serve Sharp as an intermediary?

■ **DISCUSSION**   No. The statutes prohibit appointments to only one side of the transaction. If a licensee is appointed to the buyer, a different licensee must be appointed to the seller. For example, Figure 6.5 shows the scales being maintained in balance as to the services provided by both the broker and the sales licensee (i.e., no opinions, advice, or confidential information to either side.)

The principals' interests are NOT kept in strict balance by the broker or the associate; their interests are left to each of them to protect on their own. It is a misinterpretation of the intermediary statute to turn the intermediary into an arbiter of what is right for each of the two clients. Some believe it is the intermediary's duty to balance the equities between the parties and make sure each gets a fair deal. That is a risky course of action. If one party is a superior negotiator, that party may get a far better deal. The intermediary is not a referee. The intermediary is an impartial bystander with facilitator duties to carry out the final agreement of the parties. No advice, no opinions, no advocacy, and no full disclosure of confidential information. Buyers, tenants, and owners who consent to an intermediary should be clearly informed about the drawbacks and limitations, as well as advantages of their broker/agent becoming an intermediary. Statements such as "Don't worry Mr. Seller and Ms. Buyer, we can represent you both" are at the least superficial, possibly misleading, and depending on the sophistication of the parties, border on being deceptive.

FIGURE 6.5

Intermediary Broker With One Associate and Without Appointments

■ **EXAMPLE 4**   Broker Able hires another associate, Jim Bob, who lists a home owned by seller Susan. The listing agreement authorizes Able to act as an intermediary and to make appointments, if appropriate. Sally, who represented buyer Smith in an unsuccessful attempt to purchase the Sharp property (example 3), wishes to make an offer on the Anxious property.

■ **QUESTION**   What are the potential roles of Able?

■ **DISCUSSION**   Able may complete the transaction as an intermediary, with or without making appointments.

■ **QUESTION**   If no appointments are made, what will be the roles of Sally and Jim Bob?

■ **DISCUSSION**   Sally and Jim Bob will be instructed to carry out the duties of their intermediary broker. Neither associate may give advice or opinions to the principals with whom they are working. Both principals must be treated exactly the same. Figure 6.6 illustrates this option. Note that the broker and both associates are required to keep the scale in balance. No advice or opinions are given to either party.

FIGURE 6.6

Intermediary Broker With Two Sales Associates and Without Appointments

■ **QUESTION**   If broker Able wishes to make appointments, how is this accomplished?

■ **DISCUSSION**   Able will advise Sally that she is the appointed associate for Smith and will advise Jim Bob that he is the appointed associate for Susan. In addition, both principals must receive written notification of the appointments naming the licensee appointed to both parties. (See Figure 6.2, TAR Intermediary Relationship Notice.) Keep in mind that the identities of the parties must be disclosed to each other. Common law would also dictate that the intermediary and the appointed licensees disclose any family relationships, prior business dealings, or potential conflicts of interest the brokerage and any of its agents have had or contemplate having with the either of the parties.

■ **QUESTION**   How will the appointments change the roles of Able and her associates, Sally and Jim Bob?

■ **DISCUSSION**   Able's role will not change. She will carry out her duties as an intermediary, being careful not to take any action that would favor one party over the other. However, the roles of the agents who are now the appointed licensees change. Sally will now be permitted to give advice and opinions to Smith and assist in the negotiations. Jim Bob will now be able to give similar services to Susan. Figure 6.7 depicts the intermediary transaction with appointments. Note that while the broker must continue to be impartial, the appointed licensees will be able to give advice and opinions during the negotiations. The parties and the appointed associates must be aware that the intermediary broker is prohibited from providing any advice or opinion to either party.

FIGURE 6.7

Intermediary Broker With Two Associates and with Appointments

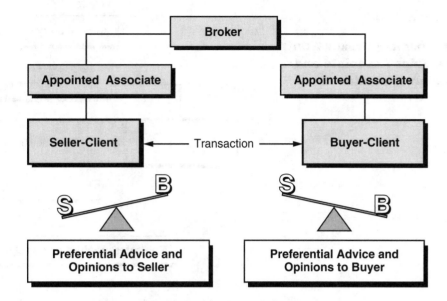

■ **EXAMPLE 5**   Sally, an agent of broker Able, is working with buyer Smith, a buyer represented by the company. Smith wishes to negotiate on a property owned by seller Jones. Sally is also the listing agent for the Jones property. Both representation contracts permit Able to act as an intermediary and to make appointments.

■ **QUESTION**   If Able wishes to conduct an intermediary transaction, what options are available regarding appointments?

■ **DISCUSSION**   If Able wished to make appointments, Sally could be appointed to either the buyer or the seller, but a different associate would have to be appointed to the other party. This would require the involvement of a new associate in the transaction, possibly causing concern for the principals. In addition, Sally might be required to share some commission with the other associate, depending on company policy. The practical solution for the broker and the associate would be not to make appointments. However, not making appointments is probably not advantageous to the two clients. The broker, to avoid legal problems later, may have to consider whether it is in the best interests of the two clients to make appointments or keep Sally in place in an impartial intermediary role. The degree of sophistication in real estate negotiations by either party could play a significant role in reaching the broker's decision to appoint or not.

■ **QUESTION**   If no appointments are made, how would this change the roles that Able and Sally could play?

■ **DISCUSSION**   Able would remain as the intermediary and instruct Sally to carry out the duties of the intermediary while working with both the buyer and the seller. No new associate would be required to enter the transaction. Figure 6.8 shows the transaction without appointments. Again, the broker and the sales licensee must keep the scales in balance relative to the services they provide and remember to be impartial. It would be best for the broker to confirm this choice with the principals to ensure that they would agree with the decision not to make appointments.

FIGURE 6.8

Intermediary Broker With One Sales Associate and Without Appointments

Status of Intermediary Brokers and Appointed Licensees

Intermediary brokerage is a relatively new concept in Texas real estate law (January 1, 1996). Consequently, many questions remain unanswered regarding the nature of this form of brokerage. Such questions relate to the nature of the agency relationship, representation issues, and fiduciary duties, if any. The general interpretation of the TREC is as follows:

- An intermediary is an agent, but with different duties from those of a single agent.
- Subject to the limitations imposed by TRELA § 1101.651(d), an intermediary **offers a limited form of representation** to the parties. This representation may be broadened somewhat by the use of "appointed associates." However, loyalty and full disclosure are sacrificed.
- As an intermediary, although the scope of agency is quite limited, certain fiduciary duties are imposed on the agent.
- The License Act has no provision for a broker to "opt out" of an agency relationship when acting as an intermediary.

Although TRELA § 1101.559(a) states that a "broker may act as an intermediary between parties to a real estate transaction if . . ." at least for the purposes of negotiating the transaction, TREC's interpretation of the word *may* is taken to be permissive rather than conditional. That is to say, the use of *may* confirms the authority of the broker to act as an agent rather than to suggest an alternative nonagency relationship. Keep in mind that these represent only interpretations of the statute. The statutory language is not clear on these issues, and perhaps the courts will ultimately be required to determine the agency capacity and fiduciary duties—if any—that accrue to the intermediary broker. Additionally, a court may have to decide what level of and extent of advice and opinion appointed licensees may give to the parties they are appointed to.

While attorneys debate the issue of agency versus nonagency status of the intermediary, brokers must grapple with the everyday application of the statute. From a practical perspective, TREC has offered some guidelines for the licensee. Until the courts, the legislature, or TREC changes these opinions, the licensee might be well advised to follow these interpretations. The label that we attach to the broker may be less important than a clear understanding of the broker's duties when act-ing as an intermediary, as described in TRELA § 1101.559; 651(d), and discussed earlier in this chapter. Remember that, in court, the important fact might be what role you played instead of the role you said you would play. Some direction is found in TRELA § 1101.561, which states that the duties of an intermediary, as described in § 1101.559; 651(d), "supersede the duties of a license holder estab-lished under any other law, including common law." **But as we have just seen, the explicit duties described in the statute are very limited**: conditional nondis-closure, honesty, and compliance with the License Act. It was initially believed that many of the questions surrounding intermediary brokerage would be resolved by the issuance of additional TREC regulations and by interpretation of this law in the courts. Yet the wording in the statute has not changed, case law remains limited, and TREC has not issued any regulations regarding intermediaries or appointed licensees. In the meantime, licensees should exercise caution when attempting to act in an intermediary role and understand the possible pitfalls, as well as the potential benefits, especially as they apply to consumers.

Keep in mind, that while the intermediary provisions of TRELA may only affect a minority of real estate transactions, the impact of a botched intermediary transac-tion can have a ripple effect of inflicting damage on buyers, owners, tenants and all the licensees involved. Only during in-house transactions involving a repre-sented buyer from the same listing firm and a represented seller will the interme-diary circumstance arise, and then only when all parties have agreed, in writing, to the arrangement. Although few of the licensee's transactions may involve the intermediary rules, if a broker attempts to undertake a single intermediary transac-tion, there should be a clear understanding as to how the broker and all affected licensees should proceed. In an attempt to clarify some of the issues surrounding the intermediary law, TREC, through its legal counsel, has compiled the list of frequently asked questions from licensees, which are found in Appendix B. The responses are those of the commissioners through the general counsel for TREC. They do not constitute legal advice, nor are they TREC Rules.

Concerns Related to Intermediary Practice

Even with the guidelines provided by statute and the rules of TREC, many brokers and attorneys feel that the specter of attempting to represent more than one party in a transaction presents too many legal and ethical problems to be practical. TREC in no way recommends intermediary practice, but neither does it recom-mend against it, and only provides certain guidelines and suggestions for brokers who choose to offer intermediary services. Remember, TREC has not passed a single rule regarding intermediary practice.

Consider, for example, that in an intermediary transaction, appointments have been made in writing to the respective parties. The appointed associates are now permitted to give advice and opinions to their party that may not be in the best interest of the other party. Still, confidential information must be kept confiden-tial. How far may the appointed associate go as a giver of opinions and advice? At what point will the associate violate confidentiality? What if one party feels that the associate appointed to the other party is more experienced or competent and that they are now at a disadvantage during negotiations? TRELA § 1101.559(c) states that the appointment of the associated licensee to the parties "is a fair and impartial act." Whether it really is in a particular case or not is apparently irrelevant because the statute has stated that it is both "fair" and "impartial." These and many other issues have yet to be resolved, and many brokers are understandably leery of this type of practice.

Certainly before attempting intermediary practice, a broker should carefully study the law and determine company policy regarding procedures. Once established, the policies and procedures should be reviewed by an attorney competent in this area of this particular area of law. Finally, a company training program should be developed and delivered to ensure that the policies and procedures are properly implemented.

■ **EXAMPLE**   Kelly, a first-time buyer, engaged Jackie, through her broker, to act as a buyer's agent. In the process of finding a suitable home, Kelly became interested in a property listed by Jackie. The buyer's representation agreement authorized Jackie's broker to act as an intermediary should the potential arise.

During the negotiations, Kelly complained to Jackie that it appeared that all the advice and opinions were being offered to the seller rather than to her. In fact, the only advice offered to the buyer was that she should pay the full price for the property and meet all other demands made by the seller. After the complaint from the buyer, Jackie told Kelly that if Kelly didn't like the way she was being represented that Kelly's broker would represent Kelly and Jackie would represent the seller.

Subsequently, Kelly's broker, by phone, informed Kelly that he would represent her interests rather than the seller's, again recommended that at least a full-price offer be tendered, and never spoke with Kelly again. After several negotiations through Jackie, Kelly ended up paying slightly more than full asking price. Later she complained again that all the emphasis seemed to be placed on the seller's need rather than her own, but she ultimately closed on the transaction, paying more than market value.

■ **QUESTION**   1. Is it permissible for a listing associate to negotiate the sale of her own listing to a buyer whom she also represents through her broker? 2. In the above example, how should the process of making appointments be handled? 3. What issues arose when the broker, in effect, appointed the listing agent to the seller and told the buyer that he would represent her interests rather than the seller's?

■ **DISCUSSION**   This example illustrates the lack of understanding of the intermediary statutes and points to the fact that brokers who do not understand the role of an intermediary should not attempt the practice.

In reference to the first question, nothing prevents a listing associate from negotiating a sale of that listing to a represented buyer. However, in this case, no appointments could be made and neither the seller nor the buyer should receive any advice or opinions that would act to the disadvantage of the other party.

If, in reference to the second question, appointments are to be made, one or more associates of the broker may be appointed to give advice and opinions to one party and one or more other associates of the broker could have been appointed to offer advice and opinions to the other party (TRELA § 1101.560; 651(d)). Once the appointments are made, both parties should receive written notification of the respective appointments naming the appointed associates. Under no circumstance should any broker attempt to appoint herself to either party.

A number of legal and ethical questions arise from this example and clearly point out the dangers of attempting to act as an intermediary without fully understanding the rules. In addition to demonstrating the lack of understanding of the fundamentals of intermediary brokerage, the broker, by claiming to represent the buyer rather than the seller in the transaction, violated fiduciary duties to the seller, whom he had originally agreed to represent in the listing contract.

■ SPECIALIZED INTERMEDIARY APPLICATIONS

The representation of more than one party is not confined to residential transactions, and brokers should be alert to the potential for undisclosed dual-representation issues arising in real estate exchanges; syndications; and farm and ranch, industrial, special-use, and commercial property transactions. Keep in mind that in any of these transactions, the statutorily required written statement in TRELA § 1101.558(d) must be given to each of the parties at the first substantive discussion involving a specific real property. The TREC IABS form may be used for these purposes, or brokers may use a form of their own choosing if the form complies with the statutory requirements as to wording and font size.

Exchanges

Some brokers help owners exchange property under the Internal Revenue Code of 1986, Section 1031, "Tax-Deferred Exchange Provisions." Clear disclosure must be made when only a single broker is involved with more than one party to an exchange. An intermediary relationship would probably best serve the interests of the parties as well as those of the broker. With one agent and two commissions at stake, the nonprofessional broker has ample temptation to compromise the interests of either or both parties. Often more than one broker is involved in an exchange.

Syndications

Possible undisclosed dual-representation problems may arise in several situations in which the general partner of a limited partnership syndication is also a broker. Examples include the following:

■ The general partner sells or leases partnership property for a fee to be paid by the partnership.
■ The general partner sells her own property to the partnership for a fee.
■ The general partner, on behalf of the partnership, buys property listed with another firm and seeks a commission split.
■ The general partner, on behalf of the partnership, buys unlisted property and seeks compensation from the seller-owner.

The general partner has fiduciary obligations to the other general partners and limited partners. The broker should represent and be paid by the partnership only, unless full disclosure is made and written consent is obtained from all principals and brokers involved.

Commercial Leasing Agent

Brokers involved in commercial real estate leasing may find themselves in situations where both parties desire representation. Leasing agents often work under exclusive-right-to-lease listings from developers or building owners. Usually, an MLS does not require the listing of commercial properties being offered for lease. In commercial leasing, a great deal of negotiation regarding lease terms and concessions frequently occurs between the owner and the potential lessee. The leasing agent is usually at the center of such negotiations and should be careful to ensure that both owner and lessee understand the role of the leasing agent.

Many times, the lessee is sophisticated and is represented by an attorney or an accountant; the lessee should not look to the owner's leasing agent for advice of a legal or financial nature. Often the principals complete their own negotiations and look to the broker as an effective go-between. The lessee looks to the leasing agent more for accurate information and figures, especially about market trends and economic factors, typically not within the attorney's field of expertise.

For those cases when the lessee has no adviser and looks to the leasing agent for negotiating advice and opinions, a cautious leasing agent will have the owner and lessee consent to an intermediary agreement permitting appointments. The broker might further recommend that the lessor and lessee each obtain legal counsel.

Leasing agents may work with lessees to locate and evaluate specific sites. It is not unusual for a leasing agent to approach the owner of an unlisted building. In these no-listing transactions, there should be a clear written understanding as to whom the leasing agent represents, regardless of which party is paying the commission. There is no difference between residential and commercial licensees regarding agency disclosure and intermediary and appointed licensee requirements.

■ INTENTIONAL VERSUS UNINTENDED DUAL REPRESENTATION

In considering the representation of more than one party to a transaction, one must determine whether such representation is intentional or unintentional. An intentional representation of more than one party as an intermediary may present some serious business risks, but it does provide the broker an opportunity to discuss the pros and cons of multiple representation and obtain written consent designed to minimize risk. In addition, the specific requirements to act as an intermediary are stated in the law.

The chief concerns, however, focus on the unintended or accidental representation of more than one party. A broker who doesn't know that multiple representation is occurring has no contractual way to minimize the risks inherent in the dual representation and by default will become an undisclosed dual agent. While any form of undisclosed agency violates the statutes, undisclosed dual agency is particularly troublesome.

Most commonly, unintended dual representation occurs in one of the following contexts:

- The listing broker or licensed associate represents both the buyer and the seller.
- Separate associates from the listing office (an in-house sale) represent the buyer and the seller.
- Another broker represents the buyer and also acts as a subagent of the seller.
- The real estate licensee acts as a buyer or a seller.
- Written agreement with the seller; only verbal agreement with the buyer.

The conduct of the listing broker's licensed associate may be such that the buyer is led to believe that the associate represents the buyer. Eager to develop rapport with the buyer prospect, the salesperson sometimes gives the buyer that impression. In its handbook *Who Is My Client?*, NAR lists the following examples of statements often used by real estate brokers that can create implied agency relationships with buyers:

- "I'll take care of everything. I'll handle the sale for you."
- "I'll see if I can get the seller to come down on the price."
- "This listing has been on the market for six months. That tells me it's overpriced. Let's offer $80,000 and see what they say."
- "I'll get you the best deal I possibly can."
- "Trust me. I'm sure the seller won't counter at that price."
- "If the seller is going to insist on a full-price sale, I think you should tell him no. Then we can try an offer on that house your wife liked so much. I'm sure those sellers will be more realistic."
- "If they insist on the full $100,000, I'll remind them that the furnace is 15 years old and the carpet is fraying. That should justify at least a $3,000 reduction." (Author's note: These were 1986 prices!)

An additional statement that could be used against a licensee today under the intermediary law is as follows: "Don't worry, we can represent you both." While technically true, it tends to mislead because of the meaning of "representation" as understood by the consumer versus the very limited meaning of the term as intended by the licensee.

Prior Relationships

Sometimes a dual representation arises based on a prior relationship between the listing broker and the buyer.

■ **EXAMPLE**   Mike of Prospect Realty lists George's house. Mike has represented Linda **on several sales and purchases of property**. Mike tells Linda about the house, and Linda wants Mike to prepare an offer at 10% below the asking price. Linda mentions that she'll pay near the asking price, if necessary.

■ **QUESTION**   Whom does Mike represent?

■ **DISCUSSION**   As the listing salesperson, Mike owes primary allegiance to George, the seller. Based on his prior relationship with Linda, however, Mike may, under implied agency principles, also be held to represent Linda. This could put Mike's firm, Prospect Realty, into an unintended dual representation role.

Mike's options are either to disclose the prior relationship and obtain consents from Linda, George, and the broker of Prospect Realty permitting an intermediary transaction or to disclaim any agency to Linda. The second option requires clarification to Linda that Mike can work with her, but only on a customer basis, because Mike would be the agent of the seller only.

If Mike is acting through his broker in an intermediary role, he has a duty to Linda not to reveal her bargaining intentions. Neither can Mike tell Linda that his other principal, George, will take $10,000 less than the listed price or reveal any of George's other bargaining intentions. These usually inappropriate duties are the norm of intermediary brokerage, and mutually exclusive duties are the dilemma of the intermediary. With clear disclosure and consents, Mike, under the first option, may be authorized to keep confidential his discussions regarding price and terms. On the other hand, if Mike disclaims an agency relationship with Linda, under the second option, he would have to tell George that Linda has expressed a willingness to increase her first offer. Had Mike followed proper information and disclosure procedures, the options would have been discussed at first contact with Linda. If the second option were selected, Linda should have been advised not to disclose any bargaining information that she did not want George to know. In either event, Mike should tell George about his prior business relationship with Linda and any contemplated future transactions where he may be representing her. If George decides to consent to the intermediary arrangement, he should "play his cards close to his vest" and not reveal any information that compromises his position. Although in an intermediary transaction, Mike would be required to keep all of George's information confidential, Mike is only human, and Linda represents repeat business if he gets her a good deal.

In-House Sale

Even though the selling salesperson working for a represented buyer in an in-house sale is someone other than the listing salesperson, a dual representation exists because the employing broker has become an intermediary or, hopefully not, an undisclosed dual agent through the conduct of the two salespersons.

■ **EXAMPLE**   Joe, a salesperson with Pacesetter Realty, lists Harry's house. Kathy, also of Pacesetter Realty, has been looking for two months to find the right house for her client, Lisa. She shows Lisa the house that Joe listed. Lisa loves it and wants Kathy to negotiate on her behalf for a lower price, a long closing period, and favorable financing terms. Lisa wants Kathy secretly to look for a resale buyer at a quick profit, ideally in a back-to-back closing.

■ **QUESTION**   Who represents whom?

■ **DISCUSSION**   Unless Pacesetter Realty has written consent to act as an intermediary, it now represents both the seller and the buyer as an undisclosed dual agent. The knowledge possessed by both Joe and Kathy will be imputed to Pacesetter Realty and to each other. Pacesetter Realty is still the broker and would, therefore, be advocating for both sides against each other. The only logical conclusion is that Pacesetter Realty has become an unlawful dual agent. The danger here is of actually trading inside information within the same office.

One attempt at an answer may lie in the intermediary transaction with appointments. Joe, the listing agent, would be appointed to give advice and opinions to seller Harry, thereby protecting Harry's interests. Kathy, working with represented buyer Lisa, would be appointed to assist Lisa with advice and opinions toward meeting her goals. Because in the intermediary agreement, both parties have agreed that certain information may be kept confidential, the fact that Lisa is hoping to resell quickly at a profit is moot. The problem is that, if the appointed licensee's character and personal ethics are not of the highest order, the fact that a regulatory "façade" exists to create a statutory version of a pretended "wall," neither dual agency nor intermediary will work for the clients, even though intermediary may work to protect the broker. Nothing works against unscrupulous or unqualified people to stop their predations on consumers before they happen. Only punishment after the fact seems to deter the truly unethical agent. As has been stated before in this text, "The purpose of the statute is to eliminate or reduce fraud that might be occasioned on the public by unlicensed, unscrupulous, or unqualified persons." [*Henry S. Miller v. TREO Enterprises*]

Some brokers are not aware that this two-salesperson situation in an in-house sale creates a dual-representation conflict and, therefore, will not attempt to obtain proper consents. The broker may believe that both buyer and seller will be treated fairly and that each will receive full representation from their respective associates.

The broker often becomes aware of the conflict for the first time when served with notice of a lawsuit. It is then that the listing broker discovers, for example, that the salesperson never told the seller that the real reason for extending the closing date was to close the sale of the buyer's home, which was also listed by the broker. The seller then claims a breach of fiduciary duty because the broker failed to point out the seller's options in agreeing to an extension (for example, as a condition for extending, the seller possibly could have asked for compensating concessions). Trying to reverse unintended dual agency by attempting to get an intermediary agreement at the point of a lawsuit comes too late to protect the broker or the parties.

Cooperating or Other Broker

The "Other Broker" (i.e., not the listing broker) in the transaction often acts as the agent of the buyer in negotiations to acquire a property listed in an MLS. If subagency is offered and the other broker fails to make clear to all parties that he represents the buyer only and not the seller, then a problem arises. If the offer of subagency is not rejected by the buyer broker, the court may deem the buyer broker to be a subagent of the seller and the implied agent of the buyer, and therefore, an undisclosed dual agent. Failure to make such representation clear to all parties is also violation of the License Act. (TRELA § 1101.652(b)(7))

■ **EXAMPLE**   Patricia of Supreme Real Estate checks the MLS book in her search for a home for Nancy. There was no expressed agreement, either written or oral, that Patricia represented Nancy. Patricia sees an interesting house and calls Jeff from South Side Realty about his listing. Patricia arranges to see the property and subsequently submits Nancy's offer. The negotiations are long and hard, but after a series of four different offers and counteroffers, the seller agrees to Nancy's offer. Before closing, Nancy gets cold feet and asks for a return of her deposit money.

■ **QUESTION**   Does Nancy have a valid claim for rescission of the contract based on undisclosed dual representation?

■ **DISCUSSION**   Even though it may have no relevance to the true reason why Nancy wants to back out of the contract, she might assert that she relied on the fact that she believed that Patricia was her agent. Later, Nancy alleges she discovered that Patricia and Supreme Real Estate were really subagents of the seller. Because of Nancy's claim that Supreme Real Estate acted as an undisclosed dual agent, Nancy argues that either the buyer or the seller can legally refuse to close, even though no damages are proven. Patricia should have clarified her agency status to both Nancy and Jeff when she first began to work with Nancy and again when she first contacted Jeff to view the property. Under typical MLS rules, if subagency is offered, according to current Texas common law, Patricia will probably be presumed to be the subagent of the seller unless she rejects the offer of subagency and declares that she is a buyer's agent. She did not declare that she represented anyone. If a subagent of the seller, Patricia must act as a subagent of the seller should have acted, taking care to protect the interest of the seller and not act as an agent of the buyer. In this case, she negotiated hard for Nancy, and it may very well be that Patricia and Supreme Real Estate were unintended agents of Nancy, as well as intended agents of the seller through the subagency rules.

Real estate licensees should note that professional liability often is based on the law of agency and the failure of a licensee to live up to the duties of an agent when held to be acting as one. Subagency may complicate this problem by creating an unintended dual representation with an inherent conflict of interest. It is important to note that not all subagents are subagents of the seller. Occasionally, a buyer broker's client will want to see properties outside of the area where the broker is knowledgeable about prices, properties, and the like. In that event, if the original buyer broker does not want to refer the business to a buyer broker in the desired area, the broker may decided to call a competent/ethical exclusive buyer broker in the area desired by the client. An oral, or preferably written, agreement for subagency is formed between the two buyer brokers. The original buyer broker maintains his buyer representation agreement with the buyer but offers the out of area broker subagency and compensation. Only a very few people in the business have ever even heard of this aspect of subagency, and even fewer have actually tried it.

Broker as Principal

Brokers should be especially alert to dual-representation problems when they or their associates or employees, licensed or otherwise, buy or sell property for their own accounts. This can happen in several contexts:

■ Broker or agent buying broker's listed properties
■ Buyer broker competing with her own buyer/client for purchase of a property
■ Broker puts own house on market, then attempts to represent buyer in purchasing it.
■ During a listing appointment, broker decides seller's house is perfect for broker's spouse and attempts to buy it instead of listing it.
■ Broker puts own house on market and fails to notify buyer that he is a broker.
■ Broker puts own house on market under an assumed name, trust, company name, or the like. Acts as buyer broker to "help" buyer buy his house without disclosing that the broker is the real owner or has a beneficial interest in the proceeds from the sale of the house.

Member of the Brokerage Buying an In-House Listing.   On occasion, a broker or one of the broker's associates decides to make an offer on one of the broker's own listings. As a rule, brokers should not purchase their own listings, especially if they are real bargains. The risks to the professional image of the broker are too great, not to mention the risks of loss of commission for breach of the duties of good faith and loyalty and loss of license under TRELA rules and regulations. To minimize exposure to liability, brokers desiring to purchase in-house listings should recommend that sellers obtain confirming appraisals and retain other consultants or advisers. To really minimize exposure to liability in this instance is to have a rigid company policy forbidding it (e.g., "Buy one of our listings. Get a new broker.")

■ **EXAMPLE**   Debra lists her home with broker Sid for $100,000. After six months of marketing, Debra has received only one offer, for $75,000. Sid offers to pay $95,000 by way of an assumption of the $80,000 first mortgage and further agrees to reduce the 7% listing fee to 3.5%. Five days before closing, Sid meets Betty, a recent arrival to town, who buys the home from Sid for $110,000 five days after closing.

■ **QUESTION**   Did Sid breach a fiduciary duty to Debra?

■ **DISCUSSION**   Sid probably did breach his fiduciary duty if he did not inform Debra immediately on learning of Betty's offer. Under 22 TAC § 535.156 (b) and (c), a broker "must put the interest of the licensee's principal above the licensee's own interest" and the broker has "an affirmative duty to keep the principal informed at all times of significant information applicable to the transaction." Under 22 TAC § 535.16, Sid is obligated "under a listing contract to negotiate the best possible transaction for the principal the broker has agreed to represent."

Even if, technically, Sid were found to have breached no fiduciary duty, the appearance of wrongdoing is there. Sid may have a difficult time proving to a jury that he acted in Debra's best interests, particularly if the home's appraised value exceeded the listing price.

At best, there will always be a doubt in Debra's mind as to whether Sid stole a profit opportunity from her. Even if Betty had not appeared until a few days after closing, Sid would have a tough time convincing a jury that he didn't knowingly underprice the house at the time of the listing, which would be not only an additional breach of fiduciary duty but also a deceptive trade practice.

Sid should offer to return to Debra all or a fair portion of the quick profit or allow Debra the opportunity to sell directly to Betty. Such an attitude enhances the broker's professional standing in the community. In fact, it may enhance the broker's reputation so much that it more than makes up for the temporary loss of revenue. However, whether it is more profitable is not an appropriate standard by which to measure moral conduct. It is easy for brokers to say they promote their clients' best interests above anyone else's, including their own. It is much more effective to demonstrate this. (See *Wilson v. Donze*, 692 S.W.2d 735 [Tex. App. 2 Dist. 1985].) In this case, the broker had a duty to obtain the best price possible, even above the asking price, because he was found to be an agent of the seller, even though he believed he was not.

When a member of the brokerage buys an in-house listing, the listing price could become a matter of dispute between the seller and the broker because the broker helps establish the list price. There is a popular misunderstanding in the industry that the seller always determines the list price. This is not quite true. The most used listing contract in Texas is called a Residential Real Estate Listing Agreement. Like almost any contract, it is an agreement, not a unilateral imposition of terms and duties. The broker and the seller must agree on the list price or there will be no listing. Few professional brokers would take a listing at just any price a seller tried to dictate. The list price is a price arrived at first by negotiation and finally by mutual agreement.

The risks of a lawsuit increase if the licensee buying an in-house listing competes against offers submitted by other licensees on behalf of buyers or by buyers' agents on behalf of their clients. The listing agent has an unfair competitive advantage over other buyers because the agent knows all the bids. TRELA § 1101.652(b)(2), which prohibits dealing in bad faith and dishonest dealings, also applies. The listing agent should reveal to other buyers the price and terms of any prior or subsequent offer made by the listing agent. Otherwise, the agent risks possible action by a buyer for breach of the general duties of fairness and honesty. Such an action could be based on failure to present the buyer's offer in a timely manner, failure to notify the buyer after the agent outbid the buyer, or failure to reveal information the buyer might have used to justify a more attractive offering price, such as a pending beneficial zoning change.

State licensing law often requires that real estate licensees disclose in writing their true position when offering to buy property listed with the broker. Although TRELA § 1101.652(b)(16) requires this disclosure, it does not require that it be in writing. Remember that although TRELA is the general law governing licensees, TREC rules may also apply. In this case, the requirement for "written" notification is addressed by TREC rule:

> **22 TAC 535.144 When Acquiring or Disposing of Own Property or Property of Spouse, Parent or Child.**
>
> (b) A licensee, when engaging in a real estate transaction on his or her own behalf, on behalf of a business entity in which the licensee is more than a 10% owner, or on behalf of the licensees spouse, parent, or child, is obligated to disclose in writing to any person with whom the licensee deals that he or she is a licensed real estate broker or salesperson acting on his or her own behalf or on behalf of the licensee's spouse, parent or child in any contract of sale or rental agreement or in any other writing given prior to entering into any contract of sale or rental agreement.

As the buyer, the listing agent must remember that unless the agency has been terminated, the broker is still a fiduciary of the seller. The agent must act primarily for the benefit of the seller and owes the seller the standard duties of full disclosure, skill, and care, in addition to honesty and fairness. There may be a question as to whether a broker can self-represent in buying a client's property and continue to place that client's interests first. A jury might also find it difficult to accept.

Buying Property Listed in an MLS   A licensee may decide to purchase a property listed in an MLS by another firm, either for themselves or for a family member (i.e., spouse, parent or child) or a business entity (more than 10% ownership interest), as previously described in 22 TAC § 535.144. The licensee should, before any offer or negotiation, immediately disclaim any subagency to the seller. Otherwise, the seller may claim that the licensee-buyer owed fiduciary duties to the seller under any MLS offer of subagency. Note that licensees are not normal consumers and may be required, under agency law, to disclose their opinions of value or of the likelihood of future appreciation (22 TAC § 535.16(c)). This area is little tricky: If you come to a prospective seller's house with the idea of listing the property or have been called by the seller to discuss listing the property, you have a particular set of duties that don't apply to the average investor buyer or prospective home buyer. If you decide, upon seeing the house, this is the house you and your spouse would love to own, you cannot switch to buyer mode without an important requirement being met. In this instance, you must give the seller an honest BPO or CMA before making an offer on the home. On the other hand, if you were driving down the street and saw a FSBO sign, presented yourself as an investor or buyer, not as potential or prospective agent for the seller, asked to see the house as a prospective purchaser, you would have no obligation to offer the seller a CMA or a BPO before making an offer. Having a real estate license does not deprive you of rights you already have as a citizen, like buying someone else's house and trying to get the best deal you can for yourself. However, you must disclose in writing that you are a real estate licensee and must not leave the impression with the owner that you are on the owner's side in any way. A good way to do that might be to say something like this:

> Good afternoon Ms. Property Owner. My name is _____. I saw your property and was wondering if you would consider selling it. Although I am a licensed real estate broker in Texas, I am not here to help you sell your house. I am here as an investor buyer who regularly tries to buy and sell or rent properties for a profit. Is today a good time to talk with you or would tomorrow be better?

A good general rule is to never try to purchase properties listed by your firm. That is an invitation for disaster for you and your broker. If you intend to buy numerous properties, you may want to consider going with a small real estate firm that does not have many listings, or buy properties in an area where your broker does not wish to list or represent buyers. You will also need to work out an arrangement with your broker about your intended investing. Your broker might have some serious questions about you buying and selling or renting your properties in competition with the brokerage's listings.

Sellers have won cases against cooperating subagent brokers who bought for their own accounts, or that of close relatives. The success of these suits has been based on failure by licensees to disclose the true market value (one week after purchase of a property, for example, a licensee listed it on a financial statement as having a $20,000 greater value) or to disclose that a simple subdivision of the property would increase its market value (in one case, by 25%). The sellers won because the other agent owed fiduciary duties to the sellers based on the rules of subagency. These cases might have turned out differently had the licensee rejected subagency from the beginning, made all proper disclosures, and documented them before proceeding.

If a commission split will occur, the listing agent should fully disclose this fact. This amount is often used as part of the down payment. The broker buying on his own account should disclose in the purchase contract that the receipt of such a split does not create an agency relationship between the buyer/licensee and the seller or the seller's broker. It is much safer for the buyer/licensee to disclaim subagency, deduct the fee from the offering price, and not participate in the fee paid by the seller.

Buying From the FSBO Licensees buying FSBO (For Sale by Owner) properties (again, either for themselves or acting on behalf of a close relative or business entity described previously) should disclaim any agency relationship with the sellers and should not approach the sellers under the guise of representing the sellers' best interests or listing the properties. Otherwise, under the law, they may be deemed agents of the sellers. If the licensees are deemed agents, they will be held to a higher standard of care with a greater duty of disclosure to sellers (22 TAC § 535.16(c)).

The ' seller often agrees to pay a reduced commission to the licensee-buyer as a courtesy fee. The seller may later argue that the payment of a fee to the licensee-buyer was enough to create an agency relationship. At a minimum, licensees buying for their own account should insert disclaimer language into the purchase offer, such as the following: "Seller acknowledges that buyer is a Texas real estate licensee buying for the licensee's own account and is not acting as an agent of the seller. Seller is not relying on the buyer/licensee for any advice or counsel regarding the sale. The buyer/licensee has advised seller that seller is free to obtain an independent consultant, attorney, or agent to advise the seller and/or represent the seller's interest."

Adopting the Buyer

If no other broker is involved, the listing agent often spends a good deal of time with the buyer both before and after the contract is signed. A clear conflict arises in a back-to-back sale if the agent signs a listing with the buyer to resell the property before an offer has been made. More likely, however, is a situation in which an agent "adopts" a buyer during the closing process, agreeing, for example, to list other properties of the buyer, to cooperatively develop a property, or to perform any other actions that may create an implied or express conflict of interest or representation agreement with the buyer.

Suppose the listing agent is asked by a buyer before closing to look for a resale buyer at $10,000 more than the contract price. While it is not illegal to take a listing from a buyer after the contract is signed, the listing agent ethically and legally must disclose the dual representation to the seller. The seller might feel, in retrospect, that the agent, before the contract was signed, failed to disclose the existence of a resale buyer and possible higher selling price so that the agent could make a double commission.

A key ingredient in all the preceding scenarios is a full and complete disclosure of the role the broker is to play and then for the broker to play that role exactly. When parties agree to allow a broker to act in any capacity that gives any principal less than the full fiduciary duties of an agent, the principals should be fully informed of the limitations and give their informed consent.

Nonagency

Some states provide for nonagency status for real estate licensees who may provide real estate services as transactional brokers, facilitators, or middlemen. A broker in Texas attempting to maintain a nonagency status will find no comfort in TRELA if a dispute arises in the transaction. Likewise, the courts have determined that brokers, while attempting to act as middlemen, may become an agent if they attempt to perform any services on behalf of a property owner. (See *West v. Touchstone*, 620 S.W.2d687 [Tex.Civ.App., Dallas 1981].)

■ SUMMARY

Statutory changes during the 1995 legislative session made sweeping changes in the area involving representation of more than one party to a transaction. Those changes became effective on January 1, 1996. Statutory dual agency was removed and replaced with intermediary brokerage. The statutory intermediary brokerage status in Texas presented an industry solution to the problems for brokers inherent in trying to represent both sides in a transaction. Many consumers and consumer advocate organizations disagreed, saying that the intermediary law benefited brokers to the disadvantage of sellers and buyers. The key distinction between the old statutory dual agent and the intermediary broker lies in the ability of the intermediary to offer a broader range of services to represented buyers and sellers during in-house transactions. These extended services are accomplished through allowing appointed licensees of the broker to give advice and opinions to the party to whom the licensee has been appointed, while the intermediary broker remains "impartial" throughout the transaction.

Undisclosed dual representation is a clear breach of an agent's fiduciary duty of loyalty. Even when an agent intends to act as an agent of both parties, such dual representation violates TRELA if adequate disclosure is not given to both the buyer and the seller and unless an agreed intermediary relationship is established under TRELA. Many dual representations are accidental and arise because of the conduct of the licensees. Brokers need to establish internal management controls to lessen the risks of both unintended and underdisclosed dual representation.

The concepts of intermediary brokerage practice are difficult to grasp for new brokers and newly licensed salespersons. FAQ's compiled by TREC are provided for review in Appendix B.

■ KEY POINTS

- A broker must agree to act as an intermediary when representing more than one party in a transaction.
- Contrary to the opinions of many in the industry, it is possible for a company to sell its own listings without creating intermediary brokerage, provided the brokerage does not establish agency relationships with the buyers, expressly or accidentally, and the buyers remain as customers, not clients.

- Intermediary brokerage, with the option of appointed licensees for each party, is authorized in Texas and became effective on January 1, 1996. Theoretically, an intermediary broker may act as an "agent" for both parties, but the intermediary broker's duties differ significantly from those the broker assumes when acting as a an agent for only one party in a transaction. The duties and obligations of the intermediary are limited to those set out in TRELA § 1101.559; .651(d). The major purpose of the statute is to reduce the liability of brokers when they conduct transactions in which both principals are represented by the same broker. This new law has yet to be interpreted by TREC regulations or by decisions of the courts.

- A broker who expects to become an intermediary should lay a foundation early by discussing the possibility of an intermediary transaction with in-house sales at the initial interviews with both the potential seller and the potential buyer. The possibility of an intermediary transaction should never be sprung on a client after a relationship is established. Consent to conduct an intermediary transaction can be authorized in the listing contract or in a buyer representation contract, but it must be authorized in writing somewhere, even by a separate agreement. The listing and buyer/tenant representation agreements are the easiest, most logical, and legal place to insert the statutory language allowing the practice.

- In comparison with single agency, the intermediary brokerage practice offers reduced services to the parties in the transaction. However, this shortcoming has been reduced slightly by the ability of the broker to appoint associates to the buyer and the seller for the intermediary transaction. These appointed associates may give advice and opinion to their respective parties during the transaction.

- Although the intermediary broker may be exposed to legal liability by failing to follow the intermediary guidelines carefully, the broker may benefit from this practice through in-house sales to represented buyers. The buyers and the sellers might not benefit as much as they would by having true agents on both sides.

■ SUGGESTIONS FOR BROKERS

A broker who is considering offering intermediary services to buyers and sellers should fully understand the requirements of the intermediary and develop a company policy regarding such practices. In addition, the broker should address the issue of appointed associates and be prepared to train associates who may be involved in such transactions before they become involved in a transaction. After the transaction has begun, the intermediary broker, sales managers, or trainers are not allowed to give the appointed licensee advice.

CHAPTER 6 QUIZ

1. An associate of a broker, while working with a nonrepresented buyer, begins to give advice and opinions to the buyer during negotiations with a seller represented by the broker. *MOST* likely the broker has become a(n)
   a. single agent of the buyer.
   b. intermediary.
   c. undisclosed dual agent.
   d. facilitator.

2. Currently, the form of dual representation known as dual agency is
   a. not permitted by TRELA.
   b. permitted under statutory rules.
   c. encouraged by TREC.
   d. permitted under common law rules.

3. The major difference between the former statutory dual agency and the current intermediary status is that with intermediary status,
   a. appointed licensees can give advice and opinions.
   b. agents have the same restrictions as the broker.
   c. the broker can give advice and opinions.
   d. confidential information can be relayed.

4. If an intermediary situation arises, the broker may *NOT* disclose
   a. the highest price the buyer might pay, until authorized to do so in writing.
   b. the minimum price a seller will take, unless authorized to do so in writing.
   c. confidential information of either party, unless the parties authorize it or law requires disclosure.
   d. any of these.

5. In a transaction involving appointed associates, which of the following is *TRUE*?
   a. Associates may be appointed to either the buyer or the seller.
   b. The broker may be appointed to the buyer, while an associate is appointed to the seller.
   c. Written notification of the intermediary transaction and the appointed associates must be given to both parties.
   d. Written notification and identification of the appointed associates must be given to both parties.

6. Broker Able's represented buyer wishes to negotiate on a property listed by broker Smith in a different firm. During this transaction, which broker(s) may act as an intermediary?
   a. Able
   b. Smith
   c. Neither Able nor Smith
   d. Both Able and Smith

7. In an intermediary transaction, if a broker appoints an associate to the seller,
   a. an associate also must be appointed to the buyer.
   b. the broker must take an appointment to the buyer.
   c. the same associate also must be appointed to the buyer.
   d. the broker must appoint someone from another firm to the buyer.

8. Unintentional dual representation can occur when
   a. another broker acts as a subagent and represents the buyer.
   b. the listing broker represents both the buyer and seller.
   c. a licensee acts as a buyer or a seller.
   d. any of these takes place.

9. A small company consists of a broker and one associate. During an intermediary transaction, the

a. broker may be appointed to one party and the associate may be appointed to the other party.
b. broker is prohibited from making appointments.
c. associate may be appointed to both parties.
d. broker may be appointed to both parties.

10. What occurs when an associate who has listed a property shows that same property to a buyer he also represents, and an intermediary transaction is agreed to?

a. The associate may be appointed to both the seller and the buyer.
b. The associate may be appointed to either the seller or the buyer.
c. The associate may not be appointed to either the seller or the buyer.
d. The associate may appoint another associate to work with the buyer.

DISCUSSION QUESTIONS

1. What are the key differences between the former statutory dual agent and the current intermediary broker?

2. Why might a broker make or not make appointments in an intermediary transaction?

3. What issues should be considered in office policy regarding appointed associates?

4. What are five advantages for a buyer or tenant in having his broker act as an intermediary instead of giving full fiduciary duties to the buyer or tenant?

5. What are five advantages for an owner in having the owner's broker act as an intermediary instead of giving full fiduciary duties to the owner?

6. What are the advantages for a broker to act as an intermediary instead of exclusively representing only one party to a transaction?

Creation and Termination of Agency

Few people, including many licensees, know the acts, conditions, expectations, and statements that can unintentionally turn an ordinary broker into an agent for one or more parties. It is in the best interests of all parties to a real estate transaction to understand the rules that govern agency. This is particularly important for licensees to enable them to establish when their responsibilities begin and which set of legal duties they owe—and to whom. Many professional publications, standards of professional conduct, and state licensing laws focus on the strict fulfillment of the rules of conduct for an agent. However, few offer exact determinations of when an agency relationship is created and to whom fiduciary duties are owed.

Licensees must know and understand the dynamics of agency and are responsible for strict compliance with the law of agency. This chapter introduces the concepts of how and when agency is created, as well as how the relationship may be terminated. This knowledge will lay the foundation for understanding one of the most vital aspects of real estate practice today.

■ **LEARNING OBJECTIVES**   *This chapter addresses the following:*

- ■ How and When Agency Is Created
  - — Express Agency
  - — Implied Agency
  - — Agency Is Transaction Specific
  - — Ostensible Agency or Agency by Estoppel
  - — Agency by Ratification
  - — Gratuitous Agency and Compensation
- ■ Important Issues
  - — Legal Effect
  - — Constructive or Imputed Notice
  - — Imputed Knowledge
  - — Professional and Ethical Responsibility
- ■ How Agency Is Terminated
  - — Lapse of Time
  - — Actions of Principals and Agents
  - — Operation of Law
- ■ Duties of Agency That Survive Termination

■ HOW AND WHEN AGENCY IS CREATED

We know that an agency relationship generally is created when one person authorizes another to act on that person's behalf and to exercise some degree of authority and discretion while acting in this capacity. In most cases, the agreement must be mutual; that is, the principal must authorize the agent to act on the principal's behalf, and the agent must agree to do so. The agent may be empowered to do many of the things the principal could do but has chosen not to do. Typically, the agency relationship is created by some spoken or written agreement between the parties, but as will be shown, agency can be created by other, less formal means. Regardless of how or when the agency relation is ultimately created, TRELA states that a broker who represents a party in a real estate transaction acts as that party's agent (§ 1101.557(a)). Furthermore, while acting as an agent for another, the broker or salesperson acting for the broker is a fiduciary (22 TAC § 531.1).

The fact that a person licensed as a real estate broker or a salesperson performs a service for a consumer is not, by itself, sufficient to create an agency relationship. A real estate licensee's role is to give valuable service both to clients and to customers. However, the motivation of the sellers to give service to a customer buyer should center on the fact that certain services to a buyer-customer are carried for the benefit of the seller/client. In other words, good service to the customer so that the customer will do what the seller-client wants the customer to do, which is to buy the seller's property at the best price and terms possible for the seller-client.

The creation of an agency relationship requires more than just giving benefits and services. **It requires consent and control**. Once created, the agency relationship requires that licensees, acting as agents, place the interests of the client above the interests of all other parties related to the transaction, including and especially above the agent's own interests in the transaction. (22 TAC § 531.1(3); § 535.156(b)). The licensee, as an agent, becomes an advocate of the principal/

client in dealing with third parties (customers) and is obligated to protect the interests of that person.

As stated earlier, an agency relationship ideally results from mutual consent between the principal and the agent. In this case, the agent agrees to act on the principal's behalf and is subject to the principal's control. Formalities are not required, however, and an agent does not need a license, written contract, or receipt of a commission or fee for an agency relationship to exist (see Figure 7.1). Keep in mind the basic definition of a "broker" in Texas. Under TRELA § 1101.002(1)(A), *broker* means "a person who, in exchange for a commission or other valuable consideration or with the expectation of receiving a commission or other valuable consideration, performs for another person one of the following acts."

TRELA goes on to list the numerous acts that would require an individual to be licensed as a real estate agent. Licensing as a broker or a salesperson is technically not required to perform any of those activities unless compensation is either received or anticipated. Compensation can come in many forms, however, ranging from cash to barter. So an individual who routinely provided the listed brokerage services for consumers would be hard-pressed to convince any court that compensation in some form was not being received for those services. In addition, the licensing requirement does not apply to myriad other individuals specifically exempted, such as Texas attorneys, onsite property managers, trustees, public officials, or individuals operating under a power-of-attorney (§ 1101.005).

While it is desirable for the agent and the principal to enter into a written agreement, nothing exists in Texas statutory or common law mandating that the agency relationship be created by written contract. Most states, however, including Texas, would require a written agreement, if the broker wants to have the option of bringing a lawsuit for a commission should the client default on the agreement (§ 1101.806(c)). Texas also requires written permission to perform specific acts, such as advertising or placing the broker's sign on the property.

Agency can be created by an oral agreement between the agent and the principal. The prudent broker will, however, establish a written contract as soon as possible. The written agreement should, at minimum, address the issues relating to the duties of the agent and principal and the expectations for compensation, and it should be sufficient to protect the interests of both parties. Remember, licensees not yet agents for a prospective client have the right to advocate for their own interests in reaching an agreement to represent the prospective client. However, after reaching agreement, the agent's interests must then be subordinated to those of the client under the terms of the agreement. The licensee's interests are protected by contract once the seller or the buyer representation agreement is signed. The licensee is free to negotiate for the client without concern for his or her own interests.

Even if the licensee is not a REALTOR®, the NAR Code of Ethics presents a strong standard of practice for the entire industry. In that Code, Article 9 states the following:

> REALTORS®, for the protection of all parties, shall assure whenever possible that all agreements related to real estate transactions including, but not limited to, listing and representation agreements, purchase contracts, and leases are in writing in clear and understandable language expressing the specific terms, conditions, obligations and commitments of the parties. A copy of each agreement shall be furnished to each party to such agreements upon their signing or initialing. (amended 1/04)

Some form of authorization (e.g., oral, written, implied, etc.) from the principal is needed for the agent to act on behalf of the principal in dealing with others. The principal must delegate authority to act to the agent and the agent must consent to act, or no agency exists. Licensees and other parties should be clear about the licensee's authority to act for others.

FIGURE 7.1

Elements Not Essential to Create an Agency Relationship

Not Essential for Agency

Specific authorization may come in different forms—express or implied—and by different means—words, actions, or, in some cases, by inaction. Agency may be classified as

- express agency,
- implied agency,
- ostensible agency or agency by estoppel,
- agency by ratification, or
- gratuitous agency.

It would be helpful for you to refer to Figure 7.2 during your study of these topics.

Express Agency

Express agency is the agency relationship created when principals engage or employ an agent to act for them. In legal terms, the word *express* means clear, definite, explicit, unmistakable, and unambiguous. In carrying out the duties of an express agency agreement, the agent acquires express authority to act for the principal.

In practice, this authority is created when principals authorize an agent to act for them by specifying certain acts, functions, or duties that the agent should perform. Remember that these instructions may be either written or oral. Generally, the more specific the agreement, the better for both the agent and the principal. Some states require such an agreement of representation to be in writing under both the licensing law and other laws relating to oral versus written contracts. In Texas, the authorization may be in writing or by an oral agreement between the principal and the broker. The obligations of the agent (broker) and the principal are the same, whether the agreement is in writing or is oral; however, if a broker wishes to have the right to bring a lawsuit for payment of a commission or fee for services, the agreement must be in writing. The agreement can be a simple note or memorandum that includes an agreement to compensate the broker for services performed.

FIGURE 7.2

How Agency Is Created

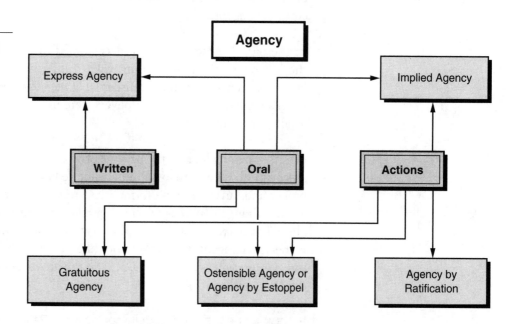

The two most common express agency agreements used by brokers in sales transactions are written listing contracts and buyer-representation contracts. Generically, these agreements are called broker employment agreements. In written listing contracts, the broker is authorized to represent a seller or a landlord in the sale or lease of that principal's property. The written buyer-tenant representation agreement employs the broker to represent the buyer or the tenant in the purchase or lease of a property. These written agency contracts are usually quite detailed. They attempt to clarify the rights and obligations of both the principal and the agent and include provisions for compensation when the agent's duties have been performed. These contracts will be discussed in detail later. Implied authority (not to be confused with implied agency) is a concept that is applicable to both express agency and implied agency (discussed in the next section). Implied authority is authority not specifically granted to the agent but necessary or customary if agents are to perform their agency duties, and it is implied by the principal's actions. Due to the varied functions required of real estate agents, it is unlikely that the entire scope of an agent's activities could be stated in an express written agreement such as a listing agreement. The agent, therefore, may also acquire certain authority to act for the principal by implied authority. For example, a listing contract may not specifically outline each and every tool that the agent may employ in marketing the property. However, when owners instruct agents to make their best efforts to sell their properties, it is implied that the agents have the authority to advertise, conduct open houses, distribute flyers, and so on. Note that this type of authority is created between the agent and the principal and does not require some third party's reliance or actions to become operational.

Implied Agency

Implied agency (not to be confused with implied authority) occurs when there is no express agreement that the broker will act as an agent for a party. The actions or words of the broker and the party may lead the party to believe that the broker is representing the party's interests. This often occurs when a licensee who is working with a buyer-customer with no intended representation makes statements or performs actions that lead the customer to believe the licensee has become the customer's agent.

In the past, licensees were not accustomed to discussing and confirming whom they represented when meeting with third parties. As a result, unrepresented buyers often assumed that licensees who were showing them properties were the buyer's representatives. Those buyers were unaware of the fact that the licensees legally represented the sellers.

Courts generally look to the actions of a broker and to the reliance by a buyer on a licensee to determine whether an implied agency relationship existed between broker and buyer. Because formalities are not required, courts may hold that an agency arrangement was implied, based on the intentions of the broker and the alleged principal, as shown by their actions and/or words. Even though a broker is the seller's agent, the broker could be held to be acting as the buyer's agent as well. Courts will ask the question, "Did the broker act under the alleged principal's direction and control?"

■ **EXAMPLE** Buyer Betty contacts Bay Realty, seeking to purchase a four-unit rental building. Here is what happens next:

1. Sally, a licensee with Bay Realty, agrees to work **with** Betty.

2. Betty signs no representation contract.

3. Sally shows 10 properties listed by her company and other real estate companies.

4. Sally negotiates unsuccessfully on two of those properties.

5. During the negotiations, Sally gives advice and opinions to Betty.

6. After the two unsuccessful attempts to negotiate a purchase, Sally tells Betty not to despair because she is sure that she can locate the "perfect property."

7. Sally continues to seek, and ultimately finds, a four-unit rental building that suits Betty's needs and qualifications.

8. Sally then obtains the listing on the four-unit building from owner Harry on behalf of Bay Realty.

9. Betty and the seller enter into a contract for the purchase of the property.

■ **QUESTIONS**

- Who was Sally's and Bay Realty's principal in actions 1 through 3?

- Was Sally Betty's principal on the first 10 properties listed by her company?

- Was Sally, and therefore Bay Realty, an intermediary or an unlawful dual agent?

- Did Betty know that Sally was not her agent regarding Bay Realty's listings?

- Did Betty think Sally was representing her on the other properties that were not Bay Realty listings?

- Was Sally a subagent of the listing brokers on the other companies' listings?

- If Sally was a subagent relative to the other brokerages, could Sally legally or ethically give advice and opinions to Betty?

- Did the other companies even offer subagency to Sally?

- Did Sally represent Betty during the negotiation on the two unsuccessful contracts?

- If so, when did her representation begin?

- Did Sally's actions imply that Sally represented Betty?

- If so, which of Sally's actions would give that impression?

- Did Sally have any knowledge about agency relationships, duties, and actions?

How many incorrect things can Sally do in one series of transactions or attempted transactions? She obviously made many missteps and mistakes and doesn't have a clear understanding of the processes involved.

Disclosure and clarification should lessen the chances of creating an implied agency. However, a licensee who behaves like a buyer's agent, even though bound to an express written agreement to represent the seller, nevertheless will be deemed an implied agent of the buyer. Licensees must be careful of their actions, **even after they disclose their agency arrangements in writing**.

Note that most licensees never disclose their agency relationship in writing to customers. Most disclose only **orally** to the customer their agency relationship to their clients and then give the customer the IABS form or its equivalent. Most licensees believe that the IABS form is the agency disclosure form. No such agency disclosure form exists, unless the individual brokerage has its own form for the purpose of disclosing whom they represent. Neither TRELA nor TREC Rules require that agency disclosure be made in writing: therefore, it usually isn't. In fact, in 1995, the industry waged a successful legislative campaign to modify TRELA so as to do away with the necessity to make the disclosure in writing. The campaign resulted in what was, in 2003, a renumbering as TRELA § 1101.558(b), which says "(b) A license holder who represents a party in a proposed real estate transaction shall **disclose, orally or in writing**, that representation at the time of the license holder's first contact with: . . ."

Any disclosure of agency must name or clearly identify the party being represented in a specific transaction, not just a general declaration of seller or buyer agency in the broad sense of a general company policy to represent a certain type client.

Agency Is Transaction Specific

Agency is always transaction specific. In each and every case, the client or principal of the agent must be clearly identified to the other party. TRELA § 1101.652(b)(7) says that it is grounds for TREC discipline if a licensee "(7) fails to make **clear to all parties** to a real estate transaction the party for whom the license holder is acting."

A broker's sign in the yard of a home being shown to a buyer may not be adequate disclosure or notice to an unsophisticated buyer that the broker represents the owner and not the buyer. When it comes to agency disclosure, take nothing for granted relative to a party's understanding of agency law and what services they can expect from you.

The conduct of the parties can result in the creation of an agency relationship, even if a written agreement asserts that no agency exists or that the parties never intended for an agency relationship to exist. The courts tend to look at the conduct or action itself, not just what the parties named or called it.

Ostensible Agency or Agency by Estoppel

The word *ostensible* means "for all appearances." In agency law, ostensible agency and agency by estoppel (when a court does not allow a principal to deny that agency existed) are based on a third party's being led to believe that a licensee was acting as an agent of another party. If the actions of a principal led reasonable persons to assume that a licensee was acting on their behalf, then ostensible agency or agency by estoppel could have occurred. In that event, a court would likely prevent the principal from denying that an agency relationship existed. In effect, if a principal allows a licensee to "walk like an agent, talk like an agent, and act like an agent," third parties will reasonably be allowed to presume that the licensee is an agent for that principal.

This concept could apply either before a formal agency agreement is created or after it expires. For example, presume that the sellers allow their "former agent" to show and advertise their property after the listing contract expires. During this period of unofficial representation, a buyer purchases the property and, after closing, discovers that the licensee has made misrepresentations regarding the property. The buyer later sues the sellers, claiming misrepresentations were made by the licensee while acting as an agent of the sellers. The sellers then claim that because the listing contract had terminated, the licensee was not the sellers' agent and the buyer cannot hold the seller liable for the misrepresentations made by the licensee. Under these circumstances, the court is likely to hold that, based on the doctrine of estoppel, the sellers cannot deny the agency relationship still existed. The sellers allowed the buyer to believe that an agency relationship continued to exist between them and the licensee, and the buyers were justified in relying on that belief.

■ **EXAMPLE**   In *Wilson v. Donze*, 692 S.W.2d 735 (Tex. Ct. App.—Fort Worth 1985), Ken Wilson, the owner of Ken/Car Investments, Inc., approached Anthony and Lena Donze in May asking if their home was for sale. The Donzes informed Wilson that they did not do business with brokers and did not pay commissions. Wilson said he would get the commission from the buyers if he could sell their home. The Donzes agreed to allow him to show the property and told him that they wanted $85,000 for the home.

On June 1, another real estate broker named Powers, acting with Wilson, wrote an offer from the Bullards for $100,000, telling the Bullards that it would probably take $115,000 to purchase the home. On June 2, Wilson presented a contract to the Donzes for $85,000, naming Ken/Car Investments, Inc., trustee or assigns, as the purchasers; the contract was accepted by the Donzes. Also on June 2, the Bullards were informed by Powers that their offer had been rejected and that it would indeed take $115,000 to purchase the property; they agreed.

The Donzes and the Bullards met only once after the contracts were signed and both assumed that the contract was between them, and not Ken/Car, even though Ken/Car Investments, Inc., trustee or assigns, was named as the purchaser on the Donzes' contract and Ken Wilson, trustee as the seller on the Bullards' contract. No one clarified to the Donzes or the Bullards that this was a pass-through transaction. Wilson believed that he had done no wrong because the Donzes received what they wanted for the sale of the property, and the Bullards were willing to pay $115,000.

The court held that Ken Wilson was a broker for the Donzes and that he breached his fiduciary duty by not obtaining the best price for them. The jury awarded $24,900 in actual damages and $35,000 in punitive damages. The court of appeals upheld the jury's decision.

■ **QUESTIONS**

1. When did Ken Wilson become an agent for the Donzes?

2. How could Ken Wilson have avoided this problem?

Agency by Ratification

Agency by ratification occurs when a principal gains some benefit from a previously unauthorized act of an agent, and the principals, on learning of the act, do not deny that the agent had authority to perform such an act on their behalf. The principals ratify the action of the agent by accepting the benefits that come from the action. Principals have an affirmative duty to reject any unauthorized acts of an agent; otherwise, the principals may be held liable for the consequences of the agent's actions. Under the ratification theory, principals are considered to have approved the agency if they accept the benefits of an agent's previously unauthorized act. This is agency after the fact. There are four elements to look for in this concept:

■ The agent performs an unauthorized act.
■ The principal subsequently learns of the act.
■ The principal does not repudiate (deny) the agent's authority to act.
■ The principal benefits from the act.

■ **EXAMPLE** Daniel, from Action Realty, tried unsuccessfully to obtain a listing on a warehouse from Harry. Daniel went to Harry one day and told him that he had a number of interested buyers, but Harry would not give him a listing. Nevertheless, Daniel showed several buyers the property. When Daniel brought an offer from a buyer, Harry accepted the offer, which contained a provision for him to pay Daniel. Harry asked Daniel to monitor the closing. Subsequently, the buyer brought a lawsuit against Harry to cancel the purchase contract because of a misrepresentation made by Daniel. Harry argued that Daniel was not his agent because he did not sign a listing agreement. A court likely would hold that Harry ratified or affirmed the agency by signing the contract of sale and asking Daniel to monitor the closing and that he is, therefore, bound by Daniel's misrepresentation.

■ **QUESTIONS** 1. What actions should Harry have taken to ensure that Daniel did not represent him? 2. What could Daniel have done to secure his position as Harry's agent?

Gratuitous Agency and Compensation

One of the most common notions of real estate agency has been frequently expressed as "You are the agent of the person who pays you", or "You work for the one who pays you." In the past, when asked to name the determining factor in creating an agency, most real estate licensees answered that it is payment of the fee. However, the payment of a commission is not the sole factor in creating an agency relationship. In fact, by contract, the seller could agree to pay all the buyer's broker's fee, just like the seller sometimes agrees to pay the loan discount points on the buyer's loan or the cost of the professional home inspection. Also, by contract, the buyer could agree to pay the brokerage fees and/or any of the seller's closing expenses. An agency relationship can exist without regard to who pays the fee: the seller, the buyer, both, or neither. Texas law, like most state agency disclosure laws, confirms the common law rule that payment of the fee does not determine agency. Remember that the IABS (which is a part of TRELA) states the following: "Your payment of a fee to a broker does not necessarily establish that the broker represents you."

The agency relationship created when the agent provides brokerage services and charges no fee is known as gratuitous agency. Thus, a gratuitous agent giving free advice, perhaps to build goodwill, could be held liable when giving the wrong advice. For example, an agent working without charge could be liable for giving legal or bad advice if the agent were asked for and gave an opinion about the buyer-client's need to obtain an inspection of the property, whether to have title insurance, or to "have the abstract covering the real estate that is the subject of the contract examined by an attorney chosen by the buyer" (TRELA § 1101.555; TRELA § 1101.652(b)(29)). If the agent's opinion were subsequently relied on and resulted in a loss to the principal, the agent could be held liable just as though a fee or commission had been charged to render the service.

Licensees are often placed in positions where they are asked their opinions regarding real estate matters. Many licensees will say that once they obtained a real estate license, they never could go to a gathering of people without someone asking their advice about real estate. While it is flattering to be asked for advice, it is also **very risky** to offer advice without being fully informed about the situation. If the advice is legal advice rather than marketing advice and the like, don't give it

Failure to advise the client in writing to have the abstract examined by an attorney of the client's choosing might subject the licensee to 1) loss of commission if the notice is not given at the time parties enter into a contract and/or 2) loss of license if the notice is not given in writing prior to closing. [TRELA § 1101.555; TRELA §1101.652(b)(29); TRELA § 1101.806(d)] TREC's One to Four Family Residential Contract (Resale) includes this notice. A licensee who doesn't use this form is still required to provide the notice and can use TREC OP-C (Notice to Prospective Buyer) for this purpose.

at all, even if the party asking is your client. This is particularly true in the arena of helping a For Sale by Owner party who says, "I only need a simple question answered."

Despite the fact that payment of the commission does not necessarily determine agency, prudent licensees should discuss and document whom they represent and who pays whom. A contract to function as an intermediary must clearly express the source of any intended compensation, or TREC will say the licensee failed to form a lawful intermediary relationship:

> TRELA § 1101.559
>
> (a) A broker may act as an intermediary between parties to a real estate transaction **if**:
>
>> (1) the broker obtains written consent from each party for the broker to act as an intermediary in the transaction; and
>>
>> (2) the written consent of the parties states the source of any expected compensation to the broker. (emphasis added)

The danger here is that if an intermediary relationship is not created properly, then what is the broker? An unlawful intermediary? A dual agent? An undisclosed dual agent? While a broker could become an accidental agent or an accidental dual agent, a broker cannot become an accidental intermediary. That relationship can be created only by following the statute exactly.

A clear disclosure can dispel any notion that the licensee represented the person who paid the broker's commission when the licensee did not represent that person. If no agency documentation exists, courts might use the commission payment as evidence of the intended agency relationship, especially if the person paying the fee is the one claiming that an agency existed. Without clear evidence to the contrary, the broker will have difficulty proving no agency existed. Note that this could apply either to a buyer who pays the commission or to a seller who pays the commission.

■ **EXAMPLE**   In *Kelly v. Roussalis*, 776 P.2d. 1016 (Wyo. 1989), John Roussalis called Gus Kelly of McNamara Realty to show him a property located on South Poplar because Gus had worked with him on several other real estate transactions. The house was listed with another firm, and the asking price was $600,000. John said that he would like to pay less and that he would need to sell his current home before purchasing another. Gus had heard that the seller was having financial problems and thought the South Poplar house might go into foreclosure. He suggested that John might be able to buy the property for less at a foreclosure sale.

Subsequently, a property in the name of the same person who owned the South Poplar property was posted for foreclosure. John asked Gus whether it was the South Poplar property that he had seen, and Gus told him that it was, without checking to verify the information.

Gus then helped John purchase the property by accompanying him to the foreclosure sale—even though Gus's company had a policy of not attending foreclosure sales. Gus bid $150,000 for John and won the final sale, obtained a check from the bank, and paid the sheriff, only to find out that the property John had been successful in buying was not the South Poplar property.

John sued Gus and McNamara Realty for negligence. Gus said he was just being a friend and not an agent. John won the suit, and Gus and McNamara Realty appealed. The state supreme court upheld the lower court's decision, saying that Gus did not exercise the care expected of real estate agents. The court also held McNamara Realty responsible for Gus's actions.

■ QUESTIONS

1. When did Gus become an agent for Roussalis?

2. How did the fact that no fee was being paid affect the outcome?

3. What steps should Gus and his broker have taken to prevent this problem?

■ IMPORTANT ISSUES

Why is it so important to determine in every case whether an agency relationship has, in fact, been created? The main reasons are legal effect, constructive or imputed notice, professional and ethical responsibility, and quality of representation.

Legal Effect

The agent stands in the shoes of the principal and carries out those duties agreed to in the agency contract. The agent speaks, listens, and acts for the principal. **This is the very essence of the word represents when used in the context of the agency relationship.**

Because the agent acts on behalf of the principal, the principal may be responsible for or bound to the agent's statements within the scope of the agency. That is, anything done to further the principal's objective to sell or purchase may be assumed to be done with the knowledge and approval of the principal. This is true whether the words or actions are fraudulent, negligent, or innocent. The statements, omissions, admissions, and misrepresentations made by the agent or the subagent may be attributed to the principal, even though the principal may be unaware of them. The reasoning behind this ruling is that principals should not be allowed to benefit from the negligent acts of their agents and subagents.

Texas contract law will not, presumably, hold principals responsible for the unauthorized acts of their agents unless they are actually aware of the acts. Likewise, there would be no liability under TRELA § 1101.805(d). There is, however, little case law to reflect how the courts interpret these changes. In any event, principals should make an informed decision regarding the agent they select for representation.

The judicial trend, however, continues to hold an agent liable in the area of negligence. Courts often base decisions on the fact that as a professional, an agent knew or should have known certain information, such as the sewer not being connected, the roof leaking, or the property's location in a flood-prone area. The listing agent's failure to discover obvious defects and disclose such defects to the buyer may be termed *negligence*. However, in Texas, the courts have found that agents who did not know of latent defects were not bound to the same extent as real estate inspectors. In fact, agents are prohibited from acting as inspectors and brokers in the same transaction. In the landmark case *Kubinsky v. Van Zandt*, the broker was found to have not known in a "should have known" situation. Some courts in the United States have held that brokers and their principals are liable for the brokers' innocent misrepresentations.

■ **EXAMPLE**   Agent Charlie lists a home in an exclusive area of town. Although near the shoreline and at a relatively low elevation, the property has never flooded. However, mortgage lenders require flood insurance when making loans in the area. Charlie finds a buyer, and the seller agrees to "owner finance" the property. Neither Charlie nor the seller advises the purchaser about the issue of possible flooding. Six months after the sale, the property floods after a torrential downpour. The new purchaser has not secured flood insurance, and the loss is devastating. Charlie claims no fault because he was not aware of the potential problem.

■ **QUESTIONS**

1. Is this something that Charlie should have known?

2. Is the seller obligated to disclose this type of information?

3. What should Charlie have done differently, if anything?

Constructive or Imputed Notice

During a real estate transaction, licensees are required to give notice to buyers and sellers regarding matters such as acceptance or rejection of offers to buy or sell, withdrawal of offers, or removal of a property from the market. Time is important in negotiations of offers, and proper notice may determine who becomes the rightful purchaser of a property—particularly when more than one offer is being negotiated and two or more contracts are formed for the same property.

It is important for everyone involved in a real estate transaction to know who is representing whom, so that when notifications are required, it may be determined when a legal notification actually occurred. In practice, licensees often find themselves involved in disputes over issues of notification to buyers and sellers, as well as to other licensees involved in the transaction.

Once the buyer and the seller have reached an agreement and all parties have signed the contract, it must be delivered to all principals, or their agents, to become enforceable. Most contracts have a number of conditions or promises that must be completed to completely perform on the contract. Frequently, there are deadlines for the delivery of inspection reports, approval of the buyer's financing, or a title commitment, et cetera.

Many licensees erroneously believe that an agent must actually tell the principal before notice is effective. In reality, the knowledge of or notice to the agent is imputed to the principal by law and deemed constructive notice, even if the information is never actually conveyed to the principal. In other words, notifying the agent is regarded as actually notifying the principal. This is called constructive or imputed notice. Some contracts, however, specifically state that notice will not be effective unless delivered in writing to a specific party in a specific manner.

The following case is somewhat complex; nevertheless, it demonstrates the importance of properly notifying each party and making sure that all parties are aware of whom each agent is representing.

■ **EXAMPLE** In *Stortroen v. Beneficial Finance Company*, 736 P.2d 391 (Colo. 1987), Beneficial Finance entered into a listing agreement with Olthoff Realty Company to sell a property it owned. Olthoff placed the property in the local multiple listing service (MLS). Mary Panio, an associate with Foremost Realty, saw the listing in the MLS and subsequently showed the home to the Stortroens, who had expressed an interest in selling their home and purchasing a larger one. After touring the home, the Stortroens asked Mary to prepare and present an offer for $105,000 to the seller. Because the Stortroens needed to sell their current home before buying another one, they made the offer contingent on selling and closing the sale of their present home. The contingency also stated that Beneficial would keep the home on the market and give the Stortroens 72 hours to remove the contingency on notification that Beneficial Finance had received another acceptable offer.

Beneficial's representative, Donald Reh, reviewed the contract and instructed Olthoff to increase the sales price to $110,000 and to state in the counteroffer that acceptance by the buyer would be "evidenced by the Purchaser's signature hereon; and if seller receives notice of such acceptance on or before 9 pm 2-3-84."

While the offer from the Stortroens was being negotiated, the Carellis also toured the home and submitted an offer for $112,000 on Friday, February 3, 1984, through their agent. Olthoff informed Beneficial's Reh of the second offer and was told by him to have the Carellis' agent bring the offer directly to him. Reh reviewed the contract and told Olthoff to withdraw the counteroffer to the Stortroens and accept the offer from the Carellis.

Olthoff tried contacting Mary Panio but was unable to speak to her personally, so he left messages at her office and her home informing her that the counteroffer with Beneficial had been withdrawn. Olthoff told Reh about the messages to Panio, whereupon Reh signed the offer from the Carellis.

Before she received the messages from Olthoff, Mary Panio presented the counteroffer to the Stortroens. The Stortroens agreed to the terms of the counteroffer and signed it at about 4:10 pm on Friday, February 3. On returning to her office with the signed counteroffer, Mary received the messages from Olthoff.

On Saturday, February 4, Mary Panio obtained a withdrawal of the contingency from the Stortroens. On Monday, February 6, Mary delivered the signed offer and the withdrawal of the contingency to Olthoff. Subsequently, the Stortroens filed their contract into record at the county clerk's office—thereby placing a cloud on the title to Beneficial's property.

The Carellis moved into the home on a month-to-month lease because they didn't want to close on the property while there was a cloud on the title. The Stortroens brought suit against Beneficial for specific performance of the contract and against the Carellis to vacate the premises. The Carellis brought suit against Beneficial and a complaint against Olthoff.

The district court found in favor of Beneficial and against the Stortroens, saying that Mary Panio was acting as a representative of the buyer. Thus, when the counteroffer and the contingency were signed by the Stortroens and given to Panio, this was not considered to be notification of acceptance to Beneficial.

The state supreme court was asked to render a decision regarding whom Mary Panio was representing. They found that she was representing Beneficial Finance through the agreement of subagency (working with the buyer but representing the seller) offered through the MLS. Therefore, when the counteroffer from Beneficial was accepted and signed by the Stortroens in the presence of Mary, constructive notice to Beneficial had been officially made. This decision made the Stortroens the prevailing party.

This case illustrates how licensees can run into enormous problems when notification is required. Even more importantly, it demonstrates the widespread ignorance of agency law and who works for whom. Technically, once all parties have signed the offer, absent any other legal impediments, the offer becomes an enforceable contract, but only when all parties or their agents have received notification (either actual or constructive notice).

If Mary Panio had been representing the buyers—not the seller through a subagency agreement—notice would have been considered effective at the time she delivered it to Olthoff Realty. No doubt the lawyers for Beneficial were otherwise competent lawyers; however they (like others in the transaction and the public at large) did not have an adequate grasp of subagency as an accepted practice in real estate at the time, nor its impact on contract formation.

Imputed Knowledge

In addition to imputed notice, both agents and clients should be familiar with the related legal concept of imputed knowledge. Although this term is sometimes considered the equivalent of imputed notice, it is more specific to information or facts known by the agent but not actually delivered or relayed to the client. In such cases, it may be deemed that such knowledge has been imputed, or constructively delivered to the client.

Thus, clients are considered to have the same information or knowledge that their agent has regarding a property or transaction. Because the agent has a duty to convey such information to the client, it is generally held that this has, in fact, occurred. Additionally, other parties involved in the transaction may presume that the principal has been (or should have been) made aware of this information or knowledge.

For example, a listing agent who tells the buyer's agent about a major drug raid on the property next door the previous evening has given notice of a material fact to the buyer through the buyer's agent. Once agency is established, it is the fiduciary duty of the agent to communicate material information to the client (TRELA § 1101.557(b)(2)).

On the other side of agency representation, consider this scenario: A buyer's broker delivers her buyer's inspection report for the property under contract to the listing agent in the listing agent's office. The listing agent refuses to touch it or acknowledge receipt. The buyer's agent politely drops the envelope containing the report on the receptionist's desk and leaves. Does the seller now have notice of the information in the envelope? Yes.

Consider this: The brokerage is engaged in an intermediary transaction. The buyer hands the inspection report to the licensee appointed by the intermediary broker to work with the buyer. Does the seller now have notice or knowledge—imputed, constructive, or otherwise—of the contents of the envelope? Seek legal counsel for an answer.

In another intermediary transaction, the licensee appointed to the seller knows the roof leaks. Is that knowledge imputed to the licensee appointed to the buyer? To the intermediary broker? To the buyer? Seek legal counsel for advice.

Professional and Ethical Responsibility

Real estate licensees acting as agents owe general duties of good faith, fairness, and honesty to all with whom they deal. But when acting as agents and subagents, licensees owe a far greater degree of care and loyalty to a principal than they do to a third person. In general, a customer is entitled to honesty, fairness, accurate information, and material facts concerning a property. A client is entitled to accurate information, opinions, and advice about the significance of facts and information, the available alternative courses of action, and the agent's recommendations. The best interests of the client must be kept in mind at all times.

■ HOW AGENCY IS TERMINATED

Except in the case of an agency coupled with a broker's interest in the transaction (partial ownership), an agency relationship may be terminated at any time for any of the following reasons:

- Lapse of the time specified in the agreement
- Lapse of a reasonable time if no time is specified
- Completion of the purpose of the agency
- Mutual rescission
- Revocation by the principal
- Agent's renunciation
- Abandonment of the agreement by the agent
- Incapacity or death of either the agent or the principal
- Bankruptcy of the owner if title is transferred to the receiver
- Condemnation or destruction of the premises
- Agent's breach of duties to the principal

Lapse of Time

The Real Estate License Act (TRELA) does not specifically address the length of time appropriate for listing or buyer-tenant agency contracts. It does, however, state that an agent may not enter into these contracts without a definite termination or expiration date that requires no action on the part of the principal (there are exceptions for certain types of property management contracts). Likewise, a contract may not automatically renew itself into perpetuity (forever). Failure to provide for a definite termination date may be grounds for revocation or suspension of the agent's real estate license (§ 1101.652(b)(12)).

Although TRELA does not limit the term of these agency agreements, it is inherent in agency law that such agreements must be for reasonable periods. In practice, the length of the listing and the buyer representation contracts are negotiated between the broker and the principal. Typically, these negotiations depend on the type of property, market conditions, and motivation of the sellers or the buyers.

Actions of Principals and Agents

The actions of a principal or agent may terminate the agency in a variety of ways. These include

- accomplishment of the agency objective,
- expiration of agency agreement,
- rescission,
- revocation,
- renunciation,
- abandonment by the agent, and
- breach of the agent's duty to the principal.

Accomplishment of the Agency Objective The agency agreement was entered into for a specific purpose. When that purpose has been accomplished, the agency terminates. The house is sold for the seller, or the prospective buyer-client purchases a property. Neither the agent nor the principal needs to take any action for the agency to end.

Expiration of the Agency Agreement Other than accomplishment of the agency objective, perhaps the most common form of agency termination occurs when the property remains unsold throughout the term of the listing agreement between the broker and the seller. This is frequently called an expired listing. Once the listing has expired, the seller may be approached by other brokerage firms and relist the property with a different broker. Typically, the broker and the seller are free of their obligations to each other under the terms of the listing agreement. Continuing obligations of the seller may include buyers who were shown the property during the listing period by the broker and registered under a protection clause, if included in the listing contract. During a protection period, if a protected buyer attempts to purchase directly from the seller after the listing expires, the seller would still be obligated to pay the broker a commission. The broker should also be aware that certain fiduciary duties may still be owed the seller after the expiration of the listing. Of primary concern would be the duty of confidentiality, which would require that all information of a confidential nature learned while acting as the agent of the seller remain confidential even after the listing terminates.

Rescission by the Parties Because these agency agreements are created by mutual consent, they may be terminated in the same way. The parties can jointly decide to rescind the agreement at any time. A seller could reasonably anticipate that the listing broker will agree to mutual rescission if the seller decides not to sell the property for whatever reason. Perhaps a job transfer fell through, family status changed, or the market value dropped below the seller's loan balance. Regardless, neither party would be held in default because of the mutual agreement to rescind.

Revocation by the Principal   The agency relationship is highly personal and requires the continuing consent of the principal and the agent. Thus a principal may unilaterally, at any time, revoke the authority of the agent to represent them. Such revocation may of course create liability to the principal for any financial damages suffered by the broker. For example, if a seller revokes the broker's agency after the broker has incurred substantial expenses relating to the marketing of the property, the broker may be entitled to recovery. Likewise, although the broker has no further authority to represent the seller, should the seller sell the property within the term of the listing contract period, the seller may owe the broker a commission, depending on the terms of the original listing contract. Keep in mind, however, that in order to receive damages, the broker would be required to sue the seller and hope the court sees the broker's case favorably. Many brokers have found such suits to be impractical at best.

Regardless, the contractual agreement between the principal and the agent traditionally distinguishes between the granting of authority to act as the principal's agent, and the how, when, where, and by whom the agent will be compensated. So continuing to offer a property for sale after revocation of agency by the principal, for example, would be cause for suspension or revocation of a licensee (§ 1101.652 (b)(18)–(20)). A listing agent should therefore immediately cease all advertising, remove For Sale/For Lease signs from the property, remove the listing from the multiple listing service (MLS), and remove all information from internet postings. The listing broker may then begin to deal with the matter of compensation as a separate contractual issue.

Renunciation by the Broker   A broker might unilaterally choose to discontinue representation of a seller during the term of a listing or a buyer representation contract. Again, agency is highly personal and consensual. The client cannot force an agent to continue providing agency duties once the agent has renounced. An excellent example would be a broker who renounces the relationship after the seller-client insists the broker not disclose a material property defect. Although the licensee has the duty of confidentiality to the client, that duty does not apply if the client is demanding that the licensee violate a legal responsibility.

Of course, a seller or a buyer who is damaged by such action of the broker may be able to seek damages against the broker. An example might include a broker who charges the sellers an up-front nonrefundable fee and later decides to renounce the listing before the end of the agreement. As a result, the sellers may believe that they were damaged by at least the amount of the nonrefundable fee. As with revocation by the principal, the issue of compensation is contractually separate from that of agency.

Abandonment by the Broker   Although a rare claim, a buyer or a seller may terminate the agency agreement if the broker takes no action to accomplish the agency objective. Examples may include a broker who is never available to show properties to a buyer represented by the broker; a broker who, having listed a property for a sale, makes no marketing effort to sell the property; or a listing associate who fails to return phone calls from a buyer's agent seeking delivery of an offer from the buyer. Remember, a broker who agrees to represent a party has accepted responsibility to provide statutorily defined minimum services to the client, including relaying material information, answering questions, and negotiating on the client's behalf (§ 1101.557(b)). Under the rules defining broker responsibility, a broker must "promptly respond to sponsored salespersons, clients, and licensees representing other parties in real estate transactions" (22 TAC § 535.2(j)). In such cases, the principals may terminate the agency because of ostensible abandonment by the broker.

Breach of the Agent's Duty to the Principal   This circumstance is related to the above example. When an agent breaches any duty to the principal, the principal may terminate the agency without recourse from the broker. Such a breach, particularly when associated with a fiduciary duty, may also expose the broker to legal liability, in addition to the termination of the agency agreement. There are virtually no restrictions relating to a seller's right to revoke due to breaches of fiduciary duties by the broker.

Operation of Law

In addition to acts of the parties to the agency relationship, certain circumstances, such as death of a principal, incapacity, supervening law, bankruptcy, or loss or destruction of the property, will cause the agency to terminate by law.

Death of the Agent or Principal   Unless the agent has an ownership or contractual interest in the property (known as agency coupled with an interest), death of the agent or principal will terminate the agency relationship. In the event of the death of a broker, all the listings held by the broker will terminate, as well as cause all the licenses of the broker's associates to become inactive. The sellers must find another broker with whom to list their properties, and the associates must secure another sponsoring broker before continuing their brokerage activities. In the event of the death of the principal, the listing agreement will terminate and the property would be subject to probate under the terms of the will or the administration of the estate by the courts in the event of an intestate death (no valid will).

Incapacity of the Agent or Principal   Unless operating under a durable power of attorney, the incapacity of the broker or the principal will also terminate the agency agreement. The term incapacity refers to an individual's lack of mental or physical capabilities, which would preclude certain legal consequences to attach to the person's actions. For example, an individual in a coma or diagnosed with Alzheimer's has incapacity to make a binding contract. The circumstances and resolutions under the insanity provisions apply in essentially the same way as described under the death provisions.

Supervening Law   Occasionally, a change in the law can result in the termination of an agency agreement. This occurs when the agency involves an activity that was legal when the agreement was entered into, but due to change of law, the activity later becomes illegal; the agency will terminate. Presume that a broker has a contract to manage a building providing adult-oriented entertainment and later a city ordinance makes the activity illegal. In this case, the management contract will terminate, provided the contract was tied to the management of the adult-oriented business.

Bankruptcy, Loss, or Destruction of Property Other reasons of termination by law include bankruptcy of the principal that results in the property being taken into receivership, the property being taken by the government through condemnation, or the physical destruction of the property.

DUTIES OF AGENCY THAT SURVIVE TERMINATION

Even though the agency relationship may have terminated by

- lapse of a reasonable time or by a contractual termination date;
- actions of the parties such as mutual rescission, breach of contract or breach of fiduciary duties; or
- operation of law, such as death or incapacity of one of the parties, bankruptcy of the principal, destruction of the property that is the subject of the agency, or impossibility of performance;

the duty of confidentiality of information remains after the termination of the agreement. The licensee acting as an agent is prohibited from disclosing confidential information gained during the course of the agency contract, even after the agency contract is terminated. As with almost all general legal principles, there are some exceptions to this widely accepted rule. TRELA § 1101.651(d)(3)(A),(B)&(C) provides the three exceptions under the Act:

> (d) A broker and any broker or salesperson appointed under Section 1101.560 who acts as an intermediary under Subchapter **L may not**:
>
> (3) **disclose** any confidential information or any information a party specifically instructs the broker or salesperson in writing not to disclose, **unless**:
>
> (A) the broker or salesperson is otherwise instructed **in a separate writing** by the respective party;
>
> (B) the broker or salesperson is required to disclose the information by this chapter or a court order; or
>
> (C) the information materially relates to the condition of the property; (emphasis added)

TREC's MCE *Broker Responsibility Manual* states the following on page 26:

> **Privacy of Personal Information**
>
> Confidentiality of information while performing as a fiduciary does not have a termination date unless this duty is released in writing, such as in a conventional listing or buyer representation agreement.

Frequently, an agent who has listed and/or sold a property for a seller subsequently is asked to show that seller other property to purchase. Whether or not the agent has a formal agency agreement with the former client, the agent cannot disclose any information gained during the previous relationship with the former client without that client's authorization.

■ **EXAMPLE** Christian, from Executive Realty, became the agent for Judy when he listed and sold one of Judy's investment homes. Three weeks after closing, Judy asks Christian to show her possible replacement properties. She does not ask to be represented by Christian. He knows that Judy has $30,000 from the sale of her other property to invest in new properties. He also knows that for personal reasons, Judy must invest this money quickly. Christian shows Judy one of his listings—one that he believes she will consider an excellent investment. She tours the property and proceeds to write an offer that is substantially below the list price.

■ QUESTIONS

1. Is Judy still Christian's client?

2. How much information is Christian allowed to give the seller about Judy?

3. Will Christian have to disclose his former agency relationship with Judy to the seller?

4. Should Christian have attempted to get a buyer representation agreement with Judy for Executive Realty before showing her any properties?

5. Should that agreement have contained the right to act as an intermediary?

6. Did Christian's listing agreements on Executive Realty's listings contain the right to be an intermediary?

7. If Executive Realty (Christian) acts as an intermediary, will either the seller-client or Judy have real representation and advocacy?

8. If Executive Realty makes appointments, should Christian be appointed to the seller or to Judy?

9. Would it matter?

10. If no appoints were made, how would that restrict Christian's ability to give advice or opinions to either party?

11. What if Christian didn't show Judy one of the company's listings that was actually better for Judy but was listed by another agent in the office?

12. If Judy bought the listing listed by the other associate, what would happen to the amount of Christian's commission?

13. Can you think of any other problems that could arise in this scenario?

An additional after-termination issue that is not often considered is the remaining duty to account. Any documents, escrow funds, et cetera that are still in possession of the agent are required to be returned to the client. After closing, listing agents and buyer agents may have documents that belong to their clients that were used for some purpose during the transaction. All of these documents, if any, should be returned to the former client immediately upon termination of the agency relationship.

Agents of parties should not continue to act as agents toward their former clients after closing. Doing so may establish a whole new agency relationship by implication and resurrect all the former fiduciary duties. Seek legal counsel about your conduct toward former clients to be sure that you have not recreated a whole new agency relationship unintentionally.

BEWARE! After closing, a buyer/customer or buyer/client will frequently call one of the agents complaining of problems with a seller not doing some of the things the seller promised to do. Or, the buyer might be complaining about misrepresentations made by the seller that they are just now finding out about after moving in. Here are some examples:

- "We had a Seller's Temporary Residential Lease, and the seller's time is up and he won't leave the property!"
- "The seller did repair the roof, but it still leaks!"
- "I just received a water bill for the month before closing. I need your seller to pay it."
- "The seller lied on the Seller's Disclosure Statement. The foundation is cracked. I want him to pay for repair."
- "We gave the buyer a Buyer's Temporary Residential Lease. He moved in two weeks before closing. The closing date was yesterday. His financing wasn't approved, and he won't close and he won't move out."

If these things happen to you and the issue does not involve a mistake, opinion, advice, or misrepresentation on your part, you should consider telling the buyer that you are not an attorney and that they should call their own legal counsel. This is true whether you were the buyer's agent or the seller's agent. Contact your broker first and see what risks he is willing to take when performing acts that could cause the creation of a new agency relationship.

■ SUMMARY

Real estate licensees need to be aware of the variety of positions relative to agency that a broker can have in a real estate transaction. Because no formalities are required to create an agency relationship, one can be found to exist even when none was intended. The existence of an agency relationship can have a significant impact on issues of liability, notice, responsibility, quality of representation, and even whether or offer has become a contract. By becoming more aware of agency issues, the real estate licensee can better define and control agency relationships, thus ensuring that working relationships intentionally created are the most effective and successful while better reducing the possibility of risk.

Subsequent chapters examine in depth each agency alternative. Brokers have to evaluate which alternative is best. Today, companies must consider many factors in developing their agency policies. One thing is certain: no perfect solution exists.

■ KEY POINTS

- The payment of a fee does not necessarily determine agency, but it could determine agency in court, if no other evidence was produced as to whose agent a licensee represented.
- An agency can be created expressly, by implication, by estoppel, or by ratification, with or without a written agreement.
- Any form of agency, without a written agreement for compensation, can result in a gratuitous agency.

- Regardless of how or when the agency relation is created, a broker who represents a party is a fiduciary (22 TAC § 531.1). (However, fiduciary duties are truncated in an intermediary situation.)
- Agency may be terminated by mutual agreement (rescission), unilaterally (renunciation or revocation), by expiration of time, by abandonment by the agent, or by operation of law.
- A customer is entitled to honesty, fair treatment, accurate information, and disclosure of material facts; a client is entitled to accurate information, fiduciary duties, opinions, and advice.
- In establishing liability and responsibility, courts look at not only the documents creating agency but also the acts of the agent and the parties.
- The duty of confidentiality continues after the termination of an agency (with some exceptions).

■ SUGGESTIONS FOR BROKERS

Develop a company policy covering which agency alternative the company prefers, which services the broker or sales and broker associates may extend to customers, and which services they must or must not provide to clients. It should be policy that any variations must be reported to the managing broker, as when a salesperson in a seller-agency-oriented firm attempts to represent a buyer in locating a property.

CHAPTER 7 QUIZ

1. Which is required to create an agency relationship?
   a. Compensation
   b. A contract
   c. A real estate license
   d. A belief that the relationship exists

2. Express agency
   a. is created by the principal's actions.
   b. is always in writing.
   c. can be an oral agreement.
   d. is ambiguous.

3. Implied authority is
   a. specifically given in a listing contract.
   b. not specifically given to an agent.
   c. the same as implied agency.
   d. a part of every contract.

4. Agency based on a third party's being led to believe that a licensee was acting as an agent of another party is
   a. express agency.
   b. implied agency.
   c. ostensible agency.
   d. agency by ratification.

5. Which statement is FALSE?
   a. A licensee who is not compensated for services is not liable.
   b. The broker and a consumer must enter into a written agreement to establish an agency relationship.
   c. The buyer must be personally notified of a property defect or the seller is liable for failure to disclose.
   d. All of these are false statements.

6. Which statement is TRUE regarding termination of agency for time?
   a. Unlike seller agency, a contract for buyer agency does not require a definite termination date.
   b. TRELA mandates a maximum of 180 days for residential listings.
   c. A contract for seller or buyer agency may not automatically renew itself into perpetuity.
   d. All property management contracts require a definite termination date.

7. You entered into an agency agreement with and successfully found a home for a buyer who purchases and closes on the purchase. To terminate the agency, you
   a. need take no action.
   b. must wait until closing.
   c. must notify the buyer in writing.
   d. must notify the seller in writing.

8. Which statement is TRUE regarding the determination of whom the broker represents?
   a. Whoever pays the commission is the principal.
   b. The principal must sign a written agreement for an agency to exist.
   c. It is important to decide whether the buyer or the seller is the broker's principal because the broker will owe the principal a higher standard of care and more extensive duties.
   d. The broker must be paid a commission for an agency to exist.

9. Notice to an agent that is considered notice to the principal is known as
   a. ostensible notice.
   b. constructive notice.
   c. implied notice.
   d. unintended notice.

10. Duties that continue after the termination of agency include the duty
    a. to continue to present offers to the seller.
    b. to continue to advertise the property.
    c. not to disclose confidential information.
    d. to offer advice and opinions.

DISCUSSION QUESTIONS

1. What two essential elements are necessary to create an agency relationship?

2. Compare and contrast implied and express agency.

3. When is gratuitous agency most likely to occur?

CHAPTER

8

Clarifying Agency Relationships

Most real estate licensees operate on the basis of high ethical standards that require fairness and honesty to customers and clients. Disclosure of their agency relationship to the buyer or the seller in a real estate transaction has been required for decades. No consensus exists among real estate professionals on the best way to discuss and document agency relationships. Texas agency disclosure laws apply to commercial licensees as well as to residential licensees and to leases as well as to sales.

In many transactions, at least one person has the wrong impression of who represents whom. While there are no easy solutions, licensees can—and must—take steps to eliminate any confusion. The purpose of this chapter is to help licensees develop workable strategies to reduce complaints and avoid possible lawsuits while at the same time enhancing their professional reputation.

■ **LEARNING OBJECTIVES** *This chapter addresses the following:*

- Disclosure Policy
  — Decide
  — Disclose
  — Document
  — Do as You Say
- Understanding and Developing a Company Policy
  — Rules and Laws Requiring Written Policy and Procedures Documentation
  — Areas to Consider for a Policies and Procedures Manual
  — Creating a Policies and Procedures Manual

■ DISCLOSURE POLICY

Much of the present confusion over agency relationships would be eliminated if licensees would

- decide in each particular transaction whether to represent the buyer or the seller, and whether intermediary brokerage is anticipated;
- disclose to the buyer or the seller whom they represent once an agency relationship is established;
- document the disclosure with an adequate and timely written confirmation; and
- do as they had declared, acting consistently with the disclosed decision.

Decide

Each transaction is different. A licensee must be prepared to decide in each transaction whom to represent and what the licensee's relationship will be to other participants. However, the licensee must take care not to proceed until a clearly defined relationship has been established. Agency is always a consensual relationship, which requires that buyers or sellers request that a broker act on their behalf with third parties in the business transaction. Additionally, it requires that the broker consent to act before an agency relationship exists. It is critical that the broker or broker associate not begin to take any actions of representation for a buyer or a seller before clearly establishing an agency relationship. A broker may decide whom to represent but must get the party's informed (and preferably written) consent to that representation.

Generally, unless the broker has no licensees functioning under the broker license, the first agency relationship that exists is the one between the broker and the salesperson who is sponsored by the broker. The broker is the principal, and the salesperson/sales associate is the agent to the broker. This relationship begins when the broker consents to sponsor the salesperson. TREC records will be maintained on both the broker and the salesperson. As long as the broker holds the sales associate's license, the agency relationship exists.

The broker is the one who establishes the forms of agency that the brokerage will consent to, and the sales associates are bound to conduct themselves exactly as the broker has described. Depending on the broker's agency policies and the transaction circumstance, the broker or broker associate may be representing only the seller, only the buyer, both the seller and the buyer, or possibly neither. The key for all brokers and their associates is to understand fully the implications and obligations of each of the wide variety of situations that may develop. Before deciding on the appropriate working relationship, the broker must define what role to play in each transaction. For example, a broker may handle new property sales differently from re-sales, commercial property differently from residential property, and first-time buyers differently from sophisticated buyers.

In any single transaction or in any relationship with a particular individual in multiple transactions, the real estate licensee can choose from the following basic working relationships:

- Agent only for buyers (exclusive buyer agency)
- Agent only for sellers (exclusive seller agency)
- Agent for **either** seller (or landlord) or buyer (or tenant), but not both in the same transaction (nonexclusive single agency)
- Intermediary broker between both buyer and seller, with the possibility of appointed licensees to each party
- Subagent for **either** buyer or seller (an agent who is working through another broker)
- Agent for neither buyer or seller (non-agency)

Some relevant questions from the listing broker's perspective include the following:

- Is the listing salesperson the only licensee from the firm who is involved in the transaction, or is this an in-house sale of another salesperson's listing or one from a branch office of the firm?
- If a licensee from another firm presents an offer, is that licensee a subagent of the seller or an agent of the buyer?
- Does the listing agent have any prior or current relationship with the buyer, such as having listed the buyer's home, having acted as the property manager on one of the buyer's rental properties, or having agreed to act as the buyer's agent in future transactions?
- Is the licensee working with a buyer who is only a customer, not a client?
- Is the agent acquiring or disposing of her own property or the property of her spouse, parent, or child? A business entity in which the agent is more than a 10% owner?

Following are some relevant questions from the perspective of a licensee from another firm:

- Is this a multiple listing service (MLS) sale?
- Is subagency being offered to other licensees?
- Is there a prior or present business relationship with the buyer? (This would be the case if, for example, the other licensee had listed the buyer's two-bedroom home and helped the buyer submit an offer on a three-bedroom home that is contingent on the sale of the buyer's two-bedroom home.)

When conducting a real estate transaction, it is critical to analyze all words and actions of the broker and sales associate. As the transaction proceeds, a broker or the broker's salesperson must be certain that the position of advocacy for the client is supported by words and actions. For example, a broker and the broker's sales associate are representing a seller and say to a prospective buyer (without the permission of the seller-client), "I know that the seller has an urgent need to sell his home. If you offer $180,000 instead of the full $200,000 list price, I know the seller will jump at the chance to sell." The broker and the sales associate have violated their fiduciary duties to the seller. The sales associate may not have meant to do so and may have even thought he was doing the seller a favor by getting the property sold quickly. But it was a violation nevertheless. When in doubt about what to say and how to act relative to agency duties and relationships, ask these questions:

- Who is our client, and what services must we perform?
- Who is our customer, and what services can we perform?
- If the transaction involves intermediary brokerage, are there appointed associates, and what services can and cannot be performed for each party?

Disclose

It is not enough for the broker to decide whom to represent. Real estate agents must discuss with prospective sellers and buyers (or landlords and tenants) all proposed agency relationships so that the principals can make informed choices. Agency is a consensual relationship, and to expressly create that relationship requires a delegation of authority by the principal and consent by the agent. Agency created ostensibly or by implication leaves one or more parties uncertain as to whether or not an agency relationship even exists. It is equally important for buyer and seller to know who will not be their agent. Buyers and sellers expressly alerted to the fact that an agent does not represent them will recognize that they must take greater responsibility throughout a transaction to protect their own interests. Timing of disclosure is therefore critical, and disclosure should occur before anyone can claim that an agency relationship already has been formed. If disclosure is delayed until closing or even until an offer is prepared, it is too late. Expectations of agency probably already have been created, and actions have been taken and confidences made in reliance on those expectations. For example, a buyer who presumes she is represented by the licensee has the expectation throughout the relationship that she is receiving advice and opinion from that licensee regarding a negotiating strategy that protects the buyer's financial interest. TRELA therefore requires the licensee to provide the written Information About Brokerage Services at the first substantive dialogue about a specific property. In addition, the licensee must orally or in writing declare which party the licensee represents at the time of the licensee's first contact with another party to the transaction or another licensee who represents another party to the transaction:

> TRELA § 1101.558(b) outlines the specific duties of licensees to disclose their agency relationships. (See TRELA Appendix A.) TRELA also requires that certain written information be given to prospective buyers, sellers, tenants, and landlords regarding the roles that a broker may assume in a transaction. Specifically § 1101.557(a) and 1101.558(b) read as follows:

> § 1101.557(a) A broker who represents a party in a real estate transaction or who lists real estate for sale under an exclusive agreement for a party is that party's agent.

§ 1101.558(b) A license holder who represents a party in a proposed real estate transaction shall disclose, orally or in writing, that representation at the time of the license holder's first contact with:

(1) another party to the transaction; or

(2) another license holder who represents another party to the transaction.

In addition to the specific requirements for agency disclosure, § 1101.558(d) requires that the licensee furnish prospective parties to a transaction a written information statement regarding the roles that the broker might be taking in the transaction. This statement must be given at the first meeting at which substantive discussion occurs regarding real property.

A substantive dialogue can occur at a face-to-face meeting or by written communication (including email) that involves a discussion relating to a specific real property. If the substantive dialogue occurs at other than a face-to-face meeting, the required written statement should be sent to the party promptly. The written statement may be produced in any format desired by the broker so long as the language is unchanged and the print is no smaller than 10-point type.

The Texas Real Estate Commission (TREC) has produced Information About Brokerage Services, a form that may be used by licensees. This form meets the statutory requirement and is shown as Figure 2.2. (Note: § 1101.558(e) allows the words tenant and *landlord* to be substituted for *buyer* and *seller*.) Many licensees mistakenly think the information statement is also a disclosure of their agency status. However, this form is not a disclosure of the broker's agency relationship with anyone. By giving the form to the buyer or the seller and, having the form signed and dated by the buyer or the seller, the broker or sales associate now has proof that the form and notification to consumers of their business choices was given, as well as evidence of the date it was given.

Consumers must then choose the level of service they desire in the transaction. However, the statute requires both the written information statement and a disclosure of any agency relationships. The agency disclosure is a separate duty; it can be either oral or written. Clearly, the careful broker will make sure the agency disclosure is written and acknowledged by the parties involved, even though Texas law does not require that agency disclosure be in writing.

TRELA § 1101.558 (c) grants certain exceptions to providing the written information about brokerage services. Exceptions occur when

- the proposed transaction is for a residential lease for not more than one year and no sale is being considered;
- the licensee meets with a party who is represented by another licensee (for example, a seller who has listed a property with another firm, but happens to be home when the buyer's agent arrives to show the listing);
- there is no substantive discussion regarding a specific property (for example, a consumer is simply inquiring about market conditions);
- the meeting occurs at an open house; or
- the meeting occurs after the parties have entered into a contract to sell, buy, or lease (for example, the seller has contracted to sell the property and

happens to be home when the buyer's agent arrives to open the house for the inspector).

Although these are the guidelines provided by TRELA, licensees may be wise to present the form early in the meeting. For example, a buyer who comes into the office to inquire about market conditions is most probably considering a future purchase. Although the conversation does not immediately turn to specific properties, the wise policy would be to present the TREC Information About Brokerage Services form (see Figure 2.2) as early as possible in the discussion. It is sometimes difficult to determine just when a conversation turns to more substantive matters that require the presentation of the written disclosure. Disclosure of information about agency relationships in general and whom the licensee currently represents, if anyone, relative to the contemplated transaction must also take place according to Texas law as described. In addition, when attempting to secure a listing, the seller and the licensee should discuss

- whether the property is to be listed in the MLS;
- whether the prospective listing broker intends to operate as an intermediary, with buyers produced from the broker's client pool;
- who will have access to listing information;
- whether other licensees will be authorized to cooperate in the search for buyers;
- whether other licensees will be subagents of the seller's or buyers' agents; and
- whether the listing broker intends to share fees with subagents or with buyers' agents.

These matters should be clearly stated in a written listing contract between the broker and the seller.

Timing of Agency Disclosure   When working with buyers or tenants, the timing of the agency disclosure is frequently a problem. Disclosure is especially difficult with respect to a first-time buyer who has no clue as to the distinction between client–level and customer-level services. The first-time buyer may have walked into the broker's office in response to a general advertisement or may have met the listing licensee at an open house where the Information About Brokerages Services form was not provided. No one seriously contends that the listing licensee should stop buyers after a friendly handshake and immediately present them with the written statutory information statement or make an agency disclosure. Normally, the prospect has a decision to make: do they or do they not desire representation? The written statutory disclosure helps the consumer make that decision. A suggestion to help that decision process would be to develop a personalized disclosure brochure that includes the statutory language required by TRELA § 1101.558 and outlines the types of working relationships your firm offers to buyers and sellers. The broker could also outline some of the customer-level services the brokerage can provide to one person while remaining the exclusive agent of the other person (see Figure 8.1).

FIGURE 8.1

Comparison of Consumer Services

With Representation (Client)	Consumer Services ↓	Without Representation (Customer)
☑	**Accountability**	☑
☑	**Disclose Material Facts**	☑
☑	**Fairness**	☑
☑	**Honesty**	☑
☑	**Act Under <u>YOUR</u> Instructions**	
☑	**Confidentiality**	
☑	**Full Disclosure**	
☑	**Help Negotiate**	
☑	**Objective Evaluation**	
☑	**Opinions and Advice**	
☑	**Price Counseling**	

Texas law, however, is quite specific and requires that a licensee who already represents a party in a proposed real estate transaction must disclose that representation at the time of the licensee's first contact with (1) another party to the transaction or (2) another licensee who represents another party to the transaction. The penalty for failure to expressly (oral or written) disclose the already established agency role under TRELA § 1101.652(b)(7) and (8) is that

> (b) the commission may suspend or revoke a license issued under this chapter or take other disciplinary action authorized by this chapter if the license holder, while acting as a broker or salesperson: . . .
>
> > (7) fails to make clear to all parties to a real estate transaction the party for whom the license holder is acting;
> >
> > (8) receives compensation from more than one party to a real estate transaction without the full knowledge and consent of all parties to the transaction.

Again, the disclosures of agency status required here may be made orally or in writing. Licensees should be cautioned that they must comply with both provisions. While § 1101.558 requires only that a licensee who already represents a party in a proposed transaction disclose that fact, § 1101.652(b)(7) requires a licensee "to make clear to all parties to a real estate transaction the party for whom the license holder is acting." The clear implication that can be drawn from that wording is that a licensee who does not represent any party in a transaction should disclose that fact as well (e.g., licensees buying or selling a property for their own account and representing only themselves; or licensees simply referring a consumer to another office but anticipating a referral fee). Otherwise, it could easily be assumed by one of the parties that the licensee represents that party or, conversely, represents the other party.

The licensee must be sensitive to the problems created if the buyer is led to reveal confidential bargaining and financial information to the licensee, who, it turns out, actually represents the seller. Because the licensee is then obligated to relay such information to the seller, the seller receives an unfair advantage over the buyer. The uninformed buyer could, for example, suddenly shift a conversation from a general advertisement or market conditions to inquiries about a specific property the office has already listed, all in the same sentence as indicating they have limited funds, will need serious assistance from the seller on closing costs, are desperate to close in 30 days, and, by the way, they have just been released from prison after serving a sentence for embezzlement! This is a buyer who seriously needs the fiduciary duty of confidentiality a buyer's agent can, and must, offer.

In practice, the real estate licensee may not, at first meeting, know whether to work with the buyer on a client or a customer basis. The first meeting might cover only general business practices, commission structures, and market area specialty, and might be designed to convince the buyer to work with the licensee. Nevertheless, proper disclosure must be made and the licensee is well advised to make the disclosures early in the conversation. If, in fact, the broker is going to represent the buyer, they should enter into a written agreement that specifies the details of the relationship.

Ambiguous Situations   There will, of course, be situations that are somewhat ambiguous, in which licensees may be unsure whether to discuss representation. Take the case of a real estate licensee who views a number of new listings of other brokers while on a company caravan tour. The licensee may not yet know whether revisiting such properties will be on behalf of a client or a customer. However, if meeting the seller face to face, the licensee must disclose agency status, particularly if the licensee is previewing the property for a prospective buyer-client. If meeting only with the seller's agent, the licensee, at a minimum, must discuss her current status and any future possibilities of an agency relationship. If, for example, that licensee has prospective buyer-clients who might be interested in purchasing that property, this discussion with the seller's agent is preparation for that situation.

A licensee must be especially careful to address squarely such undecided status in any discussions with the buyer, the seller, the tenant, the landlord, and other licensees. Agency and other working relationships should be firmed up as soon as possible in dealing with the buyer, but definitely before preparation of the buyer's offer. Licensees contemplating an agency relationship with a buyer-client should consider the amount of work they are willing to do for a buyer who has not signed a representation agreement. At that point, the buyer is not bound to any loyalty and may simply take all the information provided by the licensee and either find another licensee to work with, or represent herself and not pay the licensee anything for the licensee's time and effort.

Open Houses   Open houses have also created situations in which licensees may be unsure of disclosure policies. TREC, in an effort to clarify this circumstance, has stated that there is no requirement to give an open-house visitor the Information About Brokerage Services notice unless the party begins to ask in-depth questions or indicates an interest in making an offer on the property (§ 1101.558(a)(1)). Nevertheless, this does not relieve licensees of the duty to disclose to prospective buyers that they represent the seller—this can be done either orally or in writing.

What some listing agents do at an open house, for example, is show the property and answer general questions of a factual nature on such topics as available financing, municipal services, and estimated closing costs. Questions concerning the seller's marketing position are addressed by the seller's agent and subagents in ways designed to encourage prospective buyers to make their best offer. If the conversation begins to move into any substantive discussion regarding a transaction, the licensee should immediately provide the prospect with the Information About Brokerage Services notice and take time to discuss and identify what the working relationship will be. At this point, an agency disclosure statement should be made before going further.

Intermediary   Another disclosure issue will arise if the transaction involves intermediary brokerage. Recall that before entering into an intermediary transaction, written consent must be obtained from both parties (§ 1101.1101.559(a)). Typically, this consent will be given in the listing agreement with the seller and in the buyer representation contract with the buyer. Once consent has been obtained, the statute does not require any further notification when an intermediary transaction begins unless the broker appoints associates to the seller and the buyer. Remember that if the broker makes appointments, the parties must be informed in writing that appointments have been made, and such written notice must give the names of the appointees and identify the parties to whom they have been appointed (§ 1101.560(b)). Even if no appointments have been made, the prudent broker should ensure that the parties are clear that an intermediary transaction is occurring. The Texas Association of REALTORS® Intermediary Relationship Notice is an example of a form (see Figure 6.2) that accomplishes both notification objectives.

Document

To establish that the required disclosures have been given, the licensee should make the disclosures in writing and keep a copy of the disclosure forms signed by the buyer or the seller. This documentation will be especially important if any legal action results from the transaction. In addition, licensees should obtain written confirmation on the final contract that they have disclosed whom they represented and that the status of that representation has not changed. It is important that licensees obtain such written proof because the oral declaration of licensees in a lawsuit is given little weight in proving whom a licensee represented. It is sometimes equally important for licensees to prove that they were not agents of the buyer or the seller.

Do as You Say

If the buyer and the licensee decide that the broker will not represent the buyer but instead will show properties to the buyer as a subagent of sellers who have their properties listed in the MLS, the licensee should act as a subagent. To do this, the licensee will have to get the permission of the seller or the seller's agent, unless that permission is already given by the seller and shows up in the MLS system. A subagent for the seller has the same fiduciary duties as the seller's agent and owes the seller all the common law agency duties (obedience, loyalty, disclosure, confidentiality, accounting, and reasonable care and diligence). The subagent's advocacy is directed toward the seller and not the buyer. Sometimes it is hard for a subagent to remember for which party the subagent is advocating. The subagent generally gets to know the buyer very well. On the other hand, the subagent to the seller does not get to know the seller very well, hardly speaks with the seller, and is much more distant. Yet, the seller is the one the subagent is representing in this transaction. A subagent of the seller, for example, would not suggest that the buyer start by testing the seller with a nothing-down offer and a requirement that the seller carry back a note with interest deferred until the final balloon payment. That certainly is not advocating for the seller's best interests. Nor would a subagent of the seller suggest any negotiating strategies contrary to the best interests of the seller. However, the experienced buyer-customer could initiate any or all of these terms in submitting an offer to purchase the seller's property.

■ UNDERSTANDING AND DEVELOPING A COMPANY POLICY

In general, the objective of creating a comprehensive brokerage policy and procedures manual is to identify and clarify the operation of the brokerage that all parties working in the brokerage (whether employees or independent contractors, sales associates or broker associates) will have clear and concise direction for all activities. Each person should be required to read the manual and acknowledge by signature that they are willing to comply with the policies and procedures of the brokerage.

The legal risk of establishing and running a brokerage is formidable. Part of managing that risk is to create a thorough policy and procedures manual. It should define the terminology used on a daily basis in the real estate industry, clarify the duties and activities of each entity or person, prohibit illegal activity, include step-by-step procedures for as many scenarios as possible. These things will help reduce the broker's legal risks inherent in functioning as an agent for buyers and sellers. A well-done policy and procedures manual is never finished. It is continually updated as

- laws and rules change;
- documents become obsolete;
- conditions within the brokerage office change;
- new goals are created for the future success of the business; and
- the philosophy of relationships between the broker and the sales associates, broker associates, buyers, and sellers changes.

Rules and Laws Requiring Written Policy and Procedures Documentation

The Texas Real Estate Commission, in order to ensure good practices by brokers in Texas, created the following rule:

TREC Rules §535.2(i)

A broker shall maintain on a current basis written policies and procedures to ensure that:

(1) Each sponsored salesperson is advised of the scope of the salesperson's authorized activities subject to the Act and is competent to conduct such activities.

(2) Each sponsored salesperson maintains their license in active status at all times while they are engaging in activities subject to the Act.

(3) Any and all compensation paid to a sponsored salesperson for acts or services subject to the Act is paid by, through, or with the written consent of the sponsoring broker.

(4) Each sponsored salesperson is provided on a timely basis, prior to the effective date of the change, notice of any change to the Act Rules, or commission promulgated contract forms.

(5) In addition to completing statutory minimum continuing education requirements, each sponsored salesperson receives such additional educational instruction the broker may deem necessary to obtain and maintain on a current basis competency in the scope of the sponsored salesperson's practice subject to the Act.

(6) Each sponsored salesperson complies with the commission's advertising rules.

(7) All trust accounts, including but not limited to property management trust accounts, and other funds received from consumers are handled by the broker with appropriate controls.

(8) Records are properly maintained pursuant to subsection (h) of this section.

(j) A broker must promptly respond to sponsored salespersons, clients, and licensees representing other parties in real estate transactions.

(k) A sponsoring broker shall deliver to or otherwise provide, within a reasonable time after receipt, mail and other correspondence from the commission to their sponsored salespersons. A broker may deliver such correspondence by facsimile or email.

(l) When the broker is a business entity, the designated broker is the person responsible for the broker responsibilities under this section. (m) This section is not meant to create or require an employer/employee relationship between a broker and a sponsored salesperson.

The policy and procedures created by a broker will cover a much wider scope than just buyer representation and issues related to buyer brokerage. It is intended to outline every possible area of activity and then include details about potential issues so an employee, salesperson, or broker associate can pick up the manual, go directly to a specific policy or procedure, and find direction on how to handle a particular situation. The broker not only gives guidance for all those who work in the brokerage but also creates a document that will provide evidence that she explicitly told all licensees and employees how to conduct themselves when doing business for the brokerage.

TRELA § 1101.803 states that the broker "is liable to the commission, the public, and the broker's clients for any conduct engaged in . . . by the broker or by a salesperson associated with or acting for the broker." This law makes it imperative that the broker be precise in instruction to all those who work for the broker. The broker is responsible for any and all conduct of those persons.

With the variety of possible agency relationships available for a broker to choose from, TREC rule 22 TAC 535.2(i) states that a broker must actually maintain current written policies and procedures to ensure that "**each sponsored salesperson is advised of the scope of the salesperson's authorized activities subject to the Act and is competent to conduct such activities.**" Areas generally covered in a policy and procedures manual in response to the above law are the following: seen in the list below.

Areas to Consider for a Policies and Procedures Manual

- Definitions of general real estate terms used in the industry
  — Specifically, definitions of terms used throughout the manual

Brokerage contracts
- Independent Contractor Agreement
  — Licensees are not employees (IRS requirements)
  — Commission structure
  — Bonuses
  — Investment opportunities
  — Errors and omissions insurance

- Employee agreement
  — Compensation
- Use of unlicensed assistants
- Teams

Advertising
- Scope of authority of sales associates and broker associates
- Conduct prohibited by the broker
- Issues and costs of advertising, and necessary approval
- Electronic advertising: local, state, and federal requirements
- Clarification and requirements concerning the use of a doing-business-as, assumed name, team name, or other business entity

Fair housing issues
- Training in fair housing laws
- Promoting equal treatment
- Prohibitions relative to fair treatment under the law
- HUD regulations: advertising, testers, equal treatment

Multiple listing service (MLS)
- Proper use, rules, and regulations of MLS
- Rules on taking and maintaining listings

Management of records
- Risk management through good record keeping
- Statutory time requirement for records to be held
- Broker owns all listings and buyer representation agreements
- Where records are kept
- Computer versus paper records
- Lost or destroyed documents/records
- Confidentiality issues

Training requirements and opportunities
- Cost/no cost
- Minimum hours per year required
- State required training for license renewal

Managing money
- Trust accounts: interest bearing and non-interest bearing
- Laws pertaining to commingling of trust funds with personal account
- Authority of broker
- Laws pertaining to timing of deposit

Title company relationships and the law
- Title closing procedures
- Delivery of escrow money and contract
- Texas Department of Insurance (TDI) Rule P-53: rebates and discounts prohibited

Agency relationships, fiduciary duties, common Law agency duties, statutory requirements

- Definitions
- No agency interference-(going around the sign)
- Agency policy of representation (exclusive seller agency, exclusive buyer agency, single agency, intermediary, etc.)
- Legal duties to disclose agency relationship
- Requirement to give the written statement —Information About Brokerage Services
- Duties of the broker as agent to buyers and sellers
- Duties of sales associates through broker to sellers and buyers
- Broker price opinion (BPO), comparative market analysis (CMA) versus appraisal
- Policy of presenting offers and counter-offers
- Dealing with vendors (appraisers, inspectors, contractors, specialists in hazardous substances, etc.)
- Termination of salesperson or broker associate or change of sponsorship

Creating a Policies and Procedures Manual

As you can see, it is essential that every brokerage firm develop its own written policy manual; one segment of that manual clearly must be the written company policy regarding the types of agency representation practiced within that firm. The most effective way to establish a company policy on agency practice is to follow a simple but organized approach. Here's a suggested method.

Phase 1

Review the various agency options. Some options include

- exclusive seller agency,
- exclusive buyer agency,
- nonexclusive single agency, and
- seller-buyer agency with consensual intermediary brokerage for in-company transactions.

Phase 2

Review the advantages and disadvantages of each option as outlined previously.

Phase 3

Consider the size and experience of the office staff, the type of specialization (residential, commercial, farm and ranch, property management, apartment locating, etc.), local market opportunities, and financial expectations of the brokerage. For example, a broker in an already existing brokerage who creates a policy and procedures manual, or updates an existing one, will want to determine the company's profit base before choosing a new agency policy. If most of the brokerage income comes from the sale of other brokers' listings, exclusive seller agency is probably not the best option.

Phase 4

Write a company policy on agency. Start with a preliminary plan (see Figure 8.2), but make sure to submit the plan to key members of the brokerage staff and business and legal advisers for additional input.

A comprehensive plan should

- include a basic statement of policy;
- describe the procedures for handling common situations from the perspectives of both the listing office and the selling office;
- discuss the use of agency disclosure forms, especially the timing of oral or written agency disclosures and the furnishing of a mandatory written statement regarding representation alternatives; and
- above all, comply with all state laws.

Company plans that are developed using textbook models or borrowed from out-of-state brokers should be carefully modified to conform to the Texas environment. Policies and procedures are generally written to protect the broker and associated licensees; however, they should clearly focus on representing clients and working with customers while maintaining the highest ethical standards.

FIGURE 8.2

Sample Ingredients of a Company's Policies and Procedures Manual Regarding Agency

Basic Agency Philosophy
    Strict adherence to state disclosure laws
    Company disclosure guidelines
    Summary of company policy
Handling Common Situations
    Listing presentations
    Buyer representation presentations
    Intermediary representation without appointments
    Intermediary representation with appointments
    In-house sales without intermediary status
    Subagency representation
    Buying property for own account
    Open houses
Dealing with Outside Companies
    Cooperation regarding fee splitting, showing, presenting offers
    Offer of subagency
    Interacting with buyer's agents
Guidelines for the Use of Company Agency Forms
    When
    Why
    How
    Benefits
Common Agency Questions

For example, a policy manual may include the following section on dealing with buyers at an open house:

> - **Open House.** Meeting potential buyers at an open house offers arguably one of the most complex agency situations in real estate. When a prospect comes into your open house, your duty as the listing agent is to the seller and you must use your efforts to sell the house to the prospect. **This means that you cannot suggest other competing**

properties or offer to represent buyers until they have communicated to you that they are not interested in the property. If the buyers show interest in the property or indicate that they might like to purchase the property, **you must treat them as customers and make immediate disclosures concerning agency options and positions**, as required by state law and this policy manual, as follows:

— Confirm in writing or orally that the buyers understand that you represent the seller, and answer any questions that they might have concerning your agency relationship with the seller.

— Determine that the prospects are interested in the property.

— Before substantive discussions concerning the buyers' qualifications for buying or points of negotiation in any subsequent offer, provide the buyers with the company brochure, which contains the written statement required by TRELA § 1101.558 and Our Valued Customer letter (or other company-specific material).

Document in your file that you have delivered and discussed the written statement required by TRELA § 1101.558. Request that the buyers sign the written statement, give them the original, and retain copies for the company file on this property and a separate file on these customers. Should the buyers refuse to sign the notice, make a notation on the notice to that effect and retain copies as defined previously.

Phase 5

The broker should commence in-company training sessions and monitor the effectiveness of the policy. By using role-play and sample dialogue in training sessions, the sales staff can become more comfortable and competent in discussing agency in a way that showcases their professionalism. Rather than isolate discussions of agency, salespersons should be taught to integrate agency into their regular presentations. Finally, once you are certain your sales staff understands the policy, make sure they follow it. Be prepared to make exceptions in justified cases and to make changes to existing policy if exceptions begin to be the rule. (See Figure 8.3.)

Creating a meaningful, accurate policies and procedures manual requires knowledge, and skill. Legal counsel should be obtained to ensure the legal, ethical, moral, and substantive accuracy of all content in the manual.

■ SUMMARY

Much of the confusion about agency relationships can be eliminated as brokers become more comfortable and competent in discussing their roles in real estate transactions. Brokers should develop a company disclosure policy so they can control agency relationships and avoid unintended and illegal agencies. Creating a basic policy consists of these four steps: (1) decide, (2) disclose, (3) document, and (4) do. Without a doubt, timely and proper disclosure is the key ingredient to a successful and effective agency program.

FIGURE   8.3

Agency Office Policy

Agency Office Policy—Points to Ponder

Probably the best defense a company has today regarding problems in the area of agency is a well-reasoned written policy regarding agency relationships authorized and practiced by the company. Although the specific policy will be tailored to individual companies, an agency policy might include the issues on the following list.

How does your company address the following agency issues?

■ A definition and explanation of duties of a seller's representative

■ A definition and explanation of duties of a buyer's representative

■ A definition and explanation of duties of an intermediary

■ Statement regarding written listing agreements

■ Instructions regarding procedures and paperwork (including brokerage services, notices, and disclosures)

■ Listing fees or commissions

■ Policy regarding intermediary authorization in the listing agreement

■ Statement regarding cooperation and compensation with other brokers (subagents and buyer agents)

■ Procedures with first meeting with prospective buyers

■ Policy regarding buyer representation

■ Requirements for written buyer representation agreements

■ Policy regarding intermediary authorization in the buyer representation agreements

■ Commission or fee statements in buyer representation

■ Policy relating to working with non-represented (customers) buyers, including written Information About Brokerage Services and agency disclosure statements

■ Policy statement relating to selling other firms listings as subagents or buyer's agent

■ Policy relating to the sale of a FSBO to a buyer-client or customer

■ Policy relating to the in-house sale to a customer

■ Policy relating to the intermediary transaction

■ Policy relating to appointed associates (who and when)

■ Disclosure of previous agency relationships and working with close friends and relatives

■ Working with seller-clients in purchasing a subsequent property

■ Policy regarding working with competing buyers as customers or clients

■ Policy relating to associates purchasing of the company's listings or listings of other companies

■ Associates selling their own properties or the property owned by another associate of the company

Source: From *2000 and Beyond: An MCE Update.* Used with permission.

■ KEY POINTS

■ Because real estate transactions vary widely, a brokerage firm must decide what role the firm and its associates will play.

■ Once agency roles in a specific transaction have been decided, the licensee must give full disclosure to all participants in that transaction.

■ Throughout the transaction, the licensee should take great care to properly document all aspects of the transaction.

■ Once committed to a course of action, licensees must follow through and perform as agreed.

■ The firm must develop a written company policy outlining the basic agency philosophy, how to handle common real estate situations, dealing with other firms, and use of agency forms.

■ SUGGESTIONS FOR BROKERS

Develop a personalized disclosure brochure that includes the written statement required by TRELA § 1101.558 and outlines the types of working relationships your firm offers to buyers and sellers.

Outline some of the customer-level services you can provide to one person while remaining the exclusive agent of the other person.

Be careful not to use confusing language that might weaken the impact of meaningful agency disclosure and duties. A broker who attempts to cloud the issues may find such a brochure being used in a lawsuit. Use of the § 1101.558 written statement should help set the stage for meaningful discussions of your professional relationship and the needs of the prospect.

Although it is not required by law, attempt to get the prospective buyer or seller to sign an acknowledgment of receipt of the company form or letter, which discloses whom your brokerage represented, if anyone, at the time of first contact. If your company represents no one relative to the particular consumer being interviewed, say so in the form or letter. Also get an acknowledgment of receipt of the written information statement required by § 1101.558. Then, if a relationship with the party appears imminent, carefully discuss the anticipated type of client or customer or other relationship before reaching a written agreement or obtaining consents and beginning a working relationship.

CHAPTER 8 QUIZ

1. When should a licensee disclose to the buyer the agency status of the listing broker?
   a. On recordation of the deed
   b. At the first contact with the buyer
   c. When the purchase contract is signed
   d. When the buyer telephones the broker to arrange an introductory meeting

2. Which is the *BEST* stage of the transaction to present the required TRELA § 1101.558(d) written statement to the seller regarding agency options?
   a. Just before submission of a first offer to the seller
   b. Immediately after listing the seller's property
   c. Immediately prior to signing the listing agreement
   d. At the time of the first substantive dialogue with the seller

3. The other broker working with a buyer might represent
   a. the buyer.
   b. the seller.
   c. the listing broker.
   d. all of these.

4. The listing broker should discuss all of the following with the seller at the time the broker takes the listing *EXCEPT*
   a. offer of subagency.
   b. sharing of the listing fee.
   c. listing in the MLS.
   d. buyer's motivation.

5. If a buyer-customer tells the listing broker that the buyer will pay up to the listed price but first wants to submit an offer 10% below that price, what should the broker tell the seller?
   a. The buyer is qualified.
   b. The buyer has made a good offer.
   c. Don't risk losing the buyer by making a counteroffer.
   d. The buyer is willing to pay up to the listed price.

6. When buyers attending open houses are "merely lookers," there is
   a. no need for licensees to disclose their relationship with the seller.
   b. still a need for licensees to disclose their relationship with the seller in writing.
   c. still a need for licensees to disclose their relationship with the seller, at least orally.
   d. no need for licensees to disclose their relationship with the seller, unless a buyer asks.

7. The buyer is considered to have received the required disclosure of agency when the licensee
   a. delivers the TREC Information About Brokerage Services notice to the buyer and has the buyer sign the form.
   b. delivers the TREC Information About Brokerage Services notice to the buyer.
   c. discloses the agency relationship, either verbally or in writing, to the buyer.
   d. completes a purchase contract for the buyer.

8. There is no requirement for a licensee to deliver the written statement (information regarding brokerage services) to a buyer who is
   a. seeking to be represented by the firm.
   b. represented by another agent.
   c. referred by a former client.
   d. a friend.

9. When buyers' agents show a property listed by another firm, those buyers' agents must
   a. deliver the Information About Brokerage Services notice and disclose their representation of the buyer to the seller.
   b. verbally disclose their representation of the buyer to the seller.
   c. deliver the Information About Buyers' Services notice to the seller.
   d. assume that the seller has been informed of the representation.

10. A broker should develop company policies that outline
    a. how to handle common real estate situations.
    b. how to deal with other firms.
    c. use of agency forms.
    d. all of these.

DISCUSSION QUESTIONS

1. What are the four steps a broker should take to clarify agency relationships?

2. In deciding whether to act as an agent of a buyer, what are some relevant questions for a listing broker to ask?

3. In deciding whether to act as a subagent of a listing broker while working with a buyer, what are some relevant questions for another broker to ask?

4. What are some key areas of the prospective agency relationship that the listing broker should discuss with the seller during the listing appointment?

5. When is the best time to make the disclosure of seller agency to the buyer?

CHAPTER

Employment Issues

The extent of legal responsibility of those persons who hire someone else to act for them depends on the relationship. As a rule, the more extensively the person who contracts for a service controls the manner in which the service is performed, the greater that person's responsibility. For example, an employer has appreciable control over how an employee works. When employees act within the scope of their employment, the **employer** is responsible for any harm those employees cause. In real estate brokerage, the licensee's classification either as an independent contractor or as an employee is important for several reasons, including the establishment of agency relationships through employment contracts and listing agreements. Chapter 4 discussed, in detail, the listing agreement as the primary employment agreement between brokers and sellers. Likewise, Chapter 5 took an in-depth look at the buyer representation agreement as the primary employment agreement between brokers and buyers. This chapter explores some general employment issues and agreements as they affect brokers and licensed associates in their roles as principals and agents.

■ **LEARNING OBJECTIVES** *This chapter addresses the following:*

- ■ Independent Contractor Agreements
- ■ Employment Law
- ■ Employment Relationships Between Brokers and Principals
  - — Employment Relationships Between Brokers and Associates
  - — Definition of Broker Associate
  - — Employee Versus Independent Contractor
  - — Sales Associate and Broker Associate Compensation
- ■ Employment and Compensation of Personal Assistants
  - — Relationships Between Brokers, Agents, and Subagents
  - — Broker to Broker's Agent/Sales Associate
  - — Broker to Other Broker
  - — Broker to Other Sales Associate
  - — Sales Associate to Sales Associate Within the Same Brokerage
  - — Sales Associate of One Company to Sales Associate of Another Company
  - — Broker and Subagents
  - — MLS Subagency Agreements
  - — Non-MLS Subagency Agreements
  - — Agreements Between Brokers
- ■ Other Compensation Issues
  - — Nonlicensee Compensation
  - — Foreign Brokers or Brokers Licensed in Other States

■ INDEPENDENT CONTRACTOR AGREEMENTS

The first agency relationship that a new licensee will enter into is the one between the licensee's sponsoring broker and the licensee. The sponsoring broker is the principal in this agency relationship, and the licensee is the agent of the broker. Sales associates owe all fiduciary duties and common law agency duties to their broker.

Although not as clearly defined in real estate law, the broker acting as principal to the broker's sales associate owes his sales associate/agent the duties of 1) performance, 2) compensation, 3) indemnification, and 4) reimbursement, unless there is an agreement to the contrary or there is no written agreement to compensate.

We have discussed the agency duties owed to a principal in the broker, seller, or buyer relationship. Now the discussion will shift to the duties of the broker acting as the principal to the broker's agents:

- ■ **Performance:** The principal is required under this obligation, to do as much as possible to ensure that the purpose for which the agency was created, can be accomplished. In this situation, it relates to the broker providing information, business guidance, and availability to the broker's agent.
- ■ **Compensation:** Generally, the broker will clearly outline, in the employment agreement or a separate compensation agreement 1) the method and amount of payment due to the agent, 2) how the payment will be made, and 3) under what circumstances the payment is due and payable. Generally, the broker is paid by a seller, buyer, landlord, or tenant based on an agreement

with that entity The broker's agent does not have privity of contract with any of those entities and relies solely on the agreement for compensation with the agent's broker. If the broker does not pay the agent, the agent cannot sue the seller, buyer, landlord, or tenant directly. Consequently, the agent should have a clear and precisely written agreement covering the broker's promise to pay, and all the contingencies concerning payment.

Avoidance is when the principal avoids paying the agent. In the event the agent breaches fiduciary duties or the contract with the principal, the principal may elect to avoid any contract entered into with the agent. This means that if an agent breaches the agent's fiduciary duty, the agent's principal broker does not have to pay the agent. Consider this example:

— A sales associate, acting as an agent, breaches a contractual or fiduciary duty or causes damage or harm to a third party.
— As a result, the third party brings a lawsuit against the principal/broker.
— The third party wins the suit against the broker.
— The broker then sues the agent to seek indemnification from the agent.

Another issue to briefly explore is that of an undisclosed principal. If a real estate agent is acting on behalf of an undisclosed principal, and the agent does not disclose the identity of the principal being represented, nor does the agent disclose the agency to the third party in the transaction, the agent will be presumed to be acting on his own behalf. In that case, the agent will be liable as though a party to the contract. Agents should be careful when representing undisclosed principals. Agents may be the ones liable for their acts. It is also grounds for loss of license to act in a dual capacity as a broker and undisclosed principal in a real estate transaction. (TRELA § 1101.652 (b)(16)

- **Indemnification**: If the agent suffers a loss because of the actions of the agent's principal broker while the agent is acting on behalf of the broker and the agent bears no responsibility for the loss, the broker may have to indemnify the agent for the loss.
- **Reimbursement**: Generally, if the agent has paid for expenses on behalf of the agent's broker while working within the authority of the agency relationship with the broker, the broker owes the agent reimbursement for those expenses. For instance, the broker goes on vacation and asks his agent George to manage the office in his absence. After his broker leaves, George finds that all the copy paper has been used and the other sales associates in the office have no paper for the copy machine. George goes to the local office supply store and purchases enough cases of paper for the office to last until the broker returns. When the broker returns from his vacation, the broker will owe George reimbursement for the paper.

The Texas Real Estate Commission has not created or promulgated an independent contractor agreement for the real estate industry. TREC is not involved in the creation of agreements between the broker and the sales associate acting under the license of a broker. The Texas Association of REALTORS® (TAR) provides member benefits and includes in those benefits contract forms that meet the needs of its membership.

In Figure 9.1, at the top of the Independent Contractor Agreement for Sales Associate, it states clearly that the form was produced by TAR. It also states that the form is to be used only by members of TAR.

FIGURE 9.1

Texas Association of REALTORS® Independent Contractor Agreement for Sales Associate

TEXAS ASSOCIATION OF REALTORS®

INDEPENDENT CONTRACTOR AGREEMENT FOR SALES ASSOCIATE

USE OF THIS FORM BY PERSONS WHO ARE NOT MEMBERS OF THE TEXAS ASSOCIATION OF REALTORS® IS NOT AUTHORIZED.
©Texas Association of REALTORS®, Inc. 2007

1. **PARTIES.** The parties to this agreement are:
   Broker: _____; and
   Associate: _____.

2. **TERM:** This agreement commences on _____ (Commencement Date) and ends at such time as either party terminates this agreement in accordance with Paragraph 21.

3. **DEFINITIONS:**

   A. *"Brokerage services"* means assistance and services to prospects that are reasonably necessary to negotiate and bring about the successful closing of transactions for the sale, purchase, or lease of real estate.

   B. *"Files"* means any documents, instruments, contracts, written agreements, disclosures, memoranda, books, publications, records, correspondence, reports, data, lists, compilations, studies, surveys, images, and all other data, whether in written or electronic format, which are related to Broker's real estate business. The term "files" ❏ includes ❏ excludes Associate's prospect lists.

   C. *"Prospect"* means: (1) a buyer, prospective buyer, seller, prospective seller, landlord, prospective landlord, tenant, or prospective tenant of real estate; or (2) a client or customer of Broker or Associate.

   D. *"Real estate business"* means all business related to the acts of a real estate broker as defined by Section 1101.002, Occupations Code (the Real Estate License Act).

4. **BEST EFFORTS:** Associate will use Associate's best professional efforts to:
   A. solicit listings and prospects for Broker's real estate business; and
   B. provide brokerage services to prospects procured by or assigned to Associate.

5. **EXCLUSIVE ASSOCIATION:** Associate will perform the services contemplated by this agreement exclusively for Broker. Associate may not engage in the brokerage of businesses or in the management of property without Broker's knowledge and written consent.

6. **LEGAL AND ETHICAL COMPLIANCE:** When delivering brokerage services to prospects and when otherwise performing under this agreement, the parties agree to comply with all applicable laws and standards of practice, including but not limited to the Real Estate License Act, the Rules of the Texas Real Estate Commission, the Code of Ethics of the National Association of REALTORS®, the bylaws of the national, state, and applicable local associations of REALTORS®, any rules and regulations of any listing services to which the parties may subscribe, and any standards or policies Broker adopts.

7. **LICENSES AND TRADE ASSOCIATIONS:**

   A. Broker's License and Membership Status: Broker is a licensed real estate broker in the State of Texas and is a member of the National Association of REALTORS®, the Texas Association of REALTORS®, and the following local associations of REALTORS®:_____
   _____. Broker will maintain Broker's license and REALTOR® membership status active and in good standing at all times while this agreement is in effect.

(TAR-2301) 8-16-07   Initialed for Identification by Associate _____ and Broker _____   Page 1of 8

FIGURE 9.1

Texas Association of REALTORS® Independent Contractor Agreement for Sales Associate (continued)

Independent Contractor Agreement between_____

B. <u>Associate's License and Membership Status</u>: Associate is a licensed real estate   ❑ salesperson ❑ broker in the State of Texas and ❑ is ❑ will become a member of the National Association of REALTORS®, the Texas Association of REALTORS®, and the following local associations of REALTORS®:_____
_____.

Associate will maintain Associate's license and REALTOR® membership status active and in good standing at all times while this agreement is in effect.

8. INDEPENDENT CONTRACTOR:

A. <u>Contractor</u>: Associate is an independent contractor and is not Broker's employee. Broker will not withhold any amounts for taxes from the fees paid to Associate under this agreement, unless ordered to do so by a court of law or the Internal Revenue Service. Broker will not pay any amounts for FICA, unemployment compensation, or worker's compensation for Associate.

B. **<u>Statement of Understanding</u>: On or about the first day of _____ of each calendar year this agreement is in effect, Associate will execute and deliver to Broker a Statement of Understanding, a copy of which is attached to this agreement.**

C. <u>Not a Partnership</u>: This agreement does not create a partnership between the parties. Except as provided by this agreement, neither party is liable to the other party for any expense or obligation incurred by the other party.

9. ASSOCIATE'S AUTHORITY:

A. <u>Signing Brokerage Service Agreements</u>: Associate may sign listing agreements, buyer or tenant representation agreements, and commission agreements on Broker's behalf provided that Associate complies with Paragraph 6 and any standards and policies Broker adopts with respect to signing such agreements.

B. <u>Submission of Agreements</u>: All listings, representation agreements, commission agreements, and other agreements for brokerage services that Associate procures or signs must be taken in Broker's name and must be submitted to Broker within _____ days after the listing, representation agreement, commission agreement, or other agreement is taken by Associate.

C. <u>Cancellations or Termination of Brokerage Service Agreements</u>: Associate may not cancel, terminate, or compromise any agreement to which Broker is a party without Broker's written approval.

D. <u>Other Agreements</u>: Unless specifically authorized by this agreement or by Broker in writing, Associate may not bind or obligate Broker to any agreement or relationship.

10. FILES AND CONFIDENTIALITY OF OPERATIONS:

A. <u>Obligation to Maintain a File</u>: In any transaction related to Broker's real estate business in which Associate is involved, Associate must maintain a file at Broker's office that contains all applicable items described under the definition of "files" under Paragraph 3B. Associate will maintain the file in a format that Broker regularly maintains such files in Broker's office.

B. <u>Confidentiality of Files</u>: The parties agree that all files related to Broker's real estate business are Broker's confidential business property. Associate agrees to hold all files and information in the files confidential and not disclose such information to any person without Broker's knowledge and consent unless:
(1) required by law or a court order to disclose such information; or
(2) such information is otherwise public information.

F I G U R E 9.1

Texas Association of REALTORS® Independent Contractor Agreement for Sales Associate (continued)

Independent Contractor Agreement between_____

C. Prospects and Operations: Unless required by law or expressly permitted by Broker, Associate may not furnish any person with information about:
(1) Broker's prospects or Broker's relationship with any prospects; or
(2) Broker's policies and business operations.

D. Survival: This Paragraph 10 survives termination of this agreement.

E. NOTICE: *All Internet data that is composed, transmitted, or received on the Broker's computers or network is considered to be part of the Broker's records and, as such, is subject to: (1) Broker's review; and (2) disclosure to law enforcement agencies or as the law may otherwise require. The unauthorized use, installation, copying, or distribution of trademark or patented material on the Internet or by other means is prohibited.*

11. **OWNERSHIP OF LISTINGS AND REPRESENTATION AGREEMENTS:** All listings, representation agreements, commission agreements, and other agreements for brokerage services in which Broker is named as a party are owned exclusively by Broker.

12. **RECEIPT OF MONEY BY ASSOCIATE:**

A. Compliance with Contracts: Associate must promptly deposit all checks or funds Associate receives in trust for others in accordance with the contracts under which the checks or funds are received. Associate may not maintain a separate trust, escrow, or management account for real estate business purposes.

B. Receipt of Brokerage Fees: Unless otherwise authorized by Broker, Associate must deliver any compensation for brokerage services received from any client, customer, escrow agent, title company, prospect, or any other person to Broker for disbursement in accordance with this agreement, including but not limited to any check, credit card, debit card, draft, or any negotiable instrument made payable or issued to Associate.

13. **FACILITIES:** Broker will furnish to Associate the following office facilities at Broker's office for uses related to Broker's real estate business:_____
_____
_____
_____
_____.
Performance under this agreement does not require Associate to be present in Broker's office.

14. **ADVERTISING:**

A. All advertising related to Broker's real estate business, including brokerage services performed by Associate, may be placed only by Broker or only with Broker's knowledge and consent. Broker will, at Broker's discretion, include Associate's name in such advertising when appropriate. Associate will not cause any advertisement that is related to Broker's real estate business to be published without Broker's prior knowledge and consent.

B. "Advertising" includes any written or oral statement which is intended to induce the public to use Associate's or Broker's services, and includes without limitation all publications, newsletters, radio or television broadcasts, all electronic media including e-mail and the Internet, business stationery, business cards, signs, and billboards.

15. **ASSIGNMENT OF PROSPECTS:**

A. Definition: Under this Paragraph 15, "*assign*" means to appoint an associate to deal with a prospect on Broker's behalf.

FIGURE 9.1

Texas Association of REALTORS® Independent Contractor Agreement for Sales Associate (continued)

Independent Contractor Agreement between_____

B. <u>Assignments</u>: Broker gives to Associate the right, together with Broker, to deal with prospects that Associate procures and with prospects that Broker assigns to Associate. Broker retains the right and sole discretion to assign leads and prospects that are procured by Broker through Broker's real estate business to any of Broker's associates as Broker determines appropriate.

C. <u>Reassignments</u>: Broker may reassign a prospect with whom Associate deals to another associate if: (1) Broker determines that a reassignment of the prospect is necessary for the orderly, ethical, or lawful operation of Broker's real estate business; (2) Associate is not capable of continuing to service the prospect; or (3) this agreement terminates. This provision applies to all prospects, regardless of who procured the prospect.

D. <u>No Interference</u>: Associate may not interfere with any assignments or reassignments of prospects or leads that Broker may make.

16. ASSOCIATE'S FEES:

A. <u>Brokerage Fees are Paid to Broker</u>: All fees and compensation that Broker or Associate earn for providing brokerage services to prospects (for example, fees earned under listing agreements, buyer or tenant representation agreements, agreements between brokers) are payable to and belong to Broker.

B. <u>Amount of Associate's Fees</u>: Broker will pay Associate fees for the brokerage services that Associate provides under this agreement at the rates or in the amounts specified in:
   ❑ (1) the attached fee schedule.
   ❑ (2) _____,
        which is incorporated into this agreement.

C. <u>When Associate's Fees are Earned and Payable</u>: Associate's fees under this agreement are earned at the time Broker's fees are earned under the applicable agreements for brokerage services that Associate performs for Broker. Associate's fees under this agreement are payable when Broker receives Broker's fees under the applicable agreements for brokerage services, unless the fees are subject to arbitration, litigation, or a court order.

D. <u>Disputes between Associates</u>: If another associate of Broker claims a fee from a transaction for which Associate also claims a fee, the amount of the fee payable to Associate will be divided between Associate and the other associate claiming the fee in accordance with an agreement between them. If no such agreement is reached, the dispute will be resolved by Broker's internal dispute resolution policy; and, if no such policy exists, by arbitration. Before disbursing any fee, Broker may require written authorization from any associate claiming the fee. Associate agrees not to hold Broker liable for holding, in trust, any disputed funds between associates.

E. <u>Delinquent Brokerage Fees</u>: Broker is not liable to Associate for any fees not collected from a prospect. Broker retains complete discretion to enforce or not enforce any agreement for brokerage services with a prospect.

F. <u>Bonuses</u>: Associate may not accept any fee, bonus, or other compensation directly; whether such is in money, gift cards, credit cards, trips, or other benefits or personal property. All fees, bonuses, and other compensation must be paid to Broker for distribution in accordance with this agreement. Unless otherwise agreed in writing between the parties to this agreement, bonuses will be considered as part of the gross compensation Broker receives under the applicable agreements for brokerage services and will be disbursed in accordance with:
   ❑ (1) the attached fee schedule.
   ❑ (2) _____,
        which is incorporated into this agreement.

F I G U R E   9.1

Texas Association of REALTORS® Independent Contractor Agreement for Sales Associate (continued)

Independent Contractor Agreement between_____

G. <u>Fees upon Reassignment of Prospects</u>: If Broker reassigns a prospect with whom Associate deals to another associate or if Broker reassigns a prospect with whom another associate deals to Associate, Broker will pay Associate a fee in accordance with:
   - ❑ (1) the attached fee schedule.
   - ❑ (2) _____,
   which is incorporated into this agreement.

H. <u>Other</u>: If an attached fee schedule or other document incorporated into this agreement does not specifically address the amount of the fee or compensation due to Associate under any given circumstances, the amount of the fee or compensation will be an amount that Broker determines is reasonable and equitable.

I. <u>Assignment of Fees</u>: Associate may not assign any interest in fees or compensation due under this agreement to any other person.

17. EXPENSES:

A. <u>No Liability for Another's Expense</u>: Unless the parties agree otherwise, Broker is not liable for any expense incurred by Associate. Unless the parties agree otherwise, Associate is not liable to Broker for the expenses for the office facilities that Broker will provide under this agreement.

B. <u>Special Expenses</u>: "*Special expenses*" means expenses that Broker incurs for _____
_____
_____.
(Note: Special expenses may include items such as desk fees, transaction fees, E&O premiums, franchise fees, etc.). Special expenses will be:

   - ❑ (1) deducted from the gross fees that Broker receives under this agreement for brokerage services and paid to the providers of the special services before calculating Associate's fees payable under this agreement.

   - ❑ (2) invoiced to Associate by Broker and will become payable upon receipt of the invoice.

   - ❑ (3) charged to Associate in accordance with:
      - ❑ (a) the attached fee schedule.
      - ❑ (b) _____,
      which is incorporated into this agreement.

C. <u>License and Membership Fees</u>: Each party is responsible to pay all their respective license and membership fees. Associate must immediately reimburse Broker any fee, expense, or penalty that Broker incurs as a result of:
   (1) the parties' association; or
   (2) Associate's failure to maintain Associate's license or REALTOR® membership status as required by this agreement.

D. <u>Automobile Expenses</u>: Associate will furnish his or her own automobile and pay all such expenses. Broker is not liable or responsible for Associate's automobile or its expenses. Associate must maintain liability and property damage insurance satisfactory to Broker and must name Broker as an additional insured in any such policy. <u>Upon execution of this agreement, Associate must deliver to Broker satisfactory evidence of the insurance required by this agreement and must deliver evidence of the renewal of such insurance at the time the insurance policy is renewed.</u> If Associate fails to maintain the required insurance in full force and effect at times this agreement is in effect, Broker may:
   (1) purchase insurance that will provide Broker with the same coverage as required by this paragraph and Associate must immediately reimburse Broker for such expense; or
   (2) terminate this agreement.

FIGURE 9.1

Texas Association of REALTORS® Independent Contractor Agreement for Sales Associate (continued)

Independent Contractor Agreement between_____

E. <u>Other Expenses</u>: Associate is responsible for all of Associate's expenses necessary to perform the services required of Associate under this agreement, including but not limited to, license fees, association dues, entertainment costs, club dues, mobile phone expenses, education expenses, computer service access charges, periodical expenses, and other related expenses. Although not obligated to do so, if Broker pays any such expense for or on behalf of Associate, Associate will reimburse Broker such amount upon demand.

18. **OFFSET:** Broker retains the right of offset for all purposes. Broker may deduct amounts Associate owes Broker from any amounts Broker owes to Associate under this agreement.

19. **DEFENSE OF DISPUTES AND LITIGATION:**

A. <u>Cooperation</u>: If a dispute, litigation, or complaint against Broker or Associate occurs in a transaction in which Associate is involved and which is related to Broker's real estate business, the parties will cooperate fully with each other in defending the action.

B. <u>Insurance Deductible</u>: If Broker and Associate are named as defendants in a dispute, litigation, or complaint, any deductible for errors and omissions insurance that may cover the defense or payment of any liability under the dispute, litigation, or complaint will be paid as follows: _____
_____.

C. <u>Mutual Defense</u>: If any defense expenses are not paid by an errors and omissions insurer, Broker and Associate will share all such expenses and costs related to defend the dispute, litigation, or complaint in the same proportion as they would share the fee resulting from the transaction as if there were no dispute, litigation, or complaint; provided that both Broker and Associate are named as defendants or respondents to the dispute, litigation, or complaint. If either party determines that it cannot mutually defend a dispute, litigation, or complaint with the other party, each party will be responsible for its own costs to defend the dispute, litigation, or complaint from the time one party notifies the other of such a determination.

D. <u>Defense Management in a Mutual Defense</u>: If the parties mutually defend a dispute, litigation, or complaint, Broker maintains sole discretion to:
(1) determine whether to defend or compromise the dispute, litigation, or complaint;
(2) employ attorneys or other experts;
(3) direct the course of any defense strategy; and
(4) determine the terms and conditions of any compromise or settlement, provided that Broker may not obligate Associate to pay anything of value without Associate's written consent.

E. <u>Liability for Damages</u>: Except as provided in Paragraph 19F, each party is responsible for the payment of any amounts for which it is found liable. The sharing of defense costs provided in this Paragraph 19 does not apply to the payment of damages for which a party is found liable by a court of law, arbitrator, or state agency.

F. <u>Reimbursement and Indemnity</u>: If Broker is found to be liable by a court, arbitrator, or government agency as a result of Associate's negligence, misrepresentations, fraud, false statements, violation of the Real Estate License Act, or violation of any other state or federal statute, Associate will indemnify and reimburse Broker all such amounts and all attorney's fees, costs, and other expenses necessary to defend the action including those defense costs that were previously shared under this Paragraph 19.

G. <u>Survival</u>: This Paragraph 19 survives the termination of this agreement.

20. **PROSECUTION OF CLAIMS:** For all matters related to Broker's real estate business, Broker retains sole discretion to prosecute, complain, compromise, or settle any claim that Broker may have against any other person, including but not limited to other brokers, and Broker's or Associate's clients, customers, and prospects.

F I G U R E   9.1

Texas Association of REALTORS® Independent Contractor Agreement for Sales Associate (continued)

Independent Contractor Agreement between_____

21. TERMINATION:

    A. <u>Either Party may Terminate</u>: Either party may terminate this agreement, with or without cause, by providing written notice to the other party.

    B. <u>Entitlement to Fees</u>: Any fee to Associate that remains unpaid on the date of termination will be paid in accordance with:
      ❑ (1) the attached fee schedule.
      ❑ (2) _____,
          which is incorporated into this agreement.

    C. <u>Services to Prospects</u>: Upon termination of this agreement, all negotiations and other brokerage services with prospects commenced by Associate before termination will be assumed by Broker. Associate will cooperate with Broker to provide for an orderly transition and assumption of such service by Broker.

    D. <u>Associate's Obligations upon Termination</u>: At the time this agreement ends, Associate must:
      (1) cease all negotiations and other dealings that concern Broker's real estate business commenced by Associate before this agreement ends;
      (2) provide Broker a written list of all current listings and pending sales and leases;
      (3) turn over to Broker all files related to Broker's real estate business and that Associate may have or control; and
      (4) turn over to Broker all Broker's personal property including but not limited to keysafes, signs, equipment, supplies, manuals, forms, and keys.

    E. <u>Files</u>: Associate may not remove any files related to Broker's real estate business from Broker's office without Broker's prior knowledge and consent. Associate is entitled to copies of relevant documents concerning pending transaction in which Associate has a bona fide interest. Broker will not unreasonably withhold copies of such documents.

22. NOTICES: All notices under this agreement must be in writing and are effective when hand-delivered, mailed, sent by facsimile transmission, or sent by electronic mail from one party to the other.

23. SPECIAL PROVISIONS:

24. AGREEMENT OF THE PARTIES:

    A. <u>Addenda</u>: Attached to and incorporated into this agreement are:
      ❑ (1) the Fee Schedule dated _____;
      ❑ (2) the Statement of Understanding (which should be reviewed and signed each year);
      ❑ (3) IRS Form W-9; and
      ❑ (4) _____.

FIGURE 9.1

Texas Association of REALTORS® Independent Contractor Agreement for Sales Associate (continued)

Independent Contractor Agreement between_____

B. <u>Entire Agreement</u>: This document contains the entire agreement between the parties and may not be changed except by written agreement.

C. <u>No Assignment</u>: Neither party may assign this agreement or any interest in this agreement without the written consent of the other party.

D. <u>Heirs and Successors</u>: The parties' obligations under this agreement and the parties' entitlement to any compensation, reimbursement, or indemnity under this agreement inures to the benefit of the respective party's successors, permitted assigns, heirs, executors, and administrators.

E. <u>Controlling Law</u>: The laws of the State of Texas govern the interpretation, validity, performance, and enforcement of this agreement.

F. <u>Severable Clauses</u>: If any clause in this agreement is found to be invalid or unenforceable by a court of law, the remainder of this agreement will not be affected and all other provisions of this agreement will remain valid and enforceable.

G. <u>Waiver</u>: Waiver of any provision in this agreement by any party is effective only if the waiver is in writing. A waiver, whether in writing or otherwise, may not be construed as a waiver of any subsequent breach or failure of the same provision or any other provision of this agreement.

This is intended to be a legally binding agreement. READ IT CAREFULLY. If you do not understand the effect of this agreement, consult your attorney BEFORE signing.

Associate's Name Printed (as it appears on license)	Broker's Name Printed _____ License No.
Associate's Signature _____ Date	By:_____ Signature _____ Date
License No. _____ License Expiration Date	Title
Home Address	Office Address
City, State, Zip Code	City, State, Zip Code
Home Phone _____ Mobile Phone	Office Phone _____ Fax Number
E-mail	E-mail

Explanation of Independent Contractor Agreement

The following information clarifies what the Independent Contractor Agreement for Sales Associates says and means:

1. Parties:
   - This paragraph names the parties to the agreement.
   - The names of the parties should be clearly identified and accurately spelled.
   - If a corporation or other business entity is involved, that name should be specifically and accurately used.

2. Term:
   - The agreement has a commencement date, and references paragraph 21 for the definition of when the agreement ends.

3. Definitions:
   - This paragraph identifies exactly what certain words in the agreement mean. Every time a specifically defined word is found in the agreement, the complete and precise definition given in this section is how the word is defined.
   - For example, *files* is defined in paragraph 3B as "any documents, instruments, contracts, written agreements, disclosures, memoranda, books, publications, records, correspondence, reports, data, lists, compilations, studies, surveys, images, and all other data, whether in written or electronic format, which are related to the broker's real estate business." The term "files" ☐ includes ☐ excludes associate's prospect lists.'
   - This might differ from a dictionary definition of *files*. The point is that the definitions section of any contract provides the definition that the parties desire the word(s) to mean specific to that contract. Carefully read any definitions section and refer back to it often for clarification.

4. Best Efforts:
   - This paragraph clarifies that the associate does not promise to obtain listings and prospects, but will employ best professional efforts to solicit for listings and prospects and provide brokerage services to prospects procured by or assigned to the associate.

5. Exclusive Association:
   - The associate, by signing the agreement, promises to work exclusively for the broker named in the agreement. The associate is not allowed under TRELA to represent more than one broker at a time. If the associate desires to be sponsored by a different broker, TRELA requires a formal process in order to place a salesperson license under a different broker. Remember, when you leave one broker and move to a new broker, the listings that you may have acquired belong to the previous broker.
   - Also, the sales associate is not allowed to do the business of managing property or conducting any brokerage business without the knowledge and written consent of the broker.

■ **EXAMPLE**   Sally is a sales associate of broker Sam. Sally has a friend who would like her to manage her single-family investment home. Sally will be paid a management fee each month for her work. Sally will have to get permission from Sam to manage her friend's property, and if Sam allows her to manage the property, he may (and probably will) require Sally to pay him a percentage of the monthly management fee, or some other compensation.

6. Legal and Ethical Compliance:
   - The agreement requires that the associate comply with all applicable laws and standards of practice, including, but not limited to the following:
     — TRELA
     — Rules of TREC
     — NAR Code of Ethics
     — Bylaws of national, state, and applicable local associations of REALTORS®
     — Rules and regulations of any listing services
     — Standards or policies of the broker
7. Licenses and Trade Associations:
   - The primary purpose of paragraph A is to verify in writing that the broker is legally holding a broker license, is a member of the National Association of REALTORS®, the Texas Association of REALTORS® and a local body of REALTORS®, and will maintain all of those associations and licenses.
   - In paragraph B, the associate verifies her license status, and indicates whether she is or will become a member of NAR, TAR, and a local board of REALTORS®. In addition, the associate declares that she will maintain her license and keep REALTOR® memberships active and in good standing during the entire time she is affiliated with this broker.
8. Independent Contractor:
   - The associate agrees that he is an independent contractor.
   - The broker will not withhold any taxes or Federal Insurance Contributions Act (FICA) tax, unemployment compensation, or workers' compensation, unless ordered by a court of law or the IRS.
   - The associate must provide the broker a Statement of Understanding each year
   - The broker is not in a partnership with the associate.
9. Associate's Authority:
   - This section delineates the type of authority the associate has when acting for the broker.
   - The broker gives the authority to the associate as follows:
     — The associate may sign listing agreements, buyer or tenant representation agreements, and commission agreements on behalf of the broker.
       - The associate must comply with paragraph 6 of the agreement in order to be able to have this authority.
       - All contractual agreements (listings, representation, commission, and others) must be taken in the broker's name.
       - All of these agreements must be submitted within the time specified in the blank spaces in this paragraph.
     — The associate does not have the authority to cancel, terminate, or compromise any agreement in the broker's name without the broker's permission. If, for instance, the associate is on a listing appointment and the seller asks the associate to reduce the commission from 7% to 5%, the associate does not have the authority to do so without the authorization of the broker.
     — The associate may not bind or obligate the broker to any agreement or relationship other than those authorized in writing by the broker.

10. Files and Confidentiality of Operations:
    ■ The same concept of confidentiality that has been discussed between the broker and a seller or buyer-client is true about the relationship between the broker and the broker's agent. Unless the agent has permission from the broker to divulge confidential information to others, she must have permission from the broker/principal. The difficulty in this situation is knowing what information is confidential and what is not. To make the understanding between agent and associate clear, this section of the Independent Contractor Agreement specifies what is meant concerning confidentiality of operations.
    ■ The agent has an obligation to maintain a file. This requirement goes further and states that the file must be kept in the broker's office and must comply with the format regularly used by the broker for storing files.
    ■ The agent agrees that the files and anything related to the files will be kept in confidence and will not be shared with anyone without the knowledge and consent of the broker. There are two exceptions:
      — The law requires the revelation of the information.
      — The information is already public information.
    ■ The agreement also clarifies that the agent may not give any information, unless required by law, about 1) the broker's prospects or relationship with any prospects, or 2) the broker's policies and business operations.
    ■ Carefully consider the amount of information this requirement covers. The agent must be careful to protect the broker's industry secrets. The broker's ability to compete in the marketplace, and accomplish any financial goals may succeed or be usurped by the words of an agent. The concept is similar for the agent's broker. Anything the agent says may be overheard by the broker's competitor and be used against the broker.
    ■ Important: Paragraph 10 survives the termination of the agreement. This means that agents are responsible for keeping the broker's business secrets even after they no longer are licensed under that broker.
    ■ Note that all information composed, transmitted, or received on the broker's computer or network is considered part of the broker's records. Any enforcement agency can review it if required by law. The agent may not use, install, copy, or distribute any trademarked or patented material via the internet or by other means.
11. Ownership of Listings and Representation Agreements:
    ■ As discussed previously, the broker is the owner of all listings and representation agreements if the broker is named as a party in the contract/agreement.
12. Receipt of Money by Associate:
    ■ The associate must promptly deposit all checks or funds received in trust by the associate for others (earnest money deposits, etc.). This must be done according to the contractual requirement of the parties to the transaction.
    ■ Real estate salespersons are not allowed to maintain a separate trust account, escrow account, or management account for real estate business purposes. Only the broker may maintain a trust account for these purposes.
    ■ This area is one of the most violated areas under TRELA, either by mistake with good intentions or intentionally.

■ **EXAMPLE**   Sally is a salesperson, acting as an agent for her broker Betty is representing a seller, Sam. When an earnest money check is presented with a buyer's offer on Sam's property on Saturday morning, Sally deposits it in her personal savings account until she can get to the title company's office on Monday. This act of depositing the earnest money into her own personal account is a violation of TRELA and a violation of the independent contractor agreement she signed with her broker. Sally could lose her license, be disciplined by TREC, and be asked by the broker to leave the brokerage because of her seriousness mishandling of trust funds.

- ■ In addition, this paragraph clearly states that the agent must deliver to the broker any and all compensation for brokerage services received from any client, customer, escrow agent, title company, prospect, or any other person. Unless authorized by the broker to do otherwise, the agent must comply with this requirement. It does not matter whether the money in question is in the form of a check, credit card, draft, or any other negotiable instrument. The agent is required to give it to the broker.

13. Facilities:
    - ■ This paragraph specifically identifies any facilities at the broker's office that the broker may allow the agent to use for work related to the broker's real estate business. The allowed facility is filled in on the blank spaces. It may include the address of the office from which the associate will work on a daily basis and other locations as deemed appropriate by the broker. The agreement also clearly states that the associate is not required to be present in the broker's office.

14. Advertising:
    - ■ All advertising related to the broker's business must be placed by the broker or with the broker's knowledge and consent. The broker has sole discretion whether to include the associate's name in such advertising. The associate will always give the broker information and get the broker's consent before placing any advertisement related to the broker's real estate business.
    - ■ Improper or illegal advertising of real property has serious ramifications. Department of Housing and Urban Development (HUD) regulations, fair housing laws and rules, local/city fair housing laws, the Americans with Disabilities Act, and many other rules and regulations have specific guidelines for proper advertising. Generally, the broker or the broker's manager will review all proposed real estate advertising by the agents to determine whether any wording is incorrect or there are any violations of advertising laws.
    - ■ This paragraph also clarifies the definition of advertising. The areas of advertising included in the definition are inclusive and cover all publications, newsletters, radio or television broadcasts, electronic media (email and the internet), business stationery, business cards, signs, and billboards.

15. Assignment of Prospects:
    - ■ This paragraph refers to the definitions section to define the term *assign*. The broker has the right to appoint an agent to deal with prospects that either the associate or the broker procures.
    - ■ The broker also has sole discretion in assigning leads and prospects procured by the broker through the broker's real estate business to any of the broker's associates.

■ **EXAMPLE** Betty, a broker, receives a call at her brokerage office from Sam, a seller. Sam tells Betty he would like to list his home with her company. Betty may now give this listing lead to any sales associate in her office(s).

■ Additionally, the broker may reassign a prospect from one associate to another if
— the broker determines a reassignment of the prospect is necessary for the orderly, ethical, or lawful operation of the broker's real estate business;
— the associate who was first assigned is not able to continue to provide service to the prospect; or
— the initial associate's independent contractor agreement terminates.
■ It does not matter who procured the prospect; this applies to all prospects.

■ **EXAMPLE** Acting for her broker, salesperson Sally procures a seller prospect. Sally has a dispute with her broker. At lunch with a friend (a competing salesperson from another broker's office), Sally talks angrily about her broker and discloses some of her broker's business secrets. The broker is made aware of Sally's activities and tells Sally that she is no longer working for him.

■ The broker reassigns all the prospects Sally has been working with, as well as all the existing listings and buyer representation agreements that Sally has procured. The broker does this at his sole discretion because agency is by mutual consent only. And the wording of the independent contractor agreement that Sally signed explains that the broker has every right to take this action.
■ The last paragraph states the following: "Associate may not interfere with any assignments or reassignments of prospects or leads that Broker may make." That means if Sally has a list of 50 seller leads, the broker has the right to reassign any or all of those leads as the broker sees fit. Remember: The broker is the owner of all of the prospective buyers and sellers, and all of the listing and representation agreements, not the sales associate.

16. Associate's Fees:
■ TRELA makes it very clear that the broker is paid directly, not the salesperson working for the broker. The TAR Independent Contractor Agreement for Sales Associate restates that again. TRELA also makes it clear that the salesperson is prohibited from paying a fee directly to another person in the real estate transaction. The broker pays and receives the fees. Without specific permission from the broker, the sales associate has no authority to do anything with the money earned on behalf of the broker.

■ **EXAMPLE** Acting for her broker, salesperson Sally receives a referral from her licensed friend (who works for another broker) of the name of a buyer who is looking for property in Sally's area of listed properties. The buyer purchases one of Sally's listed properties. Once the transaction has closed, Sally directly sends her licensed friend a referral fee of $500. Sally and the friend have both violated TRELA, and in Sally's case, the TAR Independent Contractor Agreement she signed. Again, TRELA prohibits a salesperson from paying or receiving compensation other than through the broker for whom she works.

- This paragraph describes the payment that will be paid to the agent and refers to an attached fee schedule as a source for the specific percentages or amounts to be paid. In order to make the fee schedule part of the contractual agreement, the following words were added to the agreement: "which are incorporated into this agreement." This phrase, which satisfies the parol evidence rule, is designed to prevent the parol evidence rule from defeating the intent of the parties. In other words, by including this statement, it keeps the fee schedule from being extraneous material and thus not allowed as a part of the contract by the courts.

- When is the associate's fee earned and payable under this agreement?
    — Earned: At the time the broker's fees are earned under the applicable agreements for brokerage services that the associate performs for the broker.
    — Payable: At the time the broker receives broker's fees under the applicable agreements for brokerage services.
    — Exception: Unless the fees are subject to arbitration, litigation, or a court order.

- If a an associate of the broker claims a fee from a transaction for which another associate also claims a fee, the amount of the fee payable to the associate will be divided between the associate and the other associate claiming the fee in accordance with an agreement between them.

- **EXAMPLE**   Sally, a sales associate and agent for Betty, the broker, takes a listing on a seller's home. At the time of closing, John, also an associate of Betty, claims that he assisted the buyer during the transaction and wants Betty to pay him a part of the commission paid on this in-house transaction. Sally claims that she was the only one who worked with the buyer and asks her broker to pay her for both the selling side and the buying side of the transaction. The independent contractor agreement clearly spells out the following:

- "The fee payable to associate will be divided between Associate and the other associate claiming the fee in accordance with an agreement between them."

- "If no such agreement is reached, the dispute will be resolved by Broker's internal dispute resolution policy."

- If no such policy exists, then it will be decided through arbitration.

- The broker is now concerned about legal liability relative to either or both of the sales associates in this dispute. Consequently, another sentence is added to this paragraph: "Before disbursing any fee, Broker may require written authorization from any associate claiming the fee. The associate agrees not to hold the broker liable for holding, in trust, any disputed funds between associates."

- Remember, the broker has the authority to make decisions concerning listing agreements, buyer representation agreements, management agreements, and all business disputes. The agent for the broker has only the authority given by the broker. Sales associates may not think this is fair, but once the independent contractor agreement is signed, the broker has this right, whether it is perceived as fair or not.

- A broker who does not collect compensation from another broker is not liable to the associate for any fee not received. In addition, by this agreement, the broker is the one who retains complete discretion to enforce or not enforce any agreement for brokerage services with a prospect.
- Again, the associate may not accept any fee, bonus, or other compensation directly. All fees, bonuses, and other compensation must be paid to the broker for distribution in accordance with the independent contractor agreement.
- Bonuses will be considered a part of the gross compensation. The broker receives bonuses under the applicable agreements for brokerage services, unless otherwise agreed in writing between the parties to the independent contractor agreement. The attached fee schedule dictates the disbursement of the fees.
- If the broker reassigns a prospect to another associate, after the associate to this agreement deals with the prospect, the broker will pay a fee in accordance with 1) the attached fee schedule, and 2) any memorandum named in the blank space in this paragraph.
- The broker has sole discretion to divide the compensation between associates if a fee schedule is not attached to the independent contractor agreement.
- The associate does not have the right to assign any interest in fees or in compensation due under the agreement to anyone.

17. Expenses:
    - The broker is not liable for any expenses incurred by the associate. The associate is not liable to the broker for the office facilities that broker provides under the agreement. The broker and the associate have the right to contract otherwise.
    - This paragraph refers to the definition section and allows the broker to write or type in any conditions concerning special expenses.
    - Note: Special expenses may include items such as desk fees, transaction fees, errors and omissions insurance premiums, franchise fees, and the like. Special expenses will be
      — deducted from the gross fees that the broker receives and paid to the providers of the special services before calculating the associate's fees payable under the agreement;
      — invoiced to the associate by the broker and due and payable upon receipt of the invoice; and
      — charged to associate in accordance with either the attached fee schedule or some other named document.
      — Example: A sales associate owes the broker $100 for office fees. The sales associate sells one of the broker's listings. The sales associate's gross compensation due from the sale is $3,000. Before the broker disburses the $3,000 to the sales associate, the broker will subtract the $100 office fee from the $3,000 gross earnings and distribute a total of $2,900 to the sales associate.
    - Both the broker and the sales associate are responsible for their own license and membership fees. If the broker incurs a license or membership fee, that is the actual responsibility of the sales associate.

■ **EXAMPLE** A sales associate joins the local association of REALTORS® and multiple listing service. The bills for the sales associate are sent to the broker. The broker will invoice the sales associate by the terms of this agreement, and the sales associate will be required to pay the broker.

- Generally, a broker does not furnish an automobile to sales associates, and this agreement clearly states that the associate will furnish all of his own automobile expenses.
- Note: One section of this part of the agreement states the following: "Associate must maintain liability and property damage insurance satisfactory to broker and must name Broker as an additional insured in any such policy." The broker wants to ensure the ability to file a claim against the insurance policy and receive compensation from the policy if a third-party client or customer is injured while the associate is dealing with them in the course of performing a brokerage service. See example about Sally below.
- The associate is responsible for all of expenses necessary to perform the services required of the associate under the agreement. This paragraph lists items specifically, but is not limited to these items. The broker could pay any expense listed or otherwise but is not obligated to do so. If the broker does pay an expense on behalf of the associate, the associate is obligated to reimburse the broker for any amount paid, upon demand by the broker.

- **EXAMPLE**   Sally, a sales associate of broker Betty, takes a prospective buyer in her car to see one of Betty's listings. Through no fault of Sally's, another driver collides with Sally's car and the buyer is injured. The buyer sues the broker. Based on the independent contractor agreement, the broker, as a named party to Sally's insurance, may be protected financially through the policy.

In addition, if Sally does not keep the insurance up to date and allows the coverage to lapse, the broker may

- purchase insurance that will provide broker with the same coverage as required by this paragraph and associate must immediately reimburse broker for such expense; or
- terminate the independent contractor agreement.

18. Offset:
   - The broker has the right to deduct any amount owed by the associate to the broker from any amount owed by the broker to the associate.
19. Defense of Disputes and Litigation:
   - If one of the parties to a transaction that the associate is conducting complains, files a lawsuit, or brings a dispute, the broker and the broker's sales associate promise to cooperate fully with each other to defend the action.
   - Note: The broker is a separate entity, even though the sales associate is functioning as the broker's agent. The sales associate may want to consider having his own legal counsel to defend against any lawsuit or complaint filed against the sales associate or the broker.
   - Payment of any deductible amounts from errors and omissions insurance will be paid as stated in the blank space in this paragraph.
   - This agreement states the following:

     If any defense expenses are not paid by an errors and omissions insurer, Broker and Associate will share all such expenses and costs related to defend the dispute, litigation, or complaint in the same proportion as they would share the fee resulting from the transaction as if there were no dispute, litigation, or complaint; provided that both broker and Associate are named as defendants or respondents to the dispute, litigation, or complaint.

The sales associate contemplating signing any independent contractor agreement needs to pay particular attention to any promise to co-litigate or co-defend in a lawsuit.

- The associate and/or broker may determine that she cannot mutually defend a dispute, litigation, or complaint with the other party. In that case, each party will be responsible for its own costs to defend the dispute. Notification to the other party of this choice by one of the parties is required.
- If the broker and the associate agree to co-defend in the litigation or dispute, the broker has sole discretion to do the following:
  — Determine whether to defend or compromise
  — Employ attorneys or other experts
  — Direct the course of any defense strategy
  — Determine the terms and conditions of any compromise or settlement
  — Exception: The broker may not obligate the associate to pay anything of value without the associate's written consent.
- Notwithstanding paragraph 19F, the broker and the associate are each responsible for the payment of any amounts for which they are found individually liable.
- If the associate is negligent, misrepresents, commits fraud, makes false statements, violates TRELA, or violates any other state or federal statute, and the broker is found liable by a court, arbitrator, or government agency, the associate will indemnify and reimburse the broker all expenses necessary to defend against such action.
- Paragraph 19 survives the termination of the agreement.

20. Prosecution of Claims:
- The broker retains all rights to either sue or not sue, or bring a complaint, or settle any claim that the broker may have against any person. The sales associate has no authority to make this decision.

21. Termination:
- The broker and/or the associate may terminate the independent contractor agreement. Written notice to the other party must be given.
- Any fee to the associate that remains unpaid on the date of termination is to be paid in accordance with the following:
  — The attached schedule
  — Any other fee schedule mentioned in the blanks in this paragraph
- Once terminated, all negotiations and other brokerage services commenced by the associate are terminated.
- Once terminated, the associate is obligated to do the following:
  — Cease all negotiations
  — Provide the broker a written list of all current listings and pending sales and leases
  — Turn over to the broker all files related to the broker's real estate business
  — Turn over to the broker all the broker's personal property (keys, signs, equipment, supplies, manuals, forms, etc.)

- The associate may not remove any files related to the broker's real estate business from the broker's office unless the associate has the written consent of the broker.

22. Notices:
- All notices (legal communication between the parties) must be in writing and are effective when hand-delivered, mailed, sent by facsimile transmission, or sent by electronic mail from one party to the other.
- Note: If the associate wants to notify the broker, she must use one of the listed forms of notice specified by the broker. If the associate tries to use some other form of notice, the law may not recognize that the attempted notification by the sales associate to the broker took place.

23. Special Provisions:
- This blank section in the agreement is used for agreements of the parties that are not already stated in the agreement. Because both the associate and the broker are parties to this agreement, they are both allowed to write additional stated agreements in this section.

24. Agreement of the Parties:
- Once again, the fee schedule, Statement of Understanding, IRS Form W-9, and any additional form written into the blank spaces are made a part of the agreement.
- The document contains the entire agreement between the parties. It must have the agreement of both parties to be changed.
- The agreement may not be assigned to any other party except with the written agreement of the other party.
- The parties' obligations and rights become a benefit to the respective party's successors, permitted assigns, heirs, executors, and administrators.
- The laws of the State of Texas govern the interpretation, validity, performance, and enforcement of the agreement.
- If any clause is not valid or enforceable by a court of law, the remainder of the agreement will not be affected and all other provisions of the agreement remain valid and enforceable.
- Waiver of any provision in the agreement by any party is effective only if the waiver is in writing.

The final statement of the independent contractor agreement says the following: "This is intended to be a legally binding agreement. READ IT CAREFULLY. If you do not understand the effect of this agreement, consult your attorney BEFORE signing."

The last thing the associate and the broker do is sign and date the agreement. They must be sure that all the additional information requested on the last page is accurate (e.g., license number, home address, home phone, mobile phone, e-mail address).

■ EMPLOYMENT LAW

There is a difference between hiring an employee and sponsoring a salesperson who will work as an independent contractor. First, we will take a look at the *Internal Revenue Service—Employer's Supplemental Tax Guide* to establish how the IRS defines an independent contractor for the purposes of imposing taxes on both the broker and the salesperson/independent contractor.

Following are the relevant parts from the IRS's *Employer's Supplemental Tax Guide* (Publication 15-A, Cat. No. 21453T, which can be found at www.irs.gov/pub/irs-pdf/p15a.pdf):

... 2. Employee or Independent Contractor?

An employer must generally withhold federal income taxes, withhold and pay over social security and Medicare taxes, and pay unemployment tax on wages paid to an employee. **An employer does not generally have to with-hold or pay over any federal taxes on payments to independent contractors** (emphasis added).

Common law Rules

To determine whether an individual is an employee or an independent contractor under the common law, the relationship of the worker and the business must be examined. In any employee-independent contractor determination, all information that provides evidence of the degree of control and the degree of independence must be considered.

Facts that provide evidence of the degree of control and independence fall into three categories: behavioral control, financial control, and the type of relationship of the parties. These facts are discussed next.

Behavioral control. Facts that show whether the business has a right to direct and control how the worker does the task for which the worker is hired include the type and degree of:

Instructions that the business gives to the worker. An employee is generally subject to the business' instructions about when, where, and how to work. All of the following are examples of types of instructions about how to do work.

- When and where to do the work.
- What tools or equipment to use.
- What workers to hire or to assist with the work.
- Where to purchase supplies and services.
- What work must be performed by a specified individual.
- What order or sequence to follow.

The amount of instruction needed varies among different jobs. Even if no instructions are given, sufficient behavioral control may exist if the employer has the right to control how the work results are achieved. A business may lack the knowledge to instruct some highly specialized professionals; in other cases, the task may require little or no instruction. The key consideration is whether the business has retained the right to control the details of a worker's performance or instead has given up that right.

Training that the business gives to the worker. An employee may be trained to perform services in a particular manner. Independent contractors ordinarily use their own methods.

Financial control. Facts that show whether the business has a right to control the business aspects of the worker's job include:

The extent to which the worker has unreimbursed business expenses. Independent contractors are more likely to have unreimbursed expenses than are employees. Fixed ongoing costs that are incurred regardless of whether work is currently being performed are especially important. However, employees may also incur unreimbursed expenses in connection with the services that they perform for their employer.

The extent of the worker's investment. An independent contractor often has a significant investment in the facilities or tools he or she uses in performing services for someone else. However, a significant investment is not necessary for independent contractor status.

The extent to which the worker makes his or her services available to the relevant market. An independent contractor is generally free to seek out business opportunities. Independent contractors often advertise, maintain a visible business location, and are available to work in the relevant market.

How the business pays the worker. An employee is generally guaranteed a regular wage amount for an hourly, weekly, or other period of time. This usually indicates that a worker is an employee, even when the wage or salary is supplemented by a commission. An independent contractor is often paid a flat fee or on a time and materials basis for the job. However, it is common in some professions, such as law, to pay independent contractors hourly.

The extent to which the worker can realize a profit or loss. An independent contractor can make a profit or loss.

Type of relationship. Facts that show the parties' type of relationship include:

- *Written contracts describing the relationship the parties intended to create.*
- *Whether or not the business provides the worker with employee-type benefits, such as insurance, a pension plan, vacation pay, or sick pay.*
- *The permanency of the relationship.* If you engage a worker with the expectation that the relationship will continue indefinitely, rather than for a specific project or period, this is generally considered evidence that your intent was to create an employer-employee relationship.
- *The extent to which services performed by the worker are a key aspect of the regular business of the company.* If a worker provides services that are a key aspect of your regular business activity, it is more likely that you will have the right to direct and control his or her activities. For example, if a law firm hires an attorney, it is likely that it will present the attorney's work as its own and would have the right to control or direct that work. This would indicate an employer-employee relationship.

IRS help. If you want the IRS to determine whether or not a worker is an employee, file Form SS-8, Determination of Worker Status for Purposes of Federal Employment Taxes and Income Tax Withholding, with the IRS …

… Salesperson

To determine whether salespersons are employees under the usual **common law** rules, you must evaluate each individual case. If a salesperson who works for you does not meet the tests for a common law employee, discussed earlier in this section, you do not have to withhold federal income tax from his or her pay (see *Statutory Employees* in section 1). However, even if a salesperson is not an employee under the usual common law rules for income tax withholding, his or her pay may still be subject to social security, Medicare, and FUTA taxes as a statutory employee.

To determine whether a salesperson is an employee for social security, Medicare, and FUTA tax purposes, the salesperson must meet **all eight** elements of the statutory employee test. A salesperson is a statutory employee for social security, Medicare, and FUTA tax purposes if he or she:

1. Works full time for one person or company except, possibly, for sideline sales activities on behalf of some other person,

2. Sells on behalf of, and turns his or her orders over to, the person or company for which he or she works,

3. Sells to wholesalers, retailers, contractors, or operators of hotels, restaurants, or similar establishments,

4. Sells merchandise for resale, or supplies for use in the customer's business,

5. Agrees to do substantially all of this work personally,

6. Has no substantial investment in the facilities used to do the work, other than in facilities for transportation,

7. Maintains a continuing relationship with the person or company for which he or she works, and

8. Is **not** an employee under common law rules.

■ EMPLOYMENT RELATIONSHIPS BETWEEN BROKERS AND PRINCIPALS

Brokers generally enter into employment contracts with property owners through listing agreements and property management agreements. Likewise, brokers enter into employment agreements with buyers and tenants through buyer-tenant representation agreements. As discussed in previous chapters, these agreements set out the terms of employment and address issues of compensation.

Under the terms of most employment contracts with principals, brokers are responsible for the payment of brokerage expenses associated with the agreement.

In addition, the broker pays any income tax due because of any compensation received during the course of the employment.

Although brokerage fees are generally paid at the time of closing and funding of the transaction, many courts have ruled that the broker's fees are considered **earned and payable** when the broker produces a **ready, willing, and able buyer** under the terms of a listing agreement. This concept is addressed in the TAR Residential Real Estate Listing Agreement (see Figure 4.2, paragraph 5B). The basic theory is that the broker was hired to find a suitable buyer for the seller's property, and when that has been accomplished, the broker should be entitled to a commission even if the seller decides not to sell. Under TAR's Residential Buyer/Tenant Representation Agreement (see Figure 5.1 paragraph 11C), the buyer-agent fee is "earned and payable" as soon as the buyer enters into a contract to buy or lease a property and is payable even if the buyer later breaches the sales contract with the seller. It is not illegal in Texas for a broker to represent a seller or a buyer on the basis of a verbal agreement. Equally important is the fact that the broker will find little recourse against the principal who refuses to pay the broker on the strength of a verbal agreement. In order to recover compensation from the seller, the broker will be required to bring suit against the seller (there are exceptions for commercial brokers who may obtain a contractual voluntary lien for commission). For brokers to sue for a commission, TRELA § 1101.806 requires that

■ brokers prove they were duly licensed at the time the brokerage services began;
■ the agreement for compensation be in writing and signed at least by the party to be charged the commission; and
■ at the time of signing the contract to purchase, the buyer was advised in writing to have an abstract of title examined by an attorney, or to secure a policy of title insurance.

The following case illustrates the importance of obtaining a clear and concise written agreement of commission before proceeding with brokerage activities.

■ **EXAMPLE**   In *Neary v. Mikob Properties, Inc.*, 340 S.W. 316 (Tex. App. Dallas 2011), Neary and his company, St. John Holdings (SJH), filed suit to recover a brokerage fee associated with the sale of eight apartment complexes. Neary held a valid broker license at the time; however, SJH was not licensed as a business entity by TREC at the time of the transaction. The brokerage fee was not addressed in the actual purchase agreement. Instead, Neary claimed that a November 17, 2003, document titled "Term Sheet," combined with a series of emails before and after the "Term Sheet," established a contract for a brokerage fee of 2% of the sales price and that SJH was Neary's "agent for receipt of his commission." The seller claimed that the "Term Sheet" did not meet the written requirement of TRELA § 1101.806 and that since SJH was not licensed as a broker, SJH could not file suit for recovery of a commission. Although the "Term Sheet" was signed, written in above the signatures was the sentence, "This term sheet is a guideline only, and is not binding." Furthermore, the "Term Sheet" identified the purchaser as a Texas limited liability company "to be formed"; the term "seller" was used, but no seller was identified; and the property was identified as eight complexes but with no addresses or legal descriptions. The emails were between the brokers, and although several proposals were set forth, the emails did not settle on an amount the brokers were to be paid. Nowhere in the "Term Sheet" was there any indication of the relationship between Mikob Properties, Inc., and the broker allegedly signing on the company's behalf, a man named Kobernick.

■ **DISCUSSION** The court ruled that TRELA § 1101.806 (c) clearly provides that a broker cannot maintain a suit for a commission unless it is based on an agreement that has been rendered in written form and signed by the person against whom the broker seeks to enforce the commission. So the issue before the court was whether or not the combination of emails and the "Term Sheet" met the requirement for a written commission agreement. The court noted that to comply an agreement must

- be in writing and signed by the person to be charged the commission;
- promise that a definite commission will be paid or must refer to a written commission schedule;
- state the name of the broker to whom the commission is to be paid; and
- either itself or by reference to some other existing writing, identify with reasonable certainty the property to be conveyed (i.e., a legal description).

The court ruled that the sellers had signed no written agreement to pay a commission and that the "Term Sheet" and emails did not constitute a written agreement. Furthermore, the "Term Sheet" identified SJH as the broker, not Neary, and SJH was not a business entity holding a broker license in Texas at the time of the transaction.

Employment Relationships Between Brokers and Associates

In Texas, about two-thirds of all brokers work for the remaining one-third. The broker is held responsible to the state and the public for the conduct of licensees who are either licensed under the broker or working as independent contractors or employees. The responsible broker is frequently referred to as a sponsoring broker, principal broker, or designated broker. The employed, associated, or sponsored licensee is then licensed either as a salesperson or as a broker. An associate who is a broker generally is called a broker associate. Texas offers no broker associate license.

An active salesperson licensee is required to work under the sponsorship of an actively licensed broker. The broker may either be an individual or a business entity. The term *business entity* is defined in 22 TAC § 535.1(2) as "a corporation, limited liability, partnership or other entity authorized under the Texas Business Organizations Code." Under certain circumstances, the broker might even be a business entity from another state qualified to do business in Texas (22 TAC § 535.53(b)). If the broker is a business entity, however, then one of its managing officers must be licensed as an individual broker in Texas, who then acts as the designated broker for the business entity. Unlike a salesperson licensee, a person licensed as a broker may work independently or may enter into an agency relationship with another broker (broker associate) to represent that broker in dealings with the public.

Based on the TRELA and the doctrine of respondeat superior ("let the master answer"), the broker is liable to the commission, the public, and the broker's clients for any conduct engaged in under TRELA by the broker or by a licensee associated with the broker during the ordinary course of employment (§ 1101.803; 22 TAC § 535.2(a); 22 TAC § 535.141(c)). In the case of a business entity, the designated broker of the business entity is the person held liable

(22 TAC § 535.2(l)). Under general agency concepts, each of these licensed associates is the agent of the broker and represents the broker in a fiduciary capacity. Listings are made in the name of the broker, not the salesperson or the broker associate. The broker is the party responsible to the public and to clients, whether acting directly or indirectly through the broker's agents. If a broker has a listing (open or exclusive), that broker and all the licensed associates of that firm represent the seller in a fiduciary capacity. This is true of all licensed associates working in each of the listing broker's offices. (This rule, however, does not apply to franchise organizations in which each franchised brokerage firm is independently owned.)

It is important to understand that licensed salespersons cannot lawfully sell their services **directly** to the public. **Salespersons must perform all tasks under the direct supervision of a broker.** This is true even if the salesperson is, for tax purposes, an independent contractor. Under agency and licensing law and for purposes of supervision, salespersons who are licensed with a broker are agents and employees of the broker and act for the broker. The phrase *acts for*, as used in the TREC rules cited here, is equivalent to the description of an agency relationship (TRELA § 1101.351; .557; .803).

Licensed salespersons cannot legally

- list property in their own names (22 TAC § 535.154(d)(4); § 535.2(f));
- enter into buyer agency or intermediary agreements in their own names, either orally or in writing;
- sue directly sellers, buyers, landlords, or tenants for unpaid commissions (generally);
- open their own offices without hiring a broker to be responsible for all the licensees in the offices and submitting that broker's name to TREC;
- work independently without having a licensed sponsoring broker to shelter or hold each salesperson's license;
- hold a license under more than one broker at the same time;
- take listings or buyer-tenant representation agreements when they move to a new brokerage office with or without the current broker's consent (although the broker may release represented owners or buyers from their agreements and allow a salesperson's new broker to attempt to contract with the owners, buyers, or tenants);
- advertise in their own names unless the broker's name also appears, and it is clear to the public which one is the broker (TRELA § 1101.652(b)(23); 22 TAC § 535.154(d)(g));
- open their own client trust accounts for sales or rentals (22 TAC § 535.159(f));
- accept compensation directly from clients or other brokers for real estate sales and transactions without the broker's consent (TRELA § 1101.651(b); 22 TAC § 535.3); or
- pay a commission to any person except through the broker under whom they are licensed or with that broker's knowledge and consent (TRELA § 1101.651(c); 22 TAC § 535.3).

Definition of Broker Associate

A broker associate is a broker who holds a broker's license but who is with another broker in order to become an agent of, but not a partner of, the other broker.

Because they have the same state license as the principal broker, broker associates may be allowed to do virtually any of these things if the broker they work for does not prohibit a broker associate from running another brokerage operation. This practice is not the norm, however, and any broker associate attempting any of the above-listed actions without the principal broker's knowledge and consent would likely be at risk.

TREC does not regulate the broker's contractual arrangements with other brokers. The principal broker of a broker associated with the company should keep in mind—and make the associate aware—that the License Act holds the principal broker responsible for the acts of associated broker licensees (TRELA § 1101.803). In addition, in any lawsuit against the associate broker, if the plaintiff (the person bringing the suit) believes the associate acted in the name of the principal broker, will most likely name the broker in the lawsuit and the broker may be held liable for the damages caused by an associated broker. It is important to understand that when an associate of the broker secures a listing or buyer representation agreement, it is the principal broker who is employed by the buyer or the seller and acts as the direct agent of the buyer- or seller-client. The sales associate or broker associate does not directly represent the buyer or the seller, but instead, represent the principal broker and by way of the principal broker represents the buyer- or seller-client.

In Texas, it is not legally possible to construct a figurative internal wall within a brokerage firm and argue that because different licensed associates act for the buyer and the seller, no dual representation exists. In Texas, such an attempt likely would not hold up in court or at a TREC disciplinary hearing. By analogy, a large law firm could not have one of its associates on the 10th floor represent the seller of a commercial warehouse and another associate on the 11th floor represent the buyer without first obtaining from the buyer and the seller complete and detailed consent to such dual representation and agreement to receive a limited form of fiduciary representation.

Some brokerage firms advertise that they have salespersons who represent buyers and other salespersons who represent sellers. For example, Tom from Executive Realty, as the listing agent, innocently might tell an interested buyer who has expressed a desire to obtain her own agent, "I can't be your agent, but Dorothy in our branch office is very knowledgeable, loves to represent buyers, and can give you the type of representation you want."

Tom's firm must be careful to develop its company policies within the bounds of agency law. It is the principal broker, not the associates, that—by law—represents the buyer or the seller. The principal broker represents all buyers and sellers for which he has a signed listing contract or a signed buyer representation agreement. That means all of the principal broker's sales associates and the broker associates represent, through the principal broker, all of those same buyers and sellers.

Listing brokers should set up internal management controls to ensure that their associates understand these basic agency principles.

Employee Versus Independent Contractor

Brokers engage salespersons as either employees or independent contractors. Any agreements between brokers and their associates should be in the form of written contracts that define the obligations and responsibilities of the relationships. Whether an associate operates under the broker as an employee (compensation based on time) or as an independent contractor (compensation based on results) will affect the relationship between them. (See Figure 9.1.)

At minimum, TREC Rule 22 TAC § 535.2(i), requires the broker to maintain written policies and procedures to ensure the following:

1. Each sponsored salesperson is advised of the scope of the salesperson's authorized activities subject to the Act and is competent to conduct such activities.
2. Each sponsored salesperson maintains a license in active status at all times while engaged in activities subject to the Act.
3. Any and all compensation paid to the sponsored salesperson for acts or services subject to the Act is paid by, through, or with the written consent of the sponsoring broker.
4. Each sponsored salesperson is provided on a timely basis, before the effective date of the change, notice of any change to the Act, Rules, or commission promulgated contract forms.
5. In addition to completing statutory minimum continuing education requirements, each sponsored salesperson receives such additional educational instruction as the broker deems necessary to obtain and maintain on a current basis competency in the scope of the sponsored salesperson's practice.
6. Each sponsored salesperson complies with the commission's advertising rules.
7. All trust accounts . . . are handled by the broker with appropriate controls.
8. Records are properly maintained.

F I G U R E   9.1

Independent Contractor Versus Employee

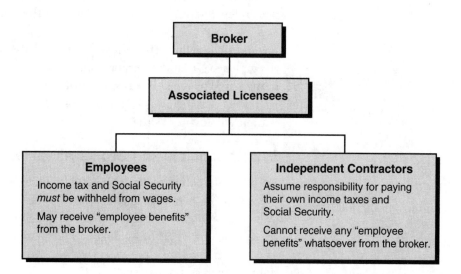

The nature of the employer-employee relationship allows a broker to exercise certain controls over associates who are employees. The broker may require that an employee adhere to regulations concerning such matters as working hours, office routine, dress, or conduct. As an employer, a broker is required by the federal government to withhold Social Security and income taxes from wages paid to employees. The broker also is required to pay unemployment compensation taxes, as required by state and federal laws. In addition, a broker may be required to provide employees with such benefits as health insurance and profit-sharing plans.

Independent contractors operate more freely than employees, and the broker may not control their activities in the same way. Crucial elements of preserving independent contractor status are that the

■ independent contractor's services must be performed under the terms of a written contract between the broker and the associate;
■ broker may control what the independent contractor does, but not how it is done; and
■ contract must state that the independent contractor assumes responsibility for paying any required income and Social Security taxes and receives nothing from the broker that could be construed as an employee benefit.

Fearful that the strictly mandated written policies and controls noted here might jeopardize the independent contractor relationship where Internal Revenue Service (IRS) is concerned, the rule states that the section was not meant to create or require an employer/employee relationship between a broker and a sponsored salesperson (22 TAC § 535.2(m)).

In Texas, brokers are not required to carry workers' compensation coverage for independent contractors.

To ensure that all licensed associates are treated by the IRS and the Texas Employment Commission as independent contractors, brokers are urged to maintain close contact with competent tax counsel and have their policies and procedures reviewed frequently for compliance. Brokers should exercise great care to ensure that independent contractors understand their personal obligations under law.

Some people believe that the difference between an independent contractor and an employee is that the former works on a commission-only basis and the employee is salaried. That may be relevant, but it is not conclusive. Many salespersons are paid on a commission basis but are considered employees because of other features of their employment situations.

Sales Associate and Broker Associate Compensation

An associate's compensation is set by mutual agreement between the broker and the associate. A broker may agree to pay a salary or a share of the commissions from transactions originated by an associate. Associates may have a drawing account against their individual earned share of commissions. In such a case, the associate should sign a note for each draw to preserve the independent contractor status, if such status is desired.

A departure from traditional compensation plans is the 100% commission plan. Generally, in a brokerage firm that has adopted this system, associates pay a monthly service charge to the broker (to cover the costs of office space, telephone service, supervision, and administration) and receive 100% of the commissions from the sales they negotiate.

■ EMPLOYMENT AND COMPENSATION OF PERSONAL ASSISTANTS

Many busy brokers and associates have found that employing personal assistants allows them to become more productive. Assistants are generally given responsibilities that do not require licensure, such as holding open houses, maintaining records, scheduling, and placing signs and lockboxes on properties. Some licensees employ assistants who are licensed so that more extensive duties can be assigned.

Employment agreements must be carefully considered. It may be difficult to employ a personal assistant as an independent contractor because the essence of the relationship is that the employer carefully directs and controls the actions of the assistant. Because an independent contractor must be able to perform duties independent of employer control or direction, it may be difficult, if not impossible, to convince the IRS that such a relationship exists with an assistant. Before entering into such an agreement, it would be wise to consult an attorney or CPA who is familiar with all aspects of employment law.

TREC has produced an excellent overview of the laws pertaining to the use of personal assistants, and added a Q&A section that answers many questions salespersons and brokers have regarding hiring a personal assistant. The following TREC Q&A can also be found at www.trec.state.tx.us/newsandpublic/publications/specialtopics/unlicensed-assistants.asp:

> **Information for Brokers and Salespersons Regarding Use of Unlicensed Assistants in Real Estate Transactions**
>
> Brokers and salespersons often use unlicensed personnel for assistance in conducting their real estate brokerage activities. Such unlicensed persons, sometimes referred to as administrative assistants, can be of great help to a busy agent. However, care must be taken to ensure that the unlicensed person does not conduct any of the activities for which real estate licensure is required. This article defines some of those activities which may and may not be legally conducted by unlicensed persons.
>
> Sections 1101.351(a) and 1101.758 of The Real Estate License Act establish that it is a crime for an unlicensed person to engage in activity for which a real estate license is required. The broker or salesperson that employs an unlicensed person might be criminally charged for the crime as well. In addition, TREC may take disciplinary action against a broker or salesperson that pays or associates with an unlicensed person who engages in activities that require a real estate license. Authority for this disciplinary action is set out in Sections 1101.652(b)(11) and (26) of the License Act. For these reasons, it is important to distinguish between those activities that do and those that do not require a real estate license. Section 1101.002(1)(A) of

the License Act sets forth a list of activities that require licensure and are worthy of a close reading.

Preliminarily, the real estate brokerage activities must be "for another" person or entity. This means that persons who are buying, selling or leasing their own property do not need a license; they are acting for themselves and not for another person. The activities must also be for a fee or something of value, or with the intention of collecting a fee or something of value. This means, for example, that an unlicensed person whose neighbor has been transferred out of state may solicit tenants and negotiate a lease on behalf of the neighbor so long as the person does not receive or expect to receive anything of value for helping.

The list of activities requiring licensure may be summarized and placed in two categories (but remember, this is a summary only and not all inclusive). First, and as used in the paragraph above, are those activities in which a person directly helps another buy, sell, or lease real property. These activities, such as negotiating a listing agreement with a property owner, spending the afternoon with a couple showing houses for sale, or negotiating a contract to buy or lease real property, obviously require licensure. These "direct" activities are seldom the subject of debate or controversy.

The second category of activities might be referred to as "indirect" activities and are more troublesome. Section 1101.002(1)(A)(viii) of the License Act requires licensure of those persons who procure or assist in procuring prospects to buy, sell, or lease property. Section 1101.002(1)(A)(ix) of the License Act requires licensure of those persons who procure or assist in procuring properties to be bought, sold, or leased. If the words "assist in" were read broadly enough, virtually everyone working in a real estate office would need a license. Common sense dictates, however, that many activities can be legally conducted in a real estate brokerage office that do not require licensure. There may sometimes exist only a thin line between those activities that require licensure and those that do not. The foregoing general rules and the following discussion of factual situations may help licensees accurately draw this line.

"Q: May an unlicensed person, identified as such, make calls to determine whether a person is interested in buying or selling property, or has property they wish to sell, and if so, make an appointment for a licensed agent to talk to them?

"A: No. Often referred to as "telemarketing," any such activities conducted in Texas must be conducted by a licensee. In Tex. Atty. Gen. Op. H-1271 (1978), the attorney general concluded that a license was required. Also, Commission Rule 535.4(e) makes it clear that all solicitation work must be conducted by licensees.

"Q: May an unlicensed person sit in on an open house?

"A: Yes, but care must be taken that the unlicensed person does not "show" the house to prospective purchasers. Commission Rule

535.4(c) makes clear that only licensed agents are allowed to show properties. On the other hand, Commission Rule 535.5(h) also specifically allows a broker to hire an unlicensed person to serve as a "host or hostess" at homes offered for sale by the broker. The Rules do not define these terms, and such a hostess should be limited to welcoming the visitors. The hostess may register the guests and refer inquiries to a licensee. Clearly, the hostess must not point out features of the home or neighborhood to visitors; however, as is the case with secretaries and receptionists discussed below, the hostess may distribute a flyer or brochure that describes the property.

"Q: May unlicensed assistants set appointments to show a listing?

"A: Yes. Under the general rules stated above, it is permissible for an assistant to call a homeowner and schedule an appointment for the broker to bring a potential buyer to see the home. If the broker then becomes tied up on other matters, can the unlicensed assistant drive the purchaser to the listing and let them in the home? Again, yes, but extreme care must be taken that the assistant does not engage in "showing" the property. The assistant should identify himself as an unlicensed assistant and explain the assistant's limited role. Any questions that arise regarding the property or the purchase of the property must be referred to a licensee.

"Q: May the unlicensed assistant place "for sale" signs; open a property or accompany inspectors; place newspaper advertisements as directed by the broker?

"A: Yes, subject to the following guidelines. Commission Rule 535.5(g) provides that answering the telephone and acts of a secretarial nature do not require licensure. Clerical employees need not be licensed so long as they do not engage in solicitation and do not hold themselves out as licensed agents. Further, Commission Rule 535.5(g) also states that an unlicensed clerical or secretarial employee, identified to callers as such, may confirm information concerning the size, price and terms of property advertised. Taken together, this means that an unlicensed person may, after identifying himself or herself as an unlicensed person, confirm information previously advertised to callers or persons dropping by. The unlicensed person should not give information about properties other than that inquired about, and should refer any requests for information regarding other properties to a licensed agent. For example, the assistant might confirm that a particular property called about has three bedrooms and one bath, as previously advertised; however, the assistant may not attempt to identify properties which instead have two baths and bring these to the attention of the caller. Such questions must be referred to a licensee. The assistant should not attempt to "qualify" the caller in any respect. Many other duties that are administrative in nature can be safely performed, such as inputting data into a computer or typing contracts, but, only as specifically directed by a licensee. Support personnel can order supplies, schedule maintenance, and all the other things that are involved in keeping the office open. Bookkeeping and office management functions may be performed by an unlicensed assistant, as discussed immediately below.

"Q: What functions may an unlicensed office manager perform?

"A: Unlicensed persons may perform administrative tasks such as training or motivating personnel, and those tasks dealing with office administration and personnel matters. In addition, Commission Rule 535.2(c) notes that who a broker designates to sign checks in the brokerage is not regulated by the Commission. Thus, an unlicensed person may serve as bookkeeper for the company and handle personnel matters. Such an office manager may also serve as a trainer. However, Commission Rule 535.4(d) further states that an unlicensed person may not direct or supervise agents in their work as licensees. Therefore, an unlicensed person may not direct or advise agents in their attempts to help others buy, sell, or lease property. They may not review contracts, or help make "deals" work. These tasks are properly conducted only by licensed persons.

"Q: May unlicensed persons assist in arranging financing?

"A: Yes; however, great care must be taken that the person acts solely in an administrative capacity. An unlicensed assistant may be directed by a broker or salesperson to assist a particular buyer in obtaining information and forms to apply for and qualify for a loan. However, these acts should be at the direction of a licensee. Mortgage brokers and loan originators are licensed by the Texas Department of Savings and Mortgage Lending, and any questions regarding the requirements for licensure for persons dealing with financing issues should be directed to that agency.

"Q: May unlicensed persons serve as property managers for rental properties?

"A: Those who hold themselves out as "property managers" for others and for compensation must be licensed, provided the person also rent or leases the property for the property owner. In addition, Section 1101.002(1)(A)(x) of the License Act requires licensure for a person who controls the acceptance or deposit of rent from a resident of a single-family residential real property unit. Section 535.4(g) of the Commission Rules provides that a person controls the acceptance or deposit of rent if the person has the authority to use the rent to pay for services related to management of the property or has the authority to deposit the rent into a trust account and sign checks or withdraw money from the account. Many property management activities, such as bookkeeping and arranging for repairs, do not generally require licensure. So long as an unlicensed person carefully limits his or her property management activities to those which do not require a license, neither criminal charges nor Commission disciplinary action would be warranted. Note that persons acting as on-site managers at apartment complexes are exempt from licensure under Section 1101.005(7) of the License Act.

"Q: What can a licensee do to avoid criminal or disciplinary actions?

"A: First, a broker should NOT let his or her license or any of the licensed associates' licenses lapse. The lapse of a license, often inadvertent, is a common basis for disciplinary action on the grounds of improper unlicensed activity. Second, analyze any new factual situation according to the rules above to determine the extent to which the unlicensed person is being allowed to act with discretion, and how close the unlicensed person is "directly" assisting others in buying, selling, or leasing property. If still troubled, contact your attorney. You may also write or email the Commission (or call in an emergency) for an informal opinion based on a particular fact situation. Managing brokers might gain some protection from disciplinary action by establishing written guidelines and training dictating to both their agents and unlicensed personnel what is allowed and not allowed of non-licensees.

"As always, you should contact your attorney regarding matters raised by this article. You may also wish to ask your attorney for advice regarding potential civil liability for acts performed by unlicensed persons. "

■ RELATIONSHIPS BETWEEN BROKERS, AGENTS, AND SUBAGENTS

Broker to Broker's Agent/Sales Associate

The relationship between brokers and their agents/sales associates is one of a broker/principal to sales associate/agent. The sales associate will generally become an independent contractor as opposed to an employee. The licensed sales associate of the broker functions at the direction of the broker, and the broker is responsible for all acts of the sales associates when acting in the capacity of agents with third parties in a real estate transaction.

Broker to Other Broker

Brokers who are brokers of different companies function in an arm's-length relationship when involved in a real estate transaction. When one broker is representing the seller and the other is representing the buyer, they are each advocates for their respective clients and will negotiate strongly to obtain the best possible price, terms, and conditions for their clients. If the brokers are REALTORS®, the Code of Ethics addresses "Duties to REALTORS®" in Articles 15–17:

Article 15: REALTORS® shall not knowingly or recklessly make false or misleading statements about other real estate professionals, their business, or their business practices (Amended 1/12)

Article 16: REALTORS® shall not engage in any practice or take any action inconsistent with exclusive representation or exclusive brokerage relationship agreements that other REALTORS® have with clients (Amended 1/04)

Article 17: In the event of contractual disputes or specific non-contractual disputes as defined in Standard of Practice 17-4 between REALTORS (principals) associated with different firms, arising out of their relationship as REALTORS®, the REALTORS® shall mediate the dispute if the Board requires its members to mediate. If the dispute is not resolved through mediation, or if mediation is not required, REALTORS® shall submit the dispute to arbitration in accordance with the policies of the Board rather than litigate the matter.

In the event clients of REALTORS® wish to mediate or arbitrate contractual disputes arising out of real estate transactions, REALTORS® shall mediate or arbitrate those disputed in accordance with the policies of the Board, provided the clients agree to be bound by any resulting agreement or award.

The obligation to participate in mediation and arbitration contemplated by this Article includes the obligation of REALTORS® (principals) to cause their firms to mediate and arbitrate and be bound by any resulting agreement or award. (Amended 1/12)

Brokers acting as agents for the buyer or seller are focused on accomplishing serious goals on behalf of the clients. They strive to be courteous to one another, cooperative, honest when sharing data without revealing confidential or strategic information of their seller or buyer-client.

Broker to Other Sales Associate

The relationship between the broker of one company and the sales associate of another company is even more removed than that of the broker-to-broker relationship. For instance, broker A of ABC Real Estate, Inc., and sales associate B of XYZ Real Estate, Inc., are in an arm's-length relationship. The sales associate functions only through her broker, and when talking with broker A, has no direct relationship with her. Meanwhile, unseen and unheard, is the broker of sales associate B. All information derived by sales associate B pertaining to a real estate transaction in which she is acting as an agent of her broker is to be transferred to her broker and her broker's client. A may not give B a fee or commission except through her broker. While the relationship is one of courtesy and respect, A and B are each advocates for their respective clients and generally have opposing goals (e.g., highest price and best terms and conditions for the seller-client versus lowest price and best terms and conditions for the buyer-client).

Sales Associate to Sales Associate Within the Same Brokerage

Sales associates working in the same brokerage are both agents for the broker of that company. All the activity each one conducts is through the authority of and at the discretion of the broker. All listing agreements and all buyer representation agreements are the property of the broker. Although the broker will most likely never set foot in one of those listed properties, the broker is the owner of the listing and controls every aspect of the relationship with the seller. The same is true of the buyer representation agreements. The broker is responsible for all the actions of each licensee operating under his broker license when the sales associate is acting on the broker's behalf in a real estate transaction, and within the authority authorized by the broker.

Sales Associate of One Company to Sales Associate of Another Company

Once again, if the sales associates are each acting on behalf of their own broker and the clients of the respective brokers, the associates are in an arm's-length relationship with one another. Each is advocating for his client (buyer or seller) and each has opposing goals. The major difference between the broker-to-broker relationship and the sales associate-to-sales-associate relationship is that the brokers have all the authority and control. The sales associates function only through, for, and at the directive of the broker. Sales associates are not allowed, under TRELA, to

- sponsor other sales or broker associates,
- take listings or buyer representation agreements in their own name,
- hold trust funds of buyers or sellers in their own name, or
- bring suit against a buyer- or seller-client over the listing agreement or buyer representation agreement.

Any area of activity under TRELA that requires a broker license is either done by the broker or through the authority and with the direction of the broker.

Broker and Subagents

Listing agreements and buyer representation agreements may, with the agreement of the principal, include a clause that allows the broker to appoint subagents. A buyer's broker, if given such permission, may appoint subagents as readily as a seller's broker.

TRELA defines a subagent as follows:

> ### Sec. 1101.002(6)-.003(a)(5)(B)
>
> (6) "Residential rental locator" means a person who offers for consideration to locate a unit in an apartment complex for lease to a prospective tenant. The term does not include an owner who offers to locate a unit in the owner's complex.
>
> (7) "Salesperson" means a person who is associated with a licensed broker for the purpose of performing an act described by Subdivision (1).
>
> (8) **"Subagent" means a license holder who:**
>
> > (A) represents a principal through cooperation with and the consent of a broker representing the principal; and
> >
> > (B) is not sponsored by or associated with the principal's broker. (emphasis added)

- **EXAMPLE**
    - Sally, a salesperson for ABC Brokerage, is working a listing for her broker. Sally is the agent of her broker and the agent, by way of her broker, for the seller-client.
    - Sam, a salesperson for XYZ Brokerage, received a call from a buyer asking whether Sam would assist him in finding a home.

- The buyer tells Sam that he is not interested in Sam representing him in the negotiations of the purchase.
- Sam notifies his broker that the buyer chooses not to be represented but wants to see several homes in the Forest Park Addition.
- Sam shows the buyer several homes, including the one listed by Sally of ABC Brokerage.
- Sam tells Sally that he would like to function as a subagent of the seller.
- Sally notifies her broker of Sam's request, and Sally's broker tells Sally to notify the seller of Sam's request.
- The seller accepts Sam's request to be her subagent.

■ **QUESTIONS:**

- What if ABC Broker and the seller had refused to allow Sam to act as a subagent? In that case, Sam would not have been able to represent the seller and would likely have done a lot of work without any compensation. (Sam would have been called a volunteer.)
- What if ABC Broker said yes to the subagency, but the seller said no? Then, Sam would still not be allowed to act as the seller's subagent. The seller, unless he agreed in writing to allow the broker to do otherwise, has the right to say no to having a subagent represent him in the sale of his home.
- What should Sam have done differently?
  - Before spending time assisting the buyer, Sam should have marketed his special knowledge and skill to the buyer to persuade him that he would attempt to negotiate strongly on the buyer's behalf to secure the best possible transaction.
  - Consider the ramifications of spending valuable time showing properties, researching data, and doing myriad other things without a buyer representation agreement to ensure compensation.
  - Complete due diligence and research the MLS system to see whether the properties the buyer is interested in offered subagency.

MLS Subagency Agreements

Under most pre-1993 multiple listing service (MLS) rules, all listings submitted to an MLS were required to contain mandatory offers of subagency to all other members. After discovering numerous potential legal problems with such a practice, and the growth of buyer-agency, most MLS systems now offer participants optional subagency; that is, the systems allow their participants to place listings that offer cooperation and compensation to either buyer-agents or subagents of the listing broker. One of the issues that can be a danger for the broker and the seller or buyer-client is the possibility of vicarious liability relative to a subagent. TRELA addresses this issue thoroughly in § 1101.805 Liability for Misrepresentation or Concealment.

Non-MLS Subagency Agreements

Any brokers, even if they are not members of an MLS, can voluntarily contract with each other to create their own broker-to-broker cooperative agreements, to cover either one property at a time or all properties in their respective inventories for any agreed period of time. Remember, a licensee cannot pursue litigation for recovery of a commission unless the agreement to compensate was in writing. It is generally accepted that compensation indicated in the MLS would constitute such an agreement between brokers. If the cooperating broker is not a member of the MLS, however, then the cooperating broker would be well advised to obtain something in writing from the listing broker designating the cooperative fee.

Agreements Between Brokers

The special block titled "Broker Information" that appears on the last page of the TREC residential sales contract has a blank where listing brokers indicate what they have agreed to pay the "other broker." It is merely a confirmation that the listing broker will compensate the other broker in a transaction by an amount specified in this abbreviated agreement, when and if the listing broker is compensated by the seller-principal.

If the buyer's broker is not protected by a buyer representation agreement, and if at the closing, the seller refuses to compensate the listing broker because of an alleged breach of fiduciary duty by the listing broker, the buyer's broker has no way to secure compensation from anyone in the transaction. Although buyer's brokers may not be fully protected by this TREC-developed compensation agreement, it can serve as a useful memorandum of the initial intent of the parties to the agreement.

Compensation to a broker operating under the terms of a buyer-tenant representation agreement is dictated by the terms of the agreement. The Texas Association of REALTORS® agreement (see Figure 5.1) permits payment to be made directly by the buyer-client to the broker or permits the broker to be compensated through funds provided by the seller. In addition, the agreement may provide that the broker receive a flat fee, hourly compensation, and/or a retainer fee. Most often, the buyer's broker will be paid through funds paid by the seller in the same way that a subagent is usually compensated. Remember that, as in listing agreements, the compensation to a buyer's broker is fully negotiable between the buyer and the broker. The fact that a listing office may be offering a cooperating fee that is less than what the buyer agreed the agent would receive is strictly a compensation issue that must be resolved between the buyer and the buyer's agent.

■ OTHER COMPENSATION ISSUES

Nonlicensee Compensation

In Texas, licensees are not permitted to share commissions with **unlicensed parties, other than a principal in the transaction, or those parties exempt from licensure pursuant to TRELA § 1101.005.** This has been construed to include cash payments of money in any amount, or any gifts exceeding $50 in value (22 TAC § 535.20(a)). Additionally, a 1990 Texas law prohibits a broker from sharing a sales commission with an attorney unless the attorney is also licensed as a broker (22 TAC § 535.31). However, an attorney may conduct real estate transactions for compensation as long as the attorney is paid directly by the principal.

Unlicensed Brokerage Owners The issue of an unlicensed person who owns all or part of a real estate company sharing in the income earned by the company is clarified in 22 TAC § 535.147(b) as follows:

> An unlicensed person may share in the income earned by a business entity licensed as a broker or exempted from the licensing requirements under the Act if the person engages in no acts for which a license is required and does not lead the public to believe that the person is in the real estate brokerage business.

Foreign Brokers or Brokers Licensed in Other States

An exception to the prohibition for compensation to individuals not licensed in Texas states that a licensed broker may pay a commission to a licensed broker of another state. This exemption is valid only if the out-of-state broker does not attempt to physically conduct in Texas any of the negotiations for which commission or other compensation is paid (TRELA § 1101.651(a)).

A second exception relates to brokers who are residents of a foreign state that does not require a person to be licensed to act as real estate broker. This addresses real estate practitioners outside the United States. The rules permit compensation to real estate professionals in other countries, even though that country may not require licensure of those persons engaged in the practice of real estate in that country (22 TAC § 535.131(b)).

■ SUMMARY

Although brokerage firms vary widely in size, few brokers perform their agency duties without the assistance of associated licensees. Consequently, much of a firm's success hinges on the broker-associate relationship. An agreement between a broker and an associate should be set in a written contract that establishes the obligations and responsibilities of each party. The salesperson may work on the broker's behalf as either an employee or an independent contractor.

A broker's compensation generally takes the form of a commission, paid either by the seller, under the terms of a listing agreement, or a buyer, under the terms of a buyer representation agreement. Generally, the broker receiving compensation may share the commissions with other brokers who are acting as subagents of the seller or as buyers' agents.

■ KEY POINTS

- Brokers enter into employment agreements with property owners, buyers, and tenants through listing and representation agreements.
- Sponsoring brokers and associated broker and salesperson licensees enter into employment agreements and conduct brokerage activities as employees of the firm or as independent contractors.
- Salesperson licensees cannot perform brokerage activities independently. All activities must be under the direction of the sponsoring broker.
- Independent contractors must (1) have a written contract with the broker, (2) be allowed to determine how they carry out brokerage functions, and (3) pay their own income and Social Security taxes.
- Brokers may contract with other brokerage firms to represent their clients in a subagency capacity. Subagency can be achieved through an MLS or directly with selected brokers for a particular property or for an agreed period of time.
- Brokers may not share compensations with unlicensed persons, other than the principals in a transaction, except as provided in TRELA.
- Brokers licensed in other states may share in a broker's compensation; however all negotiations physically conducted in Texas must be handled by Texas licensees. (TRELA § 1101.651; 22 TAC 535.131 (a)–(b))

■ SUGGESTIONS FOR BROKERS

Brokers should carefully document relationships with associates by entering into a written employment agreement with each associate. In addition, because most associates are not considered employees, the broker should understand and adhere to the strict guidelines regarding independent contract status—most importantly, the requirements relating to directing how independent contractor duties are to be performed.

CHAPTER 9 QUIZ

1. While employed by a real estate broker, a salesperson has the authority to
   a. act as an agent for the seller.
   b. assume responsibilities assigned by the broker.
   c. accept a commission from another broker.
   d. advertise the property on the salesperson's own behalf.

2. Agreements that set the employment terms of an associated licensee include
   a. listing agreements.
   b. buyer representation agreements.
   c. independent contractor agreements.
   d. property management agreements.

3. A broker has the right to dictate which of the following to an independent contractor?
   a. Number of hours worked
   b. Work schedule
   c. How duties are performed
   d. Duties

4. When a broker engages other brokers as associates of the company,
   a. the broker associate generally works under the guidance of the sponsoring broker.
   b. TREC will issue an associate broker license to the associated broker.
   c. the sponsoring broker will not incur any liability for the broker associate.
   d. broker associates will take listings in their own names.

5. Even though the broker and the associate have a written independent contractor agreement,
   a. if the broker's conduct is that of an employer, the IRS will probably not consider that an employer-employee relationship exists.
   b. if the broker's conduct is that of an employer, the IRS will probably determine that an employer-employee relationship exists.
   c. the broker associate can conduct business activities free of any guidance.
   d. the broker will reimburse associates for all expenses.

6. An associate's compensation is set by
   a. mutual agreement between the broker and the associate.
   b. the local Board of REALTORS®.
   c. TRELA.
   d. TREC.

7. Unlicensed personal assistants hired by licensees
   a. can work for broker licensees only.
   b. must be taking real estate courses.
   c. are allowed to carry out all the licensees' real estate duties.
   d. carry out limited functions that do not require a real estate license.

8. Multiple listing service (MLS) listings
   a. require that compensation be paid by the seller.
   b. all carry a mandatory offer of subagency.
   c. do not cooperate with buyers' agents.
   d. offer optional subagency.

9. Brokers who do NOT belong to an MLS can
   a. elect to reject offers of subagency.
   b. have individual agreements with other brokers.
   c. have individual agreements with other brokers for limited periods of time.
   d. do all of these.

10. The term *foreign broker* relates to a broker
    a. licensed in another state or country.
    b. licensed in another country.
    c. of foreign descent.
    d. of a different firm.

DISCUSSION QUESTIONS

1. Explain why classifying a real estate salesperson as an independent contractor does not relieve the broker of responsibility for the salesperson's actions.

2. Discuss the differences between how a broker and a salesperson are compensated.

3. Discuss the exceptions to TRELA concerning payment of fees to individuals unlicensed in Texas.

4. Discuss the function of unlicensed assistants and whether they can conduct all, or any, of the duties of the licensed sales associate or broker.

Agency, Ethics, and the Law

The expectation of legal and ethical conduct by an agent (and the principal) is fundamental to the concepts of agency law. This basic principle is at once extraordinarily simple and vexingly complex. Simple in the sense that most licensees—both brokers and sales associates—recognize the need to "do the right thing," yet it's often complex to determine exactly what the right thing is and how to communicate the individual agent's and the brokerage company's policies to the various stakeholders. Perhaps more important is the need to ensure that the plans and policies are actually implemented. This chapter will discuss Texas laws, regulations, and ethical duties more specific to the real estate licensee (separate from the Texas Deceptive Practices Act covering general consumer protection law).

■ **LEARNING OBJECTIVES** *This chapter addresses the following:*

- Corporate Values and Business Environment
- Distinctions Between Law, Ethics, and Morals
  — Law Defined
  — Ethics Defined
  — Morals Defined
  — Legal and Ethical Guidelines for Licensees
- Federal Law Relating to Conduct
  — The Sherman Antitrust Act
  — Truth in Lending Act and Regulation Z
  — Federal Fair Housing Law
  — Environmental Laws (Environmental Protection Agency)
  — Americans with Disabilities Act
  — Equal Credit Opportunity Act
  — Community Reinvestment Act
  — Home Mortgage Disclosure Act
- Texas State Law
  — Texas Fair Housing Act
  — Texas: Fraud in a Real Estate Transaction
  — Texas Property Code
  — Local Municipal Codes and Ordinances
- TRELA and Rules of the Commission
  — The Real Estate License Act
  — The Texas Real Estate Commission (TREC)
- Professional Codes of Ethics
  — TREC Canons of Professional Ethics and Conduct
  — National Association of REALTORS® Code of Ethics and Professional Standards
- Minimum Ethical Standards
  — Individual Company Policy, Procedure, and Codes of Ethics and Conduct
  — Personal Beliefs and Individual Ethics
  — Laws and Ethics in Practice
  — A Practical Guide for Everyday Practice
  — When Enough Is Not Enough
- The Bottom Line on Ethics

■ CORPORATE VALUES AND BUSINESS ENVIRONMENT

Perhaps never in history have the business and political communities faced the level of public scrutiny that they do today. Historically, we have witnessed highly publicized scandals centered on unethical conduct leading to the collapse of major companies such as the Houston-based energy company Enron and the accounting firm Arthur Anderson. The public has been further outraged by acts committed by those who have at times brought the American financial system to the brink of disaster. Individual unethical and criminal acts by Bernie Madoff and his bogus investment company, for example, may have caused financial ruin to thousands of individual investors. These pale in comparison to the colossal mortgage-backed securities debacle created in the financial institutions of this country. In essence, millions of real estate mortgages were bundled, promoted, and sold by Wall Street investment bankers as highly rated securities. In fact, large percentages of the underlying mortgage loans were made to poorly qualified borrowers. Predictably, as the borrowers were unable to meet their payment obligations, massive numbers of properties went into foreclosure and the underlying properties lacked sufficient market value to satisfy the outstanding loans. The fallout impacted millions of investors and rocked global financial markets. Ostensibly, only a U.S. federal bailout of high-profile companies such as Goldman Sachs, J.P Morgan Chase, Bank of America, AIG, Citigroup, Wells Fargo, and many others averted a potential collapse of the U.S. financial system.

Although the press and public sentiment fell squarely against these high-profile companies, one might ask where the ethical breaches actually originated. Clearly, these firms were major players, but in a larger sense many others contributed to the problems. Where did the real problem and breach of ethics begin? Was it the Wall Street banker overselling the end product, the mortgage insurers, the rating companies, or much further down the chain? Is the blame more rightly placed on the secondary market purchasers, the primary lenders and their underwriters, or perhaps the real estate broker or salesperson who may have knowingly sold properties to buyers clearly beyond their means in the long term? What about the buyer who falsified documents with the knowledge that the no-documentation or asset-based loan policies of certain lenders would probably not discover the falsification. If blame is to be placed, obviously there are plenty to share in this complex problem. On the other hand, many of those involved may argue that the role that they played was not only legal but met the ethical standards of their industry or company.

In any event, each unfolding new event lends more credence to the popular view that general moral decay and public abuse is on the rise. Support for this view may be evidenced by the more complex societal and business structures leading into uncharted ethical waters. Indeed, an ever-growing number of real estate business models and resulting menu of services are confusing to those within the industry—much less buyers and sellers on the outside. Even today with the increased governmental scrutiny and required disclosure, the typical (or sophisticated) principal has little chance of understanding the duties and obligations of the agent. Thus, a brokerage company or individual licensee willing to risk unethical behavior for bottom-line gain may still go undetected, and the public is left with only the trust that the precepts of moral behavior and ethical conduct will prevail.

Individuals, businesses, and society in general are continually faced with questions relating to conduct that may not be clearly governed by law, and certainly the practice of real estate is no different. This chapter attempts to distinguish differences between legal versus ethical conduct and introduce the student to some of the ethical/legal decisions they may face in their real estate practices.

■ DISTINCTIONS BETWEEN LAW, ETHICS, AND MORALS

Law Defined

The following definition of the term law is excerpted from *Black's Law Dictionary*, Eighth Edition (2006, p. 200):

> The aggregate of legislation, judicial precedence, and accepted legal principles; the body of authoritative grounds of judicial and administrative action; esp., the body of rules, standards, and principles that the courts of a particular jurisdiction apply in deciding controversies brought before them (the law of the land).

Ethics Defined

Although there are many attempts to define ethics, few find much comfort in a single all-comprehensive definition because ethics involves a multitude of factors or circumstances that, when viewed by different parties, results in dramatically different opinions regarding whether any specific action was ethical. As a result, many organizations have created standards of ethical conduct for their members. Again, we draw on *Black's Law Dictionary* (2006, p. 912) for the following definition of the term *legal ethics*:

> The minimum standards of appropriate conduct within the legal profession, involving the duties that its members owe one another, their clients, and the courts. Also termed etiquette of the profession.

A broader definition of the term *ethics is found in Webster's Unabridged Dictionary, Second Edition (2001)*:

> The rules of conduct recognized in respect to a particular class of human actions or a particular group, culture, etc.; medical ethics; Christian ethics.

Morals Defined

While the terms *ethical* and *moral* are often taken to be synonymous, there are subtle distinctions between the two. Once more, *Black's Law Dictionary* provides a definition (2006, p. 1030):

- ■ Private Morality: A person's ideals, character, and private conduct which are not valid governmental concerns . . .
- ■ Public Morality: The ideals or actions of an individual to the extent they affect others.

In a sense, the law represents what we are required to do and is enforceable by governmental entities. Ethics refers to commonly accepted standards of conduct or actions, are frequently refined and tailored to specific industries or companies, and may be enforced against their members or employees. Morals deal with an individual's personal beliefs or actions and can be enforced only by conscience unless those actions violate the legal rights of others (e.g., people can think, or believe, or feel as they wish as long as they do not act on those beliefs in such a way as to violate the rights of others).

It should be evident then that at times an individual may be faced with the dilemma of choosing a course of action when personal morals, professional ethics, and the law are in conflict. The final course chosen will be dictated by which of the three has the greater influence on the individual. As a result, two individuals may consider the same set of facts and respond in totally different ways. By the same token, an individual faced with two similar sets of facts may take different actions based on the particular circumstances surrounding those facts.

A great deal has been written on the subject of ethical and moral behavior, including application models for ethical decision making; however, our discussions will be limited to real estate practice with a focus on the ethical duties imposed on Texas real estate licensees acting under agency agreements.

Legal and Ethical Guidelines for Licensees

While practicing real estate, licensees in Texas may be guided by the following:

- Federal law
- Texas general civil and criminal statutes
- Local municipal codes and ordinances
- The Real Estate License Act (TRELA)
- Rules of the Texas Real Estate Commission
- Private professional codes of ethics, (e.g. the National Association of REALTORS® Code of Ethics)
- A real estate company's Code of Ethics or Policies
- Individual ethics and moral principles

■ FEDERAL LAW RELATING TO CONDUCT

Although much real estate law is governed by individual states, federal legislation plays an important role in real estate practice. These address overriding national concerns that would apply in any state. Examples of such federal regulation are as follows:

- The Sherman Antitrust Act
- Truth in Lending Act and Regulation Z
- Federal Fair Housing Laws
- Environmental Laws (Environmental Protection Agency)
- Americans with Disabilities Act
- Equal Credit Opportunity Act
- Community Reinvestment Act
- Home Mortgage Disclosure Act

Clearly, a licensee must be familiar with a number of federal rules and regulations in order to avoid practices resulting in federal litigation. These laws provide the overarching framework for real estate licensees in all states.

The Sherman Antitrust Act

The Sherman Antitrust Act prohibits conduct that unfairly inhibits competition between businesses. The Federal Trade Commission's Guide to Antitrust Laws includes a section titled "Dealings with Competitors" (www.ftc.gov/tips-advice/

competition-guidance/guide-antitrust-laws/dealings-competitors), which covers the following topics:

- Price-fixing
- Group boycotts
- Market division or customer allocation
- Other agreements among competitors

The FTC website defines each of these terms as follows:

Price Fixing

Price fixing is an agreement (written, verbal, or inferred from conduct) among competitors that raises, lowers, or stabilizes prices or competitive terms. Generally, the antitrust laws require that each company establish prices and other terms on its own, without agreeing with a competitor. When consumers make choices about what products and services to buy, they expect that the price has been determined freely on the basis of supply and demand, not by an agreement among competitors. When competitors agree to restrict competition, the result is often higher prices. Accordingly, price fixing is a major concern of government antitrust enforcement. . . .

Price fixing relates not only to prices, but also to other terms that affect prices to consumers, such as shipping fees, warranties, discount programs, or financing rates. Antitrust scrutiny may occur when competitors discuss the following topics:

- Present or future prices
- Pricing policies
- Promotions
- Bids
- Costs
- Capacity
- Terms or conditions of sale, including credit terms
- Discounts
- Identity of customers
- Allocation of customers or sales areas
- Production quotas
- R&D [Research & Development] plans

This does not mean that the principal broker of ABC Real Estate Company and all of her managers from the 20 offices in that company can't have a business meeting to discuss their current profit structure, or make business decisions to change the commission structure within the company. They are not competitors; they work for the same company. However, if that same principal broker of ABC Real Estate Company meets with one or more competing brokers to discuss changing commission structures, that may be considered a violation of the Sherman Antitrust Act.

Group Boycotts

Any company may, on its own, refuse to do business with another firm, but an agreement among competitors not to do business with targeted individuals or businesses may be an illegal boycott, especially if the group of competitors working together has market power. For instance, a group boycott may be used to implement an illegal price-fixing agreement. In this scenario, the competitors agree not to do business with others except on agreed-upon terms, typically with the result of raising prices. An independent decision not to offer services at prevailing prices does not raise antitrust concerns, but an agreement among competitors not to offer services at prevailing prices as a means of achieving an agreed-upon (and typically higher) price does raise antitrust concerns.

Market Division or Customer Allocation

Plain agreements among competitors to divide sales territories or assign customers are almost always illegal. These arrangements are essentially agreements not to compete: "I won't sell in your market if you don't sell in mine." The FTC uncovered such an agreement when two chemical companies agreed that one would not sell in North America if the other would not sell in Japan. Illegal market sharing may involve allocating a specific percentage of available business to each producer, dividing sales territories on a geographic basis, or assigning certain customers to each seller.

Other Agreements Among Competitors

Other agreements among competitors that are not inherently harmful to consumers are examined under a flexible "rule of reason" standard that attempts to determine their overall competitive effect. Here the focus is on the nature of the agreement, the harm that could arise, and whether the agreement is reasonably necessary to achieve pro-competitive benefits.

Below are a few examples of these types of dealings with competitors that may pose competitive problems.

Agreements to restrict advertising

Truthful advertising is important in a free market system because it helps consumers compare the price and quality of products offered by competing suppliers. The FTC Act itself prohibits advertising that is false or deceptive, and the FTC vigorously enforces this standard to empower consumers to make choices in the marketplace. **Competitor restrictions on the amount or content of advertising that is truthful and not deceptive may be illegal if evidence shows the restrictions have anticompetitive effects and lack reasonable business justifications.** [emphasis added]

Example: The FTC challenged a professional code adopted by a national association of arbitrators that banned virtually all forms of advertising and soliciting clients. In a consent agreement with that organization, the rules were changed so that individual members were not barred from advertising truthful information about their prices and services.

Codes of ethics

The antitrust laws do not prohibit professional associations from adopting reasonable ethical codes designed to protect the public. Such self-regulatory activity serves legitimate purposes, and in most cases can be expected to benefit, rather than to injure, competition or consumers. In some instances, however, ethical rules may be unlawful if they unreasonably restrict the ways professionals may compete. For example, a mandatory code of ethics that prevents members from competing on the basis of price or on terms other than those developed by the trade group can be an unreasonable restraint on competition.

Example: The FTC challenged an organization of store planners that sought to prevent its members from offering free or discounted design or planning services. The group's mandatory code of ethics discouraged price competition among the planners to the detriment of consumers.

Exclusive member benefits

Business associations made up of competitors can offer their members important services and benefits that improve efficiency and reduce costs. These services and benefits can range from general industry promotion to high-tech support. But when an association of competitors withholds these benefits from would-be members that offer a competitive alternative that consumers want, the restriction may harm competition and keep prices high. This problem only occurs when members of the association have a significant market presence and it is difficult for non-members to compete without access to association-sponsored benefits.

Example: Several antitrust cases have challenged realtor board rules that restricted access to Multiple Listing Services (MLS) for advertising homes for sale. The MLS system of combining the home listings of many brokers has substantial benefits for home buyers and sellers. The initial cases invalidated realtor board membership rules that excluded certain brokers from the MLS because access to the MLS was considered key to marketing homes. More recently, FTC enforcement actions have challenged MLS policies that permit access but more subtly disfavor certain types of brokerage arrangements that offer consumers a low-cost alternative to the more traditional, full-service listing agreement. For instance, some brokers offer a limited service model, listing a home on the local MLS for a fee while handing off other aspects of the sale to the seller. The FTC has challenged the rules of several MLS organizations that excluded these brokers from popular home sale web sites. These rules limited the ways in which brokers could conduct their business and denied home sellers the benefit of having different types of listings.

Real estate salespeople and brokers must be careful to avoid discussing commission structure, changing prices, allocation of customers, or markets with competitors.

Tie-In Agreements   Tie-in agreements (also known as tying agreements) are agreements to sell one product only if the buyer purchases another product as well. The sale of the first (desired) product is tied to the purchase of a second (less desirable) product. In the real estate business, this can occur if, for instance, a broker will agree to list a seller's home for sale only if the seller agrees to be represented by the broker in the purchase of a new home.

Penalties   The penalties for violating antitrust laws are severe. Under the federal Sherman Antitrust Act, the penalty for fixing prices or allocating markets is a maximum $1 million fine and 10 years in prison. For corporations, the penalty may be as high as $100 million. An individual who has suffered a loss because of an antitrust violation may sue for treble damages—three times the actual damages sustained. In addition, the injured party may recover the cost of the suit, which includes reasonable attorney fees.

Truth in Lending Act and Regulation Z

The purpose of the TILA and Regulation Z, according to the *FDIC Compliance Manual—March 2014* is as follows:

> The TILA is intended to ensure that credit terms are disclosed in a meaningful way so consumers can compare credit terms more readily and knowledgeably. Before its enactment, consumers were faced with a bewildering array of credit terms and rates. It was difficult to compare loans because they were seldom presented in the same format. Now, all creditors must use the same credit terminology and expressions of rates. In addition to providing a uniform system for disclosures, the act:
> - Protects consumers against inaccurate and unfair credit billing and credit card practices:
> - Provides consumers with rescission rights;
> - Provides for rate caps on certain dwelling-secured loans;
> - Imposes limitations on home equity lines of credit and certain closed-end home mortgages;
> - Provides minimum standards for most dwelling-secured loans; and
> - Delineates and prohibits unfair or deceptive mortgage lending practices.

Federal Fair Housing Laws

HUD defines various laws and presidential executive orders pertaining to fair housing in "Fair Housing Laws and Presidential Executive Orders" at http://portal .hud.gov/hudportal/HUD?src=/program_offices/fair_housing_equal_opp/FHLaws:

> ### Fair Housing Act
>
> Title VIII of the Civil Rights Act of 1968 (Fair Housing Act), as amended, prohibits discrimination in the sale, rental, and financing of dwellings and in other housing-related transactions based on race, color, national origin, religion, sex, familial status (including children under the age of 18 living with parents or legal custodians, pregnant women, and people securing custody of children under the age of 18), or disability.
>
> ### Title VI of the Civil Rights Act of 1964
>
> Title VI prohibits discrimination on the basis of race, color, or national origin in programs and activities receiving federal financial assistance.

Section 504 of the Rehabilitation Act of 1973

Section 504 prohibits discrimination based on disability in any program or activity receiving federal financial assistance.

Section 109 of Title I of the Housing and Community Development Act of 1974

Section 109 prohibits discrimination on the basis of race, color, national origin, sex, or religion in programs and activities receiving financial assistance from HUD's Community Development and Block Grant Program.

Title II of the Americans with Disabilities Act of 1990

Title II prohibits discrimination based on disability in programs, services, and activities provided or made available by public entities. HUD enforces Title II when it relates to state and local public housing, housing assistance, and housing referrals.

Architectural Barriers Act of 1968

The Architectural Barriers Act requires that buildings and facilities designed, constructed, altered, or leased with certain federal funds after September 1969 must be accessible to and useable by handicapped persons.

Age Discrimination Act of 1975

The Age Discrimination Act prohibits discrimination on the basis of age in programs or activities receiving federal financial assistance.

Title IX of the Education Amendments Act of 1972

Title IX prohibits discrimination on the basis of sex in education programs or activities that receive federal financial assistance.

Fair Housing-Related Presidential Executive Orders

Executive Order 11063

Executive Order 11063 prohibits discrimination in the sale, leasing, rental, or other disposition of properties and facilities owned or operated by the federal government or provided with federal funds.

Executive Order 11246

Executive Order 11246, as amended, bars discrimination in federal employment because of race, color, religion, sex, or national origin.

Executive Order 12892

Executive Order 12892, as amended, requires federal agencies to affirmatively further fair housing in their programs and activities, and provides that the Secretary of HUD will be responsible for coordinating the effort. The Order also establishes the President's Fair Housing Council, which will be chaired by the Secretary of HUD.

Executive Order 12898

Executive Order 12898 requires that each federal agency conduct its program, policies, and activities that substantially affect human health or the environment in a manner that does not exclude persons based on race, color, or national origin.

Executive Order 13166

Executive Order 13166 eliminates, to the extent possible, limited English proficiency as a barrier to full and meaningful participation by beneficiaries in all federally-assisted and federally conducted programs and activities.

Executive Order 13217

Executive Order 13217 requires federal agencies to evaluate their policies and programs to determine if any can be revised or modified to improve the availability of community-based living arrangements for persons with disabilities.

According to HUD's website, the agency's programs are governed by Title 24, Housing and Urban Development of the Code of Federal Regulations, which follows:

PART 100—DISCRIMINATORY CONDUCT UNDER THE FAIR HOUSING ACT

§ 100.1   Authority.

This regulation is issued under the authority of the Secretary of Housing and Urban Development to administer and enforce title VIII of the Civil Rights Act of 1968, as amended by the Fair Housing Amendments Act of 1988 (the Fair Housing Act).

§ 100.5   Scope.

(a) It is the policy of the United States to provide, within constitutional limitations, for fair housing throughout the United States. No person shall be subjected to discrimination because of race, color, religion, sex, handicap, familial status, or national origin in the sale, rental, or advertising of dwellings, in the provision of brokerage services, or in the availability of residential real estate-related transactions.

(b) This part provides the Department's interpretation of the coverage of the Fair Housing Act regarding discrimination related to the sale or rental of dwellings, the provision of services in connection therewith, and the availability of residential real estate-related transactions. The illustrations of unlawful housing discrimination in this part may be established by a practice's discriminatory effect, even if not motivated by discriminatory intent, consistent with the standards outlined in §100.500.

(c) Nothing in this part relieves persons participating in a Federal or Federally-assisted program or activity from other requirements applicable to buildings and dwellings.

[54 FR 3283, Jan. 23, 1989, as amended at 78 FR 11481, Feb. 15, 2013]

§ 100.10   Exemptions.

(a) This part does not:

(1) Prohibit a religious organization, association, or society, or any nonprofit institution or organization operated, supervised or controlled by or in conjunction with a religious organization, association, or society, from limiting the sale, rental or occupancy of dwellings which it owns or operates for other than a commercial purpose to persons of the same religion, or from giving preference to such persons, unless membership in such religion is restricted because of race, color, or national origin;

(2) Prohibit a private club, not in fact open to the public, which, incident to its primary purpose or purposes, provides lodgings which it owns or operates for other than a commercial purpose, from limiting the rental or occupancy of such lodgings to its members or from giving preference to its members;

(3) Limit the applicability of any reasonable local, State or Federal restrictions regarding the maximum number of occupants permitted to occupy a dwelling; or

(4) Prohibit conduct against a person because such person has been convicted by any court of competent jurisdiction of the illegal manufacture or distribution of a controlled substance as defined in section 102 of the Controlled Substances Act (21 U.S.C. 802).

(b) Nothing in this part regarding discrimination based on familial status applies with respect to housing for older persons as defined in subpart E of this part.

(c) Nothing in this part, other than the prohibitions against discriminatory advertising, applies to:

(1) The sale or rental of any single family house by an owner, provided the following conditions are met:

(i) The owner does not own or have any interest in more than three single family houses at any one time.

(ii) The house is sold or rented without the use of a real estate broker, agent or salesperson or the facilities of any person in the business of selling or renting dwellings. If the owner selling the house does not reside in it at the time of the sale or was not the most recent resident of the house prior to such sale, the exemption in this paragraph (c)(1) of this section applies to only one such sale in any 24-month period.

(2) Rooms or units in dwellings containing living quarters occupied or intended to be occupied by no more than four families living independently of each other, if the owner actually maintains and occupies one of such living quarters as his or her residence.

§ 100.20 Definitions.

The terms Department, Fair Housing Act, and Secretary are defined in 24 CFR part 5.

Aggrieved person includes any person who—

(a) Claims to have been injured by a discriminatory housing practice; or

(b) Believes that such person will be injured by a discriminatory housing practice that is about to occur.

Broker or *Agent* includes any person authorized to perform an action on behalf of another person regarding any matter related to the sale or rental of dwellings, including offers, solicitations or contracts and the administration of matters regarding such offers, solicitations or contracts or any residential real estate-related transactions.

Discriminatory housing practice means an act that is unlawful under section 804, 805, 806, or 818 of the Fair Housing Act.

Dwelling means any building, structure or portion thereof which is occupied as, or designed or intended for occupancy as, a residence by one or more families, and any vacant land which is offered for sale or lease for the construction or location thereon of any such building, structure or portion thereof.

Familial status means one or more individuals (who have not attained the age of 18 years) being domiciled with—

(a) A parent or another person having legal custody of such individual or individuals; or

(b) The designee of such parent or other person having such custody, with the written permission of such parent or other person.

The protections afforded against discrimination on the basis of familial status shall apply to any person who is pregnant or is in the process of securing legal custody of any individual who has not attained the age of 18 years.

Handicap is defined in §100.201.

Person includes one or more individuals, corporations, partnerships, associations, labor organizations, legal representatives, mutual companies, joint-stock companies, trusts, unincorporated organizations, trustees, trustees in cases under title 11 U.S.C., receivers, and fiduciaries.

Person in the business of selling or renting dwellings means any person who:

(a) Within the preceding twelve months, has participated as principal in three or more transactions involving the sale or rental of any dwelling or any interest therein;

(b) Within the preceding twelve months, has participated as agent, other than in the sale of his or her own personal residence, in providing sales or rental facilities or sales or rental services in two or more transactions involving the sale or rental of any dwelling or any interest therein; or

(c) Is the owner of any dwelling designed or intended for occupancy by, or occupied by, five or more families.

State means any of the several states, the District of Columbia, the Commonwealth of Puerto Rico, or any of the territories and possessions of the United States.

[54 FR 3283, Jan. 23, 1989, as amended at 61 FR 5205, Feb. 9, 1996]

Subpart B—Discriminatory Housing Practices

§ 100.50   Real estate practices prohibited.

(a) This subpart provides the Department's interpretation of conduct that is unlawful housing discrimination under section 804 and section 806 of the Fair Housing Act. In general the prohibited actions are set forth under sections of this subpart which are most applicable to the discriminatory conduct described. However, an action illustrated in one section can constitute a violation under sections in the subpart. For example, the conduct described in §100.60(b)(3) and (4) would constitute a violation of §100.65(a) as well as §100.60(a).

(b) It shall be unlawful to:

(1) Refuse to sell or rent a dwelling after a *bona fide* offer has been made, or to refuse to negotiate for the sale or rental of a dwelling because of race, color, religion, sex, familial status, or national origin, or to discriminate in the sale or rental of a dwelling because of handicap.

(2) Discriminate in the terms, conditions or privileges of sale or rental of a dwelling, or in the provision of services or facilities in connection with sales or rentals, because of race, color, religion, sex, handicap, familial status, or national origin.

(3) Engage in any conduct relating to the provision of housing which otherwise makes unavailable or denies dwellings to persons because of race, color, religion, sex, handicap, familial status, or national origin.

(4) Make, print or publish, or cause to be made, printed or published, any notice, statement or advertisement with respect to the sale or rental of a dwelling that indicates any preference, limitation or discrimination because of race, color, religion, sex, handicap, familial status, or national origin, or an intention to make any such preference, limitation or discrimination.

(5) Represent to any person because of race, color, religion, sex, handicap, familial status, or national origin that a dwelling is not available for sale or rental when such dwelling is in fact available.

(6) Engage in blockbusting practices in connection with the sale or rental of dwellings because of race, color, religion, sex, handicap, familial status, or national origin.

(7) Deny access to or membership or participation in, or to discriminate against any person in his or her access to or membership or participation in, any multiple-listing service, real estate brokers' association, or other service organization or facility relating to the business of selling or renting a dwelling or in the terms or conditions or membership or participation, because of race, color, religion, sex, handicap, familial status, or national origin.

(c) The application of the Fair Housing Act with respect to persons with handicaps is discussed in subpart D of this part.

§ 100.60   Unlawful refusal to sell or rent or to negotiate for the sale or rental.

(a) It shall be unlawful for a person to refuse to sell or rent a dwelling to a person who has made a *bona fide* offer, because of race, color, religion, sex, familial status, or national origin or to refuse to negotiate with a person for the sale or rental of a dwelling because of race, color, religion, sex, familial status, or national origin, or to discriminate against any person in the sale or rental of a dwelling because of handicap.

(b) Prohibited actions under this section include, but are not limited to:

(1) Failing to accept or consider a *bona fide* offer because of race, color, religion, sex, handicap, familial status, or national origin.

(2) Refusing to sell or rent a dwelling to, or to negotiate for the sale or rental of a dwelling with, any person because of race, color, religion, sex, handicap, familial status, or national origin.

(3) Imposing different sales prices or rental charges for the sale or rental of a dwelling upon any person because of race, color, religion, sex, handicap, familial status, or national origin.

(4) Using different qualification criteria or applications, or sale or rental standards or procedures, such as income standards, application requirements, application fees, credit analysis or sale or rental approval procedures or other requirements, because of race, color, religion, sex, handicap, familial status, or national origin.

(5) Evicting tenants because of their race, color, religion, sex, handicap, familial status, or national origin or because of the race, color, religion, sex, handicap, familial status, or national origin of a tenant's guest.

§ 100.65   Discrimination in terms, conditions and privileges and in services and facilities.

(a) It shall be unlawful, because of race, color, religion, sex, handicap, familial status, or national origin, to impose different terms, conditions or privileges relating to the sale or rental of a dwelling or to deny or limit services or facilities in connection with the sale or rental of a dwelling.

(b) Prohibited actions under this section include, but are not limited to:

(1) Using different provisions in leases or contracts of sale, such as those relating to rental charges, security deposits and the terms of a lease and those relating to down payment and closing requirements, because of race, color, religion, sex, handicap, familial status, or national origin.

(2) Failing or delaying maintenance or repairs of sale or rental dwellings because of race, color, religion, sex, handicap, familial status, or national origin.

(3) Failing to process an offer for the sale or rental of a dwelling or to communicate an offer accurately because of race, color, religion, sex, handicap, familial status, or national origin.

(4) Limiting the use of privileges, services or facilities associated with a dwelling because of race, color, religion, sex, handicap, familial status, or national origin of an owner, tenant or a person associated with him or her.

(5) Denying or limiting services or facilities in connection with the sale or rental of a dwelling, because a person failed or refused to provide sexual favors.

§ 100.70 Other prohibited sale and rental conduct.

(a) It shall be unlawful, because of race, color, religion, sex, handicap, familial status, or national origin, to restrict or attempt to restrict the choices of a person by word or conduct in connection with seeking, negotiating for, buying or renting a dwelling so as to perpetuate, or tend to perpetuate, segregated housing patterns, or to discourage or obstruct choices in a community, neighborhood or development.

(b) It shall be unlawful, because of race, color, religion, sex, handicap, familial status, or national origin, to engage in any conduct relating to the provision of housing or of services and facilities in connection therewith that otherwise makes unavailable or denies dwellings to persons.

(c) Prohibited actions under paragraph (a) of this section, which are generally referred to as unlawful steering practices, include, but are not limited to:

(1) Discouraging any person from inspecting, purchasing or renting a dwelling because of race, color, religion, sex, handicap, familial status, or national origin, or because of the race, color, religion, sex, handicap, familial status, or national origin of persons in a community, neighborhood or development.

(2) Discouraging the purchase or rental of a dwelling because of race, color, religion, sex, handicap, familial status, or national origin, by exaggerating drawbacks or failing to inform any person of

desirable features of a dwelling or of a community, neighborhood, or development.

(3) Communicating to any prospective purchaser that he or she would not be comfortable or compatible with existing residents of a community, neighborhood or development because of race, color, religion, sex, handicap, familial status, or national origin.

(4) Assigning any person to a particular section of a community, neighborhood or development, or to a particular floor of a building, because of race, color, religion, sex, handicap, familial status, or national origin.

(d) Prohibited activities relating to dwellings under paragraph (b) of this section include, but are not limited to:

(1) Discharging or taking other adverse action against an employee, broker or agent because he or she refused to participate in a discriminatory housing practice.

(2) Employing codes or other devices to segregate or reject applicants, purchasers or renters, refusing to take or to show listings of dwellings in certain areas because of race, color, religion, sex, handicap, familial status, or national origin, or refusing to deal with certain brokers or agents because they or one or more of their clients are of a particular race, color, religion, sex, handicap, familial status, or national origin.

(3) Denying or delaying the processing of an application made by a purchaser or renter or refusing to approve such a person for occupancy in a cooperative or condominium dwelling because of race, color, religion, sex, handicap, familial status, or national origin.

(4) Refusing to provide municipal services or property or hazard insurance for dwellings or providing such services or insurance differently because of race, color, religion, sex, handicap, familial status, or national origin.

(5) Enacting or implementing land-use rules, ordinances, policies, or procedures that restrict or deny housing opportunities or otherwise make unavailable or deny dwellings to persons because of race, color, religion, sex, handicap, familial status, or national origin.

[54 FR 3283, Jan. 23, 1989, as amended at 78 FR 11481, Feb. 15, 2013]

§ 100.75 Discriminatory advertisements, statements and notices.

(a) It shall be unlawful to make, print or publish, or cause to be made, printed or published, any notice, statement or advertisement with respect to the sale or rental of a dwelling which indicates any preference, limitation or discrimination because of race, color, religion, sex, handicap, familial status, or national origin, or an intention to make any such preference, limitation or discrimination.

(b) The prohibitions in this section shall apply to all written or oral notices or statements by a person engaged in the sale or rental of a dwelling. Written notices and statements include any applications, flyers, brochures, deeds, signs, banners, posters, billboards or any documents used with respect to the sale or rental of a dwelling.

(c) Discriminatory notices, statements and advertisements include, but are not limited to:

(1) Using words, phrases, photographs, illustrations, symbols or forms which convey that dwellings are available or not available to a particular group of persons because of race, color, religion, sex, handicap, familial status, or national origin.

(2) Expressing to agents, brokers, employees, prospective sellers or renters or any other persons a preference for or limitation on any purchaser or renter because of race, color, religion, sex, handicap, familial status, or national origin of such persons.

(3) Selecting media or locations for advertising the sale or rental of dwellings which deny particular segments of the housing market information about housing opportunities because of race, color, religion, sex, handicap, familial status, or national origin.

(4) Refusing to publish advertising for the sale or rental of dwellings or requiring different charges or terms for such advertising because of race, color, religion, sex, handicap, familial status, or national origin.

(d) 24 CFR part 109 provides information to assist persons to advertise dwellings in a nondiscriminatory manner and describes the matters the Department will review in evaluating compliance with the Fair Housing Act and in investigating complaints alleging discriminatory housing practices involving advertising.

§ 100.80 Discriminatory representations on the availability of dwellings.

(a) It shall be unlawful, because of race, color, religion, sex, handicap, familial status, or national origin, to provide inaccurate or untrue information about the availability of dwellings for sale or rental.

(b) Prohibited actions under this section include, but are not limited to:

(1) Indicating through words or conduct that a dwelling which is available for inspection, sale, or rental has been sold or rented, because of race, color, religion, sex, handicap, familial status, or national origin.

(2) Representing that covenants or other deed, trust or lease provisions which purport to restrict the sale or rental of dwellings because of race, color, religion, sex, handicap, familial status, or national origin preclude the sale of rental of a dwelling to a person.

(3) Enforcing covenants or other deed, trust, or lease provisions which preclude the sale or rental of a dwelling to any person

because of race, color, religion, sex, handicap, familial status, or national origin.

(4) Limiting information, by word or conduct, regarding suitably priced dwellings available for inspection, sale or rental, because of race, color, religion, sex, handicap, familial status, or national origin.

(5) Providing false or inaccurate information regarding the availability of a dwelling for sale or rental to any person, including testers, regardless of whether such person is actually seeking housing, because of race, color, religion, sex, handicap, familial status, or national origin.

§ 100.85   Blockbusting.

(a) It shall be unlawful, for profit, to induce or attempt to induce a person to sell or rent a dwelling by representations regarding the entry or prospective entry into the neighborhood of a person or persons of a particular race, color, religion, sex, familial status, or national origin or with a handicap.

(b) In establishing a discriminatory housing practice under this section it is not necessary that there was in fact profit as long as profit was a factor for engaging in the blockbusting activity.

(c) Prohibited actions under this section include, but are not limited to:

(1) Engaging, for profit, in conduct (including uninvited solicitations for listings) which conveys to a person that a neighborhood is undergoing or is about to undergo a change in the race, color, religion, sex, handicap, familial status, or national origin of persons residing in it, in order to encourage the person to offer a dwelling for sale or rental.

(2) Encouraging, for profit, any person to sell or rent a dwelling through assertions that the entry or prospective entry of persons of a particular race, color, religion, sex, familial status, or national origin, or with handicaps, can or will result in undesirable consequences for the project, neighborhood or community, such as a lowering of property values, an increase in criminal or antisocial behavior, or a decline in the quality of schools or other services or facilities.

§ 100.90   Discrimination in the provision of brokerage services.

(a) It shall be unlawful to deny any person access to or membership or participation in any multiple listing service, real estate brokers' organization or other service, organization, or facility relating to the business of selling or renting dwellings, or to discriminate against any person in the terms or conditions of such access, membership or participation, because of race, color, religion, sex, handicap, familial status, or national origin.

(b) Prohibited actions under this section include, but are not limited to:

(1) Setting different fees for access to or membership in a multiple listing service because of race, color, religion, sex, handicap, familial status, or national origin.

(2) Denying or limiting benefits accruing to members in a real estate brokers' organization because of race, color, religion, sex, handicap, familial status, or national origin.

(3) Imposing different standards or criteria for membership in a real estate sales or rental organization because of race, color, religion, sex, handicap, familial status, or national origin.

(4) Establishing geographic boundaries or office location or residence requirements for access to or membership or participation in any multiple listing service, real estate brokers' organization or other service, organization or facility relating to the business of selling or renting dwellings, because of race, color, religion, sex, handicap, familial status, or national origin.

Environmental Laws (Environmental Protection Agency [EPA])

The mission of EPA is to protect human health and the environment.

In order to accomplish that mission, the EPA does the following:

- *Develops and enforces regulations.* Once Congress writes environmental law, the EPA implements it by writing regulations.
- *Gives grants.* The money granted may be used for a wide variety of projects, such as scientific studies to assist in evaluating how to best help communities clean up environmental issues.
- *Studies environmental issues.* Through the use of laboratories across the country, the EPA identifies and tries to solve environmental problems. This information is often shared with other countries, private sector organizations, academic institutions, and other agencies.
- *Sponsors partnerships.* The EPA works with businesses, nonprofit organizations, and state and local governments through dozens of partnerships.
- *Teaches people about the environment and publishes information.* The agency's website, brochures, pamphlets, education programs, and other resources are used to educate the public about environmental protection.

How does this relate to the real estate licensee? As a seller's agent, the listing broker is concerned about any potential environmental issues on the property. As the buyer's broker, the agent is focused on the types of property hazards for which a buyer will want an inspection, elimination before purchase, or the ability to obtain financial resources for their remediation or elimination after the purchase is finalized. Here are a few specific environmental issues:

- **Radon:** Radon is a gas formed when radium and uranium break down. It enters a home as a gas through cracks, joints, wall spaces, the water supply, and poorly-fitted pipes. Radon gas can cause respiratory diseases, as well as cancer.

- **Asbestos:** Asbestos is made up of tiny fibers that come from minerals. Once these fibers are released into the air and breathed in, they can cause a variety of respiratory diseases, as well as cancer.
- **Lead and lead-based paint:** Lead is a metal found in the earth, and can be very dangerous when ingested. It was used in paint in the past, and the federal government passed a law, which became effective in 1995, requiring disclosure of information on real property built in1978 or before. The following is a statement from HUD:

The Lead Disclosure Rule

Congress passed the Residential Lead-Based Paint Hazard Reduction Act of 1992, also known as Title X, to protect families from exposure to lead from paint, dust, and soil. Section 1018 of this law directed HUD and EPA to require the disclosure of known information on lead-based paint and lead-based paint hazards before the sale or lease of most housing built before 1978.

What is required?

Before ratification of a contract for housing sale or lease, sellers and landlords must:

- Give an EPA-approved information pamphlet on identifying and controlling lead-based paint hazards ("Protect Your Family From Lead In Your Home" pamphlet, currently available in English, Spanish, Vietnamese, Russian, Arabic, Somali)
- Disclose any known information concerning lead-based paint or lead-based paint hazards. The seller or landlord must also disclose information such as the location of the lead-based paint and/or lead-based paint hazards, and the condition of the painted surfaces.
- Provide any records and reports on lead-based paint and/or lead-based paint hazards which are available to the seller or landlord (for multi-unit buildings, this requirement includes records and reports concerning common areas and other units, when such information was obtained as a result of a building-wide evaluation)
- Include an attachment to the contract or lease (or language inserted in the lease itself) which includes a Lead Warning Statement and confirms that the seller or landlord has complied with all notification requirements. This attachment is to be provided in the same language used in the rest of the contract. **Sellers or landlords, and agents, as well as homebuyers or tenants, must sign and date the attachment.** (emphasis added)
- Sellers must provide homebuyers a 10-day period to conduct a paint inspection or risk assessment for lead-based paint or lead-based paint hazards. Parties may mutually agree, in writing, to lengthen or shorten the time period for inspection. Homebuyers may waive this inspection opportunity.

Types of Housing Covered?

Most private housing public housing, Federally owned housing, and housing receiving Federal assistance are affected by this rule.

Effective Dates

The regulations became effective on September 6, 1996 for transactions involving owners of more than 4 residential dwellings and on December 6, 1996 for transactions involving owners of 1 to 4 residential dwellings.

Recordkeeping

Sellers and lessors must retain a copy of the disclosures for no less than three years from the date of sale or the date the leasing period begins.

What Can You Do?

If you did not receive the Disclosure of Information on Lead-Based Paint and/or Lead-Based Paint Hazards form when you bought or leased pre-1978 housing, contact 1-800-424-LEAD (5323)

TREC has approved the Addendum for Seller's Disclosure of Information on Lead-Based Paint and Lead-Based Paint Hazards as Required by Federal Law form, which can be attached to the main contract in compliance with federal disclosure requirements. See Figure 10.1.

While real estate licensees are generally not experts in lead-based paint hazards, they must be aware of the requirements and keep their clients informed of the law regarding such hazards.

■ **Mold:** Not all molds are harmful to humans. However, the one that has claimed the notorious position at the top of the list for damage to property and to humans is called *stachybotrys chartarum* or *stachybotrys atra*. Serious respiratory problems, as well as other health issues, may be caused by this mold.

The Texas Department of Insurance published the pamphlet *Protecting Your Home from Mold*, and the Texas Association of REALTORS® offers a form to its members for use when informing buyers and sellers about mold and mold-related issues (TAR-2507).

■ **Formaldehyde gas:** Formaldehyde gas is a noxious strong-smelling gas that is colorless. It can be found in paneling, particleboard, furniture, draperies, and other items used in home construction. Formaldehyde gas can cause cancer and other, less serious problems that mimic allergy symptoms.

■ **Chlorofluorocarbons:** Chlorofluorocarbons (CFCs) are nontoxic, nonflammable chemicals used as refrigerants in air conditioners, refrigerators, and freezers. CFCs are also used in aerosol sprays, paints, solvents, and foam-blowing applications. Although CFCs are safe in most applications and are inert in the lower atmosphere, once CFC vapors rise to the upper atmosphere, where they may survive from 2 to 150 years, they are broken down by ultraviolet light into chemicals that deplete the ozone layer.

F I G U R E   10.1

Addendum for Seller's Disclosure of Information on Lead-Based Paint and Lead-Based Paint Hazards as Required by Federal Law

APPROVED BY THE TEXAS REAL ESTATE COMMISSION   10-10-11

EQUAL HOUSING OPPORTUNITY

ADDENDUM FOR SELLER'S DISCLOSURE OF INFORMATION ON LEAD-BASED PAINT AND LEAD-BASED PAINT HAZARDS AS REQUIRED BY FEDERAL LAW

CONCERNING THE PROPERTY AT _____
(Street Address and City)

A. LEAD WARNING STATEMENT: "Every purchaser of any interest in residential real property on which a residential dwelling was built prior to 1978 is notified that such property may present exposure to lead from lead-based paint that may place young children at risk of developing lead poisoning. Lead poisoning in young children may produce permanent neurological damage, including learning disabilities, reduced intelligence quotient, behavioral problems, and impaired memory. Lead poisoning also poses a particular risk to pregnant women. The seller of any interest in residential real property is required to provide the buyer with any information on lead-based paint hazards from risk assessments or inspections in the seller's possession and notify the buyer of any known lead-based paint hazards. A risk assessment or inspection for possible lead-paint hazards is recommended prior to purchase."
NOTICE: Inspector must be properly certified as required by federal law.

B. SELLER'S DISCLOSURE:
1. PRESENCE OF LEAD-BASED PAINT AND/OR LEAD-BASED PAINT HAZARDS (check one box only):
☐ (a) Known lead-based paint and/or lead-based paint hazards are present in the Property (explain): _____
_____ .
☐ (b) Seller has no actual knowledge of lead-based paint and/or lead-based paint hazards in the Property.
2. RECORDS AND REPORTS AVAILABLE TO SELLER (check one box only):
☐ (a) Seller has provided the purchaser with all available records and reports pertaining to lead-based paint and/or lead-based paint hazards in the Property (list documents):_____
_____ .
☐ (b) Seller has no reports or records pertaining to lead-based paint and/or lead-based paint hazards in the Property.

C. BUYER'S RIGHTS (check one box only):
☐ 1. Buyer waives the opportunity to conduct a risk assessment or inspection of the Property for the presence of lead-based paint or lead-based paint hazards.
☐ 2. Within ten days after the effective date of this contract, Buyer may have the Property inspected by inspectors selected by Buyer. If lead-based paint or lead-based paint hazards are present, Buyer may terminate this contract by giving Seller written notice within 14 days after the effective date of this contract, and the earnest money will be refunded to Buyer.

D. BUYER'S ACKNOWLEDGMENT (check applicable boxes):
☐ 1. Buyer has received copies of all information listed above.
☐ 2. Buyer has received the pamphlet *Protect Your Family from Lead in Your Home*.

E. BROKERS' ACKNOWLEDGMENT: Brokers have informed Seller of Seller's obligations under 42 U.S.C. 4852d to: (a) provide Buyer with the federally approved pamphlet on lead poisoning prevention; (b) complete this addendum; (c) disclose any known lead-based paint and/or lead-based paint hazards in the Property; (d) deliver all records and reports to Buyer pertaining to lead-based paint and/or lead-based paint hazards in the Property; (e) provide Buyer a period of up to 10 days to have the Property inspected; and (f) retain a completed copy of this addendum for at least 3 years following the sale. Brokers are aware of their responsibility to ensure compliance.

F. CERTIFICATION OF ACCURACY: The following persons have reviewed the information above and certify, to the best of their knowledge, that the information they have provided is true and accurate.

_____   _____   _____   _____
Buyer   Date   Seller   Date

_____   _____   _____   _____
Buyer   Date   Seller   Date

_____   _____   _____   _____
Other Broker   Date   Listing Broker   Date

The form of this addendum has been approved by the Texas Real Estate Commission for use only with similarly approved or promulgated forms of contracts. Such approval relates to this contract form only. TREC forms are intended for use only by trained real estate licensees. No representation is made as to the legal validity or adequacy of any provision in any specific transactions. It is not suitable for complex transactions. Texas Real Estate Commission, P.O. Box 12188, Austin, TX 78711-2188, 512-936-3000 (http://www.trec.texas.gov)

TREC NO. OP-L

Global treaties have sought to reduce the production levels of CFCs. The manufacture of these chemicals ended for the most part in 1996, with exceptions for production in developing countries, medical products (e.g., asthma inhalers), and research.

Although newer air conditioners use a different product, older appliances may leak CFCs and should be properly disposed of to prevent further leakage. A buyer's representative may wish to advise the client to consider upgrading to newer, more energy-efficient and environmentally safe appliances.

Only EPA-certified technicians should work on refrigeration systems, especially the larger systems found in commercial and industrial buildings. Approved equipment should carry a label reading "This equipment has been certified by ARI/UL to meet EPA's minimum requirements for recycling and recovery equipment."

Americans with Disabilities Act (ADA)

According to ADA.gov, a part of the U.S. Department of Justice Civil Rights Division,

> the Americans with Disabilities Act of 1990 (ADA) prohibits discrimination and ensures equal opportunity for persons with disabilities in employment, State and local government services, public accommodations, commercial facilities, and transportation. It also mandates the establishment of TDD/telephone relay services. The current text of the ADA includes changes made by the ADA Amendments Act of 2008 (P.L. 110-325), which became effective on January 1, 2009. The ADA was originally enacted in public law format and later rearranged and published in the United States Code.

> On Friday, July 23, 2010, Attorney General Eric Holder signed final regulations revising the Department's ADA regulations, including its ADA Standards for Accessible Design. The official text was published in the Federal Register on September 15, 2010 (corrections to this text were published in the Federal Register on March 11, 2011). . . .

> These final rules went into effect on March 15, 2011, and were published in the 2011 edition of the Code of Federal Regulations (CFR).

Texas Workforce Commission The Texas Workforce Commission has a procedure for those who believe they have suffered employment discrimination related to a disability. The commission offers the following advice at www.twc.state.tx.us/crd/disability-discrimination.html:

> If you believe you may have been discriminated against in employment due to a disability and meet the requirements listed below, you may submit a discrimination complaint through the TWC Civil Rights Division. To learn more about the complaint process, see How to Submit an Employment Discrimination Complaint [www.twc.state.tx.us/crd/how-submit-employment-discrimination-complaint.html].

> Texas Labor Code Chapter 21 (Chapter 21) and the Americans with Disabilities Act (ADA) prohibit employers from discriminating

against applicants or employees with disabilities in job application, procedures, conditions and privileges of employment. Chapter 21 applies to private employers with 15 or more employees, and to all state and local governmental entities no matter how many employees they have.

A qualified individual under Chapter 21 and ADA meets one or more of these requirements:

- Has a physical or mental disability that substantially limits one or more major life activities
- Has a record of having a disability
- Is regarded as having a disability

In the sections below we provide information about common concerns or complaints.

Reasonable Accommodation

An employee with a disability must be able to perform the essential functions of their job with or without a reasonable accommodation. If you need an accommodation due to a disability, you must request it from your employer. A reasonable accommodation is a requested item or action that would enable you to perform the required functions of your job.

For example, the accommodation may be one of the following:

- Make buildings and bathrooms readily accessible to and usable by persons with disabilities
- Change your work schedule or reassign you to a vacant position you are qualified for
- Provide you with equipment or devices that will aid you in performing the essential functions of your job
- Provide additional training
- Provide qualified readers or interpreters

An employer is required to make a reasonable accommodation unless the request causes significant difficulty or expense to the employer.

An employer is not required to lower quality or production standards for disabled applicants or employees.

Equal Credit Opportunity Act

The Equal Credit Opportunity Act (ECOA) (Regulation B) is described in the law as follows:

§ 202.1   Authority, scope and purpose.

(a) *Authority and scope.* This regulation is issued by the Board of Governors of the Federal Reserve System pursuant to title VII (Equal Credit Opportunity Act) of the Consumer Credit Protection Act, as amended (15 U.S.C. 1601 *et seq.*). Except as otherwise provided herein, this regulation applies to all persons who are creditors, as defined in §202.2(1). Information collection requirements contained in this regulation have been approved by the Office of Management and Budget under the provisions of 44 U.S.C. 3501 et seq. and have been assigned OMB No. 7100-0201.

(b) *Purpose*. The purpose of this regulation is to promote the availability of credit to all creditworthy applicants without regard to race, color, religion, national origin, sex, marital status, or age (provided the applicant has the capacity to contract); to the fact that all or part of the applicant's income derives from a public assistance program; or to the fact that the applicant has in good faith exercised any right under the Consumer Credit Protection Act. The regulation prohibits creditor practices that discriminate on the basis of any of these factors. The regulation also requires creditors to notify applicants of action taken on their applications; to report credit history in the names of both spouses on an account; to retain records of credit applications; to collect information about the applicant's race and other personal characteristics in applications for certain dwelling-related loans; and to provide applicants with copies of appraisal reports used in connection with credit transactions.

As a real estate licensee, unless you have been trained in mortgage lending, you must be very careful not to cross the line by giving advice in an area where you are not qualified to offer advice. The National Association of REALTORS®, in its Code of Ethics, Article 2, states the following:

REALTORS® shall avoid exaggeration, misrepresentation, or concealment of pertinent facts relating to the property or the transaction. REALTORS® shall **not**, however, be obligated to discover latent defects in the property, **to advise on matters outside the scope of their real estate license**, or to disclose facts which are confidential under the scope of agency or non-agency relationships as defined by state law. (Amended 1/00)

Standard of Practice 2-1

REALTORS® shall only be obligated to discover and disclose adverse factors reasonably apparent to someone with expertise in those areas required by their real estate licensing authority. Article 2 does not impose upon the REALTOR® the obligation of expertise in other professional or technical disciplines. (Amended 1/96)

An agent is required to be knowledgeable and stay current in market conditions. As an agent for a buyer-client who is trying to obtain a loan, it is appropriate to make the client aware of the laws affecting real estate transactions, including lending laws operating to protect the client's interests.

Community Reinvestment Act

According to the Board of Governors of the Federal Reserve System,

the Community Reinvestment Act is intended to encourage depository institutions to help meet the credit needs of the communities in which they operate, including low- and moderate-income neighborhoods, consistent with safe and sound operations. It was enacted by the Congress in 1977 (12 U.S.C. 2901) and is implemented by

Regulation BB (12 CFR 228). The regulation was substantially revised in May 1995 and updated again in August 2005.

The CRA requires that each depository institution's record in helping meet the credit needs of its entire community be evaluated by the appropriate Federal financial supervisory agency periodically. Members of the public may submit comments on a bank's performance. Comments will be taken into consideration during the next CRA examination. A bank's CRA performance record is taken into account in considering an institution's application for deposit facilities.

Home Mortgage Disclosure Act

The Federal Financial Institutions Examination's Council at www.ffiec.gov/hmda/ describes the Home Mortgage Disclosure Act (HMDA) as follows:

> The Home Mortgage Disclosure Act (HMDA) was enacted by Congress in 1975 and was implemented by the Federal Reserve Board's Regulation C. On July 21, 2011, the rule-writing authority of Regulation C was transferred to the Consumer Financial Protection Bureau (CFPB). This regulation provides the public loan data that can be used to assist:
>
> ■ in determining whether financial institutions are serving the housing needs of their communities;
> ■ public officials in distributing public-sector investments so as to attract private investment to areas where it is needed;
> ■ and in identifying possible discriminatory lending patterns.
>
> This regulation applies to certain financial institutions, including banks, savings associations, credit unions, and other mortgage lending institutions.

■ TEXAS STATE LAW

While the federal government has a number of laws affecting real estate practitioners, state laws can vary and create the need for individual state real estate licenses. Several key Texas laws affecting licensees include the Texas Deceptive Trade Practices—Consumer Protection Act (DTPA), the Texas Fair Housing Act, and The Real Estate License Act (see Appendix A), Fraud in Real Estate and Stock Transactions(Business and Commerce Code, Chapter 23, Section 27), Texas Property Code, Texas Finance Code, and many others.

Texas Fair Housing Act

The Texas Department of Housing and Community Affairs describes on its website (www.tdhca.state.tx.us/housing-center/fair-housing/basics.htm) how Texas works to assure fair housing in the state:

> Texas also has its own Texas Fair Housing Act (www.twc.state.tx.us), which closely mirrors the Federal Fair Housing Act. The Civil Rights Division of the Texas Workforce Commission Civil Rights Division (TWCCRD) enforces the Texas Fair Housing Act. Complainants

received by TWCCRD are investigated by TWCCRD and coordinated with HUD. . . .

In addition to the Fair Housing Act, all entities that receive funding from the U.S. Department of Housing and Urban Development (HUD), or administer HUD-funded programs, have a duty to Affirmatively Further Fair Housing (AFFH - HUD.gov). HUD defines AFFH as:

- Conducting an analysis to identify impediments to fair housing choice (the AI) within the jurisdiction;
- Taking appropriate actions to overcome the effects of any impediments identified through the analysis; and
- Maintaining records reflecting the analysis and actions taken in this regard.

As part of TDHCA's AFFH efforts, all awardees must have affirmative marketing procedures (HUD.gov) to attract potential consumers or residents regardless of race, color, religion, sex, national origin, disability, or familial status, and that are primarily targeted to tenants and homebuyers who are least likely to apply for the housing. Awardees must also maintain waiting lists in a non-discriminatory manner.

In addition to the protected groups in federal and Texas fair housing laws, TRELA §1101.652 (b)(32), and TREC Rule §531.19 (a)(6) adds ancestry as an additional category to the protected classes.

The NAR Code of Ethics (as amended 1/2014) includes, in the list of classes that a REALTOR® should not discriminate against, the categories of sexual orientation and gender identity. Keep in mind, the NAR Code of Ethics, while not a law, can be used in court as a "standard of practice" for real estate brokers.

NAR Code of Ethics: Duties to the Public

Article 10

REALTORS® shall not deny equal professional services to any person for reasons of race, color, religion, sex, handicap, familial status, national origin, sexual orientation, or gender identity. REALTORS® shall not be parties to any plan or agreement to discriminate against a person or persons on the basis of race, color, religion, sex, handicap, familial status, national origin, sexual orientation, or gender identity. (*Amended 1/14*)

REALTORS®, in their real estate employment practices, shall not discriminate against any person or persons on the basis of race, color, religion, sex, handicap, familial status, national origin, sexual orientation, or gender identity. (*Amended 1/14*)

A frequently overlooked source of laws prohibiting discrimination is the municipal ordinances of particular cities. Check them out before operating in any given community.

Texas: Fraud in a Real Estate Transaction

Real estate fraud is covered in the Business and Commerce Code (Title 3, Insolvency, Fraudulent Transfers, and Fraud; Chapter 27, Fraud; § 27.01 Fraud in Real Estate and Stock Transactions):

(a) Fraud in a transaction involving real estate or stock in a corporation or joint stock company consists of a

(1) false representation of a past or existing material fact, when the false representation is

(A) made to a person for the purpose of inducing that person to enter into a contract; and

(B) relied on by that person in entering into that contract; or

(2) false promise to do an act, when the false promise is

(A) material;

(B) made with the intention of not fulfilling it;

(C) made to a person for the purpose of inducing that person to enter into a contract; and

(D) relied on by that person in entering into that contract.

■ **EXAMPLE:**

■ Sally, a broker, is representing a seller in the sale of his home.

■ Sally has the builder's plans for the seller's home, which shows that the home has 3,500 square feet of air-conditioned living space.

■ Sally was also told by the seller that the home has 3,500 square feet of air-conditioned living space.

■ When talking with Sally, the buyer/customer asks what the square footage of the house is.

■ Sally, knowing that the buyer needs 4,000 square feet of living space, says, "There are 4,000 square feet of air-conditioned living space in the home. Why don't you make your best offer today so that you don't lose the opportunity to purchase it."

■ After the sale is concluded, the buyer finds that there are only 3,500 square feet.

■ **QUESTIONS:**

■ Do you think that the buyer and the courts will find the missing 500 square feet to be material?

■ Was the information provided with the intent to deceive?

■ Was the information given by Sally to induce the buyer into a contract that he would not have entered into had the information been known?

■ Did the buyer rely on the information given by Sally to make a decision to purchase?

If the answer is yes to these questions, then the buyer's attorney will likely use this law, as well as the DTPA, to sue Sally. Additionally, Sally could be reported to

TREC for a violation of TRELA § 1101.652(b)(2) and possibly lose her license. If Sally is a REALTOR®, she could also face sanctions from NAR based on her fraudulent actions.

Texas Property Code

We can't possibly cover all the information in this textbook that appears in the Texas Property Code; however, Section 5.008 of the Texas Property Code is a good example of the impact of the Code on real estate licensees and consumers.

When explaining § 5.008 of the Code to the seller and the legal requirement to give the Seller's Disclosure of Property Condition to a prospective buyer, the agent should not give any advice or assist the seller in filling out the form. The form is given directly from the seller to a buyer prospect and is the seller's written statement concerning the condition of his property. If the agent simply gives the completed form (or one produced by the agent's brokerage that meets the Code's requirements) to the buyer and does not make any claims concerning the condition of the property, it will generally take the agent out of the loop of legal liability if later the buyer finds that the seller made misstatements of fact and is damaged as a result.

The law allows the buyer, if the buyer does not receive the form, the opportunity to terminate the contract without default and receive earnest money back. The seller's agent needs to explain this section to the seller-client, and the buyer's agent needs to make the buyer aware of the options.

According to Sec. 5.008 (Seller's Disclosure of Property Condition):,

> (a) A seller of residential real property comprising not more than one dwelling unit located in this state shall give to the purchaser of the property a written notice as prescribed by this section or a written notice substantially similar to the notice prescribed by this section which contains, at a minimum, all of the items in the notice prescribed by this section...

> (f) The notice shall be delivered by the seller to the purchaser on or before the effective date of an executory contract binding the purchaser to purchase the property. **If a contract is entered without the seller providing the notice required by this section, the purchaser may terminate the contract for any reason within seven days after receiving the notice.**

The following 11 exceptions pertain to the seller's having to give the Seller's Disclosure of Property Condition to a prospective buyer:

> § 5.008 (d) The notice shall be completed to the best of seller's belief and knowledge as of the date the notice is completed and signed by the seller. If the information required by the notice is unknown to the seller, the seller shall indicate that fact on the notice, and by that act is in compliance with this section.

> (e) **This section does not apply to a transfer** (emphasis added):

> > (1) pursuant to a court order or foreclosure sale;

(2) by a trustee in bankruptcy;

(3) to a mortgagee by a mortgagor or successor in interest, or to a beneficiary of a deed of trust by a trustor or successor in interest;

(4) by a mortgagee or a beneficiary under a deed of trust who has acquired the real property at a sale conducted pursuant to a power of sale under a deed of trust or a sale pursuant to a court ordered foreclosure or has acquired the real property by a deed in lieu of foreclosure;

(5) by a fiduciary in the course of the administration of a decedent's estate, guardianship, conservatorship, or trust;

(6) from one co-owner to one or more other co-owners;

(7) made to a spouse or to a person or persons in the lineal line of consanguinity of one or more of the transferors;

(8) between spouses resulting from a decree of dissolution of marriage or a decree of legal separation or from a property settlement agreement incidental to such a decree;

(9) to or from any governmental entity;

(10) of a new residence of not more than one dwelling unit which has not previously been occupied for residential purposes; or

(11) of real property where the value of any dwelling does not exceed five percent of the value of the property."

A licensee must not make the decision for the seller-client that an exception applies and the seller does not to give the property condition disclosure notice. It is the decision of the seller, not the agent, to elect not to give the notice. If, for instance, the seller's attorney advises the seller to abstain from filling in the property disclosure form, or giving written information to a buyer on the condition of the property, the seller's agent is obligated to make the seller aware of the § 5.008 requirement, but cannot force the seller to complete the form. This does not relieve the agent or the seller of the legal obligation to disclose any property condition that a reasonable and prudent purchaser would want to know before making the decision to purchase that property.

If it is the policy of the agent's brokerage not to take a listing without the seller filling out a Seller's Disclosure of Property Condition form, that is permissible, and the licensee can refuse to take a listing or market the property.

Although the Seller's Disclosure of Property Condition is not required of commercial property owners, commercial property brokers have found that requiring the use of similar seller disclosure notices is a prudent business practice.

Local Municipal Codes and Ordinances

Municipalities are authorized to enact local ordinances and codes, many of which have a direct impact on real estate. Specifically, zoning regulations, city building codes, habitability and occupancy codes, as well as fair housing ordinances, have major implications for the licensee, and a thorough knowledge of these codes and ordinances is essential to the practitioner. It is a wise business practice for licensees to attend city council meetings and planning and zoning committee meetings. They should also read the monthly committee minutes and stay abreast of the decisions made by these committees in the area where the licensee is active. Changes to zoning; potential new construction, ordinances, and rules; and many other areas affected by local government should be addressed by agents when working with their clients.

■ TRELA AND RULES OF THE COMMISSION

The Real Estate License Act

The DTPA illustrates how providers of goods and services (including real estate licensees) are subject to powerful consumer laws. Other laws and regulations are specific to real estate brokers and salespersons.

The Texas Legislature first began regulating practitioners in 1939 with passage of the Real Estate Dealer's Act. This was followed in 1949 with passage of The Real Estate License Act (TRELA), the creation of the Texas Real estate Commission (TREC), and a requirement for licensure. Like the federal government, Texas legislators have since passed a number of laws relating to the practice of real estate within the state, as well as modifying and substantially expanding TRELA.

TRELA establishes a baseline for actions by Texas licensees and members of the Texas Real Estate Commission. Subsection N, § 1101.651–§ 1101.655, provides a "laundry list" of specific violations that can result in revocation or suspension of the licensee, placing the licensee on probation, and/or assessing administrative penalties (fines) against the licensee. Licensees should keep in mind that a legal action against a licensee through the courts is an action separate and distinct from a complaint filed through TREC. Texas courts cannot suspend or revoke a real estate license; however, the grounds for the suit may be the basis of a complaint filed against the licensee through TREC resulting in loss of licensure. A complete copy of TRELA is included in Appendix A.

The Texas Real Estate Commission (TREC)

Subchapter B of TRELA defines the Commission as consisting of nine members appointed by the governor with the advice and consent of the senate. Six of these members must be licensed as real estate brokers, and three must be from the general public. Subchapter D of TRELA establishes the powers and duties of the Commission. TREC is empowered under TRELA to enact rules and regulations, including the regulation of individual licensees.

TREC is responsible for safeguarding the public interest and protecting consumers of real estate services. In accordance with state and federal laws, the agency oversees real estate brokerage, appraisal, inspection, home warranty, and timeshare interest providers. Through education, licensing, and regulation, the agency ensures the availability of qualified and ethical service providers, thereby facilitating economic growth and opportunity in Texas.

Adherence to The Real Estate License Act and the Rules of the Commission is the legal responsibility of every real estate licensee in Texas. The TREC publication *The Advisor* has a section devoted to licensed brokers and salespersons who have violated TRELA and who have received a reprimand, suspension, or revocation of their licenses. Licensees must be thoroughly familiar with what the law says and what it means in relation to daily activities when functioning as an agent for their broker, or when acting through their broker, as an agent for a buyer/tenant or seller/landlord client.

■ PROFESSIONAL CODES OF ETHICS

Almost without exception, businesses and professions have adopted voluntary codes of ethics for their employees or members. These codes of ethics represent the rules of professional conduct expected of their members. Typically, these codes or rules are helpful in guiding decision making and actions with the intricacies of a specific business, profession, or industry. Although these codes do not carry the weight of law, they may be enforced against association members who agree to such enforcement power as a condition of membership. Even courts of law will use industry codes in interpreting and applying legal actions against professionals.

TREC Canons of Professional Ethics and Conduct

TRELA § 1101.151(b) grants TREC the authority to establish standards of conduct and ethics for persons licensed under the act. Thus, by rule, 22 TAC § 531 (see Figure 10.2) includes the five very basic canons of professional ethics and conduct that apply to all real estate licensees.

Notice that the canons also support the federal Fair Housing Act by prohibiting discriminatory practices against protected classes. The canons are similar in content to voluntary general business ethics and common law agency principles from a variety of sources, including case law, statutory law, and the codes of ethics of many professional and trade associations.

National Association of REALTORS® Code of Ethics and Professional Standards

Perhaps the oldest and most recognized code within the real estate industry is the National Association of REALTORS® (NAR) Code of Ethics (Code). Established in 1908, NAR adopted the original Code in 1913 as a required code of conduct for the membership. Today, NAR represents one of the largest professional organizations in the country and has powerful political influence through political action committees and professional lobbyists.

In addition to NAR, Texas practitioners may be members of the Texas Association of REALTORS® (TAR) and local associations of REALTORS®—all affiliate organizations of NAR. Approximately 50% of all Texas licensees are members of these organizations and are authorized to use the professional term *REALTOR®*. Although often used generically, the word *REALTOR®* is a trademarked term and should not be used by nonmembers. Although only REALTORS® are required to adopt and subscribe to the NAR Code of Ethics, the code offers excellent guidelines for all licensees, REALTOR® or otherwise. The NAR Code of Ethics and Standards of Practice are shown in Appendix A. A thorough reading of this material is strongly encouraged.

FIGURE 10.2

Canons of Professional Ethics

TITLE 22. EXAMINING BOARDS
PART 23. TEXAS REAL ESTATE COMMISSION
CHAPTER 531. CANONS OF PROFESSIONAL ETHICS AND CONDUCT

§531.1. Fidelity. A real estate broker or salesperson, while acting as an agent for another, is a fiduciary. Special obligations are imposed when such fiduciary relationships are created. They demand:

(1) that the primary duty of the real estate agent is to represent the interests of the agent's client, and the agent's position, in this respect, should be clear to all parties concerned in a real estate transaction; that, however, the agent, in performing duties to the client, shall treat other parties to a transaction fairly;

(2) that the real estate agent be faithful and observant to trust placed in the agent, and be scrupulous and meticulous in performing the agent's functions; and

(3) that the real estate agent place no personal interest above that of the agent's client.

The provisions of this §531.1 adopted to be effective January 1, 1976; amended to be effective February 23, 1998, 23 TexReg 1568; amended to be effective May 21, 2014, 39 TexReg 3855.

§531.2. Integrity. A real estate broker or salesperson has a special obligation to exercise integrity in the discharge of the license holder's responsibilities, including employment of prudence and caution so as to avoid misrepresentation, in any wise, by acts of commission or omission.

The provisions of this §531.2 adopted to be effective January 1, 1976; amended to be effective February 23, 1998, 23 TexReg 1568; amended to be effective May 21, 2014, 39 TexReg 3855.

§531.3. Competency. It is the obligation of a real estate agent to be knowledgeable as a real estate brokerage practitioner. The agent should:

(1) be informed on market conditions affecting the real estate business and pledged to continuing education in the intricacies involved in marketing real estate for others;

(2) be informed on national, state, and local issues and developments in the real estate industry; and

(3) exercise judgment and skill in the performance of the work.

The provisions of this §531.3 adopted to be effective January 1, 1976; amended to be effective February 23, 1998, 23 TexReg 1568.

§531.18. Consumer Information.

(a) The Texas Real Estate Commission adopts by reference Consumer Information Form 1-1. This document is published by and available from the Texas Real Estate Commission, P.O. Box 12188, Austin, Texas 78711-2188, www.trec.texas.gov.

(b) Each active real estate inspector or active real estate broker licensed by the Texas Real Estate Commission shall display Consumer Information Form 1-1 in a prominent location in each place of business the broker or inspector maintains.

The provisions of this §531.18 adopted to be effective February 1, 1990, 14 TexReg 2613; amended to be effective November 1, 1991, 16 TexReg 5209; amended to be effective September 1, 2010, 35 TexReg 7797; amended to be effective May 21, 2014, 39 TexReg 3855.

§531.19. Discriminatory Practices.

(a) No real estate license holder shall inquire about, respond to or facilitate inquiries about, or make a disclosure of an owner, previous or current occupant, potential purchaser, lessor, or potential lessee of real property which indicates or is intended to indicate any preference, limitation, or discrimination based on the following:

(1) race;

(2) color;

(3) religion;

(4) sex;

(5) national origin;

(6) ancestry;

(7) familial status; or

(8) disability.

(b) For the purpose of this section, disability includes AIDS, HIV-related illnesses, or HIV infection as defined by the Centers for Disease Control of the United States Public Health Service.

The provisions of this §531.19 adopted to be effective February 19, 1990, 15 TexReg 656; amended to be effective May 21, 2014, 39 TexReg 3855.

Real estate licensees need to be aware that in addition to TRELA, rules of the commission, and both federal and state laws, the NAR Code of Ethics has been used to identify a standard of conduct for real estate licensees (definitely for members and sometimes even for nonmembers). This has been used in the past in the courts and will continue to be used in court cases against real estate licensees. Nan Roytberg, NAR Legal Affairs, wrote the following in "When Courts Look at NAR's Code of Ethics":

> In case after case, courts afford the REALTOR® Code of Ethics just as much respect as case law, statutes, and license law in determining what standard of care a real estate professional owes the public. And courts often hold all licensees to the high standards of the Code, whether or not they're members of a REALTOR® association.

■ MINIMUM ETHICAL STANDARDS

Laws in this country were instituted to protect the rights and freedoms of individuals, to create a sense of order, and to provide for the reasonable expectation of protection in the home, marketplace, and even the halls of government. There are penalties when an individual crosses the line created by society to determine decent and appropriate behavior. The law also provides recourse for persons who are injured by others. When functioning properly, individuals can depend upon the law and a jury of their peers to listen carefully to a complaint or defense to make a judgment based on the facts of the case and the laws relative to that case.

The law, then, is a minimum standard of conduct. Ethical standards and conduct allow a society to peacefully exist. They protect citizens when one or more people choose to act without regard for the rights of others.

Before entering the real estate industry, individuals must examine whether they are willing to abide by the law and the spirit of the law. In other words, they must agree to do what is ethical in any real estate situation while performing agency duties to a client or dealing with a customer.

In practical terms, how do we achieve the aspirations of codes of conduct and the law in the real estate profession? Here are some of the ways the real estate industry promotes ethical conduct of its industry members.

Individual Company Policy, Procedure, and Codes of Ethics and Conduct

TREC requires brokers to develop written policy and procedure manuals for their own companies (22 TAC § 535.2(i)). Many individual brokers include specific sections relating to codes of conduct and ethics expected of their employees and associate licensees. These serve as the guiding principles for the company and its employees, and agents are often required to sign statements indicating that they agree to abide by the policies established by the company. In many cases, the company conducts training classes for new associates to ensure that the licensee understands and is willing to meet the company's standards of practice.

Personal Beliefs and Individual Ethics

Ethics are those things that we think or believe to be the right course of action in a given circumstance after processing the legal and moral implications. These personal or core beliefs have been inculcated in the young by parents, schools, churches, communities, states, and countries. These core beliefs typically include respect for others, being truthful and honest, fulfilling promises, and honoring commitments. If, in fact, all people agreed to and adhered to the same core beliefs or a common morality, there would be no need for codes of conduct, rules and regulations, or even laws. Obviously, this is not the case and the farther one is removed from immediate family, community, or country, the more diverse will be the notion of what is moral or ethical.

On occasion, individuals may find their personal ethics in conflict with professional codes and even laws. In the final analysis, the individual's actions will illustrate which standards have the greatest influence on that individual.

Laws and Ethics in Practice

How do laws, legal ethics, rules and regulations, codes of ethics, and personal beliefs interact in the real world? The following questions and examples illustrate the relationships and potential conflicts.

■ **EXAMPLE 1:**   Agent Sally, a REALTOR®, is attempting to list a single-family home for lease through the company's property management division. The property is a large four-bedroom home with unfenced frontage on a deep-water river. The owners have indicated that they do not want to rent to a family with young children because of the unprotected waterfront posing a serious danger to small children. As a mother herself, Sally shares the concern for safety and takes the listing, agreeing to work with the owner to try and find the right tenant, even though she knows that adults with children are considered protected under the familial status provisions of fair housing laws.

Over the next few weeks, several potential tenants inquire about the property, but Sally, using various excuses as to why the subject property could not be shown, directed the prospects to other properties meeting the prospects' needs. Within a month, Sally produced a retired couple with no children living at home and secured a lease for the owner of the waterfront property.

In evaluating Sally's actions, let's look first at the laws, rules and regulations, codes, and ethics that would apply in this case:

- Federal Fair Housing Act
- Texas antidiscrimination law
- Municipal antidiscrimination ordinances
- TRELA
- TREC Rules and Regulations
- NAR COE
- Company policy
- Sally's personal beliefs

Federal Law   The basis for antidiscrimination law is rooted in the 1866 Civil Rights Act and, more specifically, in civil rights movements of the 1950s and 1960s. The resultant Fair Housing Act and subsequent amendments make it illegal to discriminate in the sale or leasing of residential properties based on race, color, religion, sex, national origin, familial status, or handicap. These are called protected classes.

Texas State Law   Individual states such as Texas have been authorized to enact and enforce state fair housing laws so long as the federally protected classes are also included in the state law. States are, however, authorized to include additional categories of protected classes, if they so choose. As a result, many states (though not Texas) have added sexual orientation, marital status, and other identifiers as additional protected classes. Thus, in Texas, compliance with the federal law conforms to compliance with Texas antidiscrimination laws.

Municipal Ordinances   Cities, like states, may also have ordinances prohibiting discrimination in housing so long as the protected classes, at minimum, include the federally protected classes, as well as any additional state-protected classes. Municipalities may add protected classes to either the federal or the state categories. The city in which Sally resides has adopted a city fair housing ordinance that mirrors the federal law.

TRELA   TRELA § 1101.652(b)(32) specifically creates grounds for suspension or revocation of a license if the license holder

> discriminates against an owner, potential buyer, landlord, or potential tenant on the basis of race, color, religion, sex, disability, familial status, national origin, or ancestry, including directing a prospective buyer or tenant interested in equivalent properties to a different area based on the race color, religion, sex, disability, familial status, national origin or ancestry of the potential owner, or tenant.

TREC Rules   TREC Rule § 531.19 states that

> no real estate licensee shall inquire about, respond to or facilitate inquires about, or make a disclosure which indicates or is intended to indicate any preference, limitation or discrimination based on the following: race, color, religion, sex, national origin, ancestry, familial status, or handicap or an owner, previous or current occupant, potential purchaser, lessor, or potential lessee of real property. For the purpose of this section, handicap includes a person who had, may have had, has, or may have AIDS, HIV-related illnesses, or HIV infection as defined by the Centers for Disease Control [CDC] of the United States Public Health Service.

Notice that the TREC rule goes further in describing the specific activities that would be considered discriminatory and potentially actionable under TRELA as grounds for suspension or revocation of a licensee by refining the definition of handicap to include AIDS or HIV-related illnesses identified by the CDC.

Up to this point, the licensee would be relying on and subject to either legal or administrative actions by the courts or by TREC. The following guidelines would be afforded by professional or private organizations:

NAR Code of Ethics   Presuming Sally is a REALTOR® member, Article 10 from the NAR Code of Ethics (Standards of Practice 10-1, 10-2, 10-3, and 10-4) would apply (see Appendix C).

Company Policy   Individual company policy may include all the protected classes noted, as well as others, and may be more directed, if desired. Sally's company policy states the following:

> No employee, or associated sales or broker licensee shall deny professional services based on race, color, religion, sex, handicap, familial status, national origin, sexual orientation, or marital status. No employee, or associated sales or broker licensee shall inquire about, respond to or facilitate inquiries about or make a disclosure which indicates or is intended to indicate any preference, limitation or discrimination based on the following: race, color, religion, sex, handicap, familial status, national origin, sexual orientation, or marital status." Sally like other sales associates was required to read and accept the company policy.

Sally's Personal Beliefs and Ethics   Agent Sally also has personal beliefs that guide her actions as a real estate professional. They are as follows:

- Be honest, practice with integrity, and be trustworthy in all circumstances.
- Give the best professional service to all clients and customers.
- Select the best properties for each individual buyer or tenant without regard to personal commission or gain.
- Never put a child in a position of potential danger or harm.
- Never compromise your personal ethics.

Considering all the stakeholders—Sally, the client, the customer, Sally's company, and the public in general—did Sally do the right thing?

Now let's consider another case.

■ **EXAMPLE 2:**   Pam, a single mother, has fallen on relatively hard times. Sales have been slow in her market, and most of her backup funds have been used up. Unless things improve soon, Pam worries that she may have to consider leaving the business—a business that she truly loves and believes that she has a great deal to offer buyers and sellers. This weekend, Pam is holding an open house on one of her better listings, a large five-bedroom home in one of the nicer subdivisions, listed at $450,000.

After a fairly slow day, a couple entered the property, and after greeting the prospects, Pam disclosed that she was the seller's agent and invited them to view the property. During the showing, the prospects exhibited a definite interest in the property and began questioning Pam about possible financing alternatives and procedures for making an offer. Pam produced the Information About Brokerage Service form and began to explain the agency options. At that point, the prospects interrupted, telling Pam that they had already seen and signed such a form with another agent from a competing company. In fact, they had been shown this house and a number of other properties last week by the other agent. After careful consideration, they had decided to make an offer on this house; however, the other agent was on vacation this week and, upon seeing the open house advertised and fearing that the property might be sold, came directly to Pam to make an offer. Upon further questioning, Pam discovers that the prospects status with the other company is that of customer and that they have not entered into a buyer representation contract. They would like to make an offer through Pam today. Pam produces the necessary paperwork and completes the offer, which was later delivered to and accepted by the seller.

The following week, the other agent, upon learning of the transaction, threatens legal action, a formal complaint to TREC, and a procuring cause complaint through the local association of REALTORS®.

Consider the levels of guidelines described in the preceding case:

- Federal law
- State law
- Local ordinances
- TRELA
- TREC
- NAR Code of Ethics
- Company code of ethics
- Pam's personal code of ethics

■ **QUESTIONS:**

- Were the other agent's threats justified?
- Did Pam do the right thing?

The examples cited in this chapter, illustrate the everyday dilemmas faced by real estate licensees across the state and country. Unfortunately, there is not always a clear answer as to what is the legal and/or ethical thing to do in a given set of circumstances. Frequently, actions are justified because of the unique circumstances and conditions under which the decision to act was made. Although sometimes justified, circumstantial ethics (sometimes called relativistic ethics) can be a dangerous road to travel. That is to say, given enough time and thought, we usually can find a way to justify our actions.

Although ethical dilemmas occur in virtually every aspect of real estate practice, those specifically relating to the agency relationship can be the most difficult to sort out. Normally, when we think of agency, we think of the various relationships the licensee broker may have with the public. Seller agency, buyer agency, and intermediary agency relationships were discussed in earlier chapters, along with the duties that accrue to each. However, the other agency relationships also exist—those relating to the relationship between sales licensees and their broker, subagency, and general duties to other cooperating brokers and sales associates in a transaction. Consider some of the following examples.

■ **EXAMPLE 3:** Tom has been an associate with Eager Realty for the past five years. His broker, Helen, recruited Tom into the business, trained him, and helped him out considerably during his trying first year. Tom recently passed his broker's test and is thinking of opening his own office. Knowing the importance of having good agents, Tom has approached several of his co-workers with his plan, and by offering generous commission splits, Tom has received commitments from two of the highest producers to move with him when he opens his own shop. They believe that they can persuade several others to move as well. Tom had made Helen aware of his ambitions to acquire a broker's license, and Helen encouraged and supported his efforts. Tom has not spoken to Helen of his plan to leave the office and open a competing firm.

■ **QUESTIONS:**

- ■ What, if any, legal or ethical duties does Tom owe to Helen?
- ■ To the agents he is attempting to recruit?
- ■ How would you suggest he proceed?

■ **EXAMPLE 4:** Judy, a sales associate, is discontented with her current brokerage company and has decided to transfer her license to a competing broker-age firm. Two of her very expensive listings are going to expire within two weeks. Judy has spoken with both sellers and convinced them not to renew with her current broker when they expire and to list them with her once she moves to her new brokerage firm. In addition, Judy is working with a represented buyer and two nonrepresented buyers, and all three have agreed to stick with her when she moves.

■ **QUESTIONS:**

- ■ What are the legal or ethical issues involved?
- ■ Is Judy doing the right thing?
- ■ If not how should this be handled?

A Practical Guide for Everyday Practice

Earlier in this chapter, reference was made to well-developed models for ethical behavior. Today, many companies invest substantial amounts of money in the formal training of their employees in ethical conduct. From some companies' perspective, such training is an attempt to truly establish an ethical company and help their employees to understand and abide by the company's code of conduct. In others, it may simply be an attempt to cover potential liability if the principals are challenged in court of legal-ethical violations.

Although many programs offer excellent decision-making models, some are quite involved and complex and may require considerable investments of time to reach a conclusion as to the proper actions to follow. Such models are often more practical and appropriate for the major decisions made by large companies that may have major implications for the long term. On the other hand, many times the real estate licensee is faced with making on-the-spot decisions without the luxury of time or input from others. Therefore, a simpler practical guide is needed for day-to-day decisions that take into consideration the following fundamental issues relating to the brokerage company and the individual licensee.

The proposed guide is centered on 10 fundamental screening questions relating to the ethical implications of the decision that is to be made. While not a guarantee of ethical behavior, this practical framework should at least help well-meaning managers do the right thing while furthering their organizational goals.

The following discussion and the "Practitioner's Quick Guide" in Figure 10.5 has been adapted for real estate licensees from "Guiding Business Decisions in

Today's Organizations."[1] The list that follows itemizes the 10 fundamental areas that should be considered by a licensee or a real estate organization when viewing a decision in the context of ethical behavior. It establishes the foundation for the more detailed "Practitioner's Quick Guide" that follows. While the list may not be exhaustive, it addresses certain key elements of the process. The user may wish to add more specifics to the guide in order to customize it to a particular industry or company.

1. **Long-term goals.** How will this action or decision affect the long-term goals of the company and/or licensee?
2. **Short-term benefits.** Are the short-term benefits (quick closing, large commission) outweighed by the effect on the long-term goals?
3. **Interests of immediate stakeholders.** How does this decision impact the interests of the immediate stakeholders (buyers, sellers, selling and cooperating brokers, and sales associates)?
4. **Consumer expectations.** What are the buyer's and the seller's expectations, and how does this decision/action meet those expectations?
5. **Organizational commitment (long and short term).** Are the company and the licensee committed to follow through with the decision (promises of intense advertising or discounted services on future transactions)?
6. **Consequences of decision/policy reversal.** How will all parties be affected if the decision must be reversed?
7. **Regulators and outside stakeholder groups.** What impact will the policy or decision have on outside stakeholder groups (TREC, lenders, appraisers, title companies, etc.)?
8. **Legality and spirit of the law.** Is the decision/action not only legal but also does it meet the spirit of the law, or does it attempt to circumvent such spirit by seeking loopholes?
9. **Existing contractual and promissory obligations.** Does this decision/action conflict with existing contractual or promissory obligations.
10. **Public scrutiny.** Will this decision/action survive the "daylight test"? How would you feel if it was published in tomorrow's edition of the local newspaper?

Each of the fundamental issues listed is addressed in the Figure 10.5 questionnaire-type "Practitioner's Quick Guide" centered on key questions. The practical outcome is a practitioner's quick and simple guide for brokers, sales associates, and other decision makers within an organization for framing ethical decisions regarding strategy, policies, and/or codes. The guide may be used for a wide variety of decision-making scenarios and throughout the chain of management down to the agent in the field. The format is streamlined so that it may be used easily and quickly and can be adapted to a wide range of business models. It should be noted that not every item will necessarily be addressed with every decision-making process. For example, a major decision such as a broker adding a full-service property management division to the broker's residential real estate company may require an exhaustive application of the entire checklist list, while a comparatively smaller decision, perhaps relating to a possible change in the company's internal bonus structure, may involve only a portion of the checklist. The guide

---

[1]   D. Peeples, P. Stokes, and M. Peeples, "Guiding Business Decisions in Today's Organizations," *Management in Practice*, Vol. 12, No. 2, Spring 2008.

could also be used by agents in the field in a number of ethics-related decisions, such as trying to decide whether to take a listing where there exists the potential for a personal conflict of interest involving a relative or close friend who may be interested in the property. Or perhaps the issue is how to deal with a property listed by the agent's company and which the agent wishes to purchase for personal use. A key value of the checklist is the flexibility and adaptability to a wide variety of ethical decision-making scenarios.

Obviously the guide in Figure 10.5 will not resolve all the issues relating to ethical decision making in all circumstances, but it is offered as a tool to help the decision maker through a logical set of screens to better decision making. If nothing else, the guide can be used as a final check before actually implementing a decision.

FIGURE 10.5

Practitioner's Quick Guide

A Practitioner's Quick-Guide for Framing Ethical Decisions Regarding Strategy, Policies, and/or Codes

_____ 1. Does the decision contribute to the long-term goals and mission of the company and the licensee?

_____ 2. Does the decision provide short-term benefits to the company and licensee?

_____ 3. Are the interests of the following stakeholders enhanced and/or protected?

    _____ A. Stockholders/Owners   _____ D. Sales associates

    _____ B. Consumers/clients   _____ E. The community

    _____ C. Management   _____ F. Employees

_____ 4. Does this decision satisfy the following consumer/stakeholder expectations?

    _____ A. Quality of service

    _____ B. Pricing

    _____ C. Appropriateness to the competency levels of the consumer/user and the licensee?

    _____ D. Risk

_____ 5. Are the company and licensee willing and able to support the decision for the long term as well as the short term?

_____ 6. How will a subsequent withdrawal or reversal of the decision affect stakeholder interests (buyers, sellers, the company, and sales associates?

_____ 7. Does the decision meet the expectations and/or regulations of other stakeholder groups?

    _____ A. Government agencies (regulatory; IRS)?

    _____ B. Independent organizations (local association of REALTORS®, TAR, NAR, etc.)?

    _____ C. General public regarding social concerns for morality, decency, and public acceptability

_____ 8. Is the decision legal–and does it also meet the intent of the law?

_____ 9. Does the decision fulfill the company's contractual and promissory obligations?

_____ 10. Will this decision withstand public scrutiny?

Source: Adapted from D. Peeples, P. Stokes, and M. Peeples, "A Practitioner's Quick-Guide for Guiding Ethical Decisions Regarding Strategy, Policies, and/or Codes" in "Guiding Business Decisions in Today's Organizations," _Management In Practice_, Vol. 12, No. 2, Spring 2008.

An Alternate Solution   Another practical answer for ethical dilemmas lies in perhaps the oldest and most widely accepted code of conduct known as the golden rule: Do unto others as you would want done unto you. Although it may sound simplistic and be dismissed by many as naïve or idealistic, the principle of the golden rule is found in almost all world religions and incorporated into almost all codes of ethics established by professional organizations or corporations. It will answer most ethical questions raised in the licensee's interactions with buyers, sellers, other licensees, business entities, and other participants related to the transaction, and the public in general. In addition, it also addresses the ethical issues of an individual's private life as well. As John C. Maxwell states in the title of his book, *There's No Such Thing as Business Ethics: There's Only One Rule for Making Decisions*, business or otherwise—the golden rule. The rule, of course, is the principal of treating others exactly as you would wish to be treated in the same circumstance. The power of the rule lies in its simplicity and broad application. A reflection on the issues of conduct covered in the earlier parts of this chapter reveals that in almost every case, the law or code of proscribed conduct is consistent with the golden rule.

Remember, however, when you are acting as an agent for a buyer or a seller, the "you" in the golden rule does not pertain to you the licensees/agent relative to the negotiations of the contract. The "you" in the golden rule, in that instance, is pertaining to the buyer and the seller. Licensees, acting as an agent for either the buyer or the seller, do not have a unilateral choice or power of deciding. They are directed by the buyer or seller-client in his performance. For instance, if Sally, the buyer's agent, takes an offer from the buyer to the seller's agent that is $10,000 below the listed price, and the seller's agent says to Sally, "My seller will not take anything less than the list price for his property. Will your buyer increase his offer? If he will, I think we have a deal." Sally, unless her buyer-client has already expressed his feelings on this issue, will need to discuss this question with her buyer-client. Sally may "feel" that her buyer has made an offer that is too low, and she may even think to herself that "if it was me, I would increase the price in the offer immediately so that I did not lose the property," but it is not Sally's privilege to reveal that information to the seller's agent, or acquiesce by stating, "I'm sure my seller will agree to increase his offer on the property. He really wants this house." In this case, the "do unto others as you would have them do unto you" decision belongs to the buyer and the seller. If, on the other hand, Sally is acting in her own behalf as the buyer of the property, she has the full authority and opportunity, to bargain any way she wishes.

When Enough Is Not Enough

Even when armed with a basic moral and ethical foundations and solid organizational codes and guidelines to follow, individuals are still put through difficult tests of their ethical mettle. In some cases, following company guidelines for reporting illegal or ethical conduct still does not pass the test of individual responsibility to act. For example, by company policy, an employee may meet the company's requirement by reporting violations to an immediate supervisor whose responsibility may be to take either disciplinary action or to report the violation to executives higher in the company hierarchy authorized to take disciplinary action. Once reported, does the employee then have an obligation to follow up to see that appropriate action was taken?

■ **EXAMPLE**   Jennifer, a new sales associate with Action Realty, overhears Andy, a senior associate with the firm, offering a cash referral fee to a nonlicensed friend for any business she or any of her friends sends to Andy. Jennifer, knowing that this violates TRELA provisions, follows company policy and reports the violation to her broker who states that she will take care of it. A few weeks later, Jennifer becomes aware that Andy is still making the offer of referral fees and has in fact paid for several referrals from his friends. Jennifer, not wanting to become further involved in the issue, takes no further action, deciding that she had done her duty by reporting Andy's conduct to her broker.

Is Jennifer's position justified, or does she have a duty to report the violation to the Real Estate Commission if the broker takes no action?

Suppose Jennifer had observed Andy stealing money from another associate's unguarded purse and became aware that, despite reporting the incident to her broker, no action was taken. Would Jennifer have an obligation to warn other associates or perhaps report the theft to law enforcement? She had, after all, reported the incident to her broker as required by company policy.

In certain circumstances, situations may arise in which agents will be able to defend certain actions by showing that they have met all legal requirements and have complied with industry rules and company policy. However, the agents are conflicted because their actions are not compatible with their personal morality.

For example, in Texas, neither an owner nor an agent is required to disclose the location of a registered sex offender living in close proximity to a listed property. Likewise, company policy might not require such disclosure; however, the agent's personal beliefs may dictate that such disclosure should be made to a potential buyer.

In the final analysis, after a potential action has been filtered through the lenses of the law, industry, professional ethical standards, and company policy, the end decision still lies with the individual's personal morality where conscience is the final arbiter.

■ THE BOTTOM LINE ON ETHICS

In general, most people will never be exposed to formal ethics training. Fortunately, in most cases, certain core beliefs have been inculcated in the young by parents, schools, churches, communities, municipalities, states, and nations. As stated earlier, these core beliefs include respect of others, being truthful and honest, fulfilling promises, and honoring commitments. Most people know the right thing to do. The problem lies in the application of that knowledge. It appears that misconduct is not generally the result of not knowing what is right, but rather in choosing not to do the right thing. Certainly every business has technical and procedural information that must be learned by the new licensee. But, once those matters are mastered, the golden rule applies in almost every case. Test it against virtually every ethical dilemma that you have faced and you will probably agree.

■ SUMMARY

Public awareness, media coverage, and governmental agencies are focused on the ethical conduct of all businesses today—not just real estate. However, the duties imposed by the law of agency in Texas go beyond the typical business/consumer transaction. Brokers and associates must be cognizant of the rules imposed by federal and state law and the rules and regulations of TRELA and TREC. Each transaction will be unique and the licensees must consider the impact of their decisions and actions on all the relative stakeholders—buyers, sellers, their own company, as well as the cooperating brokers and related service organizations such as lenders, inspectors, appraisers, and title companies.

The "Practical Guide for Ethical Decision Making" represents one relatively simple and straightforward checklist for the practitioner in the field and could be applied to almost any kind of business. In addition, reliance on the golden rule still offers a firm foundation for business ethics.

■ KEY POINTS

- The current real estate and general business environment places almost all business practitioners in the public spotlight in relation to ethical conduct.
- Ethical obligations are distinguished from legal obligations as those duties that go beyond the law and focus on not just the legal thing to do, but also the right thing to do.
- Real estate licensees are governed by numerous federal, state, and local laws, the Real Estate License Act, and the Rules of the Texas Real Estate Commission. The licensee should be familiar with current law and rules.
- nIn addition to the noted laws and regulations, licensees have a duty of ethical conduct that in some cases has been formalized by professional organizations such as NAR, TAR, local REALTOR® associations, and other professional groups.
- Decisions and actions by licensees should be reviewed in the light of long- and short-term goals of the company and the individual licensee. Consideration should be given to the impact on all relative stakeholders, the ability to follow through, as well as the negative implications should the decision be reversed in the future. All decisions and actions should be able to stand up to the light-of-day test.
- While ethics models and practical guides such as the one presented in this chapter may be useful for licensees in deciding ethical points of decisions and actions, the golden rule is still considered a baseline in the these matters.

■ SUGGESTIONS FOR BROKERS

Even though sponsored licensees may have agreed to an industry code of ethics such as the NAR COE, brokers would be well advised today to adopt and implement a written company code of conduct for sponsored licensees within the company framework. Further, all employees and associates would be required to sign statements indicating that they have read, understand, and agree to abide by the code. Such codes provide an excellent vehicle for training new agents, as well as evidence that the company is committed to good service and ethical conduct. Many companies have found these documents extremely useful during court proceedings.

CHAPTER 10 QUIZ

1. Which of the following is enforceable only by conscience?
   a. Laws
   b. Morals
   c. Ethics
   d. Rules

2. The Rules of the Texas Real Estate Commission are created by
   a. statutory law.
   b. civil law.
   c. administrative law.
   d. criminal law.

3. Disputes relating to commissions between REALTORS® are settled by
   a. an arbitration committee.
   b. civil courts.
   c. justice courts.
   d. court-appointed arbitrators.

4. Failing, within a reasonable time, to respond to inquiries from a seller regarding marketing activities or efforts on the part of the listing broker would violate
   a. legal obligations.
   b. moral obligations.
   c. ethical obligations.
   d. no obligations.

5. Broker Beta invested considerable time and effort in showing properties to a nonrepresented buyer. The buyer subsequently purchased a home Beta had been shown him previously, but he purchased directly through the listing company—excluding Beta. Beta believes he is entitled to share in the commission; the listing broker disagrees. This is an example of
   a. discrimination.
   b. contractual dispute.
   c. regulatory dispute.
   d. procuring cause dispute.

6. The quick guide for ethical decision making, which was presented in this chapter, does not consider which of the following?
   a. Existing contractual and promissory obligations
   b. Public scrutiny
   c. Commission rates
   d. Consumer expectations

7. Which of the following statements is *TRUE*?
   a. An action may be legal but unethical.
   b. An action may be ethical but illegal.
   c. An action may be immoral but legal.
   d. All of these.

8. Almost all codes of ethics include reference to which of the following?
   a. The preamble
   b. The golden rule
   c. Religious doctrine
   d. Legal doctrine

9. Given the current business environment, from a legal perspective, real estate practitioners should be keenly aware of
   a. consumer trends.
   b. housing availability.
   c. public scrutiny.
   d. alternate financing methods.

10. A sales licensee who receives an undisclosed direct bonus payment from a customer buyer would violate which of the following?
    a. Ethical behavior
    b. TRELA
    c. TREC rules
    d. All of these

DISCUSSION QUESTIONS

1. Sales associate James with Alpha Realty observed that a competitor's listing had been on the market for several months without selling. James contacted the property owners, discovered that the existing exclusive-right-to-sell listing with the other broker would expire in 10 days, and secured an appointment with the sellers that evening. James convinced the seller to sign an exclusive-right-to-sell listing with his company that would begin immediately upon expiration of the existing listing. What are the legal and/or ethical considerations of James' actions, if any?

2. Sheila, a listing agent, had prepared an offer from her own represented buyer to present to her seller-client acting under a duly authorized intermediary agreement. Subsequent to presenting the offer to the seller, a competing offer was presented to her from another brokerage company. The offers were essentially the same; however, the competing offer was for $500 more than the offer from Sheila's client. That evening Sheila presented both offers to the sellers but offered to reduce her commission by $750 in order to have her buyer's contract accepted, although no pre-existing variable-rate commission agreement was in place. The sellers accepted Sheila's offer. What are the legal and/or ethical considerations created by Sheila's actions?

3. Jim Bob, an agent with Right On Realty, decided to move his license to a competing firm. Before leaving his current company, Jim Bob contacted the sellers of his current listings, as well as all his current prospective buyers. He informed them of his upcoming move and encouraged them to contact the broker for Right On Realty and request that the broker terminate their existing contracts so that they could enter into new contracts with Jim Bob's new broker. What are the legal and/or ethical ramifications of Jim Bob's actions?

4. Broker Alex, a buyer's representative, makes an appointment through broker Betsy to show a property listed by Betsy's company. Alex discloses to Betsy that he is representing the buyer. During the conversation, Betsy tells Alex that the sellers are in the middle of a very messy divorce and are getting desperate to sell. Betsy relates this information to his buyer. The buyer as a result makes a very low offer, which is subsequently accepted by the sellers. What are the legal and/or ethical ramifications of the actions of Alex and Betsy?

5. Give an example of your opinion of the following:

    a. An act that is legal but unethical

    b. An act that is ethical but illegal

    c. An act that is legal but immoral

11 CHAPTER

Deceptive Trade Practices and Consumer Protection Act

No evidence exists that misrepresentation and fraud are more prevalent in the real estate industry than in other sectors of the economy. If, however, deceptive acts occur in a real estate transaction, they may have a greater impact than in other areas for several reasons.

First, most real estate transactions involve large sums of money; as a result, people who feel deceived are more apt to take action to assert their rights. Second, licensing laws have placed substantial supervisory responsibility on brokers for the conduct of associated licensees. Deception or fraud committed by associated licensees can subject brokers to liability, including loss of license. Finally, in many transactions, little direct contact takes place between buyer and seller. Because information is often transmitted through a third party, misunderstanding and error can result in the buyer, the seller, or both feeling that they have been deceived. In fact, Texas holds through common law that the consumer is "ignorant, unthinking, and credulous" (*Spradling v. Williams*, 566 S.W.2d 561 [Tex. 1978]). Being naïve and unknowledgeable, consumers therefore have the right to believe and to rely on information regarding a property furnished to them by sellers—or, in some cases, information given by sellers' agents.

■ **LEARNING OBJECTIVES**   *This chapter addresses the following:*

- ■ Applicability: Real Estate Broker and Salesperson Exemption from the DTPA
- ■ Fraud Versus Misrepresentation
- ■ Deceptive Trade Practices and Consumer Protection
  - — Definitions of Terms in the DTPA
  - — Deceptive Acts
  - — Verbal and Nonverbal Communications
  - — Waivers of Rights Under the DTPA
  - — Notice and Inspection
  - — Exemptions
  - — Unconscionable Action
  - — Producing Cause
- ■ Damages
  - — Relief for Consumers
- ■ Defenses
  - — Unsuccessful Defenses
  - — Groundless Lawsuits
- ■ Ethical and Legal Concerns

■ APPLICABILITY: REAL ESTATE BROKER AND SALESPERSON EXEMPTION FROM THE DTPA

In Texas, consumer rights are protected by the Texas Deceptive Trade Practices—Consumer Protection Act (DTPA). The DTPA was passed by the Texas Legislature in 1973. As the act was originally drafted, real estate transactions were excluded from coverage. In 1975, the act was amended to include transactions involving real property purchased or leased for use. As a result of allowing the DTPA to be directly applied to the professional services of brokers and salespeople, a large number of lawsuits were generated based on "acts of omission or the advice or opinion" of real estate practitioners that the consumer later believed to be in error. Although many suits were justified, many brokers and salespersons found themselves faced with lawsuits concerning circumstances over which they had no control or knowledge. Even when successful in their defenses, the economic and emotional costs could be overwhelming.

In 2011, the Texas Legislature passed SB 1353, which amended the DTPA to once again exempt real estate brokers and salespersons as follows:

> S.B. No. 1353
>
> AN ACT
>
> BE IT ENACTED BY THE LEGISLATURE OF THE STATE OF TEXAS:
>
> SECTION 1. Section 17.49, Business & Commerce Code, is amended by adding Subsection (i) to read as follows:
>
> (i) Nothing in this subchapter shall apply to a claim against a person licensed as a broker or salesperson under Chapter 1101, Occupations Code, arising from an act or omission by the person while acting as

a broker or salesperson. This exemption does not apply to: (1) an express misrepresentation of a material fact that cannot be characterized as advice, judgment, or opinion; (2) a failure to disclose information in violation of Section 17.46(b)(24); or (3) an unconscionable action or course of action that cannot be characterized as advice, judgment, or opinion.

SECTION 2. Subsection (i), Section 17.49, Business & Commerce Code, as added by this Act, applies only to a claim arising from an act or omission that occurs on or after the effective date of this Act. A claim arising from an act or omission that occurred before the effective date of this Act is governed by the law in effect on the date the act or omission occurred, and the former law is continued in effect for that purpose.

Not surprisingly, the amendment has been met with enthusiastic approval and a sense of relief by Texas practitioners. However, licensees should pay close attention to the actions to which the exemption does not apply. In essence, licensees will not be held liable for innocent acts of omission or for advice or opinion given without an attempt to defraud or deceive. It is hoped that this exemption will place a greater burden of proof of intended deception or fraud on plaintiffs in order for the DTPA to be used in a legal action against the licensee. It should be kept firmly in mind that only future case law will actually determine how helpful the exemption will prove to be. It should also be understood that purposeful acts of fraud or deception will be subject to the full force and effect of the DTPA. For these reasons, the DTPA should be studied and understood by Texas real estate licensees.

■ FRAUD VERSUS MISREPRESENTATION

Fraud is a deceptive act practiced intentionally by one person in an attempt to gain an unfair advantage over another. In fraud cases, the plaintiff must prove an intent to deceive on the part of defendant. The typical elements of a cause of action for fraud are the following:

- A material representation was made to the plaintiff by the defendant.
- The material representation was false.
- When the material representation was made, the defendant either
  — knew that the material representation was false, or
  — made the material representation recklessly, without any knowledge of its truth, and as a positive assertion.
- The defendant made the material representation with the intent that the plaintiff should act on it.
- The plaintiff to whom the material representation was made acted in reliance upon the representation.
- The plaintiff suffered injury or damage.

Because of the legal requirements to prove fraud, especially to prove the element of intent by the defendant, it is not as frequently pursued in court actions involving real estate transactions. This is also true for actions brought under the DTPA or actions for breach of fiduciary duty or other tort claims.

Misrepresentation, on the other hand, is a false statement made negligently or innocently that is a material factor in another's decision to contract. There does not have to be an intention to deceive. As will be shown later, many real estate cases involve property owners and/or licensees unintentionally making false statements regarding material facts. Showing proof of misrepresentation is considerably easier than proving fraud; thus, court actions involving real estate frequently pursue this course. See Figure 11.1 for a comparison of fraud and misrepresentation.

F I G U R E   11.1

Comparison of Actions for Fraud and Misrepresentation

Cause of Action	Factors to Be Proven	Remedies
Common law Fraud (From decisions in court cases)	Was a false statement made?	Rescission
	Was it made intentionally or negligently?	Actual damages
	Was the misstatement a material fact?	Actual damages and rescission
	Was the misstatement relied on?	Exemplary damages (to punish)
	Was anyone injured?	
Statutory Fraud (From laws enacted by the legislature)	Same factors as for common law fraud	Same remedies as for common law fraud
	Was the false promise made with intent not to perform?	Attorney fees, court costs, and expert witness fees
	Did the person who benefited from the misrepresentation know that it had been made and fail to disclose the truth?	
Deceptive Trade Practices—Consumer Protection Act	Were any specifically listed acts committed?	Economic damages
	Were any deceptive acts committed?	Damages for mental anguish
	Were any misleading statements made?	Up to 3 × economic and mental anguish damages
	Were any false statements made, including innocent misstatements?	Attorney fees and court costs
	Was an unconscionable act or course of action practiced against the victim?	
	Were any of the acts listed above the producing cause of harm to the victim?	

■ DECEPTIVE TRADE PRACTICES AND CONSUMER PROTECTION

Adopted in 1973, the DTPA is a state law that is "intended to be liberally construed and applied to promote its underlying purposes," which are to protect Texas consumers against

■ false, misleading, and deceptive business practices;
■ unconscionable actions; and
■ breaches of warranty.

This law creates a powerful weapon for consumers. It is effective for two reasons. First, proving that a deceptive act has occurred is easier under this law than under previous real estate statutes and even common law. Second, the law provides that consumers may recover more than their actual losses.

Two of the most significant aspects of the DTPA are that

■ intent need not be shown to prove a DTPA violation has occurred; and
■ that even without intent and with small damages sometimes being sought, the DTPA may allow the plaintiff to receive up to three times the plaintiff's actual economic loss plus attorney fees and court costs.

Before the Texas DTPA, when a plaintiff sought a remedy for damages of less than a few thousand dollars, the plaintiff's attorney fees and court costs made suing economically and financially impossible for the average person who was damaged by another's misrepresentations and deceptive acts.

Although an injured party can recover punitive (punishing) damages for fraud, the DTPA does not require proof that the defendant intended to deceive or mislead. The mere occurrence of a deceptive act or omission, even if done without the intent to deceive, can result in damages in excess of the actual economic loss. Ostensibly, the exemption described will protect licensees from this provision of the DTPA. Or, more specifically, the DTPA will apparently not apply unless there was an attempt to deceive by the licensee and simple acts of omission or misrepresentation would not be actionable.

From a historical perspective, the first use of the DTPA in the real estate area involved cases concerning breach of warranty in the sale of new residential properties. The initial draft of the law allowed a consumer to recover three times the amount of actual damages suffered because of defective or unworkmanlike construction in a new home purchase. This generous remedy prompted consumers to bring all breach of warranty cases under the DTPA. In recent years, the law has been used by consumers against sellers of existing homes, brokers, and lenders. The law no longer provides for the automatic trebling of damages (triple the amount of damages); however, it still allows for a recovery of triple damages in excess of actual economic loss in certain cases.

Definitions of Terms in the DTPA

The DTPA includes specific definitions of 13 words or phrases that are used in the act. As you read the following sections, you should keep in mind that if a DTPA lawsuit goes to court, the attorneys will use these definitions in an attempt to prove or disprove their cases, and the judge and/or jury will use these definitions in their conclusions. The following 13 definitions are found in Section 17.45 of the act:

1. "Goods" means tangible chattels or real property purchased or leased for use.

2. "Services" means work, labor, or service purchased or leased for use, including services furnished in connection with the sale or repair of goods.

3. "Person" means an individual, partnership, corporation, association, or other group, however organized.

4. "Consumer" means an individual, partnership, corporation, this state, or a subdivision or agency of this state who seeks or acquires by

purchase or lease, any goods or services, except that the term does not include a business consumer that has assets of $25 million or more, or that is owned or controlled by a corporation or entity with assets of $25 million or more.

5. "Unconscionable action or course of action" means an act or practice that, to a consumer's detriment, takes advantage of the lack of knowledge, ability, experience, or capacity of the consumer to a grossly unfair degree.

6. "Trade" and "commerce" mean the advertising, offering for sale, sale, lease, or distribution of any good or service, of any property, tangible or intangible, real, personal, or mixed, and any other article, commodity, or thing of value, wherever situated, and shall include any trade or commerce directly or indirectly affecting the people of this state.

7. "Documentary material" includes the original or a copy of any book, record, report, memorandum, paper, communication, tabulation, map, chart, photograph, mechanical transcription, or other tangible document or recording, wherever situated.

8. "Consumer protection division" means the antitrust and consumer protection division of the attorney general's office.

9. "Knowingly" means actual awareness, at the time of the act or practice complained of, of the falsity, deception, or unfairness of the act or practice giving rise to the consumer's claim or, in an action brought under Subdivision (2) of Subsection (a) of Section 17.50, actual awareness of the act, practice, condition, defect, or failure constituting the breach of warranty, but actual awareness may be inferred where objective manifestations indicate that a person acted with actual awareness.

10. "Business consumer" means an individual, partnership, or corporation who seeks or acquires by purchase or lease any goods or services for commercial or business use. The term does not include this state or a subdivision or agency of this state.

11. "Economic damages" means compensatory damages for pecuniary loss, including costs of repair and replacement. The term does not include exemplary damages or damages for physical pain and mental anguish, loss of consortium, disfigurement, physical impairment, or loss of companionship and society.

12. "Residence" means a building: (A) that is a single-family house, duplex, triplex, quadruplex [sic], or a unit in a multiunit residential structure in which title to the individual units is transferred to the owners under a condominium or cooperative system; and (B) that is occupied or to be occupied as the consumer's residence.

13. "Intentionally" means actual awareness of the falsity, deception, or unfairness of the act or practice, or the condition, defect, or failure constituting a breach of warranty giving rise to the consumer's claim, coupled with the specific intent that the consumer act in detrimental

reliance on the falsity or deception or in detrimental ignorance of the unfairness. Intention may be inferred from objective manifestations that indicate that the person acted intentionally or from facts showing that a defendant acted with flagrant disregard of prudent and fair business practices to the extent that the defendant should be treated as having acted intentionally.

Deceptive Acts

The act prohibits all false, misleading, and deceptive acts in the conduct of business. The law lists a number of specific activities that violate the act. Although an awareness of the enumerated prohibited acts is important, a violation of the act is not limited to those listed and could include any type of deceptive act committed in a consumer transaction. The enumerated acts in Section 17.46—commonly called the laundry list—include, among others, the

(1) passing off goods or services as those of another;

(2) causing confusion or misunderstanding as to the source, sponsorship, approval, or certification of goods or services;

(3) causing confusion or misunderstanding as to affiliation, connection or association with, or certification by another;

(4) using deceptive representations or designations of geographic origin in connection with goods or services;

(5) representing that goods or services have sponsorship, approval, characteristics, ingredients, uses, benefits, or quantities that they do not have or that a person has a sponsorship, approval, status, affiliation, or connection that he does not;

(6) representing that goods are original or new if they are deteriorated, reconditioned, reclaimed, used, or secondhand;

(7) representing that goods or services are of a particular standard, quality, or grade, or that goods are of a particular style or model, if they are of another;

(8) disparaging the goods, services, or business of another by false or misleading representation of facts;

(9) advertising goods or services with intent not to sell them as advertised;

(10) making false or misleading statements of fact concerning the reasons for, existence of, or amount of price reductions;

(11) representing that an agreement confers or involves rights, remedies, or obligations that it does not have or involve or that are prohibited by law;

(12) knowingly making false or misleading statements of fact concerning the need for parts, replacement, or repair service;

(13) misrepresenting the authority of a salesperson, representative, or agent to negotiate the final terms of a consumer transaction; . . .

(22) representing that work or services have been performed on, or parts replaced in, goods when the work or services were not performed or the parts replaced; . . .

(24) failing to disclose information concerning goods or services which was known at the time of the transaction if such failure to disclose such information was intended to induce the consumer into a transaction into which the consumer would not have entered had the information been disclosed;

(25) using the term "corporation," "incorporated," or an abbreviation of either of those terms in the name of a business entity that is not incorporated under the laws of this state or another jurisdiction; . . .

(27) taking advantage of a disaster declared by the governor under Chapter 418, Government Code, by:

> (A) selling or leasing fuel, food, medicine, or another necessity at an exorbitant or excessive price; or

> (B) demanding an exorbitant or excessive price in connection with the sale or lease of fuel, food, medicine, or another necessity.

At first glance, many of the prohibited acts listed here appear to not be applicable to real estate transactions—for instance, those sections pertaining to repairs. Real estate licensees often find that the parties require that repairs be completed before the closing of a sale or in conjunction with property management contracts. Licensees must exercise care when involved in these aspects of transactions.

Two aspects of the enumerated acts are important to remember.

First, in general application, remember that the DTPA does not require that the consumer prove the offending party intended to deceive or misrepresent the facts. In most cases, an innocent misrepresentation is as much a violation of the act as a fraudulent misrepresentation; it is not a defense to a lawsuit brought under this act that the defendant did not know that the action was illegal.

Second, the act prohibits not only misrepresentations but also misleading statements, statements that lead the consumer in the wrong direction or create a misconception of the facts. Now, because of the 2011 exemption, it is presumed that the DTPA will not apply to licensees unless it can be shown that there was an actual attempt to defraud the consumer.

Applying the laundry list of acts statutorily defined as deceptive, the following acts by licensees could still make the licensee liable for a cause of action lawsuit under the DTPA:

- Placing a listing on a webpage that is actually a listing of another firm, thus diverting a buyer's call to the licensee's office rather than directly to the listing office
- Telling a buyer that the recently installed counter is granite when in fact it is "faux" granite
- Telling the buyer that the tub in the master bath is a Jacuzzi when it is actually a generic spa

- Advertising that a property will come with a general warranty deed when in fact the seller will only convey title with a special warranty
- Telling a buyer that the seller cut the tree down because it was rubbing against the roof when in fact the tree was causing major foundation problems
- Telling the buyer that the sellers had replaced the fan on the inside air-conditioning unit when in fact they had not
- Guaranteeing an investor that a property will appreciate 20% over the next two years
- Sponsoring a lottery drawing promising the house will go to the purchaser of the winning ticket
- Failing to self-identify as acting as a subagent while showing a property to a prospective buyer, thus leading the buyer to believe that the licensee was the buyer's agent
- As a property manager, suddenly doubling the rent on apartments rented to families displaced by a recent tornado
- Telling a buyer that the new air conditioner meets the new 13 SEER requirement when it does not
- Telling the buyer that the house was built by XYZ Builder when in fact it was ABC Builders

If a licensee has been found liable in a DTPA lawsuit, the court cannot suspend or revoke a real estate license; however, The Real Estate License Act (TRELA) contains provisions for suspending or revoking a license for similar violations. Some of the provisions of TRELA § 1101.652 that address actions corresponding with the DTPA are

- conduct that constitutes dishonest dealings, bad faith, or untrustworthiness (1101.652(b)(2));
- making a material misrepresentation or failing to disclose to a potential purchaser any latent structural defect or any other defect known to the broker or salesperson. Latent structural defects and other defects do not refer to trivial or insignificant defects but refer to those defects that would be a significant factor to a reasonable and prudent purchaser in making a decision to purchase (§ 1101.652(b)(3);(4));
- pursuing a continued and flagrant course of misrepresentation or making of false promises through agents, salespersons, advertising, or otherwise (§ 1101.652(b)(6));
- failing to make clear to all parties in a transaction which party he is acting for, or receiving compensation from more than one party except with the full knowledge and consent of all parties (§ 1101.652(b)(7);(8));
- accepting, receiving, or charging an undisclosed commission, rebate, or direct profit on expenditures made for a principal (§ 1101.652(b)(13));
- soliciting, selling, or offering for sale real property under a scheme or program that constitutes a lottery or deceptive practice (§ 1101.652(b)(14); (15));
- guaranteeing, authorizing, or permitting a person to guarantee that future profits will result from a resale of real property (§ 1101.652(b)(17)); and
- inducing or attempting to induce a party to a contract of sale or lease to break the contract for the purpose of substituting in lieu thereof a new contract (§ 1101.652(b)(21)).

Verbal and Nonverbal Communications

Licensees must be aware of both verbal and nonverbal communications with customers and clients. TRELA follows and expands on many of the prohibitions of the DTPA, and licensees can assume that a customer or client who files a DTPA suit also will file a complaint with the Texas Real Estate Commission. The following case demonstrates how liability can occur, even though no verbal representation had been made to the party that claimed there had been a violation of the DTPA.

■ **EXAMPLE** In *Orkin Exterminating Co., Inc. v. LeSassier*, 688 S.W.2d 651 (Tex. Civ. App. 9 Dist. 1985), Ms. LeSassier contracted with Orkin Exterminating Co., Inc., for termite extermination services. On the date the serviceperson came to LeSassier's home, she let him in and then returned to her employment. Almost a year later, she noticed evidence of termite activity. An Orkin employee returned and treated her home. When she continued to have problems, she hired another firm of exterminators. She had the damage to her home repaired and sued Orkin, alleging violation of the DTPA in that Orkin had "represented that work or services had been performed when such work or services had not been performed." Orkin's defense was that the DTPA did not apply because Orkin made no verbal assertion that it had performed the termite treatment. The court held that the serviceperson's coming to LeSassier's home, beginning treatments, and then leaving, never to return, was a representation that all the treatments called for in the contract had been performed.

While licensees are not responsible for performing repairs, they could be named in a DTPA suit as a result of recommending a particular serviceperson or company to a client or customer who subsequently believes that the DTPA has been violated.

Waivers of Rights Under the DTPA

Under certain circumstances, consumers may wish to waive their rights under the DTPA. For example, a buyer may wish to purchase a property in obviously poor condition. The seller, however, fearful of a lawsuit related to the condition of the property after the sale, may refuse to sell the property to the buyer unless the buyer agrees to waive the right to sue the seller under the DTPA.

In this case, the buyer may be willing to waive the right in order to acquire the property. In general, however, a waiver of the right to bring action is considered to be "contrary to public policy and is unenforceable and void" (§ 17.42(a)). This prohibition of waiver of rights had been virtually absolute until 1995, when the act was amended to allow consumers to waive their rights under certain strict guidelines. A written waiver is valid and enforceable if

- it is in writing and signed by the consumer;
- the consumer is represented by an attorney, in purchasing the goods or services, who is not directly or indirectly involved in or suggested by, or identified by the defendant or the defendant's agent; and
- the consumer is not in a significantly disparate bargaining position.

The waiver is required to be in conspicuous, boldface type that is at least 10 points in size, and it must be titled "Waiver of Consumer Rights" or words of similar meaning. The body of the waiver must have wording similar to the following:

> I waive my right under the Deceptive Trade Practice Consumer Protection Act, Section 17.41 et seq., Business & Commerce Code, a law

that gives consumers special rights and protections. After consultation with an attorney of my own selection, I voluntarily consent to this waiver (Sec. 17.42(c)(3)).

One of the greatest concerns in real estate contracts has been whether a property purchased in "as is" condition is subject to the DTPA. The following case is clear as to commercial buyers.

■ **E X A M P L E**   In *The Prudential Insurance Company v. Jefferson Associates, Ltd.*, 896 S.W.2d. 156 (Texas 1995), F. B. Goldman purchased a four-story office building from Prudential Insurance in 1984 on an "as is" basis. The purchaser was allowed full access to the property to conduct inspections, which he did. In fact, Goldman had an independent engineering firm, his maintenance supervisor, and his property manager inspect the property. The inspections showed no evidence that the building contained asbestos. After the sale, Goldman conveyed the property to the limited partnership, Jefferson Associates, Ltd., of which he was a partner. Several years after the sale, it was discovered that the building had a fireproofing material that contained asbestos. Goldman sued under the DTPA.

The Supreme Court of Texas concluded that there was no evidence that Prudential had knowledge of the asbestos and therefore could not disclose its existence. They also noted that the purchase price reflected the "as is" terms and that the purchaser was responsible for accepting the risk involved in such a transaction. The court ruling stated, "A buyer who agrees, freely and without fraudulent inducement, to purchase commercial real estate 'as is' cannot recover damages from the seller when the property is later discovered not to be in as good a condition as the buyer believed it was when he inspected it before the sale." The sales contract was clear regarding the buyer's duty to satisfy himself as to condition and that he was waiving his rights to action under the DTPA.

The courts are very careful to consider all the facts in each case. It appears that courts place more responsibility on the buyer in a commercial transaction than in a residential transaction. This may be commercial buyers are assumed to be generally more knowledgeable, more likely to seek advice and opinions from experts, and better able to assess their risks than average residential buyers. However, in *Prudential v. Jefferson*, the Texas Supreme Court noted that for an "as is" agreement to be effective, it must stand up to the following tests:

1. All known defects must be disclosed by the seller.

2. The seller must not obstruct the buyer's attempts to inspect the property.

3. The "as is" clause must be an important element of the contract, not an incidental or boilerplate provision.

4. The buyer and the seller must not be in disparate (relatively unequal) bargaining positions.

Subsequently, an appellate court used the *Prudential v. Jefferson* case in deciding the following "as is" residential property case, even though the purchaser was never required to sign a waiver of his rights under the DTPA.

■ **E X A M P L E**   In *Erwin v. Smiley*, 975 S.W.2d 335 (Tex. App. 1998), Archie and Maxine Erwin sold their property to David Smiley in "as is" condition. On several occasions before entering into the purchase agreement, Smiley inspected the property. On one occasion, Smiley asked Mr. Erwin whether there had been termite problems. Mr. Erwin said that there had been termites and that they had remedied the problem. The purchase contract was drawn on a printed form showing in the "Property Condition" section that the "Buyer accepts the Property in its present condition, subject only to any lender required repairs and as is." "As is" was typed into the blank supplied on the contract.

Approximately six months after Smiley bought the house, he noticed termite trails. He had the house inspected by a termite contractor who found live termite infestation and said that he saw no evidence that the house had ever been treated for termites. The contractor also gave the opinion that the house had been infested for 5 to 10 years. Smiley sued.

The jury in the lower court found that Archie Erwin committed false, misleading, or deceptive acts or practices and awarded Smiley $15,000 to treat and/or repair the termite damage, and $30,000 in attorney's fees. The Erwins appealed.

The appellate court observed, "The validity of the 'as is' agreement is determined in light of the sophistication of the parties, the terms of the 'as is' agreement, whether the 'as is' clause was freely negotiated, whether it was an arm's length transaction, and whether there was a knowing misrepresentation or concealment of a known fact." The court went on to say, "The evidence shows that the Erwins and Smiley were similarly situated parties and that the sale was an arm's-length transaction. This transaction involved the sale of a residence. . . . Further, both parties were represented by counsel, and there was no evidence of a special relationship between the parties which would keep it from being an arm's length transaction. The evidence also shows that the 'as is' provision was freely negotiated, not merely 'boilerplate' language in the pre-printed earnest money contract form; it was specifically added. There was evidence that, during the negotiations, Archie made Smiley aware that the sale was on an 'as is' basis. Smiley consulted his attorney before signing the earnest money contract. Furthermore, Smiley testified that he did not rely on any statement that Archie Erwin made regarding the meaning of the 'as is' term." The appellate court reversed the decision of the lower court in favor of the Erwins.

This case shows that the courts are beginning to use the same standard for residential transactions as for commercial transactions. This could be because of the greater sophistication of many sellers and purchasers in today's real estate market and the greater number of principals who are seeking legal advice during the negotiating process.

The "as is" clause is now expressly stated in the TREC-promulgated contracts (paragraph 7D) and meets the requirement of the DTPA of not being "boiler plate." In fact, it requires the parties to negotiate the scope of the "as-is" provision. Pursuant to this clause, buyers accept the property "in its present condition; provided Seller, at Seller's expense, shall" complete whatever repairs or treatments the buyers specifies. Absent fraudulent inducement, a purchaser should therefore not be able to sue the seller or the broker because a property turns out not be as they expected. The burden is on the plaintiff to prove the seller or the broker had actual knowledge of a defect, as reinforced in the following recent case.

■ **EXAMPLE**   In *Boehl v. Boley*, 2011 WL 238348 (Tex. App., Amarillo, 2011), the Boehls made an offer to purchase a property owned by Boley using the TREC-promulgated One-to-Four Family Residential (Resale) Contract. Before entering into the contract, Boley indicated on the seller's disclosure that the water well had 280 feet of water in it and that he had never had any problems with the well. In paragraph 7D, the Boehls negotiated several specific repairs not related to the water well. Shortly after closing, the Boehls began experiencing problems and an inspection revealed the well was going dry and would require extensive repairs. They then sued for the DTPA violations, fraud, negligent and fraudulent representations, and breach of contract.

■ **DISCUSSION**   The court ruled in favor of the Boleys, finding that Boehls specifically negotiated the scope of the "as is" provision by specifying what repairs had to be made before they would accept the property "in its current condition." The Boehls provided no evidence that they were fraudulently induced into the contract; no evidence that they were hindered in their inspections (in fact, they did not have the well inspected, even though they paid extra for an option to withdraw); and no evidence that the Boleys or their broker knew of the actual condition of the well. Before the change to the DTPA in 2011, the Boehls might have pursued litigation against the broker for even the innocent misrepresentation regarding the water well and thus recovered at least actual damages plus court costs and legal fees. Now, the plaintiff must prove actual knowledge and intent to deceive, charges much more difficult to prove.

Notice and Inspection

Before filing a lawsuit under the DTPA, a consumer must give the would-be defendant a 60-day notice of intent to bring suit and must provide "reasonable detail of the consumer's specific complaint and the amount of economic damages, damages for mental anguish, and expenses, including attorneys' fees" (§ 17.505(a)). The defendant then may inspect the goods that are the basis of the intended action and attempt to settle the matter with the consumer.

The defendant can make an offer to settle the matter with the consumer. The law states that an offer to settle is not admission of guilt or wrongdoing. Often a defendant wants to settle just to avoid the cost and aggravation of a lawsuit.

If the defendant makes an offer to settle the matter and the consumer rejects the settlement, the defendant may file the offer with the court. If the court finds that the offer was "the same as, substantially the same as, or more than the damage found by the trier of fact [judge or jury], the consumer may not recover as damages any amount in excess of the lesser of

1. the amount of damages tendered in the settlement offer; or
2. the amount of damages found by the trier of fact" (§ 17.5052(g)).

If the court finds that the settlement offer was fair, it will determine what reasonable attorneys' fees would have been before the offer was rejected and use that amount in calculating the total settlement. The consumer could not recover the attorneys' fees incurred for representation in court.

Exemptions

In the past, most transactions could fall under the guidelines of the DTPA. The 1995 amendment provided for some exemptions important to real estate. The following exemption from prohibition against waiver under Section 17.49(f) may apply if the transaction is the result of a written contract and meets the following criteria:

- The contract relates to a transaction, a project, or a set of transactions related to the same project involving total consideration by the consumer of more than $100,000.
- In negotiating the contract, the consumer is represented by legal counsel who is not directly or indirectly identified, suggested, or selected by the defendant or an agent of the defendant.
- The contract does not involve the consumer's residence.
- All transactions, whether written or not, that have consideration that exceeds $500,000. This exemption does not include a consumer's residence (§ 17.49(g)).

There was another general DTPA exemption under Section 17.49(c) passed in 1995 that exempted conduct based on "opinion, advice, judgment, or professional skill" that led many to believe that brokers would fall under this exemption and that therefore the DTPA would not apply. Subsequent case law, however, generally disproved that theory. The loophole in the exemption was based on conduct that would constitute misrepresentation, misconduct, or negligence on the part of the agent. Virtually all consumer suits brought against brokers were DTPA suits in which the plaintiff attempted not only to prove misrepresentation or misconduct, but further, that the broker "willfully and knowingly" committed such acts.

This general exemption regarding professional services, however, has now been made specific to real estate transaction under the 2011 amendment to the DTPA noted earlier. While the general exemption in 1995 did not prove very effective in insulating real estate licensees, it is hoped that this new specific language will be more helpful. Only after the provision is tested in the courts will the true impact be determined.

The problem is the ambiguity inherent to the phrase "professional service," which is defined under the DTPA as a service that provides "advice, judgment, opinion, or similar professional skill."

■ **EXAMPLE** Mary, designated broker for Lake Country Realty, Inc., is asked to provide a competitive market analysis (CMA) for a property owned by Dr. Lang in a large subdivision. Most properties in the subdivision are of similar construction and size with three bedrooms and two baths. Over the years, however, Lang has added a small office and a half-bath to his home. So Mary obtains data on nine comparable properties in the subdivision and then makes upward adjustments to her recommended listing price based on the addition of the half-bath and office. Ultimately, the property sells for slightly more than the other properties with no half-bath or office, but considerably less than Mary had projected. Based on this scenario, Mary's services would probably not serve as the basis for a cause of action under the DTPA.

■ **E X A M P L E**   Gerald, a sales associate for Coastal Realty, is contacted by his friend Harry. Harry is in a hurry to sell but says he will list the property with Gerald if Gerald will market it for $318,000. Without conducting a CMA, Gerald takes the listing at $318,000 and does nothing more than put the listing in the MLS and place a For Sale sign on the property. Nine months later the property goes into foreclosure when Harry is unable to keep up with the mortgage payments. This service could probably serve as the basis for the DTPA claim because it does not involve matters of advice, judgment, or professional opinion.

Even if services provided by the broker fall within the DTPA definition of professional services, the exemption from liability under the DTPA do not apply to the following:

■ An express misrepresentation of a material fact that cannot be characterized as advice, judgment, or opinion
■ An unconscionable action or course of action that cannot be characterized as advice, judgment, or opinion
■ Breach of an express warranty that cannot be characterized as advice, judgment, or opinion

Unconscionable Action

The DTPA also provides that a consumer can sue if the consumer has suffered economic damages produced by unconscionable action by another. Unconscionable action is a form of deception. Equitable relief can be afforded to a person who has been tricked or swindled to such an extent that it would be unfair to allow the transaction to stand. "Unconscionable" is a difficult legal concept to grasp because it is intentionally vague. In the case that follows, the Texas Supreme Court provides some guidance in understanding the type of action prohibited.

■ **E X A M P L E**   In *Smith v. Levine*, 911 S.W.2d 427 (Tex. App. 1995), the Smiths decided to sell a property they had previously leased. The tenant was interested in purchasing the house and had a structural inspection performed. The written report stated that the foundation "has deflected to the extent that it has damaged the super-structure and therefore the foundation is defective." The tenant decided against purchasing the property; however, he offered to give the seller a copy of the report if he would reimburse him for one-half of the cost. The sellers declined and subsequently marketed the property themselves. They prepared newspaper ads and brochures claiming the property was in "excellent condition."

The Levines became interested in the home. They noticed minor cracks and a slight slope to the floor in one area; however, Mr. Smith assured them that the cracks were only superficial. They had the structure inspected; their inspector reported minor and superficial cracks in the foundation. The Levines closed the transaction, giving the Smiths full price with $25,000 at closing and a promissory note for the balance. They lived in the home for three years, until they had financial difficulties and decided to sell. They listed the home with a real estate firm, disclosing their inspection reports, and subsequently accepted an offer from David Holmes to buy the home. By coincidence, Holmes employed the same structural inspector as the former tenant; the findings were the same. Holmes demanded the return of his earnest money and termination of the contract; the Levines immediately complied.

The Levines sued under the DTPA. The Smiths then decided to call the promissory due and started foreclosure proceedings. Only a restraining order, issued three days before the foreclosure sale date, halted the foreclosure.

In the lower court, the jury found that the Smiths "knowingly engaged in a false, misleading or deceptive act or practice, as well as an unconscionable action or course of action, and both were a producing cause of damages to the Levines." They also found that the Smiths had knowingly or intentionally committed fraud. The jury's award was the difference in value of the house of $33,800, $14,400 each for the Levines' mental anguish, and punitive damages in the amount of $65,000 against Mr. Smith and $32,750 against Mrs. Smith. The Smiths appealed; the appellate court affirmed the lower court's decision.

Producing Cause

Under the DTPA, the consumer must prove that a misleading, deceptive, or fraudulent act was a producing cause of loss. A producing cause is a contributing factor that, in the ordinary sequence, produces injury or damage. In common law and statutory fraud causes of action, the injured party is required to prove that the misrepresentation was of a relevant (material) fact and that this misrepresentation directly caused economic loss. Under the DTPA, the consumer is not required to prove that the deceptive act related to material fact or that the consumer relied on that misrepresentation. Furthermore, consumers are not required to prove that the misleading or deceptive act directly caused their injury, only that they were a contributing factor.

■ **EXAMPLE** In *Cameron v. Terrell and Garrett, Inc.*, 618 S.W.2d 535 (Tex. 1981), Jerry and JoAnn Cameron purchased a house. The house had been listed for sale by the sellers with their real estate agent, Terrell and Garrett, Inc. Terrell and Garrett had listed the house in the multiple listing service (MLS) and, in doing so, included a statement that the house contained 2,400 square feet. The Camerons were shown this information about the house by their real estate agent. Subsequently, the Camerons closed the sale and moved in. The Camerons then had the house measured and discovered that it contained 2,245 square feet of heated and air-conditioned space. However, if the garage, porch and wall space were included, there was a total of 2,400 square feet. The Camerons sued Terrell and Garrett, Inc., under the DTPA, alleging misrepresentation. They claimed that Terrell and Garrett had falsely represented the number of square feet in the house. They sought actual damages of $3,419.30.

After a trial and two appeals, judgment was rendered for the Camerons. The court stated that Terrell and Garrett had misrepresented the number of square feet through the MLS and that the Camerons were consumers under the law, even though they had no contact with Terrell and Garrett. The Camerons were required to prove that they had been adversely affected by the misrepresentation.

■ **EXAMPLE** In *Weitzel v. Barnes*, 691 S.W.2d 598 (Tex. 1985), Barnes/Segraves Development Company, seller, and the Weitzels, buyers, signed a contract to purchase a remodeled home. The written contract gave the Weitzels the right to inspect, among other things, the plumbing and air-conditioning systems in the house. The contract provided that if the Weitzels were dissatisfied with the systems, they could reject the contract. A contract addendum further provided that failure of the buyers to inspect and give written notice of repairs to the seller constituted a waiver of the buyers' inspection rights and amounted to the buyers' consent to purchase the property "as is." The Weitzels did not inspect the house. Before and after signing the contract, the seller had told the Weitzels that the plumbing and air-conditioning systems complied with the Fort Worth building code specifications.

After moving into the house, the Weitzels found that the equipment did not function properly and was not in compliance with the city code. The Weitzels claimed that the oral representations were deceptive acts under the DTPA. Barnes/Segraves asserted as its defense the written contract provision regarding inspections, repairs, and waiver. The seller also argued that the buyers did not rely on the representations and, in fact, had notice prior to consummation of the sale that the city had posted a condemned notice on the house.

The court held for the Weitzels, reasoning that the buyers were not seeking to contradict the terms of the written agreement, nor were they claiming a breach of contract. Therefore, the verbal misrepresentations were admissible to prove a violation of the DTPA. Next, the court stated that the act does not require proof that the Weitzels relied on the oral misrepresentations. Reliance is not an element of producing cause. The court did point out that had the seller remained silent and not spoken to the quality or characteristics of the plumbing and air-conditioning systems, the seller would not have been liable. The contract provision regarding inspection, repairs, and waiver would have been controlling.

■ DAMAGES

Relief for Consumers

Under DTPA §Sec. 17.50 (Relief for Consumers), the following apply:

(a) A consumer may maintain an action where any of the following constitute a producing cause of economic damages or damages for mental anguish:

(1) the use or employment by any person of a false, misleading, or deceptive act or practice that is:

(A) specifically enumerated in a subdivision of Subsection (b) of Section 17.46 of this subchapter; and

(B) relied on by a consumer to the consumer's detriment;

(2) breach of an express or implied warranty;

(3) any unconscionable action or course of action by any person; or

(4) the use or employment by any person of an act or practice in violation of Chapter 541, Insurance Code.

(b) In a suit filed under this section, each consumer who prevails may obtain:

(1) the amount of economic damages found by the trier of fact. If the trier of fact finds that the conduct of the defendant was committed **knowingly**, the consumer **may also recover** damages for

mental anguish, as found by the trier of fact, and the trier of fact may award not more than three times the amount of economic damages; **or if the trier** of fact finds the conduct was committed **intentionally**, the consumer may recover damages for mental anguish, as found by the trier of fact, and the trier of fact may award not more than **three times the amount of damages for mental anguish and economic damages**.

The DTPA provides that a prevailing consumer can recover economic damages, attorney fees, and court costs. In addition, the judge or jury can award the consumer a sum of money in excess of the economic losses for mental anguish if the conduct has been committed knowingly or intentionally.

If the act is committed *knowingly*, the consumer may receive no more than three times the economic damages and damages for mental anguish.

If the act is committed *intentionally*, the consumer may receive no more than three times the amount for economic damages and three times the amount for mental anguish damages.

Let's state it differently, along with a very scary side note that may prove to be overruled later.

If a court finds that a defendant had knowingly acted, the court is limited to an award of a total of not more than three times the consumer's economic damages. However, if the court finds the defendant acted intentionally the consumer plaintiff is entitled to up to a total of triple the economic damages plus damages for mental anguish.

■ DEFENSES

How can a person limit liability for a deceptive or misleading act or practice? The DTPA specifically limits the enforceability of any waiver (written or oral) by the consumer to sue under the act. The act, however, does establish a procedure for limiting liability and for recovering damages from a consumer if the suit is filed in bad faith and if notice and settlement provisions have been satisfied. As previously mentioned, some defense can be mounted during the required 60-day notice period if the defendant makes a reasonable offer of settlement. In addition, a second defense is the giving of timely written notice to the consumer of the broker's reliance on some other written information. This can greatly assist brokers and salespersons because they frequently rely on information provided by others, such as sellers, property inspectors, appraisers, engineers, and perhaps even government agents. The key to the success of this defense depends on the following:

■ The licensee must have received the information in writing.
■ The licensee must have given written notice to the consumer before consummation of the sale that the licensee was relying on this written information.
■ The licensee must establish that the licensee did not know and could not have known that the information was false or inaccurate.

It is important for a licensee to remember that reliance on the written information must be reasonable considering the licensee's expertise in the area. However, a licensee who can prove that this defense has been met will not be liable for the consumer's damages.

In addition to protection for licensees, the following case illustrates how giving full and complete disclosure, unlimited access for the purpose of inspections, and clearly wording the terms of a purchase contract can be a defense for sellers against an unwarranted DTPA suit.

■ **EXAMPLE**   In *Zak v. Parks*, 729 S.W. 2d. 875 (Tex. App. 1987), the Zaks purchased a home with known and disclosed foundation problems from the Parks. Mr. Zak was an engineer and a licensed real estate agent and received a real estate commission from the Parks when he and his wife purchased the home. The Zaks were allowed to inspect the home and, in fact, did so four times before contracting to buy. In addition, the Zaks hired a structural expert who discovered a fracture in the foundation of the master bedroom and estimated necessary repairs to be approximately $2,000. After the inspection, an earnest money contract was drafted by Mr. Zak and signed by both Mr. and Mrs. Zak and Mr. and Mrs. Parks. It provided that the Parks would escrow funds in the amount of $2,300 "to correct structural defect of slab fracture." Any funds remaining in the escrow account after payment for repairs were to be returned to the Parks. Subsequently, the Parks placed $2,300 in an escrow account. Six weeks after closing, Mr. Zak claimed that the slab problems were greater than he had anticipated and demanded that the Parks pay $17,300 for foundation repair, $15,000 to level the house with 50 piers, and pay for numerous other unrelated repairs.

At trial, brought under the DTPA, Mr. Zak admitted that he had not used the escrowed funds to repair the foundation nor had he refunded the unused funds to the Parks. Mr. Barron, a foundation repair expert, testified that the foundation could have been repaired for less than $2,000.

The appellate court found as follows: "The written agreement limiting the Parks' liability for foundation repair, coupled with Mr. Barron's testimony, is sufficient factual evidence for the jury to decide that the lawsuit demanding that the Parks assume additional liability for foundation repair was brought in bad faith or to harass the Parks. . . . From the terms of the earnest money contract, it is clearly evident that the Zaks expressly agreed to a limit of $2,300 on the liability of the Parks for all expenses involved in repairing the slab. A lawsuit brought to recover an additional amount for repair of the slab defect is groundless as a matter of law." The court considered the case frivolous and unwarranted and entered a take-nothing judgment against Zak. In addition, Zak was ordered to pay the Parks' attorneys' fees in the amount of $42,500.

Unsuccessful Defenses

The previous case illustrates a successful defense against a DTPA claim. The following cases illustrate the powerful protection the DTPA offers to consumers and that many defenses that might have been possible under common law or statutory fraud are not available under DTPA.

■ **EXAMPLE**   In *Kennemore v. Bennett*, 755 S.W.2d 89 (Tex. 1988), Thomas and Charles Kennemore contracted with builder Bill Bennett for the construction of a home. When the Kennemores refused to pay Bennett the balance due on the contract and $4,542.55 for extras, he placed a mechanic's and a materialman's lien against the property. Bennett then sued to foreclose his liens. The Kennemores defended against Bennett's suit and counterclaimed that Bennett had failed to construct the house in a good and workmanlike manner. The Kennemores asserted this breach of warranty action under the DTPA. Prior to trial, the Kennemores paid Bennett in full but proceeded to trial on their DTPA claim against Bennett. Bennett argued that the Kennemores had waived their DTPA action by moving into the house and paying Bennett the money demanded in Bennett's lawsuit. The Texas Supreme Court held that the DTPA claim was not waived by the consumers simply because they accepted the allegedly defective home.

■ **EXAMPLE** In *Ojeda de Toca v. Wise*, 748 S.W.2d 449 (Tex. 1988), Rocio Ojeda de Toca purchased a house from Wise Developments, Inc. Approximately 11 months before the purchase, the City of Houston had recorded a document ordering that the house be demolished and placed a lien against the property for the demolition costs. Although Wise was aware of the demolition order, it did not notify Toca. While Toca was out of the country, the city demolished the house pursuant to the demolition order. Toca sued Wise for misrepresentation, fraud, and violation of the DTPA. Wise asserted in its defense that Toca had constructive notice of the demolition order under the recording statute. The court held that the Legislature, in passing the DTPA, did not intend to bar a consumer's DTPA or fraud claim because an examination of the county records could have disclosed the seller's deception. The court also held that the recording statute is not to protect perpetrators of fraud. Therefore, Toca was allowed to recover from Wise for its failure to disclose the existence of the demolition order.

■ **EXAMPLE** In *Alvarado v. Bolton*, 749 S.W.2d 47 (Tex. 1988). The Alvarados purchased 50 acres of land in Fort Bend County, Texas, from Bolton. The sales contract did not reserve any mineral rights for the seller (Bolton), but at the closing the deed specifically reserved for Bolton one-half of the mineral rights. After oil was discovered on the land, the Alvarados learned of Bolton's mineral reservations and sued to reform the deed and to receive damages under the DTPA. Bolton asserted that under the doctrine of merger, once a deed is delivered and accepted, the sales contract becomes merged into the deed and only those terms in the deed can be used to resolve disputes. Therefore, because the deed specifically reserved the mineral rights and the Alvarados accepted the deed, the Alvarados were not entitled to the mineral rights.

The court held that the doctrine of merger cannot be used to defeat a DTPA claim for breach of an express warranty made in a sales contract. Therefore, the Alvarados can prevail against Bolton if they can prove that Bolton had breached the sales contract.

Groundless Lawsuits

Brokers may be faced with groundless lawsuits that rob them of time, energy, and productive activities. The law provides that if a suit is groundless, brought in bad faith, or brought for the purpose of harassment, the defendant will be compensated for reasonable attorney fees and court costs. While this does not give compensation for lost time and energy, it can have the effect of discouraging frivolous lawsuits. One of the primary objectives of the Legislature in creating the 2011 exemption was to help prevent these types of lawsuits in the future.

■ ETHICAL AND LEGAL CONCERNS

Although we have concentrated on the DTPA, a multitude of additional legal and ethical issues faced by real estate practitioners could be the subject of an entire text. For example, many state licensing laws address specific violations that might result in revocation or suspension of the agent's license (see TRELA § 1101.652). In addition, TREC rules include Chapter 531—Canons of Professional Conduct for Real Estate Licensees, which address topics such as fidelity, integrity, and competency.

Along with these state-mandated laws and rules, many licensees have joined professional organizations such as the National Association of REALTORS® (NAR) and voluntarily subscribe to the NAR Code of Ethics.

■ SUMMARY

In 2011, the Texas legislature passed SB 1353 which amended the DTPA to once again exempt real estate brokers and salespersons unless evidence shows an attempt on part of the licensee to purposely mislead or defraud the public. Although this change to the DTPA may help brokers and salespersons, the full impact of the exemption is not yet clear and licensees are advised to become familiar with the provisions of the DTPA in order to avoid conduct that may still subject them to liability under the act.

Fraud is a deceptive act practiced deliberately by one person in an attempt to gain an unfair advantage over another. Misrepresentation is a false statement, made negligently or innocently, that is a material factor in another's decision to contract. In Texas, one of the methods for holding a person liable for fraud or misrepresentation is the DTPA, which prohibits not only false statements but also misleading statements or acts. In general, a consumer who can prove that a misleading act was the producing cause of an injury can recover economic damages, attorney fees, court costs, and additional compensation up to three times the amount of the actual losses. One defense that can be particularly useful to brokers is giving timely written notice to a buyer or a seller that the broker is relying on written information supplied by someone else. If this notice is given in a timely and proper manner, the broker may be relieved from liability for false or misleading statements contained in such written reports.

■ KEY POINTS

- The purpose of the DTPA is to protect consumers against false, misleading, and deceptive business practices, unconscionable action, and breaches of warranty.
- Under the DTPA, a consumer may not have to provide proof of an intention to deceive or mislead, only that the result of the action or inaction did deceive or mislead. Before filing a lawsuit, the consumer must give a 60-day notice, after which the would-be defendant may inspect the "goods" that are the subject of the complaint and attempt to settle the matter with the consumer.
- The consumer may recover economic damages, attorney fees, and court costs. If the act was done knowingly or intentionally, the consumer could receive up to three times the amount of the economic damages.
- The best defense is to encourage the use of information from reliable sources other than the broker, such as appraisers, engineers, property inspectors, and government sources.
- In 2011, the Texas Legislature created a specific exemption for real estate brokers and salespersons from liability under the DTPA for innocent misrepresentations, omissions, or advice or opinions as long as there was no intent to deceive or mislead the consumer.

■ SUGGESTIONS FOR BROKERS

Brokers should be particularly careful to instruct all associated licensees adequately about the proper means of obtaining information and subsequently relaying that information to clients and customers. A written policy of documenting all contacts and all sources of information could be helpful in the event of a lawsuit by a client or customer.

CHAPTER 11 QUIZ

1. The DTPA prohibits as unlawful all of the following *EXCEPT*
   a. false acts.
   b. misleading acts.
   c. deceptive acts.
   d. moral acts.

2. Which statement is *NOT* true with respect to the Texas DTPA?
   a. A licensee can safely rely on a written and signed waiver.
   b. There is no requirement that the offending party intended to deceive.
   c. To prevail, the injured party must be a consumer as defined in the act.
   d. A written offer of settlement is some defense.

3. Which is *NOT* an example of damages available under the Texas DTPA?
   a. Economic damages
   b. Mandatory four times the actual damages
   c. Court costs and attorney fees
   d. Three times the economic damages

4. In defending against a DTPA case, licensees using the timely written notice defense must include all of the following *EXCEPT*
   a. that they must have given written notice to the consumer prior to consummation of the sale that the broker was relying on this written notice.
   b. that they must have received the information in writing.
   c. that they must establish that they did not and could not know that the information was false or inaccurate.
   d. that they must produce evidence that three independent sources were consulted before the written notice was submitted to the consumer.

5. Which of the following is provided by the Texas Deceptive Trade Practices—Consumer Protection Act?
   a. A reasonable offer of settlement made within specified time limits is some defense.
   b. Transmittal of written information prepared by others, along with a written statement of reliance on such information, is a defense.
   c. Recovery of court costs and attorney fees is possible if the lawsuit is frivolous or harassing.
   d. All of the above.

6. All of the following are included in the DTPA definition of the term consumer *EXCEPT*
   a. individuals.
   b. partnerships and corporations.
   c. business consumers with assets of $25 million or more.
   d. the State of Texas.

7. To be considered a violation of the DTPA, it is
   a. not necessary for a consumer to prove that the licensee intended to deceive or misrepresent the facts.
   b. necessary for a consumer to prove that the licensee intended to deceive or misrepresent the facts.
   c. not necessary for the court to prove that the licensee intended to deceive or misrepresent the facts.
   d. necessary for the court to prove that the licensee intended to deceive or misrepresent the facts.

8. When a real estate salesperson licensee has been found guilty of a DTPA violation, the court
   a. can suspend or revoke the license of the salesperson.
   b. cannot suspend or revoke the license of the salesperson.
   c. can suspend or revoke the license of the sponsoring broker.
   d. can suspend or revoke the licenses of both the salesperson and the sponsoring broker.

9. *Unconscionable actions* in the DTPA is a vague term that allows the courts to
   a. use their discretion in deciding cases where persons have been tricked or swindled.
   b. use whatever measure they deem appropriate when deciding all DTPA cases.
   c. ignore other DTPA cases in their decisions.
   d. apply strict guidelines to DTPA cases.

10. All waivers of rights under the DTPA are
    a. automatically unenforceable by the court.
    b. automatically enforceable by the court.
    c. legal and cannot be interpreted by the court.
    d. subject to the consideration of the court.

DISCUSSION QUESTIONS

1. What types of statements might a broker make that would lead to possible innocent misrepresentations under the DTPA (e.g., saying "this is a well-maintained home" when it would be better to say "this house appears to be well maintained")?

12

Implementation and Presentation

Licensees have faced situations involving possible lawsuits in which agency status was the main issue. If the licensees had practiced preventive brokerage, they might have lessened their risk.

■ **LEARNING OBJECTIVES** *This chapter addresses the following:*

- ■ Introduction: Preventive Brokerage
- ■ The Broker Working For or With the Seller
  - — Before an Agency Relationship With the Seller (No Listing Agreement Yet)
  - — Once a Listing Agreement Is Signed
  - — Once an Offer Is Made
  - — Once There Is a Contract
- ■ The Broker Working For or With The Buyer
  - — Before a Buyer Representation Agreement Is Signed
  - — After the Buyer Representation Agreement Is Signed
  - — Making the Offer
  - — Once There Is a Signed Sales Contract
  - — Additional Relationships
- ■ A Practical Guide To Everyday Practice: Using Rehearsed Dialogue
  - — Dialogues for Brokerage Situations
- ■ Other Considerations
  - — Presentation of Offers by the Listing Broker
  - — Presentation of Multiple Offers
  - — Presentation of Subsequent or Backup Offers
  - — Retained Earnest Money in the Event of Default
  - — Commissions
  - — Written Agreements/Contract
- ■ Risk Management

■ INTRODUCTION: PREVENTIVE BROKERAGE

Whether representing the seller or the buyer, brokers should do several things:

- ■ Use written disclosures.
- ■ Clarify their role in the transaction.
- ■ Use the help of others when needed.

Brokers should recognize that the most frequent basis for complaints against real estate licensees is their failure to disclose material facts. Remember, the exemption granted to licensees under the Texas Deceptive Trade Practices—Consumer Protection Act (DTPA) does not apply in the case of an expressed misrepresentation of a material fact. The broker must therefore be prepared to prove in a legal dispute with a consumer that important information was, in fact, provided or, on the other hand, that such disclosure was prohibited by law. The Texas Property Code (TPC) dictates that certain sellers (not all) must provide the disclosure of the condition of their property in written form (§ 5.008) The wise broker, however, would assure that any disclosures provided to consumers be in written form along with a request for the consumer's signature signifying receipt of the information.

Brokers also can help protect themselves by clarifying their roles in the transaction to the buyer and the seller. Before even offering to assist consumers in a transaction, licensees should discuss openly what they can and cannot do. For example, if the licensee has never handled a tax-deferred exchange or the sale of a business opportunity, the client (or customer) should be made aware of that fact and the licensee should then suggest the possible use of other experts. Article 11 of the REALTOR® Code of Ethics and Standards of Practice (see Appendix) states the following:

> REALTORS® shall not undertake to provide specialized professional services concerning a type of property or service that is outside their field of competence unless they engage the assistance of one who is competent on such types of property or service. . . .

To present oneself as an expert not only is grounds for loss of license but also could form the basis of a lawsuit under the DTPA (TRELA § 1101.652(b)(1)). Licensees should discuss their duties and responsibilities and those of other licensees, as well as the use of subagents and the multiple listing service (MLS).

Licensees who work with the buyer should clarify to all concerned whether the buyer is the licensee's client or customer. Regardless of the relationship, however, the licensee should make sure that the buyer in the transaction understands that the licensee does not warrant the condition of the property. Notice that this fact is expressly stated in the first paragraph of the Seller's Disclosure of Property Condition (see Figure 3.2) when it says "THIS NOTICE IS . . . NOT A WARRANTY OF ANY KIND BY SELLER OR SELLERS' AGENTS." The following list describes just some of the distinctions between duties that a broker, acting as an agent for only one party in a transaction, has to a client versus the broker's duties to a customer.

- To a customer, the seller's agent points out remedies available to the seller in the event of a buyer's default on the purchase contract. To a client, the buyer's agent might discuss the meaning of liquidated damages in this context, making sure the buyer knows that the earnest money may be forfeited. (Naturally, an agent must be very careful to avoid giving legal advice [§ 1101.654]. If buyers or sellers have any questions about the standard default provisions found in the TREC- promulgated sales contract forms, they should be advised to consult an attorney.) However, if it is evident that nonjudicial alternatives would save them both money and reduce both their risks, it would be appropriate, in fact, mandatory, that the licensee make the parties aware of such alternatives.
- When the seller carries back financing, the seller's agent could negotiate or attempt to negotiate into the original offer many contract provisions that are different from those the buyer's agent might propose. Such provisions might include prepayment, due on sale, right to make improvements, nonrecourse (no personal liability), reinstatement prior to foreclosure sale, grace periods, late charges, and so on.
- To a customer, the seller's agent discloses the existence of an underground water easement. To a client, the buyer's agent goes an extra step and reviews a copy of the grant of easement, just in case any restrictions affect the buyer's expected use of the property, such as a prohibition against constructing any improvement within a certain distance of the easement.
- To a customer, the agent emphasizes the attractive features of the seller's property. To a client, the agent points out the negative features.

■ THE BROKER WORKING FOR OR WITH THE SELLER

Particularly for newly licensed or inexperienced salespersons, the broker may want to consider developing a standard list of topics that need to be addressed by the agent when first meeting a seller or a buyer prospect. Some brokers have even developed a check-off form for use by associates to assure that all topics are consistently and thoroughly covered with each prospect. The sheet can actually form the basis of documentation regarding mandatory disclosures that may be needed should questions later arise as to whether or not the topic was covered with the consumer. The following discussion should serve as a summary of the types of topics an office **acting as the seller's agent** (either listing office or subagent of the listing office) might wish to cover with **prospects**. In addition, the step-by-step procedures of the listing broker when acting on behalf of the seller-client may be helpful in understanding the day-to-day actions of a listing broker or the broker's sales associates.

A real estate broker who takes a listing on a seller's home becomes the agent of the seller. From that time forward, until the listing terminates, the broker and the seller are bound together by mutual consent in the agent-principal relationship. The broker owes all of the fiduciary and common law duties of agency to the seller (obedience, loyalty, disclosure, confidentiality, accounting, and reasonable care and diligence). The broker is not working with the seller in the legal sense, in an agency capacity, but instead is working for the seller. The agent is in an arm-around relationship with the seller, not an arm's-length relationship.

Until the agency relationship is established, the licensee is acting on behalf of the broker as the broker's agent. When soliciting a listing from a seller, and before the listing being signed, the real estate licensee is protecting the broker's interests. Once the licensee procures the listing, the licensee's broker is the agent to the seller, and by way of the broker, the licensee salesperson also becomes the agent of the seller. Therefore, the broker and the salesperson both owe fiduciary duties, common law duties of agency, and all statutory and regulatory duties to the principal/seller.

Before an Agency Relationship With the Seller (i.e., No Listing Agreement Yet)

- At the beginning of the listing appointment, but before an agency relationship is established or the listing agreement is discussed, explain and discuss in detail the brokerage company's agency disclosure form and the broker's agency position at that time, as well as the Texas Real Estate Commission's (TREC) Information About Brokerage Services (the "written statement") notice or an equivalent, as required by the Real Estate License Act (TRELA) § 1101.558(c), regarding the written statement concerning agency options.
- So the seller-prospect has a ready reference, provide a copy of a sample listing contract the brokerage uses, such as the Residential Real Estate Listing Agreement Exclusive Right to Sell (see Figure 4.2)
- Explain what subagency means (including vicarious liability) and the optional use of subagents in an MLS, and obtain the seller's authorization to use subagents if the seller desires to use subagents.

- Explain how commission fees may be split, and obtain the sellers' approval or disapproval of splitting fees with the sellers' subagents or the buyers' brokers.

- If the listing broker or associate is a member of the MLS, verify that the listing agreement contains a provision granting the seller's permission to use the MLS and to release marketing and sales data to the MLS. If the seller elects not to have the listing broker offer subagency or elects to offer it on a selective basis, a decision must be made regarding the use of an MLS.

- On the subject of compensation, explain to the seller how commissions may be split with other brokers. Because there is a big difference between authorizing the listing broker to split commissions with a buyer's broker and authorizing the broker to split with a subagent of the seller, the seller's attention should be clearly directed to this provision before signing the listing. If the listing broker decides to offer other brokers a less-than-attractive commission split, the seller should be notified because it may mean that other brokers will be less motivated to show the seller's property.

- Explain to the seller that it is customary to work with other real estate brokers or their associates to increase the likelihood of finding a suitable buyer for the seller's property.

- Explain that the listing broker's commission fee is normally a reflection of the presumption that the listing broker will be sharing the compensation with the cooperating broker in exchange for assistance in finding a buyer for the property, but that all fees or the sharing of fees between brokers are negotiable. Explain how the seller may permit the listing broker to offer a commission split to other brokers but not to offer subagency (subagency optional).

- Explain the brokerage's policies on intermediary brokerage.

- Discuss seller motivations (by what date must they sell; by what date do they want to move out) in order to estimate whether the listing is worth taking.

- Clarify the listing agreement line by line to make sure sellers understand their obligations and rights under the agreement.

- Discuss fair housing laws relative to showing and selling the property and the fact that the property will be shown to all persons in compliance with fair housing requirements.

- Walk the exterior of the property and preview the interior rooms in preparation for establishing a broker price opinion (BPO) and eventually a listing price.

- Research properties that have sold within the last six months to a year, as well as those currently on the market in the subject property's location to provide the seller with enough information to determine a list price.

- Discuss current market conditions (average time on market for location, interest rates, etc.)

- Discuss any conditions (environmental, economic, geographic, demographic) that will affect the salability of the home.

- Discuss all researched information with the seller, and establish a list price for the property.

- Answer any of the seller's questions, and ask the seller to sign the listing agreement.

Once a Listing Agreement Is Signed

- Create a marketing strategy to present to the seller for approval.
- Discuss the required Seller's Disclosure of Property Condition (included in TREC forms and TAR forms) and give to the seller to fill out (the agent does not participate in any way in filling out this form, only in explaining what it is and the statutory requirement)
- Discuss water penetration issues, fires that have occurred inside or outside to the structure, mold, pest infestations, roof or foundation problems, and any repairs that need to be made.
- Discuss staging the home for showing, and what repairs and changes will bring a return on the investment (thorough cleaning; getting all clutter out of the home; painting exterior and interior surfaces; repairing faucets, appliances, roof, et cetera. Also discuss those repair items that the seller is not willing to make.
- Discuss what personal property items (if any) go with the property (e.g., any items in paragraphs 2 B, C, and D. of the TREC One to Four Family Residential Contract (Resale) form, or other items in or on the property.
- Explain the showing procedures and get agreement with the seller concerning when and under what conditions the property may be shown.
- Show the property to potential buyers and buyer brokers.
- Give completed Seller's Disclosure of Property Condition to all buyers or the buyers' agent and ask them to sign and date, acknowledging receipt of the document.
- Discuss negotiating strategies once an offer is made.
- Keep the seller aware of all showings, questions of buyers, prospective buyer likes and dislikes, or reasons why buyers didn't make an offer. Keeping the seller informed of all issues is essential to maintaining your agency duties to your seller-client.

Once an Offer Is Made

- Be available to accept an offer on the seller's home on behalf of the seller. The law requires that the agent make the seller-client aware of "all" offers on the seller's property.
- Set an appointment to discuss each offer (or multiple offers). The offers do not need to be shown in the order they came in to the broker's office, and the seller may review each one before making any decision.
- Discuss the concepts of accepting the offer, counteroffers, rejection of the offer, using the TAR Seller's Invitation to Buyer to Submit New Offer (TAR-1926), and the potential dangers of holding all offers until the seller chooses one.
- Explain the concept of the buyer withdrawing the offer before the seller accepting the offer.
- Explain the pros and cons of each offer and let the seller make the decision concerning which is the best.. The agent's job is to continue to give the client as much accurate and pertinent information as possible so that the client is thoroughly informed before making a decision
- Discuss negotiation strategies with the seller.
- Negotiate strongly for your seller-client to get the best price, terms, and conditions possible during the negotiating period.

Once There Is a Contract

- Check to make sure the buyer or the buyer's agent has deposited the earnest money and a copy of the contract in accordance with the contractual agreement (assuming a TREC-promulgated contract form has been used, explaining that it is the buyer's duty to deposit the earnest money when an agreement has been reached).
- Carefully explain all the important dates and deadlines, and clarify the obligations of the seller according to the contractual agreement.
- Place reminders on any electronic devices you use, or if you keep a personal planner or written log, make sure you enter these dates so you can remind the seller to comply with the contract.
- Encourage the seller to make repairs in a timely manner if required by the contract or lender.
- Keep in touch with the buyer's agent for information on the loan process.
- Request to see a copy of the Settlement Statement (HUD-1) before closing, to check for errors or omissions.
- Prepare the seller for the closing and discuss lender documents for loan payoff.
- Tell the seller to bring to the closing the house keys for the buyer, paid invoices for repairs, date the utilities will be turned off, a list of personal property items to be left for buyer, photo identification, and certified funds for closing costs or a personal check up to the limit allowed by title company.
- Based on the broker's policies, attend the closing of the transaction with the seller to ensure that the transaction is completed according to the sales contract.

THE BROKER WORKING FOR OR WITH THE BUYER

A broker or associate engaged in initial contact with a buyer prospect might wish to have a checklist of topics similar to the list noted for sellers' agents. The first step is to determine which level of service (client or customer) the broker and the broker's associates will be offering to the buyer prospect.

A real estate broker who signs a buyer representation agreement with a buyer becomes the agent of the buyer. From that time forward until the agreement is terminated, the broker and the buyer are bound together by mutual consent in the agent/principal relationship. The broker owes all the fiduciary and common law duties of agency to the buyer (obedience, loyalty, disclosure, confidentiality, accounting, and reasonable care and diligence). The broker is not working with the buyer in the legal sense in an agency capacity, but instead is working for the buyer. The broker is in an arm-around relationship with the buyer, not an arm's-length relationship.

Until the agency relationship with the buyer is established, a licensee sales associate of the broker is acting on behalf of the broker as the broker's agent. When soliciting a buyer representation agreement from a buyer, and before the representation agreement is signed, the real estate licensee is protecting the broker's interests. Once the licensee procures the representation agreement, the broker is the agent to the buyer, and by way of the broker, the licensee salesperson also becomes the agent to the buyer. Therefore, the broker and the licensee salesperson, as well as all other sales associates of the broker, owe the fiduciary duties, common law duties of agency, and all statutory and regulatory duties to the principal/buyer.

The following is a step-by-step process for the dialogue a buyer's broker (or sales associate of the broker) might have with the buyer before representation has occurred. This is followed by the process of the day-to-day interaction with the buyer-client and others in the real estate transaction.

Before a Buyer Representation Agreement Is Signed

The buyer's broker or associate's dialogue with a prospective buyer-client should include the following:

- Explain to the buyer the services to be rendered by first presenting and discussing the Information About Brokerage Services (IABS) form (or the brokerage's equivalent written statement), and then explain that the broker is not the buyer's agent unless and until a consensual agreement has been reached.
- Outline the services the brokerage offers to the buyer once the buyer representation agreement is signed and the buyer becomes a client of the broker.
- Take the buyer through the buyer representation agreement and explain it line by line, asking if the prospective buyer has any questions concerning rights and obligations.
- Carefully discuss the fee structure and clarify that the buyer is responsible for the payment unless another party agrees to pay the buyer's broker (if the agreements states this). In addition, cover when the fee is earned and payable, and any additional compensation that might be earned.
- Clarify the commencement date and the termination of the agreement.
- Discuss the broker's position on becoming an intermediary, and point out the prospective buyer's choices listed in the agreement.
- Discuss the fact that the broker may represent other brokers who may be interested in the same property as this prospective buyer and that the agreement allows the broker to continue to represent existing and future buyers. In the TAR Residential Buyer/Tenant Representation Agreement, this is called the "Protection Period."
- If the representation agreement includes information on mediation, clarify what mediation is and discuss the rights and obligations of the parties to the agreement relative to mediation.
- Clarify and discuss the ramifications of other issues, such as default by either party, limitation of liability, broker cannot give legal advice—see legal counsel if needed, and any special provisions.
- Give the prospective buyer the following brochures/pamphlets/documents (and any others that are appropriate in a particular situation):
  — Information About Brokerage Services
  — Protecting Your Home from Mold
  — Information Concerning Property Insurance
  — General Information and Notice to a Buyer (form)
  — Protect Your Family from Lead in Your Home
  — Information about Special Flood Hazard Areas
  — For Your Protection: Get a Home Inspection
  — Fair Housing and You

Additional buyer brochures are available at the HUD website: http://portal.hud
.gov/hudportal/HUD?src=/topics/buying_a_home.

After consultation regarding the role of a buyer's broker and consent of the buyer
or tenant, obtain from the buyer or tenant a written, signed buyer representation
agreement.

After the Buyer Representation Agreement Is Signed

Remember, from this point forward, the broker and all the sales associates of the
broker represent the buyer. They owe the buyer fiduciary duties, common law
duties of agency, and statutory duties. They are now in an "arm around" relationship with the buyer rather than an "arm's length" relationship. They are working
"for" not "with" the buyer.

The following is a step-by-step list of suggested areas to which the broker should
pay particular attention when serving a buyer-client:

- Establish a clear profile of the buyer(s), and their property needs and desires.
  Here is some information needed by the buyer's agent in order to best serve a
  buyer-client.

  ### Buyer and Property Information Profile
  - Name of buyer(s)
  - Complete current address
  - Contact information (home phone, mobile, fax, email, etc.)
  - Citizen of United States; lawfully admitted alien; valid green card
  - If not citizen, how long living in United States
  - Photo ID (valid Texas driver's license, out of state driver's license,
    out of country driver's license)
  - Estimated move date
  - Desired possession date
  - Is buyer willing to allow seller to remain in property under a seller's
    temporary lease?
  - How does buyer desire to take title to the property (e.g., single-
    person ownership, husband and wife, tenant in common, other/
    describe)

  ### Property Information
  - Location desired
  - Price range
  - Style of home
  - Square footage
  - Number of bedrooms, bathrooms, living areas, and dining areas
  - Other rooms/amenities desired: laundry room, pantry, study, office,
    pool, game room, workshop, entertainment room, sprinkler system,
    storage shed, outdoor entertainment area, etc.
  - Type of flooring and wall treatments
  - Special needs: amenities for physically challenged family members,
    amenities for seniors, amenities for pets

Work Information
- Do you desire to live close to your work? How close?
- In what location do you work?

Schools
- What types of schools do you prefer?

Financial/Loan Information
- Maximum loan amount
- Amount of down payment
- Type of loan (conventional, conventional insured, FHA, VA, other)

Priorities
- After completing all sections of the profile sheet, rank the highest five priorities you will use to determine which property you will purchase.
- Please list any other criteria you would like me to use to find the home that best fits your needs and desires.

Once the buyer's agent gathers all the necessary information and profiles the desired property, the agent should follow these steps:

- Using the buyer/property information profile sheet, search using the parameters provided by the buyer-client. Most licensees use the multiple listing service to search for properties (MLS membership is required to use the system). In addition, this same system allows the agent to compare current properties on the market, and ones that have already sold, to establish a broker's price opinion (BPO) for an appropriate purchase price. Agents should eliminate any properties that are not in line with the buyer's desires to save time when viewing properties with the buyer.
- Once a property, or properties, has been identified, notify the buyer, learn from the buyer which ones to see, and set a date for previewing those properties.
- Contact either the listing broker, or a system like Central Showing Systems (CSS) (a company that provides the service of setting appointments for buyers and buyer's agents to view properties listed with their service) to set up appointments to preview the properties.
- Use the MLS mapping system to map the order in which the properties will be seen.
- Explain to the buyer the courtesies and procedures of viewing properties, as well as the importance of keeping confidential information confidential.
- Discuss the Sellers Disclosure of Property Condition form and all the ramifications if the buyer does not receive the form from the seller before a contract is formed.
- Discuss each property's pros and cons with the buyer, and help the buyer decide which can be eliminated from the list.
- When the buyer is ready to make an offer on a property, assist the buyer in filling in the contract form.

Making the Offer

- It is good practice to take the buyer-client through the contract form very carefully. Explain each paragraph. Be careful not to engage in the practice of law without a license to do so. This document serves to bind the buyer and the seller together in contractual agreement. The buyer needs as much information as possible in order to make an informed decision on how to structure an offer.

■ Once the offer is structured, the buyer's agent contacts the listing agent to make notification of an offer. The buyer's agent delivers a copy of the offer to the listing agent, answers any questions the listing agent has (without revealing any confidential or strategic information of the buyer), and leaves the offer in the listing agent's possession. A copy of the offer is given to the buyer and one is placed in the buyer agent's file. Note: In some instances, it may be appropriate for the buyer's agent, at the request of the buyer, to make the presentation of the offer to the seller. This would be the case if there were very detailed and complicated provisions in the offer made by the buyer to the seller. The buyer's agent would be skilled in clarifying those provisions. However, the buyer's agent should assure the listing agent that the presentation to the seller would be made in the presence of the listing agent. The buyer's agent would answer the listing agent's questions about the offer and then leave so that the listing agent and the seller could discuss the offer further. It is the option of the seller and the seller's agent to either accept or refuse this request.

■ Now, negotiations begin; offer, counteroffer, counter-counteroffer, et cetera. The skill of the licensees will partially determine who wins in the negotiations. You may have heard that in order for negotiations to be successful, they should have a win-win result. However, the agents are working as skillfully as possible to advocate for their own buyer- or seller-client to get the best price, terms, and conditions possible. At the end of the bargaining process, both parties will have conceded in some areas. Successful negotiations result in a skillfully honed agreement where both parties, with some compromise, achieve their primary goals.

Once There Is a Signed Sales Contract

■ Once the buyer and the seller have a signed sales contract with an effective date, the buyer's agent tracks all deadlines that the buyer-client must meet. Meeting deadlines is important: if the buyer (or the seller) does not meet the deadlines required by the contract, the buyer (or seller) may be in default. The buyer's agent should explain that most of the deadlines are tied to the effective date of the contract.

■ One of the first deadlines in the TAR One to Four Family Residential Contract (Resale) form is the depositing of the earnest money (if any) and a copy of the contract, with the escrow agent (generally a title company). The contract wording will clarify for the buyer and the buyer's agent when and where the contract and earnest money must be deposited.

■ Each contractual obligation of the buyer is laid out clearly, and the duty of the buyer's agent is to assist the buyer in knowing what those obligations are and by what date they must be performed (e.g., loan application/financing approval/loan approval; general inspection of the property; appraisal; termination option period, if any [a discussion of the termination option period and its ramifications is essential]; repairs; special inspections such as hazardous waste, lead-based paint, mold, water penetration issues, and pests/insect issues; survey; title commitment letter; title policy; home warranty; hazard insurance; etc.)

■ As the closing date approaches, the pressure to complete all the contractual requirements of the buyer increases. The buyer's agent is working with the title company, the contractors, the appraiser, the inspector, and the listing agent to make sure everything is accomplished by the closing date. The buyer's agent must make the buyer aware of all contingencies and then skillfully handle issues with any of them if needed.

■ The buyer agent counsels his buyer to bring to closing a photo identification and certified funds or a personal check (the title company will have a maximum amount allowed in the form of a personal check) to pay for the buyer's closing costs. In addition, the agent will request that the escrow agent provide a copy of the Settlement Statement (HUD-1) to check for any errors or omissions. The Settlement Statement will show the total closing costs to the buyer, as well as all other debits and credits to the buyer.

■ Some companies require that the buyer and seller agents attend the closing. Others leave it up to the sales associates to decide whether to be present at the closing. Benefits to the buyer and seller agents attending the closing include protecting the interests of their clients and to solve problems and answer questions of clients. There are several papers for the buyer and seller to sign: Settlement Statement (HUD-1), loan documents, mortgage or deed of trust, government disclosures, title commitment, title filing information, proof of homeowners insurance, good-faith estimate (GFE), flood certificate (if necessary), proof of mortgage insurance, copy of appraisal, copy of inspection reports, truth-in-lending (TIL) disclosure, right to cancel/rescission, and so on.

■ The title company acting as escrow agent for the closing, will disperse all monies based on the sales contract, the lender's instructions, and instructions from the seller's broker and buyer's broker. Until the transaction is funded, there is no money disbursed to any of the parties, including the buyer and seller brokers and their sales associates.

Additional Relationships

Other Broker as Buyer's Broker   If the other broker decides to act as a buyer's broker, then the other broker (at initial contact when discussing the property and the seller) should

■ disclose to all listing brokers of properties shown (or to all owners selling their own properties) the broker's status as buyer's broker, and

■ disclaim any agency or subagency relationship with the seller or the listing agent.

Immediate disclosure will enable the listing broker to represent the seller's best interests in any showing of the property to a prospective buyer.

As a practical matter, a broker may not have any particular customer or client in mind at the time of initial contact—for instance, on an MLS tour of homes. A broker who sometimes represents buyers should inform the listing broker or the seller that the other broker may later return either with a client or with a customer. Therefore, the listing broker should keep this in mind when discussing any information concerning the seller's marketing position.

Listing Broker or Associate Working With Buyer-Customer   In this case, the listing broker is functioning as the agent for the seller, but the buyer has come to this broker asking to see one of the broker's listings. The buyer does not ask for representation, but instead the broker will work with the buyer as a customer, and not for the buyer as a client. The broker owes no fiduciary or common law duties to the buyer. This is an arm's-length relationship and not an arm-around relationship with the buyer. All the broker's associates are agents for the seller of the listed property that the buyer wants to see. All sales associates will also be in an arm's-length relationship with this buyer and owe no fiduciary or common law duties to the buyer.

The buyer, then, is on his own relative to any representation. A term used as a warning to a buyer in this position is caveat emptor meaning "let the buyer beware." While the seller's broker and the broker's sales associates are bound by fiduciary duty to look out for the best interests of the seller, in this situation no one is looking out for the interests of the buyer except the buyer. The sales associate must be continually aware of language so the buyer is not inadvertently led to believe that any of the sales associates are on the buyer's side. The buyer is not called "my buyer," but rather "the buyer."

While certainly not an exhaustive list, the following information is designed to help the licensee think through the relationship between a broker, a sales associate of the broker, and a buyer when there is no representation of that buyer.

At **first contact concerning a specific property**, the listing broker or associate should present and explain to a **buyer-customer**

- the TREC Information About Brokerage Services form, or equivalent;
- the difference between a client and a customer in terms of services, duties, and appropriate expectations;
- that the broker is employed by the seller to sell the seller's property and that the broker will be representing all of the seller's interests during negotiations;
- that the buyer is free to seek and retain technical advisers;
- that if the buyer decides not to buy the listed property, the buyer may wish to use the services of the listing broker to search for another appropriate property; if so, the agency relationship and whether the buyer is a customer or a client must be clarified;
- the in-house sales practices of the listing broker; and
- that it is customary for a broker to show other listed properties to prospective buyers.

In addition, relative to buyer-customers, listing brokers may
- provide ready access to inventory, including the MLS;
- collect pertinent data on property taxes, utility costs, and general real estate values;
- provide information on municipal services and amenities;
- discuss financing alternatives;
- discuss loan qualification and processing while being careful not to give advice or opinions;
- show properties;
- make appointments and schedule conferences;

- clarify the buyer's needs versus wants and clarify the buyer's financial ability to purchase;
- evaluate the need for property management;
- arrange for and review fire or liability insurance while being careful not to overstep professional authority and expertise;
- check inventory of personal property;
- check applicable zoning and building permits;
- estimate closing costs and monthly payments;
- explain standard forms;
- explain escrow or settlement procedures;
- transmit an offer and act as liaison between the buyer and the seller (though negotiating at all times on behalf of the seller's interests);
- monitor closing and deadlines; and
- recognize the buyer's need for expert advice (An agent, in all circumstances should be careful about providing names of experts to avoid liability if the expert does not do a good job for the buyer-customer. Check with your broker for the company policy on this issue.).

The seller's agent or subagent can make appointments, show properties meeting the buyer's stated criteria, describe general features and conditions, direct the buyer to needed sources of information, complete standard forms, and transmit offers to the seller.

If the buyer decides that neither the seller's property nor any other properties listed with the broker are suitable, the agent can then discuss what further services might be provided to help the buyer locate the right property. Before beginning a search through the MLS system for suitable properties, however, a decision must be made as to whether the broker will proceed showing additional properties to the buyer while acting in a subagent capacity to all sellers of properties now listed, or change the relationship to represent the buyer in a buyer's agent capacity. Although not required, a written agreement to represent a buyer is advisable. There is at least one issue to think through carefully in this situation. Consider this scenario:

- The buyer, who was a customer when previewing broker A's listings, does not find any homes to purchase out of those properties.
- He asks A's associate to see properties listed with other brokers.
- A does not want sales associates acting as subagents to the sellers of other broker's listings and tells the buyer that A and A's sales associates will work only as the buyer's agent when showing other broker's listings.
- A and the buyer sign a buyer representation agreement and form an agency relationship.
- At this point, there is no problem. But …
- What if the buyer can't find anything after previewing other broker's listed properties and decides to go back to one of A's listings to make an offer on that home?
- The buyer was a customer when looking at A's listings the first time, and A and A's sales associates represented the sellers of those listings.
- Now, after signing a buyer representation agreement, and becoming A's buyer-client, the buyer wants to go back to one of A's listings to make an offer to purchase the home.

- If A's sales associate shows the buyer-client A's listings again, A is now in a conflict of interest. A already represents all the sellers of A's listings and owes fiduciary duties to those sellers. The buyer-client is owed those same duties by A and A's sales associates. There is no way to get the highest price and best terms and conditions for the seller and, at the same time, get the lowest price and best terms and conditions for the buyer.
- A and A's sales associates now have a dilemma. How can they continue to serve both the buyer-client and the seller-clients at the same time without a conflict of interest?

Here are some alternative solutions:

- A could ask the buyer to find another broker for representation, thus avoiding any conflict.
- A could decide to act as an intermediary if all parties have given permission and the broker follows the legally required steps. Once A becomes an intermediary, A
    — must treat all parties fairly,
    — may not disclose any confidential information,
    — may no longer give opinions and advice,
    — may not tell the buyer that the seller will take a lower price than the asking price, and
    — may not tell the seller that the buyer will pay a price higher than the offer price,
- Once A becomes an intermediary, with the written permission of both the buyer and the seller, A may appoint one or more sales associates to the seller and one or more to the buyer. From this point forward, A is prohibited from performing many of the fiduciary duties and his agency duties are very limited.

Listing Broker and Buyer's Broker   When one broker represents the seller and one broker represents the buyer in a real estate transaction, the clearest possible delineation of representation, authority, obligation, rights, and duties between parties exists. One broker represents the seller (with all the resulting agency duties owed to the seller), and one broker represents the buyer (with all the resulting agency duties owed to the buyer). Both buyer and seller have an advocate. The legal lines of representation are clearly drawn. Neither broker may cross that line without violating fiduciary duties to the client.

> In an intermediary transaction, the fiduciary duties of obedience, loyalty, and full disclosure cannot be performed because of the legal requirement of impartiality.

This form of representation is not convoluted, does not present any conflicts of interest, and is relatively simple to follow without errors or omissions.

If the listing broker receives an offer through a buyer's broker, the listing broker should

- be cooperative, while clearly maintaining the agency relationship with the seller and respecting the relationship between the buyer's broker and the buyer;
- clarify the offer that has been made with the buyer broker, asking any necessary questions before explaining the offer to the seller-client;
- present the buyer's offer to the seller-client;

- agree on how best to handle payment of commissions consistent with the authorization of both the seller and the buyer;
- communicate to the seller the buyer's intention for payment of fees relative to the buyer's broker;
- be prepared for healthy and open negotiations; and
- evaluate all terms of the buyer's offer, recognizing that they were prepared with the buyer's best interests in mind.

Listing brokers should be prepared for the likelihood that they will receive offers from other brokers submitted on behalf of buyer-clients and should welcome these offers, working with the buyers' brokers in a spirit of cooperation and goodwill. At the same time, the listing broker should respect the fact that these brokers owe undivided loyalty to their respective principal. Listing brokers generally recognize that it is in the best interests of the seller to cooperate with all brokers, one of whom may have the ultimate buyer for the seller's property. The key question, from the listing agent's and seller's perspective regarding any offer, whether from a buyer or a buyer's broker, is this: What is the net effect to the seller? The same is true for the buyer's broker and the buyer if there is a counteroffer from the seller. If both the buyer and the seller are negotiating from a position of knowledge or with advocates who are knowledgeable and skilled, then both parties are well served, and may the best negotiator win.

The individual agents are now responsible for protecting their own client through the closing of the transaction.

- The buyer's agent will focus on all the areas pertinent to the buyer: Seller's Disclosure of Property Condition revelations (foundation, roof, mold, hazardous waste, etc.), loan process, property inspection, property appraisal, repairs, survey, title commitment/title policy, homeowners insurance, home warranty, closing issues, Settlement Statement (HUD-1), other closing documents, and the buyer's temporary residential lease (if any).
- The seller's agent will focus on areas pertinent to the seller: loan payoff information, repairs required of seller, personal property items to remain with the property per the sales contract, real property items to go with the seller per sales contract, the date utilities will be turned off, the seller's temporary lease (if any), the Settlement Statement (HUD-1), and other closing documents.

Once the closing is completed and funding has occurred, the respective brokers will be paid the compensation due them according to the listing agreement and the buyer representation agreement. The sales associates will receive their compensation via their respective brokers, or it will be paid directly to them at the time of closing per the instructions of their respective brokers.

Other Broker as Subagent of Seller Instead of Buyer's Broker   In those cases in which the other broker is a subagent of the seller, the other broker must

- disclose to the buyer, either orally or in writing, that the broker is an agent of the seller;
- provide the written statement required by TRELA § 1101.558, unless the buyer or the tenant is represented by an agent or the statement is not required for some other legitimate reason;

- discuss with the buyer or the tenant what type of services the subagent can and cannot provide;
- notify the listing broker that the other broker is a subagent of the seller;
- verify each proposed commission-split arrangement;
- inquire whether there are any special instructions or new information or whether the home is already under contract;
- inquire about the listing broker's policies regarding handling earnest money deposits, using a lockbox, drafting offers, choosing an escrow company, and placing a loan; and
- act as a subagent of the seller, at all times in the best interests of the seller.

In deciding whether to represent the seller, the other broker should understand that as a subagent of the seller, the other broker may not be privy to the same information as the listing broker. Many sellers are reluctant to pass on confidential information to the other broker for fear the other broker will divulge this information to the buyer. Other brokers cooperating with the seller through the listing broker are normally viewed by sellers as conduits for the flow of facts and figures between buyers and sellers.

This can be a very difficult position for the subagent to the seller to hold throughout the entire transaction. The subagent is continually with the buyer, getting to know the buyer and the family, and even possibly buying lunch on occasion, while functioning in an arm's-length position. All discussions between the subagent and the buyer must be carefully monitored by the subagent to make sure that all real estate terminology is used correctly so the buyer is not ever led to believe that the subagent is on the buyer's side and acting for instead of with the buyer. The subagent must not advocate, at any time, for the position of the buyer. All the subagent's fiduciary and common law agency duties are owed to the seller.

Intermediary: Reduced Agency Relationship for Buyer and Seller   If the listing office offers representation to both buyers and sellers in the same transaction, the initial contact with either the buyer or the seller should address the possibility and the consequences of that situation arising. Remember, the basic requirements to establish an intermediary relationship under TRELA § 1101.559; .560 are to

- obtain the written consent of all parties in a form that meets the specific requirements set forth in TRELA § 1101.559;
- treat all parties fairly and honestly and avoid disclosure of any information that is confidential or that a party has requested not to be disclosed;
- determine whether appointments will be made and, if so, disclose in writing to all parties that such has been done; and
- comply with the provisions of TRELA.

■ A PRACTICAL GUIDE TO EVERYDAY PRACTICE: USING REHEARSED DIALOGUE

Newly licensed or inexperienced real estate associates are often uncomfortable discussing what frequently amounts to highly sensitive personal and financial information with people they do not know. Through sales and counseling training sessions that use role playing and sample dialogue, associates often overcome their initial uneasiness.

Real estate counseling and buyer's brokerage training programs stress learning the practical skills of asking effective questions and listening actively. The goal is to select from a group of prospects those who may be clients and those who may be customers.

The following section, containing possible questions and dialogue to use when discussing the agency relationship issue, can help reduce the anxiety level of real estate agents when discussing agency. Brokers should develop their own role-playing situations for use in training sessions and expand on the brief dialogue included here. Some licensees may prefer to write out these dialogues and record them to listen to later. Often, it is not what is said, but how it is said, that makes the difference in explaining an important issue.

Dialogues for Brokerage Situations

Here are some short scenarios to indicate how some brokers handle discussions of agency to enhances their professional image. Use these as guidelines to write the dialogues in your own language and style. Then, try them out, critique them, and refine them based on the concepts of agency you have learned in this text.

■ **SCENE 1** Natalie is a customer; Andrea is an associate of a firm that practices exclusive seller agency. Natalie attends an open house where Andrea is on duty for the broker. Andrea hands Natalie a fact sheet, shows her around, and asks Natalie general questions concerning her wants and needs in housing, the general price range she is considering, and her square-footage requirements. Andrea senses that Natalie is not the typical looker but is serious about purchasing a property and seems very interested in the house. Andrea decides to turn the discussion to the subject of agency before the conversation gets too specific and before Natalie begins to reveal confidences or develops unwarranted expectations of services and information.

Andrea: Has anyone explained to you, Natalie, how real estate licensees work and the agency relationships licensees are allowed to develop with clients?

Natalie: No.

Andrea: Regarding this house you're looking at, I am the agent for the seller. The reason I'm holding this open house is to expose the seller's property to the market in the hope that a buyer such as you will decide to purchase the property. As the seller's agent, I can point out the many features of the property; answer many of your questions about financing, ownership, and closing; help you prepare an offer the way you want it; and promptly present your offer to the seller. By law, I am obligated to treat you, as a customer for my seller's property, honestly and fairly in the transaction. There are, however, other services that I cannot perform for you as an agent of the seller. Before we proceed, I would like you to consider the information about brokerage services contained in our company's agency disclosure brochure. As a licensee, I am required to make clear whom I will represent in any given transaction.

After developing this dialogue as though Andrea were an exclusive seller's agent, assume that she and her broker practice nonexclusive single agency and see where the dialogue takes you. Then attempt the same process, assuming Andrea and her brokerage offer intermediary brokerage services.

■ **SCENE 2**   A buyer's broker has an advantage over other brokers in contacting a For-Sale-by-Owner (FSBO) seller. The buyer's broker does not look to the seller either for a listing or in an attempt to bargain a commission from the seller. The following dialogue might be used in a face-to-face meeting with a FSBO seller.

Kim: Good morning, Mr. Owner, I am Kim of Gold Coast Realty. I am a real estate licensee, but I am not here to ask for a listing on your home. The reason for my visit is to see if your property might fit the needs of my client. I saw your For Sale sign. Do you have a few minutes to see if you can be of help to my buyer and me?

Owner: Yes, but not a whole lot more than a few minutes. And I don't want to list my property.

Kim: I understand you're busy. I'll be very brief. My buyer, through his buyer representation agreement with me, has agreed to include enough money in any offer he might make for your property to cover any concessions he might ask you to make, including such things as roof repairs, discount points, and my fee for services to him. Therefore, I will not personally attempt to negotiate a fee for myself from you. I am the agent for the buyer, and I will not be your agent. You will not have to list your property or publicly advertise it for sale. My buyer is ready, willing, and able to pay a fair price should you and he be able to come to a mutually acceptable agreement. If you are willing to sell for an acceptable price and terms, I would appreciate the opportunity to preview your house, with or without my client, and develop a report to my client regarding your property's suitability for his needs. Then we could prepare an offer for your consideration. Could I make an appointment with you to come back and preview your property sometime today or early tomorrow?

Owner: I'm telling you right now, I'm not listing with you and I'm not paying any commissions for anybody.

Kim: I understand, Mr. Owner, and I hear your frustration. As far as the real estate fees are concerned, my agreement with my buyer-client is an enforceable written contract in which my client has agreed to pay my fee for services to him in one of two ways. He might include enough in the offer to the owner so that the owner can pay my fee and net just as much money. Or, should my client not be able to negotiate that point with the owner but still desires the property, he has agreed to compensate me in addition to whatever the final purchase price is. Let me leave with you my company's agency disclosure form, which includes information about brokerage services. This form will confirm in writing what I've just told you. Again, I would very much like to return at a time that is convenient to you. I'll also bring a state-required seller's disclosure of property condition form, discuss both forms with you for 10 to 15 minutes, and then preview your house for my client.

■ **DISCUSSION**   In this scenario, Kim practices exclusive buyer agency. If she practiced nonexclusive single agency or intermediary brokerage, consider the following:

- ■ Would her conversation with the owner be different?
- ■ Could she start talking with the owner about becoming his agent for the purchase of his next home?
- ■ What conflicts of interest could develop?
- ■ What would happen if her brokerage practiced the hybrid form of agency, where the client is required to consent to intermediary brokerage in advance should the situation require it?
- ■ Develop additional dialogues for these scenarios.

■ OTHER CONSIDERATIONS

Presentation of Offers by the Listing Broker

One of the important issues we have discussed frequently is the duty of an agent to disclose information to clients. Under the minimum service due a client from the agent is the duty to inform the client if the broker receives any material information related to the transaction, including the receipt of an offer by the broker (see § 1101.557). A listing broker (or an associate of the listing broker) will therefore be obligated to present all offers directly to the seller (or the buyer, in the case of a buyer's agent). It is not the prerogative of a broker to decide whether an offer will or will not be presented to the client, even if the broker knows (or believes) that the offer will be unacceptable to the client. Only the client has the right to accept, reject, or counter an offer. If sellers, for example, insist on considering only those offers that meet or exceed a certain price and/or terms criteria, then the licensee should obtain written instructions from the sellers stating their wishes (this should be done only after a lengthy discussion about why this is unadvisable).

It is the duty of the licensee to explain an offer to the client and to give the client an accurate estimate of the costs and net proceeds. All offers should be presented as soon as possible—once the offer is available to the agent. The offer is privileged information and should be kept confidential, and the terms of the offer should not be made available to other licensees or potential buyers. Many ethics hearings have centered on the mishandling of offers by brokers.

■ **EXAMPLE**   Martinez listed Reese's property for $175,000. Reese stated that he would only accept a full-price cash offer, and that he would not consider paying any closing costs. Several offers were submitted that did not meet Rowan's terms, and he immediately rejected them.

Carter viewed the property and thought it would be a nice investment. She asked her agent, Smith, to prepare an offer for $150,000 with the seller paying all closing costs. After Carter signed the offer, Smith presented it to Martinez. Martinez refused to present the offer, saying that he was sure Reese would not accept it, as he had turned down similar offers in the past.

■ **QUESTION**   1. Using only the facts in the example, was Martinez right to refuse to present the offer? 2. Would it be advisable for Smith to contact the local board of REALTORS® and file an ethics complaint?

■ **DISCUSSION**   It is very tempting to refuse to present an offer when you are "sure" that a seller will reject the offer and send you on your merry way. What many licensees do not recognize, however, is that circumstances can change at any time, and those changes might make the seller more receptive to price and/or terms that were previously unacceptable.

From an ethical standpoint, it is unfair to the seller to refuse to present an offer. Every offer gives the seller an opportunity to try to negotiate. Many sales that began with outrageous prices and terms have been negotiated to the satisfaction of both parties. We as licensees do not have the crystal ball that tells us which offer will result in acceptance and which will not.

Presentation of Multiple Offers

On occasion, a listing broker may have more than one offer to present to a seller. This can occur (1) when a second offer is given to the listing broker before the first offer has been presented or (2) when a seller has received an offer, but has not yet accepted it, and another offer is made by a second buyer.

In the first case, where the broker actually has two offers to present, the broker should prepare presentations of both offers with the appropriate net proceed statements for the seller. In addition, the broker should collect as much information about the prospective buyers as possible to enable the seller to make an informed decision. For example, while one offer may net a greater net dollar amount for the seller, the financial strength of the buyer, type of financing, and other terms may make the offer less desirable than another offer that provides fewer dollars to the seller but under much more favorable terms. Remember that typical residential sellers are not very sophisticated about these issues and therefore have employed brokers to represent them in these negotiations. It is the agent's duty to give the client the best advice and opinions available.

The agent should give no preference to one offer simply because it was received before another, although in some cases the seller may wish to know and consider the information in the decision-making process. The primary duty of the agent is to give the seller as much information as possible and help the seller make the best possible decision.

The second situation occurs when the agent receives a second offer while the seller is deliberating a first offer. In this instance, the agent should immediately notify the seller of a second offer and advise the seller not to accept the first offer without first also considering the second. Consider the following situation.

■ **EXAMPLE**   Sue, a broker-associate of REI Realty, has secured a listing for the sale of the Edwards' condominium for a price of $200,000. At 10 am on Tuesday, Bob, the owner of Maxheimer Realty, brings an offer for $185,000 to Sue. Sue knows that the seller will not be available until 8 pm that evening. At 2 pm the same day, Brenda, Sue's best friend, who is also an associate of REI Realty, rushes into the office, finds Sue, and exclaims, "Guess what—I have an offer on the Edwards' condo—overpriced though it is!" Brenda's customers have offered $192,000. Late in the afternoon, while preparing the offer presentations for the Edwards, Sue receives a call from Mr. Koepke, a prospect to whom Sue had shown the Edwards' property during an open house the previous Sunday. Koepke wishes to come into the office and make a written offer on the property.

Presuming that the three offers are comparable in terms and that the buyers are equally qualified, consider the questions that follow.

■ **QUESTIONS** 1. Should Sue disclose to Brenda the existence of the offer from Maxheimer Realty? 2. If so, how much information should be given to Brenda regarding the offer? 3. Should Maxheimer be made aware of the second offer? 4. If so, how much information should be given to Maxheimer regarding the offer? 5. Should Sue's customer be made aware of the other offers? 6. If so, how much information should be given to Sue's customer regarding the offers? 7. How should Sue handle securing the offer from Koepke, considering the fact that she already knows the details of the previous offers?

■ **DISCUSSION** In general, any information that is available to one party should be available to the other parties concerned. While the details of the other offer(s) should not be disclosed, the fact that other offers exist may be disclosed. In a sense of fairness to all participants, if one agent is made aware of an existing offer, all agents involved should be made aware. In the example above, if Brenda, in Sue's office, was told of Maxheimer's offer, Maxheimer should have been contacted and made aware that Sue now has another offer.

From the seller's perspective, it is beneficial for all parties to know that multiple offers have arrived. Buyers who are truly interested in winning the bid will often want to increase the price offered or make the terms more favorable to the seller, thus giving the seller a more profitable sale.

From the buyer's perspective, if the property is one that has high personal value, this information gives the buyer the opportunity to assess the original offer, determine whether it could be made more appealing to the seller, and determine whether the buyer's financial means will allow an adjustment that would have a better chance at a successful bid. This could be a win-win situation for all parties.

Sue is in a position of a potential conflict of interest if she writes a contract for Koepke. She knows too much about the offers that have already been submitted. It would be wise to bring the sponsoring broker (or a person of the broker's choice) into the transaction. This person could write the contract for Koepke and negotiate the details, if necessary. Sue would then be able to present all offers to the seller knowing that she did not have undue influence on the construction of Koepke's offer and unethically slant the outcome in her favor.

Presentation of Subsequent or Backup Offers

On occasion, a buyer wishes to make an offer to a seller, even though the seller is already under contract with another buyer. The second offer is usually called a backup offer and would become effective only if the first offer did not proceed to closing.

This can create difficult situations for both parties and the broker, particularly if the backup offer is more desirable to the seller than the first accepted offer. The parties should proceed carefully because contract law provides that the first buyer may have legal recourse if a second contract interferes with the first buyer's contract rights (called tortious interference with a contract). The seller should not entertain backup offers without permission of the first buyer because the buyer is said to have equitable title to the property. Equitable title is the buyer's right to have the property transferred once all conditions of the contract are fulfilled.

The first step in handling these issues is for the listing agent to determine whether the seller wishes to consider backup offers. The TREC one-to-four-family promulgated sales contracts provide that the seller may continue to offer the property for sale and negotiate and accept backup offers. If a buyer does not wish the seller to continue to solicit backup offers, special provisions must be added to the TREC contract offer that prohibit the seller from doing so.

Retained Earnest Money in the Event of a Default

TREC-promulgated sales contract forms do not contain a standard provision that permits the listing broker to share in a portion of the earnest money deposit retained by the seller as liquidated damages in the event the buyer defaults. However, most listing agreements (see Figure 4.2, paragraph 5D(1)) do contain such a protection for the listing broker.

Few agreements permit the other broker, as a subagent of the seller, to share in the portion allocated to the listing broker in the event of default. The "Broker Information" section of the TREC sales contract form is silent as to a subagent broker's right to share in earnest money distributions in the event of default.

Commissions

One of the most important considerations is how to handle commissions. All commissions are negotiable. For example, TREC-promulgated sales contract forms routinely indicate that "all obligations of the parties for payment of brokers' fees are contained in separate written agreements." TAR listing and buyer representation agreements, in turn, will usually give notice to the client that brokers' fees and the sharing of fees between brokers "are not fixed, controlled, recommended, suggested, or maintained by the Association of REALTORS® or any listing service." Who pays the commission does not determine who represents whom. The listing and the selling commissions normally are paid out of the sales proceeds at closing, but they do not have to be. In residential sales, brokerage commissions are usually paid from the seller's proceeds, but they do not have to be; the buyer or the tenant may pay the broker by agreement as well.

A broker has a duty to cooperate with other brokers on behalf of their client, but only when cooperation is within their client's best interest. For example, by advertising a property in the MLS, the listing broker encourages other brokers and their associates to review the property pricing and characteristics and to then bring qualified buyers to view the property. The offer to cooperate, however, does not include the obligation to compensate another broker. The duty to cooperate relates instead to the obligation to share information on the listed property. As previously discussed, a growing number of listing brokers prefer to reduce their level of risk by not allowing other brokers to represent their client (i.e., they do not offer subagency). They accomplish their objective simply by withholding any offer of compensation to subagents within the MLS.

Written Agreements

Prudent brokers should attempt to enter into written agency agreements with clients. While it is sometimes legal, it is nonetheless unwise to proceed on oral agreements. Brokers must recognize that some buyers are reluctant to sign a buyer representation agreement, even though they will be loyal customers, because

- such an arrangement has not been customary in the past,
- they fear the closing costs will increase by an additional broker fee,
- they do not want to be tied to an exclusive contract, or
- they do not understand the benefits of representation.

■ RISK MANAGEMENT

Although we have covered many key elements of risk management under the general heading of preventive brokerage, many brokers today spend considerable time and effort to minimize legal exposure with buyers and sellers. One of the most effective ways to reduce risk in the specific area of agency risk is a well-defined and carefully implemented office policy manual that addresses the agency procedures of the company. Remember, however, that TRELA holds the broker responsible for any conduct engaged in by the broker or by a salesperson associated with or acting for the broker (§ 1101.803). The broker or office manager may not be immediately available should an associate need guidance on how to proceed with a dilemma which has arisen. Whether a large or a small office, to ensure consistent compliance with office policy, the broker should therefore assure that associates have access to a readily available set of written guidelines outlining even the most routine of office policies and procedures.

The important thing is for the broker to assure that the policy and procedures manual is a dynamic document that can be easily changed when impacted by changes in TRELA, TREC rule, local REALTOR® board policy, or even technology. After all, the only constant in the real estate business is change!

The following list of topics is not all inclusive but can serve as a starting point for a broker wishing to begin developing a basic policies and procedures manual. Consider including the following outline of contents for a manual:

- Agency
- Dealing with buyers
  — The contract—getting/servicing it
  — Length of the agreement
  — Rescission/revocation/renunciation policy
  — Commission fees
  — Dealing with the buyer as a subagent
- Dealing with sellers
  — The contract—getting/servicing it
  — Types of listings permitted
  — Rescission/revocation/renunciation policy

- — Conducting open houses and property tours
- — Company signs (standardization? content? riders?)
- — Cooperative listings between associates
- ■ Showings
  - — Company listings versus co-op listings
- ■ The purchase agreement
  - — Disclosure of relationships
  - — Earnest money
  - — Making appointments to present
  - — Presenting the offer/counteroffer/multiple offers
  - — How to handle rejection of offer
- ■ Office policy regarding commission
  - — What is the scale? fixed? sliding?
  - — Referral fees
  - — Bonuses
  - — When and where is it payable to the associate?
  - — What to do in case of a dispute with another brokerage office
  - — Antitrust policy
- ■ Closing the deal
  - — What level of service/information is provided?
    - ■ Net to consumer? Estimate of closing costs/monthly payment?
    - ■ Review of final closing documents
    - ■ Presence at scheduled inspections/appraisals/contractors
  - — Attendance at closing
- ■ Internal office administrative issues
  - — Independent contract agreement versus employee
  - — Phone/copier/conference room use
  - — Additional liability insurance
  - — Vacation time
  - — Associate expenses versus broker expenses
  - — Office conduct and dress code
  - — Internet policy
  - — Protecting privacy information
  - — Buying/selling for your own account
  - — Handling relocations and referrals
  - — Do-not-call policy
- ■ Advertising (see 22 § 535.154 for TREC rules)
- ■ Personal assistants
- ■ Arbitration and mediation policy
- ■ Sexual harassment
- ■ Equal housing opportunity/discrimination

Again, this list of policy and procedures manual topics should serve only as a starting list. A broker starting from scratch might seek further guidance at the TAR or NAR Web sites.

Because it is impossible to avoid all risk in the real estate business, many brokers and sales licensees attempt to minimize the potential of financial loss by purchasing errors and omissions (E&O) insurance and suggesting that purchasers obtain home warranties. Similar to malpractice insurance in the medical and legal fields, E&O policies cover liability for errors and negligence in the listing and selling activities of a real estate broker and often the broker's sales associates. Some E&O insurance companies also offer policies directly to individual sales associates. License law in Texas requires E&O insurance for certain business entities seeking broker licensure [TRELA § 1101.355]:

> (a) To be eligible for a license under this chapter, a business entity must
>
> > (1) designate one of its managing officers as its agent for purposes of this chapter; and
> >
> > (2) provide proof that the entity maintains errors and omissions insurance with a minimum annual limit of $1 million for each occurrence if the designated agent owns less than 10 percent of the business entity.
>
> (b) A business entity may not act as a broker unless the entity's designated agent is a licensed broker in active status and good standing according to the commission's records.
>
> (c) A business entity that receives compensation on behalf of a license holder must be licensed as a broker under this chapter.

No insurance policy will protect a real estate professional from a lawsuit or prosecution arising from criminal acts. Insurance companies normally exclude coverage for fraud and violations of civil rights and antitrust laws.

Prudent brokers attempt to shift risk by suggesting that the principals rely on other experts such as attorneys, title companies, lenders, appraisers, licensed property inspectors, and surveyors, to name a few. The area of risk management is a growing concern, and several texts have been devoted to this topic in detail.

■ SUMMARY

When you become comfortable handling your relationship with both customers and clients, you will experience enhanced professional stature and esteem. You will discover a sense of freedom in being able to more actively represent the best interests of your clients, whether buyers or sellers, when you negotiate against the other side, whether represented or unrepresented.

Part of that feeling of security can also come from knowing that the broker has provided an easy reference and how-to-guide regarding matters that routinely arise during the day-to-conduct of business.

■ KEY POINTS

- In practicing preventive brokerage, brokers should use written disclosures, clarify the roles of associated licensees, develop a written set of office policy and procedures, and when needed, use the services of others in their real estate transactions.
- Licensees should carefully prepare their clients and customers for the real estate transaction by explaining the process and providing disclosures.
- Offers to purchase should be presented in a timely manner. Multiple offers should be presented together, thereby giving the seller opportunity to accept the offer that best meets the selling goals. The seller should be able to choose whether or not to accept backup offers.
- There should be an understanding of how retained earnest money will be divided in case of a buyer's default.
- Commissions are negotiable and may be paid by either a client or a customer. An agency relationship is not necessarily determined by which party in the transaction pays the commission.
- Agency agreements should be in writing; however, oral agreements can create an agency relationship (express agency can be either oral or in writing).
- Using rehearsed dialogue will help licensees overcome uneasiness with situations that are difficult for them.
- Having errors and omission insurance may be helpful in managing inevitable errors or omissions made by either brokers or their sales associates during a real estate transaction.

■ SUGGESTIONS FOR BROKERS

Practice real-life situations in your training classes and learn the most effective ways to discuss agency relationships to prepare yourself for future discussions. Then put your practice sessions to work in the field. Allow newly licensed or inexperienced associates to accompany you or an experienced associate to view a listing presentation or an interview with a buyer prospect.

CHAPTER 12 QUIZ

1. Brokers should do all of the following *EXCEPT*
   a. use written disclosures.
   b. clarify their roles in the transaction.
   c. use the help of others when needed.
   d. warrant the condition of a property.

2. Listing brokers
   a. always offer subagency to other brokers.
   b. should explain brokerage policies regarding representation of clients.
   c. are not required to use disclosures other than those in the listing contract.
   d. may assume that sellers are aware of how commissions are split with other brokers.

3. When selecting properties to show a buyer-customer, the licensee
   a. should select those properties that best match the buyer's desires.
   b. should show only the company's listings because of fiduciary duties to their sellers.
   c. should match available properties with the buyer's needs, desires, and ability to pay.
   d. always should show properties somewhat above the buyer's desired price range because buyers typically "buy up" from their initial requested price range.

4. Which term *BEST* describes a real estate licensee, working through a listing broker, who is paid a fee for working with a buyer but is not an agent of the buyer?
   a. Listing broker
   b. Subagent
   c. Finder
   d. Buyer's broker

5. A broker wishing to act as an intermediary in a transaction may do so only if
   a. all parties give written approval.
   b. the buyers give written approval.
   c. the sellers give written approval.
   d. the parties give written or verbal approval.

6. If a second offer is received by the listing broker while a seller is deliberating an offer, the broker
   a. must not present the second offer until the seller has made a decision on the first offer.
   b. must present the offer but explain to the seller that the second offer can be considered only as a backup offer and cannot be acted on until the first offer is negotiated.
   c. must present the second offer and explain that the seller is free to consider the second offer without regard to the first offer.
   d. should advise the licensee bringing the second offer that the seller is deliberating a first offer and to delay bringing a second offer until negotiations on the first offer are completed.

7. If earnest money is used to liquidate damages in a transaction, the listing broker is
   a. not entitled to share in the earnest money.
   b. entitled to share in the earnest money.
   c. entitled to share in the earnest money only if the listing agreement or purchase agreement contains such a provision.
   d. not entitled to share in the earnest money because listing agreements and purchase agreements never contain such a provision.

8. Who can pay the buyer's broker's fee?
   a. Seller
   b. Buyer
   c. Both seller and buyer
   d. Neither seller nor buyer

9. If a listing broker receives an offer from a buyer's broker in which the buyer's broker's fee is to be paid by the seller, the listing broker should
   a. reject the offer.
   b. renegotiate the offering.
   c. increase the listing fee.
   d. present the offer to the seller.

10. Which of the following is *TRUE* of E&O insurance?

    a. E&O insurance covers fraud.
    b. E&O insurance is not required of any broker.
    c. E&O insurance is required of certain types of brokers.
    d. E&O insurance issues are not addressed in TRELA.

DISCUSSION QUESTIONS

1. You are the listing agent. A buyer wants to submit an offer to buy through you. The buyer hands you three envelopes with instructions to present a certain one first. Only if the seller rejects the offer found in the first envelope are you to present the others. What should you advise your seller? Would you do anything differently if you were the other broker acting as a subagent on an MLS listing? If you were a buyer's broker?

2. A buyer asks you how much her monthly payment will be for her mortgage loan. You explain that the monthly payment is $1,400, which will be used to pay principal, interest, taxes, and insurance. The buyer neglects to obtain fire insurance because she thinks it is included in the monthly payment when, actually, the monthly payment includes only the mortgage insurance premium. The house burns down. Are you liable? Are you more likely to be liable if you are the buyer's agent than if you are the listing agent?

3. As the other broker acting in a subagency capacity with the seller, you find a buyer who purchases a home for cash at $20,000 in excess of the true market value. Nine months later, the buyer comes to you and asks you to list the property for sale. What listing price do you suggest? How do you explain that you helped the buyer acquire the property, which was clearly overpriced?

4. Sally of Bay Realty signs a listing with George on a penthouse apartment. George asks Sally to find him a bigger penthouse. Whom does Sally represent on the current penthouse? Whom does Sally represent if she shows George a Bay Realty listing that was obtained by another agent? Whom does Sally represent if she shows George a property listed with another brokerage through the MLS? How does Sally explain to George the various working relationships open to them?

5. Review and expand on the suggested list of topics that should be covered in a well-written, detailed office policy and procedures manual.

Texas Occupations Code

TEXAS OCCUPATIONS CODE

**TITLE 7. PRACTICES AND PROFESSIONS
RELATED TO REAL PROPERTY AND HOUSING**

**SUBTITLE A.
PROFESSIONS RELATED TO REAL ESTATE**

**CHAPTER 1101.
REAL ESTATE BROKERS AND SALESPERSONS**

**CHAPTER 1102.
REAL ESTATE INSPECTORS**

As Revised and in Effect on

September 1, 2012

Texas Real Estate Commission
P.O. Box 12188, Austin, Texas 78711-2188
(512) 936-3000
www.trec.texas.gov

OCCUPATIONS CODE
TITLE 7. PRACTICES AND PROFESSIONS RELATED TO REAL PROPERTY AND HOUSING
SUBTITLE A. PROFESSIONS RELATED TO REAL ESTATE
CHAPTER 1101. REAL ESTATE BROKERS AND SALESPERSONS

SUBCHAPTER A. GENERAL PROVISIONS

Sec. 1101.001. SHORT TITLE. This chapter may be cited as The Real Estate License Act.

(Added by Acts 2001, 77th Leg., ch. 1421, Sec. 2, eff. June 1, 2003.)

Sec. 1101.002. DEFINITIONS. In this chapter:

(1) "Broker":

(A) means a person who, in exchange for a commission or other valuable consideration or with the expectation of receiving a commission or other valuable consideration, performs for another person one of the following acts:

(i) sells, exchanges, purchases, or leases real estate;

(ii) offers to sell, exchange, purchase, or lease real estate;

(iii) negotiates or attempts to negotiate the listing, sale, exchange, purchase, or lease of real estate;

(iv) lists or offers, attempts, or agrees to list real estate for sale, lease, or exchange;

(v) auctions or offers, attempts, or agrees to auction real estate;

(vi) deals in options on real estate, including buying, selling, or offering to buy or sell options on real estate;

(vii) aids or offers or attempts to aid in locating or obtaining real estate for purchase or lease;

(viii) procures or assists in procuring a prospect to effect the sale, exchange, or lease of real estate;

(ix) procures or assists in procuring property to effect the sale, exchange, or lease of real estate;

(x) controls the acceptance or deposit of rent from a resident of a single-family residential real property unit; or

(xi) provides a written analysis, opinion, or conclusion relating to the estimated price of real property if the analysis, opinion, or conclusion:

(a) is not referred to as an appraisal;

(b) is provided in the ordinary course of the person's business; and

(c) is related to the actual or potential management, acquisition, disposition, or encumbrance of an interest in real property; and

(B) includes a person who:

(i) is employed by or for an owner of real estate to sell any portion of the real estate; or

(ii) engages in the business of charging an advance fee or contracting to collect a fee under a contract that requires the person primarily to promote the sale of real estate by:

(a) listing the real estate in a publication primarily used for listing real estate; or

(b) referring information about the real estate to brokers.

(1-a) "Business entity" means a "domestic entity" or "foreign entity" as those terms are defined by Section 1.002, Business Organizations Code.

(2) "Certificate holder" means a person registered under Subchapter K.

(3) "Commission" means the Texas Real Estate Commission.

(4) "License holder" means a broker or salesperson licensed under this chapter.

(5) "Real estate" means any interest in real property, including a leasehold, located in or outside this state. The term does not include an interest given as security for the performance of an obligation.

Sec. 1101.002(6)–.003(a)(5)(B)

(6) "Residential rental locator" means a person who offers for consideration to locate a unit in an apartment complex for lease to a prospective tenant. The term does not include an owner who offers to locate a unit in the owner's complex.

(7) "Salesperson" means a person who is associated with a licensed broker for the purpose of performing an act described by Subdivision (1).

(8) "Subagent" means a license holder who:

(A) represents a principal through cooperation with and the consent of a broker representing the principal; and

(B) is not sponsored by or associated with the principal's broker.

(Added by Acts 2001, 77th Leg., ch. 1421, Sec. 2, eff. June 1, 2003. Amended by Acts 2003, 78th Leg., ch. 1276, Sec. 14A.151, eff. Sept. 1, 2003.)

(Amended by: Acts 2011, 82nd Leg., R.S., Ch. 1064, Sec. 1, eff. September 1, 2011.)

Sec. 1101.003. CORE REAL ESTATE COURSES. (a) For purposes of this chapter, "core real estate courses" include:

(1) agency law, which includes the following topics:

(A) the relationship between a principal and an agent;

(B) an agent's authority;

(C) the termination of an agent's authority;

(D) an agent's duties, including fiduciary duties;

(E) employment law;

(F) deceptive trade practices;

(G) listing or buying representation procedures; and

(H) the disclosure of agency;

(2) contract law, which includes the following topics:

(A) elements of a contract;

(B) offer and acceptance;

(C) statute of frauds;

(D) remedies for breach, including specific performance;

(E) nauthorized practice of law;

(F) commission rules relating to use of adopted forms; and

(G) owner disclosure requirements;

(3) principles of real estate, which includes:

(A) an overview of:

(i) licensing as a broker or salesperson;

(ii) ethics of practice as a license holder;

(iii) titles to and conveyance of real estate;

(iv) legal descriptions;

(v) deeds, encumbrances, and liens;

(vi) distinctions between personal and real property;

(vii) appraisal;

(viii) finance and regulations;

(ix) closing procedures; and

(x) real estate mathematics; and

(B) at least three hours of classroom instruction on federal, state, and local laws relating to housing discrimination, housing credit discrimination, and community reinvestment;

(4) property management, which includes the following topics:

(A) the role of a property manager;

(B) landlord policies;

(C) operational guidelines;

(D) leases;

(E) lease negotiations;

(F) tenant relations;

(G) maintenance;

(H) reports;

(I) habitability laws; and

(J) the Fair Housing Act (42 U.S.C. Section 3601 et seq.);

(5) real estate appraisal, which includes the following topics:

(A) the central purposes and functions of an appraisal;

(B) social and economic determinants of the value of real estate;

(C) appraisal case studies;

(D) cost, market data, and income approaches to value estimates of real estate;

(E) final correlations; and

(F) reporting;

(6) real estate brokerage, which includes the following topics:

(A) agency law;

(B) planning and organization;

(C) operational policies and procedures;

(D) recruitment, selection, and training of personnel;

(E) records and control; and

(F) real estate firm analysis and expansion criteria;

(7) real estate finance, which includes the following topics:

(A) monetary systems;

(B) primary and secondary money markets;

(C) sources of mortgage loans;

(D) federal government programs;

(E) loan applications, processes, and procedures;

(F) closing costs;

(G) alternative financial instruments;

(H) equal credit opportunity laws;

(I) community reinvestment laws, including the Community Reinvestment Act of 1977 (12 U.S.C. Section 2901 et seq.); and

(J) state housing agencies, including the Texas Department of Housing and Community Affairs;

(8) real estate investment, which includes the following topics:

(A) real estate investment characteristics;

(B) techniques of investment analysis;

(C) the time value of money;

(D) discounted and nondiscounted investment criteria;

(E) leverage;

(F) tax shelters depreciation; and

(G) applications to property tax;

(9) real estate law, which includes the following topics:

(A) legal concepts of real estate;

(B) land description;

(C) real property rights and estates in land;

(D) contracts;

(E) conveyances;

(F) encumbrances;

(G) foreclosures;

(H) recording procedures; and

(I) evidence of titles;

(10) real estate marketing, which includes the following topics:

(A) real estate professionalism and ethics;

(B) characteristics of successful salespersons;

(C) time management;

(D) psychology of marketing;

(E) listing procedures;

(F) advertising;

(G) negotiating and closing;

(H) financing; and

(I) Subchapter E, Chapter 17, Business & Commerce Code; and

(11) real estate mathematics, which includes the following topics:

(A) basic arithmetic skills and review of mathematical logic;

(B) percentages;

(C) interest;

(D) the time value of money;

(E) depreciation;

(F) amortization;

(G) proration; and

(H) estimation of closing statements.

(b) The commission may designate a course as an equivalent of a course listed in Subsection (a).

Sec. 1101.003(c)—.051(a)

(c) The commission by rule may prescribe:

(1) the content of the core real estate courses listed in Subsection (a); and

(2) the title and content of additional core real estate courses.

(Added by Acts 2001, 77th Leg., ch. 1421, Sec. 2, eff. June 1, 2003. Amended by Acts 2003, 78th Leg., ch. 1276, Sec. 14A.152(a), eff. Sept. 1, 2003.)

Sec. 1101.004. ACTING AS BROKER OR SALESPERSON. A person acts as a broker or salesperson under this chapter if the person, with the expectation of receiving valuable consideration, directly or indirectly performs or offers, attempts, or agrees to perform for another person any act described by Section 1101.002(1), as a part of a transaction or as an entire transaction.

(Added by Acts 2001, 77th Leg., ch. 1421, Sec. 2, eff. June 1, 2003. Amended by Acts 2003, 78th Leg., ch. 1276, Sec. 14A.153, eff. Sept. 1, 2003.)

Sec. 1101.005. APPLICABILITY OF CHAPTER. This chapter does not apply to:

(1) an attorney licensed in this state;

(2) an attorney-in-fact authorized under a power of attorney to conduct a real estate transaction;

(3) a public official while engaged in official duties;

(4) an auctioneer licensed under Chapter 1802 while conducting the sale of real estate by auction if the auctioneer does not perform another act of a broker or salesperson;

(5) a person conducting a real estate transaction under a court order or the authority of a will or written trust instrument;

(6) a person employed by an owner in the sale of structures and land on which structures are located if the structures are erected by the owner in the course of the owner's business;

(7) an on-site manager of an apartment complex;

(8) an owner or the owner's employee who leases the owner's improved or unimproved real estate; or

(9) a transaction involving:

(A) the sale, lease, or transfer of a mineral or mining interest in real property;

(B) the sale, lease, or transfer of a cemetery lot;

(C) the lease or management of a hotel or motel; or

(D) the sale of real property under a power of sale conferred by a deed of trust or other contract lien.

(Added by Acts 2001, 77th Leg., ch. 1421, Sec. 2, eff. June 1, 2003.) (Amended by: Acts 2005, 79th Leg., Ch. 62, Sec. 1, eff. May 17, 2005. Acts 2007, 80th Leg., R.S., Ch. 297, Sec. 1, eff. September 1, 2007. Acts 2011, 82nd Leg., R.S., Ch. 1064, Sec. 2, eff. September 1, 2011.)

Sec. 1101.0055. NONAPPLICABILITY OF LAW GOVERNING CANCELLATION OF CERTAIN TRANSACTIONS. A service contract that a license holder enters into for services governed by this chapter is not a good or service governed by Chapter 601, Business & Commerce Code.

(Added by Acts 2003, 78th Leg., ch. 1276, Sec. 14A.154(a), eff. Sept. 1, 2003.) (Amended by: Acts 2007, 80th Leg., R.S., Ch. 885, Sec. 2.27, eff. April 1, 2009.)

Sec. 1101.006. APPLICATION OF SUNSET ACT. The Texas Real Estate Commission is subject to Chapter 325, Government Code (Texas Sunset Act). Unless continued in existence as provided by that chapter, the commission is abolished and this chapter, Chapter 1102, and Chapter 1303 of this code and Chapter 221, Property Code, expire September 1, 2019.

(Added by Acts 2001, 77th Leg., ch. 1421, Sec. 2, eff. June 1, 2003. Amended by Acts 2003, 78th Leg., ch. 1276, Sec. 14A.155(a), eff. Sept. 1, 2003.) (Amended by: Acts 2007, 80th Leg., R.S., Ch. 1411, Sec. 1, eff. September 1, 2007.)

SUBCHAPTER B.
TEXAS REAL ESTATE COMMISSION

Sec. 1101.051. COMMISSION MEMBER-SHIP. (a) The Texas Real Estate Commission consists of nine members appointed by the governor with the advice and consent of the senate as follows:

(1) six members who have been engaged in the brokerage business as licensed brokers as their major occupation for the five years preceding appointment; and

(2) three members who represent the public.

(b) Each member of the commission must be a qualified voter.

(c) Appointments to the commission shall be made without regard to the race, color, disability, sex, religion, age, or national origin of the appointee.

(Added by Acts 2001, 77th Leg., ch. 1421, Sec. 2, eff. June 1, 2003.)

Sec. 1101.052. PUBLIC MEMBER ELIGI-BILITY.   A person is not eligible for appointment as a public member of the commission if the person or the person's spouse:

(1) is registered, certified, or licensed by an occupational regulatory agency in the real estate industry;

(2) is employed by or participates in the management of a business entity or other organization regulated by the commission or receiving funds from the commission;

(3) owns or controls, directly or indirectly, more than a 10 percent interest in a business entity or other organization regulated by the commission or receiving funds from the commission; or

(4) uses or receives a substantial amount of tangible goods, services, or funds from the commission, other than compensation or reimbursement authorized by law for commission membership, attendance, or expenses.

(Added by Acts 2001, 77th Leg., ch. 1421, Sec. 2, eff. June 1, 2003.)

Sec. 1101.053.   MEMBERSHIP AND EMPLOYEE RESTRICTIONS. (a) In this section, "Texas trade association" means a cooperative and voluntarily joined statewide association of business or professional competitors in this state designed to assist its members and its industry or profession in dealing with mutual business or professional problems and in promoting their common interest.

(b) A person may not be a member of the commission and may not be a commission

employee employed in a "bona fide executive, administrative, or professional capacity," as that phrase is used for purposes of establishing an exemption to the overtime provisions of the federal Fair Labor Standards Act of 1938 (29 U.S.C. Section 201 et seq.) if:

(1) the person is an officer, employee, or paid consultant of a Texas trade association in the real estate industry; or

(2) the person's spouse is an officer, manager, or paid consultant of a Texas trade association in the real estate industry.

(c) A person may not serve as a commission member or act as the general counsel to the commission if the person is required to register as a lobbyist under Chapter 305, Government Code, because of the person's activities for compensation on behalf of a profession related to the operation of the commission.

(Added by Acts 2001, 77th Leg., ch. 1421, Sec. 2, eff. June 1, 2003.) (Amended by: Acts 2007, 80th Leg., R.S., Ch. 1411, Sec. 3, eff. September 1, 2007.)

Sec. 1101.054. OFFICIAL OATH. Not later than the 15th day after the date of appointment, each appointee must take the constitutional oath of office.

(Added by Acts 2001, 77th Leg., ch. 1421, Sec. 2, eff. June 1, 2003. Amended by Acts 2003, 78th Leg., ch. 285, Sec. 27, eff. Sept. 1, 2003.)

Sec. 1101.055. TERMS; VACANCY. (a) Commission members serve staggered six-year terms, with the terms of three members expiring January 31 of each odd-numbered year.

(b) If a vacancy occurs during a member's term, the governor shall appoint a person to fill the unexpired term.

(Added by Acts 2001, 77th Leg., ch. 1421, Sec. 2, eff. June 1, 2003.)

Sec. 1101.056. OFFICERS. (a) The governor shall designate a commission member who is a licensed broker as presiding officer.   The presiding officer serves in that capacity at the pleasure of the governor.

(b) At a regular meeting in February of each year, the commission shall elect an assistant presiding officer and secretary from its membership.

(Added by Acts 2001, 77th Leg., ch. 1421, Sec. 2, eff. June 1, 2003.)

Sec. 1101.057-.101(c)

Sec. 1101.057. GROUNDS FOR REMOVAL. (a) It is a ground for removal from the commission that a member:

(1) does not have at the time of appointment the qualifications required by Section 1101.051(a) or (b) or 1101.052;

(2) does not maintain during service on the commission the qualifications required by Section 1101.051(a) or (b) or 1101.052;

(3) is ineligible for membership under Section 1101.053;

(4) cannot discharge the member's duties for a substantial part of the member's term; or

(5) is absent from more than half of the regularly scheduled commission meetings that the member is eligible to attend during each calendar year, unless the absence is excused by majority vote of the commission.

(b) The validity of an action of the commission is not affected by the fact that it is taken when a ground for removal of a commission member exists.

(c) If the administrator has knowledge that a potential ground for removal exists, the administrator shall notify the presiding officer of the commission of the potential ground. The presiding officer shall then notify the governor and the attorney general that a potential ground for removal exists. If the potential ground for removal involves the presiding officer, the administrator shall notify the next highest ranking officer of the commission, who shall then notify the governor and the attorney general that a potential ground for removal exists.

(Added by Acts 2001, 77th Leg., ch. 1421, Sec. 2, eff. June 1, 2003.) (Amended by: Acts 2007, 80th Leg., R.S., Ch. 297, Sec. 2, eff. September 1, 2007. Acts 2007, 80th Leg., R.S., Ch. 1411, Sec. 4, eff. September 1, 2007.)

Sec. 1101.058. PER DIEM; REIMBURSEMENT. A commission member is entitled to receive:

(1) $75 for each day the member performs the member's official duties; and

(2) reimbursement for actual and necessary expenses incurred in performing the member's official duties.

(Added by Acts 2001, 77th Leg., ch. 1421, Sec. 2, eff. June 1, 2003.)

Sec. 1101.059. TRAINING. (a) A person who is appointed to and qualifies for office as a member of the commission may not vote, deliberate, or be counted as a member in attendance at a meeting of the commission until the person completes a training program that complies with this section.

(b) The training program must provide the person with information regarding:

(1) this chapter and other laws regulated by the commission;

(2) the programs, functions, rules, and budget of the commission;

(3) the results of the most recent formal audit of the commission;

(4) the requirements of laws relating to open meetings, public information, administrative procedure, and conflicts of interest; and

(5) any applicable ethics policies adopted by the commission or the Texas Ethics Commission.

(c) A person appointed to the commission is entitled to reimbursement for the travel expenses incurred in attending the training program regardless of whether the attendance at the program occurs before or after the person qualifies for office.

(Added by Acts 2007, 80th Leg., R.S., Ch. 1411, Sec. 5, eff. September 1, 2007.) (Amended by: Acts 2011, 82nd Leg., R.S., Ch. 1333, Sec. 2, eff. September 1, 2011.)

SUBCHAPTER C. ADMINISTRATOR AND OTHER COMMISSION PERSONNEL

Sec. 1101.101. ADMINISTRATOR AND OTHER PERSONNEL. (a) The commission shall appoint an administrator.

(b) The commission may designate a subordinate officer as assistant administrator to act for the administrator in the administrator's absence.

(c) The commission may employ other subordinate officers and employees necessary to administer and enforce this chapter and Chapter 1102, including a general counsel, attorneys, investigators, and support staff.

(d) The commission shall determine the salaries of the administrator, officers, and employees of the commission.

(Added by Acts 2001, 77th Leg., ch. 1421, Sec. 2, eff. June 1, 2003.) (Amended by: Acts 2007, 80th Leg., R.S., Ch. 1411, Sec. 6, eff. September 1, 2007. Acts 2011, 82nd Leg., R.S., Ch. 1333, Sec. 3, eff. September 1, 2011.)

Sec. 1101.102. DIVISION OF RESPONSIBILITIES.

The commission shall develop and implement policies that clearly separate the policymaking responsibilities of the commission and the management responsibilities of the administrator and the staff of the commission.

(Added by Acts 2001, 77th Leg., ch. 1421, Sec. 2, eff. June 1, 2003.) (Amended by: Acts 2007, 80th Leg., R.S., Ch. 1411, Sec. 7, eff. September 1, 2007.)

Sec. 1101.103. CODE OF ETHICS; STANDARDS OF CONDUCT.

Each member, officer, employee, and agent of the commission is subject to the code of ethics and standards of conduct imposed by Chapter 572, Government Code.

(Added by Acts 2001, 77th Leg., ch. 1421, Sec. 2, eff. June 1, 2003.)

Sec. 1101.104. QUALIFICATIONS AND STANDARDS OF CONDUCT INFORMATION.

The commission shall provide, as often as necessary, to its members and employees information regarding their:

(1) qualifications for office or employment under this chapter and Chapter 1102; and

(2) responsibilities under applicable laws relating to standards of conduct for state officers or employees.

(Added by Acts 2001, 77th Leg., ch. 1421, Sec. 2, eff. June 1, 2003.)

Sec. 1101.105. CAREER LADDER PROGRAM; PERFORMANCE EVALUATIONS.

(a) The administrator or the administrator's designee shall develop an intra-agency career ladder program. The program must require intra-agency postings of all nonentry level positions concurrently with any public posting.

(b) The administrator or the administrator's designee shall develop a system of annual performance evaluations. All merit pay for commission employees must be based on the system established under this subsection.

(Added by Acts 2001, 77th Leg., ch. 1421, Sec. 2, eff. June 1, 2003.)

Sec. 1101.106. EQUAL EMPLOYMENT OPPORTUNITY POLICY; REPORT.

(a) The administrator or the administrator's designee shall prepare and maintain a written policy statement to ensure implementation of an equal employment opportunity program under which all personnel transactions are made without regard to race, color, disability, sex, religion, age, or national origin. The policy statement must include:

(1) personnel policies, including policies relating to recruitment, evaluation, selection, appointment, training, and promotion of personnel;

(2) a comprehensive analysis of the commission workforce that meets federal and state guidelines;

(3) procedures by which a determination can be made of significant underuse in the commission workforce of all persons for whom federal or state guidelines encourage a more equitable balance; and

(4) reasonable methods to appropriately address those areas of underuse.

(b) A policy statement prepared under Subsection (a) must:

(1) cover an annual period;

(2) be updated at least annually; and

(3) be filed with the governor.

(c) The governor shall deliver a biennial report to the legislature based on the information received under Subsection (b). The report may be made separately or as a part of other biennial reports made to the legislature.

(Added by Acts 2001, 77th Leg., ch. 1421, Sec. 2, eff. June 1, 2003.)

Sec. 1101.151-.152

SUBCHAPTER D. COMMISSION POWERS AND DUTIES

Sec. 1101.151. GENERAL POWERS AND DUTIES OF COMMISSION. (a) The commission shall:

(1) administer this chapter and Chapter 1102;

(2) adopt rules and establish standards relating to permissible forms of advertising by a license holder acting as a residential rental locator;

(3) maintain a registry of certificate holders; and

(4) design and adopt a seal.

(b) The commission may:

(1) adopt and enforce rules necessary to administer this chapter and Chapter 1102; and

(2) establish standards of conduct and ethics for persons licensed under this chapter and Chapter 1102 to:

(A) fulfill the purposes of this chapter and Chapter 1102; and

(B) ensure compliance with this chapter and Chapter 1102.

(Added by Acts 2001, 77th Leg., ch. 1421, Sec. 2, eff. June 1, 2003.) (Amended by: Acts 2007, 80th Leg., R.S., Ch. 1411, Sec. 8, eff. September 1, 2007.)

Sec. 1101.152. FEES. (a) The commission shall adopt rules to charge and collect fees in amounts reasonable and necessary to cover the costs of administering this chapter, including a fee for:

(1) filing an original application for a broker license;

(2) annual renewal of a broker license;

(3) filing an original application for a salesperson license;

(4) annual renewal of a salesperson license;

(5) annual registration;

(6) filing an application for a license examination;

(7) filing a request for a branch office license;

(8) filing a request for a change of place of business, change of name, return to active status, or change of sponsoring broker;

(9) filing a request to replace a lost or destroyed license or certificate of registration;

(10) filing an application for approval of an education program under Subchapter G;

(11) annual operation of an education program under Subchapter G;

(12) filing an application for approval of an instructor of core real estate courses;

(13) transcript evaluation;

(14) preparing a license or registration history;

(15) filing an application for a moral character determination; and

(16) conducting a criminal history check for issuing or renewing a license.

(b) The commission shall adopt rules to set and collect fees in amounts reasonable and necessary to cover the costs of implementing the continuing education requirements for license holders, including a fee for:

(1) an application for approval of a continuing education provider;

(2) an application for approval of a continuing education course of study;

(3) an application for approval of an instructor of continuing education courses; and

(4) attendance at a program to train instructors of a continuing education course prescribed under Section 1101.455.

(c) Notwithstanding Subsection (a), if the commission issues an original inactive salesperson license under Section 1101.363(b) to a salesperson who is not sponsored by a licensed broker and the salesperson is subsequently sponsored by a licensed broker, the commission may not charge:

(1) the salesperson a fee for filing a request to place the salesperson license on active status; or

(2) the broker a fee for filing a request to sponsor the salesperson.

(Added by Acts 2001, 77th Leg., ch. 1421, Sec. 2, eff. June 1, 2003. Amended by Acts 2003, 78th Leg., ch. 15, Sec. 1, 2, eff. Sept. 1, 2003.) (Amended by: Acts 2005, 79th Leg., Ch. 825, Sec. 1, eff. September 1, 2005. Acts 2007, 80th Leg., R.S., Ch. 297, Sec. 3, eff. September 1, 2007. Acts 2007, 80th Leg., R.S., Ch. 1411,

Sec. 9, eff. September 1, 2007. Acts 2009, 81st Leg., R.S., Ch. 23, Sec. 1, eff. May 12, 2009. Acts 2009, 81st Leg., R.S., Ch. 23, Sec. 2, eff. May 12, 2009.)

Sec. 1101.153. FEE INCREASE. (a) The fee for filing an original application for an individual broker license and the fee for annual renewal of an individual broker license is the amount of the fee set by the commission under Section 1101.152 and a fee increase of $200.

(b) Of each fee increase collected under Subsection (a):

(1) $50 shall be transmitted to Texas A&M University for deposit in a separate banking account that may be appropriated only to support, maintain, and carry out the purposes, objectives, and duties of the Texas Real Estate Research Center;

(2) $50 shall be deposited to the credit of the foundation school fund; and

(3) $100 shall be deposited to the credit of the general revenue fund.

(Added by Acts 2001, 77th Leg., ch. 1421, Sec. 2, eff. June 1, 2003.) (Amended by: Acts 2009, 81st Leg., R.S., Ch. 23, Sec. 3, eff. September 1, 2011.)

Sec. 1101.154. ADDITIONAL FEE: TEXAS REAL ESTATE RESEARCH CENTER. (a) The fee for the issuance or renewal of a:

(1) broker license is the amount of the fee set under Sections 1101.152 and 1101.153 and an additional $20 fee;

(2) salesperson license is the amount of the fee set under Section 1101.152 and an additional $20 fee; and

(3) certificate of registration is the amount of the fee set under Section 1101.152 and an additional $20 fee.

(b) The commission shall transmit quarterly the additional fees collected under Subsection (a) to Texas A&M University for deposit in a separate banking account that may be appropriated only to support, maintain, and carry out the purposes, objectives, and duties of the Texas Real Estate Research Center.

(Added by Acts 2001, 77th Leg., ch. 1421, Sec. 2,

eff. June 1, 2003.) (Amended by: Acts 2009, 81st Leg., R.S., Ch. 23, Sec. 4, eff. May 12, 2009.)

Sec. 1101.155. RULES RELATING TO CONTRACT FORMS. (a) The commission may adopt rules in the public's best interest that require license holders to use contract forms prepared by the Texas Real Estate Broker-Lawyer Committee and adopted by the commission.

(b) The commission may not prohibit a license holder from using for the sale, exchange, option, or lease of an interest in real property a contract form that is:

(1) prepared by the property owner; or

(2) prepared by an attorney and required by the property owner.

(c) A listing contract form adopted by the commission that relates to the contractual obligations between a seller of real estate and a license holder acting as an agent for the seller must include:

(1) a provision informing the parties to the contract that real estate commissions are negotiable; and

(2) a provision explaining the availability of Texas coastal natural hazards information important to coastal residents, if that information is appropriate.

(Added by Acts 2001, 77th Leg., ch. 1421, Sec. 2, eff. June 1, 2003.)

Sec. 1101.156. RULES RESTRICTING ADVERTISING OR COMPETITIVE BIDDING. (a) The commission may not adopt a rule restricting advertising or competitive bidding by a person regulated by the commission except to prohibit a false, misleading, or deceptive practice by the person.

(b) The commission may not include in rules to prohibit false, misleading, or deceptive practices by a person regulated by the commission a rule that:

(1) restricts the use of any advertising medium;

(2) restricts the person's personal appearance or use of the person's voice in an advertisement;

Sec. 1101.156(b)(3)-.160

(3) relates to the size or duration of an advertisement used by the person; or

(4) restricts the person's advertisement under a trade name.

(Added by Acts 2001, 77th Leg., ch. 1421, Sec. 2, eff. June 1, 2003.)

Sec. 1101.157. SUBPOENA AUTHORITY. (a) The commission may request and, if necessary, compel by subpoena:

(1) the attendance of witnesses for examination under oath; and

(2) the production for inspection and copying of records, documents, and other evidence relevant to the investigation of an alleged violation of this chapter.

(b) A subpoena may be issued throughout the state and may be served by any person designated by the commission.

(c) If a person fails to comply with a subpoena issued under this section, the commission, acting through the attorney general, may file suit to enforce the subpoena in a district court in Travis County or in the county in which a hearing conducted by the commission may be held.

(d) The court shall order compliance with the subpoena if the court finds that good cause exists to issue the subpoena.

(Added by Acts 2001, 77th Leg., ch. 1421, Sec. 2, eff. June 1, 2003.)

Sec. 1101.158. ADVISORY COMMITTEES. (a) The commission may appoint advisory committees to perform the advisory functions assigned to the committees by the commission. An advisory committee under this section is subject to Section 2110, Government Code.

(b) A member of an advisory committee who is not a member of the commission may not receive compensation for service on the committee. The member may receive reimbursement for actual and necessary expenses incurred in performing committee functions as provided by Section 2110.004, Government Code.

(c) A member of an advisory committee serves at the will of the commission.

(d) An advisory committee may hold a meeting by telephone conference call or other video or broadcast technology.

(e) Advisory committee meetings are subject to Chapter 551, Government Code.

(Added by Acts 2007, 80th Leg., R.S., Ch. 1411, Sec. 10, eff. September 1, 2007.)

Sec. 1101.159. USE OF TECHNOLOGY. The commission shall implement a policy requiring the commission to use appropriate technological solutions to improve the commission's ability to perform its functions. The policy must ensure that the public is able to interact with the commission on the Internet.

(Added by Acts 2007, 80th Leg., R.S., Ch. 1411, Sec. 10, eff. September 1, 2007.)

Sec. 1101.160. NEGOTIATED RULE-MAKING AND ALTERNATIVE DISPUTE RESOLUTION PROCEDURES. (a) The commission shall develop and implement a policy to encourage the use of:

(1) negotiated rulemaking procedures under Chapter 2008, Government Code, for the adoption of commission rules; and

(2) appropriate alternative dispute resolution procedures under Chapter 2009, Government Code, to assist in the resolution of internal and external disputes under the commission's jurisdiction.

(b) The commission's procedures relating to alternative dispute resolution must conform, to the extent possible, to any model guidelines issued by the State Office of Administrative Hearings for the use of alternative dispute resolution by state agencies.

(c) The commission shall designate a trained person to:

(1) coordinate the implementation of the policy adopted under Subsection (a);

(2) serve as a resource for any training needed to implement the procedures for negotiated rulemaking or alternative dispute resolution; and

(3) collect data concerning the effectiveness of those procedures, as implemented by the commission.

(Added by Acts 2007, 80th Leg., R.S., Ch. 1411, Sec. 10, eff. September 1, 2007.)

Sec. 1101.161.   GIFTS, GRANTS, AND DONATIONS. The commission may solicit and accept a gift, grant, donation, or other item of value from any source to pay for any activity under this chapter or Chapter 1102 or 1103.

(Added by Acts 2011, 82nd Leg., R.S., Ch. 1064, Sec. 3, eff. September 1, 2011.)

SUBCHAPTER E.
PUBLIC INTEREST INFORMATION AND COMPLAINT PROCEDURES

Sec. 1101.201.   PUBLIC INTEREST IN-FORMATION.   (a)   The commission shall prepare information of public interest describing the functions of the commission.

(b) The commission shall make the information available to the public and appropriate state agencies.

(Added by Acts 2001, 77th Leg., ch. 1421, Sec. 2, eff. June 1, 2003.) (Amended by: Acts 2007, 80th Leg., R.S., Ch. 1411, Sec. 11, eff. September 1, 2007.)

Sec. 1101.202.   COMPLAINTS.   (a)   The commission by rule shall establish methods by which consumers and service recipients are notified of the name, mailing address, and telephone number of the commission for the purpose of directing a complaint to the commission.   The commission may provide for that notice:

(1) on each application for a license or certificate of registration or written contract for services of a person regulated under this chapter or Chapter 1102;

(2) on a sign prominently displayed in the place of business of each person regulated under this chapter or Chapter 1102;

(3) in a bill for services provided by a person regulated under this chapter or Chapter 1102;

(4) in conjunction with the notice required by Section 1101.615; or

(5) to be prominently displayed on the Internet website of a person regulated under this chapter or Chapter 1102.

(b) The commission shall provide to a person who files a complaint with the commission relating to a license holder and to the license holder against whom the complaint is filed:

(1) an explanation of the remedies that are available to the person under this chapter; and

(2) information about appropriate state or local agencies or officials with whom the person may file a complaint.

(Added by Acts 2001, 77th Leg., ch. 1421, Sec. 2, eff. June 1, 2003; Amended by Acts 2003, 78th Leg., ch. 15, Sec. 3, eff. Sept. 1, 2003.)

Sec. 1101.203.   COMPLAINT INFOR-MATION.   (a)   The commission shall maintain a system to promptly and efficiently act on complaints filed with the commission.   The commission shall maintain a file on each complaint.   The file must include:

(1) information relating to the parties to the complaint;

(2) the subject matter of the complaint;

(3) a summary of the results of the review or investigation of the complaint; and

(4) the disposition of the complaint.

(b) The commission shall make information available describing its procedures for complaint investigation and resolution.

(c) The commission shall periodically notify the parties to the complaint of the status of the complaint until final disposition, unless the notice would jeopardize an undercover investigation authorized under Section 1101.204.

(Added by Acts 2001, 77th Leg., ch. 1421, Sec. 2, eff. June 1, 2003.) (Amended by: Acts 2007, 80th Leg., R.S., Ch. 1411, Sec. 12, eff. September 1, 2007.)

Sec. 1101.204.   COMPLAINT INVESTI-GATION AND DISPOSITION.   (a)   The commission or commission staff may file a complaint and conduct an investigation as necessary to enforce this chapter, Chapter 1102, or a rule adopted under those chapters.

(b) The commission shall investigate the actions and records of a license holder if:

(1) a person submits a signed, written complaint; and

Sec. 1101.204(b)(2)-.252(a)(3)

(2) the complaint and any evidence presented with the complaint provide reasonable cause for an investigation.

(c) The commission may not conduct an investigation of a person licensed under this chapter or Chapter 1102 in connection with a complaint submitted later than the fourth anniversary of the date of the incident that is the subject of the complaint.

(d) The commission shall promptly provide a written notice to a person licensed under this chapter or Chapter 1102 who is the subject of an investigation unless after deliberation the commission decides against notification.

(e) Notwithstanding any other provision of this chapter, an undercover or covert investigation may not be conducted unless the commission expressly authorizes the investigation after considering the circumstances and determining that the investigation is necessary to implement this chapter.

(f) An investigation or other action against a person licensed under this chapter or Chapter 1102 may not be initiated on the basis of an anonymous complaint.

(g) Repealed by Acts 2007, 80th Leg., R.S., Ch. 1411, Sec. 59(1), eff. September 1, 2007.

(h) The commission shall ensure that the commission gives priority to the investigation of a complaint filed by a consumer and an enforcement case resulting from the consumer complaint. The commission shall assign priorities and investigate complaints using a risk-based approach based on the:

(1) degree of potential harm to a consumer;

(2) potential for immediate harm to a consumer;

(3) overall severity of the allegations in the complaint;

(4) number of license holders potentially involved in the complaint;

(5) previous complaint history of the license holder; and

(6) number of potential violations in the complaint.

(Added by Acts 2001, 77th Leg., ch. 1421, Sec. 2, eff. June 1, 2003. Amended by Acts 2003, 78th Leg., ch. 1276, Sec. 14A.154(b), 14A.157(a), eff. Sept. 1, 2003.) (Amended by: Acts 2005, 79th Leg., Ch. 825, Sec. 2, eff. September 1, 2005.

Acts 2007, 80th Leg., R.S., Ch. 1411, Sec. 13, eff. September 1, 2007. Acts 2007, 80th Leg., R.S., Ch. 1411, Sec. 59(1), eff. September 1, 2007.)

Sec. 1101.205. COMPLAINT INVESTIGATION OF CERTIFICATE HOLDER. The commission shall investigate a signed complaint received by the commission that relates to an act of a certificate holder or a person required to hold a certificate under Subchapter K.

(Added by Acts 2001, 77th Leg., ch. 1421, Sec. 2, eff. June 1, 2003.)

Sec. 1101.206. PUBLIC PARTICIPATION. (a) The commission shall develop and implement policies that provide the public with a reasonable opportunity to appear before the commission and to speak on any issue under the commission's jurisdiction.

(b) The commission shall prepare and maintain a written plan that describes how a person who does not speak English or who has a physical, mental, or developmental disability may be provided reasonable access to the commission's programs.

(Added by Acts 2001, 77th Leg., ch. 1421, Sec. 2, eff. June 1, 2003.)

SUBCHAPTER F. TEXAS REAL ESTATE BROKER-LAWYER COMMITTEE

Sec. 1101.251. DEFINITION OF COMMITTEE. In this subchapter, "committee" means the Texas Real Estate Broker-Lawyer Committee.

(Added by Acts 2001, 77th Leg., ch. 1421, Sec. 2, eff. June 1, 2003.)

Sec. 1101.252. COMMITTEE MEMBERSHIP. (a) The Texas Real Estate Broker-Lawyer Committee consists of 13 members appointed as follows:

(1) six members appointed by the commission;

(2) six members of the State Bar of Texas appointed by the president of the state bar; and

(3) one public member appointed by the

governor.

(b) Appointments to the committee shall be made without regard to the race, creed, sex, religion, or national origin of the appointee.

(Added by Acts 2001, 77th Leg., ch. 1421, Sec. 2, eff. June 1, 2003. Amended by Acts 2003, 78th Leg., ch. 1170, Sec. 38.01, eff. Sept. 1, 2003.)

Sec. 1101.253. TERMS; VACANCIES. (a) Committee members serve staggered six-year terms, with the terms of two commission appointees and two State Bar of Texas appointees expiring every two years and the term of the public member expiring every six years.

(b) A committee member shall hold office until the member's successor is appointed.

(c) If a vacancy occurs during a member's term, the entity making the original appointment shall appoint a person to fill the unexpired term.

(Added by Acts 2001, 77th Leg., ch. 1421, Sec. 2, eff. June 1, 2003. Amended by Acts 2003, 78th Leg., ch. 1170, Sec. 38.02, eff. Sept. 1, 2003.)

Sec. 1101.254. POWERS AND DUTIES. (a) In addition to other delegated powers and duties, the committee shall draft and revise contract forms that are capable of being standardized to expedite real estate transactions and minimize controversy.

(b) The contract forms must contain safeguards adequate to protect the principals in the transaction.

(Added by Acts 2001, 77th Leg., ch. 1421, Sec. 2, eff. June 1, 2003.)

SUBCHAPTER G. ACCREDITATION AND APPROVAL OF REAL ESTATE EDUCATIONAL PROGRAMS AND COURSES OF STUDY

Sec. 1101.301. ACCREDITATION OF PROGRAMS AND COURSES OF STUDY. (a) The commission, as necessary for the administration of this chapter and Chapter 1102, may:

(1) establish standards for the accreditation of educational programs or courses of study in real estate and real estate inspection conducted in this state, excluding programs and courses offered by accredited colleges and universities;

(2) establish by rule reasonable criteria for the approval of real estate and real estate inspection courses; and

(3) inspect and accredit real estate and real estate inspection educational programs or courses of study.

(b) The commission shall determine whether a real estate or real estate inspection course satisfies the requirements of this chapter and Chapter 1102.

(c) In establishing accreditation standards for an educational program under Subsection (a), the commission shall adopt rules setting an examination passage rate benchmark for each category of license issued by the commission under this chapter or Chapter 1102. The benchmark must be based on the average percentage of examinees that pass the licensing exam on the first attempt. A program must meet or exceed the benchmark for each license category before the commission may renew the program's accreditation for the license category.

(d) The commission may deny an application for accreditation if the applicant owns or controls, or has previously owned or controlled, an educational program or course of study for which accreditation was revoked.

(Added by Acts 2001, 77th Leg., ch. 1421, Sec. 2, eff. June 1, 2003.) (Amended by: Acts 2007, 80th Leg., R.S., Ch. 1411, Sec. 14, eff. September 1, 2007. Acts 2011, 82nd Leg., R.S., Ch. 1064, Sec. 4, eff. September 1, 2011.)

Sec. 1101.302. BOND REQUIRED. (a) In this section, "educational institution" means a school, excluding an accredited college or university, authorized by the commission under this chapter to offer a real estate or real estate inspection educational program or course of study.

(b) An educational institution shall maintain a corporate surety bond or other security acceptable to the commission that is:

(1) in the amount of $20,000;

(2) payable to the commission; and

(3) for the benefit of a party who suffers damages caused by the failure of the institution to fulfill obligations related to the commission's approval.

(Added by Acts 2001, 77th Leg., ch. 1421, Sec. 2, eff. June 1, 2003.) (Amended by: Acts 2007, 80th Leg., R.S., Ch. 297, Sec. 4, eff. September 1, 2007.)

Sec. 1101.303-.351

Sec. 1101.303. APPROVAL OF CONTINU-ING EDUCATION PROVIDER OR COURSE OF STUDY.

(a) If the commission determines that an applicant for approval as a continuing education provider satisfies the requirements of this subchapter or Section 1102.205 and any rule adopted under this subchapter or Section 1102.205, the commission may authorize the applicant to offer continuing education for a two-year period.

(b) If the commission determines that an applicant for approval of a continuing education course of study satisfies the requirements of this subchapter or Section 1102.205 and any rule adopted under this subchapter or Section 1102.205, the commission may authorize the applicant to offer the course of study for a two-year period.

(Added by Acts 2001, 77th Leg., ch. 1421, Sec. 2, eff. June 1, 2003.) (Amended by: Acts 2007, 80th Leg., R.S., Ch. 1411, Sec. 15, eff. September 1, 2007.)

Sec. 1101.304. EXAMINATION PASSAGE RATE DATA.

(a) The commission shall adopt rules regarding the collection and publication of data relating to examination passage rates for graduates of accredited educational programs.

(b) Rules adopted under this section must provide for a method to:

(1) calculate the examination passage rate;

(2) collect the relevant data from the examination administrator or the accredited program; and

(3) post the examination passage rate data on the commission's Internet website, in a manner aggregated by educational program and by license group.

(c) In determining the educational program a graduate is affiliated with for purposes of this section, the educational program is the program the graduate last attended.

(Added by Acts 2007, 80th Leg., R.S., Ch. 1411, Sec. 16, eff. September 1, 2007.)

Sec. 1101.305. REVIEW COMMITTEE.

(a) The commission may appoint a committee to review the performance of an educational program performing below the standards set by the commission under Section 1101.301. The committee shall consist of:

(1) at least one commission member;

(2) at least one member of the commission staff;

(3) individuals licensed under this chapter or Chapter 1102; and

(4) a representative from the Texas Real Estate Research Center.

(b) A committee formed under this section shall review and evaluate any factor causing an educational program's poor performance and report findings and recommendations to improve performance to the program and to the commission.

(c) A committee formed under this section may not revoke the accreditation of an educational program. The commission may temporarily suspend a program in the same manner as a license under Subchapter N.

(Added by Acts 2007, 80th Leg., R.S., Ch. 1411, Sec. 16, eff. September 1, 2007.)

SUBCHAPTER H.
LICENSE REQUIREMENTS

Sec. 1101.351. LICENSE REQUIRED.

(a) Unless a person holds a license issued under this chapter, the person may not:

(1) act as or represent that the person is a broker or salesperson; or

(2) act as a residential rental locator.

(a-1) Unless a business entity holds a license issued under this chapter, the business entity may not act as a broker.

(b) An applicant for a broker or salesperson license may not act as a broker or salesperson until the person receives the license evidencing that authority.

(c) A licensed salesperson may not act or attempt to act as a broker or salesperson unless the salesperson is associated with a licensed broker and is acting for that broker.

(Added by Acts 2001, 77th Leg., ch. 1421, Sec. 2, eff. June 1, 2003.) (Amended by: Acts 2011, 82nd Leg., R.S., Ch. 1064, Sec. 5, eff. September 1, 2011.)

Sec. 1101.352. LICENSE APPLICATION.

(a) Each applicant for a broker or salesperson license must submit an application on a form prescribed by the commission.

(b) Each applicant for a broker or salesperson license must disclose in the license application whether the applicant has:

(1) entered a plea of guilty or nolo contendere to a felony; or

(2) been convicted of a felony and the time for appeal has elapsed or the judgment or conviction has been affirmed on appeal.

(c) The disclosure under Subsection (b) must be provided even if an order has granted community supervision suspending the imposition of the sentence.

(d) At the time an application is submitted under Subsection (a), each applicant shall provide the commission with the applicant's current mailing address and telephone number, and e-mail address if available. The applicant shall notify the commission of any change in the applicant's mailing or e-mail address or telephone number during the time the application is pending.

(Added by Acts 2001, 77th Leg., ch. 1421, Sec. 2, eff. June 1, 2003; Amended by Acts 2003, 78th Leg., ch. 15, Sec. 4, eff. Sept. 1, 2003; Acts 2003, 78th Leg., ch. 1276, Sec. 14A.158(a), eff. Sept. 1, 2003.) (Amended by: Acts 2011, 82nd Leg., R.S., Ch. 1064, Sec. 6, eff. September 1, 2011.)

Sec. 1101.3521. CRIMINAL HISTORY RECORD INFORMATION REQUIREMENT FOR LICENSE.

(a) The commission shall require that an applicant for a license or renewal of an unexpired license submit a complete and legible set of fingerprints, on a form prescribed by the commission, to the commission or to the Department of Public Safety for the purpose of obtaining criminal history record information from the Department of Public Safety and the Federal Bureau of Investigation.

(b) The commission shall refuse to issue a license to or renew the license of a person who does not comply with the requirement of Subsection (a).

(c) The commission shall conduct a criminal history check of each applicant for a license or renewal of a license using information:

(1) provided by the individual under this section; and

(2) made available to the commission by the Department of Public Safety, the Federal Bureau of Investigation, and any other criminal justice agency under Chapter 411, Government Code.

(d) The commission may:

(1) enter into an agreement with the Department of Public Safety to administer a criminal history check required under this section; and

(2) authorize the Department of Public Safety to collect from each applicant the costs incurred by the department in conducting the criminal history check.

(Added by Acts 2007, 80th Leg., R.S., Ch. 297, Sec. 5, eff. September 1, 2007.)

Sec. 1101.353. MORAL CHARACTER DETERMINATION.

(a) If before applying for a license under this chapter a person requests that the commission determine whether the person's moral character complies with the commission's moral character requirements for licensing under this chapter and pays the fee prescribed by Section 1101.152, the commission shall make its determination of the person's moral character.

(b) Not later than the 30th day after the date the commission makes its determination, the commission shall notify the person of the determination.

(c) If a person applies for a license after receiving notice of a determination, the commission may conduct a supplemental moral character determination of the person. The supplemental determination may cover only the period after the date the person requests a moral character determination under this section.

(d) The commission may issue a provisional moral character determination. The commission by rule shall adopt reasonable terms for issuing a provisional moral character determination.

(Added by Acts 2001, 77th Leg., ch. 1421, Sec. 2, eff. June 1, 2003.) (Amended by: Acts 2005, 79th Leg., Ch. 825, Sec. 3, eff. September 1, 2005.)

Sec. 1101.354-.357(1)(B)

Sec. 1101.354. GENERAL ELIGIBILITY REQUIREMENTS.
To be eligible to receive a license under this chapter, a person must:

(1) at the time of application:

(A) be at least 18 years of age;

(B) be a citizen of the United States or a lawfully admitted alien; and

(C) be a resident of this state;

(2) satisfy the commission as to the applicant's honesty, trustworthiness, and integrity;

(3) demonstrate competence based on an examination under Subchapter I;

(4) complete the required courses of study, including any required core real estate courses prescribed under this chapter; and

(5) complete at least:

(A) three classroom hours of course work on federal, state, and local laws governing housing discrimination, housing credit discrimination, and community reinvestment; or

(B) three semester hours of course work on constitutional law.

(Added by Acts 2001, 77th Leg., ch. 1421, Sec. 2, eff. June 1, 2003.)

Sec. 1101.355. ADDITIONAL GENERAL ELIGIBILITY REQUIREMENTS FOR BUSINESS ENTITIES.
(a) To be eligible for a license under this chapter, a business entity must:

(1) designate one of its managing officers as its agent for purposes of this chapter; and

(2) provide proof that the entity maintains errors and omissions insurance with a minimum annual limit of $1 million for each occurrence if the designated agent owns less than 10 percent of the business entity.

(b) A business entity may not act as a broker unless the entity's designated agent is a licensed broker in active status and good standing according to the commission's records.

(c) A business entity that receives compensation on behalf of a license holder must be licensed as a broker under this chapter.

(Added by Acts 2001, 77th Leg., ch. 1421, Sec. 2, eff. June 1, 2003.) (Amended by: Acts 2011, 82nd Leg., R.S., Ch. 1064, Sec. 7, eff. September 1, 2011.)

Sec. 1101.356. BROKER LICENSE: EXPERIENCE AND EDUCATION REQUIREMENTS.
(a) An applicant for a broker license must provide to the commission satisfactory evidence that the applicant:

(1) has had at least four years of active experience in this state as a license holder during the 60 months preceding the date the application is filed; and

(2) has successfully completed at least 60 semester hours, or equivalent classroom hours, of postsecondary education, including:

(A) at least 18 semester hours or equivalent classroom hours of core real estate courses, two semester hours of which must be real estate brokerage; and

(B) at least 42 hours of core real estate courses or related courses accepted by the commission.

(b) Subsection (a) does not apply to an applicant who, at the time of application, is licensed as a real estate broker by another state that has license requirements comparable to the requirements of this state.

(b-1) The commission by rule shall establish what constitutes active experience for purposes of this section and Section 1101.357.

(c) Repealed by Acts 2011, 82nd Leg., R.S., Ch. 1064, Sec. 24, eff. September 1, 2011.

(Added by Acts 2001, 77th Leg., ch. 1421, Sec. 2, eff. June 1, 2003. Amended by Acts 2003, 78th Leg., ch. 1276, Sec. 14A.152(b), eff. Sept. 1, 2003.) (Amended by: Acts 2007, 80th Leg., R.S., Ch. 297, Sec. 6, eff. September 1, 2007. Acts 2011, 82nd Leg., R.S., Ch. 1064, Sec. 8, eff. September 1, 2011. Acts 2011, 82nd Leg., R.S., Ch. 1064, Sec. 24, eff. September 1, 2011.)

Sec. 1101.357. BROKER LICENSE: ALTERNATE EXPERIENCE REQUIREMENTS FOR CERTAIN APPLICANTS.
An applicant for a broker license who does not satisfy the experience requirements of Section 1101.356 must provide to the commission satisfactory evidence that:

(1) the applicant:

(A) is a licensed real estate broker in another state;

(B) has had at least four years of active experience in that state as a licensed real estate broker or salesperson during the 60 months preceding the date the application is filed; and

(C) has satisfied the educational requirements prescribed by Section 1101.356; or

(2) the applicant was licensed in this state as a broker in the year preceding the date the application is filed.

(Added by Acts 2001, 77th Leg., ch. 1421, Sec. 2, eff. June 1, 2003.) (Amended by: Acts 2011, 82nd Leg., R.S., Ch. 1064, Sec. 9, eff. September 1, 2011.)

Sec. 1101.358. SALESPERSON LICENSE: EDUCATION REQUIREMENTS.

(a) An applicant for a salesperson license must provide to the commission satisfactory evidence that the applicant has completed at least 12 semester hours, or equivalent classroom hours, of postsecondary education consisting of:

(1) at least four semester hours of core real estate courses on principles of real estate; and

(2) at least two semester hours of each of the following core real estate courses:

(A) agency law;

(B) contract law;

(C) contract forms and addendums; and

(D) real estate finance.

(b) The commission shall waive the education requirements of Subsection (a) if the applicant has been licensed in this state as a broker or salesperson within the six months preceding the date the application is filed.

(c) If an applicant for a salesperson license was licensed as a salesperson within the six months preceding the date the application is filed and the license was issued under the conditions prescribed by Section 1101.454, the commission shall require the applicant to provide the evidence of successful completion of education requirements that would have been required if the license had been maintained without interruption during the preceding six months.

(Added by Acts 2001, 77th Leg., ch. 1421, Sec. 2, eff. June 1, 2003. Amended by Acts 2003, 78th Leg., ch. 1276, Sec. 14A.152(c), eff. Sept. 1, 2003.) (Amended by: Acts 2005, 79th Leg., Ch. 825, Sec. 4, eff. September 1, 2005. Acts 2011, 82nd Leg., R.S., Ch. 1064, Sec. 10, eff. September 1, 2011.)

Sec. 1101.359. ALTERNATE EDUCATION REQUIREMENTS FOR CERTAIN LICENSE HOLDERS.

An applicant for a broker license who is not subject to the education requirements of Section 1101.356(a)(2) and an applicant for a salesperson license who is not subject to the education requirements of Section 1101.358 or 1101.454 must provide to the commission satisfactory evidence that the applicant has completed the number of classroom hours of continuing education that would have been required for a timely renewal under Section 1101.455 during the two years preceding the date the application is filed.

(Added by Acts 2001, 77th Leg., ch. 1421, Sec. 2, eff. June 1, 2003.)

Sec. 1101.360. ELIGIBILITY REQUIREMENTS FOR CERTAIN NONRESIDENT APPLICANTS.

(a) A resident of another state who is not a licensed real estate broker and who was formerly licensed in this state as a broker or salesperson may apply for a license under this chapter not later than the first anniversary of the date of the expiration of the former license.

(b) A nonresident applicant is subject to the same license requirements as a resident. The commission may refuse to issue a license to a nonresident applicant for the same reasons that it may refuse to issue a license to a resident applicant.

(c) A nonresident applicant must submit with the application an irrevocable consent to a legal action against the applicant in the court of any county in this state in which a cause of action may arise or in which the plaintiff may reside. The action may be commenced by service of process or pleading authorized by the laws of this state or by delivery of process on the administrator or assistant administrator of the commission. The consent must:

(1) stipulate that the service of process or pleading is valid and binding in all courts as if personal service had been made on the nonresident in this state;

(2) be acknowledged; and

(3) if made by a corporation, be authenticated by its seal.

Sec. 1101.360(d)-.365(a)

(d) A service of process or pleading served on the commission under this section shall be by duplicate copies. One copy shall be filed in the commission's office, and the other copy shall be forwarded by registered mail to the last known principal address recorded in the commission's records for the nonresident against whom the process or pleading is directed.

(e) A default judgment in an action commenced as provided by this section may not be granted:

(1) unless the commission certifies that a copy of the process or pleading was mailed to the defendant as provided by Subsection (d); and

(2) until the 21st day after the date the process or pleading is mailed to the defendant.

(Added by Acts 2001, 77th Leg., ch. 1421, Sec. 2, eff. June 1, 2003.)

Sec. 1101.361. ADDITIONAL ELIGIBILITY REQUIREMENTS FOR CERTAIN NONRESIDENT APPLICANTS. (a) Notwithstanding Section 1101.360, a nonresident applicant for a license who resides in a municipality whose boundary is contiguous at any point with the boundary of a municipality in this state is eligible to be licensed under this chapter in the same manner as a resident of this state if the nonresident has been a resident of that municipality for at least the 60 days preceding the date the application is filed.

(b) A person licensed under this section shall maintain at all times a place of business in the municipality in which the person resides or in the municipality in this state that is contiguous to the municipality in which the person resides. The place of business must meet all the requirements of Section 1101.552. A place of business located in the municipality in which the person resides is considered to be in this state.

(c) A person licensed under this section may not maintain a place of business at another location in this state unless the person complies with Section 1101.356 or 1101.357.

(Added by Acts 2001, 77th Leg., ch. 1421, Sec. 2, eff. June 1, 2003.)

Sec. 1101.362. WAIVER OF LICENSE REQUIREMENTS: PREVIOUS LICENSE HOLDERS. The commission by rule may waive some or all of the requirements for a license under this chapter for an applicant who

was licensed under this chapter within the six years preceding the date the application is filed.

(Added by Acts 2001, 77th Leg., ch. 1421, Sec. 2, eff. June 1, 2003.)

Sec. 1101.363. ISSUANCE OF LICENSE. (a) The commission shall issue an appropriate license to an applicant who meets the requirements for a license.

(b) The commission may issue an inactive salesperson license to a person who applies for a salesperson license and satisfies all requirements for the license. The person may not act as a salesperson unless the person is sponsored by a licensed broker who has notified the commission as required by Section 1101.367(b). Notwithstanding Section 1101.367(b), the licensed broker is not required to pay the fee required by that subsection.

(c) A license remains in effect for the period prescribed by the commission if the license holder complies with this chapter and pays the appropriate renewal fees.

(Added by Acts 2001, 77th Leg., ch. 1421, Sec. 2, eff. June 1, 2003. Amended by Acts 2003, 78th Leg., ch. 15, Sec. 5, eff. Sept. 1, 2003; Acts 2003, 78th Leg., ch. 1276, Sec. 14A.158(b), eff. Sept. 1, 2003.)

Sec. 1101.364. DENIAL OF LICENSE. (a) The commission shall immediately give written notice to the applicant of the commission's denial of a license.

(b) A person whose license application is denied under this section is entitled to a hearing under Section 1101.657.

(c) Repealed by Acts 2007, 80th Leg., R.S., Ch. 1411, Sec. 59(2), eff. September 1, 2007.

(d) Repealed by Acts 2007, 80th Leg., R.S., Ch. 1411, Sec. 59(2), eff. September 1, 2007.

(e) Repealed by Acts 2007, 80th Leg., R.S., Ch. 1411, Sec. 59(2), eff. September 1, 2007.

(Added by Acts 2001, 77th Leg., ch. 1421, Sec. 2, eff. June 1, 2003.) (Amended by: Acts 2007, 80th Leg., R.S., Ch. 1411, Sec. 17, eff. September 1, 2007. Acts 2007, 80th Leg., R.S., Ch. 1411, Sec. 59(2), eff. September 1, 2007.)

Sec. 1101.365. PROBATIONARY LICENSE. (a) The commission may issue a probationary license.

(b) The commission by rule shall adopt reasonable terms for issuing a probationary license.

(Added by Acts 2001, 77th Leg., ch. 1421, Sec. 2, eff. June 1, 2003.)

Sec. 1101.366.   INACTIVE LICENSE: BROKER. (a) The commission may place on inactive status the license of a broker if the broker:

(1) is not acting as a broker;

(2) is not sponsoring a salesperson; and

(3) submits a written application to the commission before the expiration date of the broker's license.

(b) The commission may place on inactive status the license of a broker whose license has expired if the broker applies for inactive status on a form prescribed by the commission not later than the first anniversary of the expiration date of the broker's license.

(c) A broker applying for inactive status shall terminate the broker's association with each salesperson sponsored by the broker by giving written notice to each salesperson before the 30th day preceding the date the broker applies for inactive status.

(d) A broker on inactive status:

(1) may not perform any activity regulated under this chapter; and

(2) must pay annual renewal fees.

(e) The commission shall maintain a list of each broker whose license is on inactive status.

(f) The commission shall remove a broker's license from inactive status if the broker:

(1) submits an application to the commission;

(2) pays the required fee; and

(3) submits proof of attending at least 15 classroom hours of continuing education as specified by Section 1101.455 during the two years preceding the date the application under Subdivision (1) is filed.

(Added by Acts 2001, 77th Leg., ch. 1421, Sec. 2, eff. June 1, 2003.)

Sec. 1101.367.   INACTIVE LICENSE: SALESPERSON. (a) When the association of a salesperson with the salesperson's sponsoring broker terminates, the broker shall immediately return the salesperson license to the commission. A salesperson license returned under this subsection is inactive.

(b) The commission may remove a salesperson license from inactive status under Subsection (a) if, before the expiration date of the salesperson license, a licensed broker files a request with the commission advising the commission that the broker assumes sponsorship of the salesperson, accompanied by the appropriate fee.

(c) As a condition of returning to active status, an inactive salesperson whose license is not subject to the education requirements of Section 1101.454 must provide to the commission proof of attending at least 15 hours of continuing education as specified by Section 1101.455 during the two years preceding the date the application to return to active status is filed.

(Added by Acts 2001, 77th Leg., ch. 1421, Sec. 2, eff. June 1, 2003. Amended by Acts 2003, 78th Leg., ch. 15, Sec. 6, eff. Sept. 1, 2003; Acts 2003, 78th Leg., ch. 1276, Sec. 14A.158(c), eff. Sept. 1, 2003.) (Amended by: Acts 2011, 82nd Leg., R.S., Ch. 1064, Sec. 11, eff. September 1, 2011.)

SUBCHAPTER I. EXAMINATIONS

Sec. 1101.401.   EXAMINATION RE-QUIRED. (a) The competency requirement prescribed under Section 1101.354(3) shall be established by an examination prepared or contracted for by the commission.

(b) The commission shall determine the time and place in the state for offering the examination.

(c) The examination must be of sufficient scope in the judgment of the commission to determine whether a person is competent to act as a broker or salesperson in a manner that will protect the public.

(d) The examination for a salesperson license must be less exacting and less stringent than the broker examination.

Sec. 1101.401(e)-.451(a)

(e) The commission shall provide each applicant with study material and references on which the examination is based.

(f) An applicant must satisfy the examination requirement not later than one year after the date the license application is filed.

(Added by Acts 2001, 77th Leg., ch. 1421, Sec. 2, eff. June 1, 2003.) (Amended by: Acts 2011, 82nd Leg., R.S., Ch. 1064, Sec. 12, eff. September 1, 2011.)

Sec. 1101.402. WAIVER OF EXAMINATION. The commission shall waive the examination requirement for an applicant for:

(1) a broker license if:

(A) the applicant was previously licensed in this state as a broker; and

(B) the application is filed before the first anniversary of the expiration date of that license; and

(2) a salesperson license if:

(A) the applicant was previously licensed in this state as a broker or salesperson; and

(B) the application is filed before the first anniversary of the expiration date of that license.

(Added by Acts 2001, 77th Leg., ch. 1421, Sec. 2, eff. June 1, 2003.)

Sec. 1101.403. ADMINISTRATION OF EXAMINATION; TESTING SERVICE. (a) The commission shall administer any examination required by this chapter or Chapter 1102 unless the commission enters into an agreement with a testing service to administer the examination.

(b) The commission may accept an examination administered by a testing service if the commission retains the authority to establish the scope and type of the examination.

(c) The commission may negotiate an agreement with a testing service relating to examination development, scheduling, site arrangements, administration, grading, reporting, and analysis.

(d) The commission may require a testing service to:

(1) correspond directly with license applicants regarding the administration of the examination;

(2) collect fees directly from applicants for administering the examination; or

(3) administer the examination at specific locations and specified frequencies.

(e) The commission shall adopt rules and standards as necessary to implement this section.

(Added by Acts 2001, 77th Leg., ch. 1421, Sec. 2, eff. June 1, 2003.)

Sec. 1101.404. EXAMINATION RESULTS. (a) Not later than the 30th day after the date an examination is administered, the commission shall notify each examinee of the results of the examination. If an examination is graded or reviewed by a national testing service, the commission shall notify each examinee of the results of the examination not later than the 14th day after the date the commission receives the results from the testing service.

(b) If the notice of the results of an examination graded or reviewed by a national testing service will be delayed for more than 90 days after the examination date, the commission shall notify each examinee of the reason for the delay before the 90th day.

(c) If requested in writing by a person who fails an examination, the commission shall provide to the person an analysis of the person's performance on the examination.

(Added by Acts 2001, 77th Leg., ch. 1421, Sec. 2, eff. June 1, 2003.)

Sec. 1101.405. REEXAMINATION. An applicant who fails an examination may apply for reexamination by filing a request accompanied by the proper fee.

(Added by Acts 2001, 77th Leg., ch. 1421, Sec. 2, eff. June 1, 2003.)

SUBCHAPTER J. LICENSE RENEWAL

Sec. 1101.451. LICENSE EXPIRATION AND RENEWAL. (a) The commission may issue or renew a license for a period not to exceed 24 months.

(b) The commission by rule may adopt a system under which licenses expire on various dates during the year. The commission shall adjust the date for payment of the renewal fees accordingly.

(c) For a year in which the license expiration date is changed, renewal fees payable shall be prorated on a monthly basis so that each license holder pays only that portion of the fee that is allocable to the number of months during which the license is valid. On renewal of the license on the new expiration date, the total renewal fee is payable.

(d) Except as provided by Subsection (e), a renewal fee for a license under this chapter may not exceed, calculated on an annual basis, the amount of the sum of the fees established under Sections 1101.152, 1101.154, and 1101.603.

(e) A person whose license has been expired for 90 days or less may renew the license by paying to the commission a fee equal to 1-1/2 times the required renewal fee. If a license has been expired for more than 90 days but less than six months, the person may renew the license by paying to the commission a fee equal to two times the required renewal fee.

(f) If a person's license has been expired for six months or longer, the person may not renew the license. The person may obtain a new license by submitting to reexamination and complying with the requirements and procedures for obtaining an original license.

(Added by Acts 2001, 77th Leg., ch. 1421, Sec. 2, eff. June 1, 2003.) (Amended by: Acts 2007, 80th Leg., R.S., Ch. 1411, Sec. 18, eff. September 1, 2007. Acts 2007, 80th Leg., R.S., Ch. 1411, Sec. 19, eff. September 1, 2007. Acts 2011, 82nd Leg., R.S., Ch. 1064, Sec. 13, eff. September 1, 2011.)

Sec. 1101.452. INFORMATION REQUIRED FOR LICENSE RENEWAL.

(a) To renew an active license that is not subject to the education requirements of Section 1101.454, the license holder must provide to the commission proof of compliance with the continuing education requirements of Section 1101.455.

(b) Each applicant for the renewal of a license must disclose in the license application whether the applicant has:

(1) entered a plea of guilty or nolo contendere

to a felony; or

(2) been convicted of a felony and the time for appeal has elapsed or the judgment or conviction has been affirmed on appeal.

(c) The disclosure under Subsection (b) must be provided even if an order has granted community supervision suspending the imposition of the sentence.

(Added by Acts 2001, 77th Leg., ch. 1421, Sec. 2, eff. June 1, 2003.) (Amended by: Acts 2011, 82nd Leg., R.S., Ch. 1064, Sec. 14, eff. September 1, 2011.)

Sec. 1101.4521. CRIMINAL HISTORY RECORD INFORMATION FOR RENEWAL.

An applicant for the renewal of an unexpired license must comply with the criminal history record check requirements of Section 1101.3521.

(Added by Acts 2007, 80th Leg., R.S., Ch. 297, Sec. 7, eff. September 1, 2007.)

Sec. 1101.453. ADDITIONAL RENEWAL REQUIREMENTS FOR BUSINESS ENTITIES.

(a) To renew a license under this chapter, a business entity must:

(1) designate one of its managing officers as its agent for purposes of this chapter; and

(2) provide proof that the entity maintains errors and omissions insurance with a minimum annual limit of $1 million for each occurrence if the designated agent owns less than 10 percent of the business entity.

(b) A business entity may not act as a broker unless the entity's designated agent is a licensed broker in active status and good standing according to the commission's records.

(Added by Acts 2001, 77th Leg., ch. 1421, Sec. 2, eff. June 1, 2003.) (Amended by: Acts 2011, 82nd Leg., R.S., Ch. 1064, Sec. 15, eff. September 1, 2011.)

Sec. 1101.454. SALESPERSON LICENSE RENEWAL.

(a) An applicant applying for the first renewal of a salesperson license must provide to the commission satisfactory evidence of completion of at least 18 semester hours, or equivalent classroom hours, of core real estate courses.

Sec. 1101.455)-.455(k)

(b) Repealed by Acts 2005, 79th Leg., Ch. 825, Sec. 15, eff. September 1, 2005.

(c) Repealed by Acts 2005, 79th Leg., Ch. 825, Sec. 15, eff. September 1, 2005.

(d) The commission may not waive the requirements for renewal under this section.

(Added by Acts 2001, 77th Leg., ch. 1421, Sec. 2, eff. June 1, 2003. Amended by Acts 2003, 78th Leg., ch. 1276, Sec. 14A.152(d), eff. Sept. 1, 2003.) (Amended by: Acts 2005, 79th Leg., Ch. 825, Sec. 5, eff. September 1, 2005. Acts 2005, 79th Leg., Ch. 825, Sec. 15, eff. September 1, 2005. Acts 2011, 82nd Leg., R.S., Ch. 1064, Sec. 16, eff. September 1, 2011.)

Sec. 1101.455. CONTINUING EDUCA-TION REQUIREMENTS. (a) In this section, "property tax consulting laws and legal issues" includes the Tax Code, preparation of property tax reports, the unauthorized practice of law, agency law, tax law, law relating to property tax or property assessment, deceptive trade practices, contract forms and addendums, and other legal topics approved by the commission.

(b) A license holder who is not subject to the education requirements of Section 1101.454 must attend during the term of the current license at least 15 classroom hours of continuing education courses approved by the commission.

(c) The commission by rule may:

(1) prescribe the title, content, and duration of continuing education courses that a license holder must attend to renew a license; and

(2) approve as a substitute for the classroom attendance required by Subsection (b):

(A) relevant educational experience; and

(B) correspondence courses.

(d) In addition, the commission may approve supervised video instruction as a course that may be applied toward satisfaction of the classroom hours of continuing education courses required by Subsection (b).

(e) At least six of the continuing education hours required by Subsection (b) must cover the following legal topics:

(1) commission rules;

(2) fair housing laws;

(3) Property Code issues, including landlord-tenant law;

(4) agency law;

(5) antitrust laws;

(6) Subchapter E, Chapter 17, Business & Commerce Code;

(7) disclosures to buyers, landlords, tenants, and sellers;

(8) current contract and addendum forms;

(9) unauthorized practice of law;

(10) case studies involving violations of laws and regulations;

(11) current Federal Housing Administration and Department of Veterans Affairs regulations;

(12) tax laws;

(13) property tax consulting laws and legal issues; or

(14) other legal topics approved by the commission.

(f) The remaining nine hours may be devoted to other real estate-related topics approved by the commission.

(g) The commission may consider courses equivalent to those described by Subsections (e) and (f) for continuing education credit.

(h) The commission shall automatically approve the following courses as courses that satisfy the mandatory continuing education requirements of Subsection (f):

(1) core real estate courses; and

(2) real estate-related courses approved by the State Bar of Texas for minimum continuing legal education participatory credit.

(i) The commission may not require an examination for a course under this section unless the course is a correspondence course or a course offered by an alternative delivery system, including delivery by computer.

(j) Daily classroom course segments must be at least one hour and not more than 10 hours.

(k) Notwithstanding the number of hours required by Subsection (e), a member of the legislature licensed under this chapter is only required to complete three hours of continuing education on the legal topics under Subsection (e).

(l) An online course offered under this section may not be completed in less than 24 hours.

(Added by Acts 2001, 77th Leg., ch. 1421, Sec. 2, eff. June 1, 2003. Amended by Acts 2003, 78th Leg., ch. 1276, Sec. 14A.159(a), eff. Sept. 1, 2003.) (Amended by: Acts 2005, 79th Leg., Ch. 825, Sec. 6, eff. September 1, 2005. Acts 2007, 80th Leg., R.S., Ch. 297, Sec. 8, eff. September 1, 2007. Acts 2007, 80th Leg., R.S., Ch. 1411, Sec. 20, eff. September 1, 2007. Acts 2009, 81st Leg., R.S., Ch. 87, Sec. 27.001(72), eff. September 1, 2009. Acts 2011, 82nd Leg., R.S., Ch. 1064, Sec. 17, eff. September 1, 2011.)

Sec. 1101.456. EXEMPTION FROM CONTINUING EDUCATION REQUIREMENTS FOR CERTAIN BROKERS.

Notwithstanding any other provision of this chapter, a broker who, before October 31, 1991, qualified under former Section 7A(f), The Real Estate License Act (Article 6573a, Vernon's Texas Civil Statutes), as added by Section 1.041, Chapter 553, Acts of the 72nd Legislature, Regular Session, 1991, for an exemption from continuing education requirements is not required to comply with the mandatory continuing education requirements of this subchapter to renew the broker's license.

(Added by Acts 2001, 77th Leg., ch. 1421, Sec. 2, eff. June 1, 2003.)

Sec. 1101.457. DEFERRAL OF CONTINUING EDUCATION REQUIREMENTS.

(a) The commission by rule may establish procedures under which an applicant may have the applicant's license issued, renewed, or returned to active status before the applicant completes continuing education requirements.

(b) The commission may require an applicant under this section to:

(1) pay a fee, not to exceed $200, in addition to any fee for late renewal of a license under this chapter; and

(2) complete the required continuing education not later than the 60th day after the date the license is issued, renewed, or returned to active status.

(Added by Acts 2001, 77th Leg., ch. 1421, Sec. 2, eff. June 1, 2003.) (Amended by: Acts 2007, 80th Leg., R.S., Ch. 1411, Sec. 21, eff. September 1, 2007.)

Sec. 1101.458. ADDITIONAL EDUCATION REQUIREMENTS FOR CERTAIN LICENSE HOLDERS.

(a) A broker who sponsors a salesperson, or a license holder who supervises another license holder, must attend during the term of the current license at least six classroom hours of broker responsibility education courses approved by the commission.

(b) The commission by rule shall prescribe the title, content, and duration of broker responsibility education courses required under this section.

(c) Broker responsibility education course hours may be used to satisfy the hours described by Section 1101.455(f).

(d) This section does not apply to a broker who is exempt from continuing education requirements under Section 1101.456.

(Added by Acts 2011, 82nd Leg., R.S., Ch. 1064, Sec. 18, eff. September 1, 2011.)

SUBCHAPTER K. CERTIFICATE REQUIREMENTS

Sec. 1101.501. CERTIFICATE REQUIRED.

A person may not sell, buy, lease, or transfer an easement or right-of-way for another, for compensation or with the expectation of receiving compensation, for use in connection with telecommunication, utility, railroad, or pipeline service unless the person:

(1) holds a license issued under this chapter; or

(2) holds a certificate of registration issued under this subchapter.

(Added by Acts 2001, 77th Leg., ch. 1421, Sec. 2, eff. June 1, 2003.)

Sec. 1101.502. ELIGIBILITY REQUIREMENTS FOR CERTIFICATE.

(a) To be eligible to receive a certificate of registration or a renewal certificate under this subchapter, a person must be:

(1) at least 18 years of age; and

(2) a citizen of the United States or a lawfully admitted alien.

Sec. 1101.502(b)-.552(b)

(b) To be eligible to receive a certificate of registration or a renewal certificate under this subchapter, a business entity must designate as its agent one of its managing officers who is registered under this subchapter.

(Added by Acts 2001, 77th Leg., ch. 1421, Sec. 2, eff. June 1, 2003.) (Amended by: Acts 2011, 82nd Leg., R.S., Ch. 1064, Sec. 19, eff. September 1, 2011.)

Sec. 1101.503. ISSUANCE OF CERTIFICATE.
(a) The commission shall issue a certificate of registration to an applicant who meets the requirements for a certificate of registration.

(b) The certificate remains in effect for the period prescribed by the commission if the certificate holder complies with this chapter and pays the appropriate renewal fees.

(Added by Acts 2001, 77th Leg., ch. 1421, Sec. 2, eff. June 1, 2003.)

Sec. 1101.504. CERTIFICATE EXPIRATION.
The duration, expiration, and renewal of a certificate of registration are subject to the same provisions as are applicable under Section 1101.451 to the duration, expiration, and renewal of a license.

(Added by Acts 2001, 77th Leg., ch. 1421, Sec. 2, eff. June 1, 2003.)

Sec. 1101.5041. CRIMINAL HISTORY RECORD INFORMATION REQUIREMENT FOR CERTIFICATE.
An applicant for an original certificate of registration or renewal of a certificate of registration must comply with the criminal history record check requirements of Section 1101.3521.

(Added by Acts 2011, 82nd Leg., R.S., Ch. 676, Sec. 1, eff. September 1, 2011; Ch. 1064, Sec. 20, eff. September 1, 2011.)

Sec. 1101.505. DENIAL OF CERTIFICATE.
The denial of a certificate of registration is subject to the same provisions as are applicable under Section 1101.364 to the denial of a license.

(Added by Acts 2001, 77th Leg., ch. 1421, Sec. 2, eff. June 1, 2003.)

Sec. 1101.506. CHANGE OF ADDRESS.

Not later than the 10th day after the date a certificate holder moves its place of business from a previously designated address, the holder shall:

(1) notify the commission of the move; and

(2) obtain a new certificate of registration that reflects the address of the new place of business.

(Added by Acts 2001, 77th Leg., ch. 1421, Sec. 2, eff. June 1, 2003.)

Sec. 1101.507. DISPLAY OF CERTIFICATE.
A certificate holder shall prominently display at all times the holder's certificate of registration in the holder's place of business.

(Added by Acts 2001, 77th Leg., ch. 1421, Sec. 2, eff. June 1, 2003.)

SUBCHAPTER L. PRACTICE BY LICENSE HOLDER

Sec. 1101.551. DEFINITIONS.
In this subchapter:

(1) Intermediary" means a broker who is employed to negotiate a transaction between the parties to a transaction and for that purpose may act as an agent of the parties.

(2) Party" means a prospective buyer, seller, landlord, or tenant or an authorized representative of a buyer, seller, landlord, or tenant, including a trustee, guardian, executor, administrator, receiver, or attorney-in-fact. The term does not include a license holder who represents a party.

(Added by Acts 2001, 77th Leg., ch. 1421, Sec. 2, eff. June 1, 2003.)

Sec. 1101.552. FIXED OFFICE REQUIRED; CHANGE OF ADDRESS; BRANCH OFFICES.
(a) A resident broker shall maintain a fixed office in this state. The address of the office shall be designated on the broker's license.

(b) Not later than the 10th day after the date a broker moves from the address designated on the broker's license, the broker shall submit an application, accompanied by the appropriate fee, for a license that designates the new location of the broker's office. The commission shall issue a license that designates the new location if the new location complies with the requirements of this section.

(c) A broker who maintains more than one place of business in this state shall obtain a branch office license for each additional office maintained by the broker by submitting an application, accompanied by the appropriate fee.

(d) A nonresident licensed broker is not required to maintain a place of business in this state.

(e) A license holder shall provide the commission with the license holder's current mailing address and telephone number, and e-mail address if available. A license holder shall notify the commission of a change in the license holder's mailing or e-mail address or telephone number.

(Added by Acts 2001, 77th Leg., ch. 1421, Sec. 2, eff. June 1, 2003. Amended by: Acts 2011, 82nd Leg., R.S., Ch. 1064, Sec. 21, eff. September 1, 2011.)

Sec. 1101.553. DISPLAY OF LICENSE. (a) *Repealed by Acts 2003, 78th Leg., ch. 15, Sec. 14, eff. Sept. 1, 2003.*

(b) *Repealed by Acts 2003, 78th Leg., ch. 15, Sec. 14, eff. Sept. 1, 2003.*

(c) A residential rental locator shall prominently display in a place accessible to clients and prospective clients:

(1) the locator's license;

(2) a statement that the locator is licensed by the commission; and

(3) the name, mailing address, and telephone number of the commission as provided by Section 1101.202(a).

(Added by Acts 2001, 77th Leg., ch. 1421, Sec. 2, eff. June 1, 2003. Amended by Acts 2003, 78th Leg., ch. 15, Sec. 14, eff. Sept. 1, 2003.)

Sec. 1101.554. COPY OF SALESPERSON LICENSE. The commission shall deliver or mail a copy of each salesperson license to the broker with whom the salesperson is associated.

(Added by Acts 2001, 77th Leg., ch. 1421, Sec. 2, eff. June 1, 2003. Amended by: Acts 2011, 82nd Leg., R.S., Ch. 1064, Sec. 22, eff. September 1, 2011.)

Sec. 1101.555. NOTICE TO BUYER REGARDING ABSTRACT OR TITLE POLICY. When an offer to purchase real estate in this state is signed, a license holder shall advise each buyer, in writing, that the buyer should:

(1) have the abstract covering the real estate that is the subject of the contract examined by an attorney chosen by the buyer; or

(2) be provided with or obtain a title insurance policy.

(Added by Acts 2001, 77th Leg., ch. 1421, Sec. 2, eff. June 1, 2003.)

Sec. 1101.556. DISCLOSURE OF CERTAIN INFORMATION RELATING TO OCCUPANTS. Notwithstanding other law, a license holder is not required to inquire about, disclose, or release information relating to whether:

(1) a previous or current occupant of real property had, may have had, has, or may have AIDS, an HIV-related illness, or an HIV infection as defined by the Centers for Disease Control and Prevention of the United States Public Health Service; or

(2) a death occurred on a property by natural causes, suicide, or accident unrelated to the condition of the property.

(Added by Acts 2001, 77th Leg., ch. 1421, Sec. 2, eff. June 1, 2003.)

Sec. 1101.557. ACTING AS AGENT; REGULATION OF CERTAIN TRANSACTIONS. (a) A broker who represents a party in a real estate transaction or who lists real estate for sale under an exclusive agreement for a party is that party's agent.

(b) A broker described by Subsection (a):

(1) may not instruct another broker to directly or indirectly violate Section 1101.652(b)(22);

(2) must inform the party if the broker receives material information related to a transaction to list, buy, sell, or lease the party's real estate, including the receipt of an offer by the broker; and

(3) shall, at a minimum, answer the party's questions and present any offer to or from the party.

Sec. 1101.557(c)-.558(d)

(c) For the purposes of this section:

(1) a license holder who has the authority to bind a party to a lease or sale under a power of attorney or a property management agreement is also a party to the lease or sale;

(2) an inquiry to a person described by Section 1101.005(6) about contract terms or forms required by the person's employer does not violate Section 1101.652(b)(22) if the person does not have the authority to bind the employer to the contract; and

(3) the sole delivery of an offer to a party does not violate Section 1101.652(b)(22) if:

(A) the party's broker consents to the delivery;

(B) a copy of the offer is sent to the party's broker, unless a governmental agency using a sealed bid process does not allow a copy to be sent; and

(C) the person delivering the offer does not engage in another activity that directly or indirectly violates Section 1101.652(b)(22).

(Added by Acts 2001, 77th Leg., ch. 1421, Sec. 2, eff. June 1, 2003. Amended by: Acts 2005, 79th Leg., Ch. 825, Sec. 7, eff. September 1, 2005.)

Sec. 1101.558. REPRESENTATION DISCLOSURE. (a) In this section, "substantive dialogue" means a meeting or written communication that involves a substantive discussion relating to specific real property. The term does not include:

(1) a meeting that occurs at a property that is held open for any prospective buyer or tenant; or

(2) a meeting or written communication that occurs after the parties to a real estate transaction have signed a contract to sell, buy, or lease the real property concerned.

(b) A license holder who represents a party in a proposed real estate transaction shall disclose, orally or in writing, that representation at the time of the license holder's first contact with:

(1) another party to the transaction; or

(2) another license holder who represents another party to the transaction.

(c) A license holder shall provide to a party to a real estate transaction at the time of the first substantive dialogue with the party the written statement prescribed by Subsection (d) unless:

(1) the proposed transaction is for a residential lease for not more than one year and a sale is not being considered; or

(2) the license holder meets with a party who is represented by another license holder.

(d) The written statement required by Subsection (c) must be printed in a format that uses at least 10-point type and read as follows:

"Before working with a real estate broker, you should know that the duties of a broker depend on whom the broker represents. If you are a prospective seller or landlord (owner) or a prospective buyer or tenant (buyer), you should know that the broker who lists the property for sale or lease is the owner's agent. A broker who acts as a subagent represents the owner in cooperation with the listing broker. A broker who acts as a buyer's agent represents the buyer. A broker may act as an intermediary between the parties if the parties consent in writing. A broker can assist you in locating a property, preparing a contract or lease, or obtaining financing without representing you. A broker is obligated by law to treat you honestly.

"IF THE BROKER REPRESENTS THE OWNER: The broker becomes the owner's agent by entering into an agreement with the owner, usually through a written listing agreement, or by agreeing to act as a subagent by accepting an offer of subagency from the listing broker. A subagent may work in a different real estate office. A listing broker or subagent can assist the buyer but does not represent the buyer and must place the interests of the owner first. The buyer should not tell the owner's agent anything the buyer would not want the owner to know because an owner's agent must disclose to the owner any material information known to the agent.

"IF THE BROKER REPRESENTS THE BUYER: The broker becomes the buyer's agent by entering into an agreement to represent the buyer, usually through a written buyer representation agreement. A buyer's agent can assist the owner but does not represent the owner and must place the interests of the buyer first. The owner should not tell a buyer's agent anything the owner would not want the buyer to know because a buyer's agent must disclose to the buyer any material information known to the agent.

"IF THE BROKER ACTS AS AN INTERMEDIARY: A broker may act as an intermediary between the parties if the broker complies with The Texas Real Estate License Act. The broker must obtain the written consent of each party to the transaction to act as an intermediary. The written consent must state who will pay the broker and, in conspicuous bold or underlined print, set forth the broker's obligations as an intermediary. The broker is required to treat each party honestly and fairly and to comply with The Texas Real Estate License Act. A broker who acts as an intermediary in a transaction: (1) shall treat all parties honestly; (2) may not disclose that the owner will accept a price less than the asking price unless authorized in writing to do so by the owner; (3) may not disclose that the buyer will pay a price greater than the price submitted in a written offer unless authorized in writing to do so by the buyer; and (4) may not disclose any confidential information or any information that a party specifically instructs the broker in writing not to disclose unless authorized in writing to disclose the information or required to do so by The Texas Real Estate License Act or a court order or if the information materially relates to the condition of the property. With the parties' consent, a broker acting as an intermediary between the parties may appoint a person who is licensed under The Texas Real Estate License Act and associated with the broker to communicate with and carry out instructions of one party and another person who is licensed under that Act and associated with the broker to communicate with and carry out instructions of the other party.

"If you choose to have a broker represent you, you should enter into a written agreement with the broker that clearly establishes the broker's obligations and your obligations. The agreement should state how and by whom the broker will be paid. You have the right to choose the type of representation, if any, you wish to receive. Your payment of a fee to a broker does not necessarily establish that the broker represents you. If you have any questions regarding the duties and responsibilities of the broker, you should resolve those questions before proceeding."

(e) The license holder may substitute "buyer" for "tenant" and "seller" for "landlord" as appropriate in the written statement prescribed by Subsection (d).

(Added by Acts 2001, 77th Leg., ch. 1421, Sec. 2, eff. June 1, 2003. Amended by Acts 2003, 78th Leg., ch. 15, Sec. 7, eff. Sept. 1, 2003.)

Sec. 1101.559. BROKER ACTING AS INTERMEDIARY. (a) A broker may act as an intermediary between parties to a real estate transaction if:

(1) the broker obtains written consent from each party for the broker to act as an intermediary in the transaction; and

(2) the written consent of the parties states the source of any expected compensation to the broker.

(b) A written listing agreement to represent a seller or landlord or a written agreement to represent a buyer or tenant that authorizes a broker to act as an intermediary in a real estate transaction is sufficient to establish written consent of the party to the transaction if the written agreement specifies in conspicuous bold or underlined print the conduct that is prohibited under Section 1101.651(d).

(c) An intermediary shall act fairly and impartially. Appointment by a broker acting as an intermediary of an associated license holder under Section 1101.560 to communicate with, carry out the instructions of, and provide opinions and advice to the parties to whom that associated license holder is appointed is a fair and impartial act.

(Added by Acts 2001, 77th Leg., ch. 1421, Sec. 2, eff. June 1, 2003.)

Sec. 1101.560. ASSOCIATED LICENSE HOLDER ACTING AS INTERMEDIARY. (a) A broker who complies with the written consent requirements of Section 1101.559 may appoint:

(1) a license holder associated with the broker to communicate with and carry out instructions of one party to a real estate transaction; and

(2) another license holder associated with the broker to communicate with and carry out instructions of any other party to the transaction.

(b) A license holder may be appointed under this section only if:

(1) the written consent of the parties under Section 1101.559 authorizes the broker to make

Sec. 1101.560(b)(1)-.603

the appointment; and

(2) the broker provides written notice of the appointment to all parties involved in the real estate transaction.

(c) A license holder appointed under this section may provide opinions and advice during negotiations to the party to whom the license holder is appointed.

(Added by Acts 2001, 77th Leg., ch. 1421, Sec. 2, eff. June 1, 2003.)

Sec. 1101.561. DUTIES OF INTERMEDIARY PREVAIL.

(a) The duties of a license holder acting as an intermediary under this subchapter supersede the duties of a license holder established under any other law, including common law.

(b) A broker must agree to act as an intermediary under this subchapter if the broker agrees to represent in a transaction:

(1) a buyer or tenant; and

(2) a seller or landlord.

(Added by Acts 2001, 77th Leg., ch. 1421, Sec. 2, eff. June 1, 2003. Amended by: Acts 2005, 79th Leg., Ch. 825, Sec. 8, eff. September 1, 2005.)

SUBCHAPTER M. REAL ESTATE RECOVERY TRUST ACCOUNT

Sec. 1101.601. REAL ESTATE RECOVERY TRUST ACCOUNT.

(a) The commission shall maintain a real estate recovery trust account to reimburse aggrieved persons who suffer actual damages caused by an act described by Section 1101.602 committed by:

(1) a license holder;

(2) a certificate holder; or

(3) a person who does not hold a license or certificate and who is an employee or agent of a license or certificate holder.

(b) The license or certificate holder must have held the license or certificate at the time the act was committed.

(Added by Acts 2001, 77th Leg., ch. 1421, Sec. 2, eff. June 1, 2003.)

Sec. 1101.602. ENTITLEMENT TO REIMBURSEMENT.

An aggrieved person is entitled to reimbursement from the trust account if a person described by Section 1101.601 engages in conduct described by Section 1101.652(a)(3) or (b) or 1101.653(1), (2), (3), or (4).

(Added by Acts 2001, 77th Leg., ch. 1421, Sec. 2, eff. June 1, 2003.)

Sec. 1101.603. PAYMENTS INTO TRUST ACCOUNT.

(a) In addition to other fees required by this chapter, an applicant for an original license must pay a fee of $10.

(b) In addition to other fees required by this chapter, an applicant for an original certificate of registration or renewal certificate must pay a fee of $50.

(c) The commission shall deposit to the credit of the trust account:

(1) fees collected under Subsections (a) and (b); and

(2) an administrative penalty collected under Subchapter O for a violation by a person licensed as a broker or salesperson.

(d) An administrative penalty collected under Subchapter O for a violation by a person who is not licensed under this chapter or Chapter 1102 shall be deposited to the credit of the trust account or the real estate inspection recovery fund, as determined by the commission.

(e) On a determination by the commission at any time that the balance in the trust account is less than $1 million, each license holder at the next license renewal must pay, in addition to the renewal fee, a fee that is equal to the lesser of $10 or a pro rata share of the amount necessary to obtain a balance in the trust account of $1.7 million. The commission shall deposit the additional fee to the credit of the trust account.

(f) To ensure the availability of a sufficient amount to pay anticipated claims on the trust account, the commission by rule may provide for the collection of assessments at different times and under conditions other than those specified by this chapter.

(Added by Acts 2001, 77th Leg., ch. 1421, Sec. 2, eff. June 1, 2003. Amended by Acts 2003, 78th Leg., ch. 1276, Sec. 14A.160(a), eff. Sept. 1, 2003.)

Sec. 1101.604. MANAGEMENT OF TRUST ACCOUNT. (a) The commission shall hold money credited to the trust account in trust to carry out the purpose of the trust account.

(b) Money credited to the trust account may be invested in the same manner as money of the Employees Retirement System of Texas, except that an investment may not be made that would impair the liquidity necessary to make payments from the trust account as required by this subchapter.

(c) Interest from the investments shall be deposited to the credit of the trust account.

(d) If the balance in the trust account on December 31 of a year is more than the greater of $3.5 million or the total amount of claims paid from the trust account during the preceding four fiscal years, the commission shall transfer the excess amount of money in the trust account to the credit of the general revenue fund.

(Added by Acts 2001, 77th Leg., ch. 1421, Sec. 2, eff. June 1, 2003.)

Sec. 1101.605. DEADLINE FOR ACTION; NOTICE TO COMMISSION. (a) An action for a judgment that may result in an order for payment from the trust account may not be brought after the second anniversary of the date the cause of action accrues.

(b) When an aggrieved person brings an action for a judgment that may result in an order for payment from the trust account, the license or certificate holder against whom the action is brought shall notify the commission in writing of the action.

(Added by Acts 2001, 77th Leg., ch. 1421, Sec. 2, eff. June 1, 2003.)

Sec. 1101.606. CLAIM FOR PAYMENT FROM TRUST ACCOUNT. (a) Except as provided by Subsection (c), an aggrieved person who obtains a court judgment against a license or certificate holder for an act described by Section 1101.602 may, after final judgment is entered, execution returned nulla bona, and a judgment lien perfected, file a verified claim in the court that entered the judgment.

(b) After the 20th day after the date the aggrieved person gives written notice of the claim to the commission and judgment debtor, the person may apply to the court that entered the judgment for an order for payment from the trust account of the amount unpaid on the judgment. The court shall proceed promptly on the application.

(c) If an aggrieved person is precluded by action of a bankruptcy court from executing a judgment or perfecting a judgment lien as required by Subsection (a), the person shall verify to the commission that the person has made a good faith effort to protect the judgment from being discharged in bankruptcy.

(d) The commission by rule may prescribe the actions necessary for an aggrieved person to demonstrate that the person has made a good faith effort under Subsection (c) to protect a judgment from being discharged in bankruptcy.

(Added by Acts 2001, 77th Leg., ch. 1421, Sec. 2, eff. June 1, 2003. Amended by: Acts 2009, 81st Leg., R.S., Ch. 23, Sec. 5, eff. May 12, 2009.)

Sec. 1101.607. ISSUES AT HEARING. At the hearing on the application for payment from the trust account, the aggrieved person must show:

(1) that the judgment is based on facts allowing recovery under this subchapter;

(2) that the person is not:

(A) the spouse of the judgment debtor or the personal representative of the spouse; or

(B) a license or certificate holder who is seeking to recover compensation, including a commission, in the real estate transaction that is the subject of the application for payment;

(3) that, according to the best information available, the judgment debtor does not have sufficient attachable assets in this or another state to satisfy the judgment;

(4) the amount that may be realized from the sale of assets liable to be sold or applied to satisfy the judgment; and

(5) the balance remaining due on the judgment after application of the amount under Subdivision (4).

(Added by Acts 2001, 77th Leg., ch. 1421, Sec. 2, eff. June 1, 2003. Amended by Acts 2003, 78th Leg., ch. 1276, Sec. 14A.160(b), eff. Sept. 1, 2003.)

Sec. 1101.608. COMMISSION RESPONSE. (a) On receipt of notice under Section 1101.606 and the scheduling of a hearing, the commission may notify the attorney general of the commission's desire to enter an appearance, file a response, appear at the hearing, defend the action, or take any other action the commission considers appropriate.

(b) The commission and the attorney general may act under Subsection (a) only to:

(1) protect the trust account from spurious or unjust claims; or

(2) ensure compliance with the requirements for recovery under this subchapter.

(c) The commission may relitigate in the hearing any material and relevant issue that was determined in the action that resulted in the judgment in favor of the aggrieved person.

(Added by Acts 2001, 77th Leg., ch. 1421, Sec. 2, eff. June 1, 2003.)

Sec. 1101.609. COURT ORDER FOR PAYMENT. The court shall order the commission to pay from the trust account the amount the court finds payable on the claim under this subchapter if at a hearing the court is satisfied:

(1) of the truth of each matter the aggrieved person is required by Section 1101.607 to show; and

(2) that the aggrieved person has satisfied each requirement of Sections 1101.606 and 1101.607.

(Added by Acts 2001, 77th Leg., ch. 1421, Sec. 2, eff. June 1, 2003.)

Sec. 1101.610. PAYMENT LIMITS; ATTORNEY'S FEES. (a) Payments from the trust account for claims, including attorney's fees, interest, and court costs, arising out of a single transaction may not exceed a total of $50,000, regardless of the number of claimants.

(b) Payments from the trust account for claims based on judgments against a single license or certificate holder may not exceed a total of $100,000 until the license or certificate holder has reimbursed the trust account for all amounts paid.

(c) If the court finds that the total amount of claims against a license or certificate holder

exceeds the limitations in this section, the court shall proportionately reduce the amount payable on each claim.

(d) A person receiving payment from the trust account is entitled to receive reasonable attorney's fees in the amount determined by the court, subject to the limitations prescribed by this section.

(Added by Acts 2001, 77th Leg., ch. 1421, Sec. 2, eff. June 1, 2003.)

Sec. 1101.611. APPLICATION OF JUDGMENT RECOVERY. An aggrieved person who receives a recovery on a judgment against a single defendant before receiving a payment from the trust account must apply the recovery first to actual damages.

(Added by Acts 2001, 77th Leg., ch. 1421, Sec. 2, eff. June 1, 2003.)

Sec. 1101.612. SUBROGATION. (a) The commission is subrogated to all rights of a judgment creditor to the extent of an amount paid from the trust account, and the judgment creditor shall assign to the commission all right, title, and interest in the judgment up to that amount.

(b) The commission has priority for repayment from any subsequent recovery on the judgment.

(c) The commission shall deposit any amount recovered on the judgment to the credit of the trust account.

(Added by Acts 2001, 77th Leg., ch. 1421, Sec. 2, eff. June 1, 2003.)

Sec. 1101.613. EFFECT ON DISCIPLINARY PROCEEDINGS. (a) This subchapter does not limit the commission's authority to take disciplinary action against a license or certificate holder for a violation of this chapter or a commission rule.

(b) A license or certificate holder's repayment of all amounts owed to the trust account does not affect another disciplinary proceeding brought under this chapter.

(Added by Acts 2001, 77th Leg., ch. 1421, Sec. 2, eff. June 1, 2003.)

Sec. 1101.614. WAIVER OF RIGHTS. An aggrieved person who does not comply with this subchapter waives the person's rights under this subchapter.

(Added by Acts 2001, 77th Leg., ch. 1421, Sec. 2, eff. June 1, 2003.)

Sec. 1101.615. NOTICE TO CONSUMERS AND SERVICE RECIPIENTS. (a) Each license and certificate holder shall provide notice to consumers and service recipients of the availability of payment from the trust account for aggrieved persons:

(1) in conjunction with the notice required by Section 1101.202;

(2) on a written contract for the license or certificate holder's services;

(3) on a brochure that the license or certificate holder distributes;

(4) on a sign prominently displayed in the license or certificate holder's place of business;

(5) in a bill or receipt for the license or certificate holder's services; or

(6) in a prominent display on the Internet website of a person regulated under this chapter.

(b) The notice must include:

(1) the commission's name, mailing address, and telephone number; and

(2) any other information required by commission rule.

(Added by Acts 2001, 77th Leg., ch. 1421, Sec. 2, eff. June 1, 2003. Amended by Acts 2003, 78th Leg., ch. 15, Sec. 8, eff. Sept. 1, 2003.)

SUBCHAPTER N. PROHIBITED PRACTICES AND DISCIPLINARY PROCEEDINGS

Sec. 1101.651. CERTAIN PRACTICES PROHIBITED. (a) A licensed broker may not pay a commission to or otherwise compensate a person directly or indirectly for performing an act of a broker unless the person is:

(1) a license holder; or

(2) a real estate broker licensed in another state who does not conduct in this state any of the negotiations for which the commission or other compensation is paid.

(b) A salesperson may not accept compensation for a real estate transaction from a person other than the broker with whom the salesperson is associated or was associated when the salesperson earned the compensation.

(c) A salesperson may not pay a commission to a person except through the broker with whom the salesperson is associated at that time.

(d) A broker and any broker or salesperson appointed under Section 1101.560 who acts as an intermediary under Subchapter L may not:

(1) disclose to the buyer or tenant that the seller or landlord will accept a price less than the asking price, unless otherwise instructed in a separate writing by the seller or landlord;

(2) disclose to the seller or landlord that the buyer or tenant will pay a price greater than the price submitted in a written offer to the seller or landlord, unless otherwise instructed in a separate writing by the buyer or tenant;

(3) disclose any confidential information or any information a party specifically instructs the broker or salesperson in writing not to disclose, unless:

(A) the broker or salesperson is otherwise instructed in a separate writing by the respective party;

(B) the broker or salesperson is required to disclose the information by this chapter or a court order; or

(C) the information materially relates to the condition of the property;

(4) treat a party to a transaction dishonestly; or

(5) violate this chapter.

(Added by Acts 2001, 77th Leg., ch. 1421, Sec. 2, eff. June 1, 2003.)

Sec. 1101.652. GROUNDS FOR SUSPENSION OR REVOCATION OF LICENSE. (a) The commission may suspend or revoke a license issued under this chapter or take other disciplinary action authorized by this chapter if the license holder:

Sec. 1101.652(a)(1)-.652(b)(13)

(1) enters a plea of guilty or nolo contendere to or is convicted of a felony or a criminal offense involving fraud, and the time for appeal has elapsed or the judgment or conviction has been affirmed on appeal, without regard to an order granting community supervision that suspends the imposition of the sentence;

(2) procures or attempts to procure a license under this chapter for the license holder or a salesperson by fraud, misrepresentation, or deceit or by making a material misstatement of fact in an application for a license;

(3) engages in misrepresentation, dishonesty, or fraud when selling, buying, trading, or leasing real property in the name of:

(A) the license holder;

(B) the license holder's spouse; or

(C) a person related to the license holder within the first degree by consanguinity;

(4) fails to honor, within a reasonable time, a check issued to the commission after the commission has sent by certified mail a request for payment to the license holder's last known business address according to commission records;

(5) fails or refuses to produce on request, for inspection by the commission or a commission representative, a document, book, or record that is in the license holder's possession and relates to a real estate transaction conducted by the license holder;

(6) fails to provide, within a reasonable time, information requested by the commission that relates to a formal or informal complaint to the commission that would indicate a violation of this chapter;

(7) fails to surrender to the owner, without just cause, a document or instrument that is requested by the owner and that is in the license holder's possession;

(8) fails to use a contract form required by the commission under Section 1101.155;

(9) fails to notify the commission, not later than the 30th day after the date of a final conviction or the entry of a plea of guilty or nolo contendere, that the person has been convicted of or entered a plea of guilty or nolo contendere to a felony or a criminal offense involving fraud; or

(10) disregards or violates this chapter.

(b) The commission may suspend or revoke a license issued under this chapter or take other disciplinary action authorized by this chapter if the license holder, while acting as a broker or salesperson:

(1) acts negligently or incompetently;

(2) engages in conduct that is dishonest or in bad faith or that demonstrates untrustworthiness;

(3) makes a material misrepresentation to a potential buyer concerning a significant defect, including a latent structural defect, known to the license holder that would be a significant factor to a reasonable and prudent buyer in making a decision to purchase real property;

(4) fails to disclose to a potential buyer a defect described by Subdivision (3) that is known to the license holder;

(5) makes a false promise that is likely to influence a person to enter into an agreement when the license holder is unable or does not intend to keep the promise;

(6) pursues a continued and flagrant course of misrepresentation or makes false promises through an agent or salesperson, through advertising, or otherwise;

(7) fails to make clear to all parties to a real estate transaction the party for whom the license holder is acting;

(8) receives compensation from more than one party to a real estate transaction without the full knowledge and consent of all parties to the transaction;

(9) fails within a reasonable time to properly account for or remit money that is received by the license holder and that belongs to another person;

(10) commingles money that belongs to another person with the license holder's own money;

(11) pays a commission or a fee to or divides a commission or a fee with a person other than a license holder or a real estate broker or salesperson licensed in another state for compensation for services as a real estate agent;

(12) fails to specify a definite termination date that is not subject to prior notice in a contract, other than a contract to perform property management services, in which the license holder agrees to perform services for which a license is required under this chapter;

(13) accepts, receives, or charges an

undisclosed commission, rebate, or direct profit on an expenditure made for a principal;

(14) solicits, sells, or offers for sale real property by means of a lottery;

(15) solicits, sells, or offers for sale real property by means of a deceptive practice;

(16) acts in a dual capacity as broker and undisclosed principal in a real estate transaction;

(17) guarantees or authorizes or permits a person to guarantee that future profits will result from a resale of real property;

(18) places a sign on real property offering the real property for sale or lease without obtaining the written consent of the owner of the real property or the owner's authorized agent;

(19) offers to sell or lease real property without the knowledge and consent of the owner of the real property or the owner's authorized agent;

(20) offers to sell or lease real property on terms other than those authorized by the owner of the real property or the owner's authorized agent;

(21) induces or attempts to induce a party to a contract of sale or lease to break the contract for the purpose of substituting a new contract;

(22) negotiates or attempts to negotiate the sale, exchange, or lease of real property with an owner, landlord, buyer, or tenant with knowledge that that person is a party to an outstanding written contract that grants exclusive agency to another broker in connection with the transaction;

(23) publishes or causes to be published an advertisement, including an advertisement by newspaper, radio, television, the Internet, or display, that misleads or is likely to deceive the public, tends to create a misleading impression, or fails to identify the person causing the advertisement to be published as a licensed broker or agent;

(24) withholds from or inserts into a statement of account or invoice a statement that the license holder knows makes the statement of account or invoice inaccurate in a material way;

(25) publishes or circulates an unjustified or unwarranted threat of a legal proceeding or other action;

(26) establishes an association by employment or otherwise with a person other than a license holder if the person is expected or required to act as a license holder;

(27) aids, abets, or conspires with another person to circumvent this chapter;

(28) fails or refuses to provide, on request, a copy of a document relating to a real estate transaction to a person who signed the document;

(29) fails to advise a buyer in writing before the closing of a real estate transaction that the buyer should:

(A) have the abstract covering the real estate that is the subject of the contract examined by an attorney chosen by the buyer; or

(B) be provided with or obtain a title insurance policy;

(30) fails to deposit, within a reasonable time, money the license holder receives as escrow agent in a real estate transaction:

(A) in trust with a title company authorized to do business in this state; or

(B) in a custodial, trust, or escrow account maintained for that purpose in a banking institution authorized to do business in this state;

(31) disburses money deposited in a custodial, trust, or escrow account, as provided in Subdivision (30), before the completion or termination of the real estate transaction;

(32) discriminates against an owner, potential buyer, landlord, or potential tenant on the basis of race, color, religion, sex, disability, familial status, national origin, or ancestry, including directing a prospective buyer or tenant interested in equivalent properties to a different area based on the race, color, religion, sex, disability, familial status, national origin, or ancestry of the potential owner or tenant; or

(33) disregards or violates this chapter.

(Added by Acts 2001, 77th Leg., ch. 1421, Sec. 2, eff. June 1, 2003. Amended by Acts 2003, 78th Leg., ch. 1276, Sec. 14A.154(c), eff. Sept. 1, 2003. Amended by: Acts 2005, 79th Leg., Ch. 825, Sec. 9, eff. September 1, 2005. Acts 2007, 80th Leg., R.S., Ch. 297, Sec. 9, eff. September 1, 2007. Acts 2009, 81st Leg., R.S., Ch. 23, Sec. 6, eff. May 12, 2009.)

Sec. 1101.653. GROUNDS FOR SUSPENSION OR REVOCATION OF CERTIFICATE. The commission may suspend or revoke a certificate of registration issued under this chapter if the certificate holder:

Sec. 1101.653(1)-.656(b)

(1) engages in dishonest dealing, fraud, unlawful discrimination, or a deceptive act;

(2) makes a misrepresentation;

(3) acts in bad faith;

(4) demonstrates untrustworthiness;

(5) fails to honor, within a reasonable time, a check issued to the commission after the commission has mailed a request for payment to the certificate holder's last known address according to the commission's records;

(6) fails to provide to a party to a transaction a written notice prescribed by the commission that:

(A) must be given before the party is obligated to sell, buy, lease, or transfer a right-of-way or easement; and

(B) contains:

(i) the name of the certificate holder;

(ii) the certificate number;

(iii) the name of the person the certificate holder represents;

(iv) a statement advising the party that the party may seek representation from a lawyer or broker in the transaction; and

(v) a statement generally advising the party that the right-of-way or easement may affect the value of the property; or

(7) disregards or violates this chapter or a commission rule relating to certificate holders.

(Added by Acts 2001, 77th Leg., ch. 1421, Sec. 2, eff. June 1, 2003.)

Sec. 1101.654. SUSPENSION OR REVOCATION OF LICENSE OR CERTIFICATE FOR UNAUTHORIZED PRACTICE OF LAW. (a) The commission shall suspend or revoke the license or certificate of registration of a license or certificate holder who is not a licensed attorney in this state and who, for consideration, a reward, or a pecuniary benefit, present or anticipated, direct or indirect, or in connection with the person's employment, agency, or fiduciary relationship as a license or certificate holder:

(1) drafts an instrument, other than a form described by Section 1101.155, that transfers or otherwise affects an interest in real property; or

(2) advises a person regarding the validity or legal sufficiency of an instrument or the validity of title to real property.

(b) Notwithstanding any other law, a license or certificate holder who completes a contract form for the sale, exchange, option, or lease of an interest in real property incidental to acting as a broker is not engaged in the unauthorized or illegal practice of law in this state if the form was:

(1) adopted by the commission for the type of transaction for which the form is used;

(2) prepared by an attorney licensed in this state and approved by the attorney for the type of transaction for which the form is used; or

(3) prepared by the property owner or by an attorney and required by the property owner.

(Added by Acts 2001, 77th Leg., ch. 1421, Sec. 2, eff. June 1, 2003.)

Sec. 1101.655. REVOCATION OF LICENSE OR CERTIFICATE FOR CLAIM ON ACCOUNT. (a) The commission may revoke a license, approval, or registration issued under this chapter or Chapter 1102 if the commission makes a payment from the real estate recovery trust account to satisfy all or part of a judgment against the license or registration holder.

(b) The commission may probate an order revoking a license under this section.

(c) A person is not eligible for a license or certificate until the person has repaid in full the amount paid from the account for the person, plus interest at the legal rate.

(Added by Acts 2001, 77th Leg., ch. 1421, Sec. 2, eff. June 1, 2003. Amended by: Acts 2005, 79th Leg., Ch. 825, Sec. 10, eff. September 1, 2005. Acts 2007, 80th Leg., R.S., Ch. 297, Sec. 10, eff. September 1, 2007.)

Sec. 1101.656. ADDITIONAL DISCIPLINARY AUTHORITY OF COMMISSION. (a) In addition to any other authority under this chapter, the commission may suspend or revoke a license, place on probation a person whose license has been suspended, or reprimand a license holder if the license holder violates this chapter or a commission rule.

(b) The commission may probate a suspension, revocation, or cancellation of a license under reasonable terms determined by the commission.

(c) The commission may require a license holder whose license suspension or revocation is probated to:

(1) report regularly to the commission on matters that are the basis of the probation;

(2) limit practice to an area prescribed by the commission; or

(3) continue to renew professional education until the license holder attains a degree of skill satisfactory to the commission in the area that is the basis of the probation.

(Added by Acts 2001, 77th Leg., ch. 1421, Sec. 2, eff. June 1, 2003.)

Sec. 1101.6561. SUSPENSION OR REVOCATION OF EDUCATIONAL PROGRAM ACCREDITATION.
The commission may suspend or revoke an accreditation issued under Subchapter G or take any other disciplinary action authorized by this chapter if the provider of an educational program or course of study violates this chapter or a rule adopted under this chapter.

(Added by Acts 2011, 82nd Leg., R.S., Ch. 1064, Sec. 23, eff. September 1, 2011.)

Sec. 1101.657. HEARING.
(a) If the commission proposes to deny, suspend, or revoke a person's license or certificate of registration, the person is entitled to a hearing conducted by the State Office of Administrative Hearings.

(b) *Repealed by Acts 2007, 80th Leg., R.S., Ch. 1411, Sec. 59(3), eff. September 1, 2007.*

(c) *Repealed by Acts 2007, 80th Leg., R.S., Ch. 1411, Sec. 59(3), eff. September 1, 2007.*

(d) *Repealed by Acts 2007, 80th Leg., R.S., Ch. 1411, Sec. 59(3), eff. September 1, 2007.*

(e) A hearing under this section is governed by the contested case procedures under Chapter 2001, Government Code.

(Added by Acts 2001, 77th Leg., ch. 1421, Sec. 2, eff. June 1, 2003. Amended by Acts 2003, 78th Leg., ch. 15, Sec. 9, eff. Sept. 1, 2003. Amended by: Acts 2007, 80th Leg., R.S., Ch. 1411, Sec. 22, eff. September 1, 2007. Acts 2007, 80th Leg., R.S., Ch. 1411, Sec. 59(3), eff. September 1, 2007.)

Sec. 1101.658. APPEAL.
(a) A person aggrieved by a ruling, order, or decision under this subchapter is entitled to appeal to a district court in the county in which the administrative hearing was held.

(b) An appeal is governed by the procedures under Chapter 2001, Government Code.

(Added by Acts 2001, 77th Leg., ch. 1421, Sec. 2, eff. June 1, 2003. Amended by: Acts 2007, 80th Leg., R.S., Ch. 1411, Sec. 23, eff. September 1, 2007.)

Sec. 1101.659. REFUND.
(a) Subject to Subsection (b), the commission may order a person regulated by the commission to pay a refund to a consumer as provided in an agreement resulting from an informal settlement conference or an enforcement order instead of or in addition to imposing an administrative penalty or other sanctions.

(b) The amount of a refund ordered as provided in an agreement resulting from an informal settlement conference or an enforcement order may not exceed the amount the consumer paid to the person for a service or accommodation regulated by this commission. The commission may not require payment of other damages or estimate harm in a refund order.

(Added by Acts 2007, 80th Leg., R.S., Ch. 1411, Sec. 24, eff. September 1, 2007.)

Sec. 1101.660. INFORMAL PROCEEDINGS.
(a) The commission by rule shall adopt procedures governing informal disposition of a contested case.

(b) Rules adopted under this section must:

(1) provide the complainant and the license holder, certificate holder, or regulated entity an opportunity to be heard; and

(2) require the presence of:

(A) a public member of the commission for a case involving a consumer complaint; and

(B) at least two staff members of the commission with experience in the regulatory area that is the subject of the proceeding.

(Added by Acts 2007, 80th Leg., R.S., Ch. 1411, Sec. 24, eff. September 1, 2007.)

Sec. 1101.661-.702(c)

Sec. 1101.661. FINAL ORDER. The commission may issue a final order in a proceeding under this subchapter or Subchapter O regarding a person whose license has expired during the course of an investigation or administrative proceeding.

(Added by Acts 2007, 80th Leg., R.S., Ch. 1411, Sec. 24, eff. September 1, 2007.)

Sec. 1101.662. TEMPORARY SUSPENSION. (a) The presiding officer of the commission shall appoint a disciplinary panel consisting of three commission members to determine whether a person's license to practice under this chapter should be temporarily suspended.

(b) If the disciplinary panel determines from the information presented to the panel that a person licensed to practice under this chapter would, by the person's continued practice, constitute a continuing threat to the public welfare, the panel shall temporarily suspend the license of that person.

(c) A license may be suspended under this section without notice or hearing on the complaint if:

(1) institution of proceedings for a hearing before the commission is initiated simultaneously with the temporary suspension; and

(2) a hearing is held under Chapter 2001, Government Code, and this chapter as soon as possible.

(d) Notwithstanding Chapter 551, Government Code, the disciplinary panel may hold a meeting by telephone conference call if immediate action is required and convening the panel at one location is inconvenient for any member of the panel.

(Added by Acts 2007, 80th Leg., R.S., Ch. 1411, Sec. 24, eff. September 1, 2007.)

SUBCHAPTER O.
ADMINISTRATIVE PENALTY

Sec. 1101.701. IMPOSITION OF ADMINISTRATIVE PENALTY. (a) The commission may impose an administrative penalty on a person who violates this chapter or a rule adopted or order issued by the commission under this chapter.

(b) The commission shall periodically review the commission's enforcement procedures and ensure that administrative penalty and disciplinary proceedings are combined into a single enforcement procedure.

(c) The commission may combine a proceeding to impose an administrative penalty with another disciplinary proceeding, including a proceeding to suspend or revoke a license.

(Added by Acts 2001, 77th Leg., ch. 1421, Sec. 2, eff. June 1, 2003. Amended by Acts 2003, 78th Leg., ch. 1276, Sec. 14A.160(c), eff. Sept. 1, 2003. Amended by: Acts 2007, 80th Leg., R.S., Ch. 1411, Sec. 25, eff. September 1, 2007.)

Sec. 1101.7015. DELEGATION OF ADMINISTRATOR'S AUTHORITY. The commission may authorize the administrator to delegate to another commission employee the administrator's authority to act under this subchapter.

(Added by Acts 2003, 78th Leg., ch. 1276, Sec. 14A.160(d), eff. Sept. 1, 2003.)

Sec. 1101.702. AMOUNT OF PENALTY. (a) The amount of an administrative penalty may not exceed $5,000 for each violation. Each day a violation continues or occurs may be considered a separate violation for purposes of imposing a penalty.

(1) Expired.

(2) Expired.

(b) In determining the amount of the penalty, the administrator shall consider:

(1) the seriousness of the violation, including the nature, circumstances, extent, and gravity of the prohibited acts;

(2) the history of previous violations;

(3) the amount necessary to deter a future violation;

(4) efforts to correct the violation; and

(5) any other matter that justice may require.

(c) The commission by rule shall adopt a

schedule of administrative penalties based on the criteria listed in Subsection (b) for violations subject to an administrative penalty under this section to ensure that the amount of a penalty imposed is appropriate to the violation. The rules adopted under this subsection must provide authority for the commission to suspend or revoke a license in addition to or instead of imposing an administrative penalty.

(Added by Acts 2001, 77th Leg., ch. 1421, Sec. 2, eff. June 1, 2003. Amended by Acts 2003, 78th Leg., ch. 1276, Sec. 14A.160(e), eff. Sept. 1, 2003. Amended by: Acts 2007, 80th Leg., R.S., Ch. 1411, Sec. 26, eff. September 1, 2007.)

Sec. 1101.703. NOTICE OF VIOLATION AND PENALTY.

(a) If, after investigation of a possible violation and the facts relating to that violation, the administrator determines that a violation has occurred, the administrator may issue a notice of violation stating:

(1) a brief summary of the alleged violation;

(2) the administrator's recommendation on the imposition of the administrative penalty or another disciplinary sanction, including a recommendation on the amount of the penalty; and

(3) that the respondent has the right to a hearing to contest the alleged violation, the recommended penalty, or both.

(b) *Repealed by Acts 2007, 80th Leg., R.S., Ch. 1411, Sec. 59(4), eff. September 1, 2007.*

(1) *Expired.*

(2) *Expired.*

(3) *Expired.*

(Added by Acts 2001, 77th Leg., ch. 1421, Sec. 2, eff. June 1, 2003. Amended by: Acts 2007, 80th Leg., R.S., Ch. 1411, Sec. 27, eff. September 1, 2007. Acts 2007, 80th Leg., R.S., Ch. 1411, Sec. 28, eff. September 1, 2007. Acts 2007, 80th Leg., R.S., Ch. 1411, Sec. 59(4), eff. September 1, 2007.)

Sec. 1101.704. PENALTY TO BE PAID OR HEARING REQUESTED.

(a) Not later than the 20th day after the date the person receives the notice under Section 1101.703, the person may:

(1) accept the administrator's determination, including the recommended administrative penalty; or

(2) request in writing a hearing on the occurrence of the violation, the amount of the penalty, or both.

(b) If the person accepts the administrator's determination, or fails to respond in a timely manner to the notice, the commission by order shall approve the determination and order payment of the recommended penalty or impose the recommended sanction.

(Added by Acts 2001, 77th Leg., ch. 1421, Sec. 2, eff. June 1, 2003. Amended by: Acts 2007, 80th Leg., R.S., Ch. 1411, Sec. 29, eff. September 1, 2007.)

Sec. 1101.705. HEARING; DECISION.

(a) If the person requests a hearing, the administrator shall set a hearing and give notice of the hearing to the person.

(b) An administrative law judge of the State Office of Administrative Hearings shall conduct the hearing. The administrative law judge shall:

(1) make findings of fact and conclusions of law; and

(2) promptly issue to the commission a proposal for decision regarding the occurrence of the violation and the amount of any proposed administrative penalty.

(c) Based on the findings of fact, conclusions of law, and proposal for decision of the administrative law judge, the commission by order may determine that:

(1) a violation occurred and impose an administrative penalty; or

(2) a violation did not occur.

(d) A proceeding under this section is subject to Chapter 2001, Government Code.

(e) The notice of the commission's order given to the person under Chapter 2001, Government Code, must include a statement of the person's right to judicial review of the order.

(Added by Acts 2001, 77th Leg., ch. 1421, Sec. 2, eff. June 1, 2003. Amended by Acts 2003, 78th Leg., ch. 1276, Sec. 14A.160(f), eff. Sept. 1, 2003. Amended by: Acts 2007, 80th Leg., R.S., Ch. 1411, Sec. 30, eff. September 1, 2007. Acts 2007, 80th Leg., R.S., Ch. 1411, Sec. 31, eff. September 1, 2007.)

Sec. 1101.706-.709(d)

Sec. 1101.706. NOTICE OF ORDER. The administrator shall give notice of the commission's order to the person. The notice must:

(1) include the findings of fact and conclusions of law, separately stated;

(2) state the amount of any penalty imposed;

(3) inform the person of the person's right to judicial review of the order; and

(4) include other information required by law.

(Added by Acts 2001, 77th Leg., ch. 1421, Sec. 2, eff. June 1, 2003.)

Sec. 1101.707. OPTIONS FOLLOWING DECISION: PAY OR APPEAL. (a) Not later than the 30th day after the date the commission's order becomes final, the person shall:

(1) pay the administrative penalty; or

(2) file a petition for judicial review contesting the occurrence of the violation, the amount of the penalty, or both.

(b) Within the 30-day period prescribed by Subsection (a), a person who files a petition for judicial review may:

(1) stay enforcement of the penalty by:

(A) paying the penalty to the court for placement in an escrow account; or

(B) giving the court a supersedeas bond in a form approved by the court that:

(i) is for the amount of the penalty; and

(ii) is effective until judicial review of the order is final; or

(2) request the court to stay enforcement by:

(A) filing with the court an affidavit of the person stating that the person is financially unable to pay the penalty and is financially unable to give the supersedeas bond; and

(B) giving a copy of the affidavit to the administrator by certified mail.

(c) If the administrator receives a copy of an affidavit under Subsection (b)(2), the administrator may file with the court, within five days after the date the copy is received, a contest to the affidavit.

(d) The court shall hold a hearing on the facts alleged in the affidavit as soon as practicable and shall stay the enforcement of the penalty on finding that the alleged facts are true. The person who files an affidavit has the burden of proving that the person is financially unable to pay the penalty and to give a supersedeas bond.

(Added by Acts 2001, 77th Leg., ch. 1421, Sec. 2, eff. June 1, 2003. Amended by: Acts 2007, 80th Leg., R.S., Ch. 1411, Sec. 32, eff. September 1, 2007.)

Sec. 1101.708. COLLECTION OF PENALTY. If the person does not pay the administrative penalty and the enforcement of the penalty is not stayed, the administrator may refer the matter to the attorney general for collection of the penalty.

(Added by Acts 2001, 77th Leg., ch. 1421, Sec. 2, eff. June 1, 2003.)

Sec. 1101.7085. DETERMINATION BY COURT. (a) If the court sustains the determination that a violation occurred, the court may uphold or reduce the amount of the administrative penalty and order the person to pay the full or reduced amount of the penalty.

(b) If the court does not sustain the finding that a violation occurred, the court shall order that a penalty is not owed.

(Added by Acts 2007, 80th Leg., R.S., Ch. 1411, Sec. 33, eff. September 1, 2007.)

Sec. 1101.709. REMITTANCE OF PENALTY AND INTEREST. (a) If after judicial review the administrative penalty is reduced or is not upheld by the court, the court shall remit the appropriate amount, plus accrued interest, to the person if the person paid the penalty.

(b) The interest accrues at the rate charged on loans to depository institutions by the New York Federal Reserve Bank.

(c) The interest shall be paid for the period beginning on the date the penalty is paid and ending on the date the penalty is remitted.

(d) If the person gave a supersedeas bond and the penalty is not upheld by the court, the court shall order, when the court's judgment becomes final, the release of the bond.

(e) If the person gave a supersedeas bond and the amount of the penalty is reduced, the court shall order the release of the bond after the person pays the reduced amount.

(Added by Acts 2001, 77th Leg., ch. 1421, Sec. 2, eff. June 1, 2003. Amended by: Acts 2007, 80th Leg., R.S., Ch. 1411, Sec. 34, eff. September 1, 2007.)

Sec. 1101.710. ADMINISTRATIVE PROCEDURE. A proceeding under this subchapter is subject to Chapter 2001, Government Code.

(Added by Acts 2007, 80th Leg., R.S., Ch. 1411, Sec. 35, eff. September 1, 2007.)

SUBCHAPTER P. OTHER PENALTIES AND ENFORCEMENT PROVISIONS

Sec. 1101.751. INJUNCTIVE ACTION BROUGHT BY COMMISSION. (a) In addition to any other action authorized by law, the commission may bring an action in its name to enjoin a violation of this chapter or a commission rule.

(b) To obtain an injunction under this section, the commission is not required to allege or prove that:

(1) an adequate remedy at law does not exist; or

(2) substantial or irreparable damage would result from the continued violation.

(Added by Acts 2001, 77th Leg., ch. 1421, Sec. 2, eff. June 1, 2003.)

Sec. 1101.752. ADDITIONAL INJUNCTIVE AUTHORITY. (a) In addition to any other action authorized by law, the commission, acting through the attorney general, may bring an action to abate a violation or enjoin a violation or potential violation of this chapter or a commission rule if the commission determines that a person has violated or is about to violate this chapter.

(b) The action shall be brought in the name of the state in the district court in the county in which:

(1) the violation occurred or is about to occur; or

(2) the defendant resides.

(c) An injunctive action may be brought to abate or temporarily or permanently enjoin an act or to enforce this chapter.

(d) The commission is not required to give a bond in an action under Subsection (a), and court costs may not be recovered from the commission.

(e) If the commission determines that a person has violated or is about to violate this chapter, the attorney general or the county attorney or district attorney in the county in which the violation has occurred or is about to occur or in the county of the defendant's residence may bring an action in the name of the state in the district court of the county to abate or temporarily or permanently enjoin the violation or to enforce this chapter. The plaintiff in an action under this subsection is not required to give a bond, and court costs may not be recovered from the plaintiff.

(Added by Acts 2001, 77th Leg., ch. 1421, Sec. 2, eff. June 1, 2003.)

Sec. 1101.753. CIVIL PENALTY FOR CERTAIN VIOLATIONS BY BROKER, SALESPERSON, OR CERTIFICATE HOLDER. (a) In addition to injunctive relief under Sections 1101.751 and 1101.752, a person who receives a commission or other consideration as a result of acting as a broker or salesperson without holding a license or certificate of registration under this chapter is liable to the state for a civil penalty of not less than the amount of money received or more than three times the amount of money received.

(b) The commission may recover the civil penalty, court costs, and reasonable attorney's fees on behalf of the state.

(c) The commission is not required to give a bond in an action under this section, and court costs may not be recovered from the commission.

(Added by Acts 2001, 77th Leg., ch. 1421, Sec. 2, eff. June 1, 2003.)

Sec. 1101.754. PRIVATE CAUSE OF ACTION FOR CERTAIN VIOLATIONS BY BROKER, SALESPERSON, OR CERTIFICATE HOLDER. (a) A person who receives a commission or other consideration as a result of acting as a broker or salesperson

Sec. 1101.754-.802

without holding a license or certificate of registration under this chapter is liable to an aggrieved person for a penalty of not less than the amount of money received or more than three times the amount of money received.

(b) The aggrieved person may file suit to recover a penalty under this section.

(Added by Acts 2001, 77th Leg., ch. 1421, Sec. 2, eff. June 1, 2003.)

Sec. 1101.755. APPEAL BOND EXEMPTION. The commission is not required to give an appeal bond in an action to enforce this chapter.

(Added by Acts 2001, 77th Leg., ch. 1421, Sec. 2, eff. June 1, 2003.)

Sec. 1101.756. GENERAL CRIMINAL PENALTY. (a) A person commits an offense if the person willfully violates or fails to comply with this chapter or a commission order.

(b) An offense under this section is a Class A misdemeanor.

(Added by Acts 2001, 77th Leg., ch. 1421, Sec. 2, eff. June 1, 2003.)

Sec. 1101.757. CRIMINAL PENALTY FOR CERTAIN VIOLATIONS BY RESIDENTIAL RENTAL LOCATOR. (a) A person commits an offense if the person engages in business as a residential rental locator in this state without a license issued under this chapter.

(b) An offense under this section is a Class A misdemeanor.

(Added by Acts 2001, 77th Leg., ch. 1421, Sec. 2, eff. June 1, 2003. Amended by Acts 2003, 78th Leg., ch. 1276, Sec. 14A.161(a), eff. Sept. 1, 2003.)

Sec. 1101.758. CRIMINAL PENALTY FOR CERTAIN VIOLATIONS BY BROKER, SALESPERSON, OR CERTIFICATE HOLDER. (a) A person commits an offense if the person acts as a broker or salesperson without holding a license under this chapter or engages in an activity for which a certificate of registration is required under this chapter without holding a certificate.

(b) An offense under this section is a Class A misdemeanor.

(c) to (e) *Repealed by Acts 2003, 78th Leg., ch. 1276, Sec. 14A.162(b).*

(Added by Acts 2001, 77th Leg., ch. 1421, Sec. 2, eff. June 1, 2003. Amended by Acts 2003, 78th Leg., ch. 1276, Sec. 14A.162(a), (b), eff. Sept. 1, 2003.)

Sec. 1101.759. CEASE AND DESIST ORDER. (a) If it appears to the commission that a person is violating this chapter or Chapter 1102 or a rule adopted under this chapter or Chapter 1102, the commission, after notice and opportunity for a hearing, may issue a cease and desist order prohibiting the person from engaging in the activity.

(b) A violation of an order under this section constitutes grounds for imposing an administrative penalty under Subchapter O.

(Added by Acts 2007, 80th Leg., R.S., Ch. 1411, Sec. 36, eff. September 1, 2007.)

SUBCHAPTER Q. GENERAL PROVISIONS RELATING TO LIABILITY ISSUES

Sec. 1101.801. EFFECT OF DISCIPLINARY ACTION ON LIABILITY. Disciplinary action taken against a person under Section 1101.652 does not relieve the person from civil or criminal liability.

(Added by Acts 2001, 77th Leg., ch. 1421, Sec. 2, eff. June 1, 2003.)

Sec. 1101.802. LIABILITY RELATING TO HIV INFECTION OR AIDS. Notwithstanding Section 1101.801, a person is not civilly or criminally liable because the person failed to inquire about, make a disclosure relating to, or release information relating to whether a previous or current occupant of real property had, may have had, has, or may have AIDS, an HIV-related illness, or HIV infection as defined by the Centers for Disease Control and Prevention of the United States Public Health Service.

(Added by Acts 2001, 77th Leg., ch. 1421, Sec. 2, eff. June 1, 2003.)

Sec. 1101.803. GENERAL LIABILITY OF BROKER. A licensed broker is liable to the commission, the public, and the broker's clients for any conduct engaged in under this chapter by the broker or by a salesperson associated with or acting for the broker.

(Added by Acts 2001, 77th Leg., ch. 1421, Sec. 2, eff. June 1, 2003.)

Sec. 1101.804. LIABILITY FOR PROVIDING CERTAIN INFORMATION.

A license holder or nonprofit real estate board or association that provides information about real property sales prices or the terms of a sale for the purpose of facilitating the listing, selling, leasing, financing, or appraisal of real property is not liable to another person for providing that information unless the disclosure of that information is specifically prohibited by statute.

(Added by Acts 2001, 77th Leg., ch. 1421, Sec. 2, eff. June 1, 2003.)

Sec. 1101.805. LIABILITY FOR MISREPRESENTATION OR CONCEALMENT.

(a) In this section, "party" has the meaning assigned by Section 1101.551.

(b) This section prevails over any other law, including common law.

(c) This section does not diminish a broker's responsibility for the acts or omissions of a salesperson associated with or acting for the broker.

(d) A party is not liable for a misrepresentation or a concealment of a material fact made by a license holder in a real estate transaction unless the party:

(1) knew of the falsity of the misrepresentation or concealment; and

(2) failed to disclose the party's knowledge of the falsity of the misrepresentation or concealment.

(e) A license holder is not liable for a misrepresentation or a concealment of a material fact made by a party to a real estate transaction unless the license holder:

(1) knew of the falsity of the misrepresentation or concealment; and

(2) failed to disclose the license holder's knowledge of the falsity of the misrepresentation or concealment.

(f) A party or a license holder is not liable for a misrepresentation or a concealment of a

material fact made by a subagent in a real estate transaction unless the party or license holder:

(1) knew of the falsity of the misrepresentation or concealment; and

(2) failed to disclose the party's or license holder's knowledge of the falsity of the misrepresentation or concealment.

(Added by Acts 2001, 77th Leg., ch. 1421, Sec. 2, eff. June 1, 2003.)

Sec. 1101.806. LIABILITY FOR PAYMENT OF COMPENSATION OR COMMISSION.

(a) This section does not:

(1) apply to an agreement to share compensation among license holders; or

(2) limit a cause of action among brokers for interference with business relationships.

(b) A person may not maintain an action to collect compensation for an act as a broker or salesperson that is performed in this state unless the person alleges and proves that the person was:

(1) a license holder at the time the act was commenced; or

(2) an attorney licensed in any state.

(c) A person may not maintain an action in this state to recover a commission for the sale or purchase of real estate unless the promise or agreement on which the action is based, or a memorandum, is in writing and signed by the party against whom the action is brought or by a person authorized by that party to sign the document.

(d) A license holder who fails to advise a buyer as provided by Section 1101.555 may not receive payment of or recover any commission agreed to be paid on the sale.

(Added by Acts 2001, 77th Leg., ch. 1421, Sec. 2, eff. June 1, 2003.)

APPENDIX B

Questions and Answers Regarding Disclosure of Agency and Intermediary Practice

Questions and Answers Regarding Disclosure of Agency

and Intermediary Practice

The following questions and answers have been developed to assist licensees in complying with the disclosure of agency and intermediary practice provisions (Representation Provisions) of The Real Estate License Act (TRELA or the Act). The provisions include §§1101.558-1101.561 and §1101.651(d) of the Occupations Code. These answers are intended to address general situations only and are not intended as legal opinions addressing the duties and obligations of licensees in specific transactions. What licensees say and do in a specific transaction may cause these general answers to be inapplicable or inaccurate. Licensees should consult their own attorneys for legal advice concerning the law's effect on their brokerage practices.

1. **Q: Explain how a typical intermediary relationship is created and how it would operate.**

   A: At the first substantive dialogue with a seller or a prospective buyer, the salespersons or brokers associated with a firm would provide the parties with a copy of the statutory information about agency required by TRELA. The statutory information includes an explanation of the intermediary relationship. The brokerage firm would negotiate a written listing contract with a seller and a written buyer representation agreement with a buyer. In those documents, the respective parties would authorize the broker to act as an intermediary and to appoint associated licensees to work with the parties in the event that the buyer wishes to purchase a property listed with the firm. At this point, the broker and associated licensees would be still functioning as exclusive agents of the individual parties. The listing contract and buyer representation agreement would contain in conspicuous bold or underlined print the broker's obligations set forth in Section 1101.651(d) of TRELA. When it becomes evident that the buyer represented by the firm wishes to purchase property listed with the firm, the intermediary status would come into play, and the intermediary may appoint different associates to work with the parties. The intermediary would notify both parties in writing of the appointments of licensees to work with the parties. The associates would provide advice and opinions to their respective parties during negotiations, and the intermediary broker would be careful not to favor one party over the other in any action taken by the intermediary.

2. **Q: What is an intermediary?**

   A: An intermediary is a broker who negotiates the transaction between the parties subject to the Representation Provisions of the Act. The intermediary may, with the written consent of the parties, appoint licensees associated with the intermediary to work with and advise the party to whom they have been appointed.

3. Q: Is dual agency authorized by the Representation Provisions?

A: A licensee may not represent both parties as a dual agent under revisions to the Act under S.B. 810 79th Legislature (2005), effective September 1, 2005. Occupations Code Section 1101.561(b) provides that "a broker must agree to act as an intermediary under this subchapter if the broker agrees to represent in a transaction" a buyer or tenant, and a seller or landlord. Since a broker must act as an intermediary pursuant to this new provision, a licensee cannot act as a dual agent. To the extent a dual agency relationship is created by accident or otherwise, a licensee must resolve the matter by complying with the notice and consent requirements of the Representation Provisions to act as an intermediary, or by representing one of the parties only and working with the other party as a customer.

4. Q: When must the broker act as an intermediary?

A: If the broker and associates are going to continue to work with parties they have been representing under listing contracts or buyer representation agreements, the intermediary role is the only way to handle "in-house" transactions, providing both parties the same level of service.

5. Q: If a salesperson or associated broker lists a property and has also been working with a prospective buyer under a representation agreement, how can the salesperson or associated broker sell this listing under the Representation Provisions?

A: There are three alternatives for the brokerage firm and the parties to consider:

(1) The firm, acting through the salesperson or associated broker, could represent one of the parties and work with the other party as a customer rather than as a client (realistically, this probably means working with the buyer as a customer and terminating the buyer representation agreement).

(2) If the firm has obtained permission in writing from both parties to be an intermediary and to appoint licensees to work with the parties, the salesperson or associated broker could be appointed by the intermediary to work with one of the parties. Note: **Another licensee would have to be appointed to work with the other party under this alternative. The law does not permit an intermediary to appoint the same licensee to work with both parties.**

(3) If the firm has obtained permission in writing from both parties to be an intermediary, but does not appoint different associates to work with the parties, the salesperson or broker associate could function as a representative of the firm. Since the firm is an intermediary, the

salesperson and associated broker also would be subject to the requirement not to act so as to favor one party over the other.

6. Q: If a salesperson may provide services to a party under the Representation Provisions without being appointed, why would a broker want to appoint a salesperson to work with a party?

A: Appointment following the procedures set out in the Representation Provisions would permit the salesperson to provide a higher level of service. The appointed salesperson may provide advice and opinions to the party to whom the salesperson is assigned and is not subject to the intermediary's statutory duty of not acting so as to favor one party over the other.

7. Q: Is an intermediary an agent?

A: Yes, but the duties and obligations of an intermediary are different than for exclusive, or single, agents.

8. Q: What are the duties and obligations of an intermediary?

A: The Representation Provisions require the intermediary to obtain written consent from both parties to act as an intermediary. A written listing agreement to represent a seller/landlord or a written buyer/tenant representation agreement which contains authorization for the broker to act as an intermediary between the parties is sufficient for the purposes of the Representation Provisions if the agreement sets forth, in conspicuous bold or underlined print, the broker's obligations under Section 1101.651(d), and the agreement states who will pay the broker.

If the intermediary is to appoint associated licensees to work with the parties, the intermediary must obtain written permission from both parties and give written notice of the appointments to each party. The intermediary is also required to treat the parties fairly and honestly and to comply with TRELA. The intermediary is prohibited from acting so as to favor one party over the other, and may not reveal confidential information obtained from one party without the written instructions of that party, unless disclosure of that information is required by TRELA, court order, or the information materially relates to the condition of the property. The intermediary and any associated licensees appointed by the intermediary are prohibited from disclosing without written authorization that the seller will accept a price less than the asking price or that the buyer will pay a price greater than the price submitted in a written offer.

9. Q: Can salespersons act as intermediaries?

A: Only a broker can contract with the parties to act as an intermediary between them.

In that sense, only a broker can be an intermediary. If, however, the broker intermediary does not appoint associated licensees to work with the parties in a transaction, any salesperson or broker associates of the intermediary who function in that transaction would be required to act just as the intermediary does, not favoring one party over the other.

10. Q: Can there be two intermediaries in the same transaction?

   A: No.

11. Q: Can a broker representing only the buyer be an intermediary?

   A: Ordinarily, no; the listing broker will be the intermediary. In the case of a FSBO or other seller who is not already represented by a broker, the broker representing the buyer could secure the consent of both parties to act as an intermediary.

12. Q: May an intermediary appoint a subagent in another firm to work with one of the parties?

   A: Subagency is still permitted under the law, but a subagent in another firm cannot be appointed as one of the intermediary's associated licensees under the Representation Provisions of the Act.

13. Q: May the same salesperson be appointed by the intermediary to work with both parties in the same transaction?

   A: No; the law requires the intermediary to appoint different associated licensees to work with each party.

14. Q: May more than one associated licensee be appointed by the intermediary to work with the same party?

   A: Yes.

15. Q: What is the difference between an appointed licensee working with a party and a licensee associated with the intermediary who has not been appointed to work with one party?

   A: During negotiations the appointed licensee may advise the person to whom the licensee has been appointed. An associated licensee who has not been appointed must act in the same manner as the intermediary, that is, not giving opinions and advice and not favoring one party over the other.

16. Q: Who decides whether a broker will act as intermediary, the broker or the parties?

   A: Initially, the broker, in determining the policy of the firm. If the broker does not wish to act as an intermediary, nothing requires the broker to do so. If the broker's policy is to offer services as an intermediary, both parties must authorize the broker in writing before the broker may act as in intermediary or appoint licensees to work with each of the parties.

17. **Q: When must the intermediary appoint the licensees associated with the intermediary to work with the parties?**

> **A:** This is a judgment call for the intermediary. If appointments are going to be made, they should be made before the buyer begins to receive advice and opinions from an associated licensee in connection with the property listed with the broker. If the broker appoints the associates at the time the listing contract and buyer representation agreements are signed, it should be clear that the appointments are effective only when the intermediary relationship arises. **The intermediary relationship does not exist until the parties who have authorized it are beginning to deal with each other in a proposed real estate transaction; for example, the buyer begins to negotiate to purchase the seller's property.** Prior to the creation of the intermediary relationship, the broker will typically be acting as an exclusive agent of each party. It is important to remember that **both** parties must be notified in writing of **both** appointments. If, for example, the listing agent is "appointed" at the time the listing is taken, care must be taken to ensure that the buyer is ultimately also given written notice of the appointment. When a buyer client begins to show interest in a property listed with the firm and both parties have authorized the intermediary relationship, the seller must be notified in writing as to which associate has been appointed to work with the buyer.

18. **Q: Can the intermediary delegate to another person the authority to appoint licensees associated with the intermediary?**

> **A:** The intermediary may delegate to another licensee the authority to appoint associated licensees. **If the intermediary authorizes another licensee to appoint associated licensees to work with the parties, however, that person must not appoint himself or herself as one of the associated licensees, as this would be an improper combination of the different functions of intermediary and associated licensee. It is also important to remember that there will be a single intermediary even if another licensee has been authorized to make appointments.**

19. **Q: May a broker act as a dual agent?**

> **A:** A broker may not act as a dual agent under Occupations Code Section 1101.561(b), which provides that "a broker must agree to act as an intermediary under this subchapter if the broker agrees to represent in a transaction" a buyer or tenant, and a seller or landlord.

20. **Q: What are the agency disclosure requirements for real estate licensees?**

A: To disclose their representation of a party upon the first contact with a party or a licensee representing another party.

21. **Q: Is disclosure of agency required to be in writing?**

    A: The disclosure may be oral or in writing.

22. **Q: Are licensees required to provide parties with written information relating to agency?**

    A: Yes. The Representation Provisions require licensees to provide the parties with a copy of a written statement, the content of which is specified in the statute. The form of the statement may be varied, so long as the text of the statement is in at least 10 point type.

23. **Q: Are there exceptions when the statutory statement is not required?**

    A: Yes; the statement is required to be provided when the first substantive dialogue occurs between a party and the licensee at which discussion occurs with respect to specific real property. The statement is **not** required for either of the following:

    (1) a transaction which is a residential lease no longer than one year and no sale is being considered; or

    (2) a meeting with a party represented by another licensee.

24. **Q: Are the disclosure and statutory information requirements applicable to commercial transactions, new home sales, farm and ranch sales or transactions other than residential sales?**

    A: Except as noted above, the requirements are applicable to all real estate transactions. Licensees dealing with landlords and tenants are permitted by the law to modify their versions of the statutory statement to use the terms "landlord" and "tenant" in place of the terms "seller" and "buyer."

25. **Q: What are the penalties for licensees who fail to comply with the Representation Provisions?**

    A: Failure to comply is a violation of TRELA, punishable by reprimand, by suspension or revocation of a license, or by an administrative penalty (fine).

26. **Q: In what way do the Representation Provisions prohibit or permit disclosed dual agency?**

    A: The Representation Provisions prohibit disclosed dual agency.

27. **Q: Is the licensee required under any circumstance, to provide the "written statement" to buyer prospects at properties held open for prospective buyers?**

   A: An encounter at an open house is not a meeting for the purposes of the Representation Provisions. A licensee would not be required to provide the statutory statement at the open house. However, at the first substantive dialogue thereafter with the buyer regarding a specific property and during which substantive discussions occur, the licensee will be required to provide the statement.

28. **Q: When acting as an appointed licensee what "agency" limitations does the licensee have when communicating with a buyer/tenant or seller/landlord that an agent representing one party only doesn't have?**

   A: The appointed licensee may not, except as permitted by Section 1101.651(d) of TRELA, disclose to either party confidential information received from the other party. A licensee representing one party would not be prohibited from revealing confidential information to the licensee's principal, and if the information were material to the principal's decision, would be required to reveal the information to the principal.

29. **Q: If a buyer's agent is required to disclose that licensee's agency status to a listing broker when setting up an appointment showing, must the listing broker also disclose to the buyer's agent that the listing broker represents the seller?**

   A: Yes, on the first contact with the licensee representing the buyer.

30. **Q: Does the TREC encourage brokerage companies to act for more than one party in the same transaction?**

   A: No.

31. **Q: Must the intermediary broker furnish written notice to each party to a transaction when the broker designates the appointed licensees?**

   A: Yes.

32. **Q: How is a property "showing" different from a proposed transaction?**

   A: The question appears to be "may an associate show property listed with the associate's broker while representing the buyer without first being appointed by the intermediary, and if so, why?" Yes. Only showing property does not require the associate to be appointed, because it does not require the licensee to give advice or opinions (only an appointed associate may offer opinions or advice to a party). If no appointments will be made, of course, the associate will be working with the party and will not be authorized to provide opinions or advice.

33. Q: Does TREC recommend that licensees provide a written disclosure of agency?

A: It is the licensee's choice as to whether disclosure is in writing or oral, just as it is the licensee's choice as to whether proof of disclosure will be easy or difficult.

34. Q: Our company policy requires all buyers and sellers to agree to the intermediary practice before commencing to work with them. Does the law permit a broker employment agreement to specify this practice only?

A: If by "broker employment agreement" you mean a listing contract or buyer representation agreement, yes.

35. Q: What are the differences between the duties provided to the seller or landlord by the intermediary broker and the duties provided to the buyer or tenant by the appointed licensee?

A: The intermediary and the appointed licensees do not provide duties; they perform services under certain duties imposed by the law. The intermediary is authorized to negotiate a transaction between the parties, but not to give advice or opinions to them in negotiations. The appointed licensee may provide advice or opinions to the party to which the licensee has been appointed. Both intermediary and appointed licensee are obligated to treat the parties honestly and are prohibited from revealing confidential information or other information addressed in Section 1101.651(d) of TRELA.

36. Q: Must each party's identity be revealed to the other party before an intermediary transaction can occur?

A: Yes. If associates are going to be appointed by the intermediary, the law provides that the appointments are made by giving written notice to both parties. To give notice, the intermediary must identify the party and the associate(s) appointed to that party. The law does not require notice if no appointments are going to be made. The law provides that the listing contract and buyer representation agreement are sufficient to establish the written consent of the party if the obligations of the broker under Section 1101.651(d) are set forth in conspicuous bold or underlined print.

37. Q: As a listing agent I hold open houses. If a buyer prospect enters who desires to purchase the property at that time, can I represent that buyer and, if so, must my broker designate me as an appointed licensee and provide the parties with written notice before I prepare the purchase offer?

A: As a representative of the seller, you would be obligated to disclose your representation to the buyer at the first contact. The disclosure may be in writing or oral. As an associate of the listing broker, you can enter into a buyer representation agreement for your broker to act as an intermediary in a transaction involving this buyer and the owner of the property. If the owner has similarly authorized the broker to act as an intermediary, it will depend on the firm's policy whether appointments are to be made. If appointments are not going to be made, you may proceed in the transaction as an unappointed licensee with a duty of not favoring one party over the other. If appointments are going to be made, the parties must both be notified in writing before you may provide opinions or advice to the buyer in negotiations.

38. Q: I have a salesperson's license through a broker and I also have a licensed assistant. Can that assistant be an appointed licensee under me as an intermediary?

A: Your broker, not you, will be the intermediary. The intermediary may appoint a licensed associate to work with a party. If the licensed assistant is an associate of the broker, the licensed assistant could be appointed by the intermediary to work with one of the parties. If the licensed assistant is not an associate of the broker, the licensed assistant cannot be appointed. NOTE: IF THE LICENSED ASSISTANT IS LICENSED AS A SALESPERSON, THE LICENSED ASSISTANT MUST BE SPONSORED BY, AND ACTING FOR, A BROKER TO BE AUTHORIZED TO PERFORM ANY ACT FOR WHICH A REAL ESTATE LICENSE IS REQUIRED. IF THE LICENSED ASSISTANT IS SPONSORED BY A BROKER WHO IS NOT ASSOCIATED WITH THE INTERMEDIARY, THE LICENSED ASSISTANT WOULD NOT BE CONSIDERED AN ASSOCIATE OF THE INTERMEDIARY EITHER.

39. Q: I am a listing agent and a buyer prospect wants to buy the property I have listed. How can I sell my own listing?

A: See the three alternatives discussed in the related question on page 2. You could alter the agency relationships and only represent one party, you could be appointed to work with one party and another associate could be appointed to work with the other party, or no appointments would be made, or you could work with the parties being careful not to favor one over the other or provide advice or opinions to them.

40. Q: Must the respective appointed licensees each provide an opinion of value to the respective buyer prospect and seller prospect?

A: At the time a property is listed, the licensee is obligated to advise the owner as to the licensee's opinion of the market value of the property. Once appointments have been made, the appointed associates are permitted, but not required, to provide the party to whom they have been appointed with opinions and advice during negotiations.

41. Q: How can the intermediary broker advise the seller or buyer on value, escrow deposit amount, repair expenses, or interest rates?

A: When the listing contract or buyer representation agreement has come into existence, and no intermediary status yet exists, the broker may advise the parties generally on such matters. Offers from or to parties not represented by the intermediary's firm may have made the parties knowledgeable on these matters. Once the intermediary status has been created, however, the intermediary broker may not express opinions or give advice during negotiations. Information about such matters which does not constitute an opinion or advice may be supplied in response to question. For example, the intermediary could tell the buyer what the prevailing interest rate is without expressing an opinion or giving advice. The seller's question about the amount of earnest money could be answered with the factual answer that in the broker's experience, the amount of the earnest money is usually $1,500 to $2,000, depending on the amount of the sales price. If the buyer asks what amount of money should be in the offer, the intermediary could respond with the factual statement that in the intermediary's experience, those offers closest to the listing price tend to be accepted by the seller. The intermediary also could refer the party to an attorney, accountant, loan officer or other professional for advice.

42. Q: I was the listing agent for a property that didn't sell but was listed by another broker after the expiration of my agreement. I now have a buyer client who wants to see that same property. Must the new broker, or my broker, designate me as an appointed licensee or how may I otherwise act?

A: Assuming an agreement with the listing broker as regards cooperation and compensation, you may represent the buyer as an exclusive agent. You cannot be appointed by the intermediary because you are not an associate of the listing broker, and from the facts as you describe them, no intermediary status is going to arise. Confidential information obtained from the seller when you were acting as the seller's agent, of course, could not be disclosed to your new client, the buyer.

43. Q: How is the intermediary broker responsible for the actions of appointed licensees when a difference of opinion of property value estimates is provided?

A: Brokers are responsible for the actions of their salespersons under TRELA. Opinions of property values may be different and yet not indicative of error or mistake by the salespersons. If a salesperson makes an error or mistake, the sponsoring broker is responsible to the public and to TREC under Section 1101.803 of TRELA.

44. Q: Although both the buyer and the seller initially consented to the intermediary broker practice at the time each signed a broker

employment agreement, must each party consent again to a specific transaction to ensure there are not potential conflicts?

A: TRELA does not require a second written consent. TRELA does require written notice of any appointments, and the written notice would probably cause any objection to be resolved at that point. A broker would not be prohibited from obtaining a second consent as a business practice, so that potential conflicts are identified and resolved. The sales contract, of course, would typically identify the parties and show the intermediary relationship if the broker completes the "Broker Identification and Ratification of Fee" at the end of the TREC contract form.

45. **Q: In the absence of the appointed licensees, can the intermediary broker actually negotiate a purchase offer between the parties?**

   A: Yes. See the answer to the question relating to the duties of an intermediary.

46. **Q: May a licensee include the statutory statement in a listing agreement or buyer representation agreement, either in the text of the agreement, or as an exhibit?**

   A: Yes, but the licensee should provide the prospective party with a separate copy of the statutory statement as soon as is practicable at their first substantive dialogue.

APPENDIX C

The National Association of REALTORS® Code of Ethics

Code of Ethics and Standards of Practice
of the NATIONAL ASSOCIATION OF REALTORS®
Effective January 1, 2014

Where the word REALTORS® is used in this Code and Preamble, it shall be deemed to include REALTOR-ASSOCIATE®s.

While the Code of Ethics establishes obligations that may be higher than those mandated by law, in any instance where the Code of Ethics and the law conflict, the obligations of the law must take precedence.

Preamble

Under all is the land. Upon its wise utilization and widely allocated ownership depend the survival and growth of free institutions and of our civilization. REALTORS® should recognize that the interests of the nation and its citizens require the highest and best use of the land and the widest distribution of land ownership. They require the creation of adequate housing, the building of functioning cities, the development of productive industries and farms, and the preservation of a healthful environment.

Such interests impose obligations beyond those of ordinary commerce. They impose grave social responsibility and a patriotic duty to which REALTORS® should dedicate themselves, and for which they should be diligent in preparing themselves. REALTORS®, therefore, are zealous to maintain and improve the standards of their calling and share with their fellow REALTORS® a common responsibility for its integrity and honor.

In recognition and appreciation of their obligations to clients, customers, the public, and each other, REALTORS® continuously strive to become and remain informed on issues affecting real estate and, as knowledgeable professionals, they willingly share the fruit of their experience and study with others. They identify and take steps, through enforcement of this Code of Ethics and by assisting appropriate regulatory bodies, to eliminate practices which may damage the public or which might discredit or bring dishonor to the real estate profession. REALTORS® having direct personal knowledge of conduct that may violate the Code of Ethics involving misappropriation of client or customer funds or property, willful discrimination, or fraud resulting in substantial economic harm, bring such matters to the attention of the appropriate Board or Association of REALTORS®. *(Amended 1/00)*

Realizing that cooperation with other real estate professionals promotes the best interests of those who utilize their services, REALTORS® urge exclusive representation of clients; do not attempt to gain any unfair advantage over their competitors; and they refrain from making unsolicited comments about other practitioners. In instances where their opinion is sought, or where REALTORS® believe that comment is necessary, their opinion is offered in an objective, professional manner, uninfluenced by any personal motivation or potential advantage or gain.

The term REALTOR® has come to connote competency, fairness, and high integrity resulting from adherence to a lofty ideal of moral conduct in business relations. No inducement of profit and no instruction from clients ever can justify departure from this ideal.

In the interpretation of this obligation, REALTORS® can take no safer guide than that which has been handed down through the centuries, embodied in the Golden Rule, "Whatsoever ye would that others should do to you, do ye even so to them."

Accepting this standard as their own, REALTORS® pledge to observe its spirit in all of their activities whether conducted personally, through associates or others, or via technological means, and to conduct their business in accordance with the tenets set forth below. *(Amended 1/07)*

Duties to Clients and Customers

Article 1

When representing a buyer, seller, landlord, tenant, or other client as an agent, REALTORS® pledge themselves to protect and promote the interests of their client. This obligation to the client is primary, but it does not relieve REALTORS® of their obligation to treat all parties honestly. When serving a buyer, seller, landlord, tenant or other party in a non-agency capacity, REALTORS® remain obligated to treat all parties honestly. *(Amended 1/01)*

- **Standard of Practice 1-1**
  REALTORS®, when acting as principals in a real estate transaction, remain obligated by the duties imposed by the Code of Ethics. *(Amended 1/93)*

- **Standard of Practice 1-2**
  The duties imposed by the Code of Ethics encompass all real estate-related activities and transactions whether conducted in person, electronically, or through any other means.

  The duties the Code of Ethics imposes are applicable whether REALTORS® are acting as agents or in legally recognized non-agency capacities except that any duty imposed exclusively on agents by law or regulation shall not be imposed by this Code of Ethics on REALTORS® acting in non-agency capacities.

  As used in this Code of Ethics, "client" means the person(s) or entity(ies) with whom a REALTOR® or a REALTOR®'s firm has an agency or legally recognized non-agency relationship; "customer" means a party to a real estate transaction who receives information, services, or benefits but has no contractual relationship with the REALTOR® or the REALTOR®'s firm; "prospect" means a purchaser, seller, tenant, or landlord who is not subject to a representation relationship with the REALTOR® or REALTOR®'s firm; "agent" means a real estate licensee (including brokers and sales associates) acting in an agency relationship as defined by state law or regulation; and "broker" means a real estate licensee (including brokers and sales associates) acting as an agent or in a legally recognized non-agency capacity. *(Adopted 1/95, Amended 1/07)*

- **Standard of Practice 1-3**
  REALTORS®, in attempting to secure a listing, shall not deliberately mislead the owner as to market value.

- **Standard of Practice 1-4**
  REALTORS®, when seeking to become a buyer/tenant representative, shall not mislead buyers or tenants as to savings or other benefits that might be realized through use of the REALTOR®'s services. *(Amended 1/93)*

- **Standard of Practice 1-5**
  REALTORS® may represent the seller/landlord and buyer/tenant in the

NATIONAL
ASSOCIATION *of*
REALTORS®

same transaction only after full disclosure to and with informed consent of both parties. *(Adopted 1/93)*

· **Standard of Practice 1-6**
REALTORS® shall submit offers and counter-offers objectively and as quickly as possible. *(Adopted 1/93, Amended 1/95)*

· **Standard of Practice 1-7**
When acting as listing brokers, REALTORS® shall continue to submit to the seller/landlord all offers and counter-offers until closing or execution of a lease unless the seller/landlord has waived this obligation in writing. REALTORS® shall not be obligated to continue to market the property after an offer has been accepted by the seller/landlord. REALTORS® shall recommend that sellers/landlords obtain the advice of legal counsel prior to acceptance of a subsequent offer except where the acceptance is contingent on the termination of the pre-existing purchase contract or lease. *(Amended 1/93)*

· **Standard of Practice 1-8**
REALTORS®, acting as agents or brokers of buyers/tenants, shall submit to buyers/tenants all offers and counter-offers until acceptance but have no obligation to continue to show properties to their clients after an offer has been accepted unless otherwise agreed in writing. REALTORS®, acting as agents or brokers of buyers/tenants, shall recommend that buyers/tenants obtain the advice of legal counsel if there is a question as to whether a pre-existing contract has been terminated. *(Adopted 1/93, Amended 1/99)*

· **Standard of Practice 1-9**
The obligation of REALTORS® to preserve confidential information (as defined by state law) provided by their clients in the course of any agency relationship or non-agency relationship recognized by law continues after termination of agency relationships or any non-agency relationships recognized by law. REALTORS® shall not knowingly, during or following the termination of professional relationships with their clients:
1) reveal confidential information of clients; or
2) use confidential information of clients to the disadvantage of clients; or
3) use confidential information of clients for the REALTOR®'s advantage or the advantage of third parties unless:
   a) clients consent after full disclosure; or
   b) REALTORS® are required by court order; or
   c) it is the intention of a client to commit a crime and the information is necessary to prevent the crime; or
   d) it is necessary to defend a REALTOR® or the REALTOR®'s employees or associates against an accusation of wrongful conduct.
Information concerning latent material defects is not considered confidential information under this Code of Ethics. *(Adopted 1/93, Amended 1/01)*

· **Standard of Practice 1-10**
REALTORS® shall, consistent with the terms and conditions of their real estate licensure and their property management agreement, competently manage the property of clients with due regard for the rights, safety and health of tenants and others lawfully on the premises. *(Adopted 1/95, Amended 1/00)*

· **Standard of Practice 1-11**
REALTORS® who are employed to maintain or manage a client's property shall exercise due diligence and make reasonable efforts to protect it against reasonably foreseeable contingencies and losses. *(Adopted 1/95)*

· **Standard of Practice 1-12**
When entering into listing contracts, REALTORS® must advise sellers/landlords of:
1) the REALTOR®'s company policies regarding cooperation and the amount(s) of any compensation that will be offered to subagents, buyer/tenant agents, and/or brokers acting in legally recognized non-agency capacities;

2) the fact that buyer/tenant agents or brokers, even if compensated by listing brokers, or by sellers/landlords may represent the interests of buyers/tenants; and
3) any potential for listing brokers to act as disclosed dual agents, e.g., buyer/tenant agents. *(Adopted 1/93, Renumbered 1/98, Amended 1/03)*

· **Standard of Practice 1-13**
When entering into buyer/tenant agreements, REALTORS® must advise potential clients of:
1) the REALTOR®'s company policies regarding cooperation;
2) the amount of compensation to be paid by the client;
3) the potential for additional or offsetting compensation from other brokers, from the seller or landlord, or from other parties;
4) any potential for the buyer/tenant representative to act as a disclosed dual agent, e.g., listing broker, subagent, landlord's agent, etc., and
5) the possibility that sellers or sellers' representatives may not treat the existence, terms, or conditions of offers as confidential unless confidentiality is required by law, regulation, or by any confidentiality agreement between the parties. *(Adopted 1/93, Renumbered 1/98, Amended 1/06)*

· **Standard of Practice 1-14**
Fees for preparing appraisals or other valuations shall not be contingent upon the amount of the appraisal or valuation. *(Adopted 1/02)*

· **Standard of Practice 1-15**
REALTORS®, in response to inquiries from buyers or cooperating brokers shall, with the sellers' approval, disclose the existence of offers on the property. Where disclosure is authorized, REALTORS® shall also disclose, if asked, whether offers were obtained by the listing licensee, another licensee in the listing firm, or by a cooperating broker. *(Adopted 1/03, Amended 1/09)*

· **Standard of Practice 1-16**
REALTORS® shall not access or use, or permit or enable others to access or use, listed or managed property on terms or conditions other than those authorized by the owner or seller. *(Adopted 1/12)*

Article 2

REALTORS® shall avoid exaggeration, misrepresentation, or concealment of pertinent facts relating to the property or the transaction. REALTORS® shall not, however, be obligated to discover latent defects in the property, to advise on matters outside the scope of their real estate license, or to disclose facts which are confidential under the scope of agency or non-agency relationships as defined by state law. *(Amended 1/00)*

· **Standard of Practice 2-1**
REALTORS® shall only be obligated to discover and disclose adverse factors reasonably apparent to someone with expertise in those areas required by their real estate licensing authority. Article 2 does not impose upon the REALTOR® the obligation of expertise in other professional or technical disciplines. *(Amended 1/96)*

· **Standard of Practice 2-2**
(Renumbered as Standard of Practice 1-12 1/98)

· **Standard of Practice 2-3**
(Renumbered as Standard of Practice 1-13 1/98)

· **Standard of Practice 2-4**
REALTORS® shall not be parties to the naming of a false consideration in any document, unless it be the naming of an obviously nominal consideration.

· **Standard of Practice 2-5**
Factors defined as "non-material" by law or regulation or which are expressly referenced in law or regulation as not being subject to disclosure are considered not "pertinent" for purposes of Article 2. *(Adopted 1/93)*

Article 3

REALTORS® shall cooperate with other brokers except when cooperation is not in the client's best interest. The obligation to cooperate does not include the obligation to share commissions, fees, or to otherwise compensate another broker. *(Amended 1/95)*

- **Standard of Practice 3-1**

  REALTORS®, acting as exclusive agents or brokers of sellers/ landlords, establish the terms and conditions of offers to cooperate. Unless expressly indicated in offers to cooperate, cooperating brokers may not assume that the offer of cooperation includes an offer of compensation. Terms of compensation, if any, shall be ascertained by cooperating brokers before beginning efforts to accept the offer of cooperation. *(Amended 1/99)*

- **Standard of Practice 3-2**

  Any change in compensation offered for cooperative services must be communicated to the other REALTOR® prior to the time that REALTOR® submits an offer to purchase/lease the property. After a REALTOR® has submitted an offer to purchase or lease property, the listing broker may not attempt to unilaterally modify the offered compensation with respect to that cooperative transaction. *(Amended 1/14)*

- **Standard of Practice 3-3**

  Standard of Practice 3-2 does not preclude the listing broker and cooperating broker from entering into an agreement to change cooperative compensation. *(Adopted 1/94)*

- **Standard of Practice 3-4**

  REALTORS®, acting as listing brokers, have an affirmative obligation to disclose the existence of dual or variable rate commission arrangements (i.e., listings where one amount of commission is payable if the listing broker's firm is the procuring cause of sale/lease and a different amount of commission is payable if the sale/lease results through the efforts of the seller/landlord or a cooperating broker). The listing broker shall, as soon as practical, disclose the existence of such arrangements to potential cooperating brokers and shall, in response to inquiries from cooperating brokers, disclose the differential that would result in a cooperative transaction or in a sale/lease that results through the efforts of the seller/ landlord. If the cooperating broker is a buyer/tenant representative, the buyer/tenant representative must disclose such information to their client before the client makes an offer to purchase or lease. *(Amended 1/02)*

- **Standard of Practice 3-5**

  It is the obligation of subagents to promptly disclose all pertinent facts to the principal's agent prior to as well as after a purchase or lease agreement is executed. *(Amended 1/93)*

- **Standard of Practice 3-6**

  REALTORS® shall disclose the existence of accepted offers, including offers with unresolved contingencies, to any broker seeking cooperation. *(Adopted 5/86, Amended 1/04)*

- **Standard of Practice 3-7**

  When seeking information from another REALTOR® concerning property under a management or listing agreement, REALTORS® shall disclose their REALTOR® status and whether their interest is personal or on behalf of a client and, if on behalf of a client, their relationship with the client. *(Amended 1/11)*

- **Standard of Practice 3-8**

  REALTORS® shall not misrepresent the availability of access to show or inspect a listed property. *(Amended 11/87)*

- **Standard of Practice 3-9**

  REALTORS® shall not provide access to listed property on terms other than those established by the owner or the listing broker. *(Adopted 1/10)*

- **Standard of Practice 3-10**

  The duty to cooperate established in Article 3 relates to the obligation to share information on listed property, and to make property available to other brokers for showing to prospective purchasers/tenants when it is in the best interests of sellers/landlords. *(Adopted 1/11)*

Article 4

REALTORS® shall not acquire an interest in or buy or present offers from themselves, any member of their immediate families, their firms or any member thereof, or any entities in which they have any ownership interest, any real property without making their true position known to the owner or the owner's agent or broker. In selling property they own, or in which they have any interest, REALTORS® shall reveal their ownership or interest in writing to the purchaser or the purchaser's representative. *(Amended 1/00)*

- **Standard of Practice 4-1**

  For the protection of all parties, the disclosures required by Article 4 shall be in writing and provided by REALTORS® prior to the signing of any contract. *(Adopted 2/86)*

Article 5

REALTORS® shall not undertake to provide professional services concerning a property or its value where they have a present or contemplated interest unless such interest is specifically disclosed to all affected parties.

Article 6

REALTORS® shall not accept any commission, rebate, or profit on expenditures made for their client, without the client's knowledge and consent.

When recommending real estate products or services (e.g., homeowner's insurance, warranty programs, mortgage financing, title insurance, etc.), REALTORS® shall disclose to the client or customer to whom the recommendation is made any financial benefits or fees, other than real estate referral fees, the REALTOR® or REALTOR®'s firm may receive as a direct result of such recommendation. *(Amended 1/99)*

- **Standard of Practice 6-1**

  REALTORS® shall not recommend or suggest to a client or a customer the use of services of another organization or business entity in which they have a direct interest without disclosing such interest at the time of the recommendation or suggestion. *(Amended 5/88)*

Article 7

In a transaction, REALTORS® shall not accept compensation from more than one party, even if permitted by law, without disclosure to all parties and the informed consent of the REALTOR®'s client or clients. *(Amended 1/93)*

Article 8

REALTORS® shall keep in a special account in an appropriate financial institution, separated from their own funds, monies coming into their possession in trust for other persons, such as escrows, trust funds, clients' monies, and other like items.

Article 9

REALTORS®, for the protection of all parties, shall assure whenever possible that all agreements related to real estate transactions including, but not limited to, listing and representation agreements, purchase contracts, and leases are in writing in clear and understandable language expressing the specific terms, conditions, obligations and commitments of the parties. A copy of each agreement shall be furnished to each party to such agreements upon their signing or initialing. *(Amended 1/04)*

- **Standard of Practice 9-1**

For the protection of all parties, REALTORS® shall use reasonable care to ensure that documents pertaining to the purchase, sale, or lease of real estate are kept current through the use of written extensions or amendments. *(Amended 1/93)*

- **Standard of Practice 9-2**

When assisting or enabling a client or customer in establishing a contractual relationship (e.g., listing and representation agreements, purchase agreements, leases, etc.) electronically, REALTORS® shall make reasonable efforts to explain the nature and disclose the specific terms of the contractual relationship being established prior to it being agreed to by a contracting party. *(Adopted 1/07)*

Duties to the Public

Article 10

REALTORS® shall not deny equal professional services to any person for reasons of race, color, religion, sex, handicap, familial status, national origin, sexual orientation, or gender identity. REALTORS® shall not be parties to any plan or agreement to discriminate against a person or persons on the basis of race, color, religion, sex, handicap, familial status, national origin, sexual orientation, or gender identity. *(Amended 1/14)*

REALTORS®, in their real estate employment practices, shall not discriminate against any person or persons on the basis of race, color, religion, sex, handicap, familial status, national origin, sexual orientation, or gender identity. *(Amended 1/14)*

- **Standard of Practice 10-1**

When involved in the sale or lease of a residence, REALTORS® shall not volunteer information regarding the racial, religious or ethnic composition of any neighborhood nor shall they engage in any activity which may result in panic selling, however, REALTORS® may provide other demographic information. *(Adopted 1/94, Amended 1/06)*

- **Standard of Practice 10-2**

When not involved in the sale or lease of a residence, REALTORS® may provide demographic information related to a property, transaction or professional assignment to a party if such demographic information is (a) deemed by the REALTOR® to be needed to assist with or complete, in a manner consistent with Article 10, a real estate transaction or professional assignment and (b) is obtained or derived from a recognized, reliable, independent, and impartial source. The source of such information and any additions, deletions, modifications, interpretations, or other changes shall be disclosed in reasonable detail. *(Adopted 1/05, Renumbered 1/06)*

- **Standard of Practice 10-3**

REALTORS® shall not print, display or circulate any statement or advertisement with respect to selling or renting of a property that indicates any preference, limitations or discrimination based on race, color, religion, sex, handicap, familial status, national origin, sexual orientation, or gender identity. *(Adopted 1/94, Renumbered 1/05 and 1/06, Amended 1/14)*

- **Standard of Practice 10-4**

As used in Article 10 "real estate employment practices" relates to employees and independent contractors providing real estate-related services and the administrative and clerical staff directly supporting those individuals. *(Adopted 1/00, Renumbered 1/05 and 1/06)*

Article 11

The services which REALTORS® provide to their clients and customers shall conform to the standards of practice and competence which are reasonably expected in the specific real estate disciplines in which they engage; specifically, residential real estate brokerage, real property management, commercial and industrial real estate brokerage, land brokerage, real estate appraisal, real estate counseling, real estate syndication, real estate auction, and international real estate.

REALTORS® shall not undertake to provide specialized professional services concerning a type of property or service that is outside their field of competence unless they engage the assistance of one who is competent on such types of property or service, or unless the facts are fully disclosed to the client. Any persons engaged to provide such assistance shall be so identified to the client and their contribution to the assignment should be set forth. *(Amended 1/10)*

- **Standard of Practice 11-1**

When REALTORS® prepare opinions of real property value or price they must:
1) be knowledgeable about the type of property being valued,
2) have access to the information and resources necessary to formulate an accurate opinion, and
3) be familiar with the area where the subject property is located

unless lack of any of these is disclosed to the party requesting the opinion in advance.

When an opinion of value or price is prepared other than in pursuit of a listing or to assist a potential purchaser in formulating a purchase offer, the opinion shall include the following unless the party requesting the opinion requires a specific type of report or different data set:
1) identification of the subject property
2) date prepared
3) defined value or price
4) limiting conditions, including statements of purpose(s) and intended user(s)
5) any present or contemplated interest, including the possibility of representing the seller/landlord or buyers/tenants
6) basis for the opinion, including applicable market data
7) if the opinion is not an appraisal, a statement to that effect
8) disclosure of whether and when a physical inspection of the property's exterior was conducted
9) disclosure of whether and when a physical inspection of the property's interior was conducted
10) disclosure of whether the REALTOR® has any conflicts of interest *(Amended 1/14)*

- **Standard of Practice 11-2**

The obligations of the Code of Ethics in respect of real estate disciplines other than appraisal shall be interpreted and applied in accordance with the standards of competence and practice which clients and the public reasonably require to protect their rights and interests considering the complexity of the transaction, the availability of expert assistance, and, where the REALTOR® is an agent or subagent, the obligations of a fiduciary. *(Adopted 1/95)*

- **Standard of Practice 11-3**

When REALTORS® provide consultive services to clients which involve advice or counsel for a fee (not a commission), such advice shall be rendered in an objective manner and the fee shall not be contingent on the substance of the advice or counsel given. If brokerage or transaction services are to be provided in addition to consultive services, a separate compensation may be paid with prior agreement between the client and REALTOR®. *(Adopted 1/96)*

- **Standard of Practice 11-4**

The competency required by Article 11 relates to services contracted for between REALTORS® and their clients or customers; the duties expressly imposed by the Code of Ethics; and the duties imposed by law or regulation. *(Adopted 1/02)*

Article 12

REALTORS® shall be honest and truthful in their real estate communications and shall present a true picture in their advertising, marketing, and other representations. REALTORS® shall ensure that their status as real estate professionals is readily apparent in their advertising, marketing, and other representations, and that the recipients of all real estate communications are, or have been, notified that those communications are from a real estate professional. *(Amended 1/08)*

- **Standard of Practice 12-1**
  REALTORS® may use the term "free" and similar terms in their advertising and in other representations provided that all terms governing availability of the offered product or service are clearly disclosed at the same time. *(Amended 1/97)*

- **Standard of Practice 12-2**
  REALTORS® may represent their services as "free" or without cost even if they expect to receive compensation from a source other than their client provided that the potential for the REALTOR® to obtain a benefit from a third party is clearly disclosed at the same time. *(Amended 1/97)*

- **Standard of Practice 12-3**
  The offering of premiums, prizes, merchandise discounts or other inducements to list, sell, purchase, or lease is not, in itself, unethical even if receipt of the benefit is contingent on listing, selling, purchasing, or leasing through the REALTOR® making the offer. However, REALTORS® must exercise care and candor in any such advertising or other public or private representations so that any party interested in receiving or otherwise benefiting from the REALTOR®'s offer will have clear, thorough, advance understanding of all the terms and conditions of the offer. The offering of any inducements to do business is subject to the limitations and restrictions of state law and the ethical obligations established by any applicable Standard of Practice. *(Amended 1/95)*

- **Standard of Practice 12-4**
  REALTORS® shall not offer for sale/lease or advertise property without authority. When acting as listing brokers or as subagents, REALTORS® shall not quote a price different from that agreed upon with the seller/landlord. *(Amended 1/93)*

- **Standard of Practice 12-5**
  REALTORS® shall not advertise nor permit any person employed by or affiliated with them to advertise real estate services or listed property in any medium (e.g., electronically, print, radio, television, etc.) without disclosing the name of that REALTOR®'s firm in a reasonable and readily apparent manner. This Standard of Practice acknowledges that disclosing the name of the firm may not be practical in electronic displays of limited information (e.g., "thumbnails", text messages, "tweets", etc.). Such displays are exempt from the disclosure requirement established in this Standard of Practice, but only when linked to a display that includes all required disclosures. *(Adopted 11/86, Amended 1/11)*

- **Standard of Practice 12-6**
  REALTORS®, when advertising unlisted real property for sale/lease in which they have an ownership interest, shall disclose their status as both owners/landlords and as REALTORS® or real estate licensees. *(Amended 1/93)*

- **Standard of Practice 12-7**
  Only REALTORS® who participated in the transaction as the listing broker or cooperating broker (selling broker) may claim to have "sold" the property.

Prior to closing, a cooperating broker may post a "sold" sign only with the consent of the listing broker. *(Amended 1/96)*

- **Standard of Practice 12-8**
  The obligation to present a true picture in representations to the public includes information presented, provided, or displayed on REALTORS®' websites. REALTORS® shall use reasonable efforts to ensure that information on their websites is current. When it becomes apparent that information on a REALTOR®'s website is no longer current or accurate, REALTORS® shall promptly take corrective action. *(Adopted 1/07)*

- **Standard of Practice 12-9**
  REALTOR® firm websites shall disclose the firm's name and state(s) of licensure in a reasonable and readily apparent manner.

  Websites of REALTORS® and non-member licensees affiliated with a REALTOR® firm shall disclose the firm's name and that REALTOR®'s or non-member licensee's state(s) of licensure in a reasonable and readily apparent manner. *(Adopted 1/07)*

- **Standard of Practice 12-10**
  REALTORS®' obligation to present a true picture in their advertising and representations to the public includes Internet content posted, and the URLs and domain names they use, and prohibits REALTORS® from:
  1) engaging in deceptive or unauthorized framing of real estate brokerage websites;
  2) manipulating (e.g., presenting content developed by others) listing and other content in any way that produces a deceptive or misleading result;
  3) deceptively using metatags, keywords or other devices/methods to direct, drive, or divert Internet traffic; or
  4) presenting content developed by others without either attribution or without permission, or
  5) to otherwise mislead consumers. *(Adopted 1/07, Amended 1/13)*

- **Standard of Practice 12-11**
  REALTORS® intending to share or sell consumer information gathered via the Internet shall disclose that possibility in a reasonable and readily apparent manner. *(Adopted 1/07)*

- **Standard of Practice 12-12**
  REALTORS® shall not:
  1) use URLs or domain names that present less than a true picture, or
  2) register URLs or domain names which, if used, would present less than a true picture. *(Adopted 1/08)*

- **Standard of Practice 12-13**
  The obligation to present a true picture in advertising, marketing, and representations allows REALTORS® to use and display only professional designations, certifications, and other credentials to which they are legitimately entitled. *(Adopted 1/08)*

Article 13

REALTORS® shall not engage in activities that constitute the unauthorized practice of law and shall recommend that legal counsel be obtained when the interest of any party to the transaction requires it.

Article 14

If charged with unethical practice or asked to present evidence or to cooperate in any other way, in any professional standards proceeding or investigation, REALTORS® shall place all pertinent facts before the proper tribunals of the Member Board or affiliated institute, society, or council in which membership is held and shall take no action to disrupt or obstruct such processes. *(Amended 1/99)*

- **Standard of Practice 14-1**

REALTORS® shall not be subject to disciplinary proceedings in more than one Board of REALTORS® or affiliated institute, society, or council in which they hold membership with respect to alleged violations of the Code of Ethics relating to the same transaction or event. *(Amended 1/95)*

- **Standard of Practice 14-2**

REALTORS® shall not make any unauthorized disclosure or dissemination of the allegations, findings, or decision developed in connection with an ethics hearing or appeal or in connection with an arbitration hearing or procedural review. *(Amended 1/92)*

- **Standard of Practice 14-3**

REALTORS® shall not obstruct the Board's investigative or professional standards proceedings by instituting or threatening to institute actions for libel, slander, or defamation against any party to a professional standards proceeding or their witnesses based on the filing of an arbitration request, an ethics complaint, or testimony given before any tribunal. *(Adopted 11/87, Amended 1/99)*

- **Standard of Practice 14-4**

REALTORS® shall not intentionally impede the Board's investigative or disciplinary proceedings by filing multiple ethics complaints based on the same event or transaction. *(Adopted 11/88)*

Duties to REALTORS®

Article 15

REALTORS® shall not knowingly or recklessly make false or misleading statements about other real estate professionals, their businesses, or their business practices. *(Amended 1/12)*

- **Standard of Practice 15-1**

REALTORS® shall not knowingly or recklessly file false or unfounded ethics complaints. *(Adopted 1/00)*

- **Standard of Practice 15-2**

The obligation to refrain from making false or misleading statements about other real estate professionals, their businesses, and their business practices includes the duty to not knowingly or recklessly publish, repeat, retransmit, or republish false or misleading statements made by others. This duty applies whether false or misleading statements are repeated in person, in writing, by technological means (e.g., the Internet), or by any other means. *(Adopted 1/07, Amended 1/12)*

- **Standard of Practice 15-3**

The obligation to refrain from making false or misleading statements about other real estate professionals, their businesses, and their business practices includes the duty to publish a clarification about or to remove statements made by others on electronic media the REALTOR® controls once the REALTOR® knows the statement is false or misleading. *(Adopted 1/10, Amended 1/12)*

Article 16

REALTORS® shall not engage in any practice or take any action inconsistent with exclusive representation or exclusive brokerage relationship agreements that other REALTORS® have with clients. *(Amended 1/04)*

- **Standard of Practice 16-1**

Article 16 is not intended to prohibit aggressive or innovative business practices which are otherwise ethical and does not prohibit disagreements with other REALTORS® involving commission, fees, compensation or other forms of payment or expenses. *(Adopted 1/93, Amended 1/95)*

- **Standard of Practice 16-2**

Article 16 does not preclude REALTORS® from making general announcements to prospects describing their services and the terms of their availability even though some recipients may have entered into agency agreements or other exclusive relationships with another REALTOR®. A general telephone canvass, general mailing or distribution addressed to all prospects in a given geographical area or in a given profession, business, club, or organization, or other classification or group is deemed "general" for purposes of this standard. *(Amended 1/04)*

Article 16 is intended to recognize as unethical two basic types of solicitations:

First, telephone or personal solicitations of property owners who have been identified by a real estate sign, multiple listing compilation, or other information service as having exclusively listed their property with another REALTOR® and

Second, mail or other forms of written solicitations of prospects whose properties are exclusively listed with another REALTOR® when such solicitations are not part of a general mailing but are directed specifically to property owners identified through compilations of current listings, "for sale" or "for rent" signs, or other sources of information required by Article 3 and Multiple Listing Service rules to be made available to other REALTORS® under offers of subagency or cooperation. *(Amended 1/04)*

- **Standard of Practice 16-3**

Article 16 does not preclude REALTORS® from contacting the client of another broker for the purpose of offering to provide, or entering into a contract to provide, a different type of real estate service unrelated to the type of service currently being provided (e.g., property management as opposed to brokerage) or from offering the same type of service for property not subject to other brokers' exclusive agreements. However, information received through a Multiple Listing Service or any other offer of cooperation may not be used to target clients of other REALTORS® to whom such offers to provide services may be made. *(Amended 1/04)*

- **Standard of Practice 16-4**

REALTORS® shall not solicit a listing which is currently listed exclusively with another broker. However, if the listing broker, when asked by the REALTOR®, refuses to disclose the expiration date and nature of such listing, i.e., an exclusive right to sell, an exclusive agency, open listing, or other form of contractual agreement between the listing broker and the client, the REALTOR® may contact the owner to secure such information and may discuss the terms upon which the REALTOR® might take a future listing or, alternatively, may take a listing to become effective upon expiration of any existing exclusive listing. *(Amended 1/94)*

- **Standard of Practice 16-5**

REALTORS® shall not solicit buyer/tenant agreements from buyers/tenants who are subject to exclusive buyer/tenant agreements. However, if asked by a REALTOR®, the broker refuses to disclose the expiration date of the exclusive buyer/tenant agreement, the REALTOR® may contact the buyer/tenant to secure such information and may discuss the terms upon which the REALTOR® might enter into a future buyer/tenant agreement or, alternatively, may enter into a buyer/tenant agreement to become effective upon the expiration of any existing exclusive buyer/tenant agreement. *(Adopted 1/94, Amended 1/98)*

- **Standard of Practice 16-6**

  When REALTORS® are contacted by the client of another REALTOR® regarding the creation of an exclusive relationship to provide the same type of service, and REALTORS® have not directly or indirectly initiated such discussions, they may discuss the terms upon which they might enter into a future agreement or, alternatively, may enter into an agreement which becomes effective upon expiration of any existing exclusive agreement. *(Amended 1/98)*

- **Standard of Practice 16-7**

  The fact that a prospect has retained a REALTOR® as an exclusive representative or exclusive broker in one or more past transactions does not preclude other REALTORS® from seeking such prospect's future business. *(Amended 1/04)*

- **Standard of Practice 16-8**

  The fact that an exclusive agreement has been entered into with a REALTOR® shall not preclude or inhibit any other REALTOR® from entering into a similar agreement after the expiration of the prior agreement. *(Amended 1/98)*

- **Standard of Practice 16-9**

  REALTORS®, prior to entering into a representation agreement, have an affirmative obligation to make reasonable efforts to determine whether the prospect is subject to a current, valid exclusive agreement to provide the same type of real estate service. *(Amended 1/04)*

- **Standard of Practice 16-10**

  REALTORS®, acting as buyer or tenant representatives or brokers, shall disclose that relationship to the seller/landlord's representative or broker at first contact and shall provide written confirmation of that disclosure to the seller/landlord's representative or broker not later than execution of a purchase agreement or lease. *(Amended 1/04)*

- **Standard of Practice 16-11**

  On unlisted property, REALTORS® acting as buyer/tenant representatives or brokers shall disclose that relationship to the seller/landlord at first contact for that buyer/tenant and shall provide written confirmation of such disclosure to the seller/landlord not later than execution of any purchase or lease agreement. *(Amended 1/04)*

  REALTORS® shall make any request for anticipated compensation from the seller/landlord at first contact. *(Amended 1/98)*

- **Standard of Practice 16-12**

  REALTORS®, acting as representatives or brokers of sellers/landlords or as subagents of listing brokers, shall disclose that relationship to buyers/tenants as soon as practicable and shall provide written confirmation of such disclosure to buyers/tenants not later than execution of any purchase or lease agreement. *(Amended 1/04)*

- **Standard of Practice 16-13**

  All dealings concerning property exclusively listed, or with buyer/tenants who are subject to an exclusive agreement shall be carried on with the client's representative or broker, and not with the client, except with the consent of the client's representative or broker or except where such dealings are initiated by the client.

  Before providing substantive services (such as writing a purchase offer or presenting a CMA) to prospects, REALTORS® shall ask prospects whether they are a party to any exclusive representation agreement. REALTORS® shall not knowingly provide substantive services concerning a prospective transaction to prospects who are parties to exclusive representation agreements, except with the consent of the prospects' exclusive representatives or at the direction of prospects. *(Adopted 1/93, Amended 1/04)*

- **Standard of Practice 16-14**

  REALTORS® are free to enter into contractual relationships or to negotiate with sellers/landlords, buyers/tenants or others who are not subject to   an exclusive agreement but shall not knowingly obligate them to pay more than one commission except with their informed consent. *(Amended 1/98)*

- **Standard of Practice 16-15**

  In cooperative transactions REALTORS® shall compensate cooperating REALTORS® (principal brokers) and shall not compensate nor offer to compensate, directly or indirectly, any of the sales licensees employed by or affiliated with other REALTORS® without the prior express knowledge and consent of the cooperating broker.

- **Standard of Practice 16-16**

  REALTORS®, acting as subagents or buyer/tenant representatives or brokers, shall not use the terms of an offer to purchase/lease to attempt to modify the listing broker's offer of compensation to subagents or buyer/tenant representatives or brokers nor make the submission of an executed offer to purchase/lease contingent on the listing broker's agreement to modify the offer of compensation. *(Amended 1/04)*

- **Standard of Practice 16-17**

  REALTORS®, acting as subagents or as buyer/tenant representatives or brokers, shall not attempt to extend a listing broker's offer of cooperation and/or compensation to other brokers without the consent of the listing broker. *(Amended 1/04)*

- **Standard of Practice 16-18**

  REALTORS® shall not use information obtained from listing brokers through offers to cooperate made through multiple listing services or through other offers of cooperation to refer listing brokers' clients to other brokers or to create buyer/tenant relationships with listing brokers' clients, unless such use is authorized by listing brokers. *(Amended 1/02)*

- **Standard of Practice 16-19**

  Signs giving notice of property for sale, rent, lease, or exchange shall not be placed on property without consent of the seller/landlord. *(Amended 1/93)*

- **Standard of Practice 16-20**

  REALTORS®, prior to or after their relationship with their current firm is terminated, shall not induce clients of their current firm to cancel exclusive contractual agreements between the client and that firm. This does not preclude REALTORS® (principals) from establishing agreements with their associated licensees governing assignability of exclusive agreements. *(Adopted 1/98, Amended 1/10)*

Article 17

In the event of contractual disputes or specific non-contractual disputes as defined in Standard of Practice 17-4 between REALTORS® (principals) associated with different firms, arising out of their relationship as REALTORS®, the REALTORS® shall mediate the dispute if the Board requires its members to mediate. If the dispute is not resolved through mediation, or if mediation is not required, REALTORS® shall submit the dispute to arbitration in accordance with the policies of the Board rather than litigate the matter.

In the event clients of REALTORS® wish to mediate or arbitrate contractual disputes arising out of real estate transactions, REALTORS® shall mediate or arbitrate those disputes in accordance with the policies of the Board, provided the clients agree to be bound by any resulting agreement or award.

The obligation to participate in mediation and arbitration contemplated by this Article includes the obligation of REALTORS® (principals) to cause their firms to mediate and arbitrate and be bound by any resulting agreement or award. *(Amended 1/12)*

- **Standard of Practice 17-1**

The filing of litigation and refusal to withdraw from it by REALTORS® in an arbitrable matter constitutes a refusal to arbitrate. *(Adopted 2/86)*

- **Standard of Practice 17-2**

Article 17 does not require REALTORS® to mediate in those circumstances when all parties to the dispute advise the Board in writing that they choose not to mediate through the Board's facilities. The fact that all parties decline to participate in mediation does not relieve REALTORS® of the duty to arbitrate.

Article 17 does not require REALTORS® to arbitrate in those circumstances when all parties to the dispute advise the Board in writing that they choose not to arbitrate before the Board. *(Amended 1/12)*

- **Standard of Practice 17-3**

REALTORS®, when acting solely as principals in a real estate transaction, are not obligated to arbitrate disputes with other REALTORS® absent a specific written agreement to the contrary. *(Adopted 1/96)*

- **Standard of Practice 17-4**

Specific non-contractual disputes that are subject to arbitration pursuant to Article 17 are:

1) Where a listing broker has compensated a cooperating broker and another cooperating broker subsequently claims to be the procuring cause of the sale or lease. In such cases the complainant may name the first cooperating broker as respondent and arbitration may proceed without the listing broker being named as a respondent. When arbitration occurs between two (or more) cooperating brokers and where the listing broker is not a party, the amount in dispute and the amount of any potential resulting award is limited to the amount paid to the respondent by the listing broker and any amount credited or paid to a party to the transaction at the direction of the respondent. Alternatively, if the complaint is brought against the listing broker, the listing broker may name the first cooperating broker as a third-party respondent. In either instance the decision of the hearing panel as to procuring cause shall be conclusive with respect to all current or subsequent claims of the parties for compensation arising out of the underlying cooperative transaction. *(Adopted 1/97, Amended 1/07)*

2) Where a buyer or tenant representative is compensated by the seller or landlord, and not by the listing broker, and the listing broker, as a result, reduces the commission owed by the seller or landlord and, subsequent to such actions, another cooperating broker claims to be the procuring cause of sale or lease. In such cases the complainant may name the first cooperating broker as respondent and arbitration may proceed without the listing broker being named as a respondent. When arbitration occurs between two (or more) cooperating brokers and where the listing broker is not a party, the amount in dispute and the amount of any potential resulting award is limited to the amount paid to the respondent by the seller or landlord and any amount credited or paid to a party to the transaction at the direction of the respondent. Alternatively, if the complaint is brought against the listing broker, the listing broker may name the first cooperating broker as a third-party respondent. In either instance the decision of the hearing panel as to procuring cause shall be conclusive with respect to all current or subsequent claims of the parties for compensation arising out of the underlying cooperative transaction. *(Adopted 1/97, Amended 1/07)*

3) Where a buyer or tenant representative is compensated by the buyer or tenant and, as a result, the listing broker reduces the commission owed by the seller or landlord and, subsequent to such actions, another cooperating broker claims to be the procuring cause of sale or lease. In such cases the complainant may name the first cooperating broker as respondent and arbitration may proceed without the listing broker being named as a respondent. Alternatively, if the complaint is brought against the listing broker, the listing broker may name the first cooperating broker as a third-party respondent. In either instance the decision of the hearing panel as to procuring cause shall be conclusive with respect to all current or subsequent claims of the parties for compensation arising out of the underlying cooperative transaction. *(Adopted 1/97)*

4) Where two or more listing brokers claim entitlement to compensation pursuant to open listings with a seller or landlord who agrees to participate in arbitration (or who requests arbitration) and who agrees to be bound by the decision. In cases where one of the listing brokers has been compensated by the seller or landlord, the other listing broker, as complainant, may name the first listing broker as respondent and arbitration may proceed between the brokers. *(Adopted 1/97)*

5) Where a buyer or tenant representative is compensated by the seller or landlord, and not by the listing broker, and the listing broker, as a result, reduces the commission owed by the seller or landlord and, subsequent to such actions, claims to be the procuring cause of sale or lease. In such cases arbitration shall be between the listing broker and the buyer or tenant representative and the amount in dispute is limited to the amount of the reduction of commission to which the listing broker agreed. *(Adopted 1/05)*

- **Standard of Practice 17-5**

The obligation to arbitrate established in Article 17 includes disputes between REALTORS® (principals) in different states in instances where, absent an established inter-association arbitration agreement, the REALTOR® (principal) requesting arbitration agrees to submit to the jurisdiction of, travel to, participate in, and be bound by any resulting award rendered in arbitration conducted by the respondent(s) REALTOR®'s association, in instances where the respondent(s) REALTOR®'s association determines that an arbitrable issue exists. *(Adopted 1/07)*

Explanatory Notes

The reader should be aware of the following policies which have been approved by the Board of Directors of the National Association:

In filing a charge of an alleged violation of the Code of Ethics by a REALTOR®, the charge must read as an alleged violation of one or more Articles of the Code. Standards of Practice may be cited in support of the charge.

The Standards of Practice serve to clarify the ethical obligations imposed by the various Articles and supplement, and do not substitute for, the Case Interpretations in *Interpretations of the Code of Ethics*.

Modifications to existing Standards of Practice and additional new Standards of Practice are approved from time to time. Readers are cautioned to ensure that the most recent publications are utilized.

For information about the Code's centennial go to: *www.realtor.org/coe100*

430 North Michigan Avenue • Chicago, IL 60611-4087
800.874.6500 • www.REALTOR.org

NATIONAL
ASSOCIATION *of*
REALTORS®

Glossary

accidental agency An unintended agency relationship that is created by actions or words.

agency relationship The fiduciary relationship that exists when one person (agent) represents the interests of another (principal) in dealings with others, with their consent and under their control.

agency by ratification Agency by ratification occurs when a principal gains some benefit from a previously unauthorized act of an agent, and the principal, on learning of the act, does not deny that the agent had authority to perform such an act on the principal's behalf. The principal ratifies the action of the agent by accepting the benefits that come from the action.

agent (1) A broker who represents a seller, a landlord, a buyer, or a tenant. (2) A salesperson or broker licensee who represents the broker with whom the agent is associated.

appraisal An estimate or opinion of the value of a piece of property as of a certain date.

appraiser An individual licensed under the Texas Occupation Code § 1103 to conduct appraisals that conform to those of the *Uniform Standards of Professional Appraisal Practice (USPAP)*. Real estate brokers provide a broker price opinion or comparative market analysis.

arbitration A form of alternative dispute resolution whereby a neutral third party listens to each party's position and makes a final decision.

associate A salesperson or a broker licensee who is associated with a broker.

attorney in fact A person authorized to act for another under a power of attorney. This person is not necessarily a licensed attorney.

back-up offer An offer to purchase accepted by a seller who has already accepted an early primary offer to purchase the same property. The backup offer is contingent on the first offer failing to close.

blanket offer of subagency The offer made by the listing broker on behalf of the seller to all other participants in the multiple listing service (MLS) to act as a subagent for the seller. The seller has the option of making a blanket unilateral offer of subagency or making no offer of subagency; in either case, under MLS rules, an offer to cooperate must include an offer to compensate.

broker associate A broker associated with and conducting business, all or in part, as an agent of another broker.

Broker-Lawyer Committee A committee of six licensed brokers appointed by TREC, six licensed attorneys appointed by the State Bar of Texas, and one public member appointed by the governor. This committee is responsible for drafting and revising the standardized contract forms promulgated by TREC for public and licensee use.

broker licensee An individual holding a broker's license issued by the Texas Real Estate Commission (TREC). Brokers may act independently in conducting real estate transactions or may engage other broker licensees or salesperson licensees to represent them in the conduct of their real estate business. Under TRELA, a broker may also be a business entity such as a corporation, limited liability partnership company, or partnership authorized under the Texas Business Organizations Code.

business entity Any corporation, limited liability partnership company, partnership or similar entity authorized under the Texas Business Organizations Code. If the broker is a business entity, however, then one of its managing officers must be licensed as an individual broker in Texas, who then acts as the designated broker for the business entity.

buyer's agent A broker who is representing the buyer in a real estate transaction. Also called a buyer's broker, selling broker, or selling agent.

buyer's broker A real estate broker who is employed by and represents only the buyer in the transaction, whether the commission is paid by the buyer directly or by the seller through a commission split with the listing broker. To be distinguished from brokers who represent the seller but nevertheless "works with" the buyer; these brokers are not called "buyers' brokers." They are subagents of the seller. Also, brokers acting as an intermediary for buyers and sellers are not called buyers' brokers. Buyer brokerage is one part of an exclusive or nonexclusive single agency real estate practice.

client A person, sometimes called a principal, who engages the professional advice or services of another, called an agent, and whose interests are protected by the specific duties and loyalties of an agency relationship.

commission split The sharing of the seller-paid commission between the listing broker and the selling broker. An MLS listing generally indicates the compensation being offered by the listing broker to the other MLS participants, either as a percentage of the gross selling price or as a definite dollar amount. Thus, MLS members know what they will earn on finding a suitable buyer.

common law Law that has evolved by custom or by court decisions (case law).

company policy A set of rules and principles that establishes how a brokerage company is to operate. Every firm should have a clear company policy on agency and take steps to ensure that the sales staff follows it.

consideration Anything of value given to induce another to enter into a contract, such as money, barter, promise, goods, or services.

contract A legally enforceable agreement between competent parties who agree to perform or refrain from performing certain acts for a consideration. In essence, a contract is an enforceable promise.

cooperating broker The real estate broker working with the prospective buyer on a property listed with another broker. The cooperating broker traditionally is compensated through a commission split with the listing broker. The cooperating broker, also called the selling broker, participating broker, outside broker, or other broker, may be either a subagent acting on behalf of the seller or a buyer's broker, both of whom cooperate to make a sale. In some states, the cooperating broker may act as a transaction broker or transaction coordinator.

customer A buyer or a seller in a real estate transaction being assisted by a broker, but without the benefits of an agency relationship.

dual agency The representation of two or more principals in the same transaction by the same agent. In Texas, the duties of a license holder acting as an intermediary supersede the previously accepted role of common law dual agent. Brokers in Texas are no longer permitted to act as dual agents when representing more than one party.

employee Someone who works under the control and direction of another. Compensation is generally based on time rather than results. *See* independent contractor.

ethics A system of accepted principles or standards of moral conduct.

exclusive single agency A type of agency business model adopted by a real estate broker who elects to represent only one side of a real estate transaction. That is, the broker and associates will only represent sellers in the capacity of listing broker or subagent of the listing broker; or the broker elects to only represent buyers (never sellers) in the roll of buyer's broker.

exclusive listing A written listing of real property in which the seller agrees to appoint only one broker to handle the transaction. Two types apply to the seller: (1) the exclusive-right-to-sell listing obligates the seller to pay a commission if anyone, including the seller, procures a ready, willing, and able buyer; and (2) the exclusive-agency listing reserves for the owner the right to sell the property directly without owing a commission. The exclusive agent is entitled to a commission if the buyer is procured by anyone other than the seller. A third type applies to the buyer: the exclusive-right-to-represent agreement obligates the buyer to pay a commission if the buyer agrees to buy a described type of property located by the broker, the buyer, or anyone else during the listing period.

express agency The agency relationship that is created when a principal engages or employs an agent to act for the principal by actually stating it in words, spoken or written. In legal terms, the word *express* means clear, definite, explicit, unmistakable, and unambiguous. *See* implied agency.

facilitator A person who assists the parties to a potential real estate transaction in communication and negotiation without being an advocate for any interest except the mutual interest of all parties to reach agreement. Also called a middleman, mediator, nonagent, or transaction broker.

fiduciary (1) A relationship of trust and confidence between principal and agent. The law imposes on the agent duties of loyalty, confidentiality, accounting, obedience, and full disclosure, as well as the duty to use skill, care, and diligence. A real estate agent owes complete fiduciary duties to the principal and must act in the best interests of the principal (the client) while also being competent with and honest to the other side (the customer, whether the seller or the buyer). (2) The agent is called the fiduciary—one who holds the faith, confidence, and trust of the client.

finder One who produces a buyer or locates a property—nothing more. The finder is not an agent and owes no fiduciary duties.

fraud A deceptive act practiced deliberately by one person in an attempt to gain an unfair advantage over another. There is always the intention to deceive.

FSBO For sale by owner; a property that is being offered for sale by the owner without the benefit of a real estate broker.

general agency The agent who is authorized to conduct an ongoing series of transactions for the principal and can obligate the principal to certain types of contractual agreements.

gratuitous agency The agency relationship that is created when the agent provides brokerage services and charges no fee.

implied agency An agency relationship created by the words or conduct of the agent or principal rather than by written agreement. For example, a listing agent who acts like a buyer's agent in negotiating for the buyer can become involved in an undisclosed dual agency relationship (express agent of seller and implied agent of buyer).

implied authority Not to be confused with implied agency, implied authority is a concept that is applicable to both express agency and implied agency. Implied authority is authority not specifically granted to the agent but necessary or customary if the agent is to perform the agency duties, and it is implied by the principal's actions.

independent contractor A person who contracts to do a job for another but maintains control over the task will be accomplished. Compensation is generally based on results rather than time. In real estate, brokers normally elect to subcontract with other licensees (either salespersons or broker associates) to assist in their real estate brokerage office. *See* employee.

informed consent A person's approval based on full disclosure of all the facts needed to make the decision intelligently. For example, to consent to an intermediary, the buyer and the seller need to understand the liability, the alternatives, and the roles that they and the real estate licensees will play once that relationship is established.

in-house sale A sale involving only one brokerage firm acting as both the listing and the selling agent; the listing agent is also the selling agent. Frequently, one real estate agent in the firm secures the listing and works for the seller, and a different member of the same firm finds and works either for or with the buyer (in which case, with written consent of both parties, the broker plays the role of intermediary). Assuming careful disclosure and conduct by the listing broker, however, there is nothing improper about selling a listing in-house; in fact, the seller lists the property so that the broker will find a qualified buyer.

intermediary A broker who is employed to negotiate a transaction between the parties subject to the obligations of § 1101.559 and § 1101.651(d).

landlord's agent A broker who is representing the landlord in a real estate transaction.

laundry list The enumerated acts in Section 17.46 of the Texas Deceptive Trade Practices—Consumer Protection Act (DTPA) that represent per se evidence of a false, misleading, or deceptive act or practice in the conduct of any trade or commerce.

liable Legally responsible.

licensee A person licensed by TREC to act as a broker or a salesperson in a real estate transaction.

license holder A broker or a salesperson licensed by TREC.

limited agency Limited agency authorizes the agent to perform only those acts permitted by the principal. Real estate agents are most frequently called limited or special agents; their scope of authority usually does not extend beyond the terms of a listing agreement or a buyer representation or tenant representation agreement.

listing An agreement that establishes the rights and obligations between the seller and the broker or between the buyer and the broker. A salesperson usually obtains the listing of a seller's property in the name of the broker. The broker is called the listing broker; the salesperson is sometimes called the listing agent.

listing broker In this textbook, refers to the seller's agent. A buyer's agent can also list the buyer.

material fact Any fact that is relevant to a person making a decision.

mediation A type of alternative dispute resolution where a neutral third party works with parties to a dispute with the objective of assisting or facilitating the parties to come to a mutually acceptable resolution. The mediator does not make the decision for the parties. *See* arbitration.

middleman A person who facilitates a real estate transaction by introducing a buyer to a seller, both of whom negotiate their own transaction; a finder. Provided the middleman exercises no discretion in facilitating the transaction, the middleman, in some states, may be exempted from the traditional fiduciary duties owed by an agent to a principal. Very seldom does a real estate broker conform to this middleman concept. Middleman status could occur when a buyer works with a broker but specifically refuses to authorize the broker to act as the buyer's agent; likewise, the seller does not authorize the broker to act as a subagent. *See also* facilitator.

misrepresentation A false statement made negligently or innocently that is a material factor in another's decision to contract. There does not have to be an intention to deceive.

MLS (multiple listing service) An information service, generally owned and operated by a local association of brokers, in which members pool their listings (primarily residential) and agree to share commissions with other member brokers who find purchasers. Most MLSs are affiliated with the National Association of REALTORS®, which considers the MLS to be a formal system of presenting listings in which blanket offers of cooperation and compensation are made to other MLS members.

Nonexclusive single agency The practice of representing either the buyer or the seller, but never both, in the same transaction. The nonexclusive single-agency broker may be compensated indirectly through an authorized commission split or directly by the principal who employs the agent to represent him.

offer   When one person proposes a contract to another. Once signed and accepted, the contract is binding on both parties.

one-time-showing agreement   A one-time-showing agreement allows the terms of the agreement to apply to a specific buyer only.

open listing   A listing in which the broker has the non-exclusive right to sell the property and receive a commission. If the sale results through the efforts of the seller or another broker, the open listing broker receives no commission. Controversies may arise over which broker actually was the procuring cause of the sale.

optional offer of subagency   The MLS policy that affords a seller represented by a participating member the option of offering subagency or not. The seller can choose to make a blanket offer of subagency or to offer cooperation and compensation to buyer agents, subagents, and other licensed participants in the MLS. No mandatory offer of subagency exists.

ostensible agency   Also known as agency by estoppel (when a court does not allow a principal to deny that agency existed), is based on a third party's being led to believe that a licensee was acting as an agent of another party. For example, if the buyer presumes the agent showing the buyer a property is the agent of the seller, then the agent is ostensibly the seller's agent, even though the agent never expressly self-identified as representing the seller in the transaction.

plaintiff   The party who initiates the suit in civil court; the one who sues.

power of attorney   A written authorization for one person (attorney in fact) to act as the agent of another.

principal   (1) A person who employs an agent to represent her as a client, especially if referred to with the use of a pronoun: her principal. (2) One of the primary parties to a transaction, whether or not an agency relationship is involved (i.e., the buyer or the seller, especially if called the principal).

representation   To act on another's behalf (the principal) as an agent owing fiduciary duties to such principal. There is a definite distinction between working with a buyer (who is then a customer or prospect) and representing a buyer (who is then a client). Buyers often believe they are being represented when, in fact, they either are not represented or are represented by sellers' agents in undisclosed dual agencies. While a listing broker frequently works with buyers to encourage them to buy listed properties, the listing broker should be careful that the broker's words and actions do not lead the buyers to expect that the broker represents them. It is the broker's conduct that usually forms the basis for the reasonable expectations of a buyer or a seller. If, in fact, the broker represents both buyer and seller, appropriate intermediary disclosures must be given and the informed consents of the buyer and the seller must be obtained to this form of limited representation.

promulgated contract form   Forms that TREC has publically and officially announced that are mandatory for licensee use.

REALTOR®   A real estate licensee who is an active member of the Texas and National Association of REALTORS® and usually a local board as well.

renunciation   The giving up or rejecting of something that was originally accepted, such as when a broker unilaterally chooses to discontinue representation of a seller during the term of a listing or buyer representation contract.

rescission   A mutual cancellation of a contract by all parties.

revocation   The withdrawing of a permission that was previously given, such as when a seller or a buyer revokes the broker's authority to act as the agent prior to the expiration of the agency contract.

sales associate   Salesperson licensee associated with and conducting business as an agent of the sponsoring broker.

salesperson   A person who meets the state's requirements for a salesperson's or broker's license and who works for and is licensed under a broker or a brokerage firm. Salespersons are commonly called real estate agents, even though they are not the primary agents of sellers or buyers; in essence, they are agents of agents (brokers). This is an important concept to keep in mind when discussing the in-house intermediary situation in which, for example, salesperson Alice from Bay Realty is thought to represent the seller, and salesperson Sally, also from Bay Realty, is thought to represent the buyer. In this situation, both the buyer and the seller have the same agent (Bay Realty). Separate agents do not represent the buyer and the seller. Alice is not the seller's agent, and Sally is not the buyer's agent; rather, Bay Realty is the only agent of the two clients—in this case, acting as an intermediary. Bay Realty is the primary fiduciary that owns the listing. Bay Realty is obligated by TRELA to supervise its salespersons and is responsible for and bound by their actions.

salesperson licensee   An individual holding a salesperson's license issued by TREC—an agent of the sponsoring broker. Salesperson licensees may conduct business only through their sponsoring brokers.

seller's agent   A broker who is representing the seller in a real estate transaction. Also called seller's broker, listing broker, or listing agent.

selling broker   The broker working with or representing the buyer in the purchase of a listed property. Also called the cooperating broker, participating broker, or other broker when the selling broker is a member of a firm other than the listing firm. The selling broker may be the listing broker or a cooperating broker (subagent or a buyer's agent).

special agency   Sometimes known as limited agency, authorizes the agent to perform only those acts permitted by the principal. Real estate agents are most frequently called limited or special agents; their scope of authority usually does not extend beyond the terms of a listing agreement or a buyer representation or tenant representation agreement.

statutory law   Law that is enacted by legislatures (federal, state, county, or city council).

subagency   A theory of agency law applicable to the agent of a person who already acts as an agent for a principal. In real estate, the client (usually the seller) lists with an agent who, in turn, retains the services of subagents to find a buyer. A seller may limit the authority of the broker to appoint subagents. Cooperating broker members of the MLS may reject any blanket offer of subagency.

subagent   A licensee holder not sponsored by or associated with the client's broker who is representing the client through a cooperative agreement with the client's broker. Also called the other broker.

tenant's agent   A broker who is representing a tenant in a real estate transaction.

unintended dual representation   Accidental representation of both the buyer and the seller by the same broker. This is especially prevalent when the broker does not expressly declare, and the principal does not expressly affirm, the agency status of the broker.

universal agency   A type of agency in which the agent is empowered to conduct every type of transaction that may be legally delegated by a principal to an agent.

void   Having no legal force or effect. A contract that one of the parties can make void without liability.

ANSWER KEY

Texas Real Estate Agency, Eight Edition

Answers to Textbook Chapter Quizzes

Chapter 1
1. c
2. b
3. c
4. b
5. c
6. d
7. a
8. d
9. d
10. b

Chapter 2
1. c
2. a
3. d
4. a
5. c
6. c
7. c
8. d
9. c
10. d

Chapter 3
1. a
2. d
3. c
4. a
5. b
6. a
7. c
8. d
9. b
10. d

Chapter 4
1. c
2. a
3. d
4. c
5. c
6. c
7. b
8. a
9. c
10. b

Chapter 5
1. a
2. b
3. a
4. b
5. b
6. a
7. b
8. d
9. d
10. a

Chapter 6
1. c
2. a
3. a
4. d
5. d
6. c
7. a
8. d
9. b
10. b

Chapter 7

1. d
2. c
3. b
4. c
5. d
6. c
7. a
8. c
9. b
10. c

Chapter 8

1. b
2. d
3. d
4. d
5. d
6. c
7. c
8. b
9. b
10. d

Chapter 9

1. b
2. c
3. d
4. a
5. b
6. a
7. d
8. d
9. d
10. a

Chapter 10

1. b
2. c
3. a
4. a
5. d
6. c
7. d
8. b
9. c
10. d

Chapter 11

1. d
2. a
3. b
4. d
5. d
6. c
7. b
8. b
9. a
10. d

Chapter 12

1. d
2. b
3. c
4. b
5. a
6. c
7. c
8. c
9. d
10. b

Index

Notes

Notes